Mastering ColdFusion 4.5

Mastering™ ColdFusion® 4.5

Arman Danesh
Kristin Aileen Motlagh

SYBEX®

San Francisco • Paris • Düsseldorf • Soest • London

Associate Publisher: Richard Mills
Contracts and Licensing Manager: Kristine O'Callaghan
Acquisitions & Developmental Editor: Kim Goodfriend
Editors: Elizabeth Hurley, Patrick J. Peterson
Production Editor: Shannon Murphy
Technical Editors: Shlomy Gantz, Ilan Admon
Book Designers: Robin Kibby, Kris Warrenburg
Graphic Illustrator: Tony Jonick
Electronic Publishing Specialists: Bill Gibson, Judy Fung, Susie Hendrickson
Proofreaders: Laurie O'Connell, Nancy Riddiough, Laura Schattschneider, Leslie Higbee
Indexer: Matthew Spence
CD Coordinator: Kara Schwartz
CD Technician: Ginger Warner
Cover Designer: Design Site
Cover Illustrator/Photographer: Sergie Loobkoff

To Mrs. G: thanks for all the samosas and get well soon.

–Arman Danesh

To The Boojie.

–Kristin Motlagh

ACKNOWLEDGMENTS

Even though the task of writing such long treatises now seems almost routine, this can never mask the enormous contributions of so many people in bringing projects such as these to reality.

First, I must thank the entire team brought together to make this book a reality. Notably, I am grateful to my coauthor Kristin Motlagh, our team of project managers and editors at Sybex including Kim Goodfriend, Elizabeth Hurley, Shannon Murphy, Patrick Peterson, Bill Gibson, Judy Fung, and Susie Hendrickson, as well as the book's technical editors, Shlomy Gantz and Ilan Admon, and the numerous contributing authors and the nameless many who helped in the task of producing this book.

I also want to thank all my colleagues at Landegg Academy. They tolerated extended periods of absence from the office while I rushed to meet deadlines and they deserve credit for taking up the slack I inevitably left behind at times.

Finally, three people deserve credit for tolerating the fact that I was always in front of the computer screen throughout the writing of this book: my wife, Tahirih, and my parents, Michele and Hossain.

–Arman Danesh

Well, there are certainly a lot of people to thank. J. J. and Jeremy Allaire have created a great company and a great product that have truly changed the direction of my life (for the better, of course). Many Allaire employees have been very helpful to me over this last year. They include Kim Walker Borst, Victoria Crawford, Shawna Constantine, Ben Forta (yeah, that's right…Ben Forta), Amy Gauthier, Steve Penella, Simeon Simeonov, Catherine Stirling, Jessica Wohl-Ludman, and many others. My company partners, Emily Kim and Annette Kunovic, have spared my time to work on the book and they have been the best of friends. Sybex has been absolutely wonderful to me, specifically Kim Goodfriend, Adrienne Crew, and Richard Mills. Our contributing authors were the best! Thanks to Raymond Camden for putting up with my constant stream of ICQ messages. Many, many thanks to all of you! I would also like to thank Shlomy Gantz for squeezing us into his tight schedule to do a great job tech editing the book! And, I thank Arman Danesh for this great opportunity! It has been an adventure!

Finally, I would like to thank my husband, Safa Motlagh! I couldn't have done it without him!

–Kristin Motlagh

About the Authors and Contributors

Arman Danesh is pursuing an advanced degree in computer science at Simon Fraser University in Vancouver. He also serves as the technical manager for The Bahá'í World (http://www.bahai.org/), the official Web site of the Bahá'í International Community, and is the editorial director for Juxta Publishing Limited (http://www.juxta.com/). He has been working with ColdFusion since 1997 and maintains several ColdFusion-based Web sites. Arman has written several books including *Mastering Linux*, *1001 Linux Tips*, and *Teach Yourself JavaScript in a Week*.

Kristin Aileen Motlagh is the Vice President of Business Development and cofounder of Trilemetry, Inc. (http://www.trilemetry.com). She has worked with the Internet for over six years and has developed and managed interactive Web sites and multimedia applications for clients like MCI, Nasdaq, GE, and the World Bank. These Web sites included revenue tracking systems, shopping cart applications, and custom-tailored administrative tools. Her extensive experience with ColdFusion has enabled her to serve as a member of Team Allaire, coauthor the book *Mastering ColdFusion 4*, and teach a ColdFusion course through the HTML Writers Guild. Kristin has also spoken at several conferences and local users groups. In addition, she is an accomplished multimedia programmer, graphic artist, digital restoration specialist, and trainer.

Joel Mueller is a senior software engineer at TekEdge Software. A member of Team Allaire, he has been working with ColdFusion since version 1.5, and has contributed to the development of ColdFusion through beta testing for nearly that entire time. Joel has also been involved with the development of the CF Studio integration tools included with Allaire Spectra, as well as some of the utilities included in the WDDX SDK.

Raymond Camden is a Senior Developer for Syntegra (http://www.syntegra.com). His programming skills include ColdFusion, JavaScript, and Perl. Raymond is a member of Team Allaire, an Allaire Certified Instructor, and the founder of the Hampton Roads ColdFusion User Group (http://www.hrcfug.org). Raymond has worked on numerous ColdFusion projects over the past few years and has developed numerous custom tags. Raymond has been published in the ColdFusion Developer's Journal and is one of the authors of the upcoming Allaire Spectra book. Raymond can be reached at morpheus@deathclock.com.

Emily Kim is Director of Development Solutions and cofounder of Trilemetry, Inc. (http://www.trilemetry.com), a Web site development firm that focuses on ColdFusion solutions and innovative designs. She is also a certified Allaire instructor who teaches their FastTrack to HTML, FastTrack to ColdFusion, and Advanced ColdFusion Development courses. When not teaching or creating Web sites, she writes magazine articles and is a technical and developmental editor and technical reviewer for both text and trade computer books. You can e-mail her at emily@trilemetry.com.

CONTENTS AT A GLANCE

Appendices   889

CONTENTS

INTRODUCTION

This book is designed to teach you how to develop sophisticated, dynamic, and interactive Web sites by using ColdFusion.

ColdFusion, launched in 1995 by Allaire Corporation, was the first Web application server available for Windows NT–based Web servers. ColdFusion is now at version 4.5, which is the version covered in this book.

Today, ColdFusion is used by half of Fortune 500 companies by some counts. It has grown from its modest beginnings to this wide level of industry acceptance because it offers a powerful, yet easy-to-use environment in which Web-based applications can be rapidly designed, prototyped, and deployed. ColdFusion is available for Windows NT, HPUX, and Linux.

Compared to some other Web application server products, ColdFusion offers a simplicity that often belies its powerful capabilities. These capabilities include working with data in databases, interacting with the Internet through FTP, e-mail, and HTTP, and much more.

The goal of this book is to teach Web developers how to extend their knowledge of HTML into a strong command of ColdFusion so that they can begin to develop the dynamic Web applications and interactive Web sites that are becoming common on the Internet and intranets worldwide.

The Components of ColdFusion

ColdFusion consists of several components that, when put together, create the powerful development and deployment environment for Web applications. These components are:

- ColdFusion Markup Language
- ColdFusion Application Server
- ColdFusion Studio
- ColdFusion Administrator

ColdFusion Markup Language

Learning to develop applications in ColdFusion is centered around learning the ColdFusion Markup Language or CFML.

The name of the language offers insight as to its nature. In terms of style and use, CFML is a close relative to the Hypertext Markup Language (HTML). Like HTML, it is tag based and doesn't require learning a programming language with a unique syntax in the way that JavaScript or VBScript do. However, the similarities end there: HTML is used to define the structure, and to some extent, the layout and design of a Web page. CFML is used to specify actions to take in the form of small server-based programs. As in most Web application environments, HTML and CFML are used in files that are processed by the ColdFusion server to generate complete Web pages to be displayed in users' browsers.

Application Server

The process of taking files containing CFML and HTML and converting them into completed Web pages for delivery to the user's browser is handled by the ColdFusion Application Server. The application server is an extension of the Web server that handles the processing of all files containing CFML tags and returning to the Web server pure HTML files for delivery to the user.

The ColdFusion Application Server offers numerous features that make developing and deploying reliable, robust, and high-performance Web applications and interactive Web sites possible. These include:

- Scalability features such as the capability to track client state, load balancing, and clustering.
- Open integration including support for the emerging Extensible Markup Language (XML) standard, built-in support for high-end database servers such as Oracle and Sybase, support for popular application development standards such as the Common Object Request Broker Architecture (CORBA), and the ability to extend the server's capabilities by using standard programming languages such as Visual C++.
- Security features include a comprehensive authentication system, remote development with security to allow secure control over Web site content from remote locations, and integration with Windows NT security and authentication systems. ColdFusion application security is covered in Chapter 30, "Application Security."

Studio

ColdFusion Studio is an integrated development environment (IDE) for ColdFusion. IDEs generally offer a complete graphical environment in which to develop applications.

Studio is optimized for development of ColdFusion-based Web sites and applications (although it can be used to develop static HTML Web sites that don't use any of the interactive or dynamic features of ColdFusion). Among the features of Studio that make it a valuable tool for ColdFusion development are:

Access to the ColdFusion documentation and Help   You can access complete reference information while you are developing.

Tag editors   You can build complete tags by filling in simple-to-follow forms.

Project management   You can group files into sets of related files known as projects. These projects can be managed as single entities, which allows for global tasks such as search-and-replace across whole projects.

Code snippets   You can create a library of code blocks (called snippets) that you commonly use and then quickly include them in the files you are creating.

Expression Builder   ColdFusion allows the creation of some fairly complex expressions. This is simplified in Studio through a point-and-click expression-building applet.

Visual Database tools   One of the powers of ColdFusion is that it makes accessing data stored in relational databases quite easy. You can use visual tools to create database queries, making the creation of code for accessing databases a trivial matter.

Validation tools   You can ensure that the code you have developed is valid through link validation and CFML and HTML code validation capabilities.

Code debugging   ColdFusion application development is a form of programming, and like all forms of programming, it is impossible to write 100 percent accurate code all the time. You can use debugging tools to help pinpoint bugs and errors in code, saving time and frustration.

Design layout and page preview   You can design your pages by using visual page design tools and can preview them inside an integrated browser.

A basic introduction to using Studio as a development tool can be found in Chapter 20, "ColdFusion Studio."

ColdFusion Administrator

The ColdFusion Administrator is an application that enables you to manage your ColdFusion Application Server through a simple, forms-driven Web interface.

With the ColdFusion Administrator, you can configure all aspects of your server's operation, including setting performance-related options, managing security settings, creating database connections, indexing content, and much more. The ColdFusion Administrator is covered in Chapter 35, "ColdFusion Administration."

How ColdFusion Works

ColdFusion integrates tightly with the Web server it is installed with. This allows for a quick and easy transfer of data between the Web server and the ColdFusion Application Server.

This tight integration is normally achieved through the Web server's application programming interface, or API. The API provides a way for an external product such ColdFusion to become an integral part of the operating environment of the Web server. All major Web servers including Apache, Netscape Enterprise Server, and Microsoft Internet Information Server offer APIs, and ColdFusion is designed to work with all of these.

By using the API to connect with the Web server, several benefits are automatically achieved:

- The ColdFusion server essentially becomes part of the Web server.
- A separate program is not launched each time a dynamic page is requested; instead, the pages are interpreted by the ColdFusion server and returned to the user while the ColdFusion server remains loaded and in memory as long as the Web server is running.
- Tight integration with the security and authentication model used by the Web server is possible.

For more insight into the way in which ColdFusion interacts with the Web server, refer to Appendix D, "Differences between ColdFusion and Traditional Server-Side Programming."

Requirements

To use ColdFusion in your environment, you need to meet certain hardware and software requirements. Using ColdFusion effectively also requires previous experience in certain areas of Web development. These requirements are outlined in the following sections.

Hardware

The ColdFusion Application Server for Windows has the following minimum hardware requirements, according to Allaire:

- 486 processor or higher running Windows 95, 98, or NT
- 30MB of disk space
- 32MB of RAM
- CD-ROM drive

Of course, the real hardware requirements will depend largely on your individual needs. For instance, if you are running ColdFusion on your own workstation for development purposes, you will need far less resources than running it on a heavily used production server.

As a general rule of thumb, the system on which you plan to run ColdFusion should already be running a Web server quite comfortably under the expected user load. If you already find that your Web server can't handle the number of hits you receive, then you can't expect ColdFusion to perform adequately either.

NOTE   For hardware requirements on Linux, please refer to Chapter 36, "ColdFusion for Linux."

Allaire has a different set of hardware requirements for ColdFusion Studio:

- Windows 95, 98, or NT (Studio is not available for Solaris)
- 15MB of disk space
- 32MB of RAM

The ColdFusion Administrator has no special requirements; it is simply a ColdFusion application that runs on top of the ColdFusion Application Server. If you have sufficient hardware resources to run the Application Server, then the Administrator will operate without difficulty.

Software

To run the ColdFusion Application server, you need to meet two software requirements:

- The TCP/IP networking protocol must be enabled on the system.
- A suitable Web server must be running.

Suitable Web servers include:

Apache `http://www.apache.org`; for Unix, Linux or Windows NT; free.

Microsoft Internet Information Server `http://www.microsoft.com/iis`; for Windows NT; free.

Netscape Enterprise Server `http://www.netscape.com`; for Unix or Windows NT.

O'Reilly WebSite Pro `http://website.ora.com`; for Windows NT, 98, or 95.

Microsoft Personal Web Server `http://www.microsoft.com`; for Windows NT Workstation, Windows 98, or 95; free.

Experience/Knowledge

ColdFusion is an environment for developing Web applications. As such, it is impossible to use ColdFusion effectively without first having a firm grasp of HTML, including advanced features such as tables and forms.

Without this knowledge, you cannot develop usable applications with ColdFusion. Accordingly, you should have a good grasp of HTML. If you need to review HTML, consider reading *Mastering HTML 4*, Second Edition, by Deborah S. Ray and Eric J. Ray or *HTML Complete*, both from Sybex.

In addition to having a firm grounding in HTML, at least a basic knowledge of Java-Script is useful. Since its introduction in Netscape Navigator 2, JavaScript has quickly become the standard scripting language for client-side scripting and is commonly used on Internet and intranet Web sites. Because JavaScript can be used to perform so many useful functions on Web pages and Web applications, having some knowledge of Java-Script programming will enable you to further enhance and extend the Web applications you develop with ColdFusion.

If you want to learn some JavaScript or review your knowledge, consider reading *Mastering JavaScript and Jscript* by James Jaworski or *The ABCs of JavaScript* by Leo Purcell and Mary Jane Mara.

If you plan to become a serious ColdFusion developer, you also need to understand relational databases and how they work. Specifically, you will want to understand the basics of database design and table creation as well as the basic syntax and usage of the Structured Query Language (SQL), which is commonly used to query and manipulate data stored in relational databases.

You can gain a basic understanding of databases and how they work by reading a book on using Microsoft Access such as *Access 97: No Experience Required* by Celeste Robinson or *Mastering Access 97* by Alan Simpson and Elizabeth Olson. If you want to learn or review SQL, consider reading *Understanding SQL* by Martin Gruber. A SQL reference such as *SQL Instant Reference*, also by Martin Gruber, can prove useful when developing database-driven applications in ColdFusion.

Finally, although learning ColdFusion doesn't require previous programming knowledge or experience, having some will help you to more easily grasp ColdFusion's structure and to design and deploy large, complicated applications in ColdFusion.

ColdFusion Installation

Installing a complete ColdFusion system requires three steps:

- Installing a Web Server
- Installing the ColdFusion Application Server
- Installing ColdFusion Studio

These steps are covered in Appendix A, "Installing ColdFusion," which is located at the back of this book.

How This Book Is Structured

This book is structured to take you from a quick introduction to the basics of ColdFusion (so that you can quickly begin developing applications) and then right up to mastery of advanced topics (so that you can become ColdFusion experts).

The book is divided into four parts:

- Part I teaches how to create a basic ColdFusion file (or template) and then introduces the basics of retrieving information from a database and displaying to a Web browser using CFML. This will enable you to immediately begin developing dynamic, database-driven Web pages.
- Part II teaches the core ColdFusion concepts and CFML syntax that are essential to becoming a proficient ColdFusion developer. These include working with variables, functions, and expressions; creating interactive forms; working with databases; and using the ColdFusion Web Application Framework.
- Part III concentrates on the way in which ColdFusion applications can interact with information services on the Web, including by uploading and downloading files from FTP servers, by sending and retrieving e-mail messages, and by working with LDAP directory servers.
- Part IV addresses a range of advanced concepts, including ColdFusion scripting, event scheduling, application security, and the ColdFusion Administrator. We've also included six appendices that span installation, tag references, function references, and SQL function references.

If your goal is to learn ColdFusion without any prior knowledge of ColdFusion, then you should read the chapters in order because the information presented in each chapter builds on knowledge gained in previous chapters. If you have prior ColdFusion experience, you will probably find the first three sections a good review. In this case, the book can be used as an effective reference tool when you are developing applications in ColdFusion.

Contents of the CD-ROM

The attached CD-ROM includes several items that will be useful in learning ColdFusion, including:

- Selected source code listings from the book (those with headings, such as Listing 1.1)
- Complete evaluation versions of ColdFusion Application Server 4.5 and ColdFusion Studio 4.5 for Windows
- The Apache Web server

The Basics

Learn to:

- Create your first ColdFusion template

- Pass data between ColdFusion templates

- Retrieve data from a database

chapter 1

Creating Your First ColdFusion Template

- Understanding CFML vs. HTML

- Using ColdFusion Studio

- Saving a File

- Using CFOUTPUT

- Using CFSET to Create a Variable

- Using ColdFusion Functions

- Adding Comments to Your Templates

In this chapter, you will write your first ColdFusion template and learn the basic ColdFusion code that will prepare you for the rest of this book. Once you get started, coding your first template should take you less than 15 minutes. Good luck and welcome to ColdFusion!

Get Ready...

The first thing you need to do is ensure that the following programs are installed on your computer:

- A Web server (for example, WebSite, IIS, Apache, PWS, etc.)
- ColdFusion Application Server 4.5
- ColdFusion Studio 4.5

You need to install these programs to complete the exercises in this book. If you have been through the installation procedure described in the Introduction, continue to the next section. Otherwise, please refer to Appendix A, "Installing ColdFusion," and follow the directions for installation. If you believe that you may already have these programs installed, Appendix A can also help you verify the installation.

Get Set...

Now that you have successfully installed a Web server, ColdFusion Application Server, and ColdFusion Studio, you are ready to code your first ColdFusion template.

Understanding CFML vs. HTML

Coding ColdFusion Markup Language (CFML) is very similar to coding Hypertext Markup Language (HTML). CFML and HTML are both tag-based languages that usually have beginning and ending tags. CFML has been designed to work seamlessly with HTML. *CFML is used to determine what content will appear on the page, whereas HTML is used to determine how that content will be displayed.*

TIP   It is important that you have a clear understanding of HTML and how it works before you continue with this book. If you need to learn more about HTML, refer to the book recommendations in the "Requirements" section of the Introduction.

When coding a CFML template, you will use HTML and CFML together. So, a basic HTML page will become a ColdFusion template if CFML is added to the code. Here is a basic HTML tag:

```
<BODY> </BODY>
```

Now compare this to a basic CFML tag:

```
<CFOUTPUT> </CFOUTPUT>
```

As you can see, they look very similar. Of course, they perform different tasks and that is exactly what this book will teach you.

Using ColdFusion Studio

ColdFusion templates and HTML pages are both text-based documents that can be edited in any text editor. Throughout this book, you will edit all your templates using ColdFusion Studio, Allaire's Web editor.

NOTE   Allaire's ColdFusion Studio started out as an enhanced HTML editor called Homesite, created by Nick Bradbury. In March 1997, Allaire acquired Homesite, decided to expand on Homesite's features, and created a new product: ColdFusion Studio. ColdFusion Studio is a full-fledged Web-development editing application that integrates seamlessly with ColdFusion Application Server. It enables you to track projects, add version control, preview Web pages, edit in WYSIWYG (What-You-See-Is-What-You-Get) mode, and much more. To learn more about Studio 4.5, refer to Chapter 20, "Using ColdFusion Studio."

To open ColdFusion Studio, click the Windows Start button and go to Programs ➢ ColdFusion Studio 4.5 (Program Group) ➢ ColdFusion Studio 4.5. You can also click the Windows Start button and select Run. Then, in the Open field, type **C:\Program Files\ Allaire\ColdFusion Studio4\cfstudio4.exe** or the path that corresponds to the location in which you've installed CF Studio.

You will notice that when you open Studio (see Figure 1.1), an HTML page is already provided with all the necessary head and body tags. This is the page that you will use to code your first ColdFusion template. You will also notice that many toolbars and windows are in the Studio interface. These will be explained as needed throughout the book, but if you would like more information now on these toolbars and windows, you can refer to Chapter 20.

FIGURE 1.1
Interface for ColdFusion
Studio 4.5

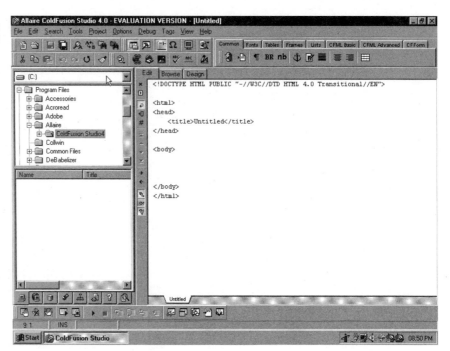

Saving a File

Before you begin coding, follow these steps to save your file to a new directory:

Go to File ➤ Save on the CF Studio menu bar

Make sure that the Look In pull-down menu displays the Web server root directory.

NOTE   The Web server root directory should be the default directory. This directory may vary according to the Web server that is installed on your system. If your Web server root directory does not appear, or if you are not sure what it is, then use the following information to find it in the directory structure. The following are the default Web server root directories for the most popular Web servers:

WebSite   `c:\website\htdocs`

IIS   `c:\inetpub\wwwroot`

PWS   `c:\webshare\wwwroot`

Apache   `c:\program files\apache group\apache\htdocs`

Now select the New Folder button to create a new folder in the Web server root directory (see Figure 1.2).

FIGURE 1.2
Creating a new folder

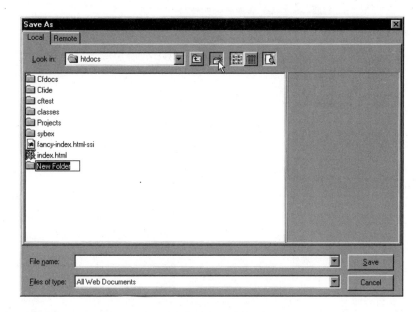

Name this folder **sybex** and then open it. Name this file home.cfm and click the Save button.

You have given this file a CFM extension so that the ColdFusion Application Server will recognize it and process all the ColdFusion tags that you will eventually add to it. For a more detailed description of how ColdFusion templates are processed, please refer to "How Does ColdFusion Work" in the Introduction.

Go!

You are now going to add some text and ColdFusion code to your new home.cfm file. At this point, just follow the example. The code will be explained in the next section. Add the code in Listing 1.1 to your new home.cfm file.

Listing 1.1

```
<!DOCTYPE HTML PUBLIC "-//W3C//DTD HTML 4.0 Transitional//EN">

<HTML>
<HEAD>
<TITLE>My Home Page</TITLE>
</HEAD>

<BODY BGCOLOR="#FFFFFF">
```

```
<DIV ALIGN="center">
<HR><B>Welcome to My Home Page!</B><HR>

<B>Today's date is:</B><BR>
<CFOUTPUT>
<CFSET today = Now()>
<I>#today#</I>
</CFOUTPUT>
</DIV>

</BODY>
</HTML>
```

You can view this file in your browser using the following URL: `http://127.0.0.1/sybex/home.cfm`. You should see a page similar to that shown in Figure 1.3.

NOTE   `http://127.0.0.1/` is the URL that points to your local Web server root directory. You can use this URL to browse any Web pages or Web sites that are stored on your local machine.

FIGURE 1.3
Your first ColdFusion template

Wasn't that easy? You have just created your first ColdFusion template! Let's take a closer look at what you did.

Using *CFOUTPUT*

In the preceding example, ColdFusion Studio provided you with the standard HTML page codes to create a basic HTML page. You then added text and included today's date. Because basic HTML does not provide a way to display dynamic (or changing) information such as the current date, you added ColdFusion code to display the date.

ColdFusion tags and HTML tags are used in a similar way. Both CFML and HTML usually have a beginning and end tag that encloses some information. Each set of beginning and end tags always has the same name, except the end tag name is preceded by a slash (/). In this case, you used one of the most basic of all ColdFusion tags, CFOUTPUT. This is one of the tags you can use when you want to display ColdFusion data. The CFOUTPUT tag tells the ColdFusion Application Server that it needs to evaluate all the ColdFusion variables between the beginning and end CFOUTPUT tags and then display it. The format for using a CFOUTPUT tag is written as the following:

```
<CFOUTPUT>
In this space you can enter HTML, text, and ColdFusion code.
</CFOUTPUT>
```

NOTE   For more information on CFOUTPUT, please refer to the "CFOUTPUT" section in Appendix B, "ColdFusion Tag Reference."

Using *CFSET* to Create a Variable

Between your CFOUTPUT tags, you created a ColdFusion variable, called today, using the CFSET tag. CFSET is used to create and modify variables. The syntax for the CFSET tag is written as the following:

```
<CFSET your_variable_name = the_value_of_your_variable>
```

NOTE   For more information on CFSET, please refer to the "CFSET" section in Appendix B.

To understand variables, think of the stock market. Every stock on the stock market has a name. For example, Allaire's stock has the name ALLR. Now, almost every time you look at the value of the ALLR stock, it will have changed. So, the name of the stock is the same, but its value changes. In the same way, variables are given names, but their values can change. For example, you could create a variable named ALLR with an initial value of 120. Over time, the value of the variable can change to 140, for example, without the name changing. At any time, the current value can be accessed through the variable name ALLR.

In the previous example, you created the variable today and assigned it the value of Now(). The value Now() is actually a ColdFusion function that returns the current timestamp (or the date and time) that is recorded on the server (functions are discussed in more detail in the next section). If you were to reload your Web page right now, you would see a new timestamp returned because the value of the variable today has changed since you last loaded the home.cfm page.

Several rules about variables are useful to know when coding your templates:

- ColdFusion variables that will be displayed in the browser usually need to be enclosed within pound (#) signs—but not always. For example, you did not have to enclose your today variable within # signs to set it, but you did have to enclose it within # signs to display it." Chapter 4, "Creating and Manipulating Variables," provides more information about when you should and should not use # signs with your variables. For now, when in doubt, use # signs.
- *When you want to display a ColdFusion variable, it needs to be inside a CFOUTPUT tag* or other similar tag (which you will learn about later in this book).
- ColdFusion variables cannot contain reserved words, spaces, special characters, or begin with a number.

NOTE   For more information on ColdFusion variables, please refer to Chapter 4.

Using ColdFusion Functions

Now that you've taken a closer look at your first template, let's make some minor modifications to it. Because the output of the today variable isn't the easiest to understand, let's change the format so that the date displayed looks something like Tuesday, September 15, 1998. Of course, the date displayed will reflect the current date. Modify your CFSET tag to look like the following:

```
<CFSET today = DateFormat(Now(), "dddd, mmmm d, yyyy")
```

Save your file and then reload the page in your browser.

Now your date is in a more useful and readable format (see Figure 1.4), but how did you do that? As explained before, the Now() function returns the current timestamp of the server but is difficult to read. To change the format so that it is easier to read, you have to modify the date returned by the Now() function. So, you used another function called the DateFormat function. The DateFormat function will modify any date passed to it to almost any format you want. Its syntax is:

```
DateFormat(date, format_of_date)
```

FIGURE 1.4
Your modified template

Table 1.1 describes the two values that the DateFormat function takes.

TABLE 1.1: DateFormat Values

Value	Description
date	A valid date that you would like to be formatted. In the preceding example, you used the function Now(), which returns the current date.
format_of_date	This is where you specify the mask that you want applied to the date (how you want the date to be formatted). In the preceding example, you used the following masks: *dddd*–Specifies the full name of the day of the week (Monday, Tuesday) *mmmm*–Specifies the full name of the month (May, June) *d*–Specifies the day of the month in a numeric value (1, 2, 3) *yyyy*–Specifies the year in four digits (1998, 1999) You can mix and match these to create different formats. For a full description of the masks used for DateFormat, refer to DateFormat in Appendix C, "ColdFusion Function Reference."

So, in the following example:

```
<CFSET today = DateFormat(Now(), "dddd, mmmm d, yyyy")>
```

the variable today returns to

```
Tuesday, September 15, 1998
```

ColdFusion functions perform an action. The Now( ) function returned the current timestamp. Other functions may, for example, format a string for you or find a character within a string. The important concept to understand is that functions perform an action and return a result. If you've used any other programming language, this may be familiar territory.

> **NOTE** For more information on ColdFusion functions, please refer to Chapter 5, "Functions."

Adding Comments to Your Templates

Comments may already be familiar to you because of your background in HTML. They can have many purposes, including the following:

- Allowing the developer to explain his/her code
- Tracking changes within a document
- Tracking who has worked on the document
- Placing reminders to make changes or additions to the code

ColdFusion comment tags are very similar to HTML comment tags. The only differences between how HTML and CFML comments are processed are the following:

- ColdFusion code within an HTML comment is processed, whereas ColdFusion code within a CFML comment is treated as plain text.
- CFML comments are not displayed in the source code of the Web page document; they are stripped out before the final HTML file is rendered.

CFML and HTML comments look similar. Here is an HTML comment:

```
<!-- add your HTML comment here -->
```

Here is another CFML comment:

```
<!--- add your CFML comment here --->
```

As you can tell, except for the extra dash (-), they are very similar. Also, CFML comments can span many lines, just like HTML comments can. It is only necessary that a CFML comment begin with <!--- and end with --->.

You are now going to add a CFML comment to your home.cfm file for the purpose of explaining your code. Modify the text between the CFOUTPUT tags in your home.cfm file to reflect the changes indicated in Listing 1.2.

Listing 1.2

```
<CFOUTPUT>

<!---
The following variable, 'today', displays the current date in the format:
Tuesday, September 15, 1998

Now() returns the current timestamp (date & time)

Dddd    = full day of week
Mmmm    = full name of month
D   = day of month
Yyyy    = year in four digits
--->

<CFSET today = DateFormat(Now(), "dddd, mmmm d, yyyy")>
<I>#today#</I>
</CFOUTPUT>
```

You will notice that this comment provided quite a bit of information and spanned many lines. Comments are used extensively in ColdFusion to make the code easier to understand. Because every developer has a different style of coding, comments are very helpful in deciphering what others were trying to do with their code. Good ColdFusion programmers always add comments to their code.

Now, if you save and reload your page in the browser, you won't see a change. If you look at the source, you still won't see a change. This is because CFML comments do not appear to the end user, even in the source. If you were to change the CFML comment to an HTML comment, it would, of course, appear in the browser's source code. CFML comments appear only to the developers who have access to the original code.

You added the comment tag so that when you refer to this file later, you will understand how you coded the today variable. ColdFusion comments can be extremely useful in documenting your code while also keeping your coding secrets private and safe from end users.

Where Do We Go from Here?

In this chapter, you created your first ColdFusion template. Although it wasn't very fancy, it showed you the basic concepts for coding ColdFusion templates. These concepts are the following:

- Understanding variables

- Creating variables
- Displaying variables
- Understanding functions
- Using functions
- Commenting your code

In the next chapter, you will learn how to pass data from one template to another using HTML forms and hyperlinks.

chapter 2

Passing Data between ColdFusion Templates

- Passing ColdFusion Parameters: An Overview

- Passing Parameters through the URL

- Evaluating Variables

- Passing Parameters through a Form

Now that you have created your first ColdFusion template, you are ready to learn how to pass values, or *parameters*, between two ColdFusion templates. This chapter will provide a basic overview of how to pass parameters between ColdFusion templates using URLs and forms. You will also learn how to control the flow of your document through the use of the CFIF tag. This chapter builds upon the HTML knowledge you already have and shows you how much more can be done with it using ColdFusion.

Passing ColdFusion Parameters: An Overview

If you're using plain HTML, there is no way to pass data between pages or store information in variables. This results in a static Web site without much interactivity. The most you can do on an interactive basis is allow the user to navigate to other pages, submit forms (which can only be sent unformatted to an e-mail address), and send an e-mail (provided the user's browser is configured appropriately).

Once you can pass data between HTML pages and store the data in variables, you can create many more interactive processes with your Web site. For example, just some of the things you can do include the following:

• Create a form that requests information from users, then display that information on the next page while also storing the information in variables for later use
• Program a quiz, evaluate user answers, and keep track of scores
• Track which pages a user has visited on your site
• Create a game of tick-tack-toe or some other puzzle
• Redirect users to different locations based on variable contents

You may already have worked with other technologies that enable you to create these types of interactions. For example, JavaScript can be used to pass data between HTML pages. You can also use Common Gateway Interface (CGI) programming, Active Server Pages, and a whole host of other technologies. ColdFusion, though, is generally much easier to work with, especially for someone who has never programmed. Also, Cold-Fusion offers advantages over all these technologies because it is easier to learn, easier to use, and allows for database interaction (which will be covered in the next chapter).

In this chapter, you will create a short quiz using variables, URL parameters, and form parameters.

NOTE   Remember, you should have a thorough understanding of HTML, URLs, and forms before continuing. If you need to learn more about HTML, URLs, or forms, refer to the book recommendations in the "Requirements" section of the Introduction.

Passing Parameters through the URL

You are already familiar with how to create a basic hypertext link that enables the user to navigate to various pages on the Web. In the next example, you will be using hypertext links to allow for user navigation while also passing parameters to the next ColdFusion template. A parameter is the value of an assigned variable that is passed to another template. This can be done through the URL or a form.

Creating a Basic ColdFusion URL

To pass a parameter to another template, you must separate the standard URL from the parameters you are passing with a question mark (?). The ? is then followed by the *name of the parameter* equal to the *value of the parameter*—in this case, `answer=1985`. The syntax for passing a parameter to the next template is as follows:

```
<A HREF="name_of_template.cfm?variable1=value1">
```

If you want to pass more than one parameter, you must separate each with an ampersand (&), as in the following example:

```
<A HREF="name_of_template.cfm?variable1=value1&variable2=value2">
```

In the `home.cfm` file that you created in Chapter 1, "Creating Your First ColdFusion Template," you can now add the code in Listing 2.1.

NOTE

In Listing 2.1, all bold lines indicate where modifications have been made in the code. You need to make changes only to these lines in your template. This convention applies throughout the book.

Listing 2.1

```
<!DOCTYPE HTML PUBLIC "-//W3C//DTD HTML 4.0 Transitional//EN">

<HTML>
<HEAD>
<TITLE>My Home Page</TITLE>
</HEAD>

<BODY BGCOLOR="#FFFFFF">

<DIV ALIGN="center">
<HR><B>Welcome to My Home Page!</B><HR>

<B>Today's date is:</B><BR>
<CFOUTPUT>
<!---
```

```
The following variable, 'today', displays the current
date in the format: Tuesday, September 15, 1998

Now() returns the current timestamp (date & time)

dddd = full day of week
mmmm = full name of month
d = day of month
yyyy = year in four digits
--->

<CFSET today = DateFormat(Now(), "dddd, mmmm d, yyyy")>
<I>#today#</I>
</CFOUTPUT>
</DIV>

<P><HR><B>Today's question is:</B>

<BR><I>In what year was ColdFusion introduced?</I>

<OL>
<LI><A HREF="quiz_results.cfm?user_answer=1985">1985</A>
<LI><A HREF="quiz_results.cfm?user_answer=1990">1990</A>
<LI><A HREF="quiz_results.cfm?user_answer=1995">1995</A>
<LI><A HREF="quiz_results.cfm?user_answer=1998">1998</A>
</OL>

</BODY>
</HTML>
```

When viewed in your browser, the file should look like Figure 2.1.

If you take a closer look at home.cfm, you will notice that the four possible answers to the quiz question all link to the same page, quiz_results.cfm. You will also notice that additional data has been appended to the standard URL, making each link slightly different. This data is the user_answer parameter that you are passing to the next template.

NOTE   *Parameters* are the values of variables passed through the URL or a form.

NOTE   *Variables* are assigned either by you (the developer) or the ColdFusion environment in a given template.

Now, to test the home.cfm page, you need to first create quiz_results.cfm. In quiz_results.cfm you will display the user's selected answer and the correct answer. Create the code in Listing 2.2 in ColdFusion Studio by selecting File ➢ New ➢ Default Template. Then save the file to the sybex directory as quiz_results.cfm.

FIGURE 2.1

Multiple-choice quiz

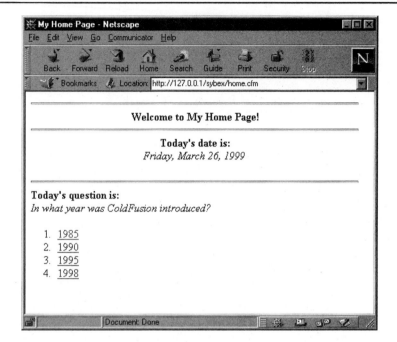

NOTE Remember that you must give your filename a **CFM** extension for it to be processed by the ColdFusion Application Server.

NOTE Remember that you must display ColdFusion variables inside a **CFOUTPUT** tag set and enclosed in pound (#) signs.

Listing 2.2

```
<!DOCTYPE HTML PUBLIC "-//W3C//DTD HTML 4.0 Transitional//EN">

<HTML>
<HEAD>
<TITLE>Quiz Results</TITLE>
</HEAD>

<BODY BGCOLOR="#FFFFFF">
```

```
<DIV ALIGN="center">
<HR><B>Quiz Results!</B><HR>
<B>Thank you for taking my short quiz!</B><P>
</DIV>

<CFOUTPUT>
<B>The question was:</B>
In what year was ColdFusion introduced?<BR>
<B>Your answer was:</B> #url.user_answer#<BR>
<B>The correct answer is:</B> 1995<P>
</CFOUTPUT>

<DIV ALIGN="center">
<I><A HREF="home.cfm">Take the quiz again?</A></I>
</DIV>

</BODY>
</HTML>
```

Now reload the home.cfm file in your browser window and select the first answer, 1985. You should be directed to the file quiz_results.cfm, which should look like Figure 2.2.

FIGURE 2.2

Your quiz results

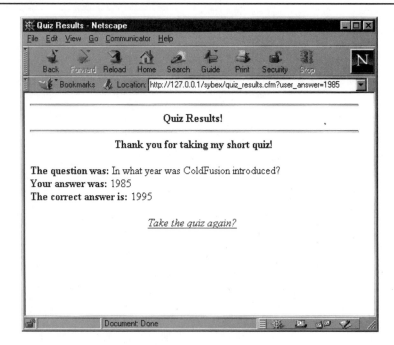

You have just passed your first parameter from one template to another through the URL. If you look at the URL in the browser's location, you will notice that it also contains the passed parameter. ColdFusion reads this URL when the template is being processed and assigns all the parameters to variable names in the following format: URL.parameter_name. You can then access the generated variable later in the template, which is exactly what you did. When you coded which year the user chose as #url.user_answer#, you accessed the variable URL.user_answer. This variable was generated by ColdFusion when it parsed the parameter in the URL.

Other types of variables are listed in Table 2.1. You will be learning about URL and form variables later in this chapter.

TABLE 2.1:   Variable Types

Other types of variables	Format	Description
URL	url.variable_name	Variables passed through the URL
Form	form.variable_name	Variables passed through a form submission
CGI	cgi.variable_name	Variables supplied by the server (contains variables such as user's IP address and user's browser version)
Cookie	Cookie.variable_name	Variables created from a browser Cookie.
Query	Query_name.variable_name	Variables created as a result of a query to a data source, such as a database or mail server.
Local	Variable_name	Variables created in a template and accessible only within the template.
Server	Server.variable_name	Variables associated with the ColdFusion server and available in all applications running on the server.
Application	Application.variable_name	Variables applied to all templates in an application
Session	session.variable_name	Variables stored during the current browser session
Client	client.variable_name	Persistent variables stored until deleted

NOTE   You can learn more about the types of variables you can set in Chapter 4, "Creating and Manipulating Variables."

This was, of course, a simple example. You passed a parameter from one template to another and then displayed the generated variable to the user. It would be much more useful if you could evaluate the value of that parameter and then display different messages based on whether the answer was correct. You will learn how to do exactly this later in this chapter.

Working with Multiple Parameters

In this section, you will expand on the previous example by passing four parameters with different characteristics through the URL. Before modifying your code, it is important to look at each of the parameters that you will pass.

In the last example, you passed only the user_answer parameter. The only real benefit gained by doing so was to display the answer to the user on the next page. Everything else on the quiz_results.cfm file was hard-coded. But what if your ultimate goal is to create a quiz with randomly generated questions or multiple questions on the first template? If that is your goal, then you cannot hard-code the question and the correct answer on your second template (as was done in the previous example) because the question and answer could be different each time.

You will be adding an additional quiz question to your home.cfm file to illustrate the preceding point. This will enable you to pass different quiz question variables through the URL. You will be modifying your code so that the following variables will be passed through each of the URLs:

question   The full text of the question the user has chosen

user_answer   The answer chosen by the user

correct_answer   The correct answer

today   The variable today that you created in Chapter 1

First, you need to create your variables in your home.cfm file. You already created the today variable in Chapter 1. The user_answer variable will be selected by the end user as part of the URL, as demonstrated in the preceding section. To create the question and correct_answer variables and to add an additional question, modify the code in your home.cfm file as shown in Listing 2.3.

Listing 2.3

```
<!DOCTYPE HTML PUBLIC "-//W3C//DTD HTML 4.0 Transitional//EN">

<HTML>
<HEAD>
<TITLE>My Home Page</TITLE>
</HEAD>

<BODY BGCOLOR="#FFFFFF">

<DIV ALIGN="center">
```

```
<HR><B>Welcome to My Home Page!</B><HR>

<B>Today's date is:</B><BR>
<CFOUTPUT>
<!---
The following variable, 'today', displays the current
date in the format: Tuesday, September 15, 1998

Now() returns the current timestamp (date & time)

dddd = full day of week
mmmm = full name of month
d = day of month
yyyy = year in four digits
--->

<CFSET today = DateFormat(Now(), "dddd, mmmm d, yyyy")>
<I>#today#</I>
</CFOUTPUT>
</DIV>

<!--- The following is code for my first quiz question --->
<CFSET question1 = "In what year was ColdFusion introduced?">
<CFSET correct_answer1 = 1995>

<P><HR><B>Today's 1st question is:</B>
<BR><I><CFOUTPUT>#question1#</CFOUTPUT></I>

<OL>
<LI><A HREF="quiz_results.cfm?user_answer=1985">1985</A>
<LI><A HREF="quiz_results.cfm?user_answer=1990">1990</A>
<LI><A HREF="quiz_results.cfm?user_answer=1995">1995</A>
<LI><A HREF="quiz_results.cfm?user_answer=1998">1998</A>
</OL>

<!--- The following is code for my second quiz question --->
<CFSET question2 = "Who developed the first version of ColdFusion?">
<CFSET correct_answer2 = "J.J. Allaire">

<P><B>Today's 2nd question is:</B>
<BR><I><CFOUTPUT>#question2#</CFOUTPUT></I>

<OL>
<LI><A HREF="quiz_results.cfm?user_answer='Kristin Motlagh'">Kristin Motlagh</A>
<LI><A HREF="quiz_results.cfm?user_answer='J.J. Allaire'">J.J. Allaire</A>
<LI><A HREF="quiz_results.cfm?user_answer='Arman Danesh'">Arman Danesh</A>
<LI><A HREF="quiz_results.cfm?user_answer='Gaio Gonzalez'">Gaio Gonzalez</A>
</OL>

</BODY>
</HTML>
```

TIP   If you are assigning a text string to a variable, you should surround the text string in quotes. You do not need to do this with numbers. For more information on variables, please refer to Chapter 4.

Here is what you just did to your template:

1. Added a comment line explaining where the code for each quiz question started
2. Set the `question1` and `correct_answer1` variables for question 1
3. Changed from displaying a hard-coded question to displaying the `question1` variable
4. Added code for the second question and repeated steps 1–3 for question 2

Now that you have all your variables set, you are ready to add them as parameters to the URLs in your home.cfm file. Let's add each parameter one at a time to the first URL in your first question. Your current URL format looks like this:

```
<A HREF="quiz_results.cfm?user_answer=1985">1985</A>
```

You are already passing the `user_answer` parameter. This parameter is hard-coded into the URL. Now you can add the `correct_answer` parameter. But, because the `correct_answer` parameter is not hard-coded, and its value is equal to the ColdFusion variable `correct_answer1` that you set earlier in the template, you will need to output it in the URL using CFOUTPUT tags. Here is the resulting code:

```
<CFOUTPUT><A HREF="quiz_results.cfm?user_answer=1985&correct_answer=
#correct_answer1#">1985</A></CFOUTPUT>
```

The `question` parameter is like the `correct_answer` parameter in that it is not hard-coded. Now, add the `question` parameter in the same manner:

```
<CFOUTPUT><A HREF="quiz_results.cfm?user_answer=1985&correct_answer=
#correct_answer1#&question=#question1#">1985</A></CFOUTPUT>
```

Finally, you can add the `today` parameter:

```
<CFOUTPUT><A HREF="quiz_results.cfm?user_answer=1985&correct_answer=
#correct_answer1#&question=#question1#&today=#today#">1985</A></CFOUTPUT>
```

You're not quite finished yet. You now need to complete the same set of steps for the other three URLs in the first question and the rest of the URLs in the second question. Remember that while you are modifying your code, you need only one CFOUTPUT tag set to surround all of your ColdFusion variables. You do not need a separate CFOUTPUT tag set for each variable.

Your final file should look like Listing 2.4.

Listing 2.4

```html
<!DOCTYPE HTML PUBLIC "-//W3C//DTD HTML 4.0 Transitional//EN">

<HTML>
<HEAD>
<TITLE>My Home Page</TITLE>
</HEAD>

<BODY BGCOLOR="#FFFFFF">

<DIV ALIGN="center">
<HR><B>Welcome to My Home Page!</B><HR>

<B>Today's date is:</B><BR>
<CFOUTPUT>
<!---
The following variable, 'today', displays the current
date in the format: Tuesday, September 15, 1998

Now() returns the current timestamp (date & time)

dddd = full day of week
mmmm = full name of month
d = day of month
yyyy = year in four digits
--->

<CFSET today = DateFormat(Now(), "dddd, mmmm d, yyyy")>
<I>#today#</I>
</CFOUTPUT>
</DIV>

<!--- The following is code for my first quiz question --->
<CFSET question1 = "In what year was ColdFusion introduced?">
<CFSET correct_answer1 = 1995>

<P><HR><B>Today's 1st question is:</B>
<CFOUTPUT>
<BR><I>#question1#</I>

<OL>
<LI><A
HREF="quiz_results.cfm?user_answer=1985&correct_answer=#correct_answer1#&question=#question1#&today=#today#">1985</A>
```

```
    <LI><A HREF="quiz_results.cfm?user_answer=1990&correct_answer=#
correct_answer1#&question=#question1#&today=#today#">1990</A>
    <LI><A
HREF="quiz_results.cfm?user_answer=1995&correct_answer=#correct_answer1#&question=#qu
estion1#&today=#today#">1995</A>
    <LI><A
HREF="quiz_results.cfm?user_answer=1998&correct_answer=#correct_answer1#&question=#qu
estion1#&today=#today#">1998</A>
    </OL>
    </CFOUTPUT>

    <!--- The following is code for my second quiz question --->
    <CFSET question2 = "Who developed the first version of ColdFusion?">
    <CFSET correct_answer2 = "J.J. Allaire">

    <P><B>Today's 2nd question is:</B>
    <CFOUTPUT>
    <BR><I>#question2#</I>

    <OL>
    <LI><A HREF="quiz_results.cfm?user_answer='Kristin Motlagh'&correct_answer=
#correct_answer2#&question=#question2#&today=#today#">Kristin Motlagh</A>
    <LI><A HREF="quiz_results.cfm?user_answer='J.J.
Allaire'&correct_answer=#correct_answer2#&question=#question2#&today=#today#">J.J.
Allaire</A>
    <LI><A HREF="quiz_results.cfm?user_answer='Arman Danesh'&correct_answer=
#correct_answer2#&question=#question2#&today=#today#">Arman Danesh</A>
    <LI><A HREF="quiz_results.cfm?user_answer='Gaio Gonzalez'&correct_answer=
#correct_answer2#&question=#question2#&today=#today#">Gaio Gonzalez</A>
    </OL>
    </CFOUTPUT>

    </BODY>
    </HTML>
```

To test your changes, you also need to make some changes to your second template, `quiz_results.cfm`. Because you are no longer hard-coding any of the quiz data on the second template, you need to remove the quiz question and answer from the second template and replace them with the variables generated from the parameters passed through the URL. The variables generated are as follows:

- `URL.user_answer`
- `URL.correct_answer`
- `URL.question`
- `URL.today`

NOTE You do not need to specify the URL prefix if there are no conflicting variable names.

Modify your `quiz_results.cfm` as shown in Listing 2.5.

Listing 2.5

```
<!DOCTYPE HTML PUBLIC "-//W3C//DTD HTML 4.0 Transitional//EN">

<HTML>
<HEAD>
<TITLE>Quiz Results</TITLE>
</HEAD>

<BODY BGCOLOR="#FFFFFF">

<DIV ALIGN="center">
<HR><B>Quiz Results!</B><HR>
<B>Thank you for taking my short quiz!</B><P>
</DIV>

<CFOUTPUT>
<B>The question was:</B> #question#<BR>
<B>Your answer was:</B> #user_answer#<BR>
<B>The correct answer is:</B> #correct_answer#<BR>
<B>You took the quiz on:</B> #today#<P>
</CFOUTPUT>

<DIV ALIGN="center">
<I><A HREF="home.cfm">Take the quiz again?</A></I>
</DIV>

</BODY>
</HTML>
```

In this file, you added the date the quiz was taken and you changed the question and correct answer from hard-coded values to the output of variables generated from the URL. Now, go to your browser and reload the `home.cfm` file (see Figure 2.3). You will notice that the value displayed in the status window when you put your mouse over the URL has changed. Select the first answer to question 1.

FIGURE 2.3

Your new quiz

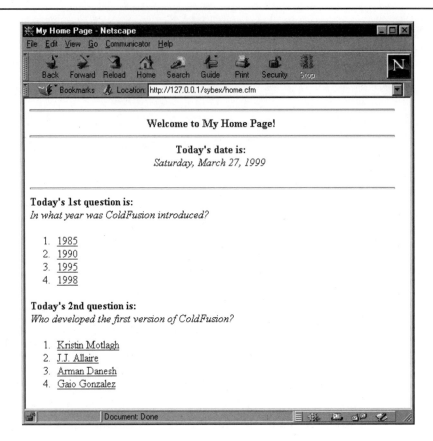

What did you see? Well, hopefully you received your first ColdFusion error. If you didn't receive an error, then recheck your code to make sure it is correct. The error should look something like this:

```
Error Diagnostic Information

Error resolving parameter TODAY

ColdFusion was unable to determine the value of the parameter. This problem is
very
  likely due to the fact that either:

    1.You have misspelled the parameter name, or
    2.You have not specified a QUERY attribute for a CFOUTPUT, CFMAIL, or
      CFTABLE tag.
```

```
The error occurred while evaluating the expression:

#today#

The error occurred while processing an element with a general identifier of
(#today#),
    occupying document position (19:31) to (19:37) in the template file
    C:\WebSite\htdocs\sybex\quiz_results.cfm.

Date/Time: 03/27/99 01:44:19
Browser: Mozilla/4.04 [en] (Win95; U)
Remote Address: 127.0.0.1
HTTP Referer: http://127.0.0.1/sybex/home.cfm
Template: C:\WebSite\htdocs\sybex\quiz_results.cfm
Query String: user_answer=1985&correct_answer=1995&question=In
```

NOTE   If you are using Internet Explorer 4 or above, spaces in URL parameters will automatically be resolved, so you will not receive an error.

That's a pretty long error message with a lot of information that, at this point, may not make a lot of sense. But it does provide all the information you need to figure out the problem. Look at the entire text of the error for a minute or so and see if you can figure out the problem for yourself.

You know from the error message that ColdFusion had a problem processing the today parameter. When the ColdFusion processor came across the variable today, it searched for the value (the one you passed through the URL) but could not find it. If you look at the last line of the error message, you will see that the today parameter was never passed. In fact, the question parameter was not completely passed either. This is because you cannot pass certain characters, such as spaces, through the URL. When you passed the question parameter through the URL, its value contained spaces, and the browser did not understand how to process it. As a result, the URL was truncated at the first space received in the URL.

To preserve the value of parameters passed through the URL, you must convert the "illegal" characters to characters that the browser can better interpret. ColdFusion enables you to do this with the function URLEncodedFormat.

NOTE   For more information on URLEncodedFormat, please refer to the "URLEncodedFormat" section in Appendix C, "ColdFusion Function Reference."

In Chapter 1 you learned a bit about ColdFusion functions. Here, the URLEncoded-Format function is used similarly to the way that the DateFormat function was used in Chapter 1. Remember that functions perform an action and return a result. You must apply the URLEncodedFormat function to the parameter you are passing in the following manner:

```
#URLEncodedFormat(parameter_name)#
```

So, if you apply this concept to your home.cfm file, the first link in your file should look like this:

```
<A HREF="quiz_results.cfm?user_answer=
#URLEncodedFormat(1985)#&correct_answer=#URLEncodedFormat(correct_answer1)#&question=
#URLEncodedFormat(question1)#&today=#URLEncodedFormat(today)#">1985</A>
```

Modify all the links in your home.cfm file as demonstrated in the preceding code. It is important that you always apply the URLEncodedFormat function to each of the parameters (even if they are hard-coded) because they could possibly be changed and contain illegal characters at some time in the future. You will also notice that the hard-coded answers for the second question contain spaces and will therefore cause an error if you do not apply the URLEncodedFormat function to them.

Now reload the home.cfm file in your browser and test the links. When you link to the quiz_results.cfm file, it should look similar to Figure 2.4.

FIGURE 2.4
Your dynamic quiz results

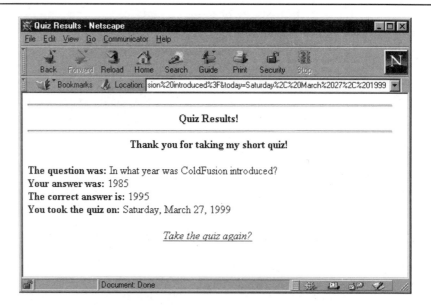

Your final template should look like Listing 2.6.

Listing 2.6

```
<!DOCTYPE HTML PUBLIC "-//W3C//DTD HTML 4.0 Transitional//EN">

<HTML>
<HEAD>
   <TITLE>My Home Page</TITLE>
</HEAD>

<BODY BGCOLOR="#FFFFFF">

<DIV ALIGN="center">
<HR><B>Welcome to My Home Page!</B><HR>

<B>Today's date is:</B><BR>
   <CFOUTPUT>
   <!---
   The following variable, 'today', displays the current date in the format:
Tuesday, September 15, 1998

   Now() returns the current timestamp (date & time)

   dddd = full day of week
   mmmm = full name of month
   d = day of month
   yyyy = year in four digits
   --->

   <CFSET today = DateFormat(Now(), "dddd, mmmm d, yyyy")>
   <I>#today#</I>
   </CFOUTPUT>
   </DIV>

   <!--- The following is code for my first quiz question --->
   <CFSET question1 = "In what year was ColdFusion introduced?">
   <CFSET correct_answer1 = 1995>

   <P><HR><B>Today's 1st question is:</B>
   <CFOUTPUT>
   <BR><I>#question1#</I>

   <OL>
   <LI><A HREF="quiz_results.cfm?user_answer=
#URLEncodedFormat(1985)#&correct_answer=#URLEncodedFormat(correct_answer1)#&question=
#URLEncodedFormat(question1)#&today=#URLEncodedFormat(today)#">1985</A>
   <LI><A HREF="quiz_results.cfm?user_answer=#URLEncodedFormat(1990)
#&correct_answer=#URLEncodedFormat(correct_answer1)#&question=#URLEncodedFormat(quest
ion1)#&today=#URLEncodedFormat(today)#">1990</A>
```

```
    <LI><A HREF="quiz_results.cfm?user_answer=#URLEncodedFormat(1995)
#&correct_answer=#URLEncodedFormat(correct_answer1)#&question=#URLEncodedFormat(quest
ion1)#&today=#URLEncodedFormat(today)#">1995</A>
    <LI><A HREF="quiz_results.cfm?user_answer=#URLEncodedFormat
(1998)#&correct_answer=#URLEncodedFormat(correct_answer1)#&question=#URLEncodedFormat
(question1)#&today=#URLEncodedFormat(today)#">1998</A>
    </OL>
    </CFOUTPUT>

    <!--- The following is code for my second quiz question --->
    <CFSET question2 = "Who developed the first version of ColdFusion?">
    <CFSET correct_answer2 = "J.J. Allaire">

    <P><B>Today's 2nd question is:</B>
    <CFOUTPUT>
    <BR><I>#question2#</I>

    <OL>
    <LI><A HREF="quiz_results.cfm?user_answer=#URLEncodedFormat('Kristin
Motlagh')#&correct_answer=#URLEncodedFormat(correct_answer2)#&question=#URLEncodedFor
mat(question2)#&today=#URLEncodedFormat(today)#">Kristin Motlagh</A>
    <LI><A HREF="quiz_results.cfm?user_answer=#URLEncodedFormat('J.J.
Allaire')#&correct_answer=#URLEncodedFormat(correct_answer2)#&question=#URLEncodedFor
mat(question2)#&today=#URLEncodedFormat(today)#">J.J. Allaire</A>
    <LI><A HREF="quiz_results.cfm?user_answer=#URLEncodedFormat('Arman
Danesh')#&correct_answer=#URLEncodedFormat(correct_answer2)#&question=#URLEncodedForm
at(question2)#&today=#URLEncodedFormat(today)#">Arman Danesh</A>
    <LI><A HREF="quiz_results.cfm?user_answer=#URLEncodedFormat('Gaio
Gonzalez')#&correct_answer=#URLEncodedFormat(correct_answer2)#&question=#URLEncodedFo
rmat(question2)#&today=#URLEncodedFormat(today)#">Gaio Gonzalez</A>
    </OL>
    </CFOUTPUT>

    </BODY>
    </HTML>
```

In this section, you have learned to pass multiple parameters through the URL. Some rules to remember when you pass parameters through the URL are:

- You must use a question mark (?) to separate your standard URL from the parameters you are passing.
- You must separate each passed parameter with an ampersand (&).
- You must always use URLEncodedFormat when passing parameters through the URL to avoid problems with illegal characters.
- You must always use pound signs (#) to surround variables included in a link.
- If you include variables in your link, you must surround the link with CFOUTPUT tags.

Evaluating Variables

At this point, you have been able to do quite a bit more with ColdFusion than you could do with basic HTML, but there is still much more that you can do. Although you have been able to provide minimal feedback to users in our quiz example, you haven't really been able to tell them how well they are doing. You haven't been able to *evaluate* the content of any variables. Being able to evaluate variables enables you to:

- Compare the value of one variable against another
- Execute a set of code based on the value of a variable or comparison of variables
- Account for nonexistent variables
- Control the flow and display of your template
- Abort the processing of a template based on the value of a variable

In this section, you will expand the quiz application to provide valuable feedback to the user about their quiz results, control what is displayed in the template based on the user's quiz results, and prevent errors by accounting for nonexistent variables.

Controlling the Display of Your Template Using *CFIF*

You will now use basic ColdFusion logic to evaluate the user's answers. If the user's answers are correct, then you will display a congratulatory statement. If they are incorrect, you will ask the user to try again. To create this interaction, you need to evaluate whether the user_answer variable is equal to the correct_answer variable. You can accomplish this by using CFIF statements.

NOTE   For more information on CFIF, please refer to the "CFIF" section in Chapter 7, "Controlling the Flow of Your Templates."

The CFIF statement has both a beginning and ending tag, and may also include the CFELSE and CFELSEIF tags. The format for using CFIF is as follows:

```
<CFIF some_expression evaluates to true>
Do this
<CFELSEIF some_other_expression evaluates to true>
Then do this
<CFELSE>
Or do this
</CFIF>
```

So, in your quiz_results.cfm file, you can evaluate whether the user's answer is the same as the correct answer by modifying your code as shown in Listing 2.7.

⟳ **Listing 2.7**

```
<!DOCTYPE HTML PUBLIC "-//W3C//DTD HTML 4.0 Transitional//EN">

<HTML>
<HEAD>
<TITLE>Quiz Results</TITLE>
</HEAD>

<BODY BGCOLOR="#FFFFFF">

<DIV ALIGN="center">
<HR><B>Quiz Results!</B><HR>
<B>Thank you for taking my short quiz!</B><P>
</DIV>

<CFIF user_answer IS correct_answer>
<B><FONT COLOR="#008000">Congratulations!!!
You are correct!</FONT></B><P>
<CFELSE>
<B><FONT COLOR="#FF0000">
I'm sorry, but that is the wrong answer.
Please try again.</FONT></B><P>
</CFIF>

<CFOUTPUT>
<B>The question was:</B> #question#<BR>
<CFIF user_answer IS NOT correct_answer>
<B>Your answer was:</B> #user_answer#<BR>

<CFELSE>

<B>The correct answer is:</B>
#correct_answer#<BR>
</CFIF>
<B>You took the quiz on:</B> #today#<P>
</CFOUTPUT>

<DIV ALIGN="center">
<I><A HREF="home.cfm">Take the quiz again?</A></I>
</DIV>

</BODY>
</HTML>
```

NOTE   Remember that you do not need to enclose variables in #'s unless you are going to display them to the user in a **CFOUTPUT** tag or other display tag.

Now reload your home.cfm file and take the quiz. When you select the correct answer, you should be congratulated. When you select the wrong answer, you should be asked to try again and the correct answer should be hidden from you (see Figure 2.5).

FIGURE 2.5
Evaluating user input

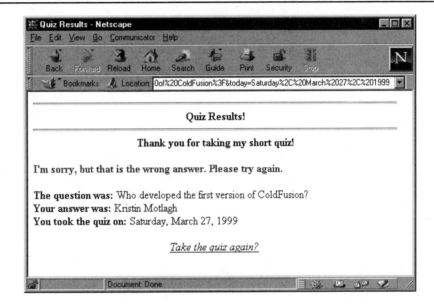

You did four things in this file to create this interaction:

1. Using **CFIF**, you evaluated whether **user_answer** was equal to **correct_answer**. If it evaluated to be **True**, then the next set of HTML and ColdFusion code was processed up until the CFELSE tag. The code following the CFELSE tag and up until the end /CFIF tag was ignored because it didn't evaluate to **True**. The opposite would be true if your initial **CFIF** statement evaluated to **False**.

2. You added color to increase the dramatic effect of correct or incorrect answers.

3. You displayed the **user_answer** variable only if the user had chosen the incorrect answer.

4. You displayed the **correct_answer** variable only if the user had chosen the correct answer. This way, a user who chooses the incorrect answer can still try again without seeing the correct answer first.

Accounting for Nonexistent Variables

Now that you are able to evaluate variables, you are also able to determine whether they exist. If a variable does not exist, but your template calls that variable, ColdFusion will produce an error. So far in the application, this has not been a problem. But this becomes a problem if someone decides to link to your quiz_results.cfm file directly without first going to the home.cfm file.

Try opening the URL http://127.0.0.1/sybex/quiz_results.cfm and you will see an error. The reason is that parameters have not been passed to the template through the URL. Even though it is unlikely that anyone will try to access this template directly, it is a possibility, and therefore you must account for it.

To account for nonexistent variables, you need to first evaluate whether the variables exist in the template. You can do this using CFIF and the ColdFusion function IsDefined.

> **NOTE**   For more information on IsDefined, please refer to the "IsDefined" section in Appendix C, "ColdFusion Function Reference".

The format used to evaluate if a variable exists is as follows:

```
<CFIF IsDefined("variable_name")>
```

The format used to evaluate if a variable does not exist is as follows:

```
<CFIF NOT IsDefined("variable_name")>
```

You can evaluate if multiple variables exist using the following syntax:

```
<CFIF NOT IsDefined("variable_name1") OR
NOT IsDefined("variable_name2") OR
NOT IsDefined("variable_name3")>
```

In the quiz, four variables are called in the quiz_results.cfm file. To evaluate if all four variables exist, add the code in Listing 2.8 to the quiz_results.cfm file immediately after the BODY tag.

Listing 2.8

```
<CFIF NOT IsDefined("user_answer") OR
NOT IsDefined("correct_answer") OR
NOT IsDefined("question") OR
NOT IsDefined("today")>
<DIV ALIGN="center">
<HR><B>Welcome!</B><HR>
<I><A HREF="home.cfm">Please take my quiz!</A></I>
</DIV>
<CFABORT>
</CFIF>
```

Now if you load `http://127.0.0.1/sybex/quiz_results.cfm`, you will see a link back to the main quiz page instead of an error (see Figure 2.6). The code you just added to the `quiz_results.cfm` template checks whether any of the four variables are missing. If even one is missing, the processing of the template is aborted. Whenever you want to abort the processing of a template, you can use the ColdFusion tag `CFABORT`.

NOTE   For more information on `CFABORT`, please refer to CFABORT in Appendix B, "ColdFusion Tag Reference.".

FIGURE 2.6
Accounting for non-existent variables

Passing Parameters through a Form

The quiz that you have created still has one major problem. You may already have noticed it: A user can view the `correct_answer` parameter in the browser's status bar when they pass their mouse over a link in the `home.cfm` file. They can also view all the parameters in the location bar of the browser when the `quiz_result.cfm` file is displayed. This is obviously a problem because giving the answers away defeats the purpose of taking a quiz. To solve this problem, you can convert your quiz to a form-based application. In a form, parameters are passed through a form submission, which does not appear in the URL location bar. Unfortunately, users can still view the correct answer by looking at the page's source code. In the next chapter you will learn how to prevent this.

So, for this example, you will use radio buttons and a submit button for each question to enable the user to take the quiz. This is a fairly simple example using your background HTML knowledge on forms. You can now modify your home.cfm file to convert each question to a separate form, as shown in Listing 2.9.

Listing 2.9

```
<!DOCTYPE HTML PUBLIC "-//W3C//DTD HTML 4.0 Transitional//EN">

<HTML>
<HEAD>
<TITLE>My Home Page</TITLE>
</HEAD>

<BODY BGCOLOR="#FFFFFF">

<DIV ALIGN="center">
<HR><B>Welcome to My Home Page!</B><HR>

<B>Today's date is:</B><BR>
<CFOUTPUT>
<!---
The following variable, 'today', displays the current date in the format: Tuesday,
September 15, 1998

Now() returns the current timestamp (date & time)

dddd = full day of week
mmmm = full name of month
d = day of month
yyyy = year in four digits
--->

<CFSET today = DateFormat(Now(), "dddd, mmmm d, yyyy")>
<I>#today#</I>
</CFOUTPUT>
</DIV>

<!--- The following is code for my first quiz question --->
<FORM ACTION="quiz_results.cfm" METHOD="post">

<CFSET question1 = "In what year was ColdFusion introduced?">
<CFSET correct_answer1 = 1995>

<P><HR><B>Today's 1st question is:</B>
<CFOUTPUT>
<BR><I>#question1#</I><P>
```

```
<INPUT TYPE="hidden" NAME="today" VALUE="#today#">
<INPUT TYPE="hidden" NAME="question" VALUE="#question1#">
<INPUT TYPE="hidden" NAME="correct_answer" VALUE="#correct_answer1#">

<INPUT TYPE="radio" NAME="user_answer" VALUE="1985"> 1985<BR>
<INPUT TYPE="radio" NAME="user_answer" VALUE="1990"> 1990<BR>
<INPUT TYPE="radio" NAME="user_answer" VALUE="1995"> 1995<BR>
<INPUT TYPE="radio" NAME="user_answer" VALUE="1998"> 1998<BR>
</CFOUTPUT>

<P><INPUT TYPE="Submit" VALUE="Score Question 1!">
</FORM>

<!--- The following is code for my second quiz question --->
<FORM ACTION="quiz_results.cfm" METHOD="post">

<CFSET question2 = "Who developed the first version of ColdFusion?">
<CFSET correct_answer2 = "J.J. Allaire">

<P><B>Today's 2nd question is:</B>
<CFOUTPUT>
<BR><I>#question2#</I><P>
<INPUT TYPE="hidden" NAME="today" VALUE="#today#">
<INPUT TYPE="hidden" NAME="question" VALUE="#question2#">
<INPUT TYPE="hidden" NAME="correct_answer" VALUE="# correct_answer2#">

<INPUT TYPE="radio" NAME="user_answer" VALUE="Kristin Motlagh"> Kristin Motlagh<BR>
<INPUT TYPE="radio" NAME="user_answer" VALUE="J.J. Allaire"> J.J. Allaire<BR>
<INPUT TYPE="radio" NAME="user_answer" VALUE="Arman Danesh"> Arman Danesh<BR>
<INPUT TYPE="radio" NAME="user_answer" VALUE="Gaio Gonzalez"> Gaio Gonzalez<BR>
</CFOUTPUT>

<P><INPUT TYPE="Submit" VALUE="Score Question 2!">
</FORM>

</BODY>
</HTML>
```

You just drastically changed your home.cfm file. In this new version, you are now passing all your parameters through form fields instead of through the URL. This also means that you no longer need to use the URLEncodedFormat function. The user_answer variable is now passed using radio buttons. The correct_answer, question, and today variables are each passed using hidden fields. In this example, you made each question its own form with its own submit button because you have not provided for the handling of multiple questions in the quiz_results.cfm file. Also, in the next chapter, you will be displaying only one randomly generated question pulled from a database, so there is no need to accommodate multiple questions now.

Test your quiz. Your home.cfm file should look like Figure 2.7, but your quiz_results .cfm file should look the same as it did before. If you had hard-coded the URL prefix to the variables in the quiz_results.cfm file, it would have produced an error now that you are using forms. When form parameters are processed by the ColdFusion server, they are assigned to variable names in the following format: form.variable_name. But, as with URL variables, you do not need to specify the prefix unless there is a conflicting variable name in the template. Therefore, ColdFusion is able to evaluate either form or URL variables in the same way.

FIGURE 2.7
Your new form-based quiz

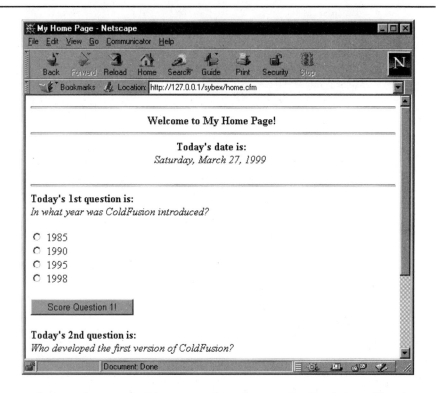

In the quiz, you have not accounted for a user choosing to submit a form without selecting a radio button. Normally, this would result in an error because all parameters would not be passed through the URL. But, because you added code to evaluate whether all variables exist in the quiz_results.cfm file, the user will not receive an error, just a pointer back to the quiz.

NOTE If you would like to learn more about form validation using ColdFusion, you can refer to Chapter 16, "Validating Form Data."

Where Do We Go from Here?

In this chapter, you created your first ColdFusion application. In creating this application, you learned the following techniques and concepts:

- Understanding the difference between parameters and variables
- Passing parameters through a URL
- Displaying parameters passed through a URL
- Using the URLEncodedFormat function to preserve URL integrity
- Evaluating variables with the CFIF tag construct
- Using the IsDefined function to evaluate the existence of a variable
- Aborting the processing of a template using CFABORT
- Passing parameters using regular HTML forms

In the next chapter, you will convert your quiz into a database-driven application that pulls all the quiz data from a database.

chapter 3

Getting Data from a Database

- Setting Up a Database

- Querying a Database

- Validating Form Input

The true power behind ColdFusion is its capability to access and manipulate database records. In this chapter, you will learn how to access a database using ColdFusion and basic Structured Query Language (SQL) to retrieve information from a database. You will be working with a Microsoft Access 97 database provided on the CD that comes with this book. It is not essential that you have Access 97 in order to continue, but it would be very useful.

Setting Up a Database

Before ColdFusion can interact with a database, you must set up a ColdFusion data source in the ColdFusion Administrator. You will have to set up a ColdFusion data source only once for each database you need to work with. A *data source* is essentially a pointer to the physical database. In a sense, it is the *source* path for the *data* you want to access. You will be working with the ColdFusion Administrator to set up the data source.

A Basic Access Database

You will use the `quiz.mdb` database for all the exercises in this chapter. It is a simple database with a table containing seven fields. If you have Access 97, you can open the database to view it. You can also see the database in Figure 3.1.

NOTE   You can also find the database on the CD provided with this book. The database is titled `quiz.mdb` and is in the `chapter3` folder. Please make sure that you save the database to the `sybex` folder in your Web server root directory.

FIGURE 3.1
`quiz.mdb` Access database

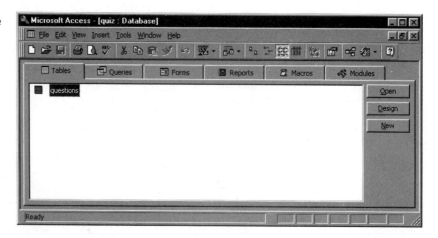

You will notice that the quiz database has a table called `questions`. This is where you will store all the data needed for the exercises during this chapter. If you are viewing the database in Access, double-click the table to open it; otherwise, look at Figure 3.2.

FIGURE 3.2
The table view in Access 97

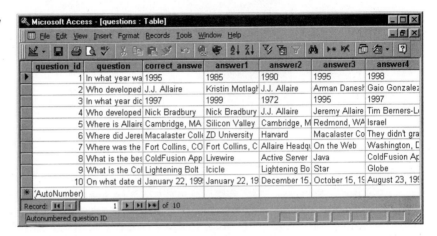

The `questions` table contains seven columns and ten rows. If you have never worked with databases, you will need a basic understanding of them before you continue. If you have worked with databases, please proceed to the section titled "Using the Administrator to Add a Data Source."

What Is a Database?

A database provides a way to store categories of information in an organized, easily accessible format. In Chapter 2, "Passing Data between ColdFusion Templates," you worked on a quiz that had the following categories of information:

- Question
- Correct Answer
- Answer 1
- Answer 2
- Answer 3
- Answer 4

If this information were stored in a database table, these categories would be called *fields* or *columns*. Each field would have its own properties (field size, default value, etc.) and would conform to a specific data type (numeric, text, etc.). In Figure 3.3, you can see that the first column of the `questions` table has been highlighted.

FIGURE 3.3

Columns, or fields, of a
database

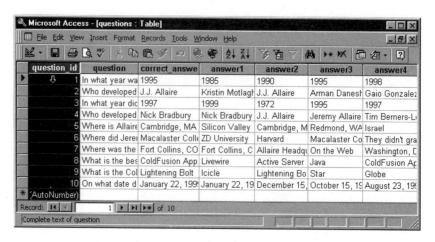

In this example, each question and all the information tied to it is called a *row* or a
record. Each question in this table has its own `correct_answer`, `answer1`, and so on. So
10 questions would constitute 10 rows, or records, in our quiz database. In Figure 3.4,
you can see that the second record has been highlighted.

FIGURE 3.4

Rows, or records, of a
database

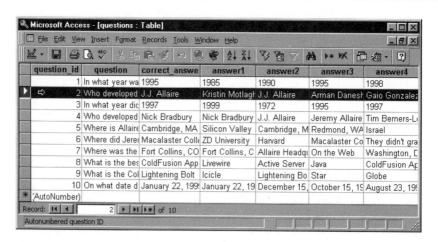

A field that you did not use in the previous chapter has been added to the `questions`
table. This field, `question_id`, is the *primary key* field (see Figure 3.3). A primary key is a
field (or combination of fields) that enables a record to be uniquely identified. Normally
a numeric value is used for the primary key. No single record in a table can have the
same primary key value as any other record. In this way you can easily distinguish,
search, and identify records. You will be using the primary key value later in this chapter to identify questions when you access the database.

Microsoft Access also enables you to view and modify the design of a table. Select View ➤ Design View, or look at Figure 3.5. This is where all the fields are defined. You will notice that the `question_id` field (the primary key) is an *autonumber* field. Autonumber means that each time a new question is added to this database table, the value for this `question_id` field is automatically generated by Access. In this way, Access ensures that no two values in this field are the same. You can also see the data types for the other fields.

FIGURE 3.5
The design view in Access 97

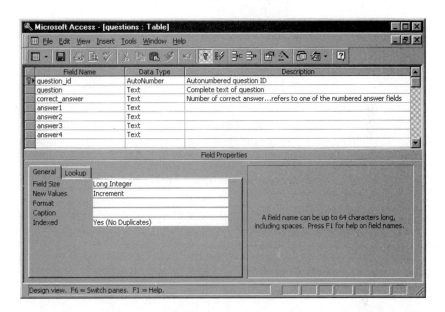

If you are using Access to view this table, please be careful about making any modifications at this time. Modifications to the table could affect the operation of the code you will write in the rest of the chapter. Of course, if you do make modifications and have difficulties, you can always copy a fresh version of the database to your hard drive from the accompanying CD.

This explanation of a database is a basic one and will hopefully get you started. You will learn more as you continue reading this book.

NOTE   If you would like to know more about working with databases, please refer to Appendix 4, "Creating Databases and Tables."

Using the Administrator to Add a Data Source

Now let's add the data source in the ColdFusion Administrator. The ColdFusion Administrator is a Web-based tool that you can access by opening the following URL in your browser:

```
http://127.0.0.1/CFIDE/administrator/index.cfm
```

You will be asked for the administrator password. This is the password that you specified during the installation of ColdFusion.

NOTE   If you have problems accessing the Administrator, please refer to "Troubleshooting Your Installation" in Appendix A.

When the administrator loads, please select the ODBC link under Data Sources on the left side (see Figure 3.6). This is the screen where you will add data sources for Open Database Connectivity (ODBC) databases. ODBC is a standard protocol used with many databases to allow for outside access (such as importing and exporting data). Microsoft Access is a database that has an ODBC driver.

First, you need to name your data source. It does not have to have the same name as the database file, although this sometimes helps in remembering what database you are referencing. In the Data Source Name field, type **quiz**. The default ODBC driver selected should be Microsoft Access Driver. If it is not, please select it. Then select Add (see Figure 3.6).

Now you are on the Create ODBC Data Source screen (see Figure 3.7). The data source name is already specified. You do not need to enter a description, but you may if you like. Now you need to specify the path where your quiz.mdb file is located. When you do this, ColdFusion will know where to go when accessing this database. Because the path will vary depending on your Web server root directory, select the Browse Server button.

FIGURE 3.6
The ColdFusion Administrator—ODBC Data Sources

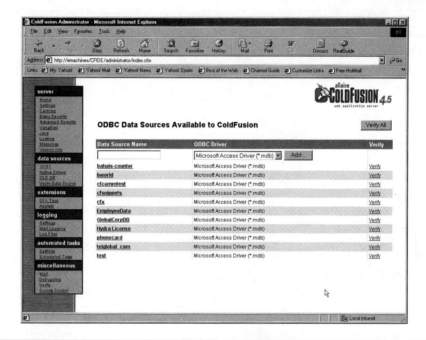

FIGURE 3.7
Creating a ColdFusion data source

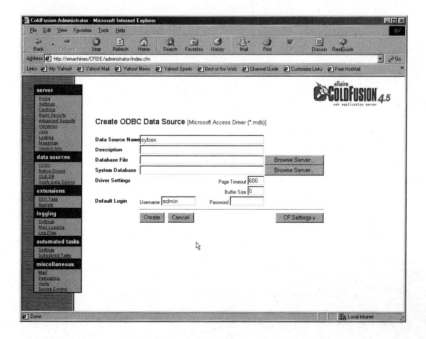

Browse your hard-drive directory structure to find the `quiz.mdb` file in the `sybex` folder of your Web server root directory. Then select OK (see Figure 3.8).

FIGURE 3.8

Finding a database

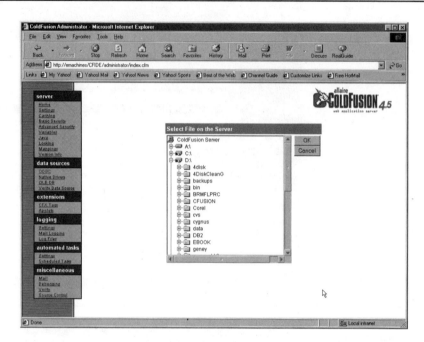

Finally, on the Create ODBC Data Source screen, select Create. You will then see the `quiz` data source listed, along with the example data sources provided by Allaire. To the far right of the screen, under the Verify column, the word *verified* should appear (see Figure 3.9). This means that the connection to the data source has been successfully established.

NOTE   If you have a problem with verifying your data source, please refer to the "Data Sources" section of Chapter 35, "ColdFusion Administration."

This is all you need to do to create a basic ODBC data source. The other available options for configuring your ODBC data source will not be discussed in this chapter. You are now ready to write ColdFusion code that will access your `quiz.mdb` database.

NOTE   If you would like to learn more about configuring Data Sources, please refer to Chapter 35.

FIGURE 3.9
A verified data source

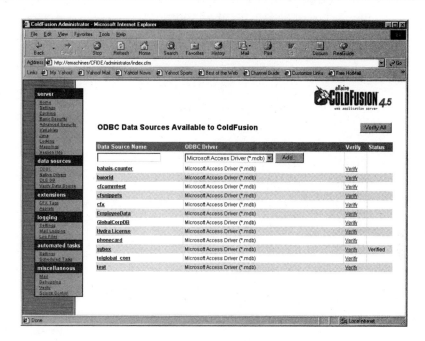

Querying a Database

Remember that in the preceding chapter you created a quiz with two questions. The user's answers as well as the correct answers were then passed through form fields. However, any user could look at the source of the home.cfm file and view the correct answers by looking at the hidden form fields. One way to solve that problem is to store all the quiz data in a database and retrieve it when needed, as opposed to passing it through URL or form parameters. In this way, the quiz information is not stored as code in your templates, which would make it accessible to the general public. The quiz.mdb file provided on the CD has all the pertinent quiz information stored for you (see Figure 3.2).

Now you just need to know how to access that information. ColdFusion makes it easy to retrieve information from a database using a basic CFQUERY tag and SQL. If you are unfamiliar with SQL, this chapter is a good place to start learning the basics. SQL is a language that is used to communicate a variety of commands to a database. Using SQL, you can do such things as retrieve data, update data, delete data, and append to existing data in a database.

Using *CFQUERY* and Basic SQL

In this section, you will use the CFQUERY tag and a basic SQL statement to retrieve all of the quiz information from the quiz database. You will no longer have to hard-code the quiz information in the template. A CFQUERY tag has both a beginning and ending tag. Between the two tags, you define your SQL statement. Look at the following example:

```
<CFQUERY NAME="myquery" DATASOURCE="name_of_datasource" DBTYPE="ODBC">
    SELECT field_name1, field_name2, field_name3
    FROM table_name
</CFQUERY>
```

Notice that the CFQUERY tag takes several attributes. The most commonly used attributes are described in Table 3.1.

TABLE 3.1:   *CFQUERY* Attributes

Attribute	Description	Required
NAME	You must give your query a name so that the results can later be referenced. The name can be anything you like as long as it begins with a letter. No spaces are allowed in the name.	Yes
DATASOURCE	This is the name of the data source that you would like to access. The data source should have already been set up in the ColdFusion Administrator.	Yes
DBTYPE	Here is where you specify the database driver that is being used. If you do not specify one, ColdFusion will assume that an ODBC driver is being used.	No

NOTE   If you would like to know more about other **CFQUERY** attributes, please see **CFQUERY** in Appendix B, "ColdFusion Tag Reference" or Chapter 10, "Using CFQUERY and SQL to Interact with the Database."

Now, look at the SQL query in the preceding example. This SQL query is a basic SELECT query, the most common type of query. It is used to retrieve data from a database. Although we will be using only a SELECT query in this chapter, you might find it useful to know what other types of queries are available. You will be using them in other parts of this book. The various query types are described in the following list:

SELECT   Used to search a database and retrieve information

DELETE   Used to delete records from a database

UPDATE   Used to change or modify information in a database

INSERT   Used to append additional records to a database

Now you can code the CFQUERY tag and SQL SELECT statement for your home.cfm file. The CFQUERY tag should look like the following:

```
<CFQUERY NAME="get_question" DATASOURCE="quiz" DBTYPE="ODBC">
```

When coding a SQL SELECT statement, you must first select the information that you would like to retrieve. First determine what information you need to display to the user. When the user views the home.cfm template, they should see each question with four possible answers. Your database table questions has the following field names that would give you this information:

- question
- answer1
- answer2
- answer3
- answer4

It is also useful to retrieve the question_id field because in the next section, you will be passing that information to the quiz_results.cfm template so that each question can be easily identified. Therefore, the first part of your SQL statement should look like this:

```
SELECT question_id, question, answer1, answer2, answer3, answer4
```

In a SELECT statement, you begin with the word *SELECT* and then follow it with the names of the fields that you wish to retrieve. The fields should be in a comma-delimited list.

WARNING   When creating your own table fields, remember that ColdFusion will not automatically resolve fieldnames with spaces

---

Now you need to tell the database which table to find the information in. The quiz database has only one table, but it is possible for a database to have many tables, so you need to specify the table to which you are referring. Because the information you need is in the questions table, your next SQL command should look like:

```
FROM questions
```

All together, your query will look like Listing 3.1.

TIP   You can find the following code on the CD provided with this book. This code is in a file titled home3a.cfm in the chapter3 folder of your CD. If you use the file on the CD, make sure that you save it to the sybex folder in your Web server root directory and that you rename it as home.cfm.

Listing 3.1: *home3a.cfm*

```
<CFQUERY NAME="get_question" DATASOURCE="quiz" DBTYPE="ODBC">
    SELECT question_id,
        question,
        answer1,
        answer2,
        answer3,
        answer4
    FROM questions
</CFQUERY>
```

The results that will be returned from this query are called a *recordset*. Add this code to the top of your home.cfm template.

You cannot test the results of your query yet because you have not added any code that would output the results into the home.cfm template. In the next section, you will learn how to output the results of your query.

Outputting Query Results

Now that you have queried the questions table, you need to output the results in your home.cfm file. You will do this using the CFOUTPUT tag. When outputting results from a query, the name of the query being referenced needs to be added to the CFOUTPUT tag by using the QUERY attribute. Your beginning CFOUTPUT tag should look like the following:

```
<CFOUTPUT QUERY="get_question">
```

The CFOUTPUT tag is then followed by HTML and CFML code. This code is used to display and format each record that is returned. ColdFusion processes this code for each record returned by the query. If the query produced 10 records, then the code inside the CFOUTPUT tag would be processed 10 times.

WARNING   Always remember to close your <CFOUTPUT> tag with </CFOUTPUT>.

When ColdFusion finishes processing all the records returned, it continues on to the rest of the code in your template.

In the preceding chapter, you hard-coded two questions in the home.cfm template. In this section, you need to provide CFML and HTML code for only one question. This code will be placed inside the CFOUTPUT tags for your get_question query. ColdFusion will then loop through this code and display as many questions as have been returned by your query. Modify your home.cfm file to reflect the changes in Listing 3.2.

TIP You can find the following code on the CD provided with this book. This code is in a file titled `home3b.cfm` in the **chapter3** folder of your CD. If you use the file on the CD, make sure that you save it to the **sybex** folder in your Web server root directory and that you rename it `home.cfm`.

TIP In the following code, all bold lines indicate where modifications have been made. You need to make changes to only these lines in your template. This applies throughout the book.

Listing 3.2: *home3b.cfm*

```
<!DOCTYPE HTML PUBLIC "-//W3C//DTD HTML 4.0 Transitional//EN">

<CFQUERY NAME="get_question" DATASOURCE="quiz" DBTYPE="ODBC">
    SELECT question_id,
        question,
        answer1,
        answer2,
        answer3,
        answer4
    FROM questions
</CFQUERY>

<HTML>
<HEAD>
    <TITLE>My Home Page</TITLE>
</HEAD>

<BODY BGCOLOR="#FFFFFF">

<DIV ALIGN="center">
    <HR><B>Welcome to My Home Page!</B><HR>

    <B>Today's date is:</B><BR>
    <CFOUTPUT>
        <!---
        The following variable, 'today', displays the current
date in the format: Tuesday, September 15, 1998

        Now() returns the current timestamp (date & time)

        dddd   = full day of week
        mmmm   = full name of month
        d    = day of month
        yyyy   = year in four digits
        --->
```

```
            <CFSET today = DateFormat(Now(), "dddd, mmmm d, yyyy")>
            <I>#today#</I>
        </CFOUTPUT>
    </DIV>

    <!--- The following is code that dynamically generates each quiz
    question --->
    <CFOUTPUT QUERY="get_question">
        <FORM ACTION="quiz_results.cfm" METHOD="post">
            <P><HR><B>Question ###currentrow# is:</B>
            <BR><I>#question#</I><P>
            <INPUT TYPE="hidden" NAME="today" VALUE="#today#">
            <INPUT TYPE="hidden" NAME="question_id"
    VALUE="#question_id#">

            <INPUT TYPE="radio" NAME="user_answer"
    VALUE="#answer1#"> #answer1#<BR>
            <INPUT TYPE="radio" NAME="user_answer"
    VALUE="#answer2#"> #answer2#<BR>
            <INPUT TYPE="radio" NAME="user_answer"
    VALUE="#answer3#"> #answer3#<BR>
            <INPUT TYPE="radio" NAME="user_answer"
    VALUE="#answer4#"> #answer4#<BR>

            <P><INPUT TYPE="Submit"
    VALUE="Score Question #currentrow#!">
        </FORM>
    </CFOUTPUT>

    </BODY>
    </HTML>
```

After you save your changes, you can view the results by opening the following URL:

```
http://127.0.0.1/sybex/home.cfm
```

NOTE   If you receive an error, make sure that your data source is set up properly in the ColdFusion Administrator. Also make sure that all your code is correct. For more help, please refer to the "Using the Administrator" section of this chapter or to Chapter 35.

You will notice that all 10 questions and their corresponding answers from the database table questions have been displayed. Imagine how much code you would have had to write if you hard-coded all 10 questions yourself!

You also made several other significant changes:

- By using the system variable currentrow, you were able to number all the questions returned. The variable currentrow is a system variable generated by ColdFusion for each record of a particular query. It is used to keep track of which record count ColdFusion is currently processing. It is not related to the primary key field in your database.

- Instead of hard-coding the answers for each question, you were able to dynamically generate them by outputting the answer fields from the query results.
- You passed the question_id field as a hidden field to the next template. In the next template, you can use it to query the database and compare the user's answer to the correct answer.

Now that you have created a dynamically generated quiz in your home.cfm template, you must also slightly modify your quiz_results.cfm template to accommodate these changes.

Retrieving a Limited Recordset

In the last section, you learned how to retrieve all records from a database using a CFQUERY tag and SQL. What if you want to retrieve only one record? Then you must limit the recordset returned by your query. You will do that in this section by adding a WHERE clause to your SQL statement. This WHERE clause will help to narrow the recordset returned by your query by making the results conditional upon some statement.

You previously coded the home.cfm template so that it would pass the following parameters to the quiz_results.cfm template:

today   The date that the quiz was taken.

question_id   The ID for the question that the user responded to.

user_answer   The answer chosen by the user for the above question_id.

This is one less parameter than you passed in the preceding chapter. You are no longer passing the correct_answer parameter because you can now pull that from the database. In the quiz_results.cfm template, you will now retrieve only the information related to the question that the user chose to answer, instead of retrieving all possible information from the database. This is where the question_id comes into play.

To pull only the data related to one record from the database, you need to add a WHERE clause to your SQL statement. The basic format is written as the following:

```
<CFQUERY NAME="myquery" DATASOURCE="name_of_datasource" DBTYPE="ODBC">
    SELECT field_name1,
        field_name2,
        field_name3
    FROM table_name
    WHERE field_name1 = "some_value"
</CFQUERY>
```

In your quiz_results.cfm template, you will need to get the following fields from the database:

question   You need to display the question chosen by the user, but because you did not pass this value through a form parameter, you need to get it from the database.

correct_answer   After the correct answer is returned from the database, you can compare it to the answer chosen by the user to see whether it was correct.

When you code your SQL statement, you want to retrieve only the record that contains the question chosen by the user. The chosen record can be identified by using the **question_id** parameter that you passed through a hidden form field. Because **question_id** is a ColdFusion variable, you need to surround it with # signs, and it will be evaluated when ColdFusion processes the query.

TIP   You do not need to use a CFOUTPUT tag inside a CFQUERY tag.

Your entire query should look like this:

```
<CFQUERY NAME="get_answer" DATASOURCE="quiz" DBTYPE="ODBC">
    SELECT question, correct_answer
    FROM questions
    WHERE question_id = #question_id#
</CFQUERY>
```

TIP   question_id does not need to be surrounded by quotes because it is a number data type. If it were a text string, your WHERE clause would look like WHERE question_id = "#question_id#". For more information on data types, please refer to Chapter 6, "Writing Expressions."

The results of this query will be limited to all records that have the field **question_id** equal to the ColdFusion variable **question_id**. For example, if the user chose a question with the **question_id** of 4, when ColdFusion processes the query, the WHERE clause that is sent to the database will be WHERE **question_id = 4.**

In your template, you will also need to output the results of this query. You have already written the code to compare the **user_answer** to the **correct_answer**, so very little modification to this file is necessary. Please make the changes indicated in Listing 3.3 to your **quiz_results.cfm** template.

TIP   You can find the following code on the CD-ROM provided with this book. This code is in a file entitled **quiz_results3a.cfm** in the **chapter3** folder of your CD-ROM. If you use the file on the CD-ROM, make sure that you save it to the **sybex** folder in your Web server root directory and that you rename it **quiz_results.cfm**.

Listing 3.3: *quiz_results3a.cfm*

```
<!DOCTYPE HTML PUBLIC "-//W3C//DTD HTML 4.0 Transitional//EN">

<HTML>
```

```
<HEAD>
    <TITLE>Quiz Results</TITLE>
</HEAD>

<BODY BGCOLOR="#FFFFFF">

<CFIF NOT ISDEFINED("Form.user_answer") OR
      NOT ISDEFINED("Form.question_id") OR
      NOT ISDEFINED("Form.today")>
    <DIV ALIGN="center">
        <HR><B>Welcome!</B><HR>
        <I><A HREF="home.cfm">Please take my quiz!</A></I>
    </DIV>
    <CFABORT>
</CFIF>

<CFQUERY NAME="get_answer" DATASOURCE="quiz" DBTYPE="ODBC">
    SELECT question, correct_answer
    FROM questions
    WHERE question_id = #Form.question_id#
</CFQUERY>

<DIV ALIGN="center">
    <HR><B>Quiz Results!</B><HR>
    <B>Thank you for taking my short quiz!</B><P>
</DIV>

<CFOUTPUT QUERY="get_answer">
    <CFIF Form.user_answer IS correct_answer>
        <B><FONT COLOR="##008000">Congratulations!!!
        You are correct!</FONT></B><P>
    <CFELSE>
        <B><FONT COLOR="##FF0000">
        I'm sorry, but that is the wrong answer.
        Please try again.</FONT></B><P>
    </CFIF>

    <B>The question was:</B> #question#<BR>
    <CFIF Form.user_answer IS NOT correct_answer>
        <B>Your answer was:</B> #Form.user_answer#<BR>
<CFELSE>
        <B>The correct answer is:</B> #correct_answer#<BR>
    </CFIF>
    <B>You took the quiz on:</B> #Form.today#<P>
</CFOUTPUT>

<DIV ALIGN="center">
    <I><A HREF="home.cfm">Take the quiz again?</A></I>
</DIV>

</BODY>
</HTML>
```

WARNING	When used as text inside of a **CFOUTPUT** tag, # signs must be escaped, or ColdFusion will produce an error. To escape a # sign in your text, just add another # sign in front of it.

Test your file by reloading the home.cfm template, and then take the quiz (see Figure 3.10).

FIGURE 3.10
Quiz results

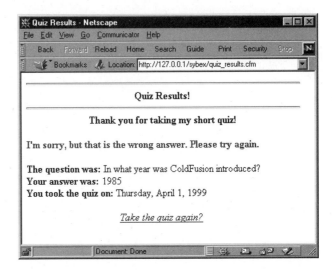

You will notice that not much seems to have changed, on the surface. But in reality, you have made the following significant changes in the way your quiz application works:

- You are no longer passing the correct answer through a hidden form field or the URL, so the user cannot cheat on the quiz.
- You are pulling all your quiz information from the database.
- You have reduced the amount of code needed to create the application.
- You can add as many questions to the database table as you wish, yet you do not need to make changes to your ColdFusion templates for your application to work.

You have learned the basics of querying a database table by using the **CFQUERY** tag and SQL. In the next sections, you will add some more functionality to your quiz application by learning to do the following:

- Display a randomly generated question
- Create SQL statements based on user input

Generating Random Results

Currently, your quiz application retrieves and displays all questions entered in the database. If you had 50 questions, all 50 would be displayed to the user on the home.cfm template. In this section, you will learn how to display one randomly generated question from all the questions available in the database.

In the preceding section, you learned how to limit the recordset returned in the quiz_results.cfm template by using the WHERE clause. In this section, you will also limit the recordset returned in the home.cfm template—but this time the record returned will be randomly generated.

First, you need to add a WHERE clause to the query in your home.cfm template. The format should be as follows:

```
WHERE question_id = randomly_generated_number
```

So how do you go about getting a randomly generated number? ColdFusion has a function that lets you generate random numbers. It is called the RandRange function. The RandRange function takes two values:

```
RandRange(number1, number2)
```

The randomly generated number will fall between the two values entered for number1 and number2. So, if number1 is 10 and number2 is 300, then the randomly generated number would have to fall somewhere between 10 and 300. In this example, the number returned could not be 8.

For the quiz application you will generate a random question_id. If you look at the questions table, you will notice that the question_id values fall between 1 and 10. You could code the WHERE clause by incorporating these numbers:

```
WHERE question_id = #RandRange(1, 10)#
```

This would work, unless you added another question to the questions table or deleted one from it (in which case the query will not return any data when question_id is 10). Any new questions you add to the table will be excluded because their question_id values would be higher than 10 (the limit you placed on the randomly generated number).

So, to accommodate the possibility of any number of questions in the table, you need to first find out how many records are in the table at any given time. To do this, you can query the database for a total count and then use that count in your existing query. This means you will have two queries in your home.cfm template.

In the new query, you will use a SQL function called **Count** to get the count. The **Count** function takes one value: the field that you want to be counted. You must then give this count a name so that ColdFusion can reference the results:

```
<CFQUERY NAME="get_count" DATASOURCE="quiz" DBTYPE="ODBC">
    SELECT count(question_id) as total_questions
    FROM questions
</CFQUERY>
```

This query returns only one value: the count of the `question_id` field. Because the `question_id` field is the primary key field, it can never be blank. So, the count of this field will always be equal to the count of records in the database. The **as** keyword places the value retrieved by the database in a variable named `total_questions` so that subsequently, the value can be referred to as `get_count.total_questions`.

Now that you have the count of records in the table, you can go back to your original query and generate a random `question_id` value like the following:

```
<CFQUERY NAME="get_question" DATASOURCE="quiz" DBTYPE="ODBC">
    SELECT question_id,
        question,
        answer1,
        answer2,
        answer3,
        answer4
    FROM questions
    WHERE question_id = #RandRange(1, get_count.total_questions)#
</CFQUERY>
```

You will notice that the total count has been referenced as `get_count.total_questions` in the RandRange function. When referencing data in a query from another query, you should always precede the variable with the name of the referenced query. In this case, `get_count` is the name of the query that returned the `total_questions` variable. Make the changes indicated in Listing 3.4 to your `home.cfm` template.

TIP   You can find the following code on the CD-ROM provided with this book. This code is in a file titled `home3c.cfm` in the **chapter3** folder of your CD-ROM. If you use the file on the CD-ROM, make sure that you save it to the **sybex** folder in your Web server root directory and that you rename it `home.cfm`.

Listing 3.4: *home3c.cfm*

```
<!DOCTYPE HTML PUBLIC "-//W3C//DTD HTML 4.0 Transitional//EN">
```

```
<CFQUERY NAME="get_count" DATASOURCE="quiz" DBTYPE="ODBC">
    SELECT count(question_id) as total_questions
    FROM questions
</CFQUERY>

<CFQUERY NAME="get_question" DATASOURCE="quiz" DBTYPE="ODBC">
    SELECT question_id,
        question,
        answer1,
        answer2,
        answer3,
        answer4
    FROM questions
    WHERE question_id = #RandRange(1, get_count.total_questions)#
</CFQUERY>

<HTML>
<HEAD>
    <TITLE>My Home Page</TITLE>
</HEAD>

<BODY BGCOLOR="#FFFFFF">

<DIV ALIGN="center">
    <HR><B>Welcome to My Home Page!</B><HR>

    <B>Today's date is:</B><BR>
    <CFOUTPUT>
        <!---
        The following variable, 'today', displays the current
date in the format: Tuesday, September 15, 1998

        Now() returns the current timestamp (date & time)

        dddd    = full day of week
        mmmm    = full name of month
        d    = day of month
        yyyy    = year in four digits
        --->
        <CFSET today = DateFormat(Now(), "dddd, mmmm d, yyyy")>
        <I>#today#</I>
    </CFOUTPUT>
</DIV>

<!--- The following is code that dynamically generates each quiz question --->
<CFOUTPUT QUERY="get_question">
    <FORM ACTION="quiz_results.cfm" METHOD="post">
        <P><HR><B>Your Question is:</B>
```

```
        <BR><I>#question#</I><P>
        <INPUT TYPE="hidden" NAME="today" VALUE="#today#">
        <INPUT TYPE="hidden" NAME="question_id"
VALUE="#question_id#">

        <INPUT TYPE="radio" NAME="user_answer"
VALUE="#answer1#"> #answer1#<BR>
        <INPUT TYPE="radio" NAME="user_answer"
VALUE="#answer2#"> #answer2#<BR>
        <INPUT TYPE="radio" NAME="user_answer"
VALUE="#answer3#"> #answer3#<BR>
        <INPUT TYPE="radio" NAME="user_answer"
VALUE="#answer4#"> #answer4#<BR>

        <P><INPUT TYPE="Submit" VALUE="Score Question!">
        <INPUT TYPE="Button" VALUE="Get New Question!"
        ONCLICK="location.href='home.cfm'">
    </FORM>
</CFOUTPUT>

</BODY>
</HTML>
```

Now view the changes in your browser (see Figure 3.11). If you receive an error, please make sure that your code matches the preceding code.

FIGURE 3.11

A randomly generated quiz question

Here's a look at what you did:

1. Determined how many records existed in the questions table.

2. Modified your query to return a random record.

3. Removed the references to the currentrow (because only one record is returned).

4. Added a form button using JavaScript in order to refresh the page and get a new quiz question. (This is needed just in case a user gets two of the same quiz questions in a row.)

Creating Dynamic SQL

In this section, you will add functionality to your quiz application that will enable the user to retake a quiz question if they gave the incorrect response. Here is the process that will occur:

1. A user goes to the home.cfm page and answers a quiz question.

2. On the quiz_results.cfm page, they are informed that their answer was incorrect.

3. A link is provided back to the same quiz question that they just answered so they can try again.

4. The process starts again until the user gets the correct answer.

You have already finished the tasks required for steps 1 and 2 to be completed. Step 3 requires that you add a link in the quiz_results.cfm template back to the home.cfm template. This link would pass the question_id parameter. Then in step 4, you need to modify the home.cfm template to determine if a new question should be displayed, or if the question that was answered incorrectly needs to be displayed.

Step 3 is easy. You just need to modify the "Please try again" text in your quiz_results.cfm template. Add the link in Listing 3.5 around this text.

TIP　You can find the following code on the CD-ROM provided with this book. This code is in a file titled quiz_results3b.cfm in the chapter3 folder of your CD-ROM. If you use the file on the CD-ROM, make sure that you save it to the sybex folder in your Web server root directory and that you rename it quiz_results.cfm.

Listing 3.5: *quiz_results3b.cfm*

```
<A HREF="home.cfm?question_id=#question_id#">Please try again.</A>
```

This link will pass the current `question_id` back to the `home.cfm` template.

The link will not retrieve the same question until you modify your `home.cfm` template. In `home.cfm` you need to determine if the `question_id` is being passed to it. Remember that in Chapter 2 you used the `IsDefined` function to determine whether a variable existed. You will now use the `IsDefined` function in the `home.cfm` template to determine whether the `question_id` has been passed to it. Modify your `home.cfm` file to reflect the changes indicated in Listing 3.6.

TIP

You can find the following code on the CD provided with this book. This code is in a file titled `home3d.cfm` in the **chapter3** folder of your CD. If you use the file on the CD, make sure that you save it to the **sybex** folder in your Web server root directory and that you rename it `home.cfm`.

Listing 3.6: *home3d.cfm*

```
<!DOCTYPE HTML PUBLIC "-//W3C//DTD HTML 4.0 Transitional//EN">

<CFIF NOT ISDEFINED("question_id")>
   <CFQUERY NAME="get_count" DATASOURCE="quiz" DBTYPE="ODBC">
      SELECT count(question_id) as total_questions
      FROM questions
   </CFQUERY>
</CFIF>

<CFQUERY NAME="get_question" DATASOURCE="quiz" DBTYPE="ODBC">
   SELECT question_id,
      question,
      answer1,
      answer2,
      answer3,
      answer4
   FROM questions
   WHERE question_id =
   <CFIF ISDEFINED("question_id")>#question_id#
   <CFELSE>#RandRange(1, get_count.total_questions)#
   </CFIF>
</CFQUERY>

<HTML>
<HEAD>
   <TITLE>My Home Page</TITLE>
</HEAD>

<BODY BGCOLOR="#FFFFFF">
```

```
<DIV ALIGN="center">
   <HR><B>Welcome to My Home Page!</B><HR>

   <B>Today's date is:</B><BR>
   <CFOUTPUT>
      <!---
      The following variable, 'today', displays the current
date in the format: Tuesday, September 15, 1998

      Now() returns the current timestamp (date & time)

      dddd   = full day of week
      mmmm   = full name of month
      d   = day of month
      yyyy   = year in four digits
      --->
      <CFSET today = DateFormat(Now(), "dddd, mmmm d, yyyy")>
      <I>#today#</I>
   </CFOUTPUT>
</DIV>

<!--- The following is code that dynamically generates each quiz
question --->
<CFOUTPUT QUERY="get_question">
   <FORM ACTION="quiz_results.cfm" METHOD="post">
      <P><HR><B>Your Question is:</B>
      <BR><I>#question#</I><P>
      <INPUT TYPE="hidden" NAME="today" VALUE="#today#">
      <INPUT TYPE="hidden" NAME="question_id"
VALUE="#question_id#">

      <INPUT TYPE="radio" NAME="user_answer"
VALUE="#answer1#"> #answer1#<BR>
      <INPUT TYPE="radio" NAME="user_answer"
VALUE="#answer2#"> #answer2#<BR>
      <INPUT TYPE="radio" NAME="user_answer"
VALUE="#answer3#"> #answer3#<BR>
      <INPUT TYPE="radio" NAME="user_answer"
VALUE="#answer4#"> #answer4#<BR>

      <P><INPUT TYPE="Submit" VALUE="Score Question!">
      <INPUT TYPE="Button" VALUE="Get New Question!"
      ONCLICK="location.href='home.cfm'">
   </FORM>
</CFOUTPUT>

</BODY>
</HTML>
```

First, you told ColdFusion that if the `question_id` variable does not exist, to run the `get_count` query. If the `question_id` variable exists, you would not need to run this query because you are not trying to retrieve a random question. You want ColdFusion to display the same question that the user answered incorrectly.

Then, in your second query, you told ColdFusion that if the `question_id` variable exists, only that particular `question_id` should be returned. The `WHERE` clause sent to the database would look like the following:

```
WHERE question_id = #question_id#
```

Otherwise, ColdFusion should get a randomly generated question.

The code you just used is called *dynamic SQL*. It is dynamic because the `WHERE` clause will vary depending on whether the conditions specified in your `CFIF` statement are met.

WARNING   It is important to note that the SQL syntax you have used in this chapter conforms to the Microsoft Access version of SQL. Other database types may use different variations of SQL.

Validating Form Input

In this final section of the chapter, you will add one last piece of code to your `home.cfm` template. This code will determine whether the user has selected a radio button. If the user wants to score their quiz, they must select one of the answer radio buttons. Otherwise, they will be redirected to start the quiz over. ColdFusion offers a simple way to validate that a form field has been selected. All you need to do is add an additional hidden form field. This hidden form field has the following format:

```
<INPUT TYPE="hidden" NAME="field_name_required" VALUE="Message to the user">
```

The form field that you want to be required is the `user_answer` form field. Using the preceding format, you would then code your hidden form field as follows:

```
<INPUT TYPE="hidden" NAME="user_answer_required" VALUE="Please select an answer!">
```

When ColdFusion processes this template, it will make sure that the `user_answer` field has been selected. If it hasn't, ColdFusion will return the message you entered in the `VALUE` attribute and prompt the user to go back and try again. Your final `home.cfm` template should reflect the changes indicated in Listing 3.7. After you have made your changes, review the results in your browser.

TIP

You can find the following code on the CD-ROM provided with this book. This code is in a file titled **home3e.cfm** in the **chapter3** folder of your CD-ROM. If you use the file on the CD-ROM, make sure that you save it to the **sybex** folder in your Web server root directory and that you rename it **home.cfm**.

Listing 3.7: *home3e.cfm*

```
<!DOCTYPE HTML PUBLIC "-//W3C//DTD HTML 4.0 Transitional//EN">

<CFIF NOT ISDEFINED("question_id")>
    <CFQUERY NAME="get_count" DATASOURCE="quiz" DBTYPE="ODBC">
        SELECT count(question_id) as total_questions
        FROM questions
    </CFQUERY>
</CFIF>

<CFQUERY NAME="get_question" DATASOURCE="quiz" DBTYPE="ODBC">
    SELECT question_id,
        question,
        answer1,
        answer2,
        answer3,
        answer4
    FROM questions
    WHERE question_id =
    <CFIF ISDEFINED("question_id")>#question_id#
    <CFELSE>#RandRange(1, get_count.total_questions)#
    </CFIF>
</CFQUERY>

<HTML>
<HEAD>
    <TITLE>My Home Page</TITLE>
</HEAD>

<BODY BGCOLOR="#FFFFFF">

<DIV ALIGN="center">
    <HR><B>Welcome to My Home Page!</B><HR>

    <B>Today's date is:</B><BR>
    <CFOUTPUT>
        <!---
        The following variable, 'today', displays the current
date in the format: Tuesday, September 15, 1998

        now() returns the current timestamp (date & time)
```

```
    dddd    = full day of week
    mmmm    = full name of month
    d   = day of month
    yyyy    = year in four digits
    --->
    <CFSET today = DateFormat(Now(), "dddd, mmmm d, yyyy")>
    <I>#today#</I>
  </CFOUTPUT>
</DIV>

<!--- The following is code that dynamically generates each quiz
question --->
<CFOUTPUT QUERY="get_question">
  <FORM ACTION="quiz_results.cfm" METHOD="post">
    <P><HR><B>Your Question is:</B>
    <BR><I>#question#</I><P>
    <INPUT TYPE="hidden" NAME="today" VALUE="#today#">
    <INPUT TYPE="hidden" NAME="question_id"
VALUE="#question_id#">

    <INPUT TYPE="radio" NAME="user_answer"
VALUE="#answer1#"> #answer1#<BR>
    <INPUT TYPE="radio" NAME="user_answer"
VALUE="#answer2#"> #answer2#<BR>
    <INPUT TYPE="radio" NAME="user_answer"
VALUE="#answer3#"> #answer3#<BR>
    <INPUT TYPE="radio" NAME="user_answer"
VALUE="#answer4#"> #answer4#<BR>

    <INPUT TYPE="hidden" NAME="user_answer_required"
    VALUE="Please select an answer!">

    <P><INPUT TYPE="Submit" VALUE="Score Question!">
    <INPUT TYPE="Button" VALUE="Get New Question!"
    ONCLICK="location.href='home.cfm'">
  </FORM>
</CFOUTPUT>

</BODY>
</HTML>
```

NOTE
For more information on form validation using ColdFusion, please refer to Chapter 16, "Validating Form Data."

Where Do We Go from Here?

You've accomplished quite a bit in this chapter. You've created your own database-driven Web application. You're now able to access a database using ColdFusion, and if you've never worked with databases or SQL, that is quite a step. You've also used some intermediate features of ColdFusion, such as generating random numbers and creating dynamic SQL. At this point, you could start coding your own basic applications for deployment over the Web. As you have also probably realized by now, Cold-Fusion is an easy language to work with, and creating Web applications with ColdFusion isn't all that difficult.

You should realize, though, that these first three chapters of the book are just the tip of the iceberg. The rest of the material in the book will be much more in depth.

The Essentials

Learn to:

- Create and manipulate variables

- Use ColdFusion functions

- Write expressions

- Control the flow of your templates

- Include outside code

- Use SQL to interact with a database

- Build dynamic queries

- Group, nest, and format outputs

- Use loops

- Work with ColdFusion data structures

chapter 4

Creating and Manipulating Variables

■ Understanding Data Types

■ Using Variable Types

■ Using CFSET

■ Using CGI Variables

■ Using URL Variables

■ Using Cookies

■ Using CFPARAM and Default Variables

Variables are the core of any programming environment. Without variables, it is impossible to abstractly refer to values by name, and it is impossible to develop logical processes that achieve specific goals.

Without variables, the value of programming of any sort, whether it is ColdFusion-style Web scripting or full-scale development of operating systems, is greatly diluted.

In this chapter, you will take a broad look at the variables used in ColdFusion. You will start by considering the types of data that can be processed in ColdFusion and then move on to an overview of the types of variables available—including user-created variables and system-created variables such as CGI, URL, and cookie variables.

In addition, you will look at two useful tags for creating variables: CFSET and CFPARAM.

Understanding Data Types

Variables act as containers for holding data that can then be referred to by name. This allows the development of programs that act in different ways based on the content of those variables and allows the creation of highly readable program code because instead of raw values, the program uses names that clarify the purpose of the data being manipulated.

To make variables useful, it is necessary to perform actions on the data in the variables. These actions can be everything from comparing two variables, to adding two variables, to concatenating two variables.

To understand these operations, which you will encounter throughout the book, you need to understand the various types of data that variables can contain.

In ColdFusion, the following basic data types exist:

- Numbers
- Strings
- Boolean values
- Date/time values
- Binary objects

In addition, several more sophisticated types are available:

- Lists
- Structures
- Arrays
- Queries
- Component Object Model (COM) objects

These more complex data types are considered elsewhere in the book. Specifically, lists, structures, and arrays are discussed in Chapter 14, "Working with ColdFusion Data Structures," and COM objects are explained in Chapter 32, "Including External Objects." Queries are discussed throughout the book, including in Chapter 3, "Getting Data from a Database," Chapter 10, "Using SQL to Interact with the Database," and Chapter 11, "Building Dynamic Using Advanced Query Techniques."

The basic data types are outlined in more detail in Chapter 6, "Writing Expressions." Most of this chapter can be read without a detailed understanding of data types. However, if you want to learn more about data types before proceeding with this chapter, review the relevant sections in Chapter 6.

Using Variable Types

ColdFusion is different from many programming environments in that it has many types of variables. These types differ from each other in terms of their sources and how they are created. There are also differences in how the variables are referenced. Nonetheless, all of these types of variables are fundamentally used in the same way: They can be used in the same expressions, they can be used to create dynamic output, and they can be used as the basis of dynamic queries.

The following list outlines the types of variables found in ColdFusion:

Local   Variables created with the CFSET tag or CFPARAM tag in a template

URL   Variables reflecting parameters appended to a URL

CGI   Variables reflecting the CGI environment variables of the context of the requested template

Cookie   Variables reflecting cookies passed to the template by the requesting browser

Query   Variables reflecting the results of a query

Form   Variables reflecting the values of the fields in a form submitted to the current template

Client   Variables used to associate data with a specific client

Server   Variables used to associate data with a specific Web server

Session   Variables used to associate data with a given client session

Application   Variables used to associate data with a specific ColdFusion application

Client, server, session, and application variables are discussed in more detail in Chapter 17, "Implementing the ColdFusion Web Application Framework." Form variables are considered in detail in Chapter 15, "Forms," and query variables are considered throughout the book as we work with different types of queries (they are first discussed in Chapter 3).

In this chapter, you will look at local, URL, CGI, and cookie variables in detail.

Using *CFSET*

The CFSET tag is the basic mechanism for creating local variables in a template. Using this tag, you can create a new variable and assign a simple value to it or to the result of a complex expression.

For instance, suppose you are developing a mathematical application that will use the value of pi throughout the application. Rather than repeatedly using the number 3.1415 (an approximation of pi) throughout the template, you can simply create a variable called PI to hold the value, and then reference that variable throughout your template. You do this with the following tag:

```
<CFSET PI = 3.1415>
```

This simple example highlights the basic structure of the CFSET tag:

```
<CFSET Variable_name = Expression>
```

The expression can be anything from a simple value such as 3.1415 to another variable to a compound expression including values, variables, and operators.

The CFSET tag is not only used in the creation of new variables. It also can be used to assign new values to a variable. For instance, if, after creating your PI variable, you want to change it to a less accurate value, such as 3.14, you simply use another CFSET tag:

```
<CFSET PI = 3.14>
```

To better understand this, consider the following segment of code:

```
<CFSET PI = 3.1415>
<CFOUTPUT>#PI#</CFOUTPUT>
<BR>
<CFSET PI=3.14>
<CFOUTPUT>#PI#</CFOUTPUT>
```

This code produces the following output:

```
3.1415
3.14
```

After you used the second CFSET tag, the value of the PI variable was changed for all subsequent lines of the template.

When assigning values to a variable, you can also use expressions. For instance, if you want to calculate the circumference of a circle with a diameter of 10, you could use the following tag:

```
<CFSET Area = PI * 10>
```

Notice the use of the PI variable to the right of the CFSET tag (in the expression).

An interesting feature of the CFSET tag is the capability to dynamically specify the variable name. As an example, consider a situation in which the name of the desired variable is stored in a variable itself. Then, say you want to assign a value to the specified variable. This situation works something like this:

```
<CFSET DesiredVariable = "PI">
<CFSET "#DesiredVariable#" = 3.1415>
```

Notice the use of "#DesiredVariable#" on the left side of the second CFSET tag to create a variable called PI, the value of DesiredVariable.

When creating your own variables using CFSET, there are some limitations to the names of the variables you create:

- Names should begin with a letter.
- Names can include numbers, letters, or the underscore character (but cannot begin with a number). All other characters are invalid in variable names. These invalid characters include spaces, dashes, and punctuation, such as dots and commas.
- Names are not case sensitive. For instance, TestName, testname, and TESTNAME all refer to the same variable.
- Names should not be the same as reserved words in ColdFusion. Reserved words include function names and operators from expressions. Functions are discussed in Chapter 5, "Functions," and expressions are discussed in Chapter 6.

Using CGI Variables

CGI variables are created every time a template is requested and returned to a browser. These are a fallback to CGI-BIN programming, which was the first mechanism for server-side scripting and automation on the World Wide Web.

NOTE   *CGI* stands for Common Gateway Interface. CGI-BIN is a standard mechanism for creating server-side applications on Web servers. CGI-BIN is, perhaps, the most commonly available mechanism for server-side programming.

Most Web servers, including those supported by ColdFusion, provide support for CGI-BIN scripts. In the world of CGI-BIN programming, Web servers create a set of standard variables that are available for use in CGI-BIN scripts. ColdFusion creates CGI variables that are available in your templates just as they would be available in CGI-BIN scripts.

These CGI variables provide information about the type of server being used, the type of browser being used to request the template, and other relevant information about the environment in which the template is being processed. The following list outlines the available CGI variables created by the server:

SERVER_SOFTWARE   The name and version of the Web server software on which Cold-Fusion is running. This takes the form name/version.

SERVER_NAME   The host name, DNS name, or IP address of the Web server.

GATEWAY_INTERFACE   The version of CGI implemented by the Web server. This value takes the form CGI/revision.

SERVER_PROTCOL   The protocol and version used to request the template. This takes the form protocol/version.

SERVER_PORT   The TCP/IP port on which the request for the template is received. On Web servers, this is generally port 80.

REQUEST_METHOD   The method used to request the template. With Web servers, this is usually Get, Post, or possibly Head.

PATH_INFO   Extra path information provided by the client.

PATH_TRANSLATED   A translated version of the PATH_INFO variable, converting virtual to physical paths.

SCRIPT_NAME   The virtual path to the requested template.

QUERY_STRING   Any query data following the question mark in the URL being used to access the template.

REMOTE_HOST   The host name of the client system requesting the template. If this information is unavailable, then the variable is not set.

REMOTE_ADDR   The IP address of the client system requesting the template.

AUTH_TYPE   The type of authentication used to validate a user if the requested template is protected.

REMOTE_USER   The username of the client user accessing a protected template (also available as AUTH_USER).

REMOTE_IDENT   The remote username retrieved from servers that support RFC 931 identification. (RFC documents are known as *request for comments* documents. These represent early definitions of proposed standards that are not yet finalized and approved by the relevant standards bodies.)

CONTENT_TYPE   The content type of attached data for requests that allow attached data (such as HTTP `Put` and `Post` requests).

CONTENT_LENGTH   The length in characters of content provided by the client.

In addition to the variables created by the server, several variables are created by the browser and passed to the server along with the request. These are outlined in the following list:

HTTP_REFERER   The URL of the document from which a link or form submission led to the requested template.

HTTP_USER_AGENT   The browser being used by the client. This takes the form `software/version library/version`.

HTTP_IF_MODIFIED_SINCE   This variable is used to support browser caching of documents. It indicates to the server the date of the version of a document in the cache so the server will only send newer documents to the browser.

NOTE   Because not all variables are supported with every combination of server and browser, ColdFusion will set unavailable variables to the empty string.

To access CGI variables, simply add `CGI.` to the front of any variable name outlined in the preceding two lists. For instance, the following template displays the page a user came from and the browser they are using:

```
<CFOUTPUT>
    <H1>Welcome</H1>
    <CFIF CGI.HTTP_REFERER is not "">
        You followed a link from #CGI.HTTP_REFERER#.
    </CFIF>
    You are using #CGI.HTTP_USER_AGENT#.
</CFOUTPUT>
```

This produces results like those in Figure 4.1.

Notice the use of the CFIF tag. You will learn about the CFIF tag in Chapter 7, "Controlling the Flow of Your Templates." In this example, you are testing whether HTTP_REFERER is the empty string. You do this because this variable is set only when the user follows a link to the current template or submits a form to the current template. Otherwise, the variable will be the empty string, and you want to output the first sentence only when the variable has a value.

NOTE   CGI variables are read-only; that is, you cannot assign values to them using CFSET.

FIGURE 4.1
Using CGI variables

TIP

From version 4.5 of ColdFusion, CGI variables are actually a standard ColdFusion structure and can be manipulated like any other structure as outlined in Chapter 14, "Working with ColdFusion Data Structures."

Using URL Variables

If you have done any amount of Web browsing, you have probably encountered long URLs with long strings of parameters following a question mark in the following form:

```
http://server/path/document?param1=value1&param2=value2&param3=value3
...
```

These URLs are built out of a basic URL (`http://server/path/document`) and a series of parameters of the form `parameter=value`. Each parameter is separated from the next by an ampersand (&), and the series of parameters is separated from the first part of the URL containing the server, path, and document by a question mark (?).

URL parameters are extremely powerful because they allow the passing of information between pages in a site through their links. This is not a browser-dependent feature (as are other techniques for passing information between pages, such as cookies, which you will look at next). For this reason, many sites rely on URL parameters as the primary mechanism for moving data between pages of a site.

The need to use URL parameters to move data between pages arises from a fundamental feature of the World Wide Web and its protocol, Hypertext Transfer Protocol (HTTP). HTTP is a stateless protocol. This means it is centered around requests: A client requests a particular URL, the resulting data is sent to the client, and the transaction is finished.

The stateless nature of HTTP means that when the user clicks a link in the page that was just sent, an entirely new request is initiated that the server has no way to associate with the previously fulfilled page. The use of URL parameters provides one means to pass information between pages and allows server-side programming environments such as ColdFusion to use the information in building the pages that are returned to the user.

Accessing these URL parameters in your templates is surprisingly easy: Simply add URL. to the front of the parameter name you want to reference. For instance, suppose you have a link to a template called url.cfm, like this:

```
<A HREF="url.cfm?Info=Information">
```

In the url.cfm template, the following code:

```
<CFOUTPUT>#URL.Info# was received</CFOUTPUT>
```

would result in the following line of output:

```
Information was received.
```

Given this capability to easily pass information along from page to page in a site, ColdFusion can be used to easily build dynamic links containing parameters. For instance, in url.cfm, you could use the following code to pass the received information along to another page:

```
<CFOUTPUT><A HREF="url2.cfm?Info=#URL.Info#"></CFOUTPUT>
```

As would be expected, the resulting output is written as follows:

```
<A HREF="url2.cfm?Info=Information">
```

NOTE   From version 4.5 of ColdFusion, URL variables are actually a standard ColdFusion structure and can be manipulated like any other structure, as outlined in Chapter 14, "Working with ColdFusion Data Structures".

Limitations of URL Parameters

For all their utility, URL parameters do have limitations. These limitations are imposed by restrictions on what is allowed in a valid URL. These restrictions include the inability to use several characters, including spaces.

This limitation is addressed by something known as *URL encoding*. URL encoding involves translating any special characters in a URL such as spaces and equal signs into two-digit hexadecimal (base 16) codes of the form %XX, where *XX* is the two-digit number.

NOTE   Hexadecimal (base 16) numbers can include the following digits: 0, 1, 2, 3, 4, 5, 6, 7, 8, 9, A, B, C, D, E, F.

Of course, it would be possible to manually translate the values of your URL parameters to URL-encoded format, but this would be difficult and time-consuming. Instead, ColdFusion provides the URLEncodedFormat function to perform the conversion for you. This function takes a single string argument. It returns the strings in URL-encoded format.

By way of example, the following code outputs the string This is a test in URL-encoded format:

```
<CFOUTPUT>#URLEncodedFormat("This is a test")#</CFOUTPUT>
```

The results look like those in Figure 4.2.

FIGURE 4.2
A URL-encoded string

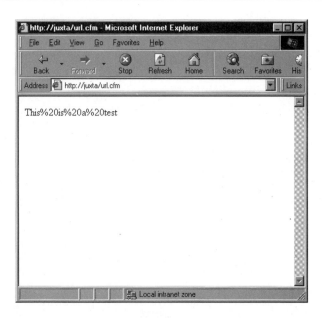

Given this, you can build your dynamic URLs with URL-encoded parameters. In the earlier example, where you built a dynamic URL with the following:

```
<CFOUTPUT><A HREF="url2.cfm?Info=#URL.Info#"></CFOUTPUT>
```

you can add `URLEncodedFormat` so that regardless of the value of the `Info` URL parameter, you can be sure that the resulting URL is valid:

```
<CFOUTPUT><A HREF="url2.cfm?Info=#URLEncodedFormat(URL.Info)#"></CFOUTPUT>
```

Using Cookies

The final type of variable that we will discuss in this chapter is the *cookie variable*. These variables reflect the HTTP cookies passed from the browser to the server along with the request for a template.

These HTTP cookies have nothing to do with their edible namesakes. Rather, they are information stored by the server in a client browser for future use.

Here's how a cookie works:

1. The client requests a template.

2. When the template returns the page, it includes commands in the header to store one or more cookies indicating which documents the template is related to and the life span of the cookies.

3. In the future, when the client requests a template for which a cookie has been set (and which hasn't expired), the cookie is sent to the server along with a request for the template.

4. The server makes the cookie available to ColdFusion for use while processing the requested template.

This means that there are two aspects to the use of cookies: setting cookies and referencing existing cookies.

NOTE   From version 4.5 of ColdFusion, cookie variables are actually a standard ColdFusion structure and can be manipulated like any other structure as outlined in Chapter 14, "Working with ColdFusion Data Structures".

Setting Cookies

The CFCOOKIE tag is used to create cookies on the browser. Before looking at the details of cookies and how to create them, consider a few of the following limitations:

- Not all browsers support cookies. Current versions of Netscape Communicator and Navigator and Microsoft Internet Explorer do, but earlier versions that are still in use don't, and other browsers still don't offer cookie support. This limits their usefulness (as compared with URL parameters) for passing information from page to page within a site in a browser-independent manner.
- There are limits on the number of cookies that can be set. A server can set only 20 cookies in a client browser with newer cookies replacing older ones as this limit is crossed. This means that if you have many applications on your server that set cookies, it is quite possible that cookies set by one application will be overwritten by another application.
- Cookies have a length limit of 4,096 characters (4KB). This length includes the value, name, and additional information, such as the expiration date. Effectively, this means the actual value stored in the cookie needs to be less than 4KB in length.

Keeping these limits in mind, we will now discuss the process of cookie creation. When creating cookies, several pieces of information can or must be provided. These are outlined in the following list:

Cookie name   This is required when creating a cookie. All cookies must have a name.

Cookie value   The value to be assigned to the cookie can be specified at the time of creation. This is optional; however, an empty cookie can be created.

Expiration date   Cookies have a life span that can be indicated at the time of creation by an expiry date. You do not have to specify an expiration date, and if you choose not to, then the cookie will expire once the client browser is closed.

Security status   It is possible to indicate that a cookie must be transmitted over Secure Sockets Layer (SSL)–encrypted Web connections.

Path   Cookies can either be related to all documents in a given Web site or can be associated with specific documents in a site.

Domain name   Cookies are associated with specific Internet domains, and the domain name ensures that cookie data is sent only to the correct servers.

These pieces of a cookie definition are translated directly into attributes of the CFCOOKIE tag. The CFCOOKIE tag takes six possible attributes:

NAME   Required attribute specifying the name of the cookie.

VALUE   Optional attribute setting a value for the cookie.

EXPIRES   Optional attribute specifying the expiration of the cookie. This can be specified as a date (such as 1/2/99), a number of days (such as 53), or as one of two keywords: NOW or NEVER. If you set the expiration to NOW for an existing cookie, you can effectively delete an existing cookie.

SECURE   Optional attribute indicating whether the cookie requires a secure connection for transmission. Possible values are YES and NO.

PATH   Optional attribute specifying a subset of documents on a server to which the cookie is associated. These are specified as paths relative to the root directory of the Web server (such as /some/path). Multiple paths can be indicated, separated by semicolons.

DOMAIN   Optional attribute specifying the domain to which the cookie can be sent. Explicit domains (such as cnn.com) should be preceded by a period (dot); for example, .cnn.com. Specific hosts are specified without the leading dot, as in www.cnn.com.

To fully understand how this works, consider the following series of CFCOOKIE tags:

```
<CFCOOKIE NAME="Cookie1" VALUE="Value1">
<CFCOOKIE NAME="Cookie2" VALUE="Value2" EXPIRES="53">
<CFCOOKIE NAME="Cookie3" VALUE="Value3" EXPIRES="22" PATH="/some/other/path">
```

So, what does this all mean? We will discuss them in the following list:

- Cookie1 will be sent with all requests for documents from the Web site that set the cookie until the user closes the browser that the cookie was originally set in.
- Cookie2 will be sent with all requests for documents from the Web site that set the cookie for 53 days from the time that it is created.
- Cookie3 will be sent with all requests for documents on the two specified paths from the Web site that set the cookie for 22 days from the time that it was created. Assuming the site that set the cookie is www.some.site, then requesting http://www.some.site/some/where.html or http://www.some.site/other/path/document.html will cause the cookie to be sent to the server, but requesting http://www.some.site/ or http://www.some.site/somewhere/else.html won't cause the cookie to be sent to the server.

Referencing Existing Cookies

Now that you know how to set cookies, you must consider how to access those variables in templates. After all, the whole point of setting cookies is to use them when the browser returns them with a request for a template. Otherwise, they serve no real purpose.

As you might expect at this point, accessing variables can be done by adding COOKIE. to the beginning of the name of the cookie. Therefore, the preceding examples can be accessed as COOKIE.Cookie1, COOKIE.Cookie2, and COOKIE.Cookie3.

CFPARAM and Default Variables

The CFPARAM tag provides a way to test whether a given variable exists and, if not, to create it and assign it a default variable. This is a useful capability.

Consider a simple example: You have created a template that may or may not be accessed with a URL parameter called Info. If the parameter exists, then it will be used in the processing of the template. If not, a default value will be used.

One way to achieve this is through the following approach:

```
<CFIF IsDefined("URL.Info)>
    <CFSET URL.Info = "Default">
</CFIF>
```

What you have done here is use the ParameterExists function to test whether URL.Info exists. If it does, the Boolean value True is returned; otherwise, False is returned. You use this function in a CFIF tag, as discussed in Chapter 7, so that if the parameter doesn't exist, you can assign a default value to the variable URL.Info.

However, this requires the use of two tags (CFIF and CFSET) and a function (ParameterExists). The same result can be achieved with the CFPARAM tag, which wraps the entire procedure into a single tag. The CFPARAM tag takes the following form:

```
<CFPARAM NAME="variable name" DEFAULT="default value">
```

Here, the value specified by the NAME attribute is the name of the variable to check, and the value of the DEFAULT attribute is the value to be assigned to the variable if it doesn't exist and needs to be created. This means that your previous three lines of code become one, to look like the following:

```
<CFPARAM NAME="URL.Info" DEFAULT="Default">
```

Where Do We Go from Here?

In this chapter, you have learned about variables. Variables are essential to the development of powerful, efficient, and easy-to-understand templates.

Having mastered creating and referencing variables, you are now in a position to use them in several ways, including as parameters to functions, as the building blocks for expressions, and as the data used to control the flow of code in your templates.

In the next chapter, you will look at functions. Common to many programming languages, functions provide a way to isolate programming code into a virtual black box which, given data as input, performs an expected action and returns the results as output.

ColdFusion offers developers a rich array of built-in functions that you will consider in the next chapter; you will also learn the mechanics of using functions in your templates.

chapter 5

Functions

■ Understanding Functions

■ Using Functions

■ Reviewing the Use of Functions in ColdFusion

Now that you know how to use variables in your ColdFusion templates, you need to consider how to leverage them in different ways, including using functions and by leveraging the power of expressions.

In this chapter, you will focus on the latter: functions. Functions are common to many programming languages and provide a way to isolate programming code into a virtual black box that, given data as input, performs an expected action and returns the results as output. In the ColdFusion context, a large number of built-in functions that provide a broad range of functionality are available to developers.

You will take a quick look at exactly which functions and how to use them in ColdFusion and then at the major groups of functions available in ColdFusion.

Understanding Functions

Functions have long been part of the vocabulary of most development environments. Functions offer a way to encapsulate a set of program code that performs a specific function on input data and provides the result as output. The function can then be assigned a name and simply referred to by that name. In effect, they are named procedures that perform a distinct purpose.

Therefore, instead of rewriting the same program code each time the particular task needs to be performed, a programmer can simply refer to the function by name and need not be concerned with the specifics of how the function performs the requested task.

Let's consider an example: taking the cube of a number. Written in plain mathematical notation, you could write:

```
number x number x number
```

Which could be used each time you want to perform the cube of a number. Alternately, you could encapsulate this detail into a function called Cube and simply call it:

```
Cube(number)
```

Of course, this doesn't seem to be a big benefit. After all, using the first option in your templates doesn't make them notably more complex than the latter. However, what if you wanted to compute an arbitrary power of a number (such as 3 to the power of 8, or 9 to the power of 7)? You can write program code to do this each time you need to, but that requires several lines of code, and the purpose of the code is not apparent at a glance while reading the template code.

Instead, the several lines needed to calculate an arbitrary power could be placed in the function Power, and 3 to the power of 8 could then be executed with:

```
Power(3,8)
```

This is far more suggestive of its purpose than several lines of obscure code.

Many programming environments offer built-in functions as well as providing the developer the ability to create their own functions. This is not the case with ColdFusion. Instead, ColdFusion offers a rich library of built-in functions covering almost every aspect of working with data in ColdFusion. The very nature of ColdFusion really precludes the need for developers to create their own functions. Instead, this ability can be achieved through the use of custom tags (see Chapter 29, "Building ColdFusion Custom Tags"). Although custom tags are not identical to functions, the same results can be achieved with both.

Using Functions

Using ColdFusion functions in your templates is not a complicated process. There are two simple aspects of functions to understand: how to provide information to functions and how to use the results.

Functions generally need input data to perform their work. This input is commonly known as parameters or *arguments*. As you will see by looking through the functions in Appendix C, "ColdFusion Function Reference," functions are defined to take these parameters in a specified order.

In ColdFusion, the syntax of passing arguments to functions is:

```
FunctionName(Argument1,Argument2,…)
```

Therefore, in our preceding Power example, the Power function takes two arguments (the base and the exponent):

```
Power(Base,Exponent)
```

All functions return a single value. This value can be of any data type (a number, a string, or even a more complex data type such as an array, which is discussed in Chapter 14, "Working with ColdFusion Data Structures").

Basically, the function call itself can be used where the data type returned can be used. For instance, our example Power function returns a number value, so it can be used wherever a number can be used:

- In a variable assignment: `<CFSET Result = Power(3,8)>`
- In an expression (see Chapter 6, "Writing Expressions"): `2 + Power(3,8)`
- As an argument to another function: `Cube(Power(3,8))`
- In dynamic output: `<CFOUTPUT>#Power(3,8)#</CFOUTPUT>`

Of course, functions aren't that useful if you can pass only literal values to them as parameters. What makes them more useful is that variables, expressions, and other functions can be passed as arguments.

Consider the following example:

```
<CFSET Base=3>
<CFSET Exponent=8>
<CFOUTPUT>#Power(Base,Exponent)#</CFOUTPUT>
```

Here, you use two variables as arguments to the function. This is a powerful ability because the data for the variables can be set anywhere in the template prior to the function call. You can even use variables derived from external information such as query results, form submissions, or URL parameters.

It is also useful to be able to pass an expression to a function. For instance, the following example uses an expression to add two variables and pass them as an argument to the function:

```
<CFSET Base=3>
<CFSET Exponent1=6>
<CFSET Exponent2=2>
<CFOUTPUT>#Power(Base,Exponent1+Exponent2)#</CFOUTPUT>
```

Effectively, this function call is the same as `Power(3,8)`.

Reviewing the Use of Functions in ColdFusion

So far, in this chapter, we have used our example `Power` function to illustrate the concepts behind functions and how to use them. However, `Power` is a function created for the purposes of this chapter. While `Power` is not a genuine ColdFusion function, Cold-Fusion does offer many functions for a variety of purposes, including the following:

- Manipulating arrays
- Working with dates and times
- Making decisions
- Formatting output
- Manipulating lists
- Working with structures
- Performing mathematical calculations
- Manipulating strings

Manipulating Arrays

Arrays are complex data structures available in ColdFusion. A large number of functions are available for working with ColdFusion arrays. We discuss arrays and the functions for manipulating them in depth in Chapter 14, "Working with ColdFusion Data Structures."

Working with Dates and Times

ColdFusion offers a variety of functions for manipulating dates and times. These include functions for creating date objects; for outputting specific information about a date, including the day of the week, the name of the month and a user-friendly format for the date; as well as for adding or subtracting time from a date.

The date functions are outlined in Appendix C.

Making Decisions

ColdFusion offers several functions that make it easy to determine, among other things, the data type of a value. For instance, it is possible to test if a value is an array, Boolean value, date, numeric value, query, or simple value. You can also use decision functions to check whether a given year is a leap year and to determine whether a user is authenticated and authorized.

The decision functions are outlined in Appendix C.

Formatting Output

With all these data types, it is useful to be able to easily format different types of data for attractive, user-friendly output. Several functions assist developers in outputting consistently formatted numbers (for instance, as currency values), to output dates in a variety of styles, and to handle outputting of HTML text in different ways.

The formatting functions are covered in Chapter 12, "Grouping, Nesting, and Formatting Output."

Manipulating Lists

Lists are complex data structures available in ColdFusion. A large number of functions are available for working with ColdFusion lists. We discuss lists in depth in Chapter 14.

Working with Structures

A *structure* is another complex data structure available in ColdFusion. A large number of functions are available for working with ColdFusion structures. We discuss structures and their related functions in depth in Chapter 14.

Performing Mathematical Calculations

As you will see in the next chapter, expressions offer the ability to perform all the basic mathematical calculations such as addition, multiplication, and division.

However, with this small vocabulary, much advanced math becomes quite difficult. To address this, ColdFusion has a wide range of mathematical functions to perform advanced calculations, including the following:

- Absolute values
- Bit-level operations
- Trigonometric calculations
- Logarithmic functions
- Rounding
- Squares

The mathematical functions are outlined in Appendix B.

Manipulating Strings

ColdFusion offers many functions for performing a range of tasks on string values, including the following:

- Comparison
- Searching
- Replacing
- Inserting characters
- Removing characters
- Justifying
- Changing case

The string functions are outlined in Appendix B.

Where Do We Go from Here?

Now that you know how to work with variables and functions, you are ready to learn how to use a fundamental building block of programming languages such as ColdFusion *expressions*.

Expressions enable you to perform complex calculations, make decisions, and generally work with data in useful ways. In the next chapter, you will look at the types of expressions available in ColdFusion, including numeric, string, and Boolean expressions; you will learn the intricacies of using the pound sign (#) in expressions; and you will look at how to use literal values, variables, and functions within your expressions.

chapter 6

Writing Expressions

- Understanding Expressions

- Using ColdFusion Data Types

- Using Operators

- Using Pound Signs Properly

- Considering Special Features of ColdFusion Expressions

Now that you have learned to use variables and functions, you will turn to a powerful tool for leveraging them: expressions.

Expressions provide a way to perform operations on one or more pieces of data. These can range from simple operations, such as addition and subtraction, to more complex operations, such as comparison and type conversion.

In this chapter, you will start with a quick overview of expressions and then consider the types of operators available for building expressions in ColdFusion. Next you will look at some of the issues surrounding the use of pound signs and quotation marks in ColdFusion expressions.

After you have a grasp of the structure of these basic building blocks of expressions, you will review the data types available in ColdFusion. These data types include string, numeric, and Boolean data, and all have different roles.

Finally, you will look at some interesting features of expressions in ColdFusion, including order of precedence rules and typeless expression evaluation.

Understanding Expressions

Expressions provide a way to build simple and complex operations to be performed on data. Expressions are built out of two essential components: data and operators.

The data used in expressions can come from many sources, including the following:

- Literal values (such as `98` or `"Hello"`)
- Variables referred to by name
- The results of a function call (such as `Exp(10)`)

Operators provide the glue that brings together multiple pieces of data, performing actions on them and providing the capabilities that make expressions useful. You will review the available ColdFusion operators in detail, but first let's discuss expressions in general a bit more.

An important aspect of an expression is that it returns a single value. By taking the data and operators that make up the expression, ColdFusion distills the logic down to a final value. As an example, consider the simple mathematical expression `1 + 1`. Here you have two pieces of data (1 and 1) plus an operator (+). This expression, as we all know, evaluates to 2.

This is an important aspect of expressions. Because they evaluate to a single value, they can effectively be used wherever a literal, variable, or other value is used in ColdFusion. For instance, you could use this expression as a parameter to a function (`Exp(1+1)`), or in a CFOUTPUT block (`<CFOUTPUT>#val(1+1)#</CFOUTPUT>`). In all cases, it is the final, evaluated value of the expression that is used as an argument to a function, or displayed to the user, or applied wherever the expression is used.

In its simplest form, an expression is a single value such as a literal (for example, 32), a variable name, or a function call (for example, Exp(32)). At the next level of complexity, expressions combine two values using a single operator:

```
Value Operator Value
```

Taking things even further, an expression can be built out of other expressions combined with an operator:

```
Expression Operator Expression
```

Expressions are differentiated by the type of data they return. Before getting into the details of operators and how they are used to build expressions, you need to consider the data types available in ColdFusion.

Using ColdFusion Data Types

ColdFusion has several data types, including the following:

- Numbers
- Strings
- Boolean values
- Date/time values
- Lists
- Arrays
- Structures
- Queries
- Component Object Model (COM) objects

Numbers, strings, Boolean values, and date/time values make up the core set of simple data types available in ColdFusion, and we will discuss them in this chapter. Lists, arrays, and structures are complex data types built from these simple data types. We discuss these three types in Chapter 14, "Working with ColdFusion Data Structures."

Similarly, queries are a complex data type that you will encounter throughout this book. However, the best place to learn about queries is in Chapter 10, "Using CFQUERY and SQL to Interact with the Database." Finally, COM objects are data types derived from working with external objects, a subject discussed in Chapter 32, "Including External Objects."

Numbers

Numeric data in ColdFusion is much simpler than in many other programming environments. Some development languages distinguish between integer and floating-point, or real, numbers. This distinction is not significant in ColdFusion. In ColdFusion, numbers can be integers or floating-point numbers and are essentially used interchangeably wherever numbers are called for in your templates.

Integers are numbers with no decimal portion. That is, they are whole numbers, such as 3, 76, and –5, with no fraction component after the decimal point. *Real* numbers, on the other hand, include a decimal component, such as -1.35 and 3.1415.

Valid numbers in ColdFusion range from -10^{300} to 10^{300}. A valid number such as 10^{300} is the same as a 1 with 300 zeros following it. Although ColdFusion supports these surprisingly small and large numbers, this does not mean it has unlimited accuracy.

When computers deal with floating-point numbers, they must deal in approximations. The level of accuracy of an environment refers to the number of digits after the decimal point that can be considered accurate. In ColdFusion, accuracy is up to 12 places after the decimal point. In practical terms, this means that if you add two numbers with 15 digits after the decimal point, only the first 12 digits after the decimal point in the result can be confidently considered accurate.

A nice feature of ColdFusion is that it supports scientific notation in indicating numbers. Scientific notation is commonly used in mathematics, engineering, and other sciences to indicate very large or very small numbers.

In traditional form, scientific notation takes the form X x 10Y, where *X* is a real number between 1.0 and 10 (but not including 10) and *Y* is an integer. In the formula shown here, the lowercase x represents multiplication.

What this means is that 250,000 could be written as 2.5 x 100,000 or, in full scientific notation, 2.5 x 105.

In ColdFusion, scientific notation is written somewhat differently than its traditional mathematical form, but the meaning is exactly the same. The ColdFusion form is XEY. Therefore, 250,000 becomes 2.5E5.

Strings

String data consists of any arbitrary series of characters (letters, numbers, punctuation, spaces, or other visible ASCII characters) surrounded by single or double quotes. Examples of strings include:

- "Hello"
- 'This is a test'
- "12345"

This last string is interesting because it looks like a number. But the quotation marks around it make it a string. Strings work somewhat differently than numbers: There are different operators for working with strings as well as different functions and different roles.

An important issue to consider when working with strings is: How do you include a quotation mark inside a string?

Well, it is not as complicated as it seems. If you enclose your string in double quotes, then you can include single quotes in your string. Therefore, the following string is valid: `"What's up?"`. Similarly, enclosing your string in single quotes allows double quotes to be used in the string, making this string valid: `'He said: "What?"'`.

But, what if you want to include a double quote inside a string enclosed with double quotes or a single quote inside one enclosed with single quotes? To do this you must use a special technique called *escaping*. This tells ColdFusion not to use the character for its special meaning (such as treating a double quote as the end of a string), but rather to include the value in the current data as if it were any other character.

In ColdFusion, characters are escaped by repeating them. Therefore, you can include single quotes in a string enclosed with single quotes by repeating the single quotes: `'What''s up?'`. You can do the same with double quotes: `"He said: ""What?"""`.

Another character requiring escaping inside strings is the pound sign. Because of its special meaning in ColdFusion, pound signs in strings must also be escaped: `"He is wearing ##3."`.

Boolean Values

Boolean values are used to express data that has an either-or state. Any value that can either be true or false is a Boolean value. Boolean data can take two possible values: `True` or `False`. These two Boolean values can also be expressed as numbers or strings, as shown in Table 6.1.

TABLE 6.1: Boolean Values

Boolean Form	Number Form	String Form
True	1	`"Yes"`
False	0	`"No"`

Date/Time Values

Date/time values are used to represent any date and time combination from A.D. 100 to A.D. 9999 (which makes ColdFusion Year 2000–compliant).

Internally, ColdFusion represents date/time values as special objects, which, if displayed to users, appear in a less than ideal form, such as:

```
{ts '1999-03-04 08:41:26'}
```

ColdFusion provides a range of functions (discussed in Appendix C, "ColdFusion Function Reference") for creating, manipulating, and displaying dates.

In addition, when a date/time value is needed in an expression or as an argument to a function, it can be expressed as a string in one of the following forms:

- `"March 21, 1999"`
- `"Mar 21, 1999"`
- `"Mar. 21, 1999"`
- `"03/21/99"`
- `"1999-21-03"`

Without times specified in a date/time value, the time is set to 12:00 A.M. To specify a time, simply include the time in one of the following forms after the date:

- `01:23:45`
- `1:23a`
- `1:23am`
- `01:23am`
- `1am`

For instance, the following are both valid date/time values:

- `"Mar 21, 1999 1:23am"`
- `"March 21, 1999 01:23:45"`

Special care needs to be taken when using two-digit year values, as in 03/21/99. Although ColdFusion can handle dates beyond the year 2000, the following rules apply to two-digit year values:

- Years from 00 to 29 are treated as being in the 21st century (such as 2001 and 2010).
- Years from 30 to 99 are treated as being in the 20th century (such as 1945 and 1999).

Using Operators

Operators are the building blocks of expressions. They enable you to combine simple values or other expressions into new expressions that return values.

The four types of operators, based on the values they return, are shown in the following list:

Arithmetic   Returns a number

String   Returns a string

Decision/comparison   Returns a Boolean value

Boolean   Returns a Boolean value

Arithmetic Operators

ColdFusion has nine *arithmetic operators*: the four basic mathematical operators of addition, subtraction, multiplication, and division, plus five other operators.

The four basic operators are outlined in Table 6.2.

TABLE 6.2:   Arithmetic Operators

Operator	Symbol	Example	Result
Addition	+	4+2	6
Subtraction	–	4–2	2
Multiplication	*	4*2	8
Division	/	4/2	2

The remaining operators can be classified into two groups: *binary* operators (those that require two values to work) and *unary* operators (those that require one value to work).

Binary Arithmetic Operators

The three binary arithmetic operators are described in the following list:

MOD   Returns the modulus (remainder) of an integer division operation. For instance, 5 divided by 3 returns 1 with a remainder of 2. In this case, 5 MOD 3 returns 2. Remember, you can't divide by zero; therefore, 5 MOD 0 is invalid.

****   Returns the result of integer division. That is, two integers are divided and the result (not the remainder) is returned. Therefore 5\3 returns 1. Again, division by zero is not possible, making 5\0 invalid.

^   Raises one number to the power of another. For instance, 5^3 returns the value of 5^3, or 125.

Unary Arithmetic Operators

There are two unary arithmetic operators used to set the sign of a number: + and -. For instance, +2 is positive 2, and –2 is negative 2 or (-1)*2. It is rare to see the + operator in use, but the – operator is seen whenever a negative number is indicated and also when the value contained in a variable is negated: -VariableName.

String Operators

ColdFusion supports one string operation: *concatenation*. This operation is indicated by the & operator.

Concatenation is the closest process to addition when working with string values. Concatenation combines two string values into a single string. For instance, "Hello" & " world" results in the value "Hello world".

Decision/Comparison Operators

Decision operators, which are also called *comparison operators*, are used to compare two values or expressions and to return a Boolean value of True or False based on a criterion for comparing the two values. As you will see in Chapter 7, "Controlling the Flow of Your Templates," these expressions are commonly used in decision-making for the CFIF tag. The eight decision operators in ColdFusion are described in Table 6.3.

TABLE 6.3: Comparison Operators

Operator	Alternative Forms	Description
IS	EQUAL, EQ	A case-insensitive comparison of two values in which True is returned if the values are identical. For instance, "hello" IS "Hello" returns True whereas 3 IS 4 returns False.
IS NOT	NOT EQUAL, NEQ	A case-insensitive comparison of two values in which True is returned if the values are not identical. For instance, "hello" IS NOT "Hello" returns False whereas 3 IS NOT 4 returns True.
CONTAINS		Returns True if the value on the left contains the value on the right. For instance, "Hello There" CONTAINS "llo" returns True but "llo" CONTAINS "Hello There" returns False.
DOES NOT CONTAIN		Returns True if the value on the left does not contain the value on the right. For instance, "abcde" DOES NOT CONTAIN "f" returns True.
GREATER THAN	GT	Returns True if the value on the left is greater than the value on the right (but not if the values are equal). For instance, 10 GREATER THAN 5 returns True whereas 5 GREATER THAN 5 and 5 GREATER THAN 10 both return False.
LESS THAN	LT	Returns True if the value on the left is smaller than the value on the right (but not if the values are equal). For instance, 5 LESS THAN 10 returns True but 5 LESS THAN 5 and 10 LESS THAN 5 both return False.

TABLE 6.3: Comparison Operators *(continued)*

Operator	Alternative Forms	Description
GREATER THAN OR EQUAL TO	GTE, GE	Returns True if the value on the left is greater than or equal to the one on the right. For instance, 10 GREATER THAN OR EQUAL TO 5 and 5 GREATER THAN OR EQUAL TO 5 both return True.
LESS THAN OR EQUAL TO	LTE, LE	Returns True if the value on the left is less than or equal to the value on the right. For instance, both 5 LESS THAN OR EQUAL TO 10 and 5 LESS THAN OR EQUAL TO 5 return True.

Boolean Operators

Both decision/comparison operators and Boolean operators return Boolean values. However, decision/comparison operators are generally used on non-Boolean values. Boolean operators can be used only on Boolean values.

There are six Boolean operators that work with one or two Boolean values and return a Boolean value as a result:

- NOT
- AND
- OR
- XOR
- EQV
- IMP

NOT

NOT is a unary Boolean operator that reverses a value from True to False or from False to True (see Table 6.4).

TABLE 6.4: Truth Table for NOT

X	NOT X
True	False
False	True

AND

AND is a binary Boolean operator that returns True only when both values are True (see Table 6.5).

TABLE 6.5:   Truth Table for AND

X	Y	X AND Y
True	True	True
True	False	False
False	True	False
False	False	False

OR

OR is a binary Boolean operator that returns True when either value is True or both are True (see Table 6.6).

TABLE 6.6:   Truth Table for OR

X	Y	X OR Y
True	True	True
True	False	True
False	True	True
False	False	False

XOR

XOR is a binary Boolean operator (commonly known as an *exclusive* OR) that returns True only when either value is True, but not when both are True (see Table 6.7).

TABLE 6.7:   Truth Table for XOR

X	Y	X XOR Y
True	True	False
True	False	True
False	True	True
False	False	False

EQV

EQV is a binary operator (commonly known as *equivalence*) that returns True when both values are True or when both values are False (see Table 6.8).

The key difference here is that the variable is used outside the string and therefore the pound signs are not needed.

As with CFOUTPUT, complex expressions containing operators cannot be used, and adjacent pound sign expressions are allowed.

One point to note is that because expressions within pound signs are evaluated before the rest of the string, any quotation marks within the pound sign expression do not need to be escaped, even though they appear within a string:

```
<CFSET Result = "The result is #Left("Test",1)#">
```

Inside Tag Attributes

Inside tag attributes, the same rules apply to the use of pound signs as within strings:

```
<CFPARAM NAME="Value" DEFAULT="The result is #Exp(1)#">
```

The only point to note is that if you are assigning the value of a single variable or function call to an attribute, it is more efficient not to enclose the pound sign expression within quotation marks:

```
<CFPARAM NAME="Value" DEFAULT=#Exp(1)#>
```

Inside Expressions

It is wise not to use pound signs when it isn't necessary to do so. For instance, within expressions, there usually isn't a need to use pound signs to evaluate a variable value or a function call.

In the following example:

```
<CFSET Value = 1>
<CFSET Result = Value + Exp(1)>
```

it is possible, but unnecessary and inefficient, to use pound signs:

```
<CFSET RESULT = #Value# + #Exp(1)#>
```

Inside Other Pound Signs

At times it may be necessary to use pound signs inside of other pound signs. This situation generally arises when an expression is somewhat complex.

Consider the following example:

```
<CFSET Value1 = "This is">
<CFSET Value2 = "a test">
<CFOUTPUT>
The string is '#Value1# #Value2#'<BR>
In reverse: #Reverse("#Value1# #Value2#")#
</CFOUTPUT>
```

This produces the following output:

```
The string is 'This is a test'
In reverse: tset a si sihT
```

Here you need to include variables inside pound signs inside a function that is already enclosed in pound signs. This is a legal use of nested pound signs.

Generally, though, it is better to take alternate approaches for the sake of clarity. There are two options. First, you can use concatenation of the variables to avoid using nested pound signs:

```
<CFSET Value1 = "This is">
<CFSET Value2 = "a test">
<CFOUTPUT>
The string is '#Value1# #Value2#'<BR>
In reverse: #Reverse(Value1 & " " & Value2)#
</CFOUTPUT>
```

Even better, though, you can assign the string to another variable:

```
<CFSET Value1 = "This is">
<CFSET Value2 = "a test">
<CFSET TheString = "#Value1# #Value2#">
<CFOUTPUT>
The string is '#TheString#'<BR>
In reverse: #Reverse(TheString)#
</CFOUTPUT>
```

A common misconception is that attributes to functions need pound signs. This is almost never the case, and will generally produce an error. For instance, #Reverse(TheString)# is valid. #Reverse(#TheString#)# is not. Only if you wanted to put the argument within quotation marks to make it part of a string would you use the pound signs, as in #Reverse("Test #TheString#")#. However, as we already discussed, there are alternatives to this that are preferable.

Considering Special Features of ColdFusion Expressions

Some additional features of ColdFusion expressions warrant consideration before we close our discussion. These are:

- Order of precedence
- Typeless expression evaluation

Order of Precedence

The order in which operators appear in complex expressions is important. Expressions are not simply evaluated from left to right, but rather follow rules of precedence. Under the rules of precedence, operators are evaluated in the following order:

1. Unary +, Unary -
2. ^
3. *, /
4. \
5. MOD
6. +, -
7. &
8. EQ, NEQ, LT, LTE, GT, GTE, CONTAINS, DOES NOT CONTAIN
9. NOT
10. AND
11. OR
12. XOR
13. EQV
14. IMP

It is important to keep this order in mind when writing your expression. For instance, consider the following expression:

```
1 + 2 * 3
```

If you write this expression expecting left-to-right evaluation, then you would expect that 1 + 2 would be evaluated to 3, and then 3 * 3 would be evaluated, resulting in 9. However, the rules of precedence tell us that first, 2 * 3 is evaluated to 6, and then 1 + 6 is evaluated, with a final result of 7.

If you want to override the rule of precedence in a particular instance, you can use parentheses. The sub-expression with parentheses will be evaluated before the rest of the expression (although within the parentheses, the rules of precedence still apply). For instance, you can make the preceding example evaluate from left to right as desired using parentheses:

```
(1 + 2) * 3
```

This expression now evaluates to 9.

Typeless Expression Evaluation

The final subject you need to consider with respect to expressions is that ColdFusion uses *typeless expression evaluation*. This refers to the capability of ColdFusion to automatically convert one data type to another data type as needed in expressions.

For instance, in many programming languages, it is not possible to add a number to a string. However, in quick-deployment scripting languages such as ColdFusion (and other Web-development languages such as Perl), this is possible.

The operator being used determines the process of converting data types in an expression. For instance, the addition operator requires two numbers to function. Therefore, ColdFusion attempts to convert both values to numbers. Similarly, the concatenation operator requires two strings, which leads ColdFusion to convert both values to strings.

In the case of functions, specific types of arguments are required for each function and, in the same way, ColdFusion converts arguments to the correct data type.

It is important to realize that not all types of data can be converted to all other types. For instance, Boolean values cannot be converted to date/time values, and converting strings to date/time values depends on rules outlined in Appendix C, where we discuss date functions.

Table 6.10 outlines the way in which most common conversions work.

TABLE 6.10:   Data Type Conversion Rules

Conversion	Notes
Boolean to Number	True becomes 1 and False becomes 0.
Number to Boolean	0 becomes False and all other numbers become True.
Boolean to String	True becomes "YES" and False becomes "NO".
String to Boolean	"YES" becomes True and "NO" becomes False. Otherwise, if the string can be converted to a number, then the Number-to-Boolean rule applies.
Number to String	The number is converted into a string using the default format (see our discussion of number formatting functions in Chapter 12, "Grouping, Nesting, and Formatting Outputs," for details of number formats).
String to Number	If the string is a number, it is converted.
String to Date	Converted if string is an ODBC date, time or timestamp value.

Where Do We Go from Here?

Now that you have learned about variables and functions and can apply them in expressions, you are ready to move on to applying this knowledge to generating templates that deploy programmatic logic.

In the next chapter, you will look at how to use expressions, combining the CFIF and CFSWITCH tags to control the flow of your templates. You will learn how to use expressions to make decisions about which portions of your templates to execute. This makes it possible to develop templates that perform many tasks based on the information provided to them from external sources such as forms, database queries, or files.

Using flow control is essential to building complex templates that are more than a simple, sequential series of tags.

chapter 7

Controlling the Flow of Your Templates

- Displaying Data Based on Conditions

- Redirecting Users to Another Template

- Using CFABORT and CFEXIT

Until this point, all your templates have been designed to execute from start to finish, without applying any decision making that could affect which tags get executed and which don't.

In this chapter, you will move into a new realm in your programming: *flow control*. Flow control refers to the ability to determine which portions of a template to execute and in what order, based on specific conditions such as the value stored in a variable. Any form of scripting or programming language, including ColdFusion, realizes its true power through a range of techniques that can be used to govern which program segments are executed under given conditions.

You will also look at the most basic flow-control structures commonly found in all scripting environments:

- If-Else constructs (using `CFIF`, `CFELSE`, and `CFELSEIF`)
- Switch-case constructs (using `CFSWITCH`, `CFCASE`, and `CFDEFAULTCASE`)

Another area you will look at, which is related to flow control, is the ability to redirect users to another template using the `CFLOCATION` tag. Finally, you will look at mechanisms for prematurely ending execution of a template or a segment of code, including the use of the `CFABORT` and `CFEXIT` tags.

Displaying Data Based on Conditions

The ability to dictate what actions are performed based on a condition is one of the most commonly used programming tools. All scripting and programming languages offer this capability, as does ColdFusion. In ColdFusion, two main constructs handle conditional decision-making:

- If-Then-Else constructs
- Switch-case constructs

If-Then-Else Decision Making

The concept of *If-Then* and *If-Then-Else* constructs is really quite simple. Written in plain English, a simple If-Then structure takes the following form: "If some condition is true, then perform a particular series of actions."

Understanding Conditions

The logical question here is: Just what is meant by a condition? Put simply, a *condition* is any expression that evaluates to a Boolean value (that is, evaluates to either `True` or `False`).

In Chapter 6, "Writing Expressions," you learned how to build expressions in Cold-Fusion. To understand conditional decision making in ColdFusion, you need to start with a quick review of the operators that enable you to build Boolean expressions.

Boolean expressions range from the simple:

- `VariableName IS Value`
- `VariableName GREATER THAN Value`
- `VariableName IS NOT Value`

to the complex:

- `VariableOne IS ValueOne AND (VariableTwo GREATER THAN ValueTwo OR VariableThree IS NOT ValueThree)`
- `NOT (VariableOne IS ValueOne AND VariableTwo GREATER THAN ValueTwo)`

At their most basic, Boolean expressions include any single operator that evaluates to `True` or `False`. These comparison operators generally compare two values, as shown in Table 7.1.

TABLE 7.1:   Comparison Operators That Return Boolean Values

Operator	Shorthand Form	Description
`IS`	`EQUAL, EQ`	Tests for equality of two values and returns `True` if the values are equal; in the case of string values, the test is case insensitive.
`IS NOT`	`NOT EQUAL, NEQ`	Tests for inequality of two values and returns `True` if the values are not equal; in the case of string values, the test is case insensitive.
`GREATER THAN`	`GT`	Tests if the value preceding the operator is greater than the value following the operator.
`LESS THAN`	`LT`	Tests if the value preceding the operator is less than the value following the operator.
`GREATER THAN OR EQUAL TO`	`GTE, GE`	Tests if the value preceding the operator is greater than or equal to the following operator.
`LESS THAN OR EQUAL TO`	`LTE, LE`	Tests if the value preceding the operator is less than or equal to the following operator.
`CONTAINS`		Tests if the value preceding the operator is contained in the value following the operator; in other words, the preceding value is tested to see if it is a substring of the following value.
`DOES NOT CONTAIN`		Tests if the value preceding the operator is not contained in the value following the operator; in other words, the preceding value is tested to see if it is not a substring of the following value.

These operators allow the creation of simple Boolean expressions that compare two values. But what happens when you want to build more complex expressions? These needs are addressed by using Boolean operators. Boolean operators work against two other expressions that already return Boolean values and return a new Boolean value as a result. Using these operators, it is possible to build complex, compound Boolean expressions.

The following list outlines the Boolean operators available in ColdFusion:

NOT   This operator takes a single expression that follows it. The operator returns the negation of its operand. If the expression against which NOT is used is True, then the compound expression returns False. Similarly, using NOT against an expression that is False returns True.

AND   Returns True when both arguments are True; otherwise, False is returned.

OR   Returns True if either argument, or both, are True.

XOR   Returns True if either argument, but not both, are True.

EQV   Returns True if both arguments are True or if both arguments are False.

IMP   A IMP B returns True if the logical statement If A Then B is True. If A is True and B is False, then A IMP B is False; otherwise, A IMP B is True.

Using the CFIF Tag

Now that you know how to build condition expressions, you are ready to use the CFIF tag to build a simple If-Then construct. Let's consider a simple example in which a variable named Price contains a value.

If the value of Price is greater than 10, you want to display a statement to that effect. Otherwise, the rest of the template proceeds normally. To do this, you use the CFIF tag, which takes the following form:

```
<CFIF Condition>
    Actions to perform/text to display if the condition is true
</CFIF>
```

Therefore, our simple example would look like this:

```
<CFIF Price greater than 10>
    <H3>The price is greater than $10</H3>
</CFIF>
```

Carrying things a bit further, you can use a compound Boolean expression to test if the value in question is between 10 and 20:

```
<CFIF Price greater than 10 AND Price less than 20>
    <H3>The price is between $10 and $20</H3>
</CFIF>
```

It is important to note that between the opening and closing CFIF tags, any code that is valid in a ColdFusion template can be used. This includes all ColdFusion tags as well as all valid HTML. In ColdFusion, CFIF will often be used to control information that is displayed in the browser, but it can also be used for ColdFusion code and tags that generate no output to the browser.

Adding the *CFELSE* Tag

Using the CFELSE tag provides a way to extend the basic If-Then structure of the CFIF tag to include code that handles all cases in which the specified condition is false. In plain English, using the CFELSE structure works like this: "If some condition is true, then perform a specific series of actions; otherwise, perform a different series of actions."

In ColdFusion, this is done by adding the CFELSE tag in the middle of the CFIF structure:

```
<CFIF Condition>
    Some Code
<CFELSE>
    Some other Code
</CFIF>
```

To see how this works, let's extend our simple example of testing a variable to see if it is between 10 and 20:

```
<CFIF Price greater than 10 and Price less than 20>
    <H3>The price is between $10 and $20</H3>
<CFELSE>
    <H3>The price is not between $10 and $20</H3>
</CFIF>
```

Going Further with *CFELSEIF*

One of the drawbacks of the basic If-Then-Else construct using CFIF and CFELSE is that it can be inefficient. For instance, consider a situation in which you need to test a number and output a message based on whether the number is between zero and nine, 10 and 19, 20 and 29, or 30 and 39.

Using CFIF, it is possible to build a simple series of CFIF tags:

```
<CFIF Price greater than 0 and Price less than 9>
    <H3>The price is between $0 and $9</H3>
</CFIF>
<CFIF Price greater than 10 and Price less than 19>
    <H3>The price is between $10 and $19</H3>
</CFIF>
<CFIF Price greater than 20 and Price less than 29>
    <H3>The price is between $20 and $29</H3>
```

```
</CFIF>
<CFIF Price greater than 30 and Price less than 39>
   <H3>The price is between $30 and $39</H3>
</CFIF>
```

It should be clear that the code will work. But, there is a problem: Even though a value meets one of the earlier conditions (for instance, it is between zero and nine), the value will still be tested in the remaining conditions and, of course, rejected. This can introduce notable inefficiency in long series of CFIF tags or in cases where this type of testing is repeated frequently.

Using the CFELSE tag, it is possible to nest a series of decisions so that less testing occurs:

```
<CFIF Price greater than 0 and Price less than 9>
   <H3>The price is between $0 and $9</H3>
<CFELSE>
<CFIF Price greater than 10 and Price less than 19>
     <H3>The price is between $10 and $19</H3>
   <CELSE>
<CFIF Price greater than 20 and Price less than 29>
       <H3>The price is between $20 and $29</H3>
     <CFELSE>
<CFIF Price greater than 30 and Price less than 39>
         <H3>The price is between $30 and $39</H3>
</CFIF>
</CFIF>
</CFIF>
</CFIF>
```

What happens here is that only when the first condition fails does the second condition get tested, and then only when the second condition fails is the next condition tested, and so on. This addresses the inefficiency issue in the first example. However, it produces awkward and hard-to-read code.

Often, though, programmers want to produce a series of conditional tests of the form If-Then-Else, If-Then-Else, If-Then-Else, and so on. This is exactly what this series of embedded CFIF and CFELSE tags produces, although with code that is awkward to read and write.

The CFELSEIF tag provides a way to combine a CFELSE tag with the subsequent CFIF condition, producing code of this form:

```
<CFIF Condition>
   Code to Execute
<CFELSEIF Other Condition>
   Other Code to Execute
<CFELSE>
   Some Other Code to Execute
</CFIF>
```

Applied to our series of consecutive CFIF statements, the resulting code looks like this:

```
<CFIF Price greater than 0 and Price less than 9>
    <H3>The price is between $0 and $9</H3>
<CFELSEIF Price greater than 10 and Price less than 19>
    <H3>The price is between $10 and $19</H3>
<CFELSEIF Price greater than 20 and Price less than 29>
    <H3>The price is between $20 and $29</H3>
<CFELSEIF Price greater than 30 and Price less than 39>
    <H3>The price is between $30 and $39</H3>
</CFIF>
```

Not only does this code address the inefficiency issues from the first example, it also eliminates the awkward appearance of the code in the second example (making it shorter and easier to read than even the first example of consecutive CFIF tags).

Multiple Comparisons: *CFSWITCH* and *CFCASE*

Sometimes, even a series of CFIF and CFELSEIF tags is too much to code and read and introduces inefficiencies of its own. For instance, consider the situation in which a variable is tested against every number from 1 to 10 and a different action is taken accordingly in each instance.

Using CFIF and CFELSEIF, the result looks something like this:

```
<CFIF TestValue is 1>
    Action 1
<CFELSEIF TestValue is 2>
    Action 2
<CFELSEIF TestValue is 3>
    Action 3
<CFELSEIF TestValue is 4>
    Action 4
<CFELSEIF TestValue is 5>
    Action 5
<CFELSEIF TestValue is 6>
    Action 6
<CFELSEIF TestValue is 7>
    Action 7
<CFELSEIF TestValue is 8>
    Action 8
<CFELSEIF TestValue is 9>
    Action 9
<CFELSEIF TestValue is 10>
    Action 10
</CFIF>
```

This seems simple and straightforward, but it is inefficient. What happens when TestValue is 10? The answer is quite simple: All 10 conditions must be tested and rejected individually. Also, the code is less than ideal; a complete, separate condition needs to be written for each value being tested.

Using CFSWITCH and CFCASE, it is possible to test a single expression against multiple possible values and to take a specific action for each value without writing multiple conditions and without causing all conditions to be tested, only to find the last one was a match.

The two tags, CFSWITCH and CFCASE, are tied together; they are not used individually. CFSWITCH specifies the expression that is being tested (in other words, the value that will be used to cause the template to switch between possible actions). CFCASE specifies each set of actions that occur when the tested expression matches specified values.

The CFSWITCH tag takes a single attribute—EXPRESSION–that specifies the expression being tested. For instance, in our preceding example, the expression is simply TestValue, so the CFSWITCH tag would read as follows:

```
<CFSWITCH EXPRESSION="TestValue">
```

CFCASE is then used to test for possible values of the expression, TestValue. The CFCASE tag must always include the VALUE attribute, which specifies the value against which to test the expression in the CFSWITCH statement. Putting this together, our series of CFIF and CFELSEIF statements becomes the following CFSWITCH/CFCASE construct:

```
<CFSWITCH EXPRESSION="#TestValue#">
   <CFCASE VALUE="1">
      Action 1
   </CFCASE>
   <CFCASE VALUE="2">
      Action 2
   </CFCASE>
   <CFCASE VALUE="3">
      Action 3
   </CFCASE>
   <CFCASE VALUE="4">
      Action 4
   </CFCASE>
   <CFCASE VALUE="5">
      Action 5
   </CFCASE>
   <CFCASE VALUE="6">
      Action 6
   </CFCASE>
   <CFCASE VALUE="7">
      Action 7
   </CFCASE>
   <CFCASE VALUE="8">
      Action 8
```

```
    </CFCASE>
    <CFCASE VALUE="9">
       Action 9
    </CFCASE>
    <CFCASE VALUE="10">
       Action 10
    </CFCASE>
 </CFSWITCH>
```

A useful feature of the switch-case structure is the ability to specify a default action, that is, an action to take if the expression fails to match any of the values specified by the CFCASE statements. This is achieved by using the CFDEFAULTCASE tag, which does not take attributes and encloses the default action.

In our example, you may want to specify an action to take when TestValue is not between one and 10:

```
<CFSWITCH EXPRESSION="#TestValue#">
   <CFCASE VALUE="1">
      Action 1
   </CFCASE>
   <CFCASE VALUE="2">
      Action 2
   </CFCASE>
   <CFCASE VALUE="3">
      Action 3
   </CFCASE>
   <CFCASE VALUE="4">
      Action 4
   </CFCASE>
   <CFCASE VALUE="5">
      Action 5
   </CFCASE>
   <CFCASE VALUE="6">
      Action 6
   </CFCASE>
   <CFCASE VALUE="7">
      Action 7
   </CFCASE>
   <CFCASE VALUE="8">
      Action 8
   </CFCASE>
   <CFCASE VALUE="9">
      Action 9
   </CFCASE>
   <CFCASE VALUE="10">
      Action 10
   </CFCASE>
```

```
   <CFDEFAULTCASE>
      Default Action
   </CFDEFAULTCASE>
</CFSWITCH>
```

Another important feature of the CFCASE tag is that it can be used to test for multiple values and to perform a single action if the expression matches any of the values. This is done by providing a list of values delimited by a separator such as a comma (which is the default delimiter). For instance, you may want to take the same action of outputting the value contained in TestValue when it is between 1 and 5 and otherwise take a default value. This can be done with one CFCASE tag and one CFDEFAULTCASE tag:

```
<CFSWITCH EXPRESSION="#TestValue#">
   <CFCASE VALUE="1,2,3,4,5">
      <CFOUTPUT><H3>The value is #TestValue#</H3></CFOUTPUT>
   </CFCASE>
   <CFDEFAULTCASE>
      <H3>The value is out of range</H3>
   </CFDEFAULTCASE>
</CFSWITCH>
```

If you need to use a delimiter other than a comma, then you need to use the DELIMIT-ERS attribute of the CFCASE tag to indicate the delimiter that you have used:

```
<CFSWITCH EXPRESSION="TestValue">
   <CFCASE VALUE="1:2:3:4:5" DELIMITERS=":">
      <CFOUTPUT><H3>The value is #TestValue#</H3></CFOUTPUT>
   </CFCASE>
   <CFDEFAULTCASE>
      <H3>The value is out of range</H3>
   </CFDEFAULTCASE>
</CFSWITCH>
```

Redirecting Users to Another Template

Indirectly related to controlling the flow of a template is the ability to redirect a user's browser to another template. This is done using the CFLOCATION tag. The CFLOCATION tag takes two attributes:

URL   Specifies the URL of the template or HTML to which the user should be redirected.

ADDTOKEN   Indicates if a client management token should be added to the specified URL. Discussion of client management takes place in Chapter 17, "Implementing the ColdFusion Web Application Framework." Possible values for the attribute are YES and NO.

For instance, to redirect the user to `newtemplate.cfm`, you could use the tag `<CFLOCATION URL="newtemplate.cfm">`.

The real question is: When would you need to redirect a user to another document? There are several applications of this technique. Just a few of them are as follows:

- After processing a form submission, you may want to redirect a user back to a home page or a default page. Forms are discussed in Chapter 15, "Forms."
- If, when processing a form submission, an error in the submitted information is wrong, you may want to redirect the user back to the original form.
- Based on the value of an expression, it may be necessary to redirect the user to different parts of the site.

Keeping in mind that after the CFLOCATION tag is executed, the remainder of the current template will not be executed, you can use multiple CFLOCATION tags within a template—for example, as part of an If-Else structure or a switch-case test:

```
<CFIF TestValue is 1>
    <CFLOCATION URL="template1.cfm">
<CFELSE>
    <CFLOCATION URL="template2.cfm">
</CFIF>
```

Using *CFABORT* and *CFEXIT*

Finally, you need to consider CFABORT and CFEXIT, which provide ways to prematurely terminate the execution of a template.

The CFABORT tag causes the execution of a template to stop and any output generated up to that point to be displayed. For this to happen, no attributes are needed: Simply use `<CFABORT>` at the appropriate place in your template.

CFABORT, though, also can be used in a slightly more complicated way. Using the SHOWERROR attribute, you can specify an error message to be displayed at the point where CFABORT caused the template to terminate. For instance, consider the following code:

```
The template is executing
<CFABORT SHOWERROR="The template has aborted.">
The rest of the template
```

This produces results like those in Figure 7.1.

FIGURE 7.1
Aborting with an error
message

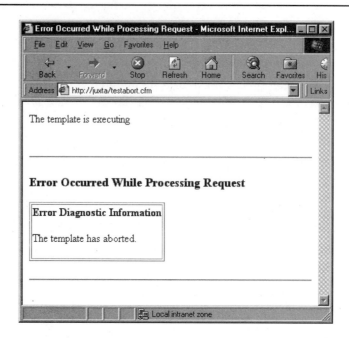

To go one step further, use the CFERROR tag. CFERROR allows the redirection to a specified error template when used with the CFABORT tag and its SHOWERROR attribute. The CFERROR tag is discussed in more detail in Chapter 18, "Implementing Error Control."

CFEXIT is, in many ways, similar to CFABORT in that it causes the premature termination of a template. Used in the context of a regular template (as opposed to a custom tag), CFEXIT has the same effect as <CFABORT>. CFEXIT, though, is designed to be used within a custom tag. Custom tags are discussed in more detail in Chapter 31, "Building ColdFusion Custom Tags."

Where Do We Go from Here?

In this chapter, you crossed an important milestone: You learned how to create templates that do more than sequentially proceed from start to finish every time. You learned how to alter the flow of a template on the basis of conditions.

This is an important ability and you will continue to build on it in Chapter 13, "Looping," which discusses another mechanism for altering the flow of a template.

In the next chapter, you will look at how it is possible to include code from other templates in a current template. This ability makes it possible to reuse segments of code in multiple templates while writing the segment only once and maintaining it in a single location. In large sites, this ability is invaluable because it eases site development and management.

chapter 8

Including Outside Code

- Including Code within the Current Template by Using CFINCLUDE

- Using CFMODULE

- Understanding Variable Scope Issues

You've probably noticed by now that ColdFusion templates can grow to be much longer and more complex than the average HTML file. In addition, just as with HTML, there will inevitably be sections of ColdFusion code that you will want to reuse repeatedly throughout an application or a Web site.

For these reasons, you need to be able to include ColdFusion code from other files in another template. In this chapter, you will look at two ways of doing this: using the CFINCLUDE tag and the CFMODULE tag. The ways in which these two tags function are different, and they are better suited to different purposes.

In considering the combining of code from different templates, it is also necessary to look at variable scope issues; that is, where does a variable exist in one or both of the templates involved?

Including Code within the Current Template by Using *CFINCLUDE*

Anyone who has done advanced work with HTML has probably encountered server-parsed HTML. With server-parsed HTML files (generally ending in the extension SHTML), it is possible to use a variety of special tags that are processed on the server side before sending the results to the browser.

Most flavors of server-parsed HTML offer one or more tags for including the contents of another HTML file in the current file. This is generally used for commonly recurring elements of pages within a site. For instance, if a site always has the same title or menu bar across the top of each page, this code could be placed in a single file and then included in every page on the site.

The great advantage of this comes in the area of site maintenance: You can modify this global page element for all pages by making changes to a single file. No longer is it necessary to edit all pages or perform global search-and-replace functions to make the necessary alterations to the site.

ColdFusion offers a similar capability. The simplest way to achieve this result is by using the CFINCLUDE tag. Although it is possible to devise ways of using your Web server's server-parsed HTML to include a ColdFusion template into an HTML file, it is generally best to stick to ColdFusion for the complete solution. This ensures that the correct parsing and processing of both files occurs.

The *CFINCLUDE* Tag

The CFINCLUDE tag is quite simple in that it has only one required parameter: TEMPLATE. This parameter indicates the logical path of another ColdFusion template to include in the current template.

The mechanics here are simple: The code of the specified template is added to the current template at the point where the CFINCLUDE tag is located and is processed as if it were part of the current page.

Let's look at how this works. Consider the following code segment. It provides a title banner and menu for a simple site. ColdFusion is used to highlight the correct menu item based on information set in the variable Chosen in the template containing the CFINCLUDE tag.

```
<H1>Using CFINCLUDE</H1>
<CFIF Chosen is 1>
    <STRONG>The Syntax</STRONG>
<CFELSE>
    <A HREF="syntax.cfm">The Syntax</A>
</CFIF> |
<CFIF Chosen is 2>
    <STRONG>Examples</STRONG>
<CFELSE>
    <A HREF="examples.cfm">Examples</A>
</CFIF> |
<CFIF Chosen is 3>
    <STRONG>Alternatives</STRONG>
<CFELSE>
    <A HREF="alternatives.cfm">Alternatives</A>
</CFIF>
<HR>
```

Of course, an immediate problem appears to exist with this template: None of the CFIF tags will work because the Chosen variable does not exist. But this is fine because the template is designed to be included in the other templates in the site. For instance, Listing 8.1 is the home page of the site that includes the menu and title template (which we will call head.cfm).

Listing 8.1: *cfinclude.cfm*

```
<CFSET Chosen=0>
<CFINCLUDE TEMPLATE="head.cfm">
This site is designed to provide reference information
about the CFINCLUDE tag. Choose an option from the
menu above.
```

The end result is that the code from the head.cfm template is included in the home page template and is processed as one large template that looks like Listing 8.2.

Listing 8.2: *head.cfm*

```
<CFSET Chosen=0>
<H1>Using CFINCLUDE</H1>
<CFIF Chosen is 1>
    <STRONG>The Syntax</STRONG>
<CFELSE>
    <A HREF="syntax.cfm">The Syntax</A>
</CFIF> |
<CFIF Chosen is 2>
    <STRONG>Examples</STRONG>
<CFELSE>
    <A HREF="examples.cfm">Examples</A>
</CFIF> |
<CFIF Chosen is 3>
    <STRONG>Alternatives</STRONG>
<CFELSE>
    <A HREF="alternatives.cfm">Alternatives</A>
</CFIF>
<HR>
This site is designed to provide reference information
about the CFINCLUDE tag. Choose an option from the
menu above.
```

The results look like those in Figure 8.1.

FIGURE 8.1

CFINCLUDE can be used to include titles and menus.

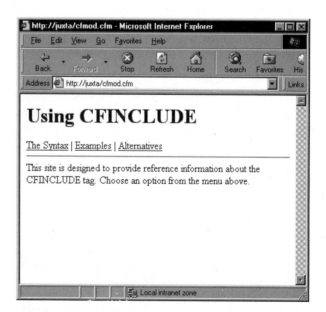

It should be noted that the code that generates the simple menu in your head.cfm template (the series of CFIF tags) is designed to highlight the current selection with a strong font if Chosen is set to 1, 2, or 3 (indicating which selection has been chosen) or to highlight no selection if the value of the variable is set to anything else.

In the home page example you just looked at, Chosen is set to 0 and the result is that all three of the menu choices are active links. By way of comparison, consider Listing 8.3, in which Chosen is set to 3.

Listing 8.3: *cfinclude.cfm*

```
<CFSET Chosen=3>
<CFINCLUDE TEMPLATE="head.cfm">
<HR>
This site is designed to provide reference information
about the CFINCLUDE tag. Choose an option from the
menu above.
```

This produces results like those in Figure 8.2. Notice how the third option in the menu is highlighted with a bold font and is not a link.

FIGURE 8.2
One menu option is highlighted and inactive.

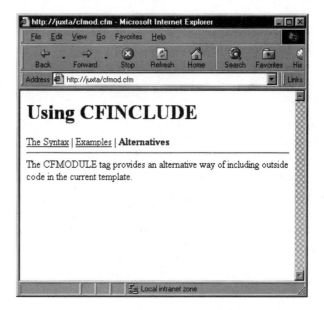

NOTE   The TEMPLATE attribute takes a logical path as a value. That is, the template to include should be specified as a relative path from the current template instead of as a complete URL. For instance, to include a template in the same directory as the current template, simply specify the file by name. To include a template in the parent directory of the one containing the current template, use the form `../template.cfm`.

Using *CFMODULE*

The CFMODULE tag is based on a different concept from that of CFINCLUDE. CFINCLUDE makes it easy to reuse the same code in multiple templates. CFMODULE, on the other hand, provides an easy way to develop custom tags.

Building custom tags can be a complicated process and is dealt with in depth in Chapter 31, "Building Custom Tags." However, CFMODULE makes it possible to quickly build custom tags. In this chapter, you will look at a simple example of a custom tag. You should refer to Chapter 31 for a detailed look at the concepts and techniques for building effective custom tags.

The idea behind a custom tag is that it provides a self-contained, reusable piece of code that implements a particular function or set of functions. Like all ColdFusion tags, you can use these tags in your templates and provide data to them through tag attributes. The custom tags process any information provided to them in attributes and then can return results which get included in the template where the tag was used.

There is a subtle, but significant, difference between this model and that of CFINCLUDE: With CFINCLUDE, you are simply adding the code contained in the included file to your template and this is processed as part of the including template. The code in the included file can refer to variables in the template that use the CFINCLUDE tag to include it. The file does not need to contain a complete, fully-functional template: the code only needs to make sense at the point at which it is being included in a template.

When you use the CFMODULE tag, you are asking ColdFusion to execute the code in the custom tag and only include the results in the template using the CFMODULE tag. The custom tag is unaware of the environment of the calling template and only uses data provided to it through attributes.

This may seem unimportant, but this encapsulation provides one key benefit: truly reusable code. A custom tag is written in such a way that it is in no way dependent on the environment in the template that invokes it with CFMODULE. This means that you can create custom tags that serve general purpose functions and you can use them in any number of applications and templates. As long as the calling template follows the correct procedures for passing data to the tag through attributes, the tag will work as expected.

Understanding *CFMODULE* Syntax

Before looking at an example, you need to consider briefly the syntax of the CFMODULE tag. The tag takes at least one of the following two attributes: TEMPLATE or NAME. In addition, any number of custom attributes can be specified, which are then accessible by the template being called.

The *TEMPLATE* Attribute

As with CFINCLUDE, the TEMPLATE attribute enables you to specify the path of the template file being called using relative paths.

The *NAME* Attribute

The NAME attribute provides an alternate way to specify the template file for your custom tag. ColdFusion provides a special CustomTags directory under the default ColdFusion directory (which is usually c:\cfusion).

This directory is used to store custom tags. Tags contained in this subdirectory can be specified by name using the NAME attribute and dotted notation. Consider the examples in Table 8.1.

TABLE 8.1: Specifying Custom Tag Locations

Custom Tag Template File Location	Value of NAME Attribute
CustomTags\mytag.cfm	NAME="mytag"
CustomTags\MyTags\example.cfm	NAME="MyTags.example"
CustomTags\MyTags\MasteringCF\Sample.cfm	NAME="MyTags.MasteringCF.Sample"

The use of the CustomTags directory is discussed in more detail in Chapter 31.

Custom Attributes

Custom attributes are used to pass information to the tag for processing. Consider a sample tag for adding two numbers (yes, ColdFusion can do this for you, but it makes for an easy example of using custom attributes).

Without writing the code for the custom tag, you can specify that the tag requires two numbers in the form of two custom attributes: A and B. In addition, you can also decide that the result of the addition will be returned to the calling template in a variable called RESULT.

With this in mind, the calling template can use CFMODULE to add the two numbers:

```
<CFMODULE NAME="add" A="1" B="2">
<CFOUTPUT>#RESULT#</CFOUTPUT>
```

This code segment calls your addition custom tag that is stored in the CustomTags directory and then displays the results using CFOUTPUT.

Creating a Sample Custom Tag with *CFMODULE*

As an example of creating a sample custom tag, let's take the simple headline and menu example used earlier when discussing CFINCLUDE. Instead of using CFINCLUDE, you will create two custom tags for generating the header and menu. The first will create the menu and output the results. The second will create the header and menu and return the results to the calling template in a variable.

For both approaches, you need to learn a little bit about how information is passed between the calling template and the custom tag.

In the code of the custom tag, the attributes being provided are accessed by using the attributes variable scope. For instance, in the preceding addition example, the A attribute is accessed in the custom tag as attributes.A and the B attribute as attributes.B.

Similarly, results can be returned to variables in the calling template by using the caller variable scope. For instance, to return the output of the addition to RESULT in the calling template, the value is assigned to caller.RESULT in the custom tag. With this knowledge in hand, let's consider both approaches to your header and menu custom tag.

Returning Output from a Custom Tag

The first approach is for the custom tag to create output, which is then included by the calling template as part of the final HTML document sent to the browser. This is similar in concept to the way in which many built-in ColdFusion tags result in specialized output in the HTML file (prime examples are the custom form control tags that you will learn about in Chapter 15, "Forms.")

First, you need to build a custom tag. The code for this tag looks like Listing 8.4.

Listing 8.4: *menu.cfm*

```
<CFSET Chosen = attributes.Section>

<H1>Using CFINCLUDE</H1>
<CFIF Chosen is 1>
    <STRONG>The Syntax</STRONG>
<CFELSE>
    <A HREF="syntax.cfm">The Syntax</A>
</CFIF> |
<CFIF Chosen is 2>
    <STRONG>Examples</STRONG>
<CFELSE>
```

```
    <A HREF="examples.cfm">Examples</A>
</CFIF> |
<CFIF Chosen is 3>
    <STRONG>Alternatives</STRONG>
<CFELSE>
    <A HREF="alternatives.cfm">Alternatives</A>
</CFIF>
<HR>
```

Fundamentally, this looks the same as the template that you used with CFINCLUDE. But there is one key difference: The first line of the template refers to attributes.Section. This means that the custom tag expects the required data to be passed in the attribute Section from the calling template. This value is assigned to the variable Chosen in the tag for easy access (Chosen requires less typing and code than attributes.Section).

The calling template for the home page would then look something like this (assuming the template for the custom tag is saved as menu.cfm in the CustomTags directory):

```
<CFMODULE NAME="menu" Section="0">
CFMODULE tag provides an alternative way of including outside code in the current
template..
```

The result is that where CFMODULE appears, the output of the CFMODULE tag will appear, producing an end result like the following:

```
<H1>Using MODULE</H1>
    <A HREF="syntax.cfm">The Syntax</A>
    <A HREF="examples.cfm">Examples</A>
    <A HREF="alternatives.cfm">Alternatives</A>
<HR>

CFMODULE tag provides an alternative way of including outside code in the current
template.
```

Functionally, this might seem to be basically the same as when you used the CFINCLUDE tag, but two different things are happening here:

- You don't have to assign a value to a variable before accessing the custom tag. This process is encapsulated into the tag itself.
- The results that are included in the calling template are not treated as ColdFusion code but rather as the result of processing ColdFusion code. This means that you can't return ColdFusion code from a custom tag and expect it to be processed as ColdFusion code within the calling template. Instead it will be treated as plain text and sent as such to the browser and displayed without processing.

Returning a Result from a Custom Tag

In this scenario, you will do things a little differently, returning a result through a variable in the calling template. Although this approach means an extra line of code is required to output the results in the calling template, it highlights the flexibility of a custom tag: Multiple values can be passed to it in a standardized way and multiple values can be returned by it in a standardized way.

Our example requires only one piece of information to be passed to the tag and only one piece of data to be returned. Listing 8.5 shows the code.

Listing 8.5: *menu2.cfm*

```
<CFSET Chosen = attributes.Section>

<CFSET Result = "<H1>Using CFINCLUDE</H1>">
<CFIF Chosen is 1>
   <CFSET Result= Result & "<STRONG>The Syntax</STRONG>">
<CFELSE>
   <CFSET Result=Result & "<A HREF=""syntax.cfm"">The Syntax</A>">
</CFIF>
<CFSET Result = Result & " | ">
<CFIF Chosen is 2>
   <CFSET Result= Result & "<STRONG>Examples</STRONG>">
<CFELSE>
   <CFSET Result=Result & "<A HREF=""examples.cfm"">Examples</A>">
</CFIF>
<CFSET Result = Result & " | ">
<CFIF Chosen is 3>
   <CFSET Result= Result & "<STRONG>Alternatives</STRONG>">
<CFELSE>
   <CFSET Result=Result & "<A HREF=""alternatives.cfm"">Alternatives</A>">
</CFIF>
<CFSET Result = Result & "<HR>">

<CFSET caller.HEADLINE = Result>
```

The calling template needs to be revised to look like this:

```
<CFMODULE NAME="menu" Section="0">
<CFOUTPUT>#HEADLINE#</CFOUTPUT>
```

CFMODULE tag provides an alternative way of including outside code in the current template.

Notice that the resulting HTML code for the header is assigned to the variable Result in the custom tag, and at the end this value is assigned to the variable HEADLINE in the calling template, which can then use CFOUTPUT to display the results.

Understanding Variable Scope Issues

In this chapter, especially in the discussion of the CFMODULE tag, you have seen examples of the implications of variable scope even if we haven't explicitly referred to them.

The concept of scope is fairly simple. *Scope* simply refers to the context in which a variable exists or doesn't. In its most simple state, a variable's scope starts when it is first declared (for instance, when a value is assigned to it using CFSET) in a template and lasts to the end of the template.

This is best understood by example. In the following example, the CFOUTPUT tag can be used to display the value of the variable SAMPLE only because the variable SAMPLE came into existence earlier in the template using the CFSET tag:

```
<CFSET SAMPLE="Some Text">
<CFOUTPUT>#SAMPLE#</CFOUTPUT>
```

However, if the order of these lines is reversed, then CFOUTPUT is trying to access the variable SAMPLE outside the scope of the variable (that is, before it has been created):

```
<CFOUTPUT>#SAMPLE#</CFOUTPUT>
<CFSET SAMPLE="Some Text">
```

In this case, an error similar to the one in Figure 8.3 will be produced.

FIGURE 8.3
Accessing a variable outside its scope produces an error.

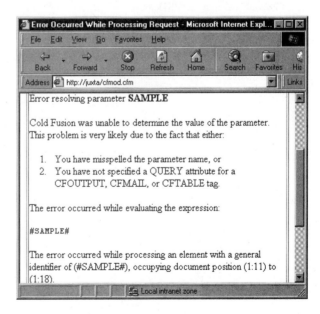

More subtleties to this exist when more than one template are involved. When you used CFINCLUDE, the code of the included template became part of the calling template. This means that it is part of the same scope. The code of the calling template can directly refer to variables contained in the code of the template being included and the other way around.

This is why, for instance, when CFINCLUDE was used, the template was able to directly reference the variable Chosen, which was used to generate the header and menu.

Using CFMODULE is more complicated, however. Because the code of the custom tag is executed independently of the code in the calling template, they have different scopes. Therefore, there is no way for the code in the custom tag to directly access values in the calling template (this can be done only indirectly through callers), and values need to be passed to the custom tag through the use of attributes.

This is an important distinction because it allows for variables to exist with the same name in both the calling template and custom tag independently of each other. They can contain different values and do not interfere with each other.

Recall our custom tag for outputting a menu and header:

```
<CFSET Chosen = attributes.Section>

<H1>Using CFINCLUDE</H1>
<CFIF Chosen is 1>
    <STRONG>The Syntax</STRONG>
<CFELSE>
    <A HREF="syntax.cfm">The Syntax</A>
</CFIF> |
<CFIF Chosen is 2>
    <STRONG>Examples</STRONG>
<CFELSE>
    <A HREF="examples.cfm">Examples</A>
</CFIF> |
<CFIF Chosen is 3>
    <STRONG>Alternatives</STRONG>
<CFELSE>
    <A HREF="alternatives.cfm">Alternatives</A>
</CFIF>
<HR>
```

Here you have created a variable called Chosen within the context of the custom tag. Consider, then, the following home-page example:

```
<CFSET Chosen="Test">
<CFMODULE NAME="menu" Section="0">
```

CFMODULE tag provides an alternative way of including outside code in the current template.

In the home page, the variable Chosen is created and assigned the value Test. Next the custom tag is called and passed the Section attribute. Within the custom tag, the value of the Section attribute is assigned to a variable called Chosen. This variable has a different scope than the one set in the calling template, however, and when the custom tag finishes executing, the variable Chosen in the calling template retains the value Test.

Taken a step further, the custom tag could even access the variable Chosen from the calling template independently of the variable Chosen created within the custom tag. That is, in the custom tag Chosen and caller.Chosen are separate and distinct variables with different values.

Where Do We Go from Here?

In this chapter, you have learned about two useful tags for combining more than one template: CFINCLUDE for including one template in another and CFMODULE for using another template as a custom tag.

In the next chapter, you will move on to an extremely important aspect of ColdFusion: creating databases and tables.

Databases are what give ColdFusion its power. With databases, ColdFusion applications can manipulate and process large amounts of information quickly and easily for the user and at the request of users. This allows the creation of sophisticated, interactive, dynamic Web sites.

chapter 9

Creating Databases and Tables

- Designing a database

- Implementing your own database

In this chapter, you will take a brief look at the process of designing a database and implementing it. The subject of designing relational database models is complex and worthy of one more book of its own. We can't hope to do justice to the subject beyond the smallest glimpse into it; a whole body of theory relates to the design of efficient databases. For most small databases, the best way to learn design is simply by doing it.

NOTE   If you would like to learn more about database creation and design, take a look at Sybex's *Mastering Access 2000* by Alan Simpson and Celeste Robinson; *Access 2000 VBA Handbook* by Susann Novalis with Jim Hobuss; and *Access 2000 Developer's Handbook, Volume 1: Desktop Edition* or *Access 2000 Developer's Handbook, Volume 2: Enterprise Edition*, both by Paul Litwin, Ken Getz, and Mike Gilbert.

You will design a small contact-management database in this chapter. You will not be creating the user interface to the database, which could be done using ColdFusion, but rather will look at the requirements of the project, and then walk through the decisions that go into designing the back-end database that would support the application.

Finally, you will walk through the implementation of the model you have designed using Microsoft Access. The process of implementing database design differs from database to database, and especially between desktop databases and full-scale client-server database systems. Still, the basic approach used in Access will help you understand what needs to be done when implementing databases on other systems.

Creating Your Database Model

For the purposes of our exercises in this section, you will walk through the design and implementation of a database to act as the back end in a simple contact-management system. The system will need to provide the following functionality:

- Track a contact's personal information, including name, age, gender, occupation, title, company, address, phone and fax numbers, e-mail address, URL, Social Security number, and customer identification number
- Ensure that state codes, telephone country codes, telephone area codes, and country names are entered in a standardized fashion
- Provide the capability to track incoming and outgoing correspondence with a given contact, including the type of correspondence (mail, fax, phone, or e-mail), the date and time of the correspondence, the direction of the correspondence (incoming or outgoing), the filename of the correspondence if it is in electronic form, indication of which other piece of correspondence it is in response to, and a summary of the correspondence

In designing this database, you need to follow several steps:

1. Gather requirements: In this stage, you look at the data you are tracking and any special issues that need to be addressed in this data.

2. Determine tables: Based on the requirements, you need to look at the specific database tables that you will create.

3. Assign primary keys: Each table needs a primary key. You will look at the data to be stored in each table to see whether there is a logical primary key, and, if not, consider how to create one.

4. Define columns: For each table you need to define the fields (or columns) to appear in the table, the data type of the field, and other limitations on the type of data stored in the field.

5. Make relationships: In the final stage, you specify relationships between tables. The whole idea behind relational database systems is that they leverage relationships between sets of data to create complex models of information.

Gathering Requirements and Determining Tables

We have already outlined the basic database requirements in our specification of application requirements. For instance, you know that you need to track personal information about each contact as well as maintain a historical log of correspondence with pointers to actual electronic documents of correspondence. One central issue is left from that definition: ensuring that "state codes, telephone country codes, telephone area codes, and country names are entered in a standardized fashion."

The standard tactic for doing this in a relational database is to maintain separate lists of countries, states, and telephone codes, and then, rather than include the state name or phone code in the personal information, simply point to an item in the list. Because all personal information records simply point to items in these country and state lists, you can ensure that every record uses a consistent spelling for country and state names, and that any required spelling changes need to be done only one place: in the separate list of countries or states.

This does raise one issue, though: It is reasonable to maintain a separate list of all countries and their telephone codes, and all states and provinces in the U.S. and Canada. However, it seems unwieldy to maintain a list of states and provinces in all countries in the world. Therefore, you will also need to provide a way to handle U.S. and Canadian addresses slightly differently from those of other countries. For U.S. and Canadian addresses, the user should be able to select an entry from the list of states and provinces, but for other addresses, the user should be able to manually enter a province or state.

This is a common tactic in many Web sites that ask for addresses in forms. They provide a drop-down list of all states and provinces in Canada and the U.S. This list, however, includes one entry along the lines of Outside the U.S. and Canada and then provides a blank text field that the user can fill in when they choose this option on the drop-down list. This type of form simply reflects the way in which data may be structured in the underlying database.

The question, then, is how all this translates into tables in your database design. You will need the following databases to store the information required by the application:

Info   A table for tracking personal information

Countries   A list of countries and their associated telephone codes and international two-letter codes

States   A list of states and provinces in the U.S. and Canada and their associated two-letter codes for addressing envelopes

Correspondence   A table for tracking correspondence with all contacts

Assigning Primary Keys

For each of these tables, you need to define a *primary key*. The primary key for a table is a table field that can be used to uniquely identify any record in the table without reference to information in the table. This means that the primary key value needs to be unique for each record in the table.

In some cases, data being tracked in the table may be suited to being the primary key. For instance, an employee identification number will be unique for each employee and therefore can serve as the primary key. However, in many tables, a field will not be suited to being the primary key. In these cases, you need to create an additional field in the table for the purposes of storing an arbitrary primary key.

When using such an arbitrary primary key, different approaches can be taken in deciding what value to use for the key. The simplest approach is to use an automatically incrementing number for the primary key; that is, with each new record, the value of the primary key increments by one, and new records can never have a primary key smaller than any used before. Therefore, if a record in the middle of the table is deleted, its primary key is not freed up for reuse by a new record.

Other approaches include deriving the primary key from information in the table based on a formula that is guaranteed to provide a unique value. This approach has advantages in terms of being able to derive the key for any record and provides a non-arbitrary relationship between the key and the data in the record.

For the purposes of small databases, if the data in a table doesn't offer a possible primary key, it is probably easiest to use an automatically-incrementing number for the primary key.

NOTE   Automatically incrementing numbers are a data type specific to the Microsoft Access database. Some databases offer this type of number and others don't. In the latter case, you need to increment a standard integer on your own, perhaps using the **CF_MAX_ID** custom tag, which can be found in the Tag Gallery on the Allaire Web site (**www.allaire.com**).

For the tables in your databases, the primary keys are outlined in Table 9.1:

TABLE 9.1:   Primary Keys for Your Database Tables

Table	Primary Key
Info	The customer identification number provides a unique value for each record and can serve as the primary key.
Countries	There is no guarantee that the country name or the country phone code will be unique (for instance, both Canada and the U.S. have 1 as their phone codes). However, there is an internationally accepted standard of unique two-letter codes for each country. These can serve as the primary key for this table.
States	The two-letter postal codes for the U.S. states and Canadian provinces provide unique ways of identifying all the records that will be stored in this table and can serve as the primary key.
Correspondence	None of the data you need to track about each item of correspondence can serve as the primary key. In this case, you need to add a separate field for an automatically incrementing primary key.

NOTE   You probably have noticed that the **Countries** and **States** tables use non-numeric primary keys. This is allowed in most database systems; primary keys can be numbers or text, as long as the data they store is unique for each record in the table. For speed and efficiency, it is generally advisable to use numeric fields instead of text fields for primary keys. Nonetheless, this doesn't mean you cannot use text fields in this capacity.

Defining Columns

Up to this point, you have considered the tables only generally, indicating the general information to be stored in each and which fields will be used as the primary keys. Now, you need to indicate the specific columns (or fields) that will make up each record in each table. For each field, you will need to clearly define the data to be stored in the field, the data type of information stored in the field, and any restrictions on data to be stored in the field.

Let's start with the personal information table, `Info`, outlined in Table 9.2.

TABLE 9.2:   Columns in the `Info` table

Field Name	Data Type	Description
CustomerID	Number	Contact's customer identification number (required; primary key)
LastName	Text	Contact's last name (required)
FirstName	Text	Contact's first name (required)
MiddleName	Text	Contact's middle name
BirthDate	Date/Time	Contact's birth data (which enables you to derive the person's age)
Gender	Text	Contact's gender (required)
Occupation	Text	Contact's occupation
Title	Text	Contact's work title
Company	Text	Contact's company
Address1	Text	First line of contact's address (required)
Address2	Text	Second line of contact's address
City	Text	Contact's city
State	Text	Code for contact's state or province
OtherState	Text	Name of state or province for non-U.S./Canada addresses
PostCode	Text	Contact's postal or ZIP code
Country	Text	Code for contact's country
PhoneCode	Number	Area code for contact's phone number (required)
PhoneNumber	Number	Contact's phone number (required)
FaxCode	Number	Area code for contact's fax number
FaxNumber	Number	Contact's fax number
MobileCode	Number	Area code for contact's mobile phone number
MobileNumber	Number	Contact's mobile phone number
Email	Text	Contact's e-mail address
URL	Text	Contact's URL
SSN	Number	Contact's Social Security number (this cannot be required because not all contacts will be from the United States and therefore may not have a Social Security number)

Note that the phone numbers have all been specified as numeric values. This is a matter of preference. As numeric fields, they can't include dashes, but they take up less space in the database than text fields. Similarly, the SSN field is numeric, which is fine because the standard places for dashes can be added when the Social Security number is displayed.

You probably noticed that there are no fields for telephone country codes. The logic here is that the country code specifies both the country name for addresses as well as the telephone code for phone numbers. Of course, an individual's phone, fax, and mobile numbers could be in different countries, but the assumption is made here that this would not be the case.

Next, consider the `Countries` table, outlined in Table 9.3.

TABLE 9.3:   Columns in the `Countries` Table

Field Name	Data Type	Description
Code	Text	Two-letter country code (required; primary key)
Phone	Number	Telephone country code (required)
Name	Text	Full country name (required)

The `States` table is similar to the `Countries` table, as shown in Table 9.4.

TABLE 9.4:   Columns in the `States` Table

Field Name	Data Type	Description
Code	Text	Two-letter state or province code (required; primary key)
Name	Text	Full state or province name (required)

Because you need to account for non-U.S./Canada addresses for which the user can manually enter a state or province name, you need to include one record in the `States` table that users from countries other than the U.S. or Canada can select.

Finally, you need to specify fields for the `Correspondence` table, outlined in Table 9.5.

TABLE 9.5:   Columns in the `Correspondence` Table

Field Name	Data Type	Description
CorrespondenceID	Automatic Number	Primary key (required)
CustomerID	Number	Customer ID of contact for correspondence (required)
CorrespondenceType	Text	Indication of the type of correspondence, such as phone, fax, or e-mail (required)
CorrespondenceDate	Date/Time	Data and time the correspondence was received or sent (required)
Direction	Text	Indication of the direction of correspondence, such as incoming or outgoing (required)
FileName	Text	Filename for electronic copies of correspondence
ResponseTo	Number	ID number of correspondence to which this is a reply
Summary	Text	Summary of the correspondence

Making Relationships

The final step in defining your database model is to specify the relationships between tables. For this purpose, you will specify individual fields in tables by using the form `TableName.FieldName`. Table 9.6 outlines the relationships between tables.

TABLE 9.6: Relationships between Tables

This Field	Contains a value chosen from this field
Info.State	States.Code
Info.Country	Countries.Code
Correspondence.Contact	Info.CustomerID
Correspondence.ResponseTo	Correspondence.CorrespondenceID

Most of these relationships should be clear. Linking `Info.State` to `States.Code` enables the full state name to be included in addresses if needed. Similarly, the `Info.Country` to `Countries.Code` link enables country names to be displayed in addresses, and telephone country codes to be provided with phone numbers. `Correspondence.Contact` is linked to `Info.CustomerID` to indicate whom the correspondence is to or from.

The final link, from `Correspondence.ResponseTo` to `Correspondence.ID`, may not make sense at first. This means that in any given correspondence record, you can't point to another correspondence record indicating that it is the item being responded to.

Deploying Your Database

Now that you have defined your database design, you are going to walk through the steps of creating this database in Access. You are not going to create Access forms or other user-interface tools such as ColdFusion templates, but rather are going to consider how to build the tables and relationships.

Creating a New Database

The first step in this process is to create a new database file. To do this in Access, choose New from the File menu. You will be presented with the New database dialog box shown in Figure 9.1.

FIGURE 9.1
Creating a new database
in Access

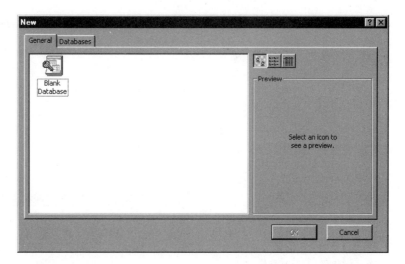

Select the General tab, click the Blank Database icon, and then click the OK button to create the database. You will be presented with a File New Database dialog box like the one in Figure 9.2, where you can specify the location and name of the database file.

FIGURE 9.2
Specifying a name and
location for a database file

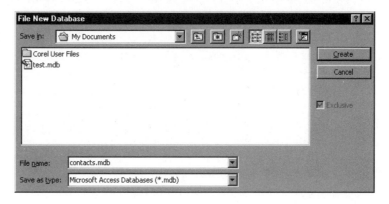

After the database is created, you will be presented with the main console for the new database. This window, shown in Figure 9.3, has tabbed pages for working with tables, queries, forms, reports, macros, and modules. These are all described in the Access documentation. In this appendix, you will stick to working with tables.

FIGURE 9.3
The main database console window

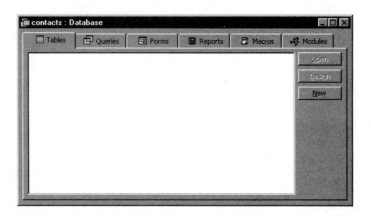

Initially, no tables will be shown in this window because the database is empty.

Creating Tables

To create a table, click the New button. To illustrate how this works, you will create the Countries table. After you click the New button, you will be prompted to specify one of the following options for creating the table:

Datasheet View   Opens an empty, new table in Datasheet View for entering data

Design View   Opens an empty, new table in Design View for defining fields

Table Wizard   Opens a wizard for creating a new table

Import Table   Imports a table from an external data source, such as another database or a spreadsheet

Link Table   Creates a table that is a link to a table in another database

You will use the Design View to enable you to create fields in your new, empty table. When Design View is selected and OK is clicked, the Design View window for the table is displayed, as in Figure 9.4.

FIGURE 9.4
The table Design View

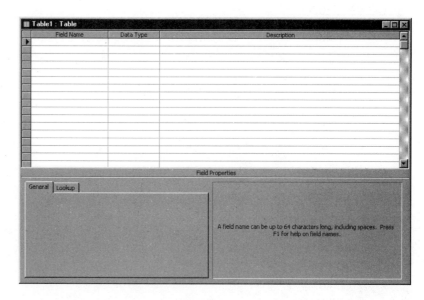

In this window you can define fields, one per row, for your table. For each field, you need to specify a field name, choose a data type from a drop-down list, and then provide an optional description of the field. The possible data types are:

Text   Text field of 1 to 255 characters

Memo   Large text field of up to roughly 64,000 characters

Number   Numeric field

Date/Time   Field containing a date/time value

Currency   Special numeric field for currencies

AutoNumber   Automatically incremented numeric field useful for primary keys

Yes/No   Boolean value field

OLE Object   Field for storing a Windows OLE object (this can be used for including external files from other applications in a database)

Hyperlink   Special text field for storing hyperlinks

In the lower part of the window, you can define field-specific options, such as default values, captions, and formats. These options are discussed in detail in the Access documentation, but are not directly relevant to the discussion in this appendix. After you define the three fields in your Countries table, the Design View window should look something like the one in Figure 9.5.

FIGURE 9.5
The Design View of the
Countries table

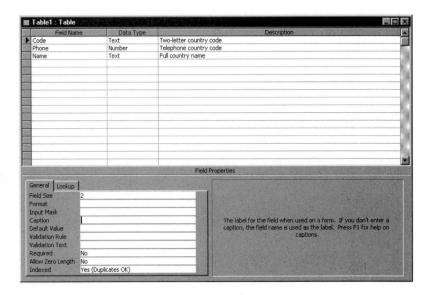

The final step is to define the primary key for the table that, in this case, is the **Code** field. To do this, right-click in the field and select Primary Key from the drop-down menu. When you do this, a small key icon will appear in the square to the left of the field name.

After you are finished defining the fields for the table, close the window. You will be prompted to indicate whether you want to save the changes to the table; select Yes and you will be prompted for a table name, as shown in the following graphic. Simply type the table name, **Countries**, and click the OK button.

As you create all the tables in your database, their names will appear in the Tables tab of the main console window.

Defining Links

After you have created all the tables, it is time to define the relationships between fields in the tables.

To do this, choose Relationships from the tools menu to open the relationship management window. The first time you do this, you will be prompted with a dialog box in which you need to select one or more tables to display in the Relationships window. Select all the tables in your database by holding down the Ctrl key and clicking each table name in the list, and then click the Add button. Next, click the Close button.

You will see the main Relationships window with four small windows displayed, each representing one of the tables in your database, as shown in Figure 9.6.

FIGURE 9.6
The Relationships window

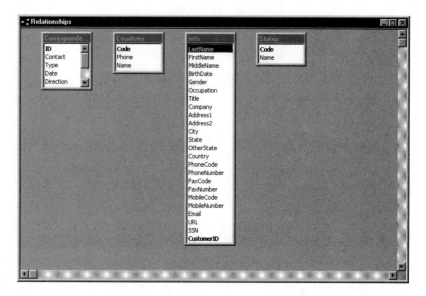

Relationships are defined graphically. You can resize and move each table window within the Relationships window. Each table window displays the names of the fields in the table and highlights the primary key in bold.

To create a relationship, you simply drag a field from one table and drop it on another field. For instance, to create the link between Info.State and States.Code, you would drag Info.State and drop it on States.Code. A window will be displayed for defining the nature of the relationship. For all links in your database, the default value is fine (refer to the Access documentation for discussions of these options). Simply click the Create button to create the link. The link will then be shown as lines between the linked items, as in Figure 9.7.

FIGURE 9.7

Links are shown as lines between items

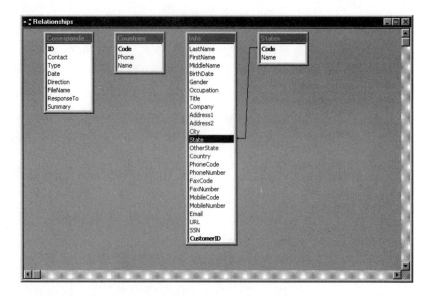

The remaining links can be created by dragging Info.Country to Countries.Code, Correspondence.Contact to Info.CustomerID, and Correspondence.ResponseTo to Correspondence.ID. To create this last link, you need to display two copies of the window for the Correspondence table. To add another copy of the window, simply right-click the background of the Relationships window and choose Show Table from the drop-down menu. Choose Correspondence in the dialog box, click the Add button, and click Close. To create the link, drag from Correspondence.ResponseTo in one of the windows to Correspondence.ID in the other.

The end results are shown in Figure 9.8.

FIGURE 9.8
All the links for the contacts database

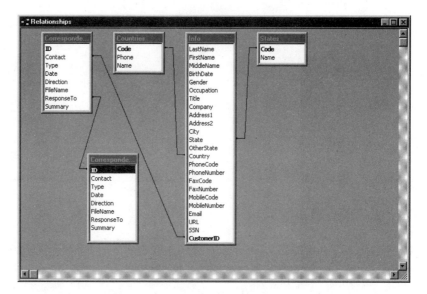

After all the links are created, simply close the window. When prompted to save the changes, click the Yes button.

Where Do We Go from Here?

Now that you know how to create databases for use with your ColdFusion applications, the next chapter will look at how the CFQUERY tag is used with the SQL database query language and how it interacts with your databases.

In particular, you will learn the basics of SQL, how to manipulate database records, and how to display the results of database query. You will also learn to use ColdFusion Studio's SQL Builder, which can allow you to graphically build SQL queries without needing to remember all the details of SQL syntax. You will also look at the CFTRANS-ACTION tag, which provides advanced capabilities for maintaining data integrity when using a database in a multi-user application.

Using *CFQUERY* and SQL to Interact with the Database

- Using CFQUERY

- Understanding SQL

- Manipulating Database Records

- Displaying Query Data

- Using ColdFusion Studio's SQL Builder

- Using CFTRANSACTION

One of ColdFusion's greatest strengths is its ability to retrieve and manipulate data stored in a database. Once you learn how to access a database through the Web, a completely new world of development will open up to you. You will be able to store, track, and manipulate the following types of data:

- User Data (interface preferences, bookmarks, personal information, login data, etc.)
- Human Resources Information (employee data, salaries, resumes, etc.)
- Product Catalogues (product descriptions, sales information, customer information, etc.)
- Financial Reports (sales information, billing, balances, credit card info, etc.)
- Educational Materials (lessons, quizzes, tests, scores, etc.)
- Any other information that can be stored in text format…

In order to begin using ColdFusion's powerful database connectivity features, there are a few things you need to be familiar with first:

1. How to design and create a database
2. Setting up a ColdFusion Datasource
3. Using Structured Query Language (SQL, pronounced 'es-que-el'—or 'sequel')

This book provides an excellent chapter on how to design and create a basic database. If you have never worked with databases before, now would be a good time to go back and read Chapter 9, "Creating Databases and Tables." While that chapter focuses mainly on developing a database using Microsoft Access 97, the concepts provided apply to development with all database applications. In Chapter 3, the section "Setting up a Database" also walks you through creating a simple database with one table.

Once you have created your database, you need to inform the ColdFusion Application Server that it exists. The section, "Using the Administrator to Add a Data Source" in Chapter 3 walks you through adding a ColdFusion data source. A data source is a pointer for ColdFusion. It explains where to find the database and what settings should be applied to it. For more detailed instructions on setting up a data source, refer to Chapter 35, "ColdFusion Administration."

After your database is created and your ColdFusion data source is defined, you are ready to start accessing your data using the ColdFusion tag CFQUERY in conjunction with SQL. SQL is the industry-standard language used to create, manipulate, and control data with all the top database management systems (DBMS). ColdFusion enables you to interact with these database systems via SQL because ColdFusion is an Open Database Connectivity (ODBC) client. ColdFusion uses ODBC as its database interface. You can also connect directly to a DBMS through native drivers.

To become a great ColdFusion developer, you really need to also be a great SQL programmer. This chapter will cover the basics of SQL and how to do the most common database interactions. You may also want to review the first half of Chapter 3, which introduces some basic SQL commands. If you want to become a SQL expert, you should buy a complete book on SQL. Some SQL book recommendations can be found in the Experience/Knowledge section of the Introduction.

NOTE   ColdFusion Application Server's Enterprise edition includes native drivers that support access to Sybase System 11, Sybase Adaptive Server 11.5, and Oracle 7.3 and 8 databases for the Windows and Solaris operating systems.

The *CFQUERY* Tag and SQL

ColdFusion allows you to connect to a variety of database applications, including (but not limited to) MS Access, SQL Server, Oracle, Sybase, Informix, and DB2. In order to connect your template to a database using ColdFusion, you need to use the CFQUERY tag. The CFQUERY tag has an opening and closing tag, takes several attributes, and is written as the following:

```
<CFQUERY NAME="name_of_query"
    DATASOURCE="name_of_datasource"
    DBTYPE="database_type"
    DBSERVER="database_management_system"
    DBNAME="database_name"
    USERNAME="database_username"
    PASSWORD="database_password"
    MAXROWS="max_rows_returned"
    BLOCKFACTOR="max_rows_fetched"
    TIMEOUT="max_timelimit_in_milliseconds"
    CACHEDAFTER="date"
    CACHEDWITHIN="timespan"
    PROVIDER="COM_provider"
    PROVIDERDSN="datasource_name"
    DEBUG="Yes/No">

    Insert SQL statement here…

</CFQUERY>
```

The CFQUERY tag attributes are described Table 10.1.

TABLE 10.1:   CFQUERY Tag Attributes

Attribute Name	Required?	Default	Description
NAME	yes	none	You must specify a name for the query. You will use this name to reference the query results later in the template. The name must not contain illegal characters (including spaces) and must begin with a letter (as opposed to a number).
DATASOURCE	yes	none	You must specify the data source name that ColdFusion should send this query to and receive results from. The data source must first be set up in the ColdFusion Administrator before you can access it.
DBTYPE	no	ODBC Driver	There are seven options to choose from (although Studio 4.0.1 only provides five in the option list). ODBC is the default if you do not specify the DBTYPE. **The options are:** ODBC–Standard Open Database Connectivity Driver. OLEDB–The OLE DB provider designated here overrides the driver type specified in the ColdFusion Administrator. Oracle73–In order to use the Oracle 7.3 native database driver the ColdFusion Server must have Oracle 7.3.4.0.0 (or greater) installed. Oracle80–In order to use the Oracle 8.0 native database driver the ColdFusion Server must have Oracle 8.0 (or greater) installed. Sybase11–In order to use the Sybase System 11 native database driver the ColdFusion Server must have Sybase 11.1.1 (or greater) installed. It is recommended that you install the Sybase patch ebf 7729. DB2–DB2 5.2 native database driver. Informix73–Informix73 native database driver.
DBSERVER	no	server specified in the datasource	If you are using native database drivers or the SQLOLEDB provider, you can specify the name of the database server machine. This setting overrides the server designated in the ColdFusion Administrator datasource settings.
DBNAME	no	default database designated in the datasource	If you are using Sybase System 11 driver or SQLOLEDB provider, you can specify the database name. This setting overrides the default database designated in the ColdFusion Administrator datasource settings.
USERNAME	no	username value designated in the datasource setup	This setting overrides the username designated in the ColdFusion Administrator datasource settings.

T A B L E 1 0 . 1 : CFQUERY Tag Attributes *(continued)*

Attribute Name	Required?	Default	Description
PASSWORD	no	password value designated in the datasource	This setting overrides the password designated in the ColdFusion Administrator datasource settings.
MAXROWS	no	none	This is the maximum number of rows returned in the query results record set.
BLOCKFACTOR	no	1	If you are using ORACLE native database drivers or ODBC drivers, this is the maximum number of rows (from 1-100) to fetch at a single time from the server. Some ODBC drivers may dynamically reduce the block factor at runtime.
TIMEOUT	no	none	A maximum number, in milliseconds, to specify how long a query should run before timing out and returning an error. Most ODBC drivers do not support this attribute or vary concerning the minimum and maximum allowable values (SQLServer 6.x and above supports **TIMEOUT**, Access does not).
CACHEDAFTER	no	none	A valid date must be used *. Cached query results will be used if 1.) The date of the original query is after the date indicated in this setting, 2.) If query caching has been enabled in the CF Administrator, and 3.) The query uses the exact same query **NAME, DATASOURCE, USERNAME, PASSWORD, DBTYPE, DBSERVER** (native drivers), **DBNAME** (Sybase), and SQL statement as the original query.
CACHED-WITHIN	no	none	The time span, from the present backward, must be entered using the ColdFusion **CreateTimeSpan()** function. Cached query results will be used if 1.) The original query date falls within the time span you define, 2.) If query caching has been enabled in the CF Administrator, and 3.) The query uses the exact same query **NAME, DATASOURCE, USERNAME, PASSWORD, DBTYPE, DBSERVER** (native drivers), **DBNAME** (Sybase), and SQL statement as the original query.
PROVIDER	no	none	You can specify a COM provider (used only with OLE-DB).
PROVIDERDSN	no	none	You can specify a datasource name for the COM provider (used only with OLE-DB).
DEBUG	no	no	Should be set to a "yes" or "no" value. When this attribute is set to "yes," the SQL statement and **recordcount** are output in the rendered template. This is useful for troubleshooting query problems.

* Years from 0 to 29 are interpreted as 21st century values. Years 30 to 99 are interpreted as 20th century values.
* When specifying a date value as a string, make sure it is enclosed in quotes.

NOTE
If you have trouble connecting to the Oracle 7.3 native driver, check out ColdFusion's Knowledge Base Article 7606 at `http://www1.allaire.com/Handlers/index.cfm?ID=7606 & Method= Full`.

When connecting to a database there are several types of interactions that can be done:

1. Data can be retrieved from a database.
2. Data can be inserted into a database.
3. Data can be updated in a database.
4. Data can be deleted from a database.
5. Tables and fields can be created in an existing database. (Discussed in Chapter 11, "Using Advanced Query Techniques.")

In all cases, you will use the CFQUERY tag to create the connection with the database.

NOTE
The exception is if you use the CFINSERT or CFUPDATE tags. Those tags will be discussed in Chapter 15, "Forms."

The type of interaction you make with the database depends on your SQL statement. The SQL statement is inserted between the opening and closing CFQUERY tags. A working example of connecting to a database using ColdFusion's CFQUERY tag and a simple SQL statement is shown in the following line of code:

```
<CFQUERY NAME="get_speaker_books"
DATASOURCE="sybex"
DBTYPE="ODBC">
SELECT    speakers.speaker_id,
speakers.speaker_first_name,
speakers.speaker_last_name
FROM      speakers
WHERE     speakers.speaker_id = 1
</CFQUERY>
```

FIGURE 10.1
Table Relationships

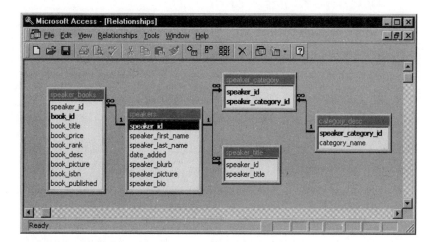

Database Tables

The database tables used in this chapter come from a scaled-down version of a database used for the Cosby Speakers Bureau Web Site (http://www.cosbybureau.com). These tables are stored in a database file (sybex.mdb) provided on the enclosed CD-ROM. To use the examples in this chapter, you need to install sybex.mdb as an ODBC data source named sybex.

The specific tables you will be looking at in this chapter are the following:

speakers　Stores information about speakers listed with the Cosby Speakers Bureau. This is the central table for the database.

speaker_title　Stores speaker job titles. This table is tied to the speakers table through the speaker_id field.

speaker_books　Stores information about books written by the speakers in the speakers table. This table is tied to the speakers table through the speaker_id field.

speaker_category　Stores the category ID's associated with each speaker. This table is tied to the speakers table through the speaker_id field and to the category_desc table through the speaker_category_id field.

Database Tables *(continued)*

category_desc Stores categories that speakers can be listed under. This table is tied to the `speaker_category` table through the `speaker_category_id field`.

These tables are all related through primary keys and foreign keys. Once you have opened the `sybex.mdb` file in Access you can see the table relationships by selecting Tools/Relationships on the Access menu bar. Also, refer back to Figure 10.1. For more information on creating databases, table relationships, and primary and foreign keys please read Chapter 9, "Creating Database and Tables."

In this CFQUERY tag, three attributes are specified. The NAME of the query, get_ speaker_books, can be used later in the template in conjunction with the CFOUTPUT tag to output the query results. The name of the DATASOURCE that has been set up in the ColdFusion Administrator, sybex, points ColdFusion to the correct database from which to retrieve records. Moreover, the type of database driver that you are connecting to, ODBC, is a driver used with Access 97, the database that has been included on the accompanying CD-ROM. The SQL statement that is included is a SELECT statement. In the next section, you will learn more about SQL SELECT statements.

Retrieving Records from a Database

When data is retrieved from a database a SELECT SQL statement should be used. To do this, you must specify in SQL which database tables and fields you would like to retrieve information from. Additionally, you can specify filtering criteria to narrow your search of the database records, and you can sort and group your data. The following sections will discuss some of the SQL keywords and clauses that can be used in a SELECT statement.

NOTE   The terms 'field' and 'column' will be used interchangeably throughout the book. The terms 'row' and 'record' will be used interchangeably throughout the book.

SELECT

The first part of the SELECT statement specifies the fields that you want returned. This is a required part of the SELECT statement. You begin the SELECT clause with the SELECT keyword followed by the names of the table fields you wish to be returned. If you are specifying more than one field, you must separate each field name with a comma. It is also a good idea to precede the field name with the table name prefix. This way, if you are retrieving data from more than one table, it will be easy to determine which table the fields come from. The code would be written as follows:

```
SELECT table_name.field_name1, table_name.field_name2
```

If you are selecting all columns, or fields in a table, then you can use the * symbol. This symbol is a wildcard that will retrieve all fields, thereby saving you from having to type out each field name. You should only use this symbol, as follows, if you want to retrieve all fields, as it puts more strain on the database connection.

```
SELECT *
```

You can also use the DISTINCT keyword to suppress the display of duplicate records where all fields in a row are the same. This might occur, for example, if you want to select all speakers that have written books, but do not want to see each book. Without DISTINCT, a speaker may be returned several times if they have written more than one book. The DISTINCT keyword, if used, would be placed immediately after the SELECT keyword and before any fields that you are selecting, as shown in the following code:

```
SELECT DISTINCT table_name.field_name1, table_name.field_name2
```

Some databases use the keyword DISTINCTROW instead.

Listing 10.1 shows an example of selecting one, several, and all fields of a particular table. When used in a ColdFusion template these SQL statements should be included inside a CFQUERY tag. You will see examples of this later in the chapter.

NOTE   The queries in Listing 10.1 will not work because they only include the SELECT clause. In order for a query to be operational, you need to also include a WHERE clause. The WHERE clause will be discussed in a later section.

Listing 10.1: *SELECT* Keyword

```
<!--- An example of selecting one field --->
SELECT    speakers.speaker_id

<!--- An example of selecting several fields --->
SELECT    speakers.speaker_id,
          speakers.speaker_first_name,
          speakers.speaker_last_name

<!--- An example of selecting all fields --->
SELECT    *
```

```
<!--- An example of selecting fields from two tables --->
SELECT    DISTINCT
                speakers.speaker_id,
                speakers.speaker_first_name,
                speakers.speaker_last_name,
                speakers.speaker_blurb,
                speakers.speaker_picture,
                speaker_books.speaker_id
```

NOTE   Table column names should not contain spaces or illegal characters. If they do, you must alias the name: SELECT ("first name") as first_name

---

FROM

The second part of your SELECT statement is where you define the table in which these fields are located. This FROM clause is also a required part of your SELECT statement. You begin this clause with the FROM keyword followed by the name(s) of the table(s) that you are selecting from. If you are selecting fields from more than one table, you should separate the table names with a comma (see Listing 10.2).

NOTE   In some versions of SQL, the FROM clause is where tables can be joined together. Joining is discussed in more detail in Chapter 11, "Using Advanced Query Techniques." For this chapter, we will only demonstrate joining in the WHERE clause. If you use Studio's Query builder, then your queries may have joins generated automatically in the FROM clause.

Listing 10.2: Adding the *FROM* Keyword

```
<!--- An example of selecting several fields --->

SELECT    speakers.speaker_id,
                speakers.speaker_first_name,
                   speakers.speaker_last_name
FROM      speakers

<!--- An example of selecting fields from two tables. This query
alone is not very useful. The results will provide every
combination of rows from each table in the results. There needs
to be a join of the two tables in a WHERE clause to provide more
usefule information. --->

SELECT    DISTINCT
                speakers.speaker_id,
                speakers.speaker_first_name,
                speakers.speaker_last_name,
                speakers.speaker_blurb,
                speakers.speaker_picture,
                speaker_books.speaker_id
```

```
FROM        speakers, speaker_books
WHERE
```

You are not required to add any more clauses to your SQL SELECT statement in order for it to work. You must realize, though, that with queries like those in Listing 10.2 all records will be returned. If you only want certain records to be returned, you must add a WHERE clause to your query. The WHERE clause allows you to define filtering criteria when selecting records from the database.

You begin a WHERE clause with the WHERE keyword followed by one or more conditions. If there is more than one condition then they need to be connected using the AND, OR, or NOT operators. All conditions included in the WHERE clause must evaluate to true or false. Listing 10.3 shows various examples of WHERE clauses and SQL conditions. SQL conditions and operators will be covered in depth later in this chapter.

Results for these queries cannot yet be shown, because you need to include the queries inside of a CFQUERY tag. Results of example queries will be shown when we discuss the CFOUTPUT tag later in this chapter.

Listing 10.3: Using the WHERE Keyword

```
<!--- In the following example all records where the
speaker_id field is equal to 1 will be returned. The three
fields: speaker_id, speaker_first_name, and speaker_last_name
will be available for use within the template. --->

SELECT    speakers.speaker_id,
          speakers.speaker_first_name,
          speakers.speaker_last_name
FROM      speakers
WHERE     speakers.speaker_id = 1


<!--- In the following example all records where the
speaker_last_name field begins with 'A' will be returned. The
% sign is a wildcard. All fields in the speakers table will be
available in the template. --->

SELECT    *
FROM    speakers
WHERE     speakers.speaker_last_name LIKE 'A%'


<!---  In the following example all records where the
speaker_id is equal to 1 and the speaker_id in the speakers
table is equal to the speaker_id in the speaker_books table
will be returned. In this example, 1 row in the speakers table
matches the criteria while 15 rows in the speaker_books table
match. So a total of 15 records will be returned. --->

SELECT    speakers.speaker_id,
          speakers.speaker_first_name,
          speakers.speaker_last_name,
          speakers.speaker_blurb,
          speaker_books.book_id,
```

```
                speaker_books.book_title,
                speaker_books.book_desc,
                speaker_books.book_picture
FROM    speaker_books, speakers
WHERE   speakers.speaker_id = speaker_books.speaker_id
AND     speakers.speaker_id = 1
```

The last example in Listing 10.3 shows how to join two tables together on the primary and foreign key fields of each table. This is one way that you can join tables. You can see visually how the two tables are joined together in Figure 10.2.

The `speaker_id` field in the `speakers` table is tied to the `speaker_id` field in the `speaker_books` table so that you can determine which books in the `speaker_books` table were written by which speakers in the `speakers` table. If the code `speakers` `.speaker_id = speaker_books.speaker_id` was not included in the statement, then the results would give every possible combination of rows in the `speakers` table matched to every row in the `speaker_books` table. This could amount to an extremely large number if your tables are quite large, and it could significantly decrease the speed and efficiency of your query. This is known as a Cartesian join. Besides, it most likely will not give you the results you are looking for.

Therefore, you need to learn how to join your tables on a related field. You can join tables as shown above, or you can learn more about joining in Chapter 11, "Using Advanced Query Techniques."

FIGURE 10.2
Joining Two Tables

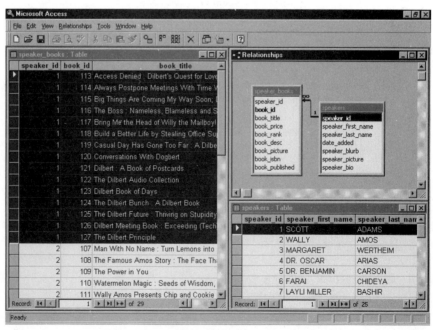

SQL commands and keywords are not case sensitive, which means you can use uppercase, lowercase, or mixed terms. However, case sensitivity is relevant for most databases when specifying data. For instance, the column names `TestColumn` and `testcolumn` are the same, but using `WHERE TestColumn = 'Hello'` is different from `WHERE TestColumn = 'HELLO'`.

NOTE   MS Access does not have case sensitivity when it comes to data.

It should also be mentioned that when strings and numbers are used in expressions, you need to be careful about the use of quotes. Strings should always be surrounded by single quotes. Numbers should not be surrounded by quotes at all, unless the field you are querying in the database is a text field. You can find more information on these topics in Chapter 11, "Using Advanced Query Techniques."

ORDER BY

The optional sorting of query results is achieved using the `ORDER BY` clause. `ORDER BY` allows you to specify which fields you would like to sort and whether the results should be sorted in ascending or descending order. The `ORDER BY` clause is also used in conjunction with the `CFOUTPUT GROUP` attribute to organize the query results into groups. CFOUTPUT will be discussed later in this chapter and in detail in Chapter 12, "Grouping, Nesting, and Formatting Outputs."

To use `ORDER BY`, you must first enter the keywords `ORDER BY` followed by the fieldname(s) you wish to sort. The default sort order is ascending. If you would like to sort the field as descending, you must add a space and then `desc` after the fieldname. Listing 10.4 shows various examples of `ORDER BY` clauses. Figure 10.3 shows the last query example in Listing 10.4 being constructed using Studio's Query Builder.

> **Listing 10.4: Using the *ORDER BY* Keyword**

```
<!--- In the following example all records where the
speaker_last_name field begins with 'A' will be returned. The
% sign is a wildcard. All fields in the speakers table will be
available in the template. The results will be in ascending order
by speaker_last_name --->

SELECT    *
FROM    speakers
WHERE    speakers.speaker_last_name LIKE 'A%'
ORDER BY speakers.speaker_last_name ASC
```

```
<!---  In the following example all records where the
speaker_id is equal to 1 and the speaker_id in the speakers
table is equal to the speaker_id in the speaker_books table
will be returned. In this example, 1 row in the speakers table
matches the criteria while 15 rows in the speaker_books table
match. So a total of 15 records will be returned. The results
will first be ordered by the speaker_id field (which can be used
in the GROUP attribute of the CFOUTPUT tag) and then descending
by the book_title --->

SELECT    speakers.speaker_id,
          speakers.speaker_first_name,
          speakers.speaker_last_name,
          speakers.speaker_blurb,
          speaker_books.book_id,
          speaker_books.book_title,
          speaker_books.book_desc,
          speaker_books.book_picture
FROM      speaker_books, speakers
WHERE     speakers.speaker_id = speaker_books.speaker_id
AND     speakers.speaker_id = 1
ORDER BY speakers.speaker_id,
speaker_books.book_title DESC
```

FIGURE 10.3
Studio Query Builder

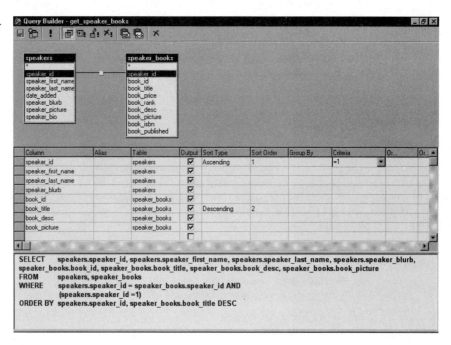

GROUP BY and Aggregate Functions

GROUP BY is used to organize related information together into groups, but is more often used in conjunction with aggregate functions. The GROUP BY clause should always be placed before the ORDER BY clause, if one is entered, and after the FROM and WHERE clauses. You cannot use the SELECT * wildcard when using GROUP BY in your query.

Aggregate functions allow you to apply certain functions to the columns retrieved in a query (the columns specified in the SELECT list) and obtain an average result for that column. When using these functions in your SELECT list you *must* always place all additional fields contained in your SELECT statement (that are not also aggregate functions) into the GROUP BY clause (as shown in Listing 10.5 and Figure 10.4). Several of the aggregate functions are listed Table 10.2. An aggregate function takes the format: FUNCTION_NAME(table_name.field_name) as aliased_name.

TABLE 10.2: Aggregate Functions

Function	Description
MAX()	Returns the maximum value of a group
MIN()	Returns the minimum value of a group
AVG()	Calculates the average value of a group
SUM()	Calculates the sum of the values in a group
COUNT()	Returns the count of rows (for the specified fieldname) that do not contain a null value in each group
COUNT(*)	Returns the total number of rows in a table when used without a WHERE clause

Listing 10.5: Aggregate Functions and *GROUP BY*

```
<!--- The results of the query will provide the total number
of books grouped by Speaker ID --->

<CFQUERY NAME="test" DATASOURCE="sybex" DBTYPE="ODBC">
SELECT    COUNT(speaker_books.book_id) as book_count,
          speaker_books.speaker_id
FROM      speaker_books
GROUP BY speaker_books.speaker_id
</CFQUERY>

<!DOCTYPE HTML PUBLIC "-//W3C//DTD HTML 4.0 Transitional//EN">

<HTML><HEAD><TITLE>Sybex - Mastering ColdFusion 4.5 -
Chapter 10 - Listing 10.5</TITLE></HEAD>

<BODY BGCOLOR="#FFFFFF">
```

```
<TABLE BORDER="1" ALIGN="center">
<TR>
<TH>Speaker ID</TH>
<TH># of books written</TH>
</TR>

<CFOUTPUT QUERY="test">
    <TR>
    <TD>#speaker_id#</TD>
    <TD>#book_count#</TD>
    </TR>
</CFOUTPUT>

</TABLE>
</BODY>
</HTML>
```

FIGURE 10.4
Using Group By to Organize Results

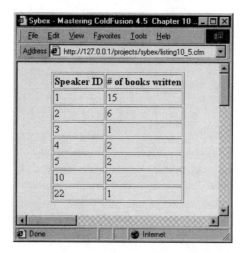

When an aggregate function is applied to a fieldname in the SELECT statement, you must give an alias to that field name so that ColdFusion knows how it should be referenced. To do that, follow the function with the as operator and then the name to be applied to the result. When referencing the result later in the template, refer to the aliased name. You can also use the following syntax for databases that will not work with the as operator:

```
SELECT    book_count=COUNT(speaker_books.book_id),
              speaker_books.speaker_id
FROM    speaker_books
GROUP BY speaker_books.speaker_id
```

NOTE For more information on using SQL aggregate functions with ColdFusion, please see Knowledge Base Article 266, "Using SQL Aggregate Functions with ColdFusion," in the Support section of the Allaire Web site at www.allaire.com.

NOTE You can also find a list of SQL Functions, including Aggregate Functions, in Appendix E, "SQL Function and Data Type Reference."

HAVING

When you use a GROUP BY clause and you want to filter the results, you should use HAVING instead of WHERE. While HAVING and WHERE can be used together in some situations, WHERE is intended to filter the records before they are grouped, and HAVING is intended to filter records after the grouping has been applied. HAVING should not be used if GROUP BY is not included in the statement. If you are trying to use HAVING, GROUP BY, and ORDER BY, or WHERE all in the same SQL statement, you may want to familiarize yourself with the complexities of SQL first by purchasing a good SQL book.

When HAVING is used with GROUP BY it should be placed after the GROUP BY clause, like the following:

```
<!--- This query will provide the total book count for the
speaker with an ID of 1 --->

SELECT    COUNT(speaker_books.book_id) as book_count,
            speaker_books.speaker_id
FROM      speaker_books
GROUP BY  speaker_books.speaker_id
HAVING    COUNT(speaker_books.book_id) > 1
```

WARNING Some versions of SQL will only allow the use of aggregate functions in the HAVING clause.

Outputting Query Results

Now that you have learned various ways to retrieve data from a database, you need to learn how to output the data in your ColdFusion template. To do this you will be using the CFOUTPUT tag. The CFOUTPUT tag has several optional attributes shown in Table 10.3.

TABLE 10.3: CFOUTPUT Attributes

Attribute Name	Description
QUERY	The name of the query that you would like to display the results of.
GROUP	A fieldname that was used in the SQL ORDER BY clause. To be used for grouping the output of the results.

TABLE 10.3: CFOUTPUT Attributes *(continued)*

Attribute Name	Description
STARTROW	The specific row to start displaying in the output block.
MAXROWS	The total number of rows to display in the output block.
GROUPCASESENSITIVE	Default is YES. Specifies whether ColdFusion should group based upon case.

In order to display query results, you must add the QUERY attribute to the CFOUTPUT tag. The name that you gave to your query in the CFQUERY tag is what should be entered for the QUERY attribute of the CFOUTPUT tag. Look at the example demonstrated in Listing 10.6 and the results shown in Figure 10.5.

Listing 10.6: Outputting Query Results

```
<!--- In the following example all records where the
speaker_last_name field begins with 'A' will be returned. The
% sign is a wildcard. All fields in the speakers table will be
available in the template. --->

<CFQUERY NAME="get_speakers" DATASOURCE="sybex" DBTYPE="ODBC">
    SELECT   *
    FROM     speakers
    WHERE    speakers.speaker_last_name LIKE 'A%'
    ORDER BY speakers.speaker_last_name
</CFQUERY>

<!DOCTYPE HTML PUBLIC "-//W3C//DTD HTML 4.0 Transitional//EN">

<HTML><HEAD><TITLE>Sybex - Mastering ColdFusion 4.5 -
Chapter 10 - Listing 10.6</TITLE></HEAD>

<BODY BGCOLOR="#FFFFFF">

<H1>Speaker List</H1>
<HR SIZE="1" NOSHADE>

<DL>
<!--- The CFOUTPUT tag will loop through the query results --->
<CFOUTPUT QUERY="get_speakers">
    <DT><B>#speaker_last_name#, #speaker_first_name#</B>
    <DD><FONT SIZE="-1">#speaker_blurb#</FONT>
</CFOUTPUT>
</DL>

</BODY>
</HTML>
```

FIGURE 10.5
Outputting Query Results

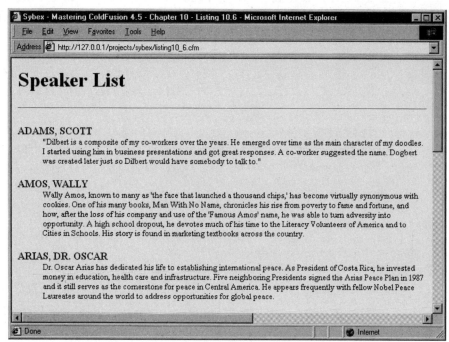

For each record returned by the query, ColdFusion will loop through the code between the opening and closing CFOUTPUT tags. In Figure 10.5, three speakers were returned, so the code was executed three times.

You can also pull data from two tables in one query. Often, when this is done, there will be one record returned from one table that is tied to multiple records returned in a second table. In this scenario, you would need to group your results so that duplicate information is not displayed. The following tables demonstrate results from an ungrouped recordset and a grouped recordset. If you do not group your output, you will get results similar to that in Table 10.4. However, if you add grouping, you can organize related information into groups as Table 10.5 shows.

TABLE 10.4: Ungrouped Recordset

AL	Anchorage
AL	Juneau
OR	Beaverton
OR	Corvallis

TABLE 10.4: Ungrouped Recordset *(continued)*

OR	Portland
WA	Bellevue
WA	Kirkland
WA	Redmond
WA	Seattle

TABLE 10.5: Grouped Recordset

AL	Anchorage
	Juneau
OR	Beaverton
	Corvallis
	Portland
WA	Bellevue
	Kirkland
	Redmond
	Seattle

In the next example, you will work with a query that pulls data from two tables in a one-to-many relationship. A one-to-many relationship means that one table has one record that is tied to multiple records in a second table through a join on a particular field (usually the primary and foreign keys). Figure 10.2 is a visual example of a one-to-many relationship between two tables. For each record in the speakers table, there are 15 records tied to it in the speaker_books table through the field speaker_id.

NOTE Please refer to Chapter 9, "Creating Databases and Tables" for more information on relational databases and primary keys. Joins will be covered in more detail later in this chapter.

Normally, when the results are returned, you receive repetitive information for each row (see Figure 10.6). Displaying grouped results via ColdFusion grouping allows you to present various levels of information that suppress the repetitive data (see Figure 10.7).

In order to group your query results using the ColdFusion grouping method (as opposed to using GROUP BY in your SQL statement), you need to make sure that the fields you wish to group on are in your SQL ORDER BY clause in the order that they should be grouped. Then, when you enter your CFOUTPUT tag, add the QUERY and GROUP attributes. The GROUP attribute should be set to the field you would like to group by (the one that was listed in your ORDER BY clause).

Then, once you have displayed your first level of grouping, you will need to nest a second CFOUTPUT tag to surround your second level of grouping. No attributes should be added unless you plan on grouping three levels deep. In that case you would need to add the GROUP attribute in the second CFOUTPUT tag set to the second-level grouping field listed in your ORDER BY clause. The last nested CFOUTPUT tag should not have a GROUP attribute. Remember to close all of your CFOUTPUT tags. Listing 10.7 provides an example of how to do two-level grouping with CFOUTPUT, and the results can be seen in Figure 10.7.

Listing 10.7: Grouping Output with *CFOUTPUT*

```
<!--- In the following example all records where the
speaker_id field in the speakers table is equal to the
speaker_id field in the speaker_books table and the speaker_id
is equal to 1 will be returned. This results in 1 record from
the speakers table and 15 records from the speaker_books
table The results are ordered by speaker_id and then
book_title --->

<CFQUERY NAME="get_speaker_books" DATASOURCE="sybex" DBTYPE="ODBC">
    SELECT    speakers.speaker_id,
              speakers.speaker_last_name,
              speakers.speaker_first_name,
              speakers.speaker_blurb,
              speaker_books.book_title,
              speaker_books.book_desc
    FROM    speakers, speaker_books
    WHERE    speakers.speaker_id = speaker_books.speaker_id
          AND speakers.speaker_id = 1
    ORDER BY speakers.speaker_id, speaker_books.book_title
</CFQUERY>

<!DOCTYPE HTML PUBLIC "-//W3C//DTD HTML 4.0 Transitional//EN">

<HTML><HEAD><TITLE>Sybex - Mastering ColdFusion 4.5 -
Chapter 10 - Listing 10.7</TITLE></HEAD>

<BODY BGCOLOR="#FFFFFF">

<!--- The CFOUTPUT tag will loop through the query results --->
<CFOUTPUT QUERY="get_speaker_books" GROUP="speaker_id">
    <H1>#speaker_first_name# #speaker_last_name#'s Books</H1>
    <HR SIZE="1" NOSHADE>

    <FONT SIZE="-1">#speaker_blurb#</FONT>

    <B>Speaker Books:</B>
    <UL>
```

```
    <CFOUTPUT><LI>#book_title#</CFOUTPUT>
    </UL>
</CFOUTPUT>

</BODY>
</HTML>
```

SELECT speakers.speaker_id, speakers.speaker_first_name, speakers.speaker_last_name, speakers.speak...

speaker_id	speaker_first_name	speaker_last_name	speaker_blurb	book_title	book_desc
1	SCOTT	ADAMS	"Dilbert is a composit	Access Denied : Dilbert's Quest for Love in the Nir	NULL
1	SCOTT	ADAMS	"Dilbert is a composit	Always Postpone Meetings With Time Wasting Mo	NULL
1	SCOTT	ADAMS	"Dilbert is a composit	Big Things Are Coming My Way Soon; Dilbert	NULL
1	SCOTT	ADAMS	"Dilbert is a composit	Bring Me the Head of Willy the Mailboy!	'Dilbert' is the most qu
1	SCOTT	ADAMS	"Dilbert is a composit	Build a Better Life by Stealing Office Supplies	NULL
1	SCOTT	ADAMS	"Dilbert is a composit	Casual Day Has Gone Too Far : A Dilbert Book	Dilbert--the world's fa
1	SCOTT	ADAMS	"Dilbert is a composit	Conversations With Dogbert	Have you ever wond
1	SCOTT	ADAMS	"Dilbert is a composit	Dilbert : A Book of Postcards	Once again, it's Dilbe
1	SCOTT	ADAMS	"Dilbert is a composit	Dilbert Book of Days	Caught in the corpora
1	SCOTT	ADAMS	"Dilbert is a composit	Dilbert Meeting Book : Exceeding (Tech) Limits	If the meetings you a
1	SCOTT	ADAMS	"Dilbert is a composit	The Boss : Nameless, Blameless and Shameless	In the newest Dilbert
1	SCOTT	ADAMS	"Dilbert is a composit	The Dilbert Audio Collection	From the New York T
1	SCOTT	ADAMS	"Dilbert is a composit	The Dilbert Bunch : A Dilbert Book	Here's a story of a ma
1	SCOTT	ADAMS	"Dilbert is a composit	The Dilbert Future : Thriving on Stupidity in the 21s	Take a look into Sco
1	SCOTT	ADAMS	"Dilbert is a composit	The Dilbert Principle	A Cubicle's-Eye View

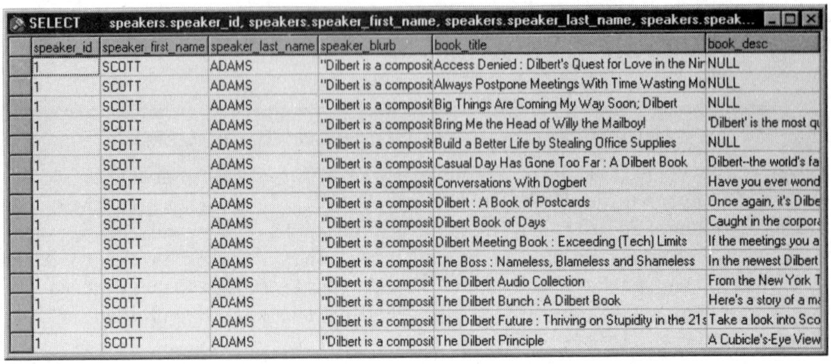

FIGURE 10.6
Results before ColdFusion Grouping

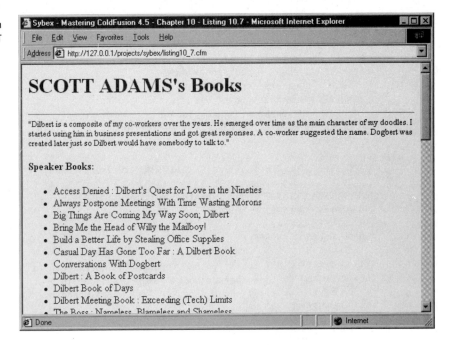

FIGURE 10.7
Grouping Output with CFOUTPUT

NOTE   More information on grouped output can be found in Chapter 12, "Grouping, Nesting, and Formatting Outputs."

Using Standard Variables Returned by the *CFQUERY* Tag

In addition to the fieldnames that you specify in your SELECT statement, ColdFusion returns several other query-related variables. They can be used in the same manner as all other returned query variables. The CFQUERY tag standard variables are:

- recordcount–provides the total number of records returned in a query result set. The number may be misleading if you are grouping your output.
- columnlist–Provides a comma-delimited list of all field names returned in a query result set. You can use List functions on this variable.
- currentrow–Stores the value of the current row number in the returned recordset.
- CFQUERY.ExecutionTime–Displays the query processing time in milliseconds. (Do not preface this variable with the query name.)

Another way that you can output query variables is by prefixing the variable with the queryname as in query_name.variable_name. This would be done inside of a CFOUTPUT tag that does not have the QUERY attribute set. In order to output the recordcount or currentrow variables without having to worry about CFOUTPUT QUERY attributes, follow the example in Listing 10.8. The code in Listing 10.8 also demonstrates a way to account for zero results in your query recordset. The results are shown in Figure 10.8.

Listing 10.8: Displaying *CFQUERY* Variables

```
<!--- In the following example all records where the
speaker_last_name field begins with 'A' will be returned. The
% sign is a wildcard. All fields in the speakers table will be
available in the template. --->

<CFQUERY NAME="get_speakers" DATASOURCE="sybex" DBTYPE="ODBC">
   SELECT   *
   FROM   speakers
   WHERE   speakers.speaker_last_name LIKE 'A%'
   ORDER BY speakers.speaker_last_name
</CFQUERY>

<!DOCTYPE HTML PUBLIC "-//W3C//DTD HTML 4.0 Transitional//EN">

<HTML><HEAD><TITLE>Sybex - Mastering ColdFusion 4.5 -
Chapter 10 - Listing 10.8</TITLE></HEAD>

<BODY BGCOLOR="#FFFFFF">
```

```
<H1>Speaker List</H1>
<HR SIZE="1" NOSHADE>

<!--- If no records are returned then the following block of
code is displayed. --->

<CFIF GET_SPEAKERS.RECORDCOUNT IS 0>
    <I>There are no speakers matching your search criteria.</I>
    </BODY>
    </HTML>
    <CFABORT>
</CFIF>

<!--- The following CFOUTPUT tag is used to display the total
number of records returned by the get_speakers query. --->

<CFOUTPUT>
    <I>There are #get_speakers.recordcount# results.
    Your query took #cfquery.ExecutionTime# milliseconds.</I>
</CFOUTPUT>
<HR SIZE="1" NOSHADE>

<!--- The CFOUTPUT tag will loop through the query results.
The currentrow variable provides the current row count. --->

<CFOUTPUT QUERY="get_speakers">
    <B>#currentrow#. #speaker_last_name#,
    #speaker_first_name#</B><BR>
</CFOUTPUT>

</BODY>
</HTML>
```

FIGURE 10.8
Using Standard Query
Variables

NOTE   CFABORT is used to stop the processing of the current template. For more information on **CFABORT** please refer to Appendix B, "ColdFusion Tag Reference."

Adding Records to the Database

Now that you have an understanding of how to retrieve and display data from a database, you may find it useful to modify data in a database. This section will discuss how to add records to tables in a database.

Using the Cosby Speakers Bureau example, you will learn how to add new speakers to the **speakers** table. Most of the time, records are added to a database based upon submitted form data. Submitting form data to a database will be covered in Chapter 15, "Forms." In this chapter, you will submit hardcoded data to the database tables. The final section of this chapter discusses more about submitting dynamic data.

In order to add records to a database, you must use the SQL INSERT statement inside of a CFQUERY tag. In the INSERT statement, you must tell ColdFusion which table and fields to add data to.

INSERT INTO

The first part of the INSERT statement is where you specify the table and fields to which you want to add data. This is a required part of the INSERT statement. You begin the INSERT statement with the INSERT INTO keywords followed by the name of the table and then the fields that you are adding data to. The format is INSERT INTO table_name (field1, field2, field3). Table fields do not need to be included in the INSERT field list unless the field requirements specify that it must not be NULL (meaning it must not be empty, it must contain a value). Then it must be present in your field list. This includes primary keys. AutoNumbered fields should not be included in the field list, as the database will automatically generate a unique value.

VALUES

The second part of the INSERT statement is where you define the values of the fields that you would like to insert. You begin this clause with the VALUES keyword followed by the values you are inserting. The order and number of values have to exactly match the order and number of fields listed in the first section of your INSERT statement. The format is INSERT INTO table_name (field1, field2, field3) VALUES (integer_value, 'text_value', 'memo_value'). If the value you are inserting is a text value, then it should be surrounded in single quotes (never use double quotes). If it is an integer, then do not put any quotes around it. The value data type must match the field data type specified in the database.

When an INSERT query is run, there are no results available for output in the template. You will know the query was unsuccessful if a ColdFusion error is returned. If you want to catch errors so they are not displayed to the user, please refer to the discussion on CFTRY and CFCATCH tags in Chapter 18, "Implementing Error Control."

An example of an INSERT query is shown in the next section under Listing 10.9.

NOTE CFINSERT can also be used to insert data into a database table. More information on CFINSERT can be found in Chapter 14, "Forms."

Retrieving the Last Inserted Record

When a record is inserted into a database, it is extremely wise to also add a field known as a primary key. The primary key is used to give the record a unique value. This makes it easier to differentiate between records and prevent duplication.

The primary key can be automatically generated (depending on your database) or you, the developer, can specify it. If you define the primary key, then you must add it to your field list in the INSERT statement. Its value must be unique and not match any other primary key value in the table. While this is not as convenient as having the database generate the number, it does make it easier to retrieve the newly inserted record from the database. Because you know the primary key value, you will easily be able to use a SELECT statement to find and return the record.

NOTE When creating your own unique primary key values you may want to consider using the function CreateUUID(). This function is described in detail in Appendix C, "ColdFusion Function Reference."

On the other hand, if the database generates the primary key value, you have no way of knowing what that is. There are several methods for finding this out.

You can query the database and select the MAX() of the primary key field. This aggregate function will give you the maximum value of the primary key field. This requires that the primary key field be numeric. There is a slight possibility, though, that User B could have inserted a record immediately following your insert and previous to your query for the maximum ID. This would result in you retrieving User B's record. To prevent this, you can surround your two queries with a CFTRANSACTION tag (see Listing 10.9 and Figure 10.9). If your database accepts it, you should set the isolation level to the value of serializable. Otherwise, the default isolation level is acceptable in most cases. Consult your database documentation for further details.

| NOTE | CFTRANSACTION is discussed later in this chapter. |

Listing 10.9: Retrieving the last inserted record ID

```
<CFTRANSACTION>

<!--- This query will insert one record and populate the
speaker_first_name and speaker_last_name fields with data.
The database will automatically populate the speaker_id
field with a unique number. All other fields will be left
blank. --->

<CFQUERY NAME="add_speaker"
DATASOURCE="sybex"
DBTYPE="ODBC">
INSERT INTO speakers (
      speaker_first_name,
      speaker_last_name
         )
VALUES (
      'Kristin',
         'Motlagh'
         )
</CFQUERY>

<!--- This query will retrieve the last inserted
speaker_id value --->

<CFQUERY NAME="get_last_record"
DATASOURCE="sybex"
DBTYPE="ODBC">
SELECT MAX(speaker_id) as new_id
FROM speakers
</CFQUERY>

</CFTRANSACTION>

<!DOCTYPE HTML PUBLIC "-//W3C//DTD HTML 4.0 Transitional//EN">

<HTML><HEAD><TITLE>Sybex - Mastering ColdFusion 4.5 -
Chapter 10 - Listing 10.9</TITLE></HEAD>

<BODY>

<CENTER>
<H2>The record has been inserted successfully!</H2>
```

```
<H3>Your new record ID is:
<CFOUTPUT QUERY="get_last_record">#new_id#</CFOUTPUT></H3>
</CENTER>

</BODY>
</HTML>
```

FIGURE 10.9

Retrieving the Last Inserted Record

Stored Procedures can be created to return the primary key value of the last inserted record as long as they are supported by your database. Defusion has several very good articles on how to do this. You can visit Defusion at www.defusion.com.

You can also retrieve the last inserted record from an Oracle or SQLServer 7.0 database by creating a trigger for all INSERT queries. This trigger would be coded as follows:

```
SELECT @@IDENTITY FROM table_name
```

Please refer to your database documentation for more detailed information on how to do this.

> **NOTE**   To learn more about database triggers please refer to a good SQL reference. SQL book recommendations can be found in the Introduction of this book.

Updating Database Records

Eventually, you may find the need to modify existing database records. Whether it is to correct an error or update old information, you need to use a SQL UPDATE statement inside of a CFQUERY tag. In the UPDATE statement, you must tell ColdFusion which table and fields to modify.

In this section, you will use the Cosby Speakers Bureau example to learn how to modify existing speaker data in the speakers table.

UPDATE

The first part of the UPDATE statement is where you specify the table that contains the record you want to modify. This is a required part of the UPDATE statement. You begin the UPDATE statement with the UPDATE keyword followed by the name of the table. The format is UPDATE table_name.

SET

The next part of your UPDATE statement requires you to define the values for the fields you are updating. You begin this clause with the SET keyword followed by the field names you are updating equal to the new field values. You can update as many fields as you wish. Just make sure that your values are the correct data type for each field that you are updating. The format for the SET clause is UPDATE table_name SET field1=value1, field2='value2', field3='value3'.

This is all that is required for an UPDATE statement to be operational. However, if you use an UPDATE statement without a WHERE clause, you will update every single record in the table. In most cases, this is not what is intended. Therefore, you should add a WHERE clause to your UPDATE statement.

WHERE

Adding a WHERE clause to an UPDATE query is just like adding a WHERE clause to a SELECT query. First, add the WHERE keyword followed by one or more expressions. The expressions must evaluate to TRUE or FALSE and be separated by AND or OR operators. The example in Listing 10.10 updates the record that was inserted in Listing 10.9. The results can be seen in Figure 10.10.

NOTE If you use the code in Listing 10.10, you need to make sure that the hardcoded speaker_id value in the UPDATE statement is the same value that was returned when running the code in Listing 10.9.

Listing 10.10: Updating a record in the speakers table

```
<!--- The following query will update the first and last name
of the speaker ID 26 in the database table speakers. --->

<CFQUERY NAME="update_speaker"
      DATASOURCE="sybex"
      DBTYPE="ODBC">
  UPDATE    speakers
  SET    speaker_first_name = 'Safa',
```

```
            speaker_last_name = 'Motlagh',
            speaker_blurb = 'Safa graduated from the University
of Maryland with a PhD in Analytical Chemistry in 1998. He has
published several papers, and is currently working on a
research project for the Bahai World Centre in Haifa, Israel'
    WHERE speakers.speaker_id = 26
</CFQUERY>

<!DOCTYPE HTML PUBLIC "-//W3C//DTD HTML 4.0 Transitional//EN">

<HTML><HEAD><TITLE>Sybex - Mastering ColdFusion 4.5 -
Chapter 10 - Listing 10.10</TITLE></HEAD>

<BODY>

<H2><CENTER>The record has been updated
successfully!</CENTER></H2>

</BODY>
</HTML>
```

FIGURE 10.10

Updating a Specific Record

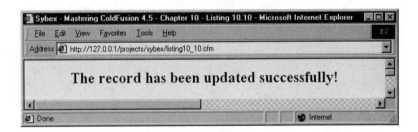

NOTE   CFUPDATE can also be used to update data in a database table. More information on CFUPDATE can be found in Chapter 15, "Forms."

Deleting Database Records

In order to delete database records, you need to use a SQL DELETE statement inside of a CFQUERY tag. In the DELETE statement, you must tell ColdFusion which table you want to delete records from as well as which record should be deleted. However, you must use this statement with caution. Deleting records is irreversible and it cannot be undone.

WARNING   If you omit the WHERE clause in your SQL DELETE statement, all data in your table will be deleted. As a rule, you should always include a WHERE clause in your DELETE statement.

In the following section, you will delete the specific record that you previously inserted and updated in the speakers table.

DELETE FROM

The first part of the DELETE statement is where you specify the table that contains the record you want to delete. This is a required part of the DELETE statement. You begin the DELETE statement with the DELETE FROM keywords followed by the name of the table. The format is DELETE FROM table_name. This is a completely valid SQL statement, but it will delete all records contained in the table specified. To specify which records should be deleted, you must add a WHERE clause.

WHERE

The WHERE clause in a DELETE statement filters which records will be deleted from a database table. Adding a WHERE clause to a DELETE query is just like adding a WHERE clause to a SELECT or UPDATE query. First, add the WHERE keyword followed by one or more expressions. The expressions must evaluate to TRUE or FALSE and be separated by AND or OR operators. The example in Listing 10.11 deletes the record that was updated in Listing 10.10. The results can be seen in Figure 10.11.

Listing 10.11: Deleting a record from the speakers table

```
<!--- The following query will delete the record with a speaker
ID of 26 in the database table speakers. --->

<CFQUERY NAME="delete_speaker"
      DATASOURCE="sybex"
      DBTYPE="ODBC">
   DELETE FROM    speakers
   WHERE speakers.speaker_id = 26
</CFQUERY>

<!DOCTYPE HTML PUBLIC "-//W3C//DTD HTML 4.0 Transitional//EN">

<HTML><HEAD><TITLE>Sybex - Mastering ColdFusion 4.5 -
Chapter 10 - Listing 10.11</TITLE></HEAD>

<BODY>

<H2><CENTER>The record has been deleted
successfully!</CENTER></H2>

</BODY>
</HTML>
```

FIGURE 10.11
Deleting a Specific Record

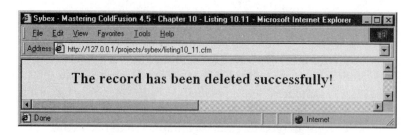

Once a DELETE query has been executed, it cannot be undone. It is therefore wise to test your query first. You can do this by making the DELETE statement a SELECT statement instead. To convert the query in Listing 10.11 to a SELECT statement you would remove the DELETE FROM keywords and replace them with the SELECT * FROM clause. The code would be written as follows:

```
<CFQUERY NAME="check_delete"
        DATASOURCE="sybex"
        DBTYPE="ODBC">
    SELECT    *
FROM    speakers
    WHERE     speakers.speaker_id = 26
</CFQUERY>
```

If the record returned in the results is the one you want to delete, then you can use the DELETE query. You can use this technique with INSERT, UPDATE, and DELETE queries.

SQL Expressions, Operators, and Functions

In order to get the most out of your queries, you need to be able to effectively and efficiently filter your query results. You do this by adding one or more conditions to your query WHERE clause. Conditions are comprised of column names, values, and operators that compare the two. You have already seen some simple SQL conditions in the section "Retrieving Records from a Database." They most often take the following format:

```
WHERE column_name operator value
```

column_name is most often the name of the field that you are evaluating. The operator tells the database how to compare the two values (column_name and value). The value is used to evaluate the column_name. The value can be hardcoded, or you can even pass variable data to it in the form of a ColdFusion variable:

```
WHERE speaker.speaker_id = #speaker_id#
```

In this scenario, you are evaluating whether the table field `speaker_id` is equal to the ColdFusion variable `speaker_id` using the `=` operator. By passing ColdFusion variables to your SQL statements, you are creating dynamic queries. Dynamic queries are discussed in the last section of this chapter.

WARNING When creating your SQL statements, you should avoid using reserved words for column names, table names, data source names, and ColdFusion variable names. A list of reserved words for SQLServer can be found at `support.microsoft.com/support/SQL/Content/ inprodhlp/_reserved_keywords.asp`. and `msdn.microsoft.com/library/sdkdoc/ daosdk/dajsql05_1hwz.htm`. For other database information, please consult your database documentation.

SQL Operators

A SQL operator is a reserved word or character used in a SQL statement. It is primarily used in the WHERE clause to do comparisons or arithmetic operations, although it can be used in other parts of your SQL statement. The four types of SQL operators that will be covered in this chapter are comparison, conditional, arithmetic, and logical. While this section does go into great depth about working with SQL, it is not comprehensive. If you would like to learn more advanced interactions using SQL, refer to Chapter 11, "Using Advanced Query Techniques," or check out the SQL book recommendations in the Introduction of this book.

Comparison Operators

Comparison operators are used to determine if the `column_name` on the left side of the operand meets the criteria defined by the value on the right side. The result returned is TRUE, FALSE, or UNKNOWN. UNKNOWN is returned if SQL finds a NULL value (see the explanation of NULL in the Conditional Operators section). UNKNOWN is often converted to FALSE by most versions of SQL. There are six comparison operators, and they are described in Table 10.6.

TABLE 10.6: Comparison Operators

Operator	Name	Description
=	Equal	Tests for values that must match exactly or no data is returned.
<>	Not-Equal	Tests for values that are not the same. Other variations of this operator include: != ^=
<	Less Than	Tests that value on the left side of the operator is less than the value on the right.

TABLE 10.6: Comparison Operators *(continued)*

Operator	Name	Description
>	Greater Than	Tests that value on the left side of the operator is greater than the value on the right.
<=	Less Than or Equal to	Tests that value on the left side of the operator is less than or equal to the value on the right.
>=	Greater Than or Equal to	Tests that value on the left side of the operator is greater than or equal to the value on the right.

Equal

The equal operator (=) has been used several times throughout this chapter. It is probably the most commonly used and most useful SQL operator. It often results in limiting your recordset more than any other operator does when comparing a primary key to a single value. You can use this operator with both strings and numerical values. The following example returns only one record:

```
SELECT *
FROM    speakers
WHERE     speakers.speaker_id = 5
```

The equal operator can also be used to join two tables on a particular field in the WHERE clause:

```
SELECT *
FROM    speakers, speaker_books
WHERE   speakers.speaker_id = speaker_books.speaker_id
```

Not-Equal

The not-equal operator (<>) is the exact opposite of the equal operator. It excludes all records that match its criteria. Again, you can use it with both strings and numerical values. Depending on your version of SQL, this operator can take any of the following formats: <>, !=, ^=. The following example returns all records except one:

```
SELECT *
FROM    speakers
WHERE   speakers.speaker_id <> 5
```

Less Than

The less than operator allows you to retrieve all records where the value to the left of the operand is less than the value to the right of the operand. You can compare both numbers and characters. If you query for all numbers less than 5, your results would be 1, 2, 3, and 4. If you query for all letters less than d, your results would be a, b, and c. Uppercase may be evaluated before lowercase characters depending on your version of SQL.

In the following query, all speakers with a last name in the first half of the alphabet up until 'm' will be returned:

```
SELECT     *
FROM       speakers
WHERE      LEFT(speaker_last_name, 1) < 'm'
ORDER BY   speakers.speaker_last_name
```

NOTE   The LEFT() SQL function is described in Appendix E, "SQL Function and Data Type Reference."

Less Than or Equal To

The less than or equal to operator is similar to the less than operator except that it includes the value to the right of the operand. You can compare both numbers and characters. If you query for all numbers less than or equal to 5, your results would be 1, 2, 3, 4, and 5. If you query for all letters less than or equal to d, your results would be a, b, c, and d. Uppercase may be evaluated before lowercase characters depending on your version of SQL. In Listing 10.12, all speakers with a last name in the first half of the alphabet up until and including 'm' will be returned. The results can be seen in Figure 10.12.

Listing 10.12: Finding Fields Less Than a Particular Value

```
<CFQUERY NAME="get_speakers" DATASOURCE="sybex" DBTYPE="ODBC">
    SELECT    *
    FROM    speakers
    WHERE    LEFT(speaker_last_name, 1) <= 'm'
    ORDER BYspeakers.speaker_last_name
</CFQUERY>

<!DOCTYPE HTML PUBLIC "-//W3C//DTD HTML 4.0 Transitional//EN">

<HTML><HEAD><TITLE>Sybex - Mastering ColdFusion 4.5 -
Chapter 10 - Listing 10.12</TITLE></HEAD>

<BODY BGCOLOR="#FFFFFF">

<H1>Speakers - A to M</H1>
<HR SIZE="1" NOSHADE>
<UL>
<CFOUTPUT QUERY="get_speakers">
<LI>#speaker_last_name#, #speaker_first_name#
</CFOUTPUT>
</UL>

</BODY>
</HTML>
```

FIGURE 10.12

Finding Fields Less Than a
Particular Value

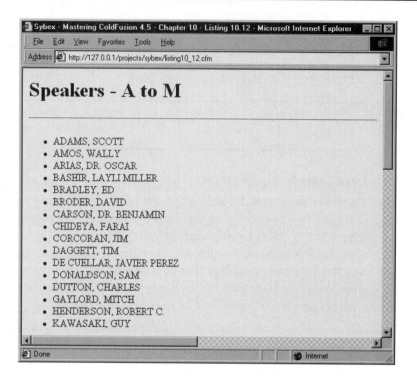

Greater Than

The greater than operator allows you to retrieve all records where the value to the left of
the operand is greater than the value to the right of the operand. You can compare both
numbers and characters. If you query for all numbers greater than 5, your results would
be 6, 7, 8, 9 and so on. If you query for all letters greater than x, your results would be y
and z. Uppercase may be evaluated before lowercase characters depending on your version of SQL. In the following query, all speakers with a last name in the second half of
the alphabet after 'n' will be returned:

```
SELECT    *
FROM      speakers
WHERE     LEFT(speaker_last_name, 1) > 'n'
ORDER BY  speakers.speaker_last_name
```

Greater Than or Equal To

The greater than or equal to operator is similar to the greater than operator except that it includes the value to the right of the operand. You can compare both numbers and characters. If you query for all numbers greater than or equal to 5, your results would be 5, 6, 7, 8, and so on. If you query for all letters greater than or equal to x, your results would be x, y, and z. Uppercase may be evaluated before lowercase characters depending on your version of SQL. In Listing 10.13, all speakers with a last name in second half of the alphabet starting with n will be returned. The results can be seen in Figure 10.13.

Listing 10.13: Finding Fields Greater Than a Particular Value

```
<CFQUERY NAME="get_speakers" DATASOURCE="sybex" DBTYPE="ODBC">
SELECT   *
FROM    speakers
WHERE    LEFT(speaker_last_name, 1) >= 'n'
ORDER BY speakers.speaker_last_name
</CFQUERY>

<!DOCTYPE HTML PUBLIC "-//W3C//DTD HTML 4.0 Transitional//EN">

<HTML><HEAD><TITLE>Sybex - Mastering ColdFusion 4.5 -
Chapter 10 - Listing 10.13</TITLE></HEAD>

<BODY BGCOLOR="#FFFFFF">

<H1>Speakers - N to Z</H1>
<HR SIZE="1" NOSHADE>
<UL>
<CFOUTPUT QUERY="get_speakers">
<LI>#speaker_last_name#, #speaker_first_name#
</CFOUTPUT>
</UL>

</BODY>
</HTML>
```

FIGURE 10.13
Finding Fields Greater Than
a Particular Value

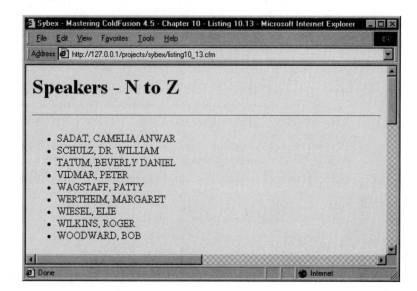

Conditional Operators

Conditional operators are used to determine if the `column_name` on the left side of the operand fulfills a particular condition. There are four basic conditional operators, and they are described in Table 10.7.

TABLE 10.7: Conditional Operators

Operator	Description
IS [NOT] NULL	Tests whether the value to the left of the operator contains a NULL value (or a non-NULL value if **NOT** is used).
BETWEEN	Tests whether the value to the left of the operator falls in the range between and including two values.
IN	Tests whether the value to the left of the operator is contained within a list of values. Can also be used to test whether a value is in the results of a subquery.
LIKE	Tests whether the value to the left of the operator matches a specific pattern. The following wildcards can be used: %, _, []

IS [NOT] NULL

IS NULL searches for fields that have no value associated with them. NULL is different than an empty string, blank, or 0; these are actual values. NULL actually means that no value or data whatsoever is associated with the field. If NOT is included in the operator, then the opposite is true. IS NOT NULL searches for fields that have some value associated with them, including empty strings, blanks, or 0's. Listing 10.14 and Figure 10.14 demonstrate using IS NULL and IS NOT NULL.

Listing 10.14: Finding NULL values

```
<CFQUERY NAME="get_books" DATASOURCE="sybex" DBTYPE="ODBC">
   SELECT   COUNT(*) as book_number
   FROM    speaker_books
   WHERE   speaker_books.book_picture IS NOT NULL
</CFQUERY>

<CFQUERY NAME="get_null_books" DATASOURCE="sybex" DBTYPE="ODBC">
   SELECT   COUNT(*) as book_null_number
   FROM    speaker_books
   WHERE   speaker_books.book_picture IS NULL
</CFQUERY>

<!DOCTYPE HTML PUBLIC "-//W3C//DTD HTML 4.0 Transitional//EN">

<HTML><HEAD><TITLE>Sybex - Mastering ColdFusion 4.5 -
Chapter 10 - Listing 10.14</TITLE></HEAD>

<BODY BGCOLOR="#FFFFFF">

<H1>Book Pictures</H1>
<HR SIZE="1" NOSHADE>

<CFOUTPUT>
<I>There are #get_books.book_number# pictures of speaker
books listed in the <CODE>speaker_books</CODE> table.
<BR>#get_null_books.book_null_number# books do not have
pictures in the <CODE>speaker_books</CODE> table.<P>

There are a total of #evaluate("get_books.book_number +
get_null_books.book_null_number")# books in the
speaker_books table.</I>
</CFOUTPUT>

</BODY>
</HTML>
```

NOTE   The aggregate function **COUNT(*)** is explained earlier in this chapter under the "**GROUP BY** and Aggregate Functions" section. The **evaluate()** function is described in Chapter 26, "Evaluating Dynamic Expressions."

FIGURE 10.14
Finding NULL values

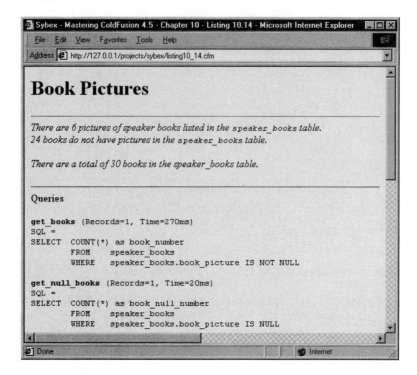

BETWEEN

If you are trying to determine whether a field value falls within the inclusive range of two values, you would use the BETWEEN operator. The following format should be used: `column_name BETWEEN value1 AND value2`. BETWEEN can be used with both numerical values and characters. Listing 10.15 and Figure 10.15 demonstrate using BETWEEN. The code in Listing 10.15 produces the exact same results as the code in Listing 10.13.

Listing 10.15: Finding a range of values

```
<CFQUERY NAME="get_speakers" DATASOURCE="sybex" DBTYPE="ODBC">
    SELECT   *
    FROM    speakers
    WHERE   LEFT(speaker_last_name, 1) BETWEEN 'n' AND 'z'
    ORDER BY speakers.speaker_last_name
</CFQUERY>

<!DOCTYPE HTML PUBLIC "-//W3C//DTD HTML 4.0 Transitional//EN">

<HTML><HEAD><TITLE>Sybex - Mastering ColdFusion 4.5 -
Chapter 10 - Listing 10.15</TITLE></HEAD>
```

```
<BODY BGCOLOR="#FFFFFF">

<H1>Speakers - N to Z</H1>
<HR SIZE="1" NOSHADE>
<UL>
<CFOUTPUT QUERY="get_speakers">
<LI>#speaker_last_name#, #speaker_first_name#
</CFOUTPUT>
</UL>

</BODY>
</HTML>
```

FIGURE 10.15
Finding a range of values

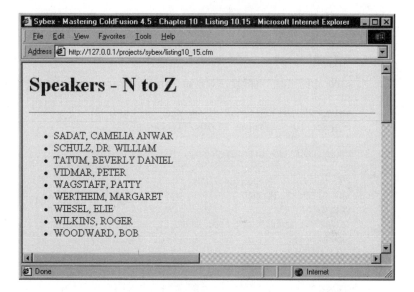

IN

If you are trying to determine whether a field value is included in a list of values or in a subquery, you should use the IN operator. The following format should be used: `column_name IN (subquery_or_list)`. Strings and numbers can be evaluated in either the list or the subquery results. If you are using strings, then each list item needs to be surrounded by single quotes. If you are using a ColdFusion variable or a form variable as the list and it contains strings instead of numbers, then you may need to use the `PreserveSingleQuotes()` function.

`PreserveSingleQuotes()` is used to ensure that the single quotes inside a list variable are not escaped by ColdFusion. This is important because SQL requires the use of unescaped single quotes when specifying string values. Please see Appendix C, "ColdFusion Function Reference" for more information.

If your list contains numbers, then you should not use any quotes. Listing 10.16 and Figure 10.16 demonstrate using IN.

Listing 10.16: Comparing a Field to a List of Values

```
<CFQUERY NAME="get_speakers" DATASOURCE="sybex" DBTYPE="ODBC">
    SELECT    *
    FROM    speakers
    WHERE    speaker_last_name IN ('Henderson', 'Bashir')
    ORDER BY speakers.speaker_last_name
</CFQUERY>

<!DOCTYPE HTML PUBLIC "-//W3C//DTD HTML 4.0 Transitional//EN">

<HTML><HEAD><TITLE>Sybex - Mastering ColdFusion 4.5 -
Chapter 10 - Listing 10.16</TITLE></HEAD>

<BODY BGCOLOR="#FFFFFF">

<H1>Bashir & Henderson</H1>
<HR SIZE="1" NOSHADE>
<UL>
<CFOUTPUT QUERY="get_speakers">
<LI>#speaker_last_name#, #speaker_first_name#<BR>
</CFOUTPUT>
</UL>

</BODY>
</HTML>
```

FIGURE 10.16

Comparing a Field to a List of Values

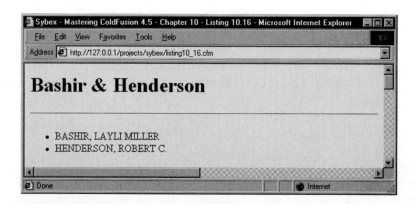

LIKE

The LIKE operator is used to match the value to the left of the operand to a string pattern combined with wildcards on the right. LIKE is case sensitive. It takes the format `column_name LIKE 'text_pattern'`. You can use the three following symbols that act as wildcards in the value to the right of the LIKE operand:

- % (Percent sign)—Use the percent sign at the beginning or ending of the value to specify that the beginning or ending of a string is variable.
- _ (Underscore sign)—Use the underscore in any location that you want to specify a single wildcard character.
- [] (Brackets)—Use brackets to provide specific matching criteria for a single character.

Look at Table 10.8 to better grasp how each wildcard can be used. An example can also be seen in Listing 10.17, with the results shown in Figure 10.17.

TABLE 10.8: Using Wildcards in SQL Queries

WHERE Clause	Result
`WHERE speakers_last_name LIKE 'Wi%'`	Displays all records in which `speakers_last_name` starts with `'Wi'`, for example, `WIESEL` and `WILKINS`.
`WHERE category_name LIKE '%management%'`	Displays all records in which `category_name` contains management, for example, `'Leadership/Management/Strategy/Ethics'`, `'Quality Management/Entrepreneurship'`, `'Communications/Negotiations & Conflict Management'`.
`WHERE speakers_first_name LIKE '%Miller'`	Displays all records in which the `speakers_first_name` field ends with `'Miller'`, for example, `'Layli Miller'`.
`WHERE speakers_first_name LIKE '_im'`	Displays all records in which the second and third positions are `'im'`, for example, `'Tim'` and `'Jim'` and `'Kim'`.
`WHERE speakers_first_name LIKE '[TK]im'`	Displays all records in which the first position starts with `'T'` or `'K'`, and the second and third positions are `'im'`, for example, `'Tim'` and `'Kim'`.

Listing 10.17: Comparing a Field to a String Pattern

```
<CFQUERY NAME="get_speakers" DATASOURCE="sybex" DBTYPE="ODBC">
    SELECT    *
    FROM    speakers
    WHERE    speaker_first_name LIKE 'Dr.%'
    ORDER BY speakers.speaker_last_name
</CFQUERY>

<!DOCTYPE HTML PUBLIC "-//W3C//DTD HTML 4.0 Transitional//EN">

<HTML><HEAD><TITLE>Sybex - Mastering ColdFusion 4.5 -
```

```
Chapter 10 - Listing 10.17</TITLE></HEAD>

<BODY BGCOLOR="#FFFFFF">

<H1>Speakers with a PhD</H1>
<HR SIZE="1" NOSHADE>
<UL>
<CFOUTPUT QUERY="get_speakers">
   <LI>#speaker_first_name# #speaker_last_name#<BR>
</CFOUTPUT>
</UL>

</BODY>
</HTML>
```

Refer to Figure 10.17 when comparing a field to a string pattern.

FIGURE 10.17

Comparing a Field to a
String Pattern

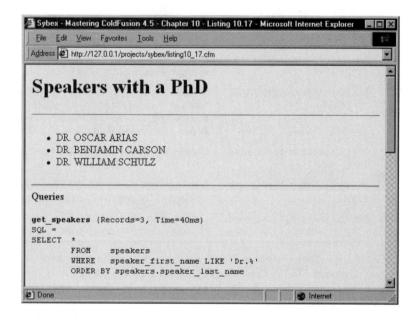

Arithmetic Operators

Arithmetic operators are used to perform mathematical calculations on fields. Some of them can also be used to work with strings. There are four arithmetic operators described here in Table 10.9.

TABLE 10.9: Arithmetic Operators

Operator	Name	Description
*	Multiply	Used to multiply two numeric values. Also used as the wildcard for selecting all fields in a table.
/	Divide	Used to divide one numeric value into another. Cannot be used with characters.
+	Add	Used to add two numeric values together or concatenate two string fields.
–	Subtract	Used to change a positive number to negative and to subtract one value from another. Cannot be used with characters.

When working with more than one arithmetic operator, there is precedence when evaluating their calculations. They are resolved in this order: multiplication, division, addition, and subtraction. Of course, you can use parentheses to override this order.

Multiply

The Multiply (*) operator is used to multiply two values. This can be done in both the SELECT and the WHERE clauses. This operator can only be used with numerical values. This symbol is also used as a wildcard for selecting all fields from a table when used with the SELECT clause. Listing 10.18 and Figure 10.18 show the use of the multiply operator in both the SELECT and the WHERE clauses. In the SELECT clause it is used to calculate a new book price that includes a 20% discount off the current price. In the WHERE clause it is used to ensure that only books that have a final price of over $10, after the discount has been applied, will be included.

Listing 10.18: Multiplying Values

```
<CFQUERY NAME="get_speakers" DATASOURCE="sybex" DBTYPE="ODBC">
   SELECT   speaker_books.book_title,
         speaker_books.book_price,
         (speaker_books.book_price * .8) as new_price
   FROM   speaker_books
   WHERE   (speaker_books.book_price * .8) > 10
</CFQUERY>

<!DOCTYPE HTML PUBLIC "-//W3C//DTD HTML 4.0 Transitional//EN">

<HTML><HEAD><TITLE>Sybex - Mastering ColdFusion 4.5 -
Chapter 10 - Listing 10.18</TITLE></HEAD>

<BODY BGCOLOR="#FFFFFF">
```

```
<H1>Speaker Books</H1>
<HR SIZE="1" NOSHADE>
<I>We give a 20% discount!</I>
<UL>
<CFOUTPUT QUERY="get_speakers">
   <LI><B>#UCASE(book_title)#</B><BR>
   <B>Amazon Price:</B> #DollarFormat(book_price)#
   <FONT COLOR="##FF0000">
   <B>Our Price:</B> #DollarFormat(new_price)#
   </FONT><P>
</CFOUTPUT>
</UL>

</BODY>
</HTML>
```

FIGURE 10.18

Multiplying Values

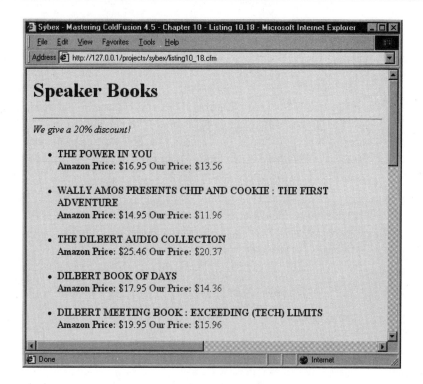

NOTE   Remember to use aliases for the fields that you perform calculations on in the SELECT clause.

Divide

The Divide (/) operator is used to divide one value into another. This can be done in both the SELECT and the WHERE clauses. This operator can only be used with numerical values. If you want to cut your book prices in half as long as the final price is over $5.00, you could use the following query:

```
SELECT    speaker_books.book_title,
          speaker_books.book_price,
          (speaker_books.book_price / 2) as half_price
FROM    speaker_books
WHERE    (speaker_books.book_price / 2) > 5
```

Add

The Add (+) operator has two main uses. The first is to add numeric values together. This can be done in both the SELECT clause and the WHERE clause. In the SELECT clause, you would most likely use it to add a set numeric value to a column. The following query would add $5.00 to every book price listed in the **speaker_books** table if the field already has a value:

```
SELECT    speaker_books.book_title,
          (speaker_books.book_price + 5) as new_price
FROM    speaker_books
WHERE    speaker_books.book_price IS NOT NULL
```

The second use of the Add (+) operator is to concatenate two string values. Again, this can be done in both the SELECT and WHERE clauses. The following example illustrates the use of the Add operator in both clauses. In the SELECT clause, it is used to concatenate the speaker's first and last name so that it is available to ColdFusion as a single field named 'full_name'. In the WHERE clause, it is used to concatenate the same two fields to see if they meet the string criteria to the right of the operand.

```
SELECT    (speakers.speaker_first_name +
speakers.speaker_last_name) as full_name,
speakers.speaker_bio
    FROM    speakers
    WHERE    (speakers.speaker_first_name +
speakers.speaker_last_name) = 'Guy Kawasaki'
```

Subtract

The Subtract (-) operator can be used to subtract one value from another. This can be done in both the SELECT and the WHERE clauses. This operator can only be used with numerical values. In the following example, $1 is subtracted from all book prices in the speaker_books table where the book_price field is not NULL:

```
SELECT    speaker_books.book_title,
             (speaker_books.book_price - 1) as new_price
    FROM   speaker_books
    WHERE  speaker_books.book_price IS NOT NULL
```

Logical/BOOLEAN/Conjunctive Operators

Logical operators are used to bind together multiple conditions in the WHERE clause. They return only the Boolean values of TRUE and FALSE. There are three logical operators, and they are described in Table 10.10.

TABLE 10.10: Logical Operators

Operator	Description
NOT	This operator is used to exclude a condition.
AND	All conditions separated by this operator must evaluate to True.
OR	At least one of the conditions separated by this operator must evaluate to True.

NOT

NOT is used in front of a condition to reverse its result. If the condition returns TRUE, then NOT changes it to FALSE. If a condition returns FALSE, then NOT changes it to TRUE. NOT can be used in front of any condition to change the results. The following example returns all records in the speaker_books table where the book_price is less than 5:

```
SELECT *
FROM Speaker_books
WHERE NOT speaker_books.book_price > 5
```

Of course, you can get the same results by just switching the greater than sign to a less than sign. NOT can also be used right alongside several of the following operators:

- NOT LIKE
- NOT IN
- IS NOT NULL
- NOT BETWEEN
- NOT EXISTS

AND

If there is more than one condition in your WHERE clause and both conditions must be fulfilled, then you would use the AND operator to join them together. A record is returned only if that record satisfies all of the conditions separated by the AND operator. The following query would return all books with a price greater than $5 and less than $10:

```
SELECT  *
FROM    speaker_books
WHERE   speaker_books.book_price > 5
AND     speaker_books.book_price < 10
```

You might think you could use the BETWEEN operator instead. However, the BETWEEN operator would include book prices that are $5 and $10. To use the BETWEEN operator and get the same results, you would need to use this WHERE clause: WHERE speaker_books.book_price BETWEEN 6 AND 9.

OR

If there is more than one condition in your WHERE clause and any of the conditions can be fulfilled to return a TRUE result, then you would use the OR operator to join the conditions together. A record is returned only if that record satisfies any of the conditions separated by the OR operator. The results for the following query and all records will be returned if the speaker_title includes any of the three words *author*, *director*, or *founder*:

```
SELECT  speaker_title.speaker_id
FROM    speaker_title
WHERE   speaker_title.speaker_title LIKE '%author%'
OR      speaker_title.speaker_title LIKE '%director%'
OR      speaker_title.speaker_title LIKE '%founder%'
```

Evaluation Precedence

When working with multiple WHERE conditions, it is important to take into account the order in which conditions are evaluated. If you are not at least aware of the order, then you might not correctly anticipate the results. Conditions are evaluated in the following order:

- Parentheses ()
- NOT
- AND
- OR

It is also helpful to note that AND operates faster than OR.

SQL Functions

SQL and ColdFusion share many similar functions. Most ColdFusion developers find it easier to just use the ColdFusion functions to format their data, as this does not require the learning of a new set of SQL functions. But, just as it is much more efficient for SQL to filter your records than it is for ColdFusion to filter them using CFIF statements; formatting your data with SQL functions is usually much faster than formatting them in your ColdFusion template with ColdFusion functions.

There are many SQL functions. A detailed list of most SQL functions can be found in Appendix E "SQL Function Reference." SQL functions can be used in both the SELECT and WHERE clauses of your SQL statement. You have already seen the use of several SQL functions when dealing with aggregate functions and the GROUP BY clause. Mainly, SQL functions are used to format data in a column before it is returned in the query results. Not all SQL functions that are available work with all versions of SQL. Check your database documentation. Listing 10.19 shows the use of two common SQL functions, UCASE() and YEAR(). UCASE() converts a string to all uppercase characters, while YEAR() extracts the year from a valid date value (see Figure 10.19).

Listing 10.19: Using SQL Functions

```
<CFQUERY NAME="get_date" DATASOURCE="sybex" DBTYPE="ODBC">
   SELECT   UCASE(speakers.speaker_first_name + ' ' +
          speakers.speaker_last_name) as full_name,
      YEAR(speakers.date_added) as year_added
   FROM    speakers
   ORDER BY speakers.date_added, speakers.speaker_last_name
</CFQUERY>

<!DOCTYPE HTML PUBLIC "-//W3C//DTD HTML 4.0 Transitional//EN">

<HTML><HEAD><TITLE>Sybex - Mastering ColdFusion 4.5 -
Chapter 10 - Listing 10.19</TITLE></HEAD>

<BODY BGCOLOR="#FFFFFF">

<H1>Speakers</H1>
<HR SIZE="1" NOSHADE>
<I>Year speaker was added to the database</I>

<DL>
<CFOUTPUT QUERY="get_date" GROUP="year_added">
   <DT><HR SIZE="1" NOSHADE><B>#year_added#</B><BR>
   <DD><FONT SIZE="-1">
   <CFOUTPUT>
      #full_name#<BR>
```

```
            </CFOUTPUT>
            </FONT>
        </CFOUTPUT>
        </DL>

        </BODY>
    </HTML>
```

FIGURE 10.19
Using SQL Functions

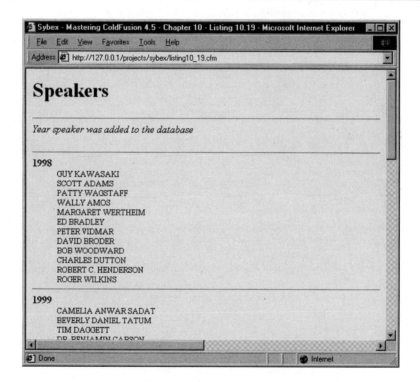

Using ColdFusion Studio's SQL Builder

Using ColdFusion Studio, you can build a SQL query without leaving the integrated development environment (IDE) for the ColdFusion development system. One of the tools available to you is the SQL Query Builder, which enables you to view the database schema and construct and test SQL operations for inclusion in your templates.

This chapter has demonstrated the basics of retrieving and manipulating data in a database. You should now be able to program your own SQL statements to retrieve records from one or more tables in a database. ColdFusion Studio's SQL query builder allows you to build more complex queries without having to learn more advanced SQL techniques. In the SQL query builder, you can visually create the joins between tables (similar to Figure 10.1) and select fieldnames that you want to retrieve. It also allows you to specify sorting orders, filtering criteria, and so on. It then dynamically builds the SQL statement for you. This tool is extremely useful and timesaving, and it produces SQL that should be operable with most databases.

Setting Up the Connection to the Data Source

ColdFusion Studio uses the Database Connection Manager in the ColdFusion Server to connect to remote data sources. Connection to these data sources requires authentication. In order to connect to your ColdFusion data sources, you should follow these procedures:

1. Click the Database tab on the lower-left side of the Studio screen, as shown in Figure 10.20.

FIGURE 10.20
The Database tab

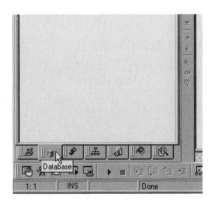

2. Click the pull-down menu as shown in Figure 10.21 and select localhost. You can add an additional RDS as well.

FIGURE 10.21
Selecting the LocalHost RDS

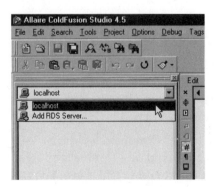

3. The Enter RDS Security Information dialogue box is displayed (see Figure 10.22). Enter the password to access the ColdFusion data sources.

FIGURE 10.22
Entering the Password

4. Click OK to set the password.

You now should be able to see all of your configured data sources (Figure 10.23) and use the SQL Builder tool.

FIGURE 10.23
Access to RDS

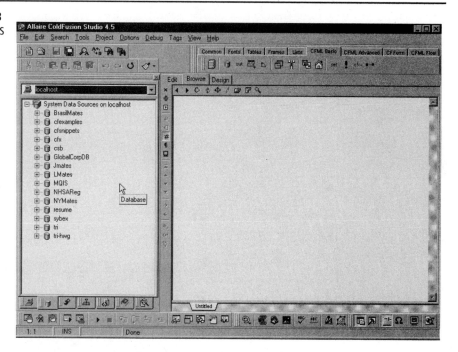

Using the SQL Builder Tool

The SQL Query Builder tool enables you to create a CFQUERY, complete with the SQL query, through a graphical interface. To create a query, follow this procedure:

1. Right-click the data source that you would like to build a new query from (see Figure 10.24).

FIGURE 10.24
Creating a New Query

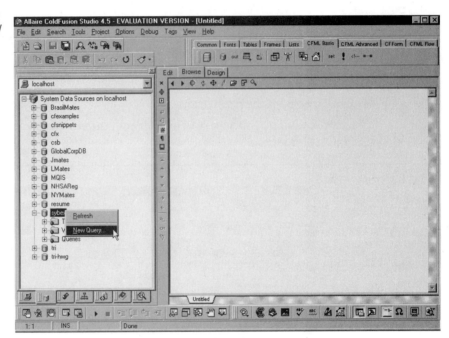

2. Select "New Query."

3. Select the desired table (see Figure 10.25).

FIGURE 10.25
Selecting a Table

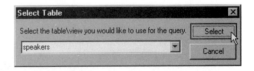

4. The Query Builder screen appears. Select and drag fields from open tables to empty cells in the column named Column (see Figure 10.26).

FIGURE 10.26

Dragging fields into a query

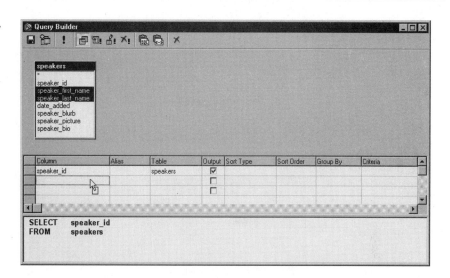

5. Notice that as you drop the new fields, the lower window, which contains the SQL statement, updates the screen to reflect the changes.

6. Add criteria (for instance, LIKE 'Dr.%') under the Criteria column of different fields. Click the exclamation mark (!) button in the toolbar to run the query (see Figure 10.27).

FIGURE 10.27

Test the Query

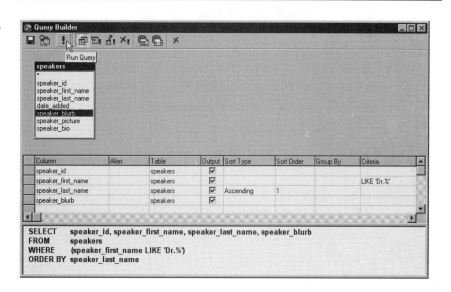

7. The result of the query is displayed in Figure 10.28.

FIGURE 10.28

Result screen

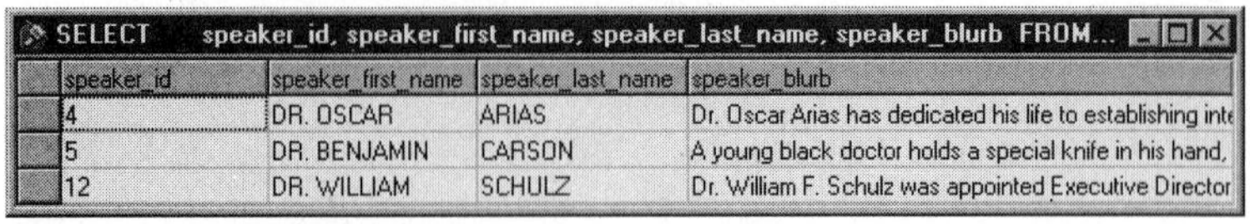

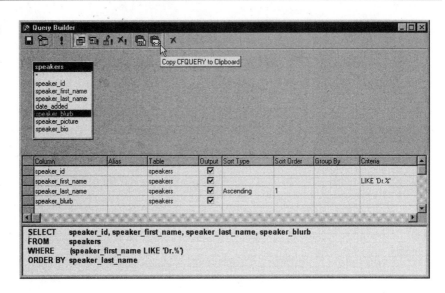

8. You can then click the Copy CFQUERY to Clipboard option, as shown in Figure 10.29.

FIGURE 10.29

Copying to the clipboard

9. Return to your main Studio Editing screen by closing the window. You are prompted to save the query. Give the query a name so you can reference it later.

10. Paste your new CFQUERY code, as shown in Figure 10.30.

FIGURE 10.30
Pasting the CFQUERY code
in the editing screen

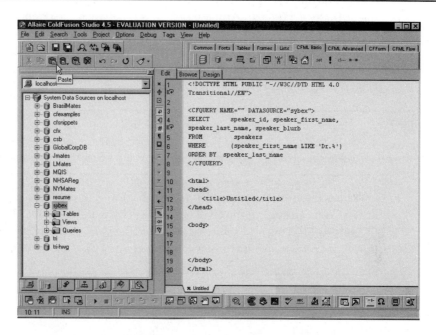

Now you can create your own CFQUERY code with more complicated SQL statements by using ColdFusion Studio's graphical SQL Builder. You never have to leave your favorite ColdFusion IDE!

CFTRANSACTION

When processing data, you sometimes will require a series of steps to complete a certain task. This is known as a *transaction*. If one of the steps is not completed, then the whole transaction should be cancelled or should be repeated from step 1. You may also require a locking mechanism while communicating with your database. You might need this to ensure that users are not overwriting each other's data. In your ColdFusion application, you can group a series of queries as a transaction and specify certain locking mechanisms. The characteristics of a transaction are:

- It must have a beginning and an end.
- If it fails in the middle of the process, no part of it can be saved.
- It must be completely saved or completely undone.

ColdFusion provides an easy way to create a transaction for multiple queries by using the CFTRANSACTION tag. Any queries placed between the opening and closing CFTRANSACTION tags are treated as a single transaction. The transaction begins at the first CFML tag connecting to a data source. None of the changes are committed to the database until all the transactions within the block are successfully executed. A rollback will occur if even one error occurs in the transaction.

WARNING   Changes to a database made with queries that create, alter, or delete tables or columns will not be rolled back if the CFTRANSACTION block fails. Creating, altering, and deleting tables or columns will be discussed in Chapter 11, "Using Advanced Query Techniques."

Transaction isolation provides you with control over database locking during a transaction. You can control the level of isolation by using the ISOLATION attribute of the CFTRANSACTION tag and setting it to one of the values listed in Table 10.11. These isolation types refer to locking schemes implemented by various ODBC drivers.

NOTE   Your database may or may not support any or all of the Isolation Levels listed in Table 10.11.

TABLE 10.11: *CFTRANSACTION* Isolation Levels

Isolation Level	Description
Read_Uncommitted	Locking of the database is not used. This can result in reading incorrect data.
Read_Committed	Default for SQL Server. Users cannot read data while it is in the process of being updated. Uses a shared lock.
Repeatable_Read	Varies according to your database. SQL Server employs all locking mechanisms to prevent inconsistent data.
Serializable	Employs all locking mechanisms.

In ColdFusion 4.5, you also have the additional optional attribute: ACTION. The three valid options for action are listed in Table 10.12.

TABLE 10.12: *CFTRANSACTION* Action Values

Actions	Description
BEGIN	Default. The beginning of a transaction block
COMMIT	Commits the current transaction
ROLLBACK	Rolls back the current transaction

The format for your CFTRANSACTION tag is:

```
<CFTRANSACTION action="action" isolation="isolation_level">
</CFTRANSACTION>
```

A very nice feature about CFTRANSACTION is the ability to use queries that interact with more than one data source. In a single transaction, you can have one query deleting data from one database and then another updating data in a second database. In order to allow this type of interaction, ColdFusion requires you to commit or rollback the transaction with a single database before moving on to a new database. You can do this by nesting a CFTRANSACTION tag with the ACTION attribute set to COMMIT or ROLLBACK:

```
<CFTRANSACTION ACTION="COMMIT"/>
```

You can also rollback:

```
<CFTRANSACTION ACTION="ROLLBACK"/>
```

If this is not done, ColdFusion will throw an error when switching to a new data source within the CFTRANSACTION tag. You will notice a trailing "/" in the CFTRANSAC-TION tags just mentioned. This is so that ColdFusion recognizes that the tags are nested; it is a required for the tag to be recognized.

NOTE The ACTION attribute of the CFTRANSACTION tag takes on a completely new meaning when you consider how it can be used in conjunction with ColdFusion Error Handling. You can base your COMMIT and ROLLBACK options on whether the database threw any errors. To do this you would need to use the CFTRY and CFCATCH tags. These tags are discussed in detail in Chapter 18, "Implementing Error Control."

When the closing CFTRANSACTION tag is encountered, ColdFusion commits the transactions to the database and terminates the transaction block.

To demonstrate the use of CFTRANSACTION, look at Listing 10.20 (a modified version of Listing 10.9) with results shown in Figure 10.31.

Listing 10.20: Using CFTRANSACTION

```
<!--- IS_PROBLEM is created to track whether database problems
have occurred. If so, the Template output will vary. --->
<CFSET IS_PROBLEM = "no">

<CFTRANSACTION ACTION="BEGIN">
    <!--- CFTRY opens a section that will be tested for errors. --->
    <CFTRY>

        <!--- The datasource specified is not a valid one,
        therefore ColdFusion should return an error. --->
```

```
<CFQUERY NAME="add_speaker"
     DATASOURCE="sybex"
     DBTYPE="ODBC">
   INSERT INTO speakers (
      speaker_first_name,
      speaker_last_name
      )
   VALUES (
      'Kristin',
      'Motlagh'
      )
</CFQUERY>

<!--- This CFCATCH tag will catch any database errors.
If there is an error, then any database connection will
be rolled back. Then the IS_PROBLEM variable is set
to yes. --->
 <CFCATCH TYPE="DATABASE">
   <CFTRANSACTION ACTION="ROLLBACK"/>
   <CFSET IS_PROBLEM = "yes">
 </CFCATCH>
</CFTRY>

<!--- If there was no database error, then the previous
query would be committed and the next query would be
executed. --->
<CFIF IS_PROBLEM IS "no">
   <CFTRANSACTION ACTION="COMMIT"/>
   <CFQUERY NAME="get_last_record"
      DATASOURCE="sybex"
      DBTYPE="ODBC">
      SELECT MAX(speaker_id) as new_id
      FROM speakers
   </CFQUERY>
</CFIF>

</CFTRANSACTION>

<!DOCTYPE HTML PUBLIC "-//W3C//DTD HTML 4.0 Transitional//EN">

<HTML><HEAD><TITLE>Sybex - Mastering ColdFusion 4.5 -
Chapter 10 - Listing 10.20</TITLE></HEAD>

<BODY>

<CENTER>

<CFIF IS_PROBLEM IS "no">
```

```
    <!--- If there was no query error --->
    <H2>The record has been inserted successfully!</H2>
    <H3>Your new record ID is:
    <CFOUTPUT QUERY="get_last_record">#new_id#</CFOUTPUT></H3>
<CFELSE>
    <!--- If there was a query error --->
    <H2>The record has not been inserted.</H2>
    <H3>Please contact your DBA for assistance.</H3>
</CFIF>
</CENTER>

</BODY>
</HTML>
```

FIGURE 10.31
Using CFTRANSACTION

Building Dynamic Queries

Once you have mastered CFQUERY and building static SQL statements, you will start wondering about how to dynamically build SQL queries within your ColdFusion application. With ColdFusion you can build these dynamic queries quite easily. You can insert dynamic parameters in your SQL statement or within your CFQUERY tag. These dynamic parameters are ColdFusion variables such as:

- Client, session, or application variables
- Form fields
- URL parameters

Any or all of these ColdFusion variables can be used as substitutes for values in the CFQUERY tag and within the SQL query. Creating dynamic queries means being able to do any of the following:

- Set your data source name as an application variable.
- Store a list of column names in a variable for the SELECT statement or for the ORDER BY clause.

- Use CFIF tags to build a column list for the SELECT statement or for building conditions in the WHERE clause or in the ORDER BY clause.
- Use IsDefined to check whether a variable is defined for inclusion in your WHERE clause or ORDER BY clause.
- Store your SQL statement in a variable, pass it around from page to page, and place it within the CFQUERY tag.

Examples of dynamic queries can be seen in later chapters of this book. For examples, please refer to the following chapters:

- Chapter 15, "Forms"
- Chapter 16, "Validating Form Data"
- Chapter 17, "Implementing the ColdFusion Web Application Framework"

Where Do We Go from Here?

You covered quite a bit of SQL in this chapter. You should have a good grasp of how to connect to a ColdFusion data source and manipulate data in a database.

In the next chapter, you will learn some more advanced techniques for communicating with databases. Some of the topics that were just touched on briefly in this chapter will be expanded upon. You will learn how to join tables, optimize your SQL, troubleshoot your queries, and much more.

Using Advanced Query Techniques

- Joining Tables and Queries

- Using Subqueries in Your SQL Statements

- Modifying Tables and Columns

- Caching Query Results

- Calling Stored Procedures by Using CFSTOREDPROC

- Working with Datatypes Using CFQUERYPARAM

- Optimizing SQL and Database Performance

- Finding Additional References for Various Databases

- Troubleshooting Common ODBC Errors

This chapter delves into some more advanced techniques for connecting your Web site to a database, optimizing your code, troubleshooting your errors, and improving your performance and speed. This is probably one of the more important chapters of the book. Once these techniques are mastered, you will have progressed from a beginner ColdFusion developer into the Intermediate to Advanced realm of development.

Working with Advanced SQL

Much of ColdFusion's robustness comes with its ability to connect to databases, so learning SQL is imperative if you want to be a great ColdFusion developer. In Chapter 10, you learned the basic SQL needed to retrieve and manipulate data in a database. This section explores some more complex SQL issues. If you want to learn even more, check out the SQL book recommendations in the introduction of this book.

NOTE The database tables used in this chapter come from a scaled-down version of a database used for the Cosby Speakers Bureau Web Site (`www.cosbybureau.com`). These tables are stored in a database file (`sybex.mdb`) provided on the enclosed CD-ROM. To use the examples in this chapter, you need to install sybex.mdb as an ODBC data source named `sybex`.

Joining

In a relational database, tables are related to each other through primary and foreign keys. The primary key field helps to uniquely identify records in a single table. The foreign key field resides in a separate table and contains data that matches the values in a primary key field. The primary and foreign keys are used to match the records between the two tables.

NOTE See Chapter 9, "Creating Databases and Tables," for more information on primary and foreign Keys.

Sooner or later (more likely sooner) you will find the need to retrieve related data from two or more tables. To do this, you will need to join the tables together on the primary and foreign key fields. There are various methods for joining tables in your SQL statements. Some of these methods depend on your style of coding while others depend on which version of SQL your database is compatible with. Depending upon the version of SQL you are working with, joining can be done in either the WHERE or the FROM clauses of your SQL statement. Both methods will be demonstrated in this chapter.

In order to learn how a join retrieves records from a database, you need to become familiar with the various types of SQL joins (Table 11.1).

TABLE 11.1: Types of SQL Joins

Join Type	Description
Inner Join	Returns all records where the data matches in the joined fields of both tables. The SELECT clause contains only non-primary and non-foreign key fields.
Equi-Join	Returns all records where the data matches in the joined fields of both tables. The SELECT clause contains both the primary and foreign key fields resulting in redundant data.
Natural Join	Returns all records where the data matches in the joined fields of both tables. The SELECT clause contains either the primary or the foreign key field.
Left Outer Join	Returns all records from the left table and only those records in the right table where the data in the joined fields match.
Right Outer Join	Returns all records from the right table and only those records in the left table where the data in the joined fields match.
Full Outer Join	Returns all records regardless of whether the data matches in the joined fields. Fields that do not match in the joined records will have NULL values.
Cross Join	Returns a Cartesian product of the two tables.
Self Join	Matches up all records in a database to itself based upon WHERE conditions.

Inner Joins

You may come across various terms used to refer to Inner Joins. They are most commonly called: Inner Joins, Equi-Joins, and Natural Joins. While these three types of Inner Joins are very similar, it is important to fully explain them so that there is not any confusion.

Inner Join

Inner Joins are used to return all records where the data in the joined fields match. There are two ways that you can code an Inner Join SQL statement. In the first example, the join will be performed in the FROM clause. This form of joining fulfills the SQL-92 ANSI standard, and is recommended for compatibility with most versions of SQL. Performing the join in the FROM clause forces your database to join the tables before evaluating any WHERE clause conditions. This can make your query performance more efficient because it limits the amount of records that the WHERE conditions will be performed on.

To create an Inner Join in the FROM clause, specify the name of the first table, then the type of join (in this case an Inner Join), followed by the name of the second table. Then enter the keyword ON, followed by the primary key of the first table equal to the related foreign key in the second table. This is the syntax: FROM table1 INNER JOIN table2 ON table1.primary_key = table2.foreign_key. In the following example, the join is indicated in bold type:

```
SELECT    speakers.speaker_first_name,
speakers.speaker_last_name,
speaker_title.speaker_title
```

```
FROM    speakers INNER JOIN speaker_title
ON      speakers.speaker_id = speaker_title.speaker_id
WHERE   (speakers.speaker_last_name LIKE 'a%')
ORDER BYspeakers.speaker_last_name,
speaker_title.speaker_title
```

The results can be seen in Figure 11.1.

To create the same results using a join in the WHERE clause, make the two joined fields equal to each other. Transact SQL (SQL Server) and PL/SQL (Oracle) support this sort of join. The following query produces the exact same results as the previous query:

```
SELECT  speakers.speaker_first_name,
speakers.speaker_last_name,
speaker_title.speaker_title
FROM    speakers, speaker_title
WHERE   speakers.speaker_id = speaker_title.speaker_id
AND     (speakers.speaker_last_name LIKE 'a%')
ORDER BY speakers.speaker_last_name,
speaker_title.speaker_title
```

Results are also shown in Figure 11.1.

FIGURE 11.1
SQL Inner Join

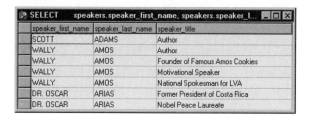

NOTE   Most versions of SQL support both methods described above. Oracle is among the databases that do not support joining in the FROM clause. Please check your database to find out which standards are supported.

Equi-Join

The second form of an Inner Join is called an Equi-Join. An Equi-Join can be described exactly the same way as an Inner Join, except that both joined fields are also included in the SQL SELECT statement.

NOTE

Because the primary and foreign keys involved in the join are often given the same column name, it is important to always prefix your field names with the corresponding table name. Then there is no confusion regarding which table a particular field belongs to.

When you output the results for an Equi-Join, you will get duplicate data for both joined fields (Figure 11.2). An Equi-join would look like this (unless, of course, you perform the join in the WHERE clause):

```
SELECT   speakers.speaker_id,
speakers.speaker_first_name,
speakers.speaker_last_name,
speaker_title.speaker_id,
speaker_title.speaker_title
FROM   speakers INNER JOIN speaker_title
ON       speakers.speaker_id = speaker_title.speaker_id
WHERE   (speakers.speaker_last_name LIKE 'a%')
ORDER BY speakers.speaker_last_name,
speaker_title.speaker_title
```

FIGURE 11.2
SQL Equi-Join

SELECT speakers.speaker_id, speaker_title.speaker_id, speakers.speaker_first_name, spea...

speaker_id	speaker_id	speaker_first_name	speaker_last_name	speaker_title
1	1	SCOTT	ADAMS	Author
2	2	WALLY	AMOS	Author
2	2	WALLY	AMOS	Founder of Famous Amos Cookies
2	2	WALLY	AMOS	Motivational Speaker
2	2	WALLY	AMOS	National Spokesman for LVA
4	4	DR. OSCAR	ARIAS	Former President of Costa Rica
4	4	DR. OSCAR	ARIAS	Nobel Peace Laureate

Natural Join

The only difference between the Equi-Join and the Natural Join is that only one of the joined fields is included in the SQL SELECT statement. This prevents duplication of data in the output of the results (see Figure 11.3). It does not matter which joined field you select. They will both contain the exact same data. The following example shows an example of a Natural Join:

```
SELECT   speakers.speaker_id,
speakers.speaker_first_name,
speakers.speaker_last_name,
speaker_title.speaker_title
FROM   speakers INNER JOIN speaker_title
ON       speakers.speaker_id = speaker_title.speaker_id
WHERE   (speakers.speaker_last_name LIKE 'a%')
ORDER BY speakers.speaker_last_name,
speaker_title.speaker_title
```

FIGURE 11.3
SQL Natural Join

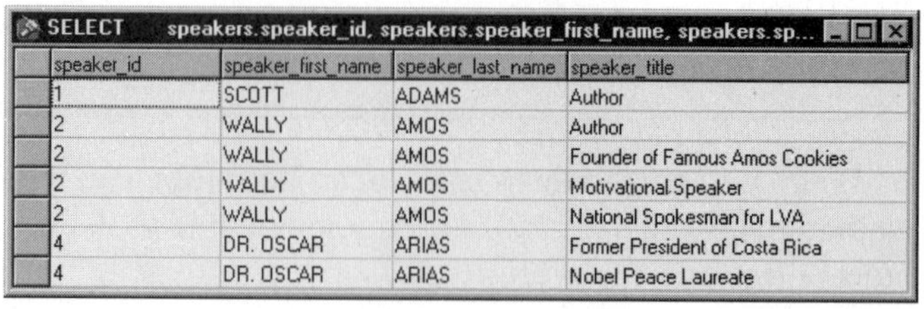

SELECT speakers.speaker_id, speakers.speaker_first_name, speakers.sp...

speaker_id	speaker_first_name	speaker_last_name	speaker_title
1	SCOTT	ADAMS	Author
2	WALLY	AMOS	Author
2	WALLY	AMOS	Founder of Famous Amos Cookies
2	WALLY	AMOS	Motivational Speaker
2	WALLY	AMOS	National Spokesman for LVA
4	DR. OSCAR	ARIAS	Former President of Costa Rica
4	DR. OSCAR	ARIAS	Nobel Peace Laureate

Outer Joins

The three types of outer joins available to you are Right Outer Join, Left Outer Join, and Full Outer Join. There are also three ways to code Outer Joins depending upon the version of SQL available to you: SQL-92 ANSI Standard, Transact SQL (T-SQL), and PL/SQL for Oracle.

NOTE The Full Outer Join is not fully supported by all versions of SQL.

Left Outer Join

A Left Join is the most common Outer Join. It returns all records from the left table and only those records in the right table where the data in the joined fields match. Any records from the left table that have no matching records in the right table are preserved and will display `NULL` values in the fields from the right table. The syntax is similar to that used with an Inner Join, except you would use the `LEFT OUTER JOIN` keywords instead: `FROM table1 LEFT OUTER JOIN table2 ON table1.primary_key = table2.foreign_key`. You can also use `LEFT JOIN` (and remove the `OUTER` keyword).

The following query would retrieve all records from `speakers` and only those records from the `speaker_books` table where the `speaker_id` matches the `speaker_id` in the `speakers` table. So, even if a speaker did not have any books tied to their record, their name would still be returned and `NULL` values would be entered in the `book_title` and `book_price` fields. This query uses the SQL-92 ANSI Standard and is written as follows:

```
SELECT   speakers.speaker_id,
speakers.speaker_first_name,
speakers.speaker_last_name,
speaker_books.book_title,
speaker_books.book_price
FROM   speakers LEFT JOIN speaker_books
ON      speakers.speaker_id = speaker_books.speaker_id
```

The results are shown in Figure 11.4.

FIGURE 11.4
SQL Left Join

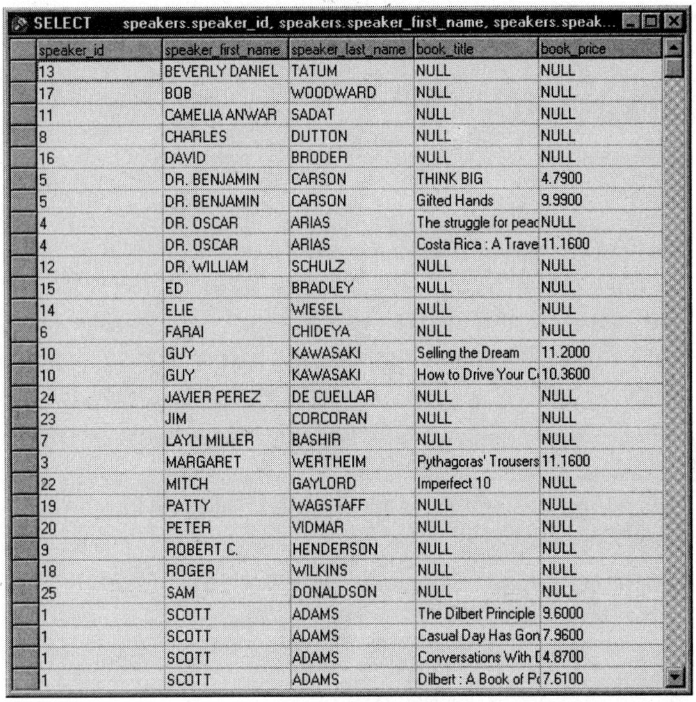

SELECT speakers.speaker_id, speakers.speaker_first_name, speakers.speak...

speaker_id	speaker_first_name	speaker_last_name	book_title	book_price
13	BEVERLY DANIEL	TATUM	NULL	NULL
17	BOB	WOODWARD	NULL	NULL
11	CAMELIA ANWAR	SADAT	NULL	NULL
8	CHARLES	DUTTON	NULL	NULL
16	DAVID	BRODER	NULL	NULL
5	DR. BENJAMIN	CARSON	THINK BIG	4.7900
5	DR. BENJAMIN	CARSON	Gifted Hands	9.9900
4	DR. OSCAR	ARIAS	The struggle for peac	NULL
4	DR. OSCAR	ARIAS	Costa Rica : A Trave	11.1600
12	DR. WILLIAM	SCHULZ	NULL	NULL
15	ED	BRADLEY	NULL	NULL
14	ELIE	WIESEL	NULL	NULL
6	FARAI	CHIDEYA	NULL	NULL
10	GUY	KAWASAKI	Selling the Dream	11.2000
10	GUY	KAWASAKI	How to Drive Your C	10.3600
24	JAVIER PEREZ	DE CUELLAR	NULL	NULL
23	JIM	CORCORAN	NULL	NULL
7	LAYLI MILLER	BASHIR	NULL	NULL
3	MARGARET	WERTHEIM	Pythagoras' Trousers	11.1600
22	MITCH	GAYLORD	Imperfect 10	NULL
19	PATTY	WAGSTAFF	NULL	NULL
20	PETER	VIDMAR	NULL	NULL
9	ROBERT C.	HENDERSON	NULL	NULL
18	ROGER	WILKINS	NULL	NULL
25	SAM	DONALDSON	NULL	NULL
1	SCOTT	ADAMS	The Dilbert Principle	9.6000
1	SCOTT	ADAMS	Casual Day Has Gon	7.9600
1	SCOTT	ADAMS	Conversations With [	4.8700
1	SCOTT	ADAMS	Dilbert : A Book of P	7.6100

The next query demonstrates using Transact SQL to create a Left Outer Join. The results would be the same as those shown in Figure 11.4 and the code would be as follows:

```
SELECT   speakers.speaker_id,
speakers.speaker_first_name,
speakers.speaker_last_name,
speaker_books.book_title,
speaker_books.book_price
FROM   speakers, speaker_books
WHERE   speakers.speaker_id *= speaker_books.speaker_id
```

The final query demonstrates using Oracle (PL/SQL) to create a Left Outer Join. Notice that the Left Outer Join symbol (+) is placed on the opposite side of the Transact SQL Left Outer Join. The results would be the same as those shown in Figure 11.4 and are written like this:

```
SELECT   speakers.speaker_id,
speakers.speaker_first_name,
speakers.speaker_last_name,
speaker_books.book_title,
```

```
speaker_books.book_price
FROM    speakers, speaker_books
WHERE   speakers.speaker_id =
speaker_books.speaker_id(+)
```

Right Outer Join

Right Outer Joins are the reverse of Left Outer Joins. They return all records from the right table and only those records in the left table where the data in the joined fields match. Any records from the right table that have no matching records in the left table will be preserved and display NULL values in the fields from the left table. The syntax is similar to that used with a Left Outer Join except you would use the Right Outer Join keywords instead: FROM `table1 RIGHT OUTER JOIN table2 ON table1.primary_key = table2.foreign_key`. You can also use Right Join (and remove the Outer keyword).

The following query would retrieve all records from `speakers_books` and only those records from the `speakers` table where the `speaker_id` matches the `speaker_id` in the `speakers_books` table. So, even if a book were not tied to any speaker, the record would be returned and NULL values would be entered in the `speaker_id`, `speaker_first_name`, and `speaker_last_name` fields. The following query uses the SQL-92 ANSI Standard:

```
SELECT  speakers.speaker_id,
speakers.speaker_first_name,
speakers.speaker_last_name,
speaker_books.book_title,
speaker_books.book_price
FROM    speakers RIGHT JOIN speaker_books
ON      speakers.speaker_id = speaker_books.speaker_id
```

The results are shown in Figure 11.5.

The next query demonstrates using Transact SQL to create a Right Outer Join. The results would be the same as those shown in Figure 11.5 and are written as follows:

```
SELECT  speakers.speaker_id,
speakers.speaker_first_name,
speakers.speaker_last_name,
speaker_books.book_title,
speaker_books.book_price
FROM    speakers, speaker_books
WHERE   speakers.speaker_id =* speaker_books.speaker_id
```

FIGURE 11.5
SQL Right Join

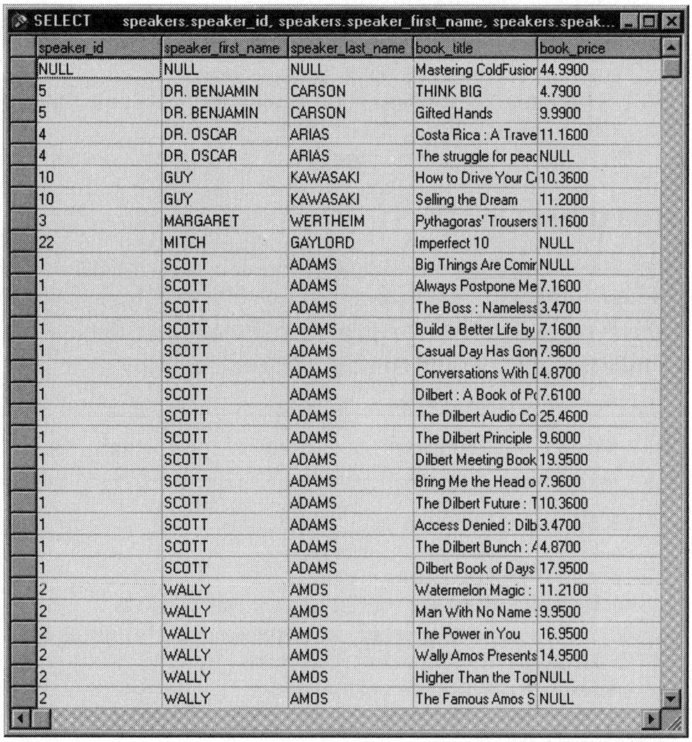
SELECT speakers.speaker_id, speakers.speaker_first_name, speakers.speak...

speaker_id	speaker_first_name	speaker_last_name	book_title	book_price
NULL	NULL	NULL	Mastering ColdFusior	44.9900
5	DR. BENJAMIN	CARSON	THINK BIG	4.7900
5	DR. BENJAMIN	CARSON	Gifted Hands	9.9900
4	DR. OSCAR	ARIAS	Costa Rica : A Trave	11.1600
4	DR. OSCAR	ARIAS	The struggle for peac	NULL
10	GUY	KAWASAKI	How to Drive Your C	10.3600
10	GUY	KAWASAKI	Selling the Dream	11.2000
3	MARGARET	WERTHEIM	Pythagoras' Trousers	11.1600
22	MITCH	GAYLORD	Imperfect 10	NULL
1	SCOTT	ADAMS	Big Things Are Comir	NULL
1	SCOTT	ADAMS	Always Postpone Me	7.1600
1	SCOTT	ADAMS	The Boss : Nameless	3.4700
1	SCOTT	ADAMS	Build a Better Life by	7.1600
1	SCOTT	ADAMS	Casual Day Has Gon	7.9600
1	SCOTT	ADAMS	Conversations With [	4.8700
1	SCOTT	ADAMS	Dilbert : A Book of P	7.6100
1	SCOTT	ADAMS	The Dilbert Audio Co	25.4600
1	SCOTT	ADAMS	The Dilbert Principle	9.6000
1	SCOTT	ADAMS	Dilbert Meeting Book	19.9500
1	SCOTT	ADAMS	Bring Me the Head o	7.9600
1	SCOTT	ADAMS	The Dilbert Future : T	10.3600
1	SCOTT	ADAMS	Access Denied : Dilb	3.4700
1	SCOTT	ADAMS	The Dilbert Bunch : /	4.8700
1	SCOTT	ADAMS	Dilbert Book of Days	17.9500
2	WALLY	AMOS	Watermelon Magic :	11.2100
2	WALLY	AMOS	Man With No Name :	9.9500
2	WALLY	AMOS	The Power in You	16.9500
2	WALLY	AMOS	Wally Amos Presents	14.9500
2	WALLY	AMOS	Higher Than the Top	NULL
2	WALLY	AMOS	The Famous Amos S	NULL

The final query demonstrates using Oracle (PL/SQL) to create a Right Outer Join. Notice that the Right Outer Join symbol (+) is placed on the opposite side of the Transact SQL Right Outer Join. The results would be the same as those shown in Figure 11.5 and would look like this:

```
SELECT   speakers.speaker_id,
speakers.speaker_first_name,
speakers.speaker_last_name,
speaker_books.book_title,
speaker_books.book_price
FROM   speakers, speaker_books
WHERE   speakers.speaker_id(+) =
speaker_books.speaker_id
```

Basically, you can get the same results from a Left Outer Join and a Right Outer Join by just flipping the tables around. For example, the following two FROM clauses produce the same results:

```
FROM    speakers LEFT JOIN speaker_books
ON         speakers.speaker_id = speaker_books.speaker_id
FROM    speaker_books RIGHT JOIN speakers
ON         speaker_books.speaker_id = speakers.speaker_id
```

Full Outer Join

A Full Outer Join is not fully supported by all versions of SQL. It combines the results of a Left and Right Outer Join. If your version of SQL does not support Full Outer Joins, then you can Union two queries together; one query would contain the Left Outer Join, while the other would contain a Right Outer Join.

> **NOTE**   UNION is discussed in the next section of this chapter.

```
SELECT   speakers.speaker_first_name,
speakers.speaker_last_name,
speaker_title.speaker_title
FROM    speakers FULL OUTER JOIN speaker_title
ON         speakers.speaker_id = speaker_title.speaker_id
ORDER BYspeakers.speaker_last_name,
speaker_title.speaker_title
```

Cross Join

A Cross Join usually occurs when a programmer has forgotten to include a join in their SQL statement. The total results from a Cross Join are calculated by multiplying the number of rows in the first table by the number of rows in the second table. This is also called a Cartesian product. Even on tables with minimal records, the result set can become quite large. On large tables, it can overload your server and cause major performance problems at the very least.

In the following query, you will notice that although the book's title "Mastering Cold-Fusion 4.0" has no author associated with it, the results have matched up every speaker as an author of this book (see Figure 11.6). The following is obviously not correct:

```
SELECT   speaker_books.book_title,
speakers.speaker_first_name,
speakers.speaker_last_name
FROM    speakers,
speaker_books
ORDER BY speaker_books.book_title
```

FIGURE 11.6
SQL Cross Join

One reason you may want to use a Cross Join is to create large amounts of test data. For example, if you needed to test a ColdFusion loop for performance, a Cross Join could provide large amounts of data for that purpose. If you do intend to use a Cross Join, you can also use the ANSI standard (if supported by your database) as shown in the following query:

```
SELECT   speaker_books.book_title,
speakers.speaker_first_name,
speakers.speaker_last_name
FROM    speakers CROSS JOIN speaker_books
ORDER BY speaker_books.book_title
```

Nesting Joins

Now what if you want to join more than two tables? You can! It is much easier to create multiple table joins using Studio's Query Builder than to attempt it yourself. Nevertheless, for the brave of heart, multiple joins will be briefly demonstrated.

If you use the SQL-92 ANSI standard to join multiple tables, you will need to nest your join statements in the FROM clause. First, look at the following query:

```
SELECT    speakers.speaker_first_name,
          speakers.speaker_last_name,
          category_desc.category_name
FROM    speakers LEFT JOIN (speaker_category LEFT JOIN category_desc ON
speaker_category.speaker_category_id = category_desc.speaker_category_id ) ON
speakers.speaker_id = speaker_category.speaker_id
    ORDER BY speakers.speaker_last_name,
          category_desc.category_name
```

If you look closely at the FROM clause you will see that three tables are involved in the join.

The outer layer of the join (underlined) is creating a Left Join between the **speakers** table and the **speaker_category** results of the nested join. This tells the database, "give me all records from **speakers**, and only those records from the nested join that match the records in **speakers**."

The nested join (in bold) is creating a left join between **speaker_category** and **category_desc**. This tells the database "give me all records from **speaker_category** and only those from **category_desc** that match." **Speaker_category** is a table that holds a **speaker_id** matched up with a **category_id**. The actual names of the categories are stored in the **category_desc** table.

The results of this join can be seen in Figure 11.7.

NOTE   Inner Joins cannot be nested in Left Outer Joins or Right Outer Joins, but Left and Right Outer Joins can be nested in an Inner Join.

If you use Transact SQL, your query might look like this:

```
SELECT speakers.speaker_first_name,
speakers.speaker_last_name,
category_desc.category_name
FROM    speakers,
speaker_category,
category_desc
WHERE    speakers.speaker_id *= speaker_category.speaker_id
AND    speaker_category.speaker_category_id *=
category_desc.speaker_category_id
ORDER BY speakers.speaker_last_name,
        category_desc.category_name
```

FIGURE 11.7
Results of Multiple Joins in
a SQL Statement

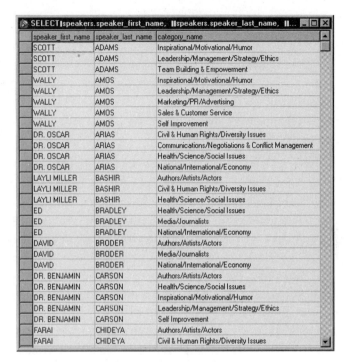

Finally, if you use PL/SQL, your query could be like this:

```
SELECT speakers.speaker_first_name,
speakers.speaker_last_name,
category_desc.category_name
FROM    speakers,
speaker_category,
category_desc
WHERE   speakers.speaker_id = speaker_category.speaker_id(+)
AND     speaker_category.speaker_category_id =
category_desc.speaker_category_id(+)
ORDER BY speakers.speaker_last_name,
category_desc.category_name
```

Subqueries

A subquery is a query nested inside of another query. It can be nested inside of a
SELECT, UPDATE, INSERT, or DELETE query in either the SELECT, FROM or WHERE clause. If
the subquery returns more than one result, it can only be used in the WHERE clause.

Subqueries can be nested many levels deep. After about the second nesting, subqueries become difficult to interpret and decipher. Usually, at that point, it is better to accomplish your task with a join. Subqueries and joins are often two different approaches to doing the same thing. What can be done in a subquery can usually be done in a join as well. In fact, joins are usually better when it comes to performance.

Subqueries are useful for returning a value to be compared, a list of values to be used with the IN operator, or a record set to be used with the EXISTS operator (discussed later in this chapter). If you are comparing a subquery to a value, the following operators can be used: =, <, >, <=, >=, and <>.

There are several rules that must be followed when using subqueries:

- The subquery must be surrounded by parentheses ().
- Subqueries cannot be used in the ORDER BY clause.
- Subqueries cannot include the following clauses: ORDER BY, SELECT INTO, COM-PUTE, GROUP BY, or HAVING (except in more advanced forms of SQL).
- The SELECT clause of a subquery cannot contain fields with the data type of text or image.

Additional rules for each type of subquery are explained in the following sections.

Subqueries and the *IN* Operator

When comparing the results of a subquery with the IN operator, the subquery can return many records but must return only one field that matches the data type of the value being compared. This subquery must be used in the WHERE clause of the parent query.

The following query demonstrates the use of a subquery in the WHERE clause using the IN operator. The results are shown in Figure 11.8. The results will show all speaker names that have books selling at a price over $5.00:

```
SELECT    speakers.speaker_first_name,
speakers.speaker_last_name
FROM      speakers
WHERE     speakers.speaker_id IN (
SELECT    speaker_books.speaker_id
FROM   speaker_books
WHERE   speaker_books.book_price > 5
)
```

FIGURE 11.8

Results of a Subquery Using
the IN Operator

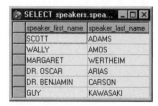

speaker_first_name	speaker_last_name
SCOTT	ADAMS
WALLY	AMOS
MARGARET	WERTHEIM
DR. OSCAR	ARIAS
DR. BENJAMIN	CARSON
GUY	KAWASAKI

Subqueries and the = Operator

If the subquery is being compared to a single value using the equal (=) operator, it must return a single value. The single value must have the same data type as the value it is being compared to. This subquery must be used in the WHERE clause of the parent query.

The following query demonstrates the use of a subquery in the WHERE clause using the = operator. The results will show all the books in the database written by Guy Kawasaki. The subquery is used to get the speaker_id of Guy.

```
SELECT    speaker_books.book_title,
speaker_books.book_price
FROM    speaker_books
WHERE    speaker_books.speaker_id = (
SELECT    speakers.speaker_id
FROM    speakers
WHERE    speaker_first_name = 'Guy'
AND    speaker_last_name = 'Kawasaki'
)
```

The results are shown in Figure 11.9.

FIGURE 11.9
Results of a Subquery Using
the = Operator

Subqueries and the *EXISTS* Operator

If the subquery is being used with the EXISTS operator, the subquery is evaluated for each row in the parent query. If the subquery has a result for that row, then it is returned. You can also use the NOT operator to only return rows in the parent query if zero rows are returned in the subquery. The subquery SELECT clause must use the * wildcard.

In the following query, a speaker is returned only if the speaker_id from the parent query is the same as the speaker_id in the subquery. Results are shown in Figure 11.10. This is also known as a correlated subquery because it references fields in the parent query:

```
SELECT    speakers.speaker_first_name,
speakers.speaker_last_name
FROM        speakers
WHERE        EXISTS (
SELECT    *
FROM    speaker_books
WHEREspeaker_books.speaker_id = speakers.speaker_id
)
```

FIGURE 11.10

Results of a Subquery Using
the EXISTS Operator

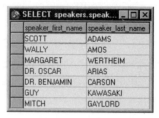

Combining Query Results

There may be cases where you need to merge the result set from one query with the result set of one or more different queries. There are three set operators that can be used to combine query result sets (see Table 11.2).

TABLE 11.2: Types of Set Operators

Operator	Description
UNION [ALL]	(UNION returns the results of two queries minus the duplicate rows.) UNION ALL works just like UNION except it does not eliminate duplicates.
MINUS	Returns records from the first query that were not available in the second query.
INTERSECT	Returns only the records found by each query.

NOTE   The UNION operator is described here. For more information on INTERSECT and MINUS, please refer to your database documentation.

In a UNION, the queries can pull data from any table as long as the SELECT list of each query contains the same number of fields, in the same order, and with the same data type. When you reference your query results in a CFOUTPUT block, you should refer to the field names in the first query. If you specify the field names from any other query in the UNION, ColdFusion will throw an error.

The query shown in Listing 11.1 actually gives the results that a FULL OUTER JOIN would give. The results can be seen in Figure 11.11. If your version of SQL does not support a FULL OUTER JOIN, you can use this method instead.

The first query returns all records from speaker_books and only those records that match in speakers. The second query returns all records from speakers and only those records that match in `speaker_books`. The final result is that all records from each table are returned with NULL values in fields that do not match. This is done because the database removes redundant data. If you want every row from each query returned regardless of whether it is a duplicate, use the UNION ALL operator instead.

Listing 11.1: The UNION Operator

```
<CFQUERY NAME="get_speaker_books" DATASOURCE="sybex">
SELECT speakers.speaker_id,
       speakers.speaker_first_name,
       speakers.speaker_last_name,
       speaker_books.book_title,
       speaker_books.book_price
FROM   speakers RIGHT JOIN speaker_books
ON     speakers.speaker_id = speaker_books.speaker_id
UNION
SELECT speakers.speaker_id,
       speakers.speaker_first_name,
       speakers.speaker_last_name,
       speaker_books.book_title,
       speaker_books.book_price
FROM   speakers LEFT JOIN speaker_books
ON     speakers.speaker_id = speaker_books.speaker_id
ORDER BY speakers.speaker_last_name desc,
         speaker_books.book_title
</CFQUERY>

<!DOCTYPE HTML PUBLIC "-//W3C//DTD HTML 4.0
Transitional//EN">

<HTML><HEAD><TITLE>Sybex - Mastering ColdFusion 4.5-
Chapter 11 - Listing 11.1</TITLE></HEAD>

<BODY BGCOLOR="#FFFFFF">

<H1>Speakers & Books</H1>

<TABLE BORDER="1" CELLPADDING="2" CELLSPACING="0">
<TR>
<TD><B>Speaker Name</B></TD>
<TD><B>Book Title & Price</B></TD>
</TR>

<CFOUTPUT    QUERY="get_speaker_books"
GROUP="speaker_last_name">
    <TR VALIGN="top">
    <TD> <B>#speaker_first_name#
```

```
#speaker_last_name#</B></TD>
   <TD>
<CFOUTPUT>
#book_title#
<CFIF book_price IS NOT  "">
- #DollarFormat(book_price)#
</CFIF>
<BR>
</CFOUTPUT>
</TD>
   </TR>
</CFOUTPUT>
</TABLE>

</BODY>
</HTML>
```

FIGURE 11.11
Results of a UNION

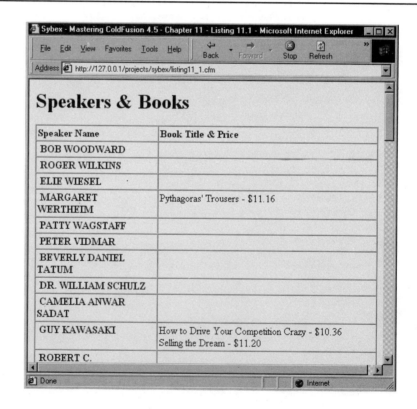

When using the ORDER BY clause, you can sort the results of both queries together. The ORDER BY clause only needs to be used on the second query.

Some things to consider before choosing the UNION operator:

- You cannot use DISTINCT in any of your query SELECT clauses. Because duplicates are removed anyway, it is unnecessary.
- Fields with the data type of memo, image, or any other BLOB type cannot be used in a UNION.
- You can only use an INTO clause in the first query.
- GROUP BY and HAVING clauses cannot be applied to all results. They can only be used on each individual query.

Creating and Changing Tables via SQL

In some cases, developers do not have easy access to the database that their Web Application connects to. In such a situation, one may think that it would be impossible for a developer to add, modify, or delete tables and columns in a database. Quite the contrary. You can add, modify, and delete tables and columns from a database using the CREATE, SELECT INTO, ALTER, and DROP clauses in a CFQUERY SQL statement.

Creating Tables

The CREATE clause can be used to create a variety of different database objects including tables, columns, views, procedures, triggers, etc. In this section, you will learn how to create empty tables and columns.

NOTE   To learn how to create views, procedures, and triggers, please consult your database documentation.

To create a new table, begin your SQL statement with the CREATE TABLE keywords followed by the name of the new table. Table names must follow these three attributes:

- They cannot begin with numbers
- They cannot include illegal characters
- They must be unique

You should consult your database documentation for what table-naming conventions are supported. After adding the table name, specify the columns you would like to add. First, specify the column name, then its data type and length, and then any constraints that you may want to add to the column. The syntax for creating a new table is CREATE TABLE table_name (column_name data_type[(length)] [constraint] [...]). When brackets are used in the syntax, it indicates an optional element.

The column name should be unique and follow the naming conventions as described in your database documentation.

The data type is used to define what kind of data the column will be storing. If you specify the incorrect data type, you will have to drop the column and add it again. You cannot modify the columns properties once set. Some databases may only allow you to add certain data type columns when the table is first created. Consult your database documentation for additional information.

> **NOTE** When specifying the column data type, you can use the data types provided in Appendix E, "SQL Function and Data Type Reference." Your version of SQL may support variations of these, so check your database documentation.

The length of a column can be specified depending upon data type. If it is not necessary, just remove that section of the query.

The constraint portion is also purely optional. A constraint is a rule that you are applying to the new column. Various constraints that you can apply to a column are listed in Table 11.3.

TABLE 11.3: Column Constraints

Constraint	Description
NULL | NOT NULL	Indicates whether a column must contain data. If a column is set to NOT NULL, and data for that column is not supplied when adding a record, an error will be thrown. If NULL is set then data is not required. The default is usually NULL. Consult your database documentation for more information.
IDENTITY	Indicates to SQL server that the field is an auto-incrementing field. You need to specify the step and the beginning value: IDENTITY (1,1).
UNIQUE	Indicates that all records must have unique values in this column.
PRIMARY KEY	Indicates that the specified column should be the primary key. If two columns are to be indicated as the primary key, you should not use this method. You should instead add this statement to the end of your query: PRIMARY KEY (column1, column2, ...).
CHECK ()	Performs a condition on the data being inserted into the column. For example, CHECK (book_price > 5). If the data does not pass the condition, an error will be thrown.
DEFAULT	Indicates the column default value; i.e., DEFAULT = 5.
FOREIGN KEY	Indicates that a column is the foreign key of a specific table and primary key. For example, FOREIGN KEY REFERENCES table_name (primary_key_column_name).
INDEX	Indicates that the column should be indexed.

When a column is defined, a constraint can be applied to it directly or it may be applied at the end of the column definition in a CONSTRAINT clause. Listing 11.2 shows the creation of an Access table. The field data types will vary depending upon your version of SQL. For example, the data type COUNTER would be IDENTITY in SQL Server. In Listing 11.2, various data type columns are created. Then the primary key value is applied to two columns using the CONSTRAINT clause. In the CONSTRAINT clause, customer_pk is the name given to the primary key. This is required in order to create the primary key. If you specify the primary key in a column definition, you do not need to give the primary key a name. When Listing 11.2 is run through the browser, you will get results like those shown in Figure 11.12. The resulting table in Access will look like Figure 11.13.

Listing 11.2: Creating a Table

```
<CFQUERY NAME="new_table" DATASOURCE="sybex">
   CREATE TABLE customers (
      customer_id counter,
      customer_name varchar(50) NOT NULL,
      customer_age smallint,
      customer_income currency NOT NULL,
      customer_comments memo,
      date_modified timestamp,
      customer_kids logical,
      CONSTRAINT customers_pk PRIMARY KEY
      (customer_id, customer_name)
   )
</CFQUERY>

<!DOCTYPE HTML PUBLIC "-//W3C//DTD HTML 4.0
Transitional//EN">

<HTML><HEAD><TITLE>Sybex - Mastering ColdFusion 4.5-
Chapter 11 - Listing 11.2</TITLE></HEAD>

<BODY BGCOLOR="#FFFFFF">

<H1>Customers Table Created!</H1>

</BODY>
</HTML>
```

FIGURE 11.12

Results of Create Table

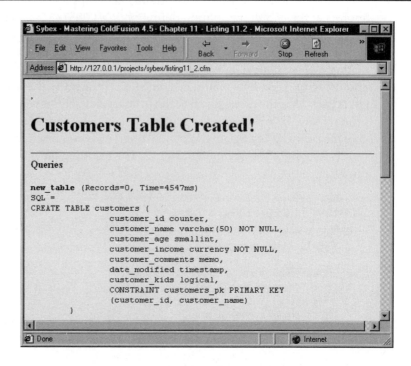

FIGURE 11.13

New Table in Access

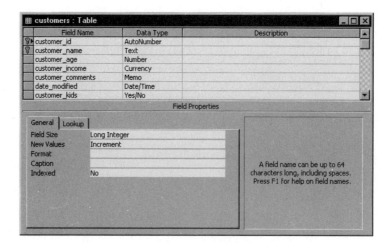

You can also create indexes using the CREATE clause. The syntax is: `CREATE [UNIQUE] INDEX index_name ON table_name (column_list)`.

SELECT INTO

You can also use `SELECT INTO` to create tables populated with data pulled from a `SELECT` statement. The syntax for a `SELECT INTO` query is the following:

```
SELECT    column_list
INTO      new_table_name
FROM      table_list
WHERE       search_criteria
```

The new table name must be unique and follow the table-naming conventions for your database. The column names for the new table will be the same as the columns pulled from the select list.

Listing 11.3 creates a new table called `doctors` and populates it with data pulled from the `speakers` table. Results are shown in Figures 11.14 and 11.15.

Listing 11.3: Creating a Populated Table

```
<CFQUERY NAME="new_table" DATASOURCE="sybex">
   SELECT    speaker_first_name,
             speaker_last_name,
             speaker_picture
   INTO   doctors
   FROM   speakers
   WHERE   speakers.speaker_first_name LIKE 'dr.%'
</CFQUERY>

<!DOCTYPE HTML PUBLIC "-//W3C//DTD HTML 4.0
Transitional//EN">

<HTML><HEAD><TITLE>Sybex - Mastering ColdFusion 4.5-
Chapter 11 - Listing 11.3</TITLE></HEAD>

<BODY BGCOLOR="#FFFFFF">

<H1>Doctors Table Created and Data Inserted!</H1>

</BODY>
</HTML>
```

FIGURE 11.14
New Table in Access

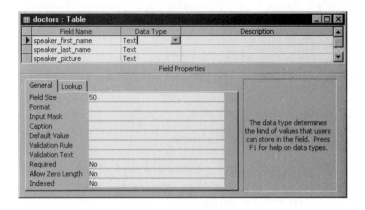

FIGURE 11.15
Data in New Access Table

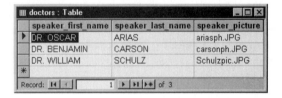

ALTER

If you would like to alter an existing table, you may do so with the ALTER clause. The syntax for the alter clause is ALTER TABLE table_name ADD|DROP|MODIFY (column_definitions). The pipe (|) sign is used in the syntax to indicate that you can use any of the keywords: ADD, DROP, or MODIFY. You would not actually use the pipe sign in your clause. The column definitions would be the same as described in the "Create Table" section of this chapter.

Listing 11.4 modifies the table structure that was created in Listing 11.3. The resulting table is shown in Figure 11.16.

Listing 11.4: Altering a Table

```
<CFQUERY NAME="add_pk" DATASOURCE="sybex">
ALTER TABLE doctors
ADD COLUMN doctor_id counter PRIMARY KEY
</CFQUERY>

<CFQUERY NAME="drop_picture" DATASOURCE="sybex">
```

```
ALTER TABLE doctors
DROP speaker_picture
</CFQUERY>

<!DOCTYPE HTML PUBLIC "-//W3C//DTD HTML 4.0
Transitional//EN">

<HTML><HEAD><TITLE>Sybex - Mastering ColdFusion 4.5-
Chapter 11 - Listing 11.4</TITLE></HEAD>

<BODY BGCOLOR="#FFFFFF">

<H1>Doctors Table Modified!</H1>

</BODY>
</HTML>
```

FIGURE 11.16
Altered Table in Access

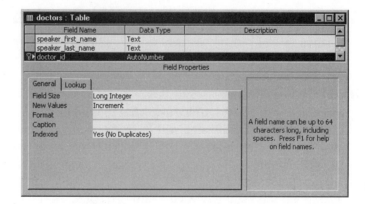

DROP

DROP is used to remove entire tables from a database. Once this command has been executed, there is no way to retrieve the table. The syntax for dropping a table is DROP TABLE table_name. The code in Listing 11.5 drops both tables created in this section.

Listing 11.5: Altering a Table

```
<CFTRANSACTION>
<CFQUERY NAME="drop_doctors" DATASOURCE="sybex">
DROP TABLE doctors
</CFQUERY>

<CFQUERY NAME="drop_customers" DATASOURCE="sybex">
```

```
DROP TABLE customers
</CFQUERY>
</CFTRANSACTION>

<!DOCTYPE HTML PUBLIC "-//W3C//DTD HTML 4.0
Transitional//EN">

<HTML><HEAD><TITLE>Sybex - Mastering ColdFusion 4.5-
Chapter 11 - Listing 11.5</TITLE></HEAD>

<BODY BGCOLOR="#FFFFFF">

<H1>Doctors and Customers Tables Dropped!</H1>

</BODY>
</HTML>
```

Using Advanced *CFQUERY* Features

Chapter 10 covered the basics of using CFQUERY. In this section, you will learn some of the more advanced features of CFQUERY and other complimentary ColdFusion tags.

Persistent Queries

Starting with version 4, ColdFusion has offered the capability to use cached query data. This means that ColdFusion will store the results of a query in the cache to limit the connections to the database. This is useful in reducing the load on the database and the processing time of the query. This option is most useful for queries that return fairly static data. For example, let's say you populate a select drop-down list with items from a table and this list is always the same except for periodic modification by a developer. You can query the table at the start of the day to retrieve the drop-down list results and have the results available in the cache for the rest of the day. This is an example of a persistent query.

To create a persistent query, you need to specify one of the following attributes in your CFQUERY tag:

- CACHEDAFTER
- CACHEDWITHIN

CACHEDAFTER is used to specify a certain date and time to use cached query data. ColdFusion will use cached query data if the date of the original query is after the date specified.

CACHEDWITHIN is used to specify a timespan for using the cached query data. For example, you can specify that the cached data will be used for a span of 15 minutes. To create a timespan, use ColdFusion's CreateTimeSpan function.

You can implement a CACHEDWITHIN attribute and still have the option of not using the cache, as shown in Listing 11.6.

LISTING 11.6: Using *CACHEDWITHIN*

```
<CFPARAM NAME="URL.ForceRead" DEFAULT="N">

<CFPARAM NAME="speaker_list" DEFAULT="'Amos', 'Henderson',
'Bashir'">

<CFIF URL.ForceRead IS "Y">
   <CFQUERY NAME="GetSpeakers" DATASOURCE="sybex">
SELECT    speakers.speaker_first_name,
          speakers.speaker_last_name,
          speakers.speaker_id
FROM      speakers
WHERE     speakers.speaker_last_name IN
(#PreserveSingleQuotes(speaker_list)#)
   </CFQUERY>
<CFELSE>
   <CFQUERY NAME="GetSpeakers" DATASOURCE="sybex"
    CACHEDWITHIN="#CreateTimeSpan(0,0,10,0)#">
SELECT    speakers.speaker_first_name,
speakers.speaker_last_name,
speakers.speaker_id
     FROM      speakers
     WHERE     speakers.speaker_last_name IN
(#PreserveSingleQuotes(speaker_list)#)
</CFQUERY>
</CFIF>

<!DOCTYPE HTML PUBLIC "-//W3C//DTD HTML 4.0
Transitional//EN">

<HTML><HEAD><TITLE>Sybex - Mastering ColdFusion 4.5 -
Chapter 10 - Listing 10.6</TITLE></HEAD>

<BODY>

<CFOUTPUT QUERY="GetSpeakers">
   <B>#speaker_id#.</B> #speaker_first_name#
#speaker_last_name#<BR>
</CFOUTPUT>

</BODY>
</HTML>
```

The variable ForceRead enables you to optionally do a direct read against the speaker table instead of the cached query data. You would call the template as follows:

http://127.0.0.1/sybex/listing11_6.cfm?ForceRead=Y

Figure 11.17 displays the result without the CACHEDWITHIN parameter. Notice that the time to query is 30ms and the page processing time is 120ms.

FIGURE 11.17
Query result without
CACHEDWITHIN

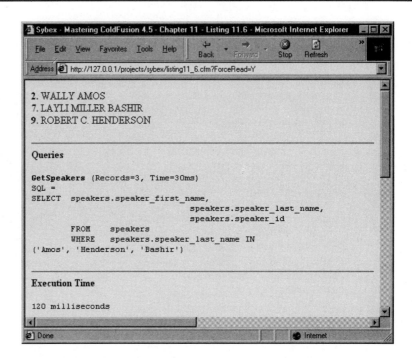

If you remove the ForceRead parameter, ColdFusion retrieves the cached data. If you have Show Processing Time turned on in the debug settings of your ColdFusion server, the time of processing will be Cached Query. This will be your indicator that the cached data was retrieved. You should also notice that the page processing time is much shorter. See Figure 11.18.

FIGURE 11.18

The cached data has been retrieved.

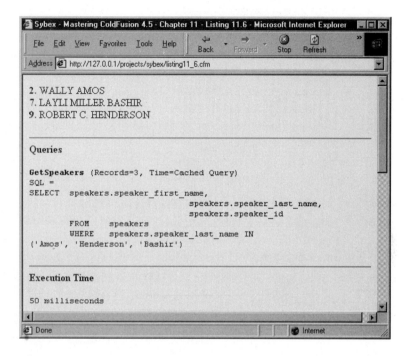

The CreateTimeSpan() function is covered more thoroughly in Appendix C, "ColdFusion Function Reference."

If you want up-to-the-minute, real-time information from your database, then you should not use CACHEDAFTER or CACHEWITHIN. For example, you would not want to cache your latest Internet stock prices because then when users request stock prices, they will receive data that is no longer current.

Calling Stored Procedures by Using *CFSTOREDPROC*

When SQL statements are executed on a regular basis, it is wise to create a stored procedure, provided that your database supports it. *Stored procedures* are compiled SQL statements that are permanently stored in the database in executable format. These compiled SQL statements are known as functions and subprograms. Stored procedures are pre-parsed, compiled, and ready to be invoked by the database user.

The advantages of using stored procedures are as follows:

- Response time is quicker.
- Statements are pre-parsed and in executable format.
- Stored procedures may call other procedures and functions.
- Stored procedures support modular programming structures.
- Stored procedures are more secure, separating the CF environment from the Database Activity. Even if someone hacks and executes CF code on your server they will not be able to do more that what is defined in the stored procedure.

ColdFusion enables you to call a stored procedure through an ODBC or native connection to a database by using the CFSTOREDPROC tag. You can call a stored procedure within your ColdFusion application in one of two ways:

- Using CFQUERY and specifying call parameters
- Using CFSTOREDPROC, CFPROCPARAM, and CFPROCRESULT

The simplest way of calling a stored procedure is by using the CFQUERY tag. The following is an example of code calling a stored procedure:

```
<CFQUERY NAME="ProcessProducts" DATASOURCE="Products">
    { call BookDB.dbo.sp_process_product( '#p_name#' ) }
</CFQUERY>
```

The code required varies depending upon your database. Consult your database documentation for more details.

You need to use CFSTOREDPROC, CFPROCPARAM, and CFPROCRESULT when calling a stored procedure that requires you to do the following:

- You need to specify input and/or output parameters for the query.
- You need to capture the return value.
- You need to select from multiple result sets in a stored procedure.

CFSTOREDPROC

The CFTOREDPROC tag is used to connect to a database and a related stored procedure. The attributes are described in Table 11.4. The following code example has several attributes, many of which you may already be familiar with after using CFQUERY:

```
<CFSTOREDPROC PROCEDURE="procedure_name"
     DATASOURCE="datasource_name"
     USERNAME="user_name"
     PASSWORD="password"
     DBSERVER="databas_server_name"
     DBNAME="database_name"
     BLOCKFACTOR="block_size"
```

```
PROVIDER="COM_Provider"
PROVIDERDSN="datasource"
DEBUG="Yes/No"
RETURNCODE="Yes/No">
```

Use CFPROCRESULT and CFPROCPARAM here.

```
</CFSTOREDPROC>
```

TABLE 11.4: CFSTOREDPROC Attributes

Attribute Name	Required?	Default	Description
PROCEDURE	yes	none	You must specify a name for the stored procedure. You use this name to reference the procedure results with **CFPROCRESULT**.
DATASOURCE	yes	none	You must specify the ODBC or native data source name that the stored procedure is stored on. The data source must first be set up in the ColdFusion Administrator before you can access it.
DBSERVER	no	server specified in the datasource	If you are using native database drivers, you can specify the name of the database server. This setting overrides the server designated in the ColdFusion Administrator datasource settings.
DBNAME	no	default database designated in the datasource	If you are using Sybase System 11 driver you can specify the database name. This setting overrides the default database designated in the ColdFusion Administrator datasource settings.
USERNAME	no	username value designated in the datasource setup	This setting overrides the username designated in the ColdFusion Administrator datasource settings.
PASSWORD	no	password value designated in the datasource	This setting overrides the password designated in the ColdFusion Administrator datasource settings.
BLOCKFACTOR	no	1	If you are using Oracle native database drivers or ODBC drivers, this is the maximum number of rows (from 1-100) to fetch at a single time from the server. Some ODBC drivers may dynamically reduce the block factor during runtime.
PROVIDER	no	none	You can specify a COM provider (used only with OLE-DB).
PROVIDERDSN	no	none	You can specify a data source name for the COM provider (used only with OLE-DB).

TABLE 11.4:   CFSTOREDPROC Attributes *(continued)*

Attribute Name	Required?	Default	Description
DEBUG	no	no	Should be set to a **yes** or **no** value. When this attribute is set to **yes** the SQL statement and **record-count** are output in the rendered template. This is useful for troubleshooting query problems.
RETURNCODE	no	no	Should be set to a **yes** or **no** value. If set to **yes** the variable **CFSTOREDPROC.STATUSCODE** will contain the status code returned by the stored procedure. The value and meaning of the status code varies depending upon database.

The CFSTOREDPROC also returns a variable CFSTOREDPROC.ExecutionTime. This variable provides the execution time of the stored procedure in milliseconds.

In order for CFSTOREDPROC to be useful, you need to also use the CFPROCRESULT and CFPROCPARAM tags nested inside the CFSTOREDPROC tag set.

CFPROCRESULT

Using the CFPROCRESULT tag allows you to access the data returned by the CFSTORED-PROC tag by defining a name for the result set. The CFPROCRESULT tag is nested within the CFSTOREDPROC tag. Because stored procedures can return multiple result sets you can specify multiple CFPROCRESULT tags. They are described in Table 11.5. CFPROCRE-SULT has several attributes, as you will see in the following code example:

```
<CFPROCRESULT  NAME="query_name"
RESULTSET="number_of_resultset"
MAXROWS="maxrows">
```

TABLE 11.5:   CFPROCRESULT Attributes

Attribute Name	Required?	Default	Description
NAME	yes	none	The name of the procedure as specified in the **CFSTOREDPROC** tag
RESULTSET	no	1	Indicates which result set from the **CFSTOREDPROC** tag should be used if there is more than 1. If you use this tag more than once and specify the same **RESULTSET**, the first **CFPROCRESULT** will be overwritten.
MAXROWS	no	returns all rows	This is the maximum number of rows returned in the **CFSTOREDPROC** results record set.

CFPROCPARAM

CFPROCPARAM is used to identify and check the data type of the parameter being passed to the stored procedure. CFPROCPARAM takes several attributes (see Table 11.6):

```
<CFPROCPARAM TYPE="IN/OUT/INOUT"
VARIABLE="variable_name"
DBVARNAME="DB_variable_name"
VALUE="parameter_value"
CFSQLTYPE="parameter_datatype"
MAXLENGTH="length"
SCALE="decimal_places"
NULL="yes/no">
```

TABLE 11.6: CFPROCPARAM Attributes

Attribute Name	Required?	Default	Description
TYPE	no	in	Options are in, out, and inout. This attribute specifies whether the passed variable is the type input, output or input/output.
VARIABLE	maybe	none	If the TYPE specified is out or inout this attribute is required. Specifies the ColdFusion variable name used to refer to the value of the output parameter.
DBVARNAME	maybe	none	If using named notation this attribute is required. Specifies the name of a parameter in the stored procedure.
VALUE	maybe	none	If the TYPE specified is in or inout this attribute is required. Specifies the value that ColdFusion passed to the stored procedure.
CFSQLTYPE	yes	none	Specifies the data type of the parameter. The available values are: CF_SQL_BIGINT, CF_SQL_BIT, CF_SQL_CHAR (Default), CF_SQL_DATE, CF_SQL_DECIMAL, CF_SQL_DOUBLE, CF_SQL_FLOAT, CF_SQL_IDSTAMP, CF_SQL_INTEGER, CF_SQL_LONGVARCHAR, CF_SQL_MONEY, CF_SQL_MONEY4, CF_SQL_NUMERIC, CF_SQL_REAL, CF_SQL_REFCURSOR, CF_SQL_SMALLINT, CF_SQL_TIME, CF_SQL_TIMESTAMP, CF_SQL_TINYINT, CF_SQL_VARCHAR
MAXLENGTH	no	none	Specifies the maximum length of the parameter.
SCALE	no	none	Specifies the parameter decimal places.
NULL	no	none	Options are yes and no. Specifies whether to pass the parameter as a NULL. If yes is indicated then the VALUE attribute is ignored.

A separate CFPROCPARAM tag is required for each procedure parameter. If the TYPE attribute is set to in or inout, you can refer to the resulting variable by the name specified in the VARIABLE attribute.

If you are using positional notation in your stored procedure, then you must add your CFPROCPARAM tags in the exact order required by the stored procedure. Alternatively, if you are using named notation, you need to specify the DBVARNAME attribute and make sure it corresponds to the name in the stored procedure.

An example of what a stored procedure call might look like if using CFSTOREDPROC is shown in Listing 11.7.

Listing 11.7: Calling Stored Procedures

```
<CFSTOREDPROC PROCEDURE="speakers"
DATASOURCE="sybex"
USERNAME="administrator"
PASSWORD="drowssap"
DBSERVER="motlagh"
DBNAME="sybex"
DEBUG="Yes"
RETURNCODE="Yes">

<CFPROCRESULT NAME="speakers_1" RESULTSET="1">
<CFPROCRESULT NAME="speakers_2" RESULTSET="2">

<CFPROCPARAM TYPE="In"
CFSQLTYPE="CF_SQL_NUMERIC"
DBVARNAME="speaker_id"
VALUE="#form.speaker_id#"
NULL="No">
</CFSTOREDPROC>

<!DOCTYPE HTML PUBLIC "-//W3C//DTD HTML 4.0
Transitional//EN">

<HTML><HEAD><TITLE>Sybex - Mastering ColdFusion 4.5 -
Chapter 10 - Listing 10.6</TITLE></HEAD>

<BODY>

<CENTER>
<H2>Speakers - Top 1000 Book Sales Rank</H2>

<CFOUTPUT>
There are #speakers_1.recordcount# results.
</CFOUTPUT>
```

```
<CFOUTPUT QUERY="speakers_1">
#speaker_name# - #book_sales#
</CFOUTPUT>

<H2>Speakers - Top 1000-10000 Book Sales Rank</H2>

<CFOUTPUT>
There are #speakers_2.recordcount# results.
</CFOUTPUT>

<CFOUTPUT QUERY="speakers_2">
#speaker_name# - #book_sales#
</CFOUTPUT>

</CENTER>

</BODY>
</HTML>
```

Stored procedures are generally found when working with enterprise database systems such as Oracle and SQL Server. Throughout this book you will be working with Microsoft Access and will not encounter stored procedures. While stored procedures can be used with Access, it is highly uncommon. For more information about creating and using stored procedures, consult your database system's documentation and the ColdFusion documentation.

NOTE CFPROCRESULT will not work for Oracle drivers because Oracle does not return result sets. You will need to return arrays of output parameters in your stored procedure. Please see Knowledge Base Article 8353, "Arrays of Output Parameters from Oracle Stored Procedures Using ColdFusion 4.01," which can be accessed from the Support section of the Allaire Web site at www.allaire.com.

NOTE To create and call a stored procedure for Sybase, see Knowledge Base Article 924, "SYBASE—How to Create and Call a Stored Procedure."

CFQUERYPARAM

CFQUERYPARAM is used to check what the data type of the query parameter is. It can be used for data validation and conversion of data types. It can also be used to update long text fields when used in a SQL UPDATE statement. CFQUERYPARAM is placed in your SQL statement where the value you want to verify or validate is located. CFQUERYPARAM has several attributes (see Table 11.7) and would be written as follows:

```
<CFQUERYPARAM VALUE="parameter_value"
      CFSQLType="parameter_type"
      MAXLENGTH="maximum_length"
      SCALE="decimal_places"
NULL="Yes/No"
LIST="YES/NO"
SEPARATOR="list_separator_character">
```

TABLE 11.7: CFQUERYPARAM Attributes

Attribute	Description
VALUE	This required attribute specifies the value that is placed to the right of the operand in a WHERE condition.
CFSQLType	This optional attribute specifies the SQL type that the parameter should be. The available values are: CF_SQL_BIGINT, CF_SQL_BIT, CF_SQL_CHAR (Default), CF_SQL_DATE, CF_SQL_DECIMAL, CF_SQL_DOUBLE, CF_SQL_FLOAT, CF_SQL_IDSTAMP, CF_SQL_INTEGER, CF_SQL_LONGVARCHAR, CF_SQL_MONEY, CF_SQL_MONEY4, CF_SQL_NUMERIC, CF_SQL_REAL, CF_SQL_REFCURSOR, CF_SQL_SMALLINT, CF_SQL_TIME, CF_SQL_TIMESTAMP, CF_SQL_TINYINT, CF_SQL_VARCHAR
MAXLENGTH	This optional attribute specifies in numbers the maximum length of the parameter value. The default is the length of the value specified in the VALUE attribute. You can use this attribute with decimal data types. When used with the LIST attribute, it specifies the maximum length for each list item and not the list as a whole.
SCALE	This optional attribute specifies in numbers the amount of decimal places in the parameter value. The default is zero. You can use this attribute with the data types: CF_SQL_NUMERIC and CF_SQL_DECIMAL.
NULL	This optional attribute specifies whether the parameter should be a NULL value. Available options are Yes or No. No is the default. If Yes is specified then the VALUE attribute is ignored. You can use this attribute with decimal data types.
LIST	This optional attribute specifies whether the VALUE parameter is a list. Available options are Yes or No. No is the default. Each list item is given a SQL parameter and validated.
SEPARATOR	This optional attribute is used with the LIST attribute to specify the list delimiter. The default delimiter is ,.

The following CFSQLType values can be converted to numbers: CF_SQL_SMALLINT, CF_SQL_INTEGER, CF_SQL_REAL, CF_SQL_FLOAT, CF_SQL_DOUBLE, CF_SQL_TINYINT, CF_SQL_MONEY, CF_SQL_MONEY4, CF_SQL_DECIMAL, CF_SQL_NUMERIC, and CF_SQL_BIGINT.

The following CFSQLType values can be converted to date values: CF_SQL_DATE, CF_SQL_TIME and CF_SQL_TIMESTAMP.

If a value cannot be converted to numeric data, ColdFusion will throw an error. An example of using CFQUERYPARAM is shown in Listing 11.8. Figure 11.19 shows how the data appears in Access.

Listing 11.8: Using CFQUERYPARAM

```
<CFTRANSACTION>

<!--- This query adds a new speaker to the speakers table --->

<CFQUERY NAME="add_speaker"
DATASOURCE="sybex"
DBTYPE="ODBC">
INSERT INTO speakers (
speaker_first_name,
speaker_last_name ,
date_added
)
VALUES (
'Kristin',
'Motlagh',
<CFQUERYPARAM VALUE="#CreateODBCDate(Now())#"
CFSQLTYPE="CF_SQL_DATE">
)
</CFQUERY>

<!--- This query will retrieve the last inserted
speaker_id value --->

<CFQUERY NAME="get_last_record"
DATASOURCE="sybex"
DBTYPE="ODBC">
SELECT MAX(speaker_id) as new_id
FROM speakers
   </CFQUERY>

<!--- This query adds a new book to the speaker_books table --->

<CFQUERY NAME="add_speaker_book"
DATASOURCE="sybex"
DBTYPE="ODBC">
INSERT INTO speaker_books (
speaker_id,
book_title,
book_price,
book_rank,
book_desc,
book_picture,
book_isbn,
book_published
)
```

```
VALUES (
#get_last_record.new_id#,
'Mastering ColdFusion 4',
<CFQUERYPARAM VALUE="35.99" CFSQLTYPE="CF_SQL_MONEY4">,
1246,
<CFQUERYPARAM VALUE="Allaire's Cold Fusion is the
leading development tool for building complex,
interactive Web sites (it competes with Microsoft Visual
InterDev). Mastering Cold Fusion is aimed at experienced
HTML programmers who need to learn the ins and outs of
the software, as well as upgraders to the new version.
One of the authors, Kristin Motlagh, is a member of Team
Allaire, a select group of Cold Fusion experts, and she
understands what new users need to know to get up to
speed with this complex product. The book includes
information on both the Cold Fusion Application Server
and CF Studio, as well as reference material on Cold
Fusion tags, SQL, and other topics. The companion CD
comes with an evaluation version of the product, an
exensive collection of custom tags created by the
authors, and a wide variety of sample applications and
code from the book." CFSQLTYPE="CF_SQL_LONGVARCHAR">,
'http://images.amazon.com/images/P/0782124526.01.LZZZZZZZ.gif',
'0782124526',
<CFQUERYPARAM VALUE="#CreateODBCDate("6/1/1999")#"
CFSQLTYPE="CF_SQL_DATE">
)
</CFQUERY>

</CFTRANSACTION>

<!DOCTYPE HTML PUBLIC "-//W3C//DTD HTML 4.0 Transitional//EN">

<HTML><HEAD><TITLE>Sybex - Mastering ColdFusion 4.5-
Chapter 10 - Listing 10.7</TITLE></HEAD>

<BODY>

<CENTER>
<H2>The record has been inserted successfully!</H2>
<H3>Your new record ID is:
<CFOUTPUT QUERY="get_last_record">#new_id#</CFOUTPUT></H3>
</CENTER>

</BODY>
</HTML>
```

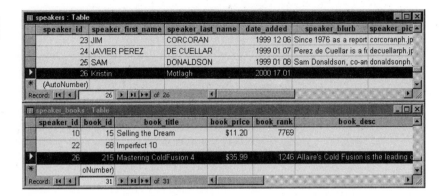

FIGURE 11.19
Data added using
CFQUERYPARAM

NOTE   In ColdFusion 4.5, **CFQUERYPARAM** does not insert data correctly on Informix using the native driver.

Query Functions

There are seven query-related functions that can be used in the development of your applications. They are as follows:

- `IsQuery()` returns TRUE if the value is a query and FALSE if it is not.
- `QuerySetCell()` resets the value of a column cell.
- `QueryAddColumn()` adds a query column populating it with values from a one-dimensional array.
- `QuotedValueList()` returns a list of values for each record with each list item enclosed in quotes.
- `QueryAddRow()` adds rows to an existing query result set.
- `ValueList()` returns a list of values for each record.
- `QueryNew()` returns an empty query.

More detailed information on these functions can be found in Appendix C, "ColdFusion Function Reference."

Optimizing Your Connection

When your ColdFusion application starts to slow down, especially during queries, then it is time to analyze and improve your application's performance. You can optimize the performance of your queries by making modifications to your SQL statements, Administrator and data source settings, and your database configuration.

SQL Suggestions

Optimizing your SQL queries means that elements in your queries are organized and referenced properly. Most importantly, you have to analyze the elements in your FROM and WHERE clauses. Here are some basic guidelines for optimizing your SQL queries:

- In the FROM clause, list the larger tables last.
- In the WHERE clause, list the most restrictive condition first. The most restrictive condition yields the least number of rows of data.

NOTE   If you are using Oracle, list the most restrictive conditions last. Oracle reads the WHERE clause from the bottom up.

- Limit the amount of columns included in a GROUP BY clause.
- Avoid using the HAVING clause.
- Avoid using the OR operator and use IN instead.
- Avoid using the LIKE operator and wildcards frequently.
- Convert recurring SQL statements to stored procedures for faster execution.
- Text fields and other unbound data columns should be placed last in the SELECT statement.
- Try to use COUNT(*) and not COUNT(column_name).
- If you are performing large queries on your database, you should frequently use the CFTRANSACTION tag to commit or rollback the results.

Remember, these guidelines are not cut and dried. You will still need to experiment, run tests, and time the executions to make sure that your optimizing procedure works.

NOTE   Allaire provides some additional information on optimizing ColdFusion queries. You can find this information at www1.allaire.com/Handlers/index.cfm?ID=1614&Method=Full.

Data Source/Administrator Settings

In order to get the best performance out of your applications it is wise to make sure the settings in your ColdFusion administrator are optimized. Here are some suggestions to keep in mind:

- For each Access ODBC data source, set the following in the EDIT ODBC Data source—CF Settings screen:
  - Buffer Size = 0
  - Page Timeout = 600
  - Limit Connections should be checked
  - Enable Limit of _simultaneous connections should be set to 1
  - Maintain Database Connections should not be checked
- Better yet, do not use ODBC to connect to an Access database. Instead, use OLE DB (requires MDAC 2.1), which is more robust and scalable.

NOTE Allaire provides information on setting up your Access database using an OLE DB connection: `www1.allaire.com/Handlers/index.cfm?ID=1540&Method=Full`.

- In the ColdFusion Administrator under Server Settings, set "Limit Simultaneous Requests" to 5-7.
- Install the most recent ODBC or OLE DB Drivers from Microsoft.

NOTE The most recent ODBC and OLE DB drivers can be found at `www.microsoft.com/data`.

- Each night, cycle your ColdFusion services using the cycle.bat file located in the \cfusion\bin directory of your server's root directory.

Database Optimization

Database optimization means doing something to your database to improve its performance. It may also mean restructuring the database and the design and layout of the tables. One of the first things that you should check is the index. What should be indexed? Obviously, the primary keys in your tables, foreign keys, and columns that are used for table joins. Other candidates for indexing are columns that are referenced by ORDER BY or GROUP BY clauses. Columns frequently used in WHERE clauses should also be considered. The best way to accomplish this is to run a test with or without certain indexes. With your ColdFusion debug turned on, you can see how long it takes to process queries.

While we have provided the following suggestions here, you should always check your database documentation for more assistance:

- When you expect the heaviest traffic on the database, avoid running very large processing queries.
- Do not run batch-processing queries while your table is indexed. Indexes can slow down queries that are accessing most of the table records.
- Do not create indexes on small tables.
- Try to minimize the size of the database.
- Store the database transaction log on another drive.
- Add processors to your computer to allow for parallel processing.
- Add RAM as much as possible, but not less than 256.
- If possible, store tables and indexes on separate drives.

Troubleshooting

Inevitably, you will run across errors during the development of any application. These errors could be due to numerous problems. They could stem from problems with your SQL statements, problems with your database setup, problems with your ColdFusion code, or a variety of other issues.

To assist you in troubleshooting these problems and to help prevent them from ever occurring, many of them have been detailed here. If you are not finding what you need here, you can search the Allaire Forums (`http://forums.allaire.com`), check out the resources detailed at the end of this chapter, or if all else fails, you can contact Allaire's support desk.

SQL Problems

Incorrect SQL code is usually the cause of most application problems. This may partially be because many ColdFusion developers are not database or SQL experts. At the same time, if this is your problem, it is probably much easier to fix than if your database has been corrupted, or is not configured properly.

Using Quotes

When using quotes in your SQL statements within your CFQUERY tags, you should use the following guidelines:

- Place single quotes (') around a field's argument if it is a text or memo field type.
- Place single quotes around dates for Microsoft SQL Server data fields.
- Do not place quotes around numeric, auto number, and binary field types.
- Do not place quotes around MS Access dates.
- Never use double quotes (").

If you need to use single quotes in your SQL statement and want to preserve the single quotes instead of having them automatically escaped by ColdFusion, use the PreserveSingleQuotes() function.

Varying Data Types

When you are inserting or updating data in your database, you need to make sure that the data being passed to the database fits the field type specified in the database. If you try to insert text into a numeric field, you will receive an error. To assist in validating data types use the CFQUERYPARAM tag described earlier in this chapter.

Null and Zero-Length Strings

Fields in the database can be defined so that a NULL value will not be accepted. If you try to insert a new record into a database and do not pass data for NOT NULL fields, you will receive an error. There are several ways to deal with this.

First, you can remove the NOT NULL limitation from the field. If you do not have access to the database, then you can use the ALTER clause to drop the particular field and then redefine it as a NULL field. Altering tables is discussed earlier in this chapter.

Second, you can pass data to the field. This can even be a space if necessary.

Versions of SQL

You have already seen in Chapter 10 and in this chapter how SQL can vary depending upon the backend database. Always try to use ANSI standard SQL that is supported by most databases. Unfortunately, there is no one way of coding your SQL that will always work with all databases. For information on other databases, please consult that database's documentation. Some of the differences between Access and SQL server are described here:

- DELETE * FROM is not supported by SQL Server; use DELETE FROM instead.
- DISTINCTROW is not supported by SQL Server; use DISTINCT instead.
- ORDER BY is not supported by SQL Server in a subquery.

- GROUP BY cannot contain more than 16 fields when used with SQL Server.
- WHERE field_name = true is not supported by SQL Server; use WHERE field_name = 1 instead.
- WHERE field_name = NULL is not supported by SQL Server; use WHERE field_name IS NULL instead.
- Concatenating fields with the ampersand (&) is not supported in SQL Server; use the plus (+) operator instead.
- If you plan to convert your Access database to SQL Server review the following article at www.defusion.com/articles/index.cfm?ArticleID=31.
- Bit fields default to no in Access. There is no default in SQL Server; you must always specify a value. You can change this by adding a default value to the field in SQL Server.
- To create an autonumber field in Access, use the counter data type. In SQL Server, use the identity data type set to unique.
- SQL Server 7 has a limit of 2,147,483,647 bytes for text data types.
- If you are not using ANSI standard SQL, your application may throw errors when switching from ODBC to OLE DB.

ColdFusion Query Problems

This section details both problems related to using CFQUERY and useful techniques for solving those problems.

Using *DEBUG* and *REQUESTTIMEOUT*

While your applications are in development, it is a good idea to turn on all of the debug settings in the ColdFusion Administrator. The debug information is useful for interpreting error messages and what went wrong. The SQL query will be displayed along with specific error messages related to ColdFusion or your database. Check the ODBC Errors section later in this chapter for more information.

If you do not have access to the Administrator, then use the DEBUG attribute of the CFQUERY tag. You can also append the following parameter to a URL in order to timeout a query that is taking too long to execute: REQUESTTIMEOUT=seconds.

CFSQL Obsolete

If, by chance, you come across the CFSQL tag, you should know that it has been obsolete since very early versions of ColdFusion. You will need to convert all CFSQL tags to CFQUERY tags.

ODBC Errors

The following are some common ODBC errors encountered while developing ColdFusion applications:

- `ODBC Error Code = 07001 (Wrong number of parameters)`
  `[Microsoft][ODBC Microsoft Access 97 Driver] Too few parameters.`
  `Expected`

This error can be due to improper use of the quotes within your SQL statement.

- `ODBC Error Code = IM002, IM003 or IM004`

NOTE   See the "Using Quotes" section earlier in this chapter for details on the proper use of quotes in SQL.

These types of errors are usually related to path issues or mismatched versions of database client files.

NOTE   See Knowledge Base Article 6564 at **www.allaire.com/Support/KnowledgeBase/ SearchForm.cfm** for more information on path issues and mismatched database client files.

- `ODBC Error Code = S1011 (Operation invalid at this time)`

If you have ColdFusion 4, this ODBC error shows up for the `CFTRANSACTION` tag where the database isolation level is always being set to `Read_Committed` even if this attribute is not set in the tag. This error does not occur in the 3.1 release and has been fixed for the 4.01 release.

- `ODBC Error Code = 37000 (Syntax error or access violation)`
  `[Microsoft][ODBC Microsoft Access 97 Driver] Syntax error (missing`
  `operator) in query expression...`

This error is a general syntax error. Be sure to check the syntax of your SQL query. It may mean that you have an extra comma, a missing comma, an extra quote, or a missing quote.

NOTE   See the "Using Quotes" section earlier in this chapter for details on the use of quotation marks in SQL.

- `ODBC Error Code = 23000 (Integrity constraint violation)`

This error indicates that you are trying to insert or update an index or primary key by using a duplicate value already listed in the table.

Useful Functions

You should consider using the following functions to help you build your SQL queries and solve SQL problems you might come across:

- ParagraphFormat()
- PreserveSingleQuotes()
- Trim()
- Val()
- IsDefined()
- DateFormat()
- CreateODBCDate()

NOTE   These functions are described in detail in Appendix C, "ColdFusion Function Reference."

Y2K Patch for Oracle Stored Procedures

If you are using CFSTOREDPROC and Oracle 7.3 and 8.x, there is a patch available to fix a problem in interpreting the year 2000. The patch can be found at www.allaire.com/handlers/index.cfm?ID=13202&Method=Full.

Finding Additional References for the Various Databases

There is much more to learn about the various databases that you will be using for your ColdFusion application. The best place to start is the free ColdFusion Support Forum located at http://forums.allaire.com/

You can post your questions and concerns there and you can also search for certain topics that interest you. The forum is divided into topics. For topics covered in this chapter, check out the "Database Access and Query Building" area.

ColdFusion's Web site also has a section called the Knowledge Base. It is a compilation of topics that include problem discussion and analysis and workarounds. It is located at www1.allaire.com/Support/KnowledgeBase/SearchForm.cfm. Some Knowledge Base articles relevant to this chapter are:

- Article 7606, "Connecting with Oracle 7.3 Native Driver"

- Article 1114, "Optimizing ColdFusion Queries"
- Article 580, "Using ColdFusion with Oracle"
- Article 564, "Microsoft Access ODBC Driver Performance Enhancement Setting"
- Article 255, "The Use of Single Quotes in CFQUERY"
- Article 13697, "CFQUERY Results Are Limited To 255 Characters"
- Article 13303, "Allaire's native Oracle driver for 4.01 Y2K Patch"
- Article 11328, "Troubleshooting Data Sources/Database Connectivity in Solaris"

Here are some other references:

- ODBC reference in ODBC Software Developers' Kit (SDK) at `www.microsoft.com/data/odbc/`.
- Oracle ODBC drivers can be found at their FTP site. (The Oracle ODBC drivers come bundled with a test tool. This is an excellent tool for testing ODBC connections, testing your SQL statements, and instantly viewing the result of your query.) The sites are as follows:
  - For Oracle 7.x, `ftp://ftp.oracle.com/pub/www/odbc_o7`
  - For Oracle 8.x, `ftp://ftp.oracle.com/pub/www/odbc_o8/`
  - Sybase Transact SQL Performance tips at `www.sybase.com/products/whitepapers/performance_tips.html`
  - `www.sqlmag.com`

Where Do We Go from Here?

We've covered a lot of territory in this chapter. We learned how to use advanced query techniques including joining tables together on primary and foreign key fields, using nested subqueries, and how to combine our query results. We also delved into CFQUERY features and how to incorporate them into our databases. Finally, we found out how to troubleshoot query problems.

In the next chapter, we will discuss grouping, nesting, and formatting outputs.

chapter 12

Grouping, Nesting, and Formatting Outputs

- Using CFOUTPUT

- Nesting and Grouping Output

- Formatting Output

In this chapter, you will take a deeper look at a tag you first visited in Chapter 3, "Getting Data from a Database," and then revisited in Chapter 10, "Using CFQUERY and SQL to Interact with the Database." This tag is the CFOUTPUT tag.

The CFOUTPUT tag is the key to producing dynamic output. Without this capability, ColdFusion would have limited use. In this chapter, you will take a detailed look at using CFOUTPUT to output the results of queries—including how to nest output, how to output limited parts of a result set, and how to format output.

You will also consider the limitations of the CFOUTPUT tag, including restrictions on which other ColdFusion tags can be used between the opening and closing CFOUTPUT tags.

Using *CFOUTPUT*

In Chapter 3, you first encountered the notion of using CFOUTPUT to output the results of a database query. You saw simple examples of taking a query result, specifying its name, and outputting every record in the result set in a specified way:

```
<CFOUTPUT QUERY="queryname">
    Code for the output of results
</CFOUTPUT>
```

Here you used a single attribute of the CFOUTPUT tag: QUERY. This attribute specified the name of the query that was to be output. Specifying the query in this way caused the code for outputting the results to be executed once for each row, or record, in the query result.

Let's look at a specific example. Consider a simple database table called Employees in a database with the data source name EmployeeData and the following fields:

EmployeeID   Employee ID

LastName   Last name of the employee

FirstName   First name of the employee

Gender   Gender of the employee (*M* for Male or *F* for Female)

If you want to output a list of employees and their ID numbers in alphabetical order by last name, you simply use a SQL SELECT statement followed by a CFOUTPUT tag, as shown in Listing 12.1.

NOTE   Many of the examples in this chapter require the database **employeedata.mdb**, which is included on the CD that comes with this book. To use this database, you need to install it as a data source using the ColdFusion Administrator. The steps required to do this are described in Chapter 35, "ColdFusion Administration."

Listing 12.1: cfoutput1.cfm

```
<CFQUERY NAME="Employees" DATASOURCE="EmployeeData">
    SELECT    EmployeeID, LastName, FirstName
    FROM      Employees
    ORDER BY  LastName, FirstName
</CFQUERY>

<TABLE BORDER=0>
<CFOUTPUT QUERY="Employees">
    <TR>
        <TD>#EmployeeID#</TD>
        <TD>
            <STRONG>#LastName#,</STRONG> #FirstName#
        </TD>
    </TR>
</CFOUTPUT>
</TABLE>
```

This produces output similar to that shown in Figure 12.1.

FIGURE 12.1
Using CFOUTPUT to pro-
duce an employee list

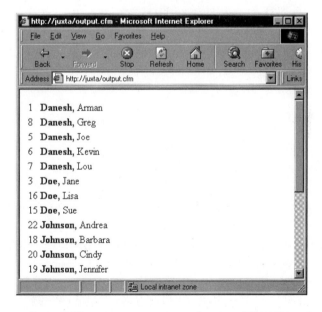

What happened here is that a SQL query was executed using CFQUERY and given the
name Employees. CFOUTPUT was then used to output the result of the query in the order
in which it was retrieved from the database. Within the CFOUTPUT tag, each column in
the current record being displayed from the query result was accessed by the name
inside pound signs.

Displaying Partial Record Sets

Often, a query result will generate many records. However, up until this point, all our examples of CFOUTPUT have displayed all records in a query result set.

Using the STARTROW and MAXROWS attributes, you can limit the number of records that are displayed by CFOUTPUT. This is especially useful when displaying a query result portion by portion (for instance, 20 records at a time).

STARTROW specifies the row at which to start displaying the records. The row number indicates the row in the resulting query and is affected by the sort order of the query. This is in contrast to the order of records as they are stored in the database. MAXROWS indicates the maximum number of rows to display.

Listing 12.2 is a simple example of using these attributes to display up to the first five records of a result set.

Listing 12.2: cfoutput2.cfm

```
<CFQUERY NAME="Employees" DATASOURCE="EmployeeData">
    SELECT   EmployeeID, LastName, FirstName
    FROM      Employees
    ORDER BY   LastName, FirstName
</CFQUERY>

<TABLE BORDER=0>
<CFOUTPUT QUERY="Employees" STARTROW=1 MAXROWS=5>
    <TR>
        <TD>#EmployeeID#</TD>
        <TD>
            <STRONG>#LastName#,</STRONG> #FirstName#
        </TD>
    </TR>
</CFOUTPUT>
</TABLE>
```

There are two significant points to understand about this example using STARTROW and MAXROWS:

- It is possible to use STARTROW on its own: The output will start at the specified row of the result set and will continue to the last record in the query result.
- MAXROWS simply specifies the maximum number of rows to display. If MAXROWS is set to 5 and there are only three records available to display, then only those three records will be displayed.

Grouping Output

At times, the data in a table being queried will contain duplicates in a certain field. For instance, consider the employee table in the preceding example. What you want to produce is a list of family names of employees.

At first glance, it seems like you could generate a list of family names with the code in Listing 12.3.

Listing 12.3: cfoutput3.cfm

```
<CFQUERY NAME="Employees" DATASOURCE="EmployeeData">
    SELECT    LastName
    FROM    Employees
    ORDER BY    LastName
</CFQUERY>

<CFOUTPUT QUERY="Employees">
    #LastName#<BR>
</CFOUTPUT>
```

However, in a large organization this code may produce numerous duplicate rows in the final output, as shown in Figure 12.2.

FIGURE 12.2
Duplicates may be
unwanted in output.

This repetition can render the list practically useless because it results in a list that is too long, making it difficult to find each distinct name.

Using the GROUP attribute of the CFOUTPUT tag, you can eliminate this problem. This attribute specifies the name of a result column under which to group output, and thereby eliminates duplicates. For instance, in outputting your list of employee last names, you need to add GROUP="LastName" to the CFOUTPUT tag to eliminate the duplicates. Adding the attribute results in the following CFOUTPUT tag: <CFOUTPUT QUERY="Employees" GROUP="LastName", which produces output like that shown in Figure 12.3.

FIGURE 12.3
Grouping output elimi-
nates duplicate

The grouping is typically done in a case-sensitive manner. However, with the release of ColdFusion 4.5, you can force ColdFusion to perform case-insensitive grouping with the GROUPCASESENSITIVE tag. If you use GROUPCASESENSITIVE =FALSE then all group-ing performed by the CFOUTPUT tag will be case insensitive.

Nesting and Grouping Output

The power of CFOUTPUT becomes even more apparent when you start to look at *nesting*, or embedding, one CFOUTPUT tag within another. This technique ties in closely with the GROUP attribute that you just looked at and shows the real power of grouping.

Although it is useful to be able to eliminate duplicates, consider the following example. You want to output an employee list organized by gender without repeating the gender with each record. Instead, you want results that look something like the following lines of code:

```
GENDER: M
    ID    LastName    FirstName
    ID    LastName    FirstName
    Etc.

GENDER: F
    ID    LastName    FirstName
    ID    LastName    FirstName
```

The first inclination of many people will be to achieve this result by using two queries, as shown in Listing 12.4.

Listing 12.4: cfoutput4.cfm

```
<CFQUERY NAME="Female" DATASOURCE="EmployeeData">
    SELECT    EmployeeID, LastName, FirstName, Gender
    FROM    Employees
    WHERE    Gender='F'
    ORDER BY    LastName, FirstName
</CFQUERY>

<H3>GENDER: F</H3>
<TABLE BORDER=0>
<CFOUTPUT QUERY="Female">
    <TR>
        <TD>#EmployeeID#</TD>
        <TD>
            <STRONG>#LastName#,</STRONG> #FirstName#
        </TD>
    </TR>
</CFOUTPUT>
</TABLE>

<CFQUERY NAME="Male" DATASOURCE="EmployeeData">
    SELECT    EmployeeID, LastName, FirstName, Gender
    FROM    Employees
    WHERE    Gender='M'
    ORDER BY    LastName, FirstName
</CFQUERY>

<H3>GENDER: M</H3>
<TABLE BORDER=0>
```

```
<CFOUTPUT QUERY="Male">
    <TR>
        <TD>#EmployeeID#</TD>
        <TD>
            <STRONG>#LastName#,</STRONG> #FirstName#
        </TD>
    </TR>
</CFOUTPUT>
</TABLE>
```

Using two queries works fine because the Gender field has only two possible values. But what if you were grouping by a field with an unlimited number of possible values? Then this approach breaks down.

This problem is solved using the GROUP attribute with nested CFOUTPUT tags. Let's consider the gender example; to use GROUP, you need do the following:

1. Sort your query result first by the Gender field (and then by any other fields you want).

2. Use a nested CFOUTPUT statement: The outer CFOUTPUT displays the gender, and the inner CFOUTPUT displays each record within the specified gender group.

Completing these steps results in the ColdFusion template shown in Listing 12.5.

Listing 12.5: cfoutput5.cfm

```
<CFQUERY NAME="Employees" DATASOURCE="EmployeeData">
    SELECT   EmployeeID, LastName, FirstName, Gender
    FROM     Employees
ORDER BY   Gender, LastName, FirstName
</CFQUERY>

<CFOUTPUT QUERY="Employees" GROUP="Gender">
<H3>GENDER: #Gender#</H3>
<TABLE BORDER=0>
    <CFOUTPUT>
        <TR>
            <TD>#EmployeeID#</TD>
            <TD>
                <STRONG>#LastName#,</STRONG> #FirstName#
        </TD>
        </TR>
    </CFOUTPUT>
</TABLE>
</CFOUTPUT>
```

Here, the outer CFOUTPUT tag groups the results by gender and displays the title for each gender. The inner CFOUTPUT tag then displays each record from within the gender group currently being displayed by the outer CFOUTPUT tag. The results look like those in Figure 12.4.

There are a couple of important points to note here:

- You must sort by the fields that are being grouped. Otherwise, problems occur. Figure 12.5 shows the results of the previous grouped and nested output in which the query result is not sorted by gender.
- You must use the GROUP attribute to nest CFOUTPUT tags. Without the GROUP attribute in the outer tag, ColdFusion will generate an error like the one in Figure 12.6 when nesting CFOUTPUT tags.

FIGURE 12.5

It is necessary to sort output when grouping.

FIGURE 12.6

The GROUP attribute is necessary when nesting CFOUTPUT tags.

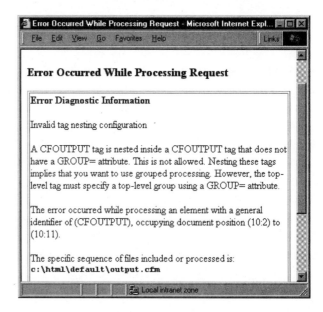

Multiple Levels of Nesting

It is possible to group and nest output more than one level deep, as you have already done. Let's extend our gender example one level further. How would you group output first by gender and then by last name to produce output like these following lines of code:

```
GENDER: F
- Last Name: Last Name
- ID    First Name
- ID    First Name
- Etc.
- Last Name: Last Name
- ID    First Name
- ID    First Name
- Etc.
- Etc.

GENDER: M
- Last Name: Last Name
- ID    First Name
- ID    First Name
- Etc.
- Last Name: Last Name
- ID    First Name
- ID    First Name
- Etc.
- Etc.
```

To achieve this, these two following things need to happen:

1. The query result needs to be sorted, in order, by gender and last name.
2. A third CFOUTPUT tag needs to be nested in the output, and the second-level CFOUTPUT tag needs to include the attribute GROUP="LastName".

The result looks like the code in Listing 12.6.

Listing 12.6: cfoutput6.cfm

```
<CFQUERY NAME="Employees" DATASOURCE="EmployeeData">
    SELECT    EmployeeID, LastName, FirstName, Gender
    FROM    Employees
ORDER BY    Gender, LastName, FirstName
</CFQUERY>

<CFOUTPUT QUERY="Employees" GROUP="Gender">
<H3>GENDER: #Gender#</H3>
<UL>
<CFOUTPUT GROUP="LastName">
```

```
<LI><STRONG>#LastName#
<UL>
<CFOUTPUT>
<LI>#EmployeeID#: #FirstName#
</CFOUTPUT>
</UL>
</CFOUTPUT>
</UL>
</CFOUTPUT>
```

This code produces results like those in Figure 12.7.

FIGURE 12.7
Multiple-level nesting and
grouping

Notice that the first (outer) CFOUTPUT tag groups by gender; the second, inner tag groups by last name; and the third has no GROUP attribute and displays all records that match the current gender and last-name grouping.

Formatting Output

In addition to being able to quickly and easily output the results of queries, you can easily format different types of data for output by using numerous tags and functions provided by ColdFusion.

For instance, let's consider dates. ColdFusion stores dates in a special format, which when displayed produces results that are less than desirable. For instance, displaying a date variable produces output that looks like this:

```
{ts '1999-02-10 17:50:17'}
```

The DateFormat function, however, makes it possible to output the same date in numerous ways, including the following:

```
10-Feb-99
Wednesday, February 10, 1999
10/02/99
02-10-99
Feb. 10, 1999
```

Other functions exist to easily format decimal numbers, currencies, numbers, HTML code, and times.

In addition to these tags for formatting data output, ColdFusion also provides the CFSETTING tag, which enables you to gain some control over how templates are turned into output.

Formatting Your Data Using ColdFusion Functions

Let's start by considering functions that enable you to format the output of different types of data. These data types are the following:

- Dates
- Decimal numbers
- Currencies
- Numbers
- HTML code
- Times
- Boolean values

Formatting Dates

You have already been introduced to the purpose of the DateFormat function. This function takes dates stored in ColdFusion's default format and displays them in a user-readable format.

The DateFormat function takes two arguments: DateFormat(Date, Mask). As would be expected, the date should be a value in ColdFusion's date format and is necessary for the function to work. The mask, on the other hand, is an optional argument that specifies how the resulting output should be formatted.

By default, when no mask is provided, DateFormat outputs dates in the form dd-mmm-yy; the day and year are displayed as two-digit numbers and the month is displayed as a three-letter abbreviation.

For instance, the following ColdFusion code:

```
<CFOUTPUT>
    #DateFormat(Now())#
</CFOUTPUT>
```

produces the following result:

```
10-Feb-99
```

NOTE   Notice the use of the Now function to provide a date to the DateFormat function. The Now function returns the current date and time as a ColdFusion date value. This makes it easy to provide a date to the DateFormat function for the purposes of experimenting and learning.

The mask is what makes the DateFormat function interesting. Using a mask, it is possible to specify in great detail how the date should be displayed. A mask generally consists of spaces, punctuation, and special characters, as listed in Table 12.1.

TABLE 12.1: Special Characters for Date Masks

Special Characters	Resulting Output
d	Day of the month as a number with no leading zeros on single-digit numbers
dd	Day of the month as a number with a leading zero on single-digit numbers
ddd	Day of the week as a three-letter abbreviation
dddd	Day of the week in unabbreviated form
m	Month as a number with no leading zeros on single-digit numbers
mm	Month as a number with a leading zero on single-digit numbers
mmm	Month as a three-letter abbreviation
mmmm	Month as an unabbreviated name
y	Year as a number reflecting the last two digits of the year with no leading zeros on single-digit numbers
yy	Year as a number reflecting the last two digits of the year with a leading zero on single-digit numbers
yyyy	Year as a full four-digit number

By way of example, Table 12.2 shows how to produce different types of date formats and the masks that produce those results.

TABLE 12.2: Examples of Date Masks

Desired Output	Required Mask
Wednesday, February 10, 1999	`"dddd, mmmm d, yyyy"`
10/02/99	`"dd/mm/yy"`
02-10-99	`"mm-dd-yy"`
Feb. 10, 1999	`"mmm. dd, yyyy"`

NOTE   Notice the use of the double quotes around the masks. Double quotes are used because the mask argument is provided as a string value to the `DateFormat` function.

Formatting Decimal Numbers

The `DecimalFormat` function performs a simple task: It returns a decimal number formatted as a decimal with two places following the decimal point and a comma used as a thousands separator.

The function tags a single argument: `DecimalFormat(Number)`. For instance, the following ColdFusion code:

```
<CFOUTPUT>#DecimalFormat(123456789.0123456789)#</CFOUTPUT>
```

produces the following result:

```
123,456,789.01
```

Formatting Currencies

ColdFusion provides the `DollarFormat` function to display a number as a currency formatted with two decimal places, a comma as a thousands separator, and a dollar sign. Negative values are placed in parentheses.

Like `DecimalFormat`, `DollarFormat` takes a single argument: `DollarFormat(Number)`. Therefore, `DollarFormat(123456.789)` produces the following output:

```
$123,456.79
```

Using a negative number, such as `DollarFormat(-123456.789)`, produces a number surrounded by parentheses:

```
($123,456.79)
```

Formatting Numbers

ColdFusion provides two useful functions for formatting numeric values:

FormatBaseN(Number,Base)   Returns a number as a string in the specified base

NumberFormat(Number,Mask)   Returns a number as a custom formatted string

Using *FormatBaseN*

FormatBaseN is a simple function: Given a number in base 10 and a base, it returns the number in that base. Table 12.3 shows examples of the function and the results that are returned.

T A B L E   1 2 . 3 :   Examples of Formatting Numbers in Different Bases

Function	Result
FormatBaseN(10,16)	A
FormatBaseN(10,8)	12
FormatBaseN(10,2)	1010

Using *NumberFormat*

NumberFormat is a flexible function for outputting numeric values. Given a number and an optional mask, a custom formatted number is returned. Without a mask, the number is returned as an integer with a comma as a thousands separator.

The mask can be built out of the following characters:

_ or 9   A digit placeholder used to define the number of digits to display and their placement. (Optional)

.   Specifies the location of the decimal point. (Required)

0   Used to the left or right of the decimal point; forces padding with zeros. (Optional)

()   Places parentheses around the number when it is less than zero. (Optional)

+   Places a plus sign in front of positive numbers and a minus sign in front of negative numbers. (Optional)

−   Places a space in front of positive numbers and a minus sign in front of negative numbers. (Optional)

,   Separates thousands with commas. (Optional)

L   Specifies left justification of the number within the width of the mask. Must appear as the first character of the mask. (Optional)

C   Specifies center justification of the number within the width of the mask. Must appear as the first character of the mask. (Optional)

$ Places a dollar sign in front of the number. Must appear as the first character of the mask. (Optional)

^   Separates left formatting from right formatting. (Optional)

This may all sound complex, but it's not. Let's start with a simple example: You want to display a number as a currency with up to five digits before the decimal place and two after, and you want decimal places to line up when multiple numbers are displayed in a column.

To format numbers as described, you need to use the $_____.__. mask in a series of numbers like this:

```
<PRE><CFOUTPUT>
    #NumberFormat(123.45,"$_____.__")#
    #NumberFormat(2345.567,"$_____.__")#
    #NumberFormat(3.4,"$_____.__")#
    #NumberFormat(45678,"$_____.__")#
</CFOUTPUT></PRE>
```

The result is shown in Figure 12.8.

FIGURE 12.8
Using NumberFormat

What happens if you don't want all the dollar signs to line up at the left but instead to appear immediately next to each number? Allaire's documentation indicates that this can be done by placing an underscore to the left of the dollar sign in the mask: _$_____.__. Used in our example above, this produces results like those in Figure 12.9.

FIGURE 12.9

Placing an underscore at
the left of a mask

The same rule holds true when using + or – in your masks. A note is required with regard to aligning a list of positive and negative numbers: If no sign is specified for a mask (that is, no + or – in the mask), then numbers will not line up in a column. For instance, the following code:

```
<PRE><CFOUTPUT>
    #NumberFormat(123.45,"___.__")#
    #NumberFormat(-123.45,"___.__")#
</CFOUTPUT>
```

produces the following output:

```
123.45
-123.45
```

To line up the decimal places, you can use a + in the mask ("+___.__"), as follows:

```
+123.45
-123.45
```

or you can use a – in the mask ("-___.__"):

```
123.45
-123.45
```

Formatting HTML Code

At times it is necessary to display HTML code rather than allow it to be parsed by the browser. For instance, normally the following HTML code:

```
<HR>
<H1>This is a test</H1>
Just Testing.
<HR>
```

produces output similar to that in Figure 12.10.

FIGURE 12.10
HTML parsed by the browser

What would happen, though, if you wanted to display a code sample and then show how it would appear on the same page? To display the HTML code rather than allow the browser to interpret it, you must escape the code. For instance, the < character needs to be converted to < and > to >. In our example, this would mean that the HTML would need to be converted to the following:

```
&lt;HR&gt;
&lt;H1&gt;This is a test&lt;/H1&gt;
Just Testing.
&lt;HR&gt;
```

In addition, you either need to add line breaks in the form of <BR> or surround the code by <PRE> and </PRE> to separate the lines in the final browser display.

However, this is no small feat for a large HTML file. ColdFusion provides the HTML-CodeFormat and HTMLEditFormat functions to address this need. These functions work slightly differently:

HTMLCodeFormat   Escapes the string (that is, converts < to <, and so on), surrounds the string in <PRE> and </PRE>, and removes all carriage returns from the string

HTMLEditFormat   Escapes the string and removes all carriage returns from the string

Both functions take two arguments: a string as the first argument and an optional version indicating the version of HTML to use in escaping special characters. The version can be one of the following values:

-1   Indicates the latest version of HTML.

2.0   Indicates HTML 2. (This is the default value when a version is not provided.)

So, how does this all differ? If the HTML code you used in the preceding example is stored in the string variable SampleHTML, then HTMLCodeFormat(SampleHTML) produces output like that in Figure 12.11, whereas HTMLEditFormat(SampleHTML) produces output like that in Figure 12.12.

FIGURE 12.11
Using HTMLCodeFormat

FIGURE 12.12
Using HTMLEditFormat

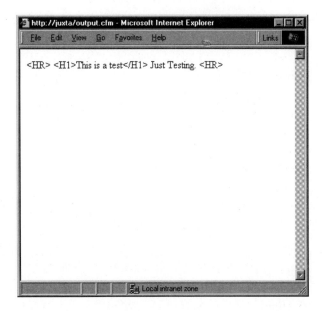

ColdFusion also provides two functions for manipulating the carriage returns in a body of text: `ParagraphFormat` and `StripCR`.

`ParagraphFormat` takes a string that may or may not include HTML code and converts single newlines into spaces and double newlines into <P> tags to create paragraph breaks. In this way, a body of text like the following:

```
This is line one.
This is line two.

This is line three.
```

that normally would be displayed by a browser as:

```
This is line one. This is line two. This is line three.
```

can be converted into valid HTML:

```
This is line one. This is line two.
<P>
This is line three.
```

To use `ParagraphFormat`, simply provide a string as the single argument to the function: `ParagraphFormat(String)`.

StripCR does what the name suggests: it strips carriage returns out of a string of text. This can be useful when displaying text using <PRE> that has been entered in the TEXTAREA field of a form. To use StripCR, simply provide a string as an argument: StripCR(String).

Formatting Times

Just as you used DateFormat to convert ColdFusion's internal dates into user-readable formats, you can use TimeFormat to do the same for times. By default, the ColdFusion date format stores information about both date and time, and these same values are used by TimeFormat to produce user-friendly strings.

TimeFormat takes two arguments: TimeFormat(Time,Mask). By default, when no mask is provided, times are output in the form 07:35 AM or 11:52 PM.

Aside from using relevant punctuation such as a colon, masks are built from the following special characters:

h   Displays the hour as a number from the 12-hour clock with no leading zero on single-digit numbers

hh   Displays the hour as a number from the 12-hour clock with a leading zero on single-digit numbers

H   Displays the hour as a number from the 24-hour clock with no leading zero on single-digit numbers

HH   Displays the hour as a number from the 24-hour clock with a leading zero on single-digit numbers

m   Displays the minutes with no leading zero on single-digit numbers

mm   Displays the minutes with a leading zero on single-digit numbers

s   Displays the seconds with no leading zero on single-digit numbers

ss   Displays the seconds with a leading zero on single-digit numbers

t   Displays a single character, A or P, indicating AM or PM

tt   Displays AM or PM

Formatting Boolean Values

Boolean values (those that are true or false, or 1 or 0) are usually viewed by users in yes-no terms. That is, a true value equates to yes and a false value equates to no.

The YesNoFormat function returns YES or NO as appropriate based on a Boolean or numeric argument: YesNoFormat(Value). True values and nonzero numbers cause YES to be returned. False values and zero cause NO to be returned.

Handling International Locales

You have probably noticed the U.S.-centric nature of the functions we have discussed for formatting data. For instance, the `DollarFormat` function is clearly aimed at North America and the default formats for many functions are also American-centric (consider the default 12-hour clock format of the `TimeFormat` function).

ColdFusion provides a series of formatting functions that result in output that is dependent on the current locale of the server. When ColdFusion starts, it generates a list of supported locales for ColdFusion and the operating system. ColdFusion supports the following locales listed in this table.

Dutch (Belgian)	German (Standard)
Dutch (Standard)	German (Swiss)
English (Australian)	Italian (Standard)
English (Canadian)	Italian (Swiss)
English (New Zealand)	Norwegian (Bokmal)
English (U.K.)	Norwegian (Nynorsk)
English (U.S.)	Portuguese (Brazilian)
French (Belgian)	Portuguese (Standard)
French (Canadian)	Spanish (Mexican)
French (Standard)	Spanish (Modern)
French (Swiss)	Spanish (Standard)
German (Austrian)	Swedish

The `SetLocale` function can be used to set a new locale as the current locale (for instance, `SetLocale("English (US)"`). `GetLocale` returns the current locale.

Table 12.4 provides an outline of the international formatting functions, their corresponding standard functions, and their descriptions and usage.

T A B L E 1 2 . 4 : International Formatting Functions

International Function	Standard Function	Description and Usage
LSCurrencyFormat	DollarFormat	Returns a number formatted as a currency for the current locale. An optional type specifies which version of the currency format to display. Possible types are none (such as 10.00), local (such as SFr. 10.00; this is the default), and international (such as USD10.00). Usage: LSCurrencyFormat(Number,Type); the type is optional.
LSDateFormat	DateFormat	Returns a formatted date based on a date value and an optional mask. Without the mask, the default format for the locale is used. Usage: DateFormat(Date,Mask); the mask is optional.

TABLE 12.4: International Formatting Functions *(continued)*

International Function	Standard Function	Description and Usage
LSNumberFormat	NumberFormat	Returns a formatted number based on a numeric value and an optional mask. Locale-specific conventions are used. Without a mask, a formatted integer is returned. Usage: NumberFormat(Number,Mask); the mask is optional.
LSTimeFormat	TimeFormat	Returns a formatted time based on a time value and an optional mask. Without the mask, the default format for the locale is used. Usage: TimeFormat(Time,Mask); the mask is optional.

Using *CFSETTING*

The CFSETTING tag takes the following two possible attributes, both of which are relevant to output:

ENABLECFOUTPUTONLY   This is a required attribute. If set to YES, it indicates that only subsequent output within CFOUTPUT tags should be displayed. This state continues until another CFSETTING tag sets the value of ENABLECFOUTPUTONLY to NO.

SHOWDEBUGOUTPUT   This is an optional attribute. When set to NO, it suppresses debugging information that is displayed at the end of pages when errors occur. By default, the value is YES.

What concerns us is the ENABLECFOUTPUTONLY attribute. The main advantage of this tag is that it is used to eliminate excess source code from the HTML generated by a template. For instance, the following template:

```
<CFSET A=1>
<CFSET B=2>
<CFSET C=A + B>
<CFOUTPUT>
The result is #C#
</CFOUTPUT>
```

generates source code that has a blank line for each line of purely ColdFusion code. That means there are four blank lines before the one line of output and one blank line after it in the source code:

```
The result is #C#
```

In large templates, this can mean many blank lines in a large block of ColdFusion code. By setting ENABLECFOUTPUTONLY to YES, you require all output destined to be in the final source code to appear between beginning and ending CFOUTPUT tags. This eliminates excess blank lines caused by the processing of ColdFusion code so that the following lines of code:

```
<CFSETTING ENABLECFOUTPUTONLY=YES>
<CFSET A=1>
<CFSET B=2>
<CFSET C=A + B>
<CFOUTPUT>
The result is #C#
</CFOUTPUT>
```

will have only one excess blank line in the source code output (that being the line of the CFSETTING tag itself):

```
The result is 3
```

NOTE   There is a caveat about the use of ENABLECFOUTPUTONLY. This attribute can be used multiple times in a template to enable and disable the requirement for all output to appear in CFOUPUT blocks. If you set it multiple times to YES, each YES must be matched by a tag setting it to NO to return to normal operation, in which normal HTML code is visible by the browser.

Where Do We Go from Here?

This chapter has been far reaching, covering many advanced aspects of output—from grouping and nesting the results of queries to easily formatting a variety of data formats by using ColdFusion functions.

In the next chapter, you will learn about a central programming concept: loops. In a sense, you have already learned about loops while learning to use CFOUTPUT, which effectively enables you to loop through a query result and perform the same action each time through the loop.

In the next chapter, though, you will learn about the CFLOOP tag, which provides much more power than CFOUTPUT (in fact, CFLOOP can be used to recreate the exact behavior of CFOUTPUT and more). CFLOOP is less restricted in terms of the types of actions that can be performed on the data that is being looped through and it can be used in many more circumstances.

chapter 13

Looping

- Understanding Loops

- Using a Basic Loop with the CFLOOP Tag

- Creating Additional Types of Loops

- Nesting Loops

Loops provide a mechanism that you can use to perform repeated actions without having to write repeated sections of program codes. This concept should already be familiar: You saw basic loops when you learned how to use CFOUTPUT to produce output for each row in a query result.

In this chapter, you will look at loops in a more general sense. Using the CFLOOP tag, you can produce a wide range of loops, many of which will be familiar to those who have experience with other programming languages, such as C, Perl, or Java. These loops include index loops, conditional loops, and query loops.

Understanding Loops

Loops are a basic part of any programmer's vocabulary. They enable programmers to repeat the same action multiple times without needing to write the same section of program code multiple times.

Loops are used for several purposes, including the following:

- Repeating a specific action a set number of times—for instance, printing the same output exactly 10 times
- Repeating a specific action while a given condition holds true—for instance, repeatedly displaying the value of a given variable until the variable contains a specific value
- Repeating a series of actions for each item in a list or array—for instance, looking at each element in an array, performing a mathematical formula on the value, and displaying the results

If you come from a traditional programming background, such as C, Java, or Perl, you will be familiar with a range of commands used to create different types of loops, including commands such as `for`, `foreach`, `while,` and `repeat`. In ColdFusion templates, however, all these types of loops are achieved using the CFLOOP tag. The different flavors of loops are achieved using different attributes and values for the tag.

Using a Basic Loop with the *CFLOOP* Tag

The most basic type of loop is the *index loop*. This is a loop that repeats once for every value between a start value and an end value. In other words, an index loops counts. For instance, a loop that counts from 1 to 10 and repeats specific actions for each integer value between 1 and 10 is an index loop. Similarly, a loop that counts down from 87 to 23 in decrements of 2 (in other words: 87, 85, 83, 81…27, 25, 23) and performs specific actions for each value is an index loop.

The name index loop comes from the loop having a range of numeric values. An index is a named variable associated with the loop. For each iteration of the loop, a new value is assigned to the variable, and this variable can be used like any other variable for any of the actions performed in the loop.

Without getting into the specifics of the code, let's consider the basic steps required to use an index loop to output the times table for the number 7 (we'll do the first 10 entries in the times table). The steps look something like this:

```
For each integer between 1 and 10, perform the following steps:
    Assign the current integer to the index variable X
    Multiply 7 by the value contained in the variable X and store the result in the
        variable Y
    Output the result stored in Y
End of loop
```

The logic isn't complicated, but it is easy to see how the code is more compact, easier to write, and even easier to read than it would be without a loop. Without a loop, the algorithm would look like this:

```
Multiple 7 by 1 and store the result in the variable Y
Output the result stored in Y
Multiple 7 by 2 and store the result in the variable Y
Output the result stored in Y
Multiple 7 by 3 and store the result in the variable Y
Output the result stored in Y
Multiple 7 by 4 and store the result in the variable Y
Output the result stored in Y
Multiple 7 by 5 and store the result in the variable Y
Output the result stored in Y
Multiple 7 by 6 and store the result in the variable Y
Output the result stored in Y
Multiple 7 by 7 and store the result in the variable Y
Output the result stored in Y
Multiple 7 by 8 and store the result in the variable Y
Output the result stored in Y
Multiple 7 by 9 and store the result in the variable Y
Output the result stored in Y
Multiple 7 by 10 and store the result in the variable Y
Output the result stored in Y
```

Understanding *CFLOOP* Basics

Now, you need to consider how to use the CFLOOP tag to create an index loop. The CFLOOP tag can take many attributes, but the essential ones for an index loop are the following:

INDEX   Specifies the name of the index variable for the loop

FROM   Specifies the starting value for the loop

TO   Specifies the ending value for the loop

It should be fairly clear how this works. To implement the loop for the 7 times table discussed earlier in this chapter, the CFLOOP tag would look like this:

```
<CFLOOP INDEX="X" FROM=1 TO=10>
```

The CFLOOP closing tag is used to specify the end of the code to perform for each iteration of the loop. The result is that our entire 7 times table code looks like this:

```
<CFLOOP INDEX="X" FROM=1 TO=10>
    <CFSET Y = 7 * X>
    <CFOUTPUT>7 * #X# = #Y#<BR></CFOUTPUT>
</CFLOOP>
```

Of course, this code isn't that useful, because it performs only the 7 times table, and only for a specified range (from 1 to 10). It should be clear that you could leverage this code to produce any times table:

```
<CFSET TABLE=7>
<CFLOOP INDEX="X" FROM=1 TO=10>
    <CFSET Y = #TABLE# * X>
    <CFOUTPUT>#TABLE# * #X# = #Y#<BR></CFOUTPUT>
</CFLOOP>
```

Here all you have done is replace the literal 7 with the variable TABLE, which represents the times table you are supposed to be calculating. Then, all you need to do is assign a value to the TABLE variable to specify which times table you want to view. To produce the 5 times table, the code would look like the following:

```
<CFSET TABLE=5>
<CFLOOP INDEX="X" FROM=1 TO=10>
    <CFSET Y = Table * X>
    <CFOUTPUT>#Table# * #X# = #Y#<BR></CFOUTPUT>
</CFLOOP>
```

Similarly, the 12 times table would use the following code:

```
<CFSET TABLE=12>
<CFLOOP INDEX="X" FROM=1 TO=10>
    <CFSET Y = Table * X>
    <CFOUTPUT>#Table# * #X# = #Y#<BR></CFOUTPUT>
</CFLOOP>
```

This can be taken a step further, specifying the number of entries to be specified through a variable. The following code creates the first 15 entries of the 11 times table by using a variable to specify the TO value in the CFLOOP tag:

```
<CFSET TABLE=11>
<CFSET ENTRIES=15>
<CFLOOP INDEX="X" FROM=1 TO=#Entries#>
    <CFSET Y = Table * X>
    <CFOUTPUT>#Table# * #X# = #Y#<BR></CFOUTPUT>
</CFLOOP>
```

Setting the Step

You may have noticed that the preceding index loops suffer from a major limitation: They count upward only in increments of 1. Of course, there are likely to be times when it is necessary to count by different increments. This is where the STEP attribute comes into play.

The STEP attribute specifies the size of the increment for the loop and needs to be used for any increment other than the default of 1.

For instance, to count even numbers, it is necessary to use an increment of 2. To count all even numbers from 2 to 100, the following CFLOOP tag could be used: <CFLOOP INDEX="X" FROM=2 TO=100 STEP=2>. Similarly, you could count multiples of 5 from 5 to 500 with <CFLOOP INDEX="X" FROM=5 TO=500 STEP=5>.

In addition to counting up by increments other than 1, the STEP attribute can be used to count down. To do this, just use a negative number as the value of the STEP attribute. For instance, to count down from 10 to 1, use the tag <CFLOOP INDEX="X" FROM=10 TO=1 STEP=-1>.

Creating Additional Types of Loops

So far, you've learned about index loops. Index loops are the most basic type of loop and are found in every type of programming language. The CFLOOP tag, however, can be used to create several other types of loops. These include the following:

- Conditional loops
- Query loops
- List loops

Conditional Loops

Conditional loops are designed to repeat as long as a specific condition is true and to end when the condition becomes false. This corresponds to the while loops found in many programming languages. Even if you haven't used other programming environments, understanding the basic structure of the `while` loop makes it easy to understand the concept of a conditional loop.

The basic structure of a `while` loop is as follows:

```
While condition is true
    Actions to perform
End of loop
```

What happens here is that before the loop even executes, the condition is checked. If it is false, the loop is skipped. If it is true, the actions inside the loop are performed once. The condition is then checked again, and, if true, the actions are repeated. This process continues until the condition is false.

Using the `CFLOOP` tag to create a conditional loop requires the use of only one attribute: `CONDITION`. This attribute specifies the condition to be tested for each iteration of the loop.

To understand how index loops and conditional loops compare, let's implement our times table code as a conditional loop. Our original index loop was as follows:

```
<CFSET TABLE=11>
<CFSET ENTRIES=15>
<CFLOOP INDEX="X" FROM=1 TO=#Entries#>
    <CFSET Y = Table * X>
    <CFOUTPUT>#Table# * #X# = #Y#<BR></CFOUTPUT>
</CFLOOP>
```

To translate this to a conditional loop, you need to consider the condition. The condition needs to test the value of the *X* variable to see if it is out of range. For instance, you can set *X* to 1 before the loop and then use the condition X `greater than Entries`. This suggests a loop that looks like this:

```
<CFSET TABLE=11>
<CFSET ENTRIES=15>
<CFSET X=1>
<CFLOOP CONDITION="X greater than Entries">
    <CFSET Y = Table * X>
    <CFOUTPUT>#Table# * #X# = #Y#<BR></CFOUTPUT>
</CFLOOP>
```

At first glance, this loop looks good. However, it has a major flaw: The value of *X* never changes. This means that the condition will always be true and the loop will repeat forever, creating an endless loop. Endless loops are the bane of programming because they create programs, scripts, or templates that never end and may eventually consume all the memory in a computer, causing it to crash.

This means you need to add an additional step to the loop: incrementing the value stored in the variable *X*:

```
<CFSET TABLE=11>
<CFSET ENTRIES=15>
<CFSET X=1>
<CFLOOP CONDITION="X greater than Entries">
    <CFSET Y = Table * X>
    <CFOUTPUT>#Table# * #X# = #Y#<BR></CFOUTPUT>
    <CFSET X = X + 1>
</CFLOOP>
```

This need to set the value of *X* before the loop and then increment it inside the loop highlights the major difference between index and conditional loops: Conditional loops do not have indexes. To use a conditional loop to count requires manually adding code to perform the counting.

Query Loops

The idea behind a *query loop* should already be familiar. In Chapter 3, "Getting Data from a Database," you saw how to use CFOUTPUT to loop over a query result from a database and display the results.

CFOUTPUT provides a limited way to loop over a query result, however. Inside a CFOUTPUT loop, only a small range of tags can be used. This constrains the use of CFOUT-PUT in performing complex tasks on a query result set.

The CFLOOP tag, however, can be used to loop through a query result set and perform any valid ColdFusion operations on the information, including outputting the result data, just as with the CFOUTPUT tag.

When using CFLOOP to loop over a query, the following attributes are available:

QUERY   The name of the query to use for the loop.

STARTROW   The row in the query result to start the loop at. By default, this value is 1.

ENDROW   The row in the query result to end the loop at. By default, this value is the last row in the query result.

To get a sense of how to use the query result, you will work against a simple Microsoft Access database containing a list of names and phone numbers. The database contains a single table, called Contacts, with two fields: Name and Phone.

In all examples you will look at, assume the following ColdFusion query has been performed:

```
<CFQUERY NAME="Contacts" DATSOURCE="ContactList">
    SELECT    *
    FROM      Contacts
    ORDER BYName
</CFQUERY>
```

As you already know, it would be simple to output the results using CFOUTPUT as follows:

```
<CFOUTPUT QUERY="Contacts">
    #Name#: #Phone#<BR>
</CFOUTPUT>
```

The CFLOOP tag can be used to produce similar results:

```
<CFLOOP QUERY="Contacts">
    <CFOUTPUT>#Name#: #Phone#<BR></CFOUTPUT>
</CFLOOP>
```

When using the CFLOOP tag, you are free to use any ColdFusion tags and functions that you want to within the loop. For instance, within the CFOUTPUT tag, it isn't possible to use the CFINCLUDE tag to include outside code in each iteration of the loop. This can be done with the CFLOOP tag.

List Loops

You will learn more about lists in Chapter 14, "Working with Cold Fusion Data Structures." For now, you need to understand that a list is a series of items (numbers or strings, usually) separated by a common delimiter such as a comma, a colon, or a special series of characters (such as -+-).

For instance, the following are both examples of lists:

```
John,Barbara,Lucy,Pete,William
987:345:235:87:1
```

In both cases, the lists have five elements. In the first list the delimiter is a comma; in the second the delimiter is a colon.

Using CFLOOP, you can iterate through a list, repeating the loop once for each item in the list. *List loops* resemble index loops in that each item in the list is assigned to an index variable in each iteration of the loop.

When creating a list loop, the following attributes are required in the CFLOOP tag:

INDEX   The name of the index variable for the list.

LIST   The list that is to be used for the loop.

DELIMITER   The character or characters that act as the delimiter between items in the list. This character is assumed to be a comma.

To see how this works, let's perform simple loops to output the two preceding list examples. First, you will output the list of names as follows:

```
<CFLOOP INDEX="Item" LIST="John,Barbara,Lucy,Pete,William">
    <CFOUTPUT>#Item#<BR></CFOUTPUT>
</CFLOOP>
```

Notice that you can use the index variable inside the loop just as you did with index loops.

Similarly, you can output the list of numbers as follows:

```
<CFLOOP INDEX="Item" LIST="987:345:235:87:1" DELIMITER=":">
<CFOUTPUT>#Item#<BR></CFOUTPUT>
</CFLOOP>
```

The critical difference here is that you have specified the delimiter with the DELIMITER attribute.

However, specifying the list and delimiter as literal values can be a constraint. You can add flexibility by using variables to specify the list and delimiter like this:

```
<CFSET List="987:345:235:87:1">
<CFSET Delimiter=":">
<CFLOOP INDEX="Item" LIST="#List#" DELIMITER="#Delimiter#">
    <CFOUTPUT>#ITEM#<BR></CFOUTPUT>
</CFLOOP>
```

With this structure, the list and delimiter variables can be created in any way, including by using CFSET, from a query, or from the user who provides them through a form.

Other Types of Loops

Two other types of loops can be created using CFLOOP: collection loops that allow you to loop over COM/DCOM objects and structure loops. COM/DCOM loops will be outlined in Chapter 32, "Including External Objects," and structure loops will be considered when we discuss ColdFusion's structure functions in Chapter 14.

Nesting Loops

Loops offer an additional powerful capability: nesting. *Nesting* refers to the technique of embedding one loop inside another. For instance, using nesting, you can repeat one loop for each iteration of another loop. This capability has already been visited in Chapter 12, "Grouping, Nesting, and Formatting Output," in the context of the CFOUTPUT tag.

To better understand how this works, let's consider an extension of our basic times table code:

```
<CFSET TABLE=11>
<CFSET ENTRIES=15>
<CFLOOP INDEX="X" FROM=1 TO=#Entries#>
    <CFSET Y = Table * X>
    <CFOUTPUT>#Table# * #X# = #Y#<BR></CFOUTPUT>
</CFLOOP>
```

What would happen if you wanted to output a series of times tables? For instance, what if you wanted to output every times table from the 1 times table to the 9 times table and output 15 entries for each table? You could nest two index loops as follows:

```
<CFSET Entries=15>
<CFLOOP INDEX="Table" FROM=1 TO=9>
    <CFOUTPUT><H1>The #Table# Times Table</H1></CFOUTPUT>
    <CFLOOP INDEX="X" FROM=1 TO=#Entries#>
        <CFSET Y= Table * X>
        <CFOUTPUT>#Table# * #X# = #Y#<BR></CFOUTPUT>
    </CFLOOP>
</CFLOOP>
```

What exactly is happening here? Well, the outer loop (the one with the index variable Table) contains the inner loop (the one with the index variable *X*). The outer loop iterates once for each times table you want to output. The index variable Table contains the number of the current table you want to output.

The inner loop is our now-familiar loop for outputting the times table specified in a variable called Table. It will run once for each iteration of the outer loop, outputting the appropriate times table based on the value of the Table variable.

It is important to note that when nesting loops, you can have the duration of the inner loop be dependent on the outer loop. An ideal example of this is a set of nested loops for calculating factorials. A *factorial* is a series of multiplication based on a specific number. For instance, factorial 4 (written as 4!) is the value 4 * 3 * 2 * 1, and 9! is 9 * 8 * 7 * 6 * 5 * 4 * 3 * 2 * 1.

A simple loop can calculate a factorial:

```
<CFSET Number=6>
<CFSET Factorial = 1>
<CFLOOP INDEX="X" FROM=#Number# TO=1 STEP=-1>
   <CFSET Factorial = Factorial * X>
</CFLOOP>
<CFOUTPUT>#Number#! = #Factorial#</CFOUTPUT>
```

The assumption here is that the number against which to calculate the factorial is stored in the variable Number. The result is stored in the variable Factorial.

Now, if you want to produce multiple factorials (for instance, for each number from 5 to 15), you need to nest two loops:

```
<CFLOOP INDEX="Number" FROM=5 TO=15>
<CFSET Factorial = 1>
   <CFLOOP INDEX="X" FROM=#Number# TO=1 STEP=-1>
      <CFSET Factorial = Factorial * X>
   </CFLOOP>
   <CFOUTPUT>#Number#! = #Factorial#<BR></CFOUTPUT>
</CFLOOP>
```

The important point here is that the inner loop's length is dependent on the value of the index variable of the outer loop (the variable Number determines how many times the inner loop will iterate).

This ability to adjust the length of one nested loop based on values from another loop raises a danger: The chance of producing endless loops is greater. This is especially true if the inner loop is a conditional loop, and the condition is based on the index variable from the outer loop. It is important to think through the logic of your loops when nesting them to be sure to avoid endless loops.

NOTE   It is possible to nest loops multiple levels deep. The two-level nested loops you have seen here are the most common, but you can often find loops nested three or four levels deep.

Where Do We Go from Here?

Up to this point, you have learned the basics of using ColdFusion to produce dynamic pages. However, the real interactive power of the Web and of ColdFusion to enhance that process with dynamic data comes from HTML forms.

In the next chapter, you will learn how forms integrate into ColdFusion, allowing the dynamic population of form fields as well as the creation of more sophisticated dynamic forms using the CFFORM tag. The chapter will include a discussion of the special Java form controls included with ColdFusion, such as tree controls, grid controls, and sliders.

In Chapter 15, "Forms," you will look at an important issue: form validation. This chapter addresses a fundamental concern with forms: How can you be sure the data entered by a user meets the criteria you expect?

chapter 14

Working with ColdFusion Data Structures

- Understanding and Using Lists: More than Just Strings

- Understanding and Using Arrays

- Understanding and Using Structures and Associative Arrays

So far in the book, you have worked with simple data types: numbers, strings, Boolean values, and the like. ColdFusion, however, supports a collection of more advanced data types common to most programming languages.

In ColdFusion, these more sophisticated data types are lists, arrays, and structures. In all cases, these data types combine collections of simpler data types into a more complex, structured relationship.

For instance, a list is just that, a list of strings in a predefined order. An array is an ordered collection of any data type, including numbers, strings, Boolean values, and lists.

Structures were introduced in ColdFusion 4. They offer the capability to create sets of relationships by mapping one set of values to its counterpart in another set of values.

Applying these data types opens the door to new possibilities in your ColdFusion templates.

Understanding and Using Lists: More Than Just Strings

You have already had a brief introduction to lists. In Chapter 7, "Controlling the Flow of Your Templates," you encountered lists as the value of the VALUE attribute of the CFCASE tag in a switch-case construct.

A list is simply a string value structured in a special way; it is a series of shorter strings separated by a delimiter. For instance, the following are all lists:

```
"A,B,C,D,E,F,G,H,I,J,K,L,M,N,O,P,Q,R,S,T,U,V,W,X,Y,Z"
"1;2;3;4;5;6;7;8;9;0"
"ab|c|defg|h|ijkl|mn|o|pqrstuvwzy|z"
```

In all cases, the lists have a delimiter (the three used here are a comma, a semicolon, and a vertical bar or pipe). These delimiters separate list elements that consist of one or more characters other than the delimiter character.

Lists can also contain more than one delimiter character. For instance, the following list can be interpreted in several ways:

```
"1,2|3,4"
```

There are three ways to break up this list, depending on the selection of the delimiter character:

- A two-element list ("1,2" and "3,4") with a vertical bar as the delimiter.
- A three-element list ("1" and "2|3" and "4") with a comma as the delimiter.
- A four-element list ("1" and "2" and "3" and "4") with both commas and vertical bars as delimiters.

Another aspect of lists is that delimiters can be more than one character long. For instance, in the list `"ab,|cd"`, if both commas and vertical bars are valid delimiter characters, then the list has two elements: `"ab"` and `"cd"`.

NOTE   When working with lists, you can generally assume that the delimiter is a comma unless otherwise specified. In most of the functions and tags that work with lists, a comma is treated as the default delimiter unless others are specified.

Working with Lists

ColdFusion provides several functions that you can use to create and manipulate the contents of lists. You will take a close look at the following functions in this section:

- ListLen
- ListFirst
- ListLast
- ListRest
- ListAppend
- ListPrepend
- ListChangeDelims
- ListGetAt
- ListInsertAt
- ListSetAt
- ListDeleteAt
- ListFind
- ListFindNoCase
- ListContains
- ListContainsNoCase

ListLen

Because a list consists of a series of elements, when working with lists you need to be able to determine the number of elements in a list. The `ListLen` function returns the number of elements in a list passed as an argument: `ListLen(List,Delimiters)`. If delimiters are not specified, the default comma is assumed to be the delimiter.

For instance, the following code:

```
<CFOUTPUT>
    #ListLen("1,2|3,4","|")#<BR>
    #ListLen("1,2|3,4")#<BR>
    #ListLen("1,2|3,4",",|")#
</CFOUTPUT>
```

produces the following output:

```
2
3
4
```

Notice the use of the second argument to specify delimiters in the first and last lines of the output. The last line specifies multiple delimiters (the comma and the vertical bar) by simply including them in the string that is the delimiter argument. In the second line of the output, a delimiter is not specified, which means that a comma is the delimiter.

ListFirst

ListFirst returns the first element in a list given an argument and an optional delimiter definition: ListFirst(List[,Delimiters]). As an example, the following code:

```
<CFOUTPUT>
    #ListFirst("1,2|3,4","|")#<BR>
    #ListFirst("1,2|3,4")#<BR>
    #ListFirst("1,2|3,4",",|")#
</CFOUTPUT>
```

produces the following output:

```
1,2
1
1
```

ListLast

As would be expected, ListLast performs the opposite job of ListFirst: It returns the last element in a list. ListLast takes the form ListLast(List, Delimiters).

ListRest

As a corollary to ListFirst, ListRest returns a given list except for the first element. Used together, ListFirst and ListRest return all elements in a list. As would be expected, ListRest takes the form ListRest(List[, Delimiters]).

NOTE   Many of the examples in this chapter require the database **mailist.mdb**, which is included on the CD that comes with this book. To use this database, you need to install it as a data source using the ColdFusion Administrator. The steps required to do this are described in Chapter 35, "ColdFusion Administration."

Listing 14.1 shows the complementary roles of ListFirst and ListRest.

Listing 14.1: `listrest.cfm`

```
<CFSET TheList  = "1,2|3,4">

<TABLE BORDER=1>
    <TR>
        <TD>DELIMITER</TD>
        <TD>FIRST</TD>
        <TD>REST</TD>
    </TR>
    <TR>
<CFOUTPUT>
    <TD>|</TD>
    <TD>#ListFirst("1,2|3,4","|")#</TD>
    <TD>#ListRest("1,2|3,4","|")#</TD>
</CFOUTPUT>
    </TR>
    <TR>
<CFOUTPUT>
    <TD>,</TD>
    <TD>#ListFirst("1,2|3,4")#</TD>
    <TD>#ListRest("1,2|3,4")#</TD>
</CFOUTPUT>
    </TR>
    <TR>
<CFOUTPUT>
    <TD>,|</TD>
    <TD>#ListFirst("1,2|3,4",",|")#</TD>
    <TD>#ListRest("1,2|3,4",",|")#</TD>
</CFOUTPUT>
    </TR>
</TABLE>
```

This code produces results like those in Figure 14.1.

FIGURE 14.1
Using ListRest

ListAppend

Up to this point, you've looked at functions that enable you to obtain information about a list and its elements. ListAppend performs a different role: It alters the contents of a list. Specifically, ListAppend adds an element to the end of the list using the form ListAppend(List, Element, Delimiters). The delimiter argument is optional and needed only if your list requires delimiters other than the default comma. The list and element arguments are required.

For instance, consider the list "A;B;C;D". To add "E" to the end of the list, use ListAppend("A;B;C;D","E",";"). This will return a new list: "A;B;C;D;E".

ListPrepend

ListPrepend plays the opposite role of ListAppend in that it adds a new element to the start of a list using the syntax ListPrepend(List, Element, Delimiters).

As an example, ListPrepend("B,C,D,E","A") returns the list "A,B,C,D,E".

ListChangeDelims

ListChangeDelims is a function whose utility is immediately apparent. The function is used to change existing delimiters in a list to a new character or set of characters.

The question here is: Why might this be useful? Consider some possible sources of lists: Users submitting forms may provide information in lists, or outside applications (such as Microsoft Excel) may generate lists in a file, which you then use in your Cold-Fusion applications.

In some cases, however, the default delimiter in these lists from outside sources won't meet your needs. For instance, if a list has commas for delimiters and you want to add an element that includes a comma, you will have a problem. The only way around this is to change the delimiter in the original list before adding the new element.

That's where ListChangeDelims comes in. The function takes the form ListChange-Delims(List, NewDelimiter[, Delimiters]). The last argument, specifying the existing delimiters, is not necessary unless the list uses a delimiter other than the default comma.

> **NOTE**   When using ListChangeDelims, it is important to note that your original list may have several possible delimiters, and not all delimiters in the list will be identical. After using ListChangeDelims, all delimiters in the list will be identical and will match the new delimiter specified as an argument to the function.

ListGetAt

Until now, most of the functions you have looked at have manipulated lists or returned elements from a list in a limited manner.

ListGetAt, however, is the first of a series of functions we are presenting that enable you to retrieve or manipulate single elements in a specific fashion. With ListGetAt, you can retrieve a single element from a list by specifying its numerical position in the list. The function is used as follows: ListGetAt(List, Position[, Delimiters]). As usual, the delimiter argument is optional if the list uses the default delimiter.

The position is specified numerically with 1 being the first element in the list, 2 the second element, 3 the third element, and so on until the last element in the list. The easiest way to understand how this works is to consider a list of the letters of the alphabet: "A,B,C,D,E,F,G,H,I,J,K,L,M,N,O,P,Q,R,S,T,U,V,W,X,Y,Z". Table 14.1 shows examples of how ListGetAt works if this list is stored in the variable Alphabet.

TABLE 14.1: Using ListGetAt

Example	Value returned by function
ListGetAt(Alphabet,1)	A
ListGetAt(Alphabet,5)	E
ListGetAt(Alphabet,26)	Z

If you choose a position that is out of the list's range (for instance, in the preceding example, both 0 and 27 are out of range—0 is too small and there is no 27th element in the list), then ColdFusion will generate an error.

ListInsertAt

Like ListGetAt, ListInsertAt uses numerical references to indicate the place in the list to insert a new element. This function provides more flexibility than ListAppend and ListPrepend, which can add elements only at the beginning or end of a list.

ListInsertAt allows the insertion of an element immediately before a specified element using the form ListInsertAt(List, Position, NewElement, Delimiters).

For instance, building on our previous example using ListGetAt, ListInsertAt (Alphabet,5,"1") would insert the element 1 immediately before the element E in the list—producing a list that starts with: A,B,C,D,1,E,F,G,….

There are two caveats to note when using ListInsertAt:

- If your list includes multiple delimiters, then the extra delimiter that will be added with the new element will be the first character in the list of delimiters you provide as an argument to ListInsertAt.
- If you are using a list generated by another application, you may find that the elements are organized as follows: element1, element2, element3, element4. Although it appears that commas act as delimiters in this list, in reality both commas and blank spaces are acting as delimiters. If you don't specify both spaces and commas as delimiters when adding a new element with ListInsertAt, the result will look something like this: element1,newelement, element2, element3, element4. If you specify the spaces as delimiters as well as commas, then your results will look like this: element1, newelement,element2, element3, element4. When using ListInsertAt in this scenario, you need to decide which approach best suits your needs.

ListSetAt

ListSetAt is closely akin to ListInsertAt in that it changes the contents of a list. However, rather than adding an element, it changes the value of an existing element. The function takes the form ListSetAt(List, Position, NewValue, Delimiters).

For instance, if instead of inserting a new element before E in our alphabet list, you want to replace the E, you simply use ListSetAt(Alphabet,5,"1") and the resulting list will start with A,B,C,D,1,F,G,….

ListDeleteAt

After learning about ListGetAt, ListInsertAt, and ListSetAt, you should find the role of ListDeleteAt fairly obvious: To delete an element from a list that is specified by its numeric position and to return the new list. And the structure of the function should be clear: ListDeleteAt(List,Position,Delimiters).

So, to delete the E from our alphabet list, you would use: ListDeleteAt(Alphabet,5).

ListFind

To make lists really useful, you need to be able to check whether a given value matches any element in the list. ListFind provides one way to do this. This function returns the numeric position of the list's first element that matches a specified value. To find a value, use the form ListFind(List,Value,Delimiters).

How does this work? It is quite simple. The function compares the first element to the value. If it matches, the position is returned. If not, then the function proceeds to the next element and repeats the same process. This continues until there is a match or all elements in the list fail to match. If no element matches, then 0 is returned.

Because the numeric position of an element is returned, the function provides more utility than simply determining whether an element is in a list. The resulting numeric position can subsequently be used with ListGetAt, ListInsertAt, ListSetAt, and ListDeleteAt.

With respect to the way in which matches occur, ListFind performs a case-sensitive match on entire elements. This means that matches to substrings inside elements are not found.

For instance, in the previous alphabet example, you can use ListFind(Alphabet,"E") to see whether the character E is in the list. This will return a value of 5. Because the search is case sensitive, this means ListFind(Alphabet, "e") will fail to find a match.

As another example, consider the following list: `"one,two,three,four,five"`. Table 14.2 shows how different examples of the `ListFind` function will work with this list.

TABLE 14.2: Using `ListFind`

Function	Result
ListFind("one,two,three,four,five","three")	Returns a value of 3.
ListFind("one,two,three,four,five","thr")	No match is found.
ListFind("one,two,three,four,five","Three")	No match is found.

ListFindNoCase

`ListFindNoCase` is a simple extension of `ListFind`. The difference is that the search is case insensitive. Therefore, `ListFindNoCase(Alphabet,"E")` and `ListFindNoCase(Alphabet,"e")` will both produce matches, as will `ListFindNoCase("one,two, three,four,five","three")` and `ListFindNoCase("one,two,three,four, five","Three")`.

ListContains

`ListContains` is also similar to `ListFind`, but the difference lies not in the treatment of uppercase and lowercase characters but rather substrings. `ListContains` matches not only complete elements but substrings as well.

Therefore, in our examples with the list `"one,two,three,four,five"`, both `ListContains("one,two,three,four,five","three")` and `ListContains ("One, two, three,four,five","thr")` generate matches for position 3. Like `ListFind`, `ListContains` uses case-sensitive searches.

ListContainsNoCase

`ListContainsNoCase` extends `ListContains` to include case-insensitive searches. Therefore, all these examples produce matches:

- `ListContainsNoCase(Alphabet,"E")`
- `ListContainsNoCase(Alphabet,"e")`
- `ListContainsNoCase("one,two,three,four,five","three")`
- `ListContainsNoCase("one,two,three,four,five","thr")`
- `ListContainsNoCase("one,two,three,four,five","Three")`

Putting It All Together

Now that you have a firm grasp of all the functions related to a list, let's look at a small example of how to use these capabilities in an application.

For example, say a list of comma-delimited e-mail addresses has been provided by a user (don't concern yourself with how the list is provided because this is addressed in Chapter 15, "Forms"). Each element in this list is assumed to be an e-mail address. You want to add each address to a simple database table only if the address is not currently in the table.

Step by step, you need to do the following:

1. Determine the number of elements in the list.

2. Display the number of addresses in the list.

3. For each element in the list, do the following:

   a. Check if the address is in the database.

   b. If it is not in the database, add it to the database.

   c. Display a message indicating the action taken.

For the purposes of your ColdFusion code, you will make the following assumptions:

- The list is already stored in a variable called `newusers`.
- Commas are the only delimiters in the list.
- The desired database table is in a data source called `mailist`.
- The table itself is called `users`.
- The table contains a single text field called `email` that is used to store the e-mail addresses.

Now, for the code, see Listing 14.2.

Listing 14.2: `email.cfm`

```
<!--- Get the length of the list --->
<CFSET Length = ListLen(newusers)>

<!--- Output the length of the list --->
<CFOUTPUT>
   <STRONG>The list contains #Length# elements</STRONG><BR>
</CFOUTPUT>

<!--- Loop through each element in the list --->
<CFLOOP INDEX="element" FROM=1 TO=#Length#>

   <!--- Get the specified element --->
   <CFSET currentuser = ListGetAt(newusers,element)>
```

```
<!--- Check if the element is in the database --->
<CFQUERY NAME="Check" DATASOURCE="maillist">
    SELECT    *
    FROM    users
    WHERE    email='#currentuser#'
</CFQUERY>

<!--- Perform the appropriate action --->
<CFIF Check.RecordCount greater than 0>
    <CFOUTPUT>#currentuser# is already in the
database and has not been added<BR></CFOUTPUT>
  <CFELSE>
    <CFQUERY NAME="Add" DATASOURCE="maillist">
        INSERT INTO    users
        VALUES        ('#currentuser#')
    </CFQUERY>
    <CFOUTPUT>#currentuser# has been added to
the database.<BR></CFOUTPUT>
  </CFIF>

</CFLOOP>
```

This code produces results like those in Figure 14.2.

FIGURE 14.2

Adding e-mail addresses to a database

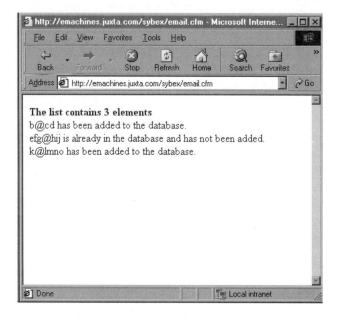

Let's walk through this template section by section. You start by using `ListLen` to obtain the number of elements to display in the list, which you then display. Knowing the number of elements in the list, you can use `CFLOOP` to perform a series of actions on each element in the list. You do this by using 1 as the starting value for the loop index and by using the number of elements in the list as the ending value for the loop.

Within the loop, you use `ListGetAt` to extract the element at the position indicated by the index of loop, `element`. After you have the element, you have two jobs: Check whether the element is already in the database and then take the appropriate action.

You use a SQL `SELECT` statement to retrieve from the database any records that match the element. Then in your `CFIF` statement, you use the `RecordCount` property of your query result to see whether any records were retrieved. If `RecordCount` is greater than zero, then you know that a record already in the database matches the current element, and you don't add it to the database again. Otherwise, you use a SQL `INSERT` statement to add a record to the database.

Understanding and Using Arrays

Arrays are data structures common to all robust programming languages, and Cold-Fusion is no exception. Conceptually, arrays are quite simple.

In its most basic form, a one-dimensional array is very close in concept to a list: a series of elements, each with a numerical place in the list. The difference lies in how elements are referred to and manipulated.

Generally, arrays are named, ordered collections of elements. Let's look at a simple example: a list of students in a class. Here you can use an array to keep track of the students' names. For instance, if you have five students in a class, you can create an array called `students` and then the elements, numbered one to five, would be as follows:

1. Student name 1
2. Student name 2
3. Student name 3
4. Student name 4
5. Student name 5

NOTE If you have programmed in other languages, you probably noticed that the first element in the preceding example is numbered 1 (that is, has an index of 1, in more traditional terms) instead of 0. Most programming languages number array elements starting at 0, so that a 10-element array has arrays numbered 0 to 9. In ColdFusion, an array element number starts at 1.

At a practical level in ColdFusion, a numerical element within an array is referred to by placing the numerical index (or position) of the element in square brackets after the name of the array. In this case, that means the five elements are referred to as the following:

```
students[1]
students[2]
students[3]
students[4]
students[5]
```

These element names can be used in the same way as regular variable names anywhere in your templates, including in CFSET tags and CFOUPUT blocks. For instance, you can use the following:

```
<CFSET CurrentStudent=students[3]>
```

to assign the name of a specific student to another variable, or you can output a name by using:

```
<CFOUTPUT>Student Name: #students[4]#</CFOUTPUT>
```

Like other variables, new values can be assigned to specific elements in an array with CFSET:

```
<CFSET students[2]="New Name">
```

Another valuable aspect of arrays is that the numeric index, or position, of an element does not have to be explicitly specified as in the preceding examples; it can be specified with a variable:

```
<CFSET index=4>
<CFSET students[index] = "NewName">
```

This approach can be extended in that entire expressions can serve to indicate the index of an array element. For instance, continuing this example, you could access the fifth element of the students array with the following:

```
<CFSET students[index+1] = "NewName2">
```

Understanding Multiple Dimensions

Up to this point, you have looked at one-dimensional arrays. These arrays can best be thought of as a single row of multiple cells, with each cell having a number—as shown in Figure 14.3.

Cells

Each cell stores a separate value

However, arrays can have more than one dimension in ColdFusion. In ColdFusion, arrays can have one, two, or three dimensions. For instance, consider a two-dimensional array: This is really a data structure of multiple rows, with each row having multiple cells. See Figure 14.4.

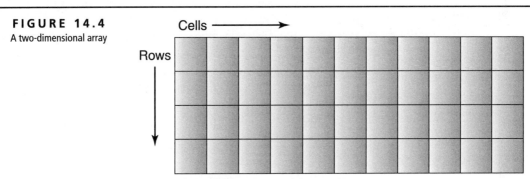

Cells

Rows

Each cell stores a separate value

Here you see multiple rows and multiple cells. In ColdFusion, an individual cell can be referenced by two numeric indexes, each in square brackets following the array name in the form `arrayname[row][cell]`. Therefore, to reference the third cell in the second row of the array shown in Figure 14.4, you would use something like `arrayname[2][3]`.

ColdFusion also provides support for three-dimensional arrays (but not higher dimensions). This simply adds another dimension to the puzzle (making it hard to show graphically). But, if you think of a cube built out of smaller cubes, then you can see the picture of multiple panes, each with a row consisting of multiple cells. To reference the individual cells, simply use three numeric indexes: `arrayname[plane][row][cell]`.

NOTE

Those familiar with conventional programming in languages such as C will probably think of multiple-dimension arrays in terms such as `array[x][y]`, which signifies the x and y dimensions in two-dimensional space. These x and y dimensions directly correspond to the model of row and cell being used here to help visualize arrays.

Creating Arrays

Arrays are created using the `ArrayNew` function. This function takes a single argument: The number of dimensions of the array (1, 2, or 3). It returns an empty array of the number of dimensions specified.

NOTE

Unlike other programming languages such as C, the number of elements in a ColdFusion array does not need to be specified when the array is created. Instead, ColdFusion arrays grow as needed to accommodate new elements, which can be added anytime after the array is created. This is important because each row in a two-dimensional array can contain a different number of elements.

For instance, our array of student names is a one-dimensional array. You create this array by using CFSET to assign the array returned by `ArrayNew` to the name `students`:

```
<CFSET students=ArrayNew(1)>
```

Similarly, to create a two-dimensional array called `array2d`, you would use the following:

```
<CFSET array2d=ArrayNew(2)>
```

Populating an Array

After an array is created, you must populate it. That is, you need to assign whatever values you want to elements in the array. You do this with a standard CFSET tag. For instance, our `students` array can be populated with a series of CFSET tags like these:

```
<CFSET students[1] = "Student name 1">
<CFSET students[2] = "Student name 2">
<CFSET students[3] = "Student name 3">
etc.
```

Our two-dimensional array could be populated with the following:

```
<CFSET array2d[1][1] = "Value 1/1">
<CFSET array2d[1][2] = "Value 1/2">
<CFSET array2d[1][3] = "Value 1/3">
<CFSET array2d[2][1] = "Value 2/1">
<CFSET array2d[2][2] = "Value 2/2">
etc.
```

At times, you may want to populate a large number of cells with a default value. For one-dimensional arrays, this can be done with the `ArraySet` function, which, given an array, fills a specified range of cells with the same value. The function is used as follows: `ArraySet(Array,StartCell,EndCell,Value)`.

For instance, if you want the first 10 elements of our `students` array to be set with a default value of `"No Name"`, you could use `ArraySet(students,1,10,"NoName")`.

Understanding Dynamic Array Sizes

The capability of ColdFusion arrays to change size dynamically has some implications that need to be understood. The essential issue is this: An array is a continuous series of elements, with the first index being 1 and no gaps in the series of element indexes.

What does this mean? First, an array with the following elements (and no other elements) is a valid array:

```
NameofArray[1]
NameofArray[2]
NameofArray[3]
```

However, an array with the following elements (and no other elements) is not valid:

```
NameofArray[1]
NameofArray[2]
NameofArray[4]
```

The latter is not valid because a gap exists in the index numbering: Where is `NameofArray[3]`?

This distinction is important when manipulating arrays. For instance, consider an array with the following elements:

```
NameofArray[1]="One"
NameofArray[2]="Two"
NameofArray[3]="Three"
NameofArray[4]="Four"
```

What happens if you delete the third element (you will learn to do this later in this chapter when we discuss the `ArrayDeleteAt` function)? First, the element is deleted. Next, all subsequent indexes are adjusted by 1 so that no gaps exist in the numerical sequence of the indexes:

```
ArrayName[1]="One"
ArrayName[2]="Two"
ArrayName[3]="Four"
```

Using Array Functions

As with lists, ColdFusion offers several functions for working with and manipulating arrays. You have already seen the `ArrayNew` and `ArraySet` functions in action, but the following functions are also available:

- `ArrayAppend`
- `ArrayPrepend`
- `ArrayDeleteAt`
- `ArrayInsertAt`
- `ArrayMax`
- `ArrayMin`
- `ArraySum`
- `ArrayAvg`
- `ArraySwap`
- `ArraySort`
- `ArrayClear`
- `ArrayResize`
- `ArrayIsEmpty`
- `IsArray`
- `ListToArray`
- `ArrayToList`

Some of these functions should be familiar because of the corresponding list functions you learned about earlier; these array functions are described in Table 14.3.

TABLE 14.3:   Common Array Functions

Function	Usage	Description
`ArrayAppend`	`ArrayAppend(Array,Value)`	Adds an element to the end of the array
`ArrayPrepend`	`ArrayPrepend(Array,Value)`	Adds an element to the start of the array
`ArrayDeleteAt`	`ArrayDeleteAt(Array,Position)`	Deletes the element at the specified point in the array
`ArrayInsertAt`	`ArrayInsertAt(Array,Position)`	Inserts an element at the specified position in the array and shifts all elements from that point on in the original array one element to the right (effectively lengthening the array by one element)

The remaining functions don't have direct parallels among the list functions. You will consider them in more detail in the following sections.

Functions for Processing Values Stored in an Array

There are several functions for processing the values stored in an array. These are:

ArrayMax   Returns the largest numerical value stored in an array

ArrayMin   Returns the smallest numerical value stored in an array

ArraySum   Returns the sum of all numerical values stored in an array

ArrayAvg   Returns the average of all numerical values stored in an array

The syntax of all these functions is simple, taking the form `FunctionName(Array)`.

An important point to understand is that only arrays with strictly numerical values can be processed by these four functions. Any attempt to process an array with one or more non-numeric values will generate an error.

Therefore, the following three-element array can be processed by these four functions:

```
ArrayName[1] = 1
ArrayName[2] = 2
ArrayName[3] = 3
```

but the following array cannot be handled by these functions because of the string value in the second element:

```
ArrayName[1] = 1
ArrayName[2] = "two"
ArrayName[3] = 3
```

Table 14.4 shows the results returned by each function when processing the following array:

```
ArrayName[1] = 1
ArrayName[2] = 3
ArrayName[3] = 2
```

TABLE 14.4: Using Functions for Processing Array Values

Function	Result
ArrayMax(ArrayName)	3
ArrayMin(ArrayName)	1
ArraySum(ArrayName)	6
ArrayAvg(ArrayName)	2

Functions for Adjusting the Position of Elements in an Array

Two functions are available to change the place of elements in an array:

ArraySwap   Swaps two elements in an array

ArraySort   Sorts the elements in an array

Because these two functions work in notably different ways, we will explain them separately.

ArraySwap

The ArraySwap function swaps the contents of two elements in an array. For instance, consider an array with the following elements and values:

```
ArrayName[1]=1
ArrayName[2]=2
ArrayName[3]=3
ArrayName[4]=4
```

If you swap the second and fourth elements, the resulting array has element values as follows:

```
ArrayName[1]=1
ArrayName[2]=4
ArrayName[3]=3
ArrayName[4]=2
```

To do this, ArraySwap expects the array name and the indexes of the two elements to swap: ArraySwap(Array,Position1,Position2). The ArraySwap function directly alters the specified array and then returns the Boolean value of True upon successful completion of the swap.

Therefore, you execute the preceding swap with the following code:

```
<CFSET Result = ArraySwap(ArrayName,2,4)>
```

The swapped array is still called ArrayName.

ArraySort

The ArraySort function enables the elements of an array to be sorted in different ways, including numerically and alphabetically and in ascending or descending order. To make this happen, the function takes three arguments: an array name, a sort type, and an optional sort order. The function directly manipulates the specified array. The syntax for the function is ArraySort(Array,SortType,SortOrder).

The sort type must be one of the following three values:

numeric   Sorts numerically

text   Sorts alphabetically, placing uppercase before lowercase

textnocase   Sorts alphabetically, ignoring case

The most significant distinction is between text and textnocase. In the first instance, elements are sorted alphabetically for all uppercase letters and then for all lowercase letters, so the following series of elements:

a
b
A
B

ends up as follows when sorted with the text sort type:

A
B
a
b

In contrast, textnocase ignores case, and the resulting sorted series would be:

a
A
b
B

Let's consider an example: Say you want to sort the list of students from our earlier example, ignoring case. You would use the following:

```
<CFSET Result = ArraySort(students,"textnocase")>
```

Like ArraySwap, ArraySort directly alters the array and then returns the Boolean value of True upon successful completion of the sorting.

Another aspect of sorting is the sort order. By default, all sorting is done in ascending order. However, you have the choice of directly specifying one of two sorting orders as follows:

asc   Sort in ascending order

desc   Sort in descending order

Therefore, to sort the same array of students in descending order, you would use:

```
<CFSET Result = ArraySort(students,"textnocase","desc")>
```

Other Array Functions

In addition to the functions we have already covered, there are several other array functions that don't fit together in any clear grouping. These are as follows:

ArrayClear   Deletes all data in an array

ArrayResize   Resizes an array to a specified minimum number of elements

ArrayIsEmpty   Checks whether an array is empty

IsArray   Checks whether a given data structure is an array and, optionally, whether it is an array of a specified dimension

ListToArray   Converts a list to an array

ArrayToList   Converts an array to a list

ArrayClear

The `ArrayClear` function deletes all elements in an array. That is, it actually removes all elements from the array (as opposed to assigning some default value such as the empty string or zero). The result is a string of length zero in all dimensions. The function takes a single argument: `ArrayClear(Array)`.

A Boolean value of `True` is returned upon successful completion of the deletions.

ArrayResize

`ArrayResize` resizes an array to a specified minimum number of elements. The key word here is *minimum*. For instance, to resize an existing array with four elements to three elements has no effect because you are resizing to a minimum of three elements and the existing four elements already exceed three elements. However, resizing the same array to seven elements results in a seven-element array.

This resizing process leaves new elements in an unusable empty state, and the elements still need values assigned to them to be used. Allaire recommends using `ArrayResize` to create the elements of a large array before assigning values to the elements. This process is supposed to provide performance gains on arrays of more than 500 elements, as compared to enabling ColdFusion to create each element with each CFSET statement that assigns an initial value to an element.

To use `ArrayResize`, simply provide the name of the array and the minimum number of elements as arguments: `ArrayResize(Array,Size)`.

This function returns the Boolean value of `True` upon successful completion of the resizing.

ArrayIsEmpty

`ArrayIsEmpty` is a simple function; it tests whether an array is completely empty and returns `True` if it is and `False` if it is not. The function is used as follows: `ArrayIsEmpty(Array)`.

Consider the following example: Imagine you have a three-element array called Test-Array with values assigned to each element in the array. The following code assigns the value False to Before and the value True to After:

```
<CFSET Before = ArrayIsEmpty(TestArray)>
<CFSET Result = ArrayClear(TestArray)>
<CFSET After = ArrayIsEmpty(TestArray)>
```

IsArray

As the name suggests, the IsArray function tests whether a given data structure is an array. The data structure to test is passed as an argument to the function and the function returns the Boolean value True if the data structure is an array and False if it isn't.

Optionally, the function can also test whether a data structure is an array of a specified dimension. The syntax of the function is IsArray(Array, Dimension) where the dimension argument is optional.

ListToArray and ArrayToList

The final functions you will look at are ListToArray and ArrayToList, which are used to convert data structures between lists and arrays.

ListToArray takes a list and an optional delimiter specification as arguments and returns a single-dimensional array with each array element containing a single list element from the original list: ListToArray(List,Delimiter). The resulting array is returned by the function.

ArrayToList works in reverse. Given a one-dimensional array and an optional delimiter, the elements in the array are copied into a list delimited by the specified delimiter character (the default delimiter is, of course, a comma): ArrayToList(Array,Delimiter). The resulting list is returned by the function.

Understanding and Using Structures and Associative Arrays

ColdFusion offers another complex data structure: structures. Some developers, including those familiar with JavaScript, will know structures as *associative arrays*.

Where standard arrays were used to create a numerically indexed group of elements, associative arrays create key-value pairs. That is, they associate one value with another where neither the key nor the value needs to be an arbitrary numeric value. This type of association is also similar to the properties of objects in object-oriented and object-based programming languages such as Java, C++, and JavaScript.

In fact, ColdFusion offers three ways to refer to elements in a structure:

- Using ColdFusion functions
- Using associative-array style notation
- Using object-property style notation

In this section, you will consider all three ways to work with structures, but first you will take a quick look at exactly how key-value pairs work and can be used.

Understanding the Concept of Key-Value Pairs

In an associative array, each entry in the array has as its index a value that is usually a string or number and then takes as its value any valid ColdFusion data type.

For instance, consider an array that you want to use to associate Social Security numbers with people's names. This would be difficult with regular arrays because they take only numeric indexes, and the indexes must be sequential starting at one.

But, with a structure, you can directly associate the Social Security numbers with the names, creating a data structure that performs mappings like those in Table 14.5.

TABLE 14.5: Mapping Values with Associative Arrays

This Value	Is Mapped to This Value
123-45-6789	Joe Smith
098-76-5432	Jane Doe

This ability to associate two values can be used in several ways. For instance, you could manipulate employee records for a company by using a structure to track a single employee: entries in the structure might include last name, first name, gender, salary, employee identification number, Social Security number, and more.

Using Structure Functions

By now, most of the functions for manipulating structures will perform familiar tasks because of their similarities to functions you have already encountered for manipulating lists and arrays.

ColdFusion provides the functions outlined in Table 14.6 for working with structures.

TABLE 14.6: Functions for Working with Structures

Function	Syntax	Description
StructNew	StructName = StructNew()	Creates a new, empty structure
StructInsert	StructInsert(Structure,Key,Value, AllowOverwrite)	Inserts an element into a structure; returns a Boolean value indicating success of the insertion

TABLE 14.6:   Functions for Working with Structures *(continued)*

Function	Syntax	Description
StructUpdate	StructUpdate(Structure,Key,Value)	Updates the value of an element in a structure; returns a Boolean value
StructDelete	StructDelete(Structure,Key,Indicate-NotExisting)	Deletes an element from a structure; returns a Boolean value
StructClear	StructClear(Structure)	Deletes all elements in a structure; returns a Boolean value
StructCopy	NewStructure = StructCopy(Structure)	Creates a copy of a structure
StructCount	NumKeys = StructCount(Structure)	Counts the number of keys (or elements) in a structure
StructFind	Value = StructFind(Structure,Key)	Returns the value associated with a specified key in the structure
StructKeyExists	StructKeyExists(Structure,Key)	Checks whether a specified key exists in a structure; returns an appropriate Boolean value
StructIsEmpty	StructIsEmpty(Structure)	Checks whether a structure is empty; returns an appropriate Boolean value
IsStruct	IsStruct(DataStructure)	Checks whether a given data structure is a structure type; returns an appropriate Boolean value

For most of these functions, their purpose and use is fairly straightforward. However, the meaning of a few arguments needs further discussion.

The AllowOverWrite argument of StructInsert is an optional argument that governs the behavior of the function when it tries to insert a key-value pair where the key already exists in the structure. If AllowOverWrite is True, then the key's value is replaced; otherwise, it isn't and an error occurs. By default, AllowOverWrite is assumed to be False.

For example, if you want to insert the key-value pair "123-45-6789", "Joe Smith" and allow overwriting of existing values in the structure, you simply use StructInsert-(StructureName, "123-45-6789", "Joe Smith", True).

The StructDelete function has an optional argument, IndicateNotExisting. The purpose of this argument determines the behavior of the function when the key specified for deletion does not exist. If IndicateNotExisting is True, then the function ignores the fact that the specified key doesn't exist and causes StructDelete to return True, indicating successful completion of the deletion.

By contrast, if the value is False and the specified key doesn't exist, then the function fails and StructDelete returns False.

Putting It All Together

To better understand how to use these functions together to work with structures, let's create a simple template to display the contents of a Social-Security-number template of the type discussed earlier in this chapter. The template should empty the structure as it displays its contents.

This template has four necessary stages:

1. Create and populate a structure.
2. Display the number of elements in the structure.
3. Display the contents of the structure while deleting each element.
4. Display the number of elements in the structure to verify that it is empty.

You achieve this process with the template in Listing 14.3.

Listing 14.3: ssn.cfm

```
<!--- 1. Create and populate a structure --->
<CFSET SSN = StructNew()>
<CFSET Result = StructInsert(SSN,"123-45-6789","Joe Smith")>
<CFSET Result = StructInsert(SSN,"987-65-4321","Jane Doe")>
<CFSET Result = StructInsert(SSN,"845-87-2345","Daryl Someone")>

<!--- 2. Display the number of elements in the structure --->
<CFOUTPUT>
<H3>There are #StructCount(SSN)# Social Secutiry
Number entries.,/H3.
</CFOUTPUT>
<HR>

<!--- 3. Display the contents of the structure while deleting each element --->
<UL>
<CFLOOP COLLECTION=#SSN# ITEM="socsec">
   <CFOUTPUT><LI>#socsec#: #StructFind(SSN,socsec)#</CFOUTPUT>
   <CFSET Result = StructDelete(SSN,socsec)>
</CFLOOP>
</UL>
```

```
<!--- 4. Display the number of elements in the structure --->
<HR>
<CFOUTPUT>
<H3>There are #StructCount(SSN)# Social Security
Number entries.</H3>
</CFOUTPUT>
```

This produces results like those in Figure 14.5.

FIGURE 14.5

Using the structure functions

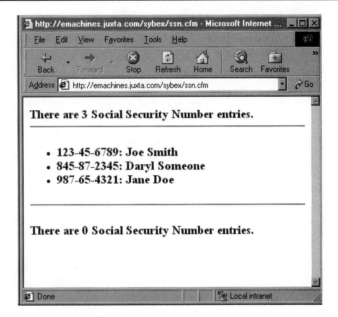

In this template, you have done the following:

- Used StructNew to create a structure called SSN.
- Used StructInsert to add three elements to the structure with Social Security numbers as keys and names as values.
- Used StructCount to display the number of elements in SSN.
- Used CFLOOP to loop through each entry in the structure. The COLLECTION attribute provides the contents of a structure (hence the use of #SSN# as opposed to simple SSN). The ITEM attribute specifies the variable name to which the key from the structure should be assigned on each iteration through the loop.
- Used StructFind to output the value for each key in the loop.
- Used StructDelete to delete key-value pairs from the structure.

Accessing Structures Using Associative-Array Syntax

The associative-array syntax for accessing elements in a structure is designed to reflect the syntax used to access elements of standard arrays. This syntax uses square brackets around the index or key. Therefore, in our social security number structure, you could assign a key-value pair to the structure with the following:

```
<CFSET SSN["123-45-6789"] = "Joe Smith">
```

In fact, several parts of the template you just used to display and delete entries from the social security number structure could be written using associative-array syntax rather than using the functions, as shown in Listing 14.4.

Listing 14.4: ssn2.cfm

```
<!--- 1. Create and populate a structure --->
<CFSET SSN = StructNew()>
<CFSET SSN["123-45-6789"]="Joe Smith">
<CFSET SSN["987-65-4321"]="Jane Doe">
<CFSET SSN["845-87-2345"]="Daryl Someone">

<!--- 2. Display the number of elements in the structure --->
<CFOUTPUT>
<H3>There are #StructCount(SSN)# Social Security
Number entries.</H3>
</CFOUTPUT>
<HR>

<!---  3. Display the contents of the structure while deleting each element --->
<UL>
<CFLOOP COLLECTION=#SSN# ITEM="socsec">
   <CFOUTPUT><LI>#socsec#: #SSN[socsec]#</CFOUTPUT>
   <CFSET Result = StructDelete(SSN,socsec)>
</CFLOOP>
</UL>

<!--- 4. Display the number of elements in the structure --->
<HR>
<CFOUTPUT>
<H3>There are #StructCount(SSN)# Social Secutiry
Number entries</H3>.
</CFOUTPUT>
```

You keep `StructNew`, `StructCount`, and `StructDelete` because these functions perform tasks that require the use of functions. However, you replace `StuctInsert` with the use of an assignment such as `SSN["987-65-4321"] = "Jane Doe"`. Similarly, `StructFind` is replaced with a simple reference to an element in the structure: `SSN[socsec]`.

Using Object-Property Notation

The third alternative for accessing elements in a structure is object-property notation, which is borrowed from object-oriented programming languages such as Java and C++. In these languages, objects can have properties that can be referred to with:

```
Objectname.propertyname
```

In the context of ColdFusion structures, the object corresponds to the structure and the property name corresponds to the key of a key-value pair. Therefore, where you used the following syntax:

```
Structure["Key"] = Value
```

you can also use:

```
Structure.Key = Value
```

This syntax has a limitation: The key cannot contain special characters such as numbers, spaces, or punctuation. The keys should be plain text strings.

Therefore, our social security number example as written cannot be altered to use object-property notation. This is because the keys contain hyphens. If you try to use object-property notation—for instance, by using the following assignment:

```
SSN.123-45-6789 = "Joe Smith"
```

you will get an error.

Where Do We Go from Here?

In this chapter, you have covered the last major types of data structures available in ColdFusion. These included the types first discussed in Chapter 4, "Creating and Manipulating Variables," as well as the lists, arrays, and structures introduced in this chapter.

In the next chapter, you will move into a major area of interactivity: forms in ColdFusion. You will learn how to build forms using special ColdFusion tags as well as how to process the data from form submissions.

It is this capability to easily create, populate, and process forms that makes Cold-Fusion a powerful tool for developing interactive applications. It enables you to obtain information from the user for the purpose of returning dynamic content, and it enables users to interact with, and even alter, data.

chapter 15

Forms

- Creating Dynamically Populated Forms

- Using Information from Forms

- Understanding the Power of Check Boxes and
  Multiple Select Lists

- Using CFFORM

In this chapter, you will move beyond the simple ability to create dynamic pages and process data into the realm of interactivity. You will look at standard HTML forms and the way they can be integrated with ColdFusion's capabilities to create fully interactive, Web-based applications.

The use of forms with ColdFusion can fulfill several needs, including the ability to search, edit, and add information to databases; to read and send e-mail; to create sophisticated search engines for Web sites; and more. Because ColdFusion is so commonly used to integrate Web-based interfaces with information stored in databases, we will present database examples throughout this chapter. Still, the fundamental principles apply to any type of interactive data access, and you will see many examples of using forms to manipulate information from other sources throughout this book.

You will start by learning how easy it is to use regular HTML tags to create forms that are populated with dynamic information. From there, you will look at how to work with data submitted from forms and at more advanced topics related to the use of check boxes and multiple select lists.

Finally, you will look at dynamic ColdFusion forms created using the CFFORM tag and a series of related ColdFusion tags such as CFINPUT, CFGRID, and CFTREE. These forms make it even easier to create a dynamically populated form, provide features lacking in a basic HTML form for data validation, and offer input controls such as hierarchical trees and grids.

Creating Dynamically Populated Forms

In many parts of this chapter you will work with a table of employee data called Employees in a data source called EmployeeData. This database is outlined in Table 15.1.

TABLE 15.1: The fields in the Employees table in the EmployeeData database

Field	Description
EmployeeID	Employee ID
LastName	Employee's last name
FirstName	Employee's first name
Gender	Employee's gender as M or F
Salary	Employee's monthly salary in dollars

To begin, you need to learn how to dynamically populate form-based data from a database. To do this, you will create a form that reflects the data in this table. But first you need to consider what the empty form looks like. Listing 15.1 creates a simple form.

Listing 15.1: *form1.cfm*

```
<H1>Employee Data: Employee #</H1>
<FORM METHOD=POST ACTION=doform.cfm ><TABLE BORDER=0 CELLSPACING=5>
<TR>
    <TD>Last Name</TD>
    <TD><INPUT TYPE=text NAME=LastName SIZE=20></TD>
</TR>
<TR>
    <TD>First Name</TD>
    <TD><INPUT TYPE=text NAME=FirstName SIZE=20></TD>
</TR>
<TR>
    <TD>Gender</TD>
    <TD><INPUT TYPE=text NAME=Gender SIZE=1></TD>
</TR>
<TR>
    <TD>Monthly Salary</TD>
    <TD><INPUT TYPE=text NAME=Salary SIZE=10></TD>
</TR>
</TABLE>
</FORM>
```

This code produces a form that looks like the one in Figure 15.1.

FIGURE 15.1
Our empty employee
data form

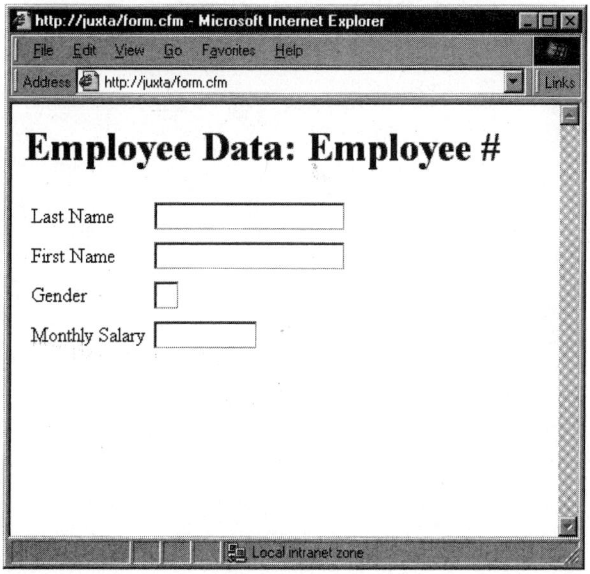

As the next step in developing your employee data form, you need to populate it with data from your database. As an example, populate it with information for the employee with ID 1. There are two steps to doing this:

1. Obtain the data from the database by using CFQUERY.

2. Use CFOUTPUT to set default values for the fields.

The process is fairly straightforward, as shown in Listing 15.2.

Listing 15.2: *form2.cfm*

```
<CFQUERY NAME="Employee" DATASOURCE="EmployeeData">
    SELECT   *
    FROM      Employees
    WHERE     ID=1
</CFQUERY>
<CFOUTPUT QUERY="Employee" MAXROWS=1>
<H1>Employee Data: Employee #ID#</H1>
<FORM METHOD=POST ACTION=doform.cfm >
<TABLE BORDER=0 CELLSPACING=5>
<TR>
        <TD>Last Name</TD>
        <TD><INPUT TYPE=text NAME=LastName SIZE=20 VALUE="#LastName#"></TD>
</TR>
<TR>
        <TD>First Name</TD>
        <TD><INPUT TYPE=text NAME=FirstName SIZE=20 VALUE="#FirstName#"></TD>
</TR>
<TR>
        <TD>Gender</TD>
        <TD><INPUT TYPE=text NAME=Gender SIZE=1 VALUE="#Gender#"></TD>
</TR>
<TR>
        <TD>Monthly Salary</TD>
        <TD><INPUT TYPE=text NAME=Salary SIZE=10 VALUE="#Salary#"></TD>
</TR>
</TABLE>
</FORM>
</CFOUTPUT>
```

This code results in the form shown in Figure 15.2, in which you queried the database for the desired employee and then used CFOUTPUT to put data from the database into the form fields by including it in the VALUE attribute of your INPUT tags.

FIGURE 15.2
A dynamically
populated form

To create a truly useful form, though, you need to be able to pass along an employee ID number and then have the data for the relevant employee displayed. To do this, you can use URL parameters to pass the ID, using a URL such as form.cfm?ID=1 to request a form for the employee with ID 1.

Simply adjust your query as follows:

```
<CFQUERY NAME="Employee" DATASOURCE="EmployeeData">
    SELECT    *
    FROM      Employees
    WHERE     ID=#URL.ID#
</CFQUERY>
```

The main problem is that if no URL parameter named ID is available, then you will get an error like the one in Figure 15.3.

This problem is easily fixed using the CFPARAM tag that you learned about in Chapter 4, "Creating and Manipulating Variables." Using this tag, you specify a default value for the URL.ID parameter, should it not exist:

```
<CFPARAM NAME="URL.ID" DEFAULT="1">
<CFQUERY NAME="Employee" DATASOURCE="EmployeeData">
    SELECT    *
    FROM      Employees
    WHERE     ID=#URL.ID#
</CFQUERY>
```

FIGURE 15.3
You get an error if the URL
parameter does not exist.

Of course, now that you are allowing users to specify which employee record to request from the database, you need to make sure that an employee exists. To do that, you can use CFIF and CFELSE tags and test the value of `Employee.RecordCount` to see whether any employee records existed in the database for the specified ID number. Listing 15.3 provides the code.

Listing 15.3: *form3.cfm*

```
<CFPARAM NAME="URL.ID" DEFAULT="1">
<CFQUERY NAME="Employee" DATASOURCE="EmployeeData">
   SELECT    *
   FROM      Employees
   WHERE     ID=#URL.ID#
</CFQUERY>

<CFIF Employee.RecordCount greater than 0>
<CFOUTPUT QUERY="Employee" MAXROWS=1>
<H1>Employee Data: Employee #ID#</H1>
<FORM METHOD=POST ACTION=doform.cfm >
<TABLE BORDER=0 CELLSPACING=5>
<TR>
        <TD>Last Name</TD>
        <TD><INPUT TYPE=text NAME=LastName SIZE=20 VALUE="#LastName#"></TD>
</TR>
```

```
<TR>
        <TD>First Name</TD>
        <TD><INPUT TYPE=text NAME=FirstName SIZE=20 VALUE="#FirstName#"></TD>
</TR>
<TR>

        <TD>Gender</TD>
        <TD><INPUT TYPE=text NAME=Gender SIZE=1 VALUE="#Gender#"></TD>
</TR>
<TR>

        <TD>Monthly Salary</TD>
        <TD><INPUT TYPE=text NAME=Salary SIZE=10 VALUE="#Salary#"></TD>
</TR>
</TABLE>
</FORM>
</CFOUTPUT>
<CFELSE>
   <H1>Sorry</H1>
   The requested employee does not exist.
</CFIF>
```

Now you can request different employees by simply using a URL parameter. For instance, ID=2 requests the employee with ID 2, as shown in Figure 15.4.

FIGURE 15.4
You can specify any
employee ID.

If no ID is specified, the default is to display the employee with ID 1. If the specified employee does not exist, then a message like the one in Figure 15.5 is displayed.

FIGURE 15.5
When the employee does
not exist, the user is
informed.

Further Refinements

Although the form you have created is useful, some refinement could make it better. Specifically, the selection of gender can be better presented as either a select field or a radio button field.

This is fairly simple. Let's start with the select field alternative. The basic syntax of a select field is

```
<SELECT NAME="Gender">
    <OPTION VALUE="F">Female
    <OPTION VALUE="M">Male
</SELECT>
```

Put into your previous template, this code generates a drop-down list like the one shown in Figure 15.6.

However, a default value is not selected, which means that regardless of the data in the database, the first item in the list is selected. You can resolve this problem with a combination of the following CFIF tags:

```
<SELECT NAME="Gender">
    <OPTION VALUE="F"<CFIF Gender is "F"> SELECTED</CFIF>>Female
    <OPTION VALUE="M"<CFIF Gender is "M"> SELECTED</CFIF>>Male
</SELECT>
```

FIGURE 15.6
Using a drop-down list for
specifying gender

The logic here is fairly simple: For each entry in the list, check whether the person's gender in the database matches, and if it does, add the SELECTED attribute to the OPTION tag. Therefore, for a male employee, the appropriate entry is automatically selected, as in Figure 15.7.

Similarly, you can use the same approach to use radio buttons for gender. The basic code would look something like this:

```
<INPUT TYPE=radio VALUE="F">Female
<INPUT TYPE=radio VALUE="M">Male
```

If you put this code into your template, then the set of radio buttons comes up unselected—that is, a value is not selected. You can apply the same CFIF logic to force selection of the correct option:

```
<INPUT TYPE=radio NAME=Gender VALUE="F"<CFIF Gender is "F"> CHECKED</CFIF>>Female
<INPUT TYPE=radio NAME=Gender VALUE="M"<CFIF Gender is "M"> CHECKED</CFIF>>Male
```

The results are shown in Figure 15.8.

FIGURE 15.7
Automatically selecting an
entry in a select field

FIGURE 15.8
Using radio buttons instead
of a select field

NOTE	Both of the preceding approaches have a serious limitation in that they require a separate CFIF statement to correctly set the initial value of the form. Using CFFORM with other ColdFusion form tags makes this much easier to do for options with numerous choices. You will learn about these tags later in this chapter.

Using Information from Forms

Although it is nice to be able to dynamically populate, the real value of these forms comes from being able to use the data in useful ways. When working with database information, for instance, you may want to use forms to insert new data into a database or to update an existing entry in a database table.

You can do this in two ways:

- Automatically add to or update the database with CFINSERT or CFUPDATE. Allaire recommends these tags no longer be used but continues to support them for backward compatibility with earlier versions of ColdFusion.
- Manually build a SQL INSERT or UPDATE statement and use CFQUERY to execute the command.

Before diving into both these approaches, let's consider the basics of accessing form data. When you submit a form to a ColdFusion template, a series of form variables are created: one for each field in the form.

These form variables take the name of the fields in the original form and are accessed as follows: Form.FieldName. Therefore, in your employee data template, if you submit the form to a ColdFusion template, you could use the following form variables in that template:

- Form.LastName
- Form.FirstName
- Form.Gender
- Form.Salary

Let's build a small example. Extend the final version of your template, including radio buttons, to be submitted to another template called doform.cfm. The code is shown in Listing 15.4.

Listing 15.4: *form4.cfm*

```
<CFPARAM NAME="URL.ID" DEFAULT="1">
<CFQUERY NAME="Employee" DATASOURCE="EmployeeData">
    SELECT    *
    FROM      Employees
    WHERE       ID=#URL.ID#
</CFQUERY>

<CFIF Employee.RecordCount greater than 0>
<CFOUTPUT QUERY="Employee" MAXROWS=1>
<H1>Employee Data: Employee #ID#</H1>
<FORM METHOD=POST ACTION=doform.cfm>
<TABLE BORDER=0 CELLSPACING=5>
<TR>
        <TD>Last Name</TD>
        <TD><INPUT TYPE=text NAME=LastName SIZE=20 VALUE="#LastName#"></TD>
</TR>
<TR>
        <TD>First Name</TD>
        <TD><INPUT TYPE=text NAME=FirstName SIZE=20 VALUE="#FirstName#"></TD>
</TR>
<TR>
        <TD>Gender</TD>
        <TD>
           <INPUT TYPE=radio NAME=Gender VALUE="F"<CFIF Gender is "F"> CHECKED</
CFIF>>Female
           <INPUT TYPE=radio NAME=Gender VALUE="M"<CFIF Gender is "M"> CHECKED</
CFIF>>Male
   </TD>
   </TR>
<TR>
        <TD>Monthly Salary</TD>
        <TD><INPUT TYPE=text NAME=Salary SIZE=10 VALUE="#Salary#"></TD>
</TR>
<TR>
   <TD></TD>
   <TD><INPUT TYPE=SUBMIT></TD>
</TR>
</TABLE>
</FORM>
</CFOUTPUT>
<CFELSE>
   <H1>Sorry</H1>
   The requested employee does not exist.
</CFIF>
```

This produces a form that looks like the one in Figure 15.9.

FIGURE 15.9
Preparing the employee
data form for submitting

Now you can build the template to which the form is submitted. To demonstrate how to access the information from the form fields, you will simply display the content from the form:

```
<H1>Form Submission</H1>
You submitted a form with the following information:
<UL>
<CFOUTPUT>
<LI>Last Name: #Form.LastName#
<LI>First Name: #Form.FirstName#
<LI>Gender: #Form.Gender#
<LI>Salary: #Form.Salary#
</CFOUTPUT>
</UL>
```

Therefore, when you submit the form, you get a result that looks like Figure 15.10.

FIGURE 15.10
Submitting the form

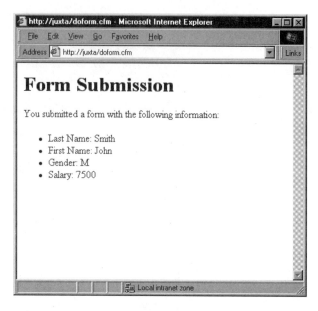

Now that you have a grasp of how data from a form can be accessed in a template, you will look at two approaches to moving data from a form into a database table.

Using *CFINSERT* and *CFUPDATE*

In the first approach, you use CFINSERT and CFUPDATE to add and change information in the database. You learned about these tags in Chapter 10, "Using CFQUERY and SQL to Interact with the Database."

Let's quickly review, though, the key requirements for using these tags:

- The names of the fields in the form being submitted must correspond to the names of the fields in the table being added to or updated.
- The form must contain a field corresponding to the primary key of the table being altered.

This means that if you want to use your employee data for updating or inserting, you need to add a hidden field containing the employee ID. Listing 15.5 provides the code.

Listing 15.5: *form5.cfm*

```
<CFPARAM NAME="URL.ID" DEFAULT="1">
<CFQUERY NAME="Employee" DATASOURCE="EmployeeData">
   SELECT    *
   FROM      Employees
   WHERE     ID=#URL.ID#
</CFQUERY>
```

```
<CFIF Employee.RecordCount greater than 0>
<CFOUTPUT QUERY="Employee" MAXROWS=1>
<H1>Employee Data: Employee #ID#</H1>
<FORM METHOD=POST ACTION=doform.cfm>
<INPUT TYPE=hidden NAME=ID VALUE=#ID#>
<TABLE BORDER=0 CELLSPACING=5>
<TR>
        <TD>Last Name</TD>
        <TD><INPUT TYPE=text NAME=LastName SIZE=20 VALUE="#LastName#"></TD>
</TR>
<TR>
        <TD>First Name</TD>
        <TD><INPUT TYPE=text NAME=FirstName SIZE=20 VALUE="#FirstName#"></TD>
</TR>
<TR>
        <TD>Gender</TD>
        <TD>
           <INPUT TYPE=radio NAME=Gender VALUE="F"<CFIF Gender is "F"> CHECKED</
CFIF>>Female
           <INPUT TYPE=radio NAME=Gender VALUE="M"<CFIF Gender is "M"> CHECKED</
CFIF>>Male
        </TD>
</TR>
<TR>
        <TD>Monthly Salary</TD>
        <TD><INPUT TYPE=text NAME=Salary SIZE=10 VALUE="#Salary#"></TD>
</TR>
<TR>
    <TD></TD>
        <TD><INPUT TYPE=SUBMIT></TD>
</TR>
</TABLE>
</FORM>
</CFOUTPUT>
<CFELSE>
    <H1>Sorry</H1>
    The requested employee does not exist.
</CFIF>
```

To fully leverage CFINSERT and CFUPDATE, let's put together a template that performs the following actions. The form is designed to submit its contents back to the same template; that means your template will be designed to perform multiple tasks. Let's review those tasks:

- When the template is not loaded with a form submission, a blank form should be presented for inserting a new record in the database.

- When an insertion form is submitted to the template, the record should be inserted and then displayed in a form for updating.
- When the template is loaded with a form submission requesting a particular record, that record should be displayed in a form for updating.
- When an update form is submitted to the template, the record should be updated and then displayed again in a form for updating.

For this to work, you first need to address a question: How will the template know which of these four actions to perform? You can use a URL attribute called Action and act in one of the following ways:

- If Action does not exist, then your default action is to present a blank for insertion. You'll call this action New.
- If Action is set to Insert, then you will use CFINSERT to create a new record based on the form submitted.
- If Action is set to Load, then you will load the record identified by a form submission and display it for editing in a form.
- If Action is set to Update, then you will use CFUPDATE to update a record based on the form submitted.

For all this to happen, you need to perform the following steps:

1. Determine the action being requested.
2. Execute the necessary queries, updates, and insertions.
3. Set default form values.
4. Display the form.

We'll present each of these in turn.

Step 1: Determine the Action Being Requested

This is fairly simple. Using CFPARAM, you can set the default value of Action to New in case the parameter is not specified:

```
<CFPARAM NAME="URL.Action" DEFAULT="New">
```

This ensures that URL.Action always has a value so that step 2 can take place.

Step 2: Execute the Necessary Queries, Updates, and Insertions

In this section, you need to work through all four possible actions and you need to prepare for the following alternatives:

- Loading an existing record for editing
- Inserting a new record
- Updating an existing record

The fourth alternative, displaying a form for inserting a new record, doesn't require any preparatory SQL queries or updating or inserting.

Loading an Existing Record

First you have to load existing records, which is done when URL.Action is Load. Loading an existing record is simple: You need to use CFQUERY to select the record from the database, assuming the ID number of the record is in Form.ID (which, as you will see later when you build the form, is exactly where it will be). The query looks like this:

```
<CFQUERY NAME="TheRecord" DATASOURCE="EmployeeData">
    SELECT    *
    FROM    Employees
    WHERE    ID=#Form.ID#
</CFQUERY>
```

Inserting a New Record

Inserting a new record requires two steps:

1. Insert the record.

2. Recall the record in preparation for displaying it for further editing and updating.

First you insert the record using CFQUERY:

```
<CFQUERY NAME="insertRecord" DATASOURCE="EmployeeData">
    INSERT INTO Employees (LastName, FirstName, Gender, Salary)
    VALUES ('#Form.LastName#','#Form.FirstName#','#Form.Gender#',#Form.Salary#)
</CFQUERY>
```

The syntax details for the CFQUERY tag can be found in Chapter 10.

After you have inserted the record, you need to recall it with the following query:

```
<CFQUERY NAME="TheRecord" DATSOURCE="EmployeeData">
    SELECT        *
    FROM          Employees
    WHERE          LastName = '#Form.LastName#'
    AND          FirstName = '#Form.FirstName#'
    AND          Gender = '#Form.Gender#'
    AND          Salary = #Form.Salary#
    ORDER BY      ID
</CFQUERY>
```

Of course, it is entirely possible that more than one record has the same last name, first name, gender, and salary. Therefore, you have still more work to do: You need to check whether more than one record exists and, if it does, re-query based on the ID number of the last record in the result (the one with the highest ID value). This is done as follows:

```
<CFIF TheRecord.RecordCount greater than 1>
    <CFLOOP QUERY="TheRecord" STARTROW=#TheRecord.RecordCount#
ENDROW=#TheRecord.RecordCount#>
        <CFQUERY NAME="TheRecord" DATASOURCE="EmployeeData" MAXROWS=1>
            SELECT    *
            FROM    Employees
            WHERE    ID=#ID#
        </CFQUERY>
    </CFLOOP>
</CFIF>
```

A simpler method to achieve the same results is to combine transactions with the SQL max function:

```
<CFTRANSACTION>
    <CFQUERY NAME="insertRecord" DATASOURCE="EmployeeData">
        INSERT INTO Employees (LastName, FirstName, Gender, Salary)
        VALUES ('#Form.LastName#','#Form.FirstName#','#Form.Gender#',#Form.Salary#)
    </CFQUERY>
    <CFQUERY NAME="getMax" DATASOURCE="EmployeeData">
        Select max(ID) AS maxID from Employees
    </CFQUERY>
</CFTRANSACTION>
```

Here, the CFTRANSACTION block prevents other updates to the database while the two queries are executed. The second query uses the max function obtain the maximum ID from the table and returns it in the maxID in the query result. This approach uses more advanced features of ColdFusion and SQL but is the cleaner, preferred approach.

Using the second approach, the total code for inserting a new record looks like Listing 15.6.

Listing 15.6: *form6.cfm*

```
<!--- Insert the new record --->
<CFQUERY NAME="insertRecord" DATASOURCE="EmployeeData">
    INSERT INTO Employees (LastName, FirstName, Gender, Salary)
    VALUES ('#Form.LastName#','#Form.FirstName#','#Form.Gender#',#Form.Salary#)
</CFQUERY>


<!--- Retrieve matching records --->
<CFQUERY NAME="TheRecord" DATSOURCE="EmployeeData">
    SELECT        *
    FROM        Employees
    WHERE        LastName = '#Form.LastName#'
    AND          FirstName = '#Form.FirstName#'
```

```
    AND         Gender = '#Gender#'
    AND         Salary = #Salary#
    ORDER BY        ID
</CFQUERY>

<!--- Check if this is the only available record --->
<CFIF TheRecord.RecordCount greater than 1>
    <CFLOOP QUERY="TheRecord" STARTROW=#TheRecord.RecordCount#
ENDROW=#TheRecord.RecordCount#>
        <CFQUERY NAME="TheRecord" DATASOURCE="EmployeeData">
            SELECT    *
            FROM    Employees
            WHERE    ID=#ID#
        </CFQUERY>
    </CFLOOP>
</CFIF>
```

Updating an Existing Record

Updating an existing record follows a pattern similar to that of inserting a new record:

1. Update the record.

2. Recall the record in preparation for displaying it for further editing and updating.

The logic is the same as for insertion: You change the value of URL.Action to ensure that the rest of the template behaves in the correct fashion.

Next you recall the record. This is easier than with insertion because you know the exact ID number of the record in question (it would have been submitted with the update form data):

```
<CFQUERY NAME="TheRecord" DATASOURCE="EmployeeData">
    SELECT    *
    FROM    Employees
    WHERE    ID=#Form.ID#
</CFQUERY>
```

Finally, you reset URL.Action:

```
<CFSET URL.Action = "Load">
```

The final result looks like this:

```
<!--- Update the record --->
<CFQUERY NAME="updateRecord" DATASOURCE="EmployeeData">
    UPDATE Employees
    SET
    LastName = '#Form.LastName#',
    FirstName = '#Form.FirstName#',
    Gender = '#Form.Gender#',
    Salary = #Form.Salary#
    WHERE
    ID = #Form.ID#
</CFQUERY>
```

```
<!--- Recall the record --->
<CFQUERY NAME="TheRecord" DATASOURCE="EmployeeData">
   SELECT   *
   FROM    Employees
   WHERE   ID=#Form.ID#
</CFQUERY>
```

Putting It All Together

Of course, you need some way to select which of these three steps to take. You can do this using CFSWITCH and CFCASE, as shown in Listing 15.7.

Listing 15.7: *form7.cfm*

```
<CFSWITCH EXPRESSION="#URL.Action#">

   <CFCASE VALUE="Load">
<CFQUERY NAME="TheRecord" DATASOURCE="EmployeeData">
   SELECT   *
   FROM    Employees
   WHERE   ID=#Form.ID#
</CFQUERY>
   </CFCASE>

   <CFCASE VALUE="Insert">
<!--- Insert the new record --->
   <CFQUERY NAME="insertRecord" DATASOURCE="EmployeeData">
      INSERT INTO Employees (LastName, FirstName, Gender, Salary)
      VALUES ('#Form.LastName#','#Form.FirstName#','#Form.Gender#',#Form.Salary#)
   </CFQUERY>


<!--- Retrieve matching records --->
<CFQUERY NAME="TheRecord" DATSOURCE="EmployeeData">
   SELECT      *
   FROM        Employees
   WHERE        LastName = '#Form.LastName#'
   AND         FirstName = '#Form.FirstName#'
   AND         Gender = '#Gender#'
   AND         Salary = #Salary#
   ORDER BY    ID
</CFQUERY>

<!--- Check if this is the only available record --->
<CFIF TheRecord.RecordCount greater than 1>
   <CFLOOP QUERY="TheRecord" STARTROW=#TheRecord.RecordCount#
ENDROW=#TheRecord.RecordCount#>
      <CFQUERY NAME="TheRecord" DATASOURCE="EmployeeData">
         SELECT    *
```

```
         FROM    Employees
         WHERE   ID=#ID#
      </CFQUERY>
   </CFLOOP>
</CFIF>
   </CFCASE>

   <CFCASE VALUE="Update">
<!--- Update the record --->
<CFQUERY NAME="updateRecord" DATASOURCE="EmployeeData">
   UPDATE Employees
   SET
   LastName = '#Form.LastName#',
   FirstName = '#Form.FirstName#',
   Gender = '#Form.Gender#',
   Salary = #Form.Salary#
   WHERE
   ID = #Form.ID#
</CFQUERY>

<!--- Recall the record --->
<CFQUERY NAME="TheRecord" DATASOURCE="EmployeeData">
   SELECT    *
   FROM    Employees
   WHERE    ID=#Form.ID#
</CFQUERY>
   </CFCASE>

</CFSWITCH>
```

Step 3: Set Default Form Values

The next step is to set a series of variables for default form values. First you need four
variables for the default values of the user-editable fields in the table: LastName, First-
Name, Gender, and Salary.

If the query result set TheRecord exists (and it will only when URL.Action was
Insert, Update, or Load), then you want to use the values of the record in TheRecord to
set your default form variables. If TheRecord doesn't exist, then URL.Action must have
been New and your default values should be the empty string because you want to create
an empty form.

In addition to these four default values, you need to decide whether a hidden field for
the ID number is necessary. A hidden field is necessary if you are updating a record but
not if you are inserting a new one. On this basis, you need to create a fifth variable that
contains the entire INPUT tag or the empty string as needed.

Finally, a sixth field will provide the text to display in the main form's submit button, and a seventh field will provide the value to place in the URL.Action parameter of the URL for the form submission.

The code to set all these default values is a combination of CFIF, CFSET, and, finally, CFPARAM. You use the ParameterExists function to check whether TheRecord exists:

```
<CFIF IsDefined("TheRecord")>
    <CFSET LastName = TheRecord.LastName>
    <CFSET FirstName = TheRecord.FirstName>
    <CFSET Gender = TheRecord.Gender>
    <CFSET Salary = TheRecord.Salary>
    <CFSET IDField = "<STRONG>Employee #TheRecord.ID#</STRONG><INPUT TYPE=HIDDEN
NAME=ID VALUE=#TheRecord.ID#>">
    <CFSET Submit = "UPDATE">
    <CFSET FormAction = "Update">
</CFIF>
<CFPARAM NAME="LastName" DEFAULT="">
<CFPARAM NAME="FirstName" DEFAULT="">
<CFPARAM NAME="Gender" DEFAULT="">
<CFPARAM NAME="Salary" DEFAULT="">
<CFPARAM NAME="IDField" DEFAULT="">
<CFPARAM NAME="Submit" DEFAULT="INSERT">
<CFPARAM NAME="FormAction" DEFAULT="Insert">
```

Step 4: Display the Form

The final step is to display your form. Actually, there are two forms to display: One is a form prompting for the ID number of a record to update, and the second is a form for updating a record or inserting a new record. Finally, you need to display a link for users to indicate that they wish to insert a new record.

The first form, for updating an existing record, looks like this:

```
<FORM METHOD=POST ACTION="form.cfm?Action=Load">
ID TO UPDATE: <INPUT TYPE=TEXT NAME=ID SIZE=3>
<INPUT TYPE=SUBMIT VALUE="LOAD">
</FORM>
```

Notice the use of Action=Load as a parameter to the template. This example makes the assumption that your template is called form.cfm.

Next, you need the editing and insertion form itself. This is based on the employee data form you have used throughout this chapter:

```
<CFOUTPUT>
<FORM METHOD=POST ACTION=form.cfm?Action=#FormAction#>
#IDField#
<TABLE BORDER=0 CELLSPACING=5>
```

```
        <TR>
                <TD>Last Name</TD>
                <TD><INPUT TYPE=text NAME=LastName SIZE=20 VALUE="#LastName#"></TD>
        </TR>
        <TR>
                <TD>First Name</TD>
                <TD><INPUT TYPE=text NAME=FirstName SIZE=20 VALUE="#FirstName#"></TD>
        </TR>
        <TR>
                <TD>Gender</TD>
                <TD>
                    <INPUT TYPE=radio NAME=Gender VALUE="F"<CFIF Gender is "F">
CHECKED</CFIF>>Female
                    <INPUT TYPE=radio NAME=Gender VALUE="M"<CFIF Gender is "M">
CHECKED</CFIF>>Male
        </TD>
        </TR>
        <TR>
                <TD>Monthly Salary</TD>
                <TD><INPUT TYPE=text NAME=Salary SIZE=10 VALUE="#Salary#"></TD>
        </TR>
        <TR>
            <TD></TD>
                <TD><INPUT TYPE=SUBMIT></TD>
        </TR>
        </TABLE>
        </FORM>
        </CFOUTPUT>
```

Finally, your link for the creation of new records is as follows:

```
<A HREF="form.cfm?Action=New">Create a New Record</A>
```

Put It All Together

Put all together, your template will look like Listing 15.8.

Listing 15.8: *form8.cfm*

```
<!--- Make sure URL.Action has a value --->
<CFPARAM NAME="URL.Action" DEFAULT="New">

<CFSWITCH EXPRESSION="#URL.Action#">

    <CFCASE VALUE="Load">
<CFQUERY NAME="TheRecord" DATASOURCE="EmployeeData">
    SELECT    *
    FROM      Employees
    WHERE     ID=#Form.ID#
</CFQUERY>
    </CFCASE>
```

```
    <CFCASE VALUE="Insert">
<!--- Insert the new record --->
    <CFQUERY NAME="insertRecord" DATASOURCE="EmployeeData">
        INSERT INTO Employees (LastName, FirstName, Gender, Salary)
        VALUES ('#Form.LastName#','#Form.FirstName#','#Form.Gender#',#Form.Salary#)
    </CFQUERY>


<!--- Retrieve matching records --->
<CFQUERY NAME="TheRecord" DATASOURCE="EmployeeData">
    SELECT      *
    FROM        Employees
    WHERE       LastName = '#Form.LastName#'
    AND         FirstName = '#Form.FirstName#'
    AND         Gender = '#Gender#'
    AND         Salary = #Salary#
    ORDER BY    ID
</CFQUERY>


<!--- Check if this is the only available record --->
<CFIF TheRecord.RecordCount greater than 1>
    <CFLOOP QUERY="TheRecord" STARTROW=#TheRecord.RecordCount#
ENDROW=#TheRecord.RecordCount#>
        <CFQUERY NAME="TheRecord" DATASOURCE="EmployeeData">
            SELECT    *
            FROM    Employees
            WHERE    ID=#ID#
        </CFQUERY>
    </CFLOOP>
</CFIF>
    </CFCASE>


    <CFCASE VALUE="Update">
<!--- Update the record --->
<CFQUERY NAME="updateRecord" DATASOURCE="EmployeeData">
    UPDATE Employees
    SET
    LastName = '#Form.LastName#',
    FirstName = '#Form.FirstName#',
    Gender = '#Form.Gender#',
    Salary = #Form.Salary#
    WHERE
    ID = #Form.ID#
</CFQUERY>

<!--- Recall the record --->
```

```
<CFQUERY NAME="TheRecord" DATASOURCE="EmployeeData">
    SELECT   *
    FROM   Employees
    WHERE   ID=#Form.ID#
</CFQUERY>
    </CFCASE>

</CFSWITCH>

<CFIF IsDefined("TheRecord")>
    <CFSET LastName = TheRecord.LastName>
    <CFSET FirstName = TheRecord.FirstName>
    <CFSET Gender = TheRecord.Gender>
    <CFSET Salary = TheRecord.Salary>
    <CFSET IDField = "<STRONG>Employee #TheRecord.ID#</STRONG><INPUT TYPE=HIDDEN
NAME=ID VALUE=#TheRecord.ID#>">
    <CFSET Submit = "UPDATE">
    <CFSET FormAction = "Update">
</CFIF>
<CFPARAM NAME="LastName" DEFAULT="">
<CFPARAM NAME="FirstName" DEFAULT="">
<CFPARAM NAME="Gender" DEFAULT="">
<CFPARAM NAME="Salary" DEFAULT="">
<CFPARAM NAME="IDField" DEFAULT="">
<CFPARAM NAME="Submit" DEFAULT="INSERT">
<CFPARAM NAME="FormAction" DEFAULT="Insert">

<FORM METHOD=POST ACTION="form.cfm?Action=Load">
ID TO UPDATE: <INPUT TYPE=TEXT NAME=ID SIZE=3>
<INPUT TYPE=SUBMIT VALUE="LOAD">
</FORM>

<HR>

<CFOUTPUT>
<FORM METHOD=POST ACTION=form.cfm?Action=#FormAction#>
#IDField#
<TABLE BORDER=0 CELLSPACING=5>
<TR>
            <TD>Last Name</TD>
            <TD><INPUT TYPE=text NAME=LastName SIZE=20 VALUE="#LastName#"></TD>
</TR>
<TR>
            <TD>First Name</TD>
            <TD><INPUT TYPE=text NAME=FirstName SIZE=20 VALUE="#FirstName#"></TD>
</TR>
<TR>
            <TD>Gender</TD>
            <TD>
```

```
                    <INPUT TYPE=radio NAME=Gender VALUE="F"<CFIF Gender is "F">
CHECKED</CFIF>>Female
                    <INPUT TYPE=radio NAME=Gender VALUE="M"<CFIF Gender is "M">
CHECKED</CFIF>>Male
    </TD>
    </TR>
    <TR>
            <TD>Monthly Salary</TD>
            <TD><INPUT TYPE=text NAME=Salary SIZE=10 VALUE="#Salary#"></TD>
    </TR>
    <TR>
        <TD></TD>
            <TD><INPUT TYPE=SUBMIT VALUE="#Submit#"></TD>
    </TR>
    </TABLE>
    </FORM>
    </CFOUTPUT>

    <HR>

    <A HREF="form.cfm?Action=New">Create a New Record</A>
```

This code produces a form like the one in Figure 15.11 when initially loaded and not producing a value for URL.Action.

FIGURE 15.11

The default insertion form

If you enter data and click the Insert button, the new record will be created and then displayed in an update form like the one in Figure 15.12. Similarly, entering an employee ID number in the ID to Update field and clicking the Load button causes a record to be loaded and displayed, as shown in Figure 15.12.

FIGURE 15.12
Editing a record

At this point you can change the data in the form and click the Update button to commit the changes to the database, and then reload the record in a new update form.

Understanding the Power of Check Boxes and Multiple Select Lists

So far, in this chapter, you have seen simple examples of select fields in which a single item was chosen. However, HTML select fields allow for multiple selections. In addition, groups of check boxes also allow for multiple items to be selected. For instance, Figure 15.13 shows both types of fields with multiple items selected.

This ability to select multiple items can be particularly useful in ColdFusion. The reason for this is that when multiple items are selected by using either type of field, the value associated with the field when the form is submitted is a comma-delimited list of the values of all selected entries.

FIGURE 15.13
Select and check box fields
allow multiple items to be
selected.

There are several ways to leverage the resulting data, including:

- Using the wide range of List functions available in ColdFusion. These functions are discussed in detail in Chapter 14, "Working with ColdFusion Data Structures."
- Using the SQL IN operator to match multiple items in a comma-delimited list.

Because working with lists is covered in such detail in Chapter 14, this chapter will focus on the second way to take advantage of multiple selections.

First, you need to review how to create multiple select fields and check boxes. The multiple select field is created by using the attribute MULTIPLE="YES" as well as by setting the number of visible rows to a size greater than 1 using the SIZE attribute. For instance, the following field displays five lines of the selection list and allows the selection of multiple elements in the list the following:

```
<SELECT NAME="Example" MULTIPLE="Yes" SIZE=5>
    <OPTION>1
    <OPTION>2
    <OPTION>3
    <OPTION>4
    <OPTION>5
</SELECT>
```

By contrast, a group of related check boxes is created using a series of INPUT tags with the same name:

```
<INPUT TYPE=checkbox NAME="EXAMPLE" VALUE=1> 1<BR>
<INPUT TYPE=checkbox NAME="EXAMPLE" VALUE=2> 2<BR>
<INPUT TYPE=checkbox NAME="EXAMPLE" VALUE=3> 3<BR>
<INPUT TYPE=checkbox NAME="EXAMPLE" VALUE=4> 4<BR>
<INPUT TYPE=checkbox NAME="EXAMPLE" VALUE=5> 5
```

How, then, do you use these types of form fields to search for multiple records in a database? Let's turn again to the simple employee database. Consider an example in which you want to give users the choice of 10 employees whose names they can display. They should be able to select any number of IDs from a list and then submit the form to another template that proceeds to find all the names and display them.

The template for displaying the form would look like this:

```
<H1>Select Employees</H1>
<FORM METHOD=POST ACTION=display.cfm>
<SELECT NAME="IDS" SIZE=10 MULTIPLE >
    <OPTION>1
    <OPTION>2
    <OPTION>3
    <OPTION>4
    <OPTION>5
    <OPTION>6
    <OPTION>7
    <OPTION>8
    <OPTION>9
    <OPTION>10
</SELECT><BR>
<INPUT TYPE=SUBMIT>
</FORM>
```

This code produces a form like the one in Figure 15.14.

After the user selects the desired employees and submits the form, the following template is executed. It uses the SQL IN operator. The IN operator has slightly different requirements with strings than with numbers; we will discuss numbers first.

FIGURE 15.14

Selecting multiple
employees

The IN operator is used in place of other comparison operators such as = when searching for one specific record by using SELECT statements. For instance, to search your employee database for two records at once, employee ID 1 and employee ID 2, you could use

```
SELECT    *
FROM    Employees
WHERE    ID IN ( 1,2 )
```

Notice that the ID numbers are in a comma-delimited list inside parentheses. Because your form returns a comma-delimited list, you can use this list inside the parentheses of the SELECT statement in your template:

```
<CFQUERY NAME="Results" DATASOURCE="EmployeeData">
    SELECT    *
    FROM    Employees
    WHERE    ID in ( #Form.IDS# )
</CFQUERY>

<CFOUTPUT QUERY="Results">
    #LastName#, #FirstName#
    <HR>
</CFOUTPUT>
```

This code produces results like those in Figure 15.15.

FIGURE 15.15
Selecting multiple records

However, working with string values requires a little extra attention. When using values of string fields in SQL, you need to wrap those values in single quotation marks. This applies to the comma-delimited list with the IN operator as well: ('Value One','Value Two','Value Three', etc.).

This means that if you want to build selection lists or check boxes to search for string values in a database, you need to make sure that the single quotes are part of the form values so the comma-delimited list that gets submitted has the appropriate single quotation marks.

For instance, if you want to select names to display on the basis of last names, you might think that the following form would work:

```
<H1>Select Employees</H1>
<FORM METHOD=POST ACTION=display.cfm>
<SELECT NAME="Names" SIZE=4 MULTIPLE=YES>
    <OPTION>Danesh
    <OPTION>Doe
    <OPTION>Johnson
    <OPTION>Smith
</SELECT><BR>
<INPUT TYPE=SUBMIT>
</FORM>
```

But if you try to use this to search for employees using the following query, you will get an error:

```
<CFQUERY NAME="Results" DATASOURCE="EmployeeData">
   SELECT  *
   FROM   Employees
   WHERE  LastName in ( #Form.Names# )
</CFQUERY>
```

To address this error, you need to adjust your form so that the value submitted includes the single quotation marks but the value displayed doesn't:

```
<H1>Select Employees</H1>
<FORM METHOD=POST ACTION=display.cfm>
<SELECT NAME="Names" SIZE=4 MULTIPLE=YES>
   <OPTION VALUE="'Danesh'">Danesh
   <OPTION VALUE="'Doe'">Doe
   <OPTION VALUE="'Johnson'">Johnson
   <OPTION VALUE="'Smith'">Smith
</SELECT><BR>
<INPUT TYPE=SUBMIT>
</FORM>
```

You also need to use the `PreserveSingleQuotes` function when building the SQL statement; otherwise, ColdFusion will escape the quotes and they will be lost in the SQL statement, leading to another error:

```
<CFQUERY NAME="Results" DATASOURCE="EmployeeData">
   SELECT  *
   FROM   Employees
   WHERE  LastName in ( #PreserveSingleQuotes(Form.Names)# )
</CFQUERY>
```

Using *CFFORM*

You've come a long way and now you will look how ColdFusion can further enhance HTML forms, making them easier to build and extending their capabilities with custom Java controls.

You will start with `CFINPUT`. This tag provides an easy way to create dynamically populated, automatically validated text, check-box, and radio-button entry fields. This tag can replace most uses of the HTML `INPUT` tag.

Next you will look at `CFSELECT`, which provides an easy way to create dynamic select fields. Then you will look at `CFTEXTINPUT`, `CFSLIDER`, `CFGRID`, and `CFTREE`, which are tags for adding specialized Java form controls to forms.

Before considering all these controls and fields, you need to look at the CFFORM tag. The CFFORM tag is the ColdFusion alternative to the FORM tag and needs to be used when you plan to use the ColdFusion tags we are about to discuss to put together your form.

The CFFORM tag is used similarly to the HTML FORM tag and takes the following attributes:

ACTION   The filename of the template to which the form should be submitted. This is a required attribute.

ENCTYPE   The MIME type of data submitted with the POST method. By default, this value is application/x-www-form-urlencoded, and there is usually no reason to change the value of this optional attribute.

ENABLECAB   This attribute indicates whether Java controls in the form should be made available as Microsoft cabinet files for users of Microsoft Internet Explorer. This is an optional attribute and takes YES or NO as possible values.

NAME   The name of the form. This is an optional attribute that should be used when you will need to access the form by name in scripts within the Web page.

ONSUBMIT   The JavaScript function to execute after form validation is complete. This is an optional attribute.

TARGET   The name of the frame or window in which the file specified by the ACTION attribute should be opened. This is an optional attribute, and if not specified, then the file will open in the same frame and window as the form.

PASSTHROUGH   Optional. HTML attributes that are not explicitly supported by CFFORM. If you specify an attribute and its value, the attribute and value are passed to the HTML code that is generated for the CFINPUT tag. See the Usage section for more information about specifying values.

NOTE   In addition to these attributes, any attributes not supported by CFFORM are passed to the HTML code generated by the tag.

These attributes should appear similar to those used with the FORM tag with the exception of the METHOD attribute, which is not used with the CFFORM tag. Therefore, in its simplest usage, if you had planned to use the following tags to create a form like the following:

```
<FORM NAME="FormName" METHOD="POST" ACTION="submit.cfm">
   ...
</FORM>
```

then you could use these ColdFusion tags for creating your form fields and elements:

```
<CFFORM NAME="FormName" ACTION="submit.cfm">
    ...
</CFFORM>
```

Within opening and closing CFFORM tags, you can use both ColdFusion and HTML form tags. Within opening and closing FORM tags, only HTML form tags can be used. If you attempt to use ColdFusion form tags in an HTML form, you will get an error like the one in Figure 15.16.

FIGURE 15.16
ColdFusion form tags cannot be used in an HTML form.

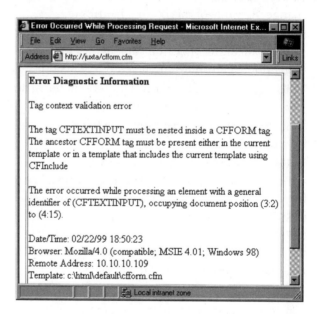

Using *CFINPUT*

CFINPUT is the ColdFusion alternative to the standard INPUT tag; it can be used to create simple text entry fields as well as password fields, check boxes, and radio buttons.

At its most basic, the tag can be used in the same way as its standard HTML counterpart. For instance, the following three tags

```
<INPUT TYPE="Text" NAME="TextField" SIZE=20 VALUE="Value">
<INPUT TYPE="checkbox" NAME="CheckBoxField" VALUE="Value">
<INPUT TYPE="radio" NAME="RadioButtonField" VALUE="Value">
```

would work in the same way as the following ColdFusion alternatives

```
<CFINPUT TYPE="Text" NAME="TextField" SIZE=20 VALUE="Value">
<CFINPUT TYPE="checkbox" NAME="CheckBoxField" VALUE="Value">
<CFINPUT TYPE="radio" NAME="RadioButtonField" VALUE="Value">
```

NOTE   The NAME attribute is required for CFINPUT whereas it is optional for INPUT. This is because JavaScript is associated with fields created with CFINPUT and the field name is necessary for correct functioning of the JavaScript scripts.

However, the reason to use CFINPUT is its extra capabilities. These capabilities lie in the area of validation that is discussed in detail in Chapter 16, "Validating Form Data."

The important fact to remember about the CFINPUT tag is that it generates regular HTML and JavaScript code to be sent to the browser. For instance, the following Cold-Fusion code

```
<CFFORM NAME="Test" ACTION="docfform.cfm">

<CFINPUT TYPE="Text" NAME="TextField" SIZE=20>
<CFINPUT TYPE="checkbox" NAME="CheckBoxField" VALUE="Value">
<CFINPUT TYPE="radio" NAME="RadioButtonField" VALUE="Value">

</CFFORM>
```

causes the following HTML code to be sent to the browser:

```
<script LANGUAGE=JAVASCRIPT>

<!--

function _CF_checkTest(_CF_this)

    {

    return true;

    }


//-->

</script>

<FORM NAME="Test" ACTION="docfform.cfm" METHOD=POST onSubmit="return
_CF_checkTest(this)">

<INPUT TYPE="Text" NAME="TextField" SIZE=20>
<INPUT TYPE="checkbox" NAME="CheckBoxField" VALUE="Value">
<INPUT TYPE="radio" NAME="RadioButtonField" VALUE="Value">

</FORM>
```

Because the result is valid HTML and JavaScript, the resulting form is usable with any browser, including those that don't support Java and those that don't support JavaScript (JavaScript is ignored by those browsers that don't support it).

Using *CFSELECT* to Create Selection Lists

The CFSELECT tag is another that corresponds closely to an HTML tag (in this case SELECT) and generates regular HTML to be sent to the browser.

At its most basic, the CFSELECT tag can replace the SELECT tag and take the expected attributes: NAME (required), SIZE (required), and MULTIPLE (optional).

You can create select fields using the CFSELECT tag with standard OPTION tags:

```
<CFSELECT NAME="SelectField" SIZE=1 MULTIPLE="No">
    <OPTION VALUE="1">One
    <OPTION VALUE="2">Two
    <OPTION VALUE="3">Three
    <OPTION VALUE="4">Four
    <OPTION VALUE="5">Tive
</CFSELECT>
```

This code results in the following HTML and JavaScript:

```
<script LANGUAGE=JAVASCRIPT>

<!--

function _CF_checkTest(_CF_this)

    {

    return true;

    }


//-->

</script>

<FORM NAME="Test" ACTION="docfform.cfm" METHOD=POST onSubmit="return
_CF_checkTest(this)">
    <SELECT NAME="SelectField" SIZE=1>
        <OPTION VALUE="1">One
        <OPTION VALUE="2">Two
        <OPTION VALUE="3">Three
        <OPTION VALUE="4">Four
        <OPTION VALUE="5">Five
    </SELECT>
</FORM>
```

The end result is a select field like the one in Figure 15.17.

FIGURE 15.17
Using CFSELECT to create
a select field

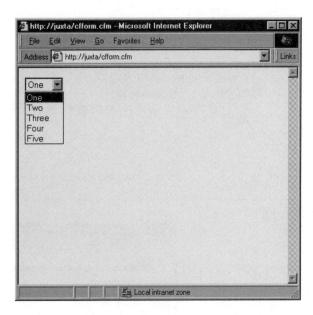

However, the dynamic aspects of the CFSELECT tag are what make it useful. Two groups of additional attributes are available for the CFSELECT tag: those for validation, which will be discussed in Chapter 16, and those for dynamically creating and populating the select field. We will discuss the latter in this chapter.

You dynamically populate select fields with query result sets, and use the following three attributes:

QUERY   Specifies a query to use to populate the select field

VALUE   Specifies the name of the query column that should be the value submitted with the form (in other words, the value to be assigned to the VALUE attribute of the OPTION tag in the resulting select field)

DISPLAY   Specifies the name of the query column that should be used to create the text displayed in the select field

You need to consider an example to fully understand the power of this tag's capability to dynamically create select fields. To do this, let's return to the employee database. Using a traditional SELECT tag, how would you go about producing a drop-down list of all employees?

Using a traditional HTML form, you could do this as follows:

```
<CFQUERY NAME="Employees" DATASOURCE="EmployeeData">
    SELECT       *
    FROM       Employees
    ORDER BY       LastName, FirstName
</CFQUERY>

<FORM METHOD="POST" ACTION="submit.cfm" NAME="EmployeeList">
    <SELECT NAME="Employee" SIZE=1>
        <CFOUTPUT QUERY="Employees">
            <OPTION VALUE="#ID#">#LastName#, #FirstName#
        </CFOUTPUT>
    </SELECT>
</FORM>
```

This code produces a drop-down list like the one in Figure 15.18.

FIGURE 15.18

A list of employees

However, using the CFSELECT tag, you can avoid the entire CFOUTPUT section of your template and automatically create the drop-down list, as follows:

```
<CFSELECT NAME="Employee" SIZE=1 QUERY="Employees" VALUE="ID" DISPLAY="LastName">
</CFSELECT>
```

This code produces results like those in Figure 15.19.

FIGURE 15.19
Using CFSELECT for an
employee list

There are some problems here, though. First, even if no OPTION tags are being used, you must use the closing CFSELECT tag. Without it, ColdFusion generates an error. Second, the VALUE attribute of the CFSELECT tag can be used to specify only a single field name from the query result set. This poses a difficulty: With the query as written, you can display either the first name or the last name or both in the drop-down list. This makes the list of little use because of invariable duplicates in first and last names.

You can use some advanced SQL techniques to address this problem. For instance, SQL allows concatenation of multiple string fields into a single field to be returned by the query. In Microsoft Access, this is done using the + or & operator and the AS keyword. For instance, to combine LastName and FirstName and return them in a single field called EmployeeName, you could use LastName + FirstName AS EmployeeName in your SELECT statement.

Of course, this produces results that aren't ideal, such as DaneshArman and Smith-Jane. Fortunately, the concatenation operator can also be used to concatenate string operators with data from fields in a table. Therefore, you can use LastName + ", " + FirstName AS EmployeeName. The end result is

```
<CFQUERY NAME="Employees" DATASOURCE="EmployeeData">
    SELECT   ID, LastName + ', ' + FirstName AS EmployeeName
    FROM    Employees
    ORDER BY   LastName, FirstName
</CFQUERY>
```

```
<CFFORM ACTION="submit.cfm" NAME="EmployeeList">
<CFSELECT NAME="Employee" SIZE=1 QUERY="Employees" VALUE="ID"
DISPLAY="EmployeeName">
</CFSELECT>
</CFFORM>
```

This code produces a drop-down list that appears identical to the one you created using SELECT and OPTION. In fact, the resulting HTML source code looks similar to what you would expect your form to have looked like when you created it using SELECT, OPTION, and CFOUTPUT (except that the formatting is not the most ideal for reading purposes):

```
<script LANGUAGE=JAVASCRIPT>

<!--

function  _CF_checkEmployeeList(_CF_this)

    {

    return true;

    }


//-->

</script>


<FORM NAME="EmployeeList" ACTION="submit.cfm" METHOD=POST onSubmit="return
_CF_checkEmployeeList(this)">
    <SELECT NAME="Employee" SIZE=1><OPTION VALUE="1">Danesh, Arman<OPTION
VALUE="8">Danesh, Greg<OPTION VALUE="5">Danesh, Joe<OPTION VALUE="6">Danesh,
Kevin<OPTION VALUE="7">Danesh, Lou<OPTION VALUE="3">Doe, Jane<OPTION VALUE="16">Doe,
Lisa<OPTION VALUE="15">Doe, Sue<OPTION VALUE="22">Johnson, Andrea<OPTION
VALUE="18">Johnson, Barbara<OPTION VALUE="20">Johnson, Cindy<OPTION
VALUE="19">Johnson, Jennifer<OPTION VALUE="4">Johnson, Mary<OPTION
VALUE="21">Johnson, Nancy<OPTION VALUE="17">Johnson, Sharon<OPTION VALUE="13">Smith,
Ben<OPTION VALUE="12">Smith, Charles<OPTION VALUE="2">Smith, John<OPTION
VALUE="9">Smith, Larry<OPTION VALUE="10">Smith, Moe<OPTION VALUE="11">Smith,
Samuel<OPTION VALUE="14">Smith, Wes
    </SELECT>
    </FORM>
```

Using *CFTEXTINPUT*

CFTEXTINPUT is the first tag you are going to look at that enables you to extend the basic functionality of HTML forms with special Java applets. The CFTEXTINPUT tag enables a form to include a more flexible single-line text entry field than traditional INPUT and CFINPUT tags.

Among the features of this Java-based field are the capabilities to specify the font of text inside the fields as well as the color and size.

The basic use of the tag is the same as that of INPUT. You can specify a name with the NAME attribute, a size in number of characters with the SIZE attribute, a maximum length for the data being entered in the field with the MAXLENGTH attribute, and a default value for the field with the VALUE attribute.

Beyond this, though, are the validation features of the CFTEXTINPUT tag, which will be discussed in the next chapter, and text formatting features, which we cover here.

Several attributes can be used to format the text in a field created with CFTEXTINPUT:

FONT   Specifies the font for text displayed or entered in the field. This value should be a standard font name such as Arial or Helvetica. This is an optional field.

FONTSIZE   Specifies the point size of the text displayed in the field. This is an optional field.

ITALIC   Indicates whether the text should be italic. It takes the value YES or NO and is an optional field. By default the value is NO.

BOLD   Indicates whether the text should be bold. It takes the value YES or NO and is an optional field. By default the value is NO.

HEIGHT   Specifies the height of the field in pixels. This is an optional attribute, and by default the height of the field will be determined by the specified font size.

WIDTH   Specifies the width of the field in pixels. This is an optional attribute, and by default the width of the field is set to a standard size of 200 pixels.

BGCOLOR   Specifies a background color for the text field. Possible colors are BLACK, MAGENTA, CYAN, ORANGE, DARKGRAY, PINK, GRAY, WHITE, LIGHTGRAY, YELLOW, or a hexadecimal Red-Green-Blue (RGB) triplet in the form ##XXXXXX where the Xs represent the hexadecimal digits. Alternately, the hexadecimal triplet can be used without the double pound signs in the form *XXXXX*.

TEXTCOLOR   Specifies a text color for the text field. Possible color values are the same as those for the BGCOLOR attribute.

Using these attributes should be fairly straightforward because they resemble the values seen in HTML tags such as BODY and FONT. Consider the following series of CFTEX-TINPUT tags:

```
<CFTEXTINPUT NAME="Test1" VALUE="Test Value"><HR>
<CFTEXTINPUT NAME="Test2" VALUE="Test Value" FONT="TimesRoman" FONTSIZE=14
ITALIC=YES><HR>
<CFTEXTINPUT NAME="Test3" VALUE="Test Value" FONT="Arial" BOLD=YES><HR>
<CFTEXTINPUT NAME="Test4" VALUE="Test Value" FONT="Arial" FONTSIZE=24
BGCOLOR="black" TEXTCOLOR="FFFFFF" WIDTH=200><HR>
<CFTEXTINPUT NAME="Test5" VALUE="Test Value" FONT="TimesRoman" FONTSIZE=10
HEIGHT=100 WIDTH=300>
```

This code produces the text fields shown in Figure 15.20.

FIGURE 15.20
Using CFTEXTINPUT

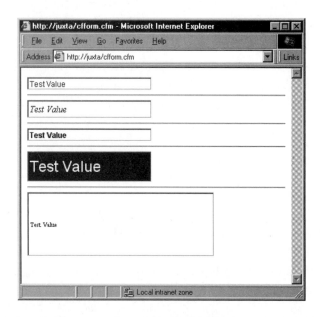

When a form containing fields created with CFTEXTINPUT is submitted, the value of the field is available through a form variable with a name corresponding to the name of the field. For instance, if you add a submit button to your form, you can access the values of the fields in submit.cfm with Form.Test1, Form.Test2, Form.Test3, Form.Test4, and Form.Test5.

A final issue needs to be addressed: What happens if a browser without Java support or with Java support disabled loads a page with a form containing a field that was created with the CFTEXTINPUT tag? As mentioned earlier, the field is actually a Java applet.

The following is an example of the HTML and JavaScript source code generated by a form with a single CFTEXTINPUT tag:

```
<script LANGUAGE=JAVASCRIPT>

<!--


function _CF_getText(textInstance)
    {
    return textInstance.cf_getText();
    }


function  _CF_checkTest(_CF_this)

    {

    _CF_this.__CFTEXT__Test__Test1.value = _CF_getText(document.Test1 );

    return true;

    }


//-->

</script>

<FORM NAME="Test" ACTION="submit.cfm" METHOD=POST onSubmit="return
_CF_checkTest(this)">
    <APPLET NAME="Test1" CODE="allaire.controls.CFTextApplet" CODEBASE="/CFIDE/classes/
" HEIGHT=200 WIDTH=200> <param NAME="ApplicationClass"
VALUE="allaire.controls.cftext">

    <param NAME="_CF_text_param" VALUE="Test Value">

<B>Browser must support Java to <Br>view ColdFusion Java Applets!</B><Br>

</APPLET>
<INPUT TYPE="HIDDEN" NAME="__CFTEXT__Test__Test1"> </FORM>
```

Notice the use of the APPLET tag to include the Java applet for the field. Between the opening and closing APPLET tags is text that is displayed if the browser does not support Java for any reason. However, it is possible to specify an alternate text for these browsers by using the NOTSUPPORTED attribute. For instance, the following attribute

```
NOTSUPPORTED="<H1>Sorry!</H1>
You need Java to use this form."
```

produces an applet block with different text for the non-Java browser:

```
<APPLET NAME="Test1" CODE="allaire.controls.CFTextApplet" CODEBASE="/CFIDE/classes/
" HEIGHT=20 WIDTH=200> <param NAME="ApplicationClass"
VALUE="allaire.controls.cftext">

<param NAME="_CF_text_param" VALUE="Test Value">

<h1>Sorry!</H1>
You need Java to use this form.

</APPLET>
```

Using *CFSLIDER* to Create Slider Controls

The next Java-based form field you will look at is created with the CFSLIDER tag. This tag builds a slider control that is ideal for selecting a value from a numerical range (such as ages, weights, and sizes). Figure 15.21 shows a sample slider control.

FIGURE 15.21

A slider control

Aside from attributes used for form validation, which we will cover in Chapter 16, the CFSLIDER tag uses several attributes to control its behavior and visual appearance. These attributes are described in the following sections.

Controlling a Slider's Behavior

A slider control's behavior is determined by the numeric range supported by the control and the increments by which the control can change the value of the field. For instance, a control may have a numeric range from 0 to 100 but could then have an increment of 10 (which means there are 11 possible values for the field: 0, 10, 20, 30, 40, 50, 60, 70, 80, 90, and 100) or it could have an increment of 1 (which would mean that the field has 101 possible values—every integer from 0 to 100 inclusive).

These two values are specified using the following attributes:

RANGE   Specifies the left and right values of the slider range. The numbers should be separated by a comma. For instance, the range 0 to 100 (which is the default range if none is specified) is indicated with RANGE="0,100".

SCALE   Specifies the increment for the control. By default the increment is 1.

Therefore, in the preceding examples, the first control with an increment of 10 would use the attributes RANGE="0,100" SCALE="10" whereas the second control would use RANGE="0,100" SCALE="1".

You need to consider some practicalities of combining range and increment settings. The basic rule is this: The left and right values of the range preferably should each be a multiple of the increment value. For instance, the range RANGE="24,100" with an increment SCALE=12 will work properly for the left value of the range: 24 is a multiple of 12. This displays as shown in the following graphic.

However, notice how the right value of the slider is 96, the closest multiple of 12 that is less than the specified right value of the range, as shown in the following graphic.

Similarly, the same issues apply to the left value of the range. If you change the increment to SCALE=11, then suddenly the left value of the range becomes 22, the closest multiple of 11 that is less than the specified left value of range (see the following graphic).

NOTE   By default, the slider will load with the control placed at the specified left value of the range. However, as the preceding slider shows, the control can be dragged to the left, in this case to 22.

In addition to specifying the range and increment of a control, you can also specify a default initial value using the VALUE attribute. Generally, you will want to make this value a multiple of the increment within the specified range. If the value specified doesn't meet these criteria, then the slider will display the default value (even if it is out of range). But after the slider is moved, then it is not possible to return it to the specified value.

By way of example, the following attributes

```
RANGE="24,96" SCALE=12 VALUE=36
```

work well and initially appear with the value shown in the following graphic.

However, if you set the value to 10,

```
RANGE="24,96" SCALE=12 VALUE=10
```

then the initial value of the slider will be 10 even though this is out of range (as shown in the following graphic). However, as soon as the slider is moved, the value will immediately be within the specified range, and it will be impossible to drag the slider back to the default value of 10.

Setting a Slider's Appearance

The sliders you have seen so far have a fairly bland appearance with a dark gray slider groove and a light gray background. By default this is the way that sliders look: gray with no label or display of the slider's current value. For instance, the tag <CFSLIDER NAME="SliderTest"> produces the results shown in the following graphic.

As the samples you have already seen show, it is possible to include a text label for a slider. This is done with the LABEL attribute. When a label is specified, the label will be displayed, immediately followed by the current value of the slider. Therefore, the tag <CFSLIDER NAME="SliderTest" LABEL="Test Slider"> produces the results shown in the following slider.

Notice, however, that the current value of the slider appears immediately next to the last letter of the label. This can be easily addressed by adding the necessary spaces to the end of `the label: <CFSLIDER NAME="SliderTest" LABEL="Test Slider: ">`. The end result is shown in the following slider.

Labels offer one additional feature: You can display the current value in the middle of the label text. To do this, use `%value%` at the place in your label where you want the current value to appear. For instance, the tag `<CFSLIDER NAME="SliderTest" LABEL= "Value is %value% percent.">` produces the following slider.

But, what about situations where you want to label a slider without displaying the current value? With the LABEL attribute alone, this isn't possible. However, you can use the REFRESHLABEL attribute to achieve the desired result. According to the definition of this attribute in the ColdFusion documentation, the purpose of this attribute is to indicate whether the label should be refreshed as the slider is moved. Possible values are YES or NO (the default value is YES).

The effective result of setting REFRESHLABEL to NO is that the current value of the slider is not displayed in the label. Therefore, in the first label example that has the current value immediately next to the label, adding `REFRESHLABEL="NO"` produces acceptable results. In other words, `<CFSLIDER NAME="SliderTest" LABEL="TestSlider" REFRESHLABEL="NO">` produces the results shown in the following graphic.

When using a label, it can also be useful to be able to specify a font, size, and color for the label. This can help make the sliders more attractive and fit the style into the overall look and feel of the form and Web site in question. Just as with the CFTEXTINPUT tag, font type and size is specified with the FONT and FONTSIZE attributes. In addition, the BOLD and ITALIC attributes enable these style features to be specified.

For instance, in the slider you just created, you could change the font to Times, change the size to 14 points, and make the text bold with the following tag:

```
<CFSLIDER NAME="SliderTest" LABEL="TestSlider" REFRESHLABEL="NO" FONT="TimesRoman"
FONTSIZE=14 BOLD="YES">
```

This tag produces the following slider.

In the examples you have seen so far, all the sliders have been of a default size, regardless of the range and increment being used. For instance, the two sliders

```
<CFSLIDER NAME="Slider1" RANGE="0,100" LABEL="Value: "><BR>
<CFSLIDER NAME="Slider2" RANGE="0,1000" LABEL="Value: ">
```

produce the two identically sized controls shown below.

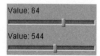

This default size is 144 pixels wide by 40 pixels deep. However, you can override these defaults by using the WIDTH and HEIGHT attributes, which specify the desired size of a slider in pixels. For instance, you can make the second slider twice as wide as the first by adding WIDTH=288 to the tag:

```
<CFSLIDER NAME="Slider1" RANGE="0,100" LABEL="Value: "><BR>
<CFSLIDER NAME="Slider2" RANGE="0,1000" LABEL="Value: " WIDTH=288>
```

This addition results in the following sliders.

Similarly, the height of the same slider can be doubled using HEIGHT=80 to create the slider shown below.

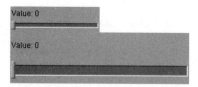

The vertical and horizontal space around a control can be specified using VSPACE and HSPACE. Therefore, if you don't want the two controls in our example to be right next to each other, you can add five pixels of vertical space to the second slider with VSPACE=5. The end result is the following ColdFusion code:

```
<CFSLIDER NAME="Slider1" RANGE="0,100" LABEL="Value: "><BR>
<CFSLIDER NAME="Slider2" RANGE="0,1000" LABEL="Value: " WIDTH=288 HEIGTH=80 VSPACE=5>
```

This code produces two sliders with space between them, as shown below.

Another group of attributes controls the colors of the slider: GROOVECOLOR, BGCOLOR, and TEXTCOLOR. All three of these can take hexadecimal RGB triplets in the form ##XXXXXX or XXXXXX as values or one of the following color names:

- BLACK
- MAGENTA
- CYAN
- ORANGE
- DARKGRAY
- PINK
- GRAY
- WHITE
- LIGHTGRAY
- YELLOW

The GROOVECOLOR attribute defines the color of the groove in the center of the slider. The BGCOLOR attribute specifies the color of the background of the entire element (including the label), and the TEXTCOLOR attribute indicates the color of the text.

For instance, the tag

```
<CFSLIDER NAME="TestSlider" LABEL="Test Value: " GROOVECOLOR="Yellow"
BGCOLOR="Black" TEXTCOLOR="White">
```

produces the following slider.

Finally, you need to look at two attributes that enable you to use an image inside the groove of the slider rather than a simple solid color. This is done with the IMG and IMG-STYLE attributes.

IMG specifies the image file to use in the groove. IMGSTYLE indicates how to display the image. There are three possible values for the IMGSTYLE attribute:

Centered   The image is shown in the center of the groove.

Tiled   The image is repeated, in a tiled fashion, in the groove.

Scaled   The image is stretched to fit in the groove. This is the default value for the IMGSTYLE attribute.

NOTE   CFSLIDER is a Java control. As with the CFTEXTINPUT control, it has a default message for non-Java browsers, and you can specify your own message using the NOTSUPPORTED attribute.

When using the CFSLIDER tag in your forms, the value of the slider is available in the template that the form is submitted to in the same way as any other standard form field: through a form variable with a name corresponding to the field name. Throughout this chapter you have used the same name for your sliders (SliderTest). Therefore, in the template processing the form submission, you can use Form.SliderTest to access the value of the slider at the time of submission.

Using *CFGRID* to Create Grids

The next Java-based field to look at is created with the CFGRID tag. The CFGRID tag is used to create a grid control, or rows and columns, which resembles a spreadsheet or a word processor table.

Grids are ideally suited to displaying the results of a query because they enable the presentation of multiple fields from multiple records in a query. In addition, grids provide an easy way to enable the editing of multiple records from a database when used in conjunction with the CFGRIDUPDATE tag.

Figure 15.22 provides an example of a grid control.

These grids can be used in several ways:

- Data presentation
- Data selection
- Data editing

You will consider each of these in turn and then look at additional features of grid controls such as those that control the appearance of elements in the grid.

FIGURE 15.22

A grid control

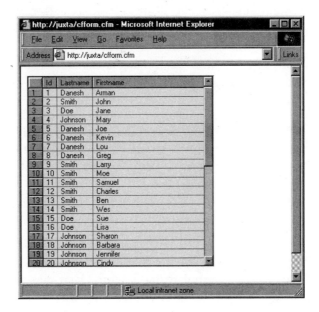

Data Presentation

The first step in using a grid control is to present query data in a useful way for browsing. When used in this way, data in the grid cannot be selected, and when the form containing the grid is submitted, no data is sent from the grid field.

This is the ideal place to start working with grids because it enables you to learn the mechanics of building grids from your queries without having to deal with some of the complexities inherent in using grids for data selection and editing.

Because grids are useful when working with query result sets, we need to start our discussion of creating grids with a query that you can use in your examples. Because you have used the employee data database throughout this chapter, continue to use it here with the following query:

```
<CFQUERY NAME="Employees" DATASOURCE="EmployeeData">
    SELECT      *
    FROM        Employees
    ORDER BY    ID
</CFQUERY>
```

Given this query, you can build a simple grid for browsing the data in this query result by using the CFGRID and CFGRIDCOLUMN tags. CFGRID is used to create the grid by specifying at a minimum the name of the grid, the query to use, and a selection mode. In the case of a grid for displaying data for browsing, you want to use SELECTMODE="Browse", which indicates that the grid is for viewing data and that selection is not possible:

```
<CFGRID NAME="GridTest" QUERY="Employees" SELECTMODE="Browse">
```

Next you need to indicate which fields to display in the grid and in which order. You use CFGRIDCOLUMN to do this because the fields are displayed in columns with each record taking a single row. For each field you want to display, you use a single CFGRID-COLUMN tag. Therefore, to display a person's ID number, last name, and first name, you would use the following tags:

```
<CFGRIDCOLUMN NAME="ID">
<CFGRIDCOLUMN NAME="LastName">
<CFGRIDCOLUMN NAME="FirstName">
```

Here the NAME attribute specifies the name of the field from the query result set that should be used to populate the column. The results are shown earlier in Figure 15.22. The complete code for the grid looks like this:

```
<CFGRID NAME="GridTest" QUERY="Employees" SELECTMODE="Browse">
<CFGRIDCOLUMN NAME="ID">
<CFGRIDCOLUMN NAME="LastName">
<CFGRIDCOLUMN NAME="FirstName">
</CFGRID>
```

Similarly, if you want a person's names and salary to be displayed, you might use

```
<CFGRID NAME="GridTest" QUERY="Employees" SELECTMODE="Browse">
<CFGRIDCOLUMN NAME="LastName">
<CFGRIDCOLUMN NAME="FirstName">
<CFGRIDCOLUMN NAME="Salary">
</CFGRID>
```

and you would get results like those in Figure 15.23.

The first thing you probably noticed in both grids is that the column headers are the names of the fields. This can be less than ideal. For instance, Lastname and Firstname should appear as Last Name and First Name, and Salary might be more descriptive as Monthly Salary.

FIGURE 15.23

Displaying employee information in a grid

These changes can be achieved by using the HEADER attribute of the CFGRIDCOLUMN tag to specify alternate column headers:

```
<CFGRID NAME="GridTest" QUERY="Employees" SELECTMODE="Browse">
<CFGRIDCOLUMN NAME="LastName" HEADER="Last Name">
<CFGRIDCOLUMN NAME="FirstName" HEADER="First Name">
<CFGRIDCOLUMN NAME="Salary" HEADER="Monthly Salary">
</CFGRID>
```

This code produces the grid shown in Figure 15.24.

Another problem with the salary grid is the way in which the numeric values in the salary column are displayed. Numeric values should be aligned to the right side of the column so that the digits align correctly. This is achieved by using the CFGRIDCOLUMN tag's DATAALIGN attribute, which can specify three possible alignments for the data in a column: Left, Center, and Right. The default alignment for a column is left aligned.

FIGURE 15.24
Using alternate column
headers

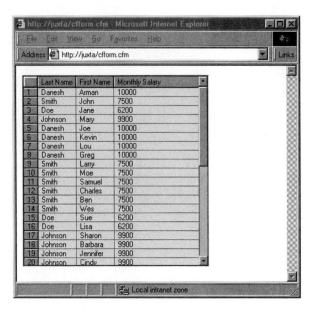

For the salary column, you will want to use the following tag:

```
<CFGRIDCOLUMN NAME="Salary" HEADER="Monthly Salary" DATAALIGN="Right">.
```

Another aspect of presenting the salaries is to present them in proper currency format, such as $1000.00. You can achieve this by using the NUMBERFORMAT attribute of the CFGRIDCOLUMN tag. This attribute takes as its value a mask defining how the number should be displayed. This mask uses the same syntax and special characters as the NumberFormat function discussed in Chapter 12, "Grouping, Nesting, and Formatting Output."

To present your salaries in a standardized currency format, you could use the numeric mask $___,___.00. Therefore, your final tag is

```
<CFGRIDCOLUMN NAME="Salary" HEADER="Monthly Salary" DATAALIGN="Right"
NUMBERFORMAT="$___,___.00">
```

This produces the grid in Figure 15.25.

FIGURE 15.25

Formatting numbers with a mask

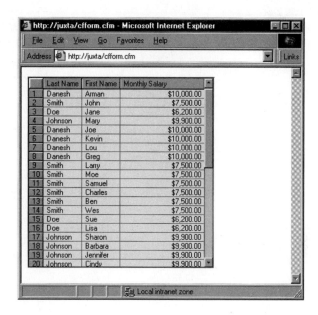

Although it is usually more desirable to specify data alignment on a per-column basis, you can change the default data alignment for the entire grid by using the GRIDDATAALIGN attribute of the CFGRID tag. The value specified with this attribute can be overridden with the DATAALIGN attribute of the CFGRIDCOLUMN tag.

By default, the rows of the grid reflect the order in which the records are returned in the query result set (in our case, the query is ordered by employee ID number). However, grids can dynamically sort presented data based on the data in any column. To enable this feature, you need to enable sorting using the SORT attribute of the CFGRID tag. This attribute can be set to YES or NO (NO is the default value) and when set to YES causes ascending and descending sort buttons to be displayed, as shown in Figure 15.26.

To sort a column, click the column's header; this selects and highlights all elements in
the column, as shown in Figure 15.27.

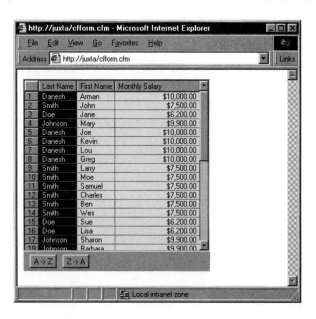

The next step is to click the appropriate sort button. For instance, to sort in descending order based on the data in the selected column, simply click the Z -> A button.

The buttons used to select ascending or descending order for sorting can use custom text instead of the default A -> Z and Z -> A. Alternate text is specified using the SOR-TASCENDINGBUTTON attribute and the SORTDESCENDINGBUTTON attribute. Therefore, the CFGRID tag

```
<CFGRID NAME="GridTest" QUERY="Employees" SELECTMODE="Browse" SORT="Yes"
SORTASCENDINGBUTTON="Ascending" SORTDESCENDINGBUTTON="Descending">
```

produces a grid with the custom sort buttons shown in Figure 15.28.

FIGURE 15.28
Sort buttons can use customized labels.

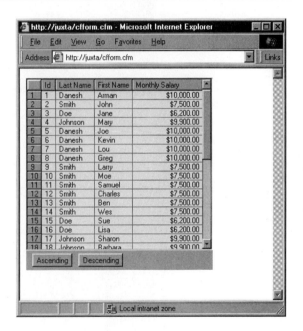

Data Selection

The next step in working with grids is to move from browsing data to selecting data. You can specify three data selection modes by using the SELECTMODE attribute of the CFGRID tag. The three modes are:

Single Allows selection of a single cell in the grid. Figure 15.29 shows a single cell being selected.

Column Allows selection of an entire column in the grid. Figure 15.30 shows a column being selected.

Row Allows selection of an entire row in the grid. Figure 15.31 shows a row being selected.

FIGURE 15.29
Selecting a single cell

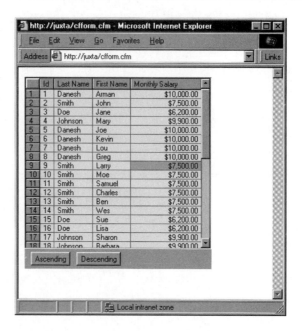

FIGURE 15.30
Selecting an entire column

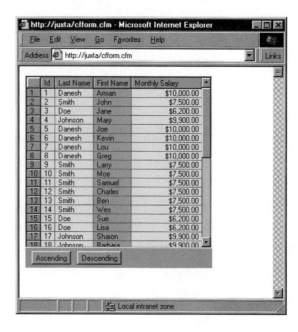

FIGURE 15.31
Selecting an entire row

Commonly, grid controls are used for selecting entire rows because this action represents the selection of a record from a database. Therefore, we will explain this in detail. Refer to the ColdFusion documentation for more information on selecting single cells or columns.

The CFGRID tag for selecting entire rows requires the use of the SELECTMODE="Row" attribute. When the form containing this type of selection grid is submitted, the selected data becomes accessible through form variables that reflect the column names from the grid. Each column's data for the selected record is reflected through the variable Form.GridName.ColumnName.

For example, consider the employee data examples. If you have a grid containing columns for all the fields in your table and the grid is named GridTest, then you can access the selected row's fields with the following five variables:

```
Form.GridTest.ID
Form.GridTest.LastName
Form.GridTest.FirstName
Form.GridTest.Gender
Form.GridTest.Salary
```

Data Editing

The last major application for grid controls is data editing. When using SELECTMODE= "Edit", you can allow users to edit the contents of a displayed grid and then process the information after the form is submitted, either by reflecting the changes back into the database used to create the grid or by performing other relevant actions.

When using this select mode, the user can highlight and change the values stored in the individual cells of the grid. Figure 15.32 shows a cell being edited.

FIGURE 15.32
Editing a grid cell

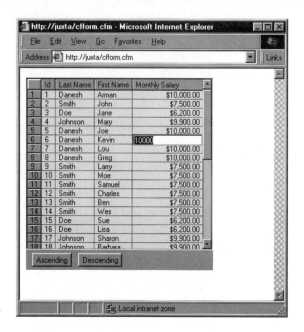

In addition to simply updating existing content, you can also allow users to add and delete rows from the grid and then have these changes reflected back to the database. The ability to add and delete rows is enabled by setting the INSERT and DELETE attributes to YES. By default, they are NO. Setting these attributes to YES produces the results shown in Figure 15.33 with Insert and Delete buttons next to the sort buttons we discussed earlier.

FIGURE 15.33

It is possible to insert and
delete rows in a grid.

When inserting a row, it is inserted as the last row of the grid, as shown in Figure 15.34.

FIGURE 15.34

New rows are added
after the existing last row
in the grid.

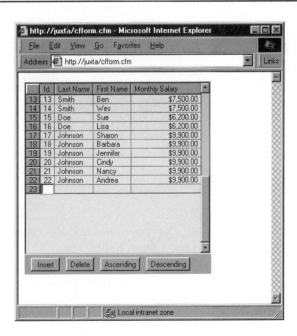

> **WARNING** The Delete function acts without asking for confirmation. This can be problematic but not as dangerous as it sounds because the user has to submit the form to cause the deletion to be reflected back to the database.

As with sort buttons, it is possible to customize the Insert and Delete buttons using the INSERTBUTTON and DELETEBUTTON attributes. For instance, using INSERTBUTTON="Add Row" and DELETEBUTTON="Del. Row" in the CFGRID tag produces the buttons shown in Figure 15.35.

FIGURE 15.35
Customizing button labels

The primary purpose of editing grid data is to allow the user to directly edit data stored in a database. Given this, you need a way to reflect these changes back to the database when the form is submitted. This can be achieved in two ways:

- Using the CFGRIDUPDATE tag
- Using CFQUERY tags

Before looking at the process of moving user changes into the database, you need to consider the issue of key values. In order for our different methods of moving changes into the database to work, you need to be able to conclusively determine which records have been edited. The easiest way to do this is by being sure that you include the primary key of the table in question in your grid.

You included the primary key of your employee table in all the grid examples in this section. However, there may be compelling reasons to prevent display of a column while still including the values in the grid and the data submitted with the form. This is done by using the DISPLAY attribute of the CFGRIDCOLUMN tag. When the attribute is set to NO, a column can be included in the grid but not displayed. By default, the DISPLAY attribute is set to YES.

For instance, if you use

```
<CFGRIDCOLUMN NAME="ID" DISPLAY="NO">
```

in producing your grid, you can produce a grid with the ID column hidden like the one in Figure 15.36, but which includes the value of the ID fields from the database table.

FIGURE 15.36
You can hide the primary key from being displayed in the grid.

Updating with the *CFGRIDUPDATE* Tag

Using the CFGRIDUPATE tag, you can quickly and easily reflect changes—including edits, additions, and deletions—back to a database. This tag should be used in the template to which the form containing the grid is being submitted.

The CFGRIDUPDATE tag makes the job of processing multiple changes by a user easy, but it has some limitations:

- It is designed to update a single table. More complex grids may be built out of a query that draws data from multiple tables. CFGRIDUPDATE cannot update all these tables in a single tag.
- CFGRIDUPDATE is not ideally suited to handling changes that are likely to cause errors. When an error is encountered, all updating stops, leaving some changes made but others undone without any easy way to determine the state in which the data in the database has been left.
- With the CFGRIDUPDATE tag, you have no control over the order in which changes are made: Row deletions happen first, row insertions next, and finally updates to existing rows are executed.

At its most basic, three attributes are required to make CFGRIDUPDATE work:

GRID Name of the grid to be processed

DATASOURCE Data source containing the table to be altered

TABLENAME Name of the table to update

Therefore, if you use the employee example, the following template creates a form with a grid for editing employee data:

```
<CFQUERY NAME="employees" DATASOURCE="EmployeeData">
   SELECT   *
   FROM    Employees
   ORDER BY   ID
</CFQUERY>

<CFFORM ACTION="submit.cfm" NAME="Test" METHOD=GET>
<CFGRID NAME="GridTest" QUERY="Employees" SELECTMODE="Edit" INSERT="YES"
DELETE="YES" INSERTBUTTON="Add Row" DELETEBUTTON="Del. Row" SORT="Yes"
SORTASCENDINGBUTTON="Ascending" SORTDESCENDINGBUTTON="Descending">
   <CFGRIDCOLUMN NAME="ID" DISPLAY="NO">
   <CFGRIDCOLUMN NAME="LastName" HEADER="Last Name">
   <CFGRIDCOLUMN NAME="FirstName" HEADER="First Name">
   <CFGRIDCOLUMN NAME="Gender">
   <CFGRIDCOLUMN NAME="Salary" HEADER="Monthly Salary" DATAALIGN="Right"
NUMBERFORMAT="$___,___.00">
   </CFGRID>
   <BR>
   <INPUT TYPE=submit>
   </CFFORM>
```

This template produces the form and grid shown in Figure 15.37.

FIGURE 15.37
A form with a grid ready for editing and submission

Next, in the `submit.cfm` template to which the form is being submitted, you can reflect all user changes back to the employee database by using the following tag:

```
<CFGRIDUPDATE GRID="GridTest" DATASOURCE="EmployeeData" TABLENAME="Employees">
```

The subject of how CFGRIDUPDATE handles updates to existing records needs to be addressed. As you know from using the SQL UPDATE statement, to effectively update a single record in a database you need to be able to identify it uniquely by using one or more fields in the record. Generally, this is done using the primary key that is usually unique for each record in the table.

However, there may be times when identifying a record strictly by the primary key is insufficient. By default, CFGRIDUPDATE uses only the primary key value to identify the record being updated. However, you can alter this behavior with the KEYONLY attribute, which is NO by default. Setting it to YES causes records being updated to be identified by keys as well as by the original values of any fields that are being changed in the record.

The CFGRIDUPDATE tag can also take other optional attributes, which may be needed at times but which are not used in most cases:

DBTYPE   Specifies which type of database is being used (ODBC, Oracle73 for Oracle 7.3 native driver, Oracle80 for Oracle 8 native driver, or Sybase11 for Sybase System 11 native driver)

DBSERVER   Overrides the specified database server for the data source when using native drivers

DBNAME   Overrides the specified database name for the data source when using native drivers

USERNAME   Overrides the specified username for the data source when using an ODBC data source

PASSWORD   Overrides the specified password for the data source when using an ODBC data source

TABLEOWNER   Specifies the table owner for the data source that supports table ownership

TABLEQUALIFIER   Specifies the table qualifier for data sources that support qualifiers

PROVIDER   Specifies the COM provider for OLE-DB

PROVIDERDSN   Specifies the data source name for the COM provider for OLE-DB

KEYONLY   When set to YES, specifies that in the update action, the WHERE criteria is limited to key values. When set to NO, indicates that key values plus the original values of changes fields are included in the WHERE criteria. The default value is YES.

If you are doing your development and testing against Microsoft Access databases as you are doing in this book, it is unlikely that you will need to use any of these attributes. If you are working against databases that support these features (such as Oracle or SQL Server), consult the documentation for the database system to clarify such subjects as table ownership and table qualifiers.

Updating with CFQUERY Tags

Although the CFGRIDUPDATE tag is easy to use, at times it is beneficial to work through your own CFQUERY tags to handle the deletions, insertions, and updates. Among other benefits, using CFQUERY tags makes it possible to build more complex SQL statements and effectively handle grid data drawn from multiple tables in a database.

To work manually with the data provided by a grid when a form is submitted, you first need to understand how to access information from an editable grid.

When an editable grid is submitted, three types of arrays become available in the receiving template, as indicated in the following list.

Form.GridName.ColumnName[RowIndex]   Reflects the new values of cells for a particular column.

Form.GridName.Original.ColumnName[RowIndex]   Reflects the original value of cells for a particular column.

Form.GridName.RowStatus.Action[RowIndex]   Reflects the type of change made to a particular row. Possible values are U for updates, I for inserts, and D for deletions.

By combining the information from these three arrays, it is possible to do the following:

- Determine edits made to particular cells
- Determine which records are new
- Determine which records need deleting
- Build SQL statements to execute all the changes

For instance, in our employee example, if `Form.GridTest.RowStatus.Action[1]` is set to `Update` and `Form.GridTest.LastName[1]` differs in value from `Form.GridTest .Original.LastName[1]`, then we know that the user has edited the `Last Name` field of the record in the first row of the grid. You can then build an effective SQL query to update the record:

```
UPDATE    Employees
SET       LastName='#Form.GridTest.LastName[1]#'
WHERE     ID=#Form.GridTest.Original.ID[1]#
AND       LastName='#Form.GridTest.Original.LastName[1]#'
```

To further highlight how to build these queries, the following template generates the necessary updates to our employee database using CFQUERY tags and SQL statements:

```
<CFLOOP INDEX="Row" FROM="1" TO=#ArrayLen(Form.GridTest.RowStatus.Action)#>

    <CFSWITCH EXPRESSION="#Form.GridTest.RowStatus.Action[Row]#">

        <CFCASE VALUE="D">
            <CFQUERY NAME="Delete" DATASOURCE="EmployeeData">
                DELETE FROM    Employees
                WHERE          ID=#Form.GridTest.Original.ID[Row]#
            </CFQUERY>
        </CFCASE>

        <CFCASE VALUE="U">
            <CFQUERY NAME="Update" DATASOURCE="EmployeeData">
                UPDATE    Employees
                SET       LastName='#Form.GridTest.LastName[Row]#',
                          FirstName='#Form.GridTest.FirstName[Row]#',
                          Gender='#Form.GridTest.Gender[Row]#',
                          Salary=#Form.GridTest.Salary[Row]#
                WHERE     ID=#Form.GridTest.Original.ID[Row]#
            </CFQUERY>
        </CFCASE>

        <CFCASE VALUE="I">
            <CFQUERY NAME="Insert" DATASOURCE="EmployeeData">
                INSERT INTO    Employees
                (LastName,FirstName,Gender,Salary)
                VALUES
('#Form.GridTest.LastName[Row]#','#Form.GridTest.FirstName[Row]#','#Form.GridTest.Gen
der[Row]#',#Form.GridTest.Salary[Row]#)
```

```
        </CFQUERY>
      </CFCASE>

   </CFSWITCH>

</CFLOOP>
```

The concept here is really quite simple. You loop through all the rows from the grid by using `ArrayLen`, which determines how many rows are in the grid by testing `Form.GridTest.RowStatus.Action`. Within the loop, you use a switch-case construct to handle all three possible actions: delete, update, and insert.

Grid Formatting

Now that you have finished with the heart of grids—creating them, populating them with useful information, and then allowing the user to work with the information—you will turn to the cosmetic: attributes that enable you to control the appearance of grids.

These attributes don't require detailed descriptions to master because most of them are quite clear and they are the same as tags used to format other form controls. Let's start by looking at attributes that can be used in the CFGRID tag:

HEIGHT   Specifies the height of the entire control in pixels

WIDTH   Specifies the width of the entire control in pixels

VSPACE   Specifies vertical space around the control in pixels

HSPACE   Specifies horizontal space around the control in pixels

FONT   Specifies the font to use for all data in the grid control

FONTSIZE   Specifies the font size in points for text in the control

ITALIC   Indicates whether text in the grid should be italic (possible values are YES and NO)

BOLD   Indicates whether text in the grid should be bold (possible value are YES and NO)

ROWHEIGHT   Specifies minimum row height in pixels

ROWHEADERALIGN   Indicates text alignment for row headers (possible values are LEFT, RIGHT, or CENTER)

ROWHEADERFONT   Specifies the font to use for row headers

ROWHEADERFONTSIZE   Specifies the font size in points for row headers

ROWHEADERITALIC   Indicates whether row headers should be italic (possible values are YES and NO)

ROWHEADERBOLD   Indicates whether row headers should be bold (possible values are YES and NO)

ROWHEADERWIDTH   Specifies the width in pixels of row headers

COLHEADERS   Indicates whether column headers should be displayed (possible values are YES and NO)

COLHEADERALIGN   Indicates text alignment for column headers (possible values are LEFT, RIGHT, or CENTER)

COLHEADERFONT   Specifies the font to use for column headers

COLHEADERFONTSIZE   Specifies the font size in points for column headers

COLHEADERITALIC   Indicates whether column headers should be italic (possible values are YES and NO)

COLHEADERBOLD   Indicates whether column headers should be bold (possible values are YES and NO)

BGCOLOR   Specifies a background color for the control as a hexadecimal RGB triplet in the form ##XXXXXX or *XXXXXX* or as a color name from the following list: BLACK, MAGENTA, CYAN, ORANGE, DARKGRAY, PINK, GRAY, WHITE, LIGHTGRAY, or YELLOW

SELECTCOLOR   Specifies the background color for a selected item as a hexadecimal RGB triplet or a color name

PICTUREBAR   Indicates whether image buttons should be used for insert, delete, and sort buttons (possible values are YES and NO)

These appearance attributes are further enhanced by attributes for the CFGRIDCOLUMN tag related to appearance and formatting:

WIDTH   Specifies the width of the column in pixels

FONT   Specifies the font to use for all data in the grid control

FONTSIZE   Specifies the font size in points for text in the control

ITALIC   Indicates whether text in the grid should be italic (possible values are YES and NO)

BOLD   Indicates whether text in the grid should be bold (possible value are YES and NO)

HEADERALIGN   Indicates text alignment for the column header (possible values are LEFT, RIGHT, or CENTER)

HEADERFONT   Specifies the font to use for the column header

HEADERFONTSIZE   Specifies the font size in points for the column header

HEADERITALIC   Indicates whether the column header should be italic (possible values are YES and NO)

HEADERBOLD   Indicates whether the column header should be bold (possible values are YES and NO)

Other Features

Some other features of grid controls warrant brief discussion:

- Associating URLs with grid items
- Including images in grid cells
- Manually populating grids

Associating URLs with Grid Items

When building grid controls, you can associate a URL with the cells in a column by using the HREF attribute. You can do this in two ways: by specifying a URL or by specifying another column from the query result that contains URLs.

In either case, the entries in the particular column will be presented as clickable URLs, and a URL attribute called CFGRIDKEY will be added to the end of the URL containing information that is dependent on the selection mode being used in the grid. Table 15.2 shows possible selection modes and their effect on the CFGRIDKEY URL attribute.

TABLE 15.2:   Selection Modes and the CFGRIDKEY URL Attribute

SELECTMODE value	CFGRIDKEY value
Single	Value of the selected cell
Row	Comma-separated list of values from the cells in the selected row in left-to-right order as displayed in the grid
Column	Comma-separated list of values from the cells in the selected column in top-to-bottom order as displayed in the grid

When a user clicks a URL, the relevant value is then passed to the template that can access it in the same way that any other URL attribute is accessed.

Entries in a grid are converted into URLs by using the HREF attribute of the CFGRID-COLUMN tag. This attribute can specify an absolute URL, a relative URL, or the name of a query column containing URLs.

For instance, if in our employee examples you have a template called employee-details.cfm that displays an employee's details, then you can useHREF=employeedetails.cfm" in the appropriate column's CFGRIDCOLUMN tag to create the URLs. For instance, consider the following form template:

```
<CFQUERY NAME="employees" DATASOURCE="EmployeeData">
    SELECT    *
    FROM      Employees
    ORDER BY  ID
</CFQUERY>
```

```
<CFFORM ACTION="submit.cfm" NAME="Test">
<CFGRID NAME="GridTest" QUERY="Employees" SELECTMODE="Row" SORT="Yes">
<CFGRIDCOLUMN NAME="ID" HREF="employeedetails.cfm">
<CFGRIDCOLUMN NAME="LastName" HEADER="Last Name">
<CFGRIDCOLUMN NAME="FirstName" HEADER="First Name">
<CFGRIDCOLUMN NAME="Gender">
<CFGRIDCOLUMN NAME="Salary" HEADER="Monthly Salary" DATAALIGN="Right"
NUMBERFORMAT="$___,___.00">
</CFGRID>
</CFFORM>
```

In this template, the grid column for the employee ID uses the HREF tag to make it into a URL. The results look like those in Figure 15.38.

FIGURE 15.38

URLs in a grid

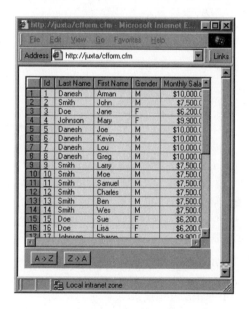

If you look carefully, you can see that each of the entries in the ID column is an underlined link as opposed to plain text. Each is a link to the employeedetails.cfm template:

```
<H1>Employee #<CFOUTPUT>#ListGetAt(URL.CFGRIDKEY,1)#</CFOUTPUT></H1>
<STRONG>Last Name</STRONG>: <CFOUTPUT>#ListGetAt(URL.CFGRIDKEY,2)#</CFOUTPUT><BR>
<STRONG>First Name</STRONG>: <CFOUTPUT>#ListGetAt(URL.CFGRIDKEY,3)#</CFOUTPUT><BR>
<STRONG>Gender</STRONG>: <CFOUTPUT>#ListGetAt(URL.CFGRIDKEY,4)#</CFOUTPUT><BR>
<STRONG>Salary</STRONG>: $<CFOUTPUT>#ListGetAt(URL.CFGRIDKEY,5)#</CFOUTPUT>
```

Notice the use of ListGetAt here to obtain individual values from URL.CFGRIDKEY. Because this URL attribute contains a comma-separated list of values in the selected row, you can treat it as a regular list variable and pull individual values out of it using ListGetAt. Details of working with lists are covered in Chapter 14.

When you click one of the links in the grid, the `employeedetails.cfm` template opens and displays the selected data, as shown in Figure 15.39.

Another use of the HREF attribute is to link a record in a grid to a URL stored with it in the database. For instance, if your employee database table had another column called `HomePage` containing the URL of the employee's home page, you could link their records to their home page with the following `CFGRIDCOLUMN` tag:

```
<CFGRIDCOLUMN NAME="ID" HREF="HomePage">
```

Because `HomePage` is a field in your query result now, the value of this field will be treated as the URL for the link. The `CFGRIDKEY` attribute will still be appended to the URL.

Including Images in Grid Cells

When using grids, it is possible to have a cell's contents interpreted as an image and displayed accordingly. ColdFusion does this by attempting to interpret the field's content and display either a built-in image or a custom image accordingly.

If the specified field contains one of the following values, then a built-in image is displayed in the cell that matches the meaning suggested by the value: `cd`, `computer`, document, `element`, `floppy`, `folder`, `fixed`, `remote`. Figure 15.40 shows a grid demonstrating these images.

FIGURE 15.40
Built-in grid images

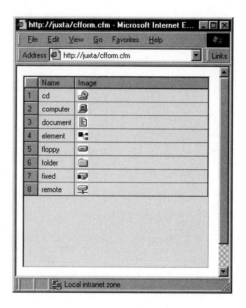

You can include your own images in two ways: Specify the complete path to the image relative to the location of the default images (which is usually `web_root\cfide\classes\images\`) or place the image in this directory and then it can be specified by name without extension.

One issue to watch out for is that row heights will not automatically adjust to accommodate the height of the image. For instance, when the icons shown in Figure 15.40 are displayed in a grid with the default row height, all the icons are cut off at the bottom, as shown in Figure 15.41.

You need to specify a minimum row height using the `ROWHEIGHT` attribute of the `CFGRID` size to ensure that your row height will accommodate the images you plan to display.

FIGURE 15.41
Row heights don't adjust.

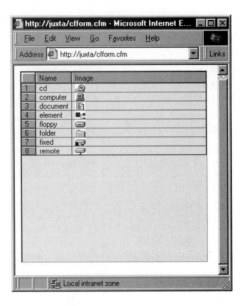

Manually Populating Grids

The last aspect of grids you will look at is how to create grids from data other than query results. The CFGRIDROW tag enables data to be manually inserted into a grid.

There are three steps to manually populating a grid. First, you need to create your grid by using CFGRID. However, because the grid will be manually populated, no query needs to be specified:

```
<CFGRID NAME="GridTest">
```

Second, you need to define the columns that will be displayed in the grid by using CFGRIDCOLUMN. For instance, to create a two-column grid for displaying first and last names, you could use

```
<CFGRIDCOLUMN NAME="LastName" HEADER="Last Name">
<CFGRIDCOLUMN NAME="FirstName" HEADER="First Name">
```

In this case, the NAME attribute doesn't specify the query column to display but rather specifies the column name for use after the form is submitted and it is necessary to process the selections in the grid.

Finally, you need to populate the grid with rows of data. For each row, one CFGRIDROW tag should be used. The tag takes a single attribute called DATA, which takes as its value a comma-separated list of values. The list should contain the same number of elements as there are columns in the grid, and entries in the list should reflect the order of columns in the grid.

For instance, you can populate the grid you have just created with three rows, as follows:

```
<CFGRIDROW DATA="Danesh,Arman">
<CFGRIDROW DATA="Smith,John">
<CFGRIDROW DATA="Doe,Jane">
```

Put together, the code for the grid looks like this:

```
<CFGRID NAME="GridTest">
<CFGRIDCOLUMN NAME="LastName" HEADER="Last Name">
<CFGRIDCOLUMN NAME="FirstName" HEADER="First Name">
<CFGRIDROW DATA="Danesh,Arman">
<CFGRIDROW DATA="Smith,John">
<CFGRIDROW DATA="Doe,Jane">
</CFGRID>
```

The resulting grid is shown in Figure 15.42.

FIGURE 15.42
Grids can be manually
populated with data.

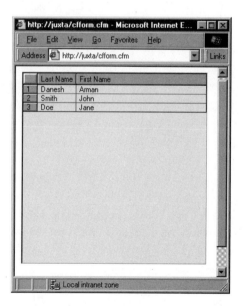

Using *CFTREE* to Create Trees

The final Java control you will look at is the CFTREE control. Using CFTREE, you can build a Windows Explorer–like hierarchical tree like the one shown in Figure 15.43.

FIGURE 15.43

A ColdFusion tree control

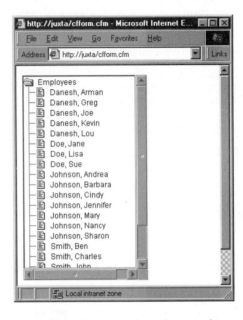

Generally, trees are built out of queries, but they don't have to be, as you will see as you work through the examples in this section. For most of the examples, you will work with simple queries from our employee database.

Let's build the tree shown in Figure 15.43. First, you need a query that obtains the last name–first name combination:

```
<CFQUERY NAME="Employees" DATASOURCE="EmployeeData">
    SELECT      LastName + ', ' + FirstName AS Name
    FROM        Employees
    ORDER BY    LastName, FirstName
</CFQUERY>
```

Next, you use the CFTREE tag to define your tree. The only required attribute of CFTREE is NAME, which specifies the name of the field for later processing of the submitted form:

```
<CFTREE NAME="TreeTest">
```

Next, you use the CFTREEITEM tag to define the entries in the tree. With this tag, The following attributes are available:

VALUE   Specifies the query column to use to create a series of items in the tree

QUERY   Specifies the query to use to create the items in the tree

QUERYASROOT   Indicates whether the item being created is the root level of the tree

IMG   Specifies a built-in image for each level of the tree

IMGOPEN   Specifies a built-in image for open tree items

HREF   Specifies a URL to associate with the tree item

TARGET   Specifies the target for a URL associated with the tree item

DISPLAY   Specifies a label to display for the tree item

PARENT   Specifies the value of the tree item's parent

EXPAND   Specifies if the tree item should be expanded by default. Possible values are YES and NO

In this particular case, you will use the following tag:

```
<CFTREEITEM VALUE="Name" QUERY="Employees" QUERYASROOT="Yes" IMG="folder,document">
```

Here, you specify that the Name value from the query named Employees should be used to create an entry in the tree, and that the entry is the root level of the tree. The IMG tag indicates that a folder icon should be used for the first level and a document icon for the sub-entries under first-level items.

This use of folder and document icons corresponds to the figure: The root item of the tree is labeled with the query name and this item has as its children the values of the Name field in the result set.

Using trees, though, you can create somewhat more complex, grouped structures. For instance, suppose you want to group the employees in the tree by gender. First, you adjust your query to include the gender of employees:

```
<CFQUERY NAME="Employees" DATASOURCE="EmployeeData">
    SELECT     Gender, LastName + ', ' + FirstName AS Name
    FROM       Employees
    ORDER BY   Gender, LastName, FirstName
</CFQUERY>
```

Next, you need to adjust your CFTREEITEM tag to handle the extra complexity:

```
<CFTREEITEM VALUE="Gender,Name" QUERY="Employees" QUERYASROOT="Yes"
IMG="folder,folder,document">
```

In this tag, the VALUE attribute takes two values that indicate the first and second level of children in the item. This adds a level to the item's hierarchy that also requires an extra entry in the list of images. The end result looks like Figure 15.44.

FIGURE 15.44
Grouped tree items

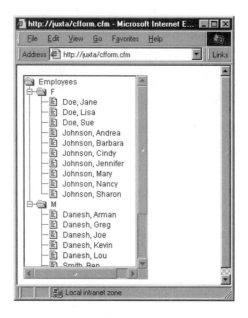

Submitting Forms with Trees

When you submit a form containing a tree, two form variables are created:

Form.TreeName.node   Contains the node the user has selected without the path to the node

Form.TreeName.path   Contains the complete path to the selected node, such as root\node1\node2\node3

You will probably notice that the root node is included in the `Form.TreeName.path` variable in the table. This is optional. By default, the path will exclude the root node. However, if the COMPLETEPATH attribute of the CFTREE tag is set to YES, then the root node will be included.

Referring back to your gender-grouped tree, let's consider the form variables that are created if the form is submitted with Doe, Sue selected. As the tree is currently defined, the variables will have values as follows:

Form.TreeTest.node   Doe, Sue

Form.TreeTest.path   F\Doe, Sue

Adding COMPLETEPATH="YES" to the CFTREE tag changes the latter to `Employees\` F\Doe, Sue.

Displaying Alternate Values

Sometimes, it will not be ideal to display the same value as is actually stored in a node of the tree. That is, sometimes you need to have the value displayed for a node differ from the value submitted by that node.

To do this, you use the DISPLAY attribute of the CFTREEITEM tag to indicate query fields to use for display purposes. Like the VALUE attribute, this can be a comma-separated list of values and should contain the same number of entries as the VALUE attribute in the same tag.

Therefore, if you want to display the employee name, but store and submit the employee ID number, you would first add the ID to your query as follows:

```
<CFQUERY NAME="Employees" DATASOURCE="EmployeeData">
    SELECT      Gender, LastName + ', ' + FirstName AS Name, ID
    FROM        Employees
    ORDER BY    Gender, LastName, FirstName
</CFQUERY>
```

Then you would change your last CTREEITEM tag to

```
<CFTREEITEM VALUE="Gender,ID" DISPLAY="Gender,Name" QUERY="Employees"
QUERYASROOT="Yes" IMG="folder,folder,document">
```

Notice that the first element in the list is the same in both the VALUE and DISPLAY attributes because the displayed and the stored values can be the same for the gender, but the second entry differs.

Although the resulting tree looks the same, when you submit the form the resulting variables are:

Form.TreeTest.node 15
Form.TreeTest.path Employees\F\15

Using URLs with Trees

As you saw with grids, it is possible for tree items to be associated with URLs and to become clickable links. You do this by specifying a URL in the HREF attribute of the CFTREEITEM tag. For instance, with the following tag

```
<CFTREEITEM VALUE="Gender,ID" DISPLAY="Gender,Name" QUERY="Employees"
QUERYASROOT="Yes" IMG="folder,folder,document" HREF=",,employeedetails.cfm">
```

you link entries to an employee details template to produce results like those in Figure 15.45.

FIGURE 15.45

Creating linked entries in a tree

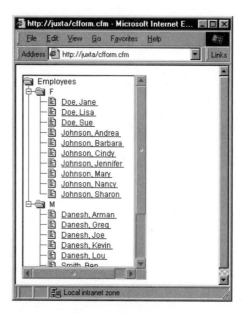

Notice the use of commas in the HREF attribute. The HREF attribute indicates a URL for each level of the item, just as the IMG attribute indicates an image for each level of the item. To indicate that a level in the tree is not a link, simply leave its space blank. This explains why the HREF value has a list with the first two entries blank: Only the nodes at the bottom level of the tree (where the names are) need to be displayed as links.

When these links are created, a URL attribute called CFTREEITEMKEY is appended to the URL with the selected value as its value. This can be used in the template you link to for processing purposes.

Formatting Trees

Several attributes are available for the CFTREE tag that control the appearance of a tree. These are outlined in the following list:

FONT   Specifies the font for the tree

FONTSIZE   Specifies the font size for the tree in points

ITALIC   Indicates whether the tree text should be in italics (possible values are YES and NO)

BOLD   Indicates whether the tree text should be bold (possible values are YES and NO)

HEIGHT   Indicates the height of the tree in pixels

WIDTH   Indicates the width of the tree in pixels

VSPACE   Indicates the vertical space around the tree in pixels

HSPACE   Indicates the horizontal space around the tree in pixels

BORDER   Indicates whether a border should be drawn around the tree (possible values are YES and NO)

HSCROLL   Indicates whether horizontal scrolling is allowed (possible values are YES and NO)

VSCROLL   Indicates whether vertical scrolling is allowed (possible values are YES and NO)

As an example, if you adjust your CFTREE tag as follows:

```
<CFTREE NAME="TreeTest" COMPLETEPATH="YES" FONT="TimesRoman" FONTSIZE=14 BOLD="Yes"
ITALIC="Yes">
```

you end up with the tree in Figure 15.46.

FIGURE 15.46
Controlling the formatting
of a tree

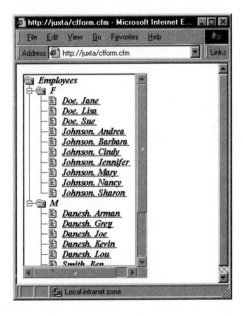

As with the other Java controls we have discussed, the NOTSUPPORTED attribute can be used to specify custom text to be displayed for browsers that do not support Java.

Where Do We Go from Here?

This has been a large but essential chapter. In it, you learned how to integrate forms—even the most basic HTML forms—into ColdFusion to create useful, interactive templates. You also learned how ColdFusion extends forms with interactive Java-based controls that allow the creation of much more sophisticated forms.

In the next chapter you will take things one step further and look at form validation. Validation is a vital part of the effective use of forms. It is through validation that the data provided by a user is checked for integrity: Required fields are checked to make sure they aren't blank and fields requiring specially formatted data are checked to make sure the entered data meets the required format. If the user has failed to enter data correctly, they are informed so that they can fix the problem.

Normally, this is a tedious process combining tedious JavaScript programming with CGI-BIN scripting. ColdFusion eliminates most of this work and automates much of the validation process.

chapter 16

Validating Form Data

- Validating Form Data Using HTML FORMS

- Validating Form Data Using CFFORM

When working with forms, you often need to *validate* the data in the form—that is, you need to make sure that required fields are filled in and that the data in the fields is consistent with the requirements of the application.

For instance, if you have a form for inserting data into a table in a database, you wouldn't want a user to provide a string value for insertion into a numeric field because if you tried to insert the string value into the database, an error would be generated. The way to avoid this problem is to validate the data entered in a form prior to using the information.

In this chapter, you will consider several approaches to validation. First you will look at traditional techniques that are not dependent on ColdFusion and work with traditional HTML forms (not with CFFORM). One method requires the use of server-side programming (in ColdFusion or any other server-side environment, including CGI-BIN). In this approach, the data in the form is submitted to a template, or script, which checks the data validity. If any data is unacceptable, a new form is generated for the user to fix the data before final processing of the information.

However, this approach requires data to be submitted to the server for validation, and then an extra form has to be sent to the user if there is invalid data. Using JavaScript, however, you can perform some validation in the client before the form is ever submitted. Putting client and server validation together, you can create a robust validation scheme using both.

ColdFusion, however, makes validation easier by providing automatically-generated JavaScript validation of many form elements generated with CFFORM. In this chapter, you will look at ColdFusion validation and consider how to leverage it to create effective validation systems for your applications.

Validating Form Data Using HTML Forms

Validating data from traditional HTML forms can be fairly straightforward, especially when using server-side validation. You will start by looking at basic server-side validation, using ColdFusion to perform this validation. Following that, you will move on to client-side validation and consider the basic JavaScript skills needed for this to work.

Server-Side Validation

The process of server-side validation is not complex:

1. The user fills in a form and submits it to a script or template on the server.
2. The script or template checks the data submitted. If all the data is valid, it is processed.

3. If the data is not valid, a new form asking for more information is presented to the user, who fills it in and submits it to the same script or template. Step 2 is then repeated.

Let's walk through these steps one by one.

Creating the Original Form

You can use any form to learn form validation. Therefore, let's work with something basic: a form asking for a person's name, phone number, and e-mail address. To make things simple, you will enforce the following validation rules when you process the form data:

- The name and phone number are required fields. The e-mail address is optional.
- The name should be no more than 50 characters in length.
- The phone number should be a seven-digit phone number in the form XXX–XXXX.
- If entered, the e-mail address should be of the form `user@host.domain`. The `host.domain` portion of the address should, at a minimum, include a single dot.
- The e-mail address should be no more than 30 characters in length.

Creating the form itself is simple, as shown in Listing 16.1.

Listing 16.1: form1.cfm

```
<FORM METHOD="POST" ACTION="submit.cfm">
<TABLE BORDER=0 CELLPADDING=5>
    <TR>
        <TD>Name</TD>
        <TD><INPUT TYPE=TEXT NAME="Name" SIZE=30 MAXLENGTH=50></TD>
    </TR>
    <TR>
        <TD>Phone</TD>
        <TD><INPUT TYPE=TEXT NAME="Phone" SIZE=8 MAXLENGTH=8></TD>
    </TR>
    <TR>
        <TD>E-mail</TD>
        <TD><INPUT TYPE=TEXT NAME="Email" SIZE=20 MAXLENGTH=30></TD>
    </TR>
    <TR>
        <TD></TD>
        <TD><INPUT TYPE=SUBMIT></TD>
    </TR>
</TABLE>
</FORM>
```

This code produces the form shown in Figure 16.1. Even before you get into server-side validation, you started the validation process in the form by using the MAXLENGTH attribute of the INPUT tag to ensure that the text entered in the fields doesn't exceed the specified maximum lengths.

FIGURE 16.1

A basic HTML form

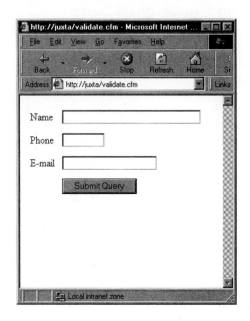

Validating the Data

Validation of the data is done in the submit.cfm template to which the data is submitted. At its most basic, the following steps need to occur:

1. Check all the fields to see if they are valid.

2. If any field is invalid, re-present the form.

Let's try this, as shown in Listing 16.2.

Listing 16.2: form2.cfm

```
<CFSET Valid = True>
<CFSET Error = "">

<!--- Check if a name has been provided --->
<CFIF Len(Form.Name) is 0>
   <CFSET Valid = False>
   <CFSET Error = Error & "A Name is required.<BR>">
</CFIF>
```

```
<!--- Check if a phone number has been provided --->
<CFIF Len(Form.Phone) is 0>
   <CFSET Valid = False>
   <CFSET Error = Error & "A Phone Number is required.<BR>">
</CFIF>

<!--- Check if the phone number is valid --->
<CFIF (Len(Form.Phone) is not 0) and (not IsNumeric(Replace(Form.Phone,"-",""))) or
Len(Replace(Form.Phone,"-",""))) is not 7)>
   <CFSET Valid = False>
   <CFSET Error = Error & "The Phone Number is invalid.<BR>">
</CFIF>

<!--- Check if the e-mail address is valid --->
<CFSET Dot = 0>
<CFSET At2 = 0>
<CFSET At = Find("@",Form.Email)>
<CFIF At greater than 0>
   <CFSET At2 = Find("@",Form.Email,At+1)>
   <CFSET Dot = Find(".",Form.Email,At+1)>
</CFIF>
<CFIF (Len(Form.Email) is not 0) and (At is 0 or At2 greater than 0 or Dot is 0)>
   <CFSET Valid = False>
   <CFSET Error = Error & "The E-mail Address is invalid.<BR>">
</CFIF>

<!--- Check if the form is valid or not --->
<CFIF not Valid>
   <STRONG>Sorry. An error occurred.</STRONG><HR>
   <CFOUTPUT>#Error#</CFOUTPUT>
   <EM>Please correct the error</EM>
   <FORM METHOD="POST" ACTION="submit.cfm">
      <TABLE BORDER=0 CELLPADDING=5>
         <TR>
            <TD>Name</TD>
            <TD><INPUT TYPE=TEXT NAME="Name" SIZE=30 MAXLENGTH=50></TD>
         </TR>
         <TR>
            <TD>Phone</TD>
            <TD><INPUT TYPE=TEXT NAME="Phone" SIZE=8 MAXLENGTH=8></TD>
         </TR>
         <TR>
            <TD>E-mail</TD>
            <TD><INPUT TYPE=TEXT NAME="Email" SIZE=20 MAXLENGTH=30></TD>
         </TR>
         <TR>
            <TD></TD>
            <TD><INPUT TYPE=SUBMIT></TD>
```

```
        </TR>
      </TABLE>
    </FORM>
<CFELSE>
    <!--- Place normal form-processing code here --->
    <H1>The Form is Valid!</H1>
</CFIF>
```

This template may seem long, but it is really rather simple. The first step is to set two variables, Valid and Error, to default values. Valid is a Boolean value indicating whether the form contains valid data. By default, the assumption is made that the form is completely valid, and the variable is set to True. Error is a string variable that will hold any error messages that need to be displayed for the user. You are assuming that the form is valid and that there are no errors to display, so initially the Error variable is the empty string.

Next you walk through a series of CFIF tags, which check all possible cases in which data would be invalid. In all cases, if the data being checked is invalid, Valid is set to False and an error message is concatenated to the Error variable by using the & operator. If more than one problem with the data exists, concatenating the errors results in all errors being displayed for the user.

You need to give some consideration to the last two CFIF tags and their conditions. First, you check whether the phone number is valid with the following CFIF tag:

```
<CFIF (Len(Form.Phone) is not 0) and (not IsNumeric(Replace(Form.Phone,"-",""")) or
Len(Replace(Form.Phone,"-",""))) is not 7)>
```

You start by making sure that the length of the phone number is not zero. This is the first condition in the CFIF tag. If the phone number is not the empty string, then two more of the following conditions are tested to check for a valid phone number in the form *XXX-XXXX*:

1. You use the Replace function to replace the dash in the phone number with the empty string, effectively deleting the dash. Then you use IsNumeric to check whether the result is a numeric value. A phone number with its dash eliminated should be a numeric value.

2. Next, you again use the Replace function to remove the dash in the phone number and then check that the length is seven digits long. All phone numbers in this example should have seven digits.

After completing these steps, you check whether the e-mail address is valid. This is a little more complicated:

```
<CFSET Dot = 0>
<CFSET At2 = 0>
<CFSET At = Find("@",Form.Email)>
<CFIF At greater than 0>
    <CFSET At2 = Find("@",Form.Email,At+1)>
    <CFSET Dot = Find(".",Form.Email,At+1)>
</CFIF>
```

```
<CFIF (Len(Form.Email) is not 0) and (At is 0 or At2 greater than 0 or Dot is 0)>
```

To check the e-mail address, you first set some default variables to zero. You will use these variables in the process of building your decision, as you will see later. Dot reflects the presence of a dot in the e-mail address whereas At2 indicates whether there is more than one at (@) symbol in the address, rendering it invalid.

Next, you use Find to search for the first occurrence of the @ symbol in the string and store the location in the At variable. Now you will check the value of the At variable. If it is greater than zero, then you may have a valid e-mail address. Therefore, you perform two more searches using the Find function. You first search from the location after the previous @ symbol for another and store the location, if found, in At2. Similarly, you search for a dot from the location after the first @ symbol and store the location, if found, in Dot.

The last step is to check whether the e-mail field is empty and if it isn't, to check whether either At or Dot is zero or whether At2 is greater than zero. If any of these three conditions are True, then you have an invalid e-mail address.

After you finish checking all the data for validity, you check the value of Valid. If it is False, you display the final error message stored in Error and then redisplay the form. Otherwise, you are free to process the data in any way you like. You won't actually process the code in this example because at this time you are concerned with the validation process and not what to do with the data once it is valid.

The end result of all of this is that if errors exist in the form, the user will be presented with the form shown in Figure 16.2.

FIGURE 16.2

If the data is invalid, the user is informed and asked to reenter the information.

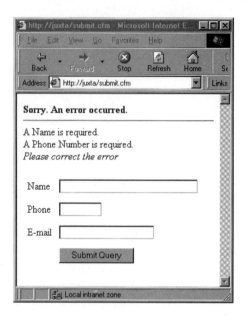

A problem needs to be addressed with this template, though. The form presented to the user for reentering information is completely blank. However, presenting a form already filled in with the user's original input is a good idea so that the user only has to alter the information already entered to make it valid instead of having to reenter all the data.

This is done quite simply by using the form variables to set the VALUE attributes of the INPUT tags in the form, as shown in Listing 16.3.

Listing 16.3: form3.cfm

```
<FORM METHOD="POST" ACTION="submit.cfm">
  <TABLE BORDER=0 CELLPADDING=5>
    <TR>
      <TD>Name</TD>
      <TD><INPUT TYPE=TEXT NAME="Name" SIZE=30 MAXLENGTH=50
VALUE="<CFOUTPUT>#Form.Name#</CFOUTPUT>"></TD>
    </TR>
    <TR>
      <TD>Phone</TD>
      <TD><INPUT TYPE=TEXT NAME="Phone" SIZE=8 MAXLENGTH=8
VALUE="<CFOUTPUT>#Form.Phone#</CFOUTPUT>"></TD>
    </TR>
```

```
            <TR>
                <TD>E-mail</TD>
                <TD><INPUT TYPE=TEXT NAME="Email" SIZE=20 MAXLENGTH=30
VALUE="<CFOUTPUT>#Form.Email#</CFOUTPUT>"></TD>
            </TR>
            <TR>
                <TD></TD>
                <TD><INPUT TYPE=SUBMIT></TD>
            </TR>
        </TABLE>
    </FORM>
```

Now, when data is invalid, the form re-presented to the user is filled in with the data they originally entered.

Of course, by presenting the user with fields to fill in, you are making it possible for them to change valid data and introduce new validity errors that weren't there in the original data.

Instead, you can present only the fields containing erroneous data to the user and store valid data in hidden fields in the new form. This requires some rethinking of your approach. Listing 16.4 illustrates the new approach you will take.

Listing 16.4: submit.cfm

```
<CFSET Valid = True>
<CFSET Error = "">
<CFSET Name = "#Form.Name#<INPUT TYPE=HIDDEN NAME=""Name"" VALUE=""#Form.Name#""">
<CFSET Phone = "#Form.Phone#<INPUT TYPE=HIDDEN NAME=""Phone""
VALUE=""#Form.Phone#""">
<CFSET Email = "#Form.Email#<INPUT TYPE=HIDDEN NAME=""Email""
VALUE=""#Form.Email#""">

<!--- Check if a name has been provided --->
<CFIF Len(Form.Name) is 0>
    <CFSET Valid = False>
    <CFSET Error = Error & "A Name is required.<BR>">
    <CFSET Name = "<INPUT TYPE=TEXT NAME=""Name"" SIZE=30 MAXLENGTH=50
VALUE=""#Form.Name#""">
</CFIF>

<!--- Check if a phone number has been provided --->
<CFIF Len(Form.Phone) is 0>
    <CFSET Valid = False>
    <CFSET Error = Error & "A Phone Number is required.<BR>">
    <CFSET Phone = "<INPUT TYPE=TEXT NAME=""Phone"" SIZE=8 MAXLENGTH=8
VALUE=""#Form.Phone#""">
</CFIF>

<!--- Check if the phone number is valid --->
<CFIF (Len(Form.Phone) is not 0) and (not IsNumeric(Replace(Form.Phone,"-",""")) or
Len(Replace(Form.Phone,"-",""")) is not 7)>
    <CFSET Valid = False>
```

```
      <CFSET Error = Error & "The Phone Number is invalid.<BR>">
      <CFSET Phone = "<INPUT TYPE=TEXT NAME=""Phone"" SIZE=8 MAXLENGTH=8
VALUE=""#Form.Phone#""">
   </CFIF>

   <!--- Check if the e-mail address is valid --->
   <CFSET Dot = 0>
   <CFSET At2 = 0>
   <CFSET At = Find("@",Form.Email)>
   <CFIF At greater than 0>
      <CFSET At2 = Find("@",Form.Email,At+1)>
      <CFSET Dot = Find(".",Form.Email,At+1)>
   </CFIF>
   <CFIF (Len(Form.Email) is not 0) and (At is 0 or At2 greater than 0 or Dot is 0)>
      <CFSET Valid = False>
      <CFSET Error = Error & "The E-mail Address is invalid.<BR>">
      <CFSET Email = "<INPUT TYPE=TEXT NAME=""Email"" SIZE=20 MAXLENGTH=30
VALUE=""#Form.Email#""">
   </CFIF>

   <!--- Check if the form is valid or not --->
   <CFIF not Valid>
      <STRONG>Sorry. An error occurred.</STRONG><HR>
      <CFOUTPUT>#Error#</CFOUTPUT>
      <EM>Please correct the error</EM>
      <FORM METHOD="POST" ACTION="submit.cfm">
         <TABLE BORDER=0 CELLPADDING=5>
            <TR>
               <TD>Name</TD>
               <TD><CFOUTPUT>#Name#</CFOUTPUT></TD>
            </TR>
            <TR>
               <TD>Phone</TD>
               <TD><CFOUTPUT>#Phone#</CFOUTPUT></TD>
            </TR>
            <TR>
               <TD>E-mail</TD>
               <TD><CFOUTPUT>#Email#</CFOUTPUT></TD>
            </TR>
            <TR>
               <TD></TD>
               <TD><INPUT TYPE=SUBMIT></TD>
            </TR>
         </TABLE>
      </FORM>
   <CFELSE>
      <!--- Place normal form-processing code here --->
      <H1>The Form is Valid!</H1>
   </CFIF>
```

What you've done here is simpler than it looks at first glance. First, you use three variables to contain the HTML code to be displayed in the form for each field. You assume that the data is all valid, so the three variables (Name, Phone, and Email) contain hidden fields with default values set to the original information entered by the user. In addition to the hidden fields, you also display the original data.

The idea here is that if the user enters valid data, a hidden form field is used to include the data in any new form you have to display to correct other information. However, you want the user to know what they have already entered, so you will display valid values in plain text so the user cannot edit them.

Then, if you encounter invalid data as you are checking each field for validity, you can change the value of the variable corresponding to that field to an editable text field containing the original data entered by the user as the default value.

Finally, in the form itself, you simply display the value of the appropriate variable in each row of the table. If there is invalid data, the resulting form has fields only for the invalid data but still displays valid data for the user's reference. The result is like that shown in Figure 16.3. Here the name field is valid so it is displayed as plain text rather than an editable form field.

FIGURE 16.3
Using hidden form fields to track valid data

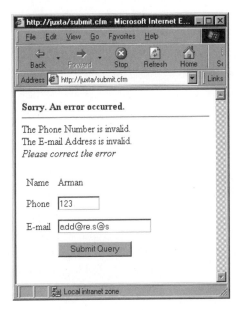

Client-Side JavaScript Validation

Server-side validation of the sort you have considered so far is an essential part of any effective validation scheme. However, the emergence of JavaScript as a de facto standard for client-side scripting makes it possible to perform some validation at the client end before submitting the form to the server.

This helps prevent unnecessary round trips to the client to fix invalid data. To build full-scale validation systems in JavaScript, you must gain a strong grasp of JavaScript. To do this, consider consulting a JavaScript book such as *Mastering JavaSript* by James Jaworski (Sybex Inc.).

Because you can't hope to learn JavaScript in the midst of a chapter on form validation, you will simply learn as you build a basic client-side validation example. If you want to build full-scale, robust, client-side validation systems for standard HTML forms, consider learning JavaScript in detail.

For the purposes of this chapter, let's turn back to our original form:

```
<FORM METHOD="POST" ACTION="submit.cfm">
<TABLE BORDER=0 CELLPADDING=5>
    <TR>
        <TD>Name</TD>
        <TD><INPUT TYPE=TEXT NAME="Name" SIZE=30 MAXLENGTH=50></TD>
    </TR>
    <TR>
        <TD>Phone</TD>
        <TD><INPUT TYPE=TEXT NAME="Phone" SIZE=8 MAXLENGTH=8></TD>
    </TR>
    <TR>
        <TD>E-mail</TD>
        <TD><INPUT TYPE=TEXT NAME="Email" SIZE=20 MAXLENGTH=30></TD>
    </TR>
    <TR>
        <TD></TD>
        <TD><INPUT TYPE=SUBMIT></TD>
    </TR>
    </TABLE>
</FORM>
```

For our validation purposes, you will simply check whether the two required fields are filled in. It is possible, in JavaScript, to perform the more complex checks on the phone number and e-mail address formats, but for the purpose of understanding the concept, you will just look at checking whether required fields contain data.

The process of client-side validation with JavaScript requires two steps:

1. Developing a validation function

2. Ensuring that the function is called before submitting the form

You will look at these in reverse order.

Calling a JavaScript Function When Submitting a Form

JavaScript extends basic HTML to include event handlers. *Event handlers* specify Java-Script code to execute when the user performs specific actions, including submitting a form.

To specify a function to call when submitting a form, you use the ONSUBMIT attribute of the FORM tag:

```
<FORM METHOD="POST" ACTION="submit.cfm" ONSUBMIT="return validate(this)">
```

Here you use ONSUBMIT to call a function called validate, which you will develop in the next section of this chapter. You pass a special keyword to the function, this, which effectively passes the form to the function.

The only requirement of the function is that it should return True if the data is valid and can be submitted, or False if the data is not valid and the form cannot be submitted.

Developing a Validation Function

Now you need to turn to your validation function. The first thing to consider is how to include SCRIPT tags:

```
<SCRIPT LANGUAGE="JavaScript1.2">
<!-- HIDE SCRIPT FROM OTHER BROWSERS

    Script goes here

// END OF SCRIPT -->
</SCRIPT>
```

You specify the language of the script with the LANGUAGE attribute of the SCRIPT tag. You also enclose the script inside HTML comments so that browsers that don't support JavaScript don't display the text of the script.

The function itself is built as follows:

```
function validate(testform) {

    JavaScript validation code

}
```

The `function` keyword indicates that you are defining a function. This keyword is followed by the name of the function, followed by parameters to the function in parentheses. Here you have one parameter called `testform`. This means that throughout the function you can refer to the object form passed as an argument as `testform`.

Now, you turn to the code of the function itself. The logic you will use is outlined in the following steps:

1. Test the `Name` field to see whether it is filled. If it isn't, ask the user to fill in the field and return `false` to prevent the form from being submitted.

2. Test the `Phone` field to see whether it is filled. If it isn't, ask the user to fill in the field and return `false` to prevent the form from being submitted.

3. When both `Name` and `Phone` are filled in, return `true` to allow the form to be submitted.

Let's work through this procedure. First you test the `Name` field:

```
if (testform.Name.value == "") {
    window.alert("Please fill in a Name.");
    return false;
}
```

The `if` statement tests the value of the `Name` field in the form and compares it to the empty string. If it is empty, an alert dialog box like the one shown in the following graphic is displayed.

If the `Name` field is not empty, then the function will move on to test the `Phone` field:

```
if (testform.Phone.value == "") {
    window.alert("Please fill in a Phone Number.");
    return false;
}
```

This code works in the same way as when you tested the `Name` field.

Finally, if you get past both `if` statements (in other words, both fields contain text), then you return `true`, allowing the form to be submitted:

```
return true;
```

The end result is the following complete document shown in Listing 16.5.

Listing 16.5: form5.cfm

```
<SCRIPT LANGUAGE="JavaScript1.2">
<!-- HIDE SCRIPT FROM OTHER BROWSERS

function validate(testform) {

    if (testform.Name.value == "") {
        window.alert("Please fill in a Name.");
        return false;
    }

    if (testform.Phone.value == "") {
        window.alert("Please fill in a Phone Number.");
        return false;
    }

    return true;

}

// END OF SCRIPT -->
</SCRIPT>

<FORM METHOD="POST" ACTION="submit.cfm" ONSUBMIT="return validate(this)">
<TABLE BORDER=0 CELLPADDING=5>
    <TR>
        <TD>Name</TD>
        <TD><INPUT TYPE=TEXT NAME="Name" SIZE=30 MAXLENGTH=50></TD>
    </TR>
    <TR>
        <TD>Phone</TD>
        <TD><INPUT TYPE=TEXT NAME="Phone" SIZE=8 MAXLENGTH=8></TD>
    </TR>
    <TR>
        <TD>E-mail</TD>
        <TD><INPUT TYPE=TEXT NAME="Email" SIZE=20 MAXLENGTH=30></TD>
    </TR>
    <TR>
        <TD></TD>
        <TD><INPUT TYPE=SUBMIT></TD>
    </TR>
</TABLE>
</FORM>
```

The nice thing about JavaScript, though, is that it allows for even more interactivity. For instance, you can use JavaScript to display a dialog box prompting the user to enter the required data, as shown in the following graphic.

This type of dialog box is achieved using the JavaScript `prompt` function:

```
window.prompt("Please fill in a Name.","");
```

The function returns the value entered by the user and therefore should be assigned to a variable:

```
testform.Name.value = window.prompt("Please fill in a Name.","");
```

Applied to your function, the logic changes slightly:

```
function validate(testform) {

    while (testform.Name.value == "") {
        testform.Name.value = window.prompt("Please fill in a Name.","");
    }


    while (testform.Phone.value == "") {
        testform.Phone.value = window.prompt("Please fill in a Phone Number.","");
    }

    return true;


}
```

What you are doing here is using `while` loops to force the user to provide the required data. For instance, the first `while` loop, translated into plain English, says: As long as the value in the Name field in the form is the empty string, continue prompting the user for a name and store the name provided in the Name field of the form. This means that as long as the user continues to respond to the prompt by providing no data, they will continue to be prompted for data; they can't avoid providing some information for the required fields.

Validating Form Data Using *CFFORM*

Nothing that you have seen so far in this chapter requires the use of ColdFusion-specific capabilities. For instance, all the server-side validation you did could just as easily have been done in Perl, JavaScript, or C++. Similarly, the JavaScript-based client-side validation you did requires no use of ColdFusion.

However, ColdFusion provides its own mechanisms for validating form data in ColdFusion-based forms built out of the CFFORM tag. This doesn't mean that validation can be 100 percent automated with ColdFusion, but it can come close, especially when a form uses basic form elements such as text fields.

You will look at the following aspects of ColdFusion validation:

- Ensuring that required fields are filled in
- Ensuring that text fields contain properly formatted data
- Enhancing validation with JavaScript

Ensuring That Required Fields Are Filled In

All the ColdFusion form tags (CFINPUT, CFSELECT, CFTABLE, and so on) with the exception of CFGRID and CFSLIDER provide two attributes that allow client-side validation of required fields. These attributes are REQUIRED and MESSAGE. Much like our attempts at JavaScript code to ensure that required fields are filled in, these attributes cause ColdFusion to generate the JavaScript code needed to validate any and all required form fields.

Let's start with our original form converted to ColdFusion tags, as shown in Listing 16.6.

Listing 16.6: cfform1.cfm

```
<CFFORM METHOD="POST" ACTION="submit.cfm">
<TABLE BORDER=0 CELLPADDING=5>
    <TR>
        <TD>Name</TD>
        <TD><CFINPUT TYPE=TEXT NAME="Name" SIZE=30 MAXLENGTH=50></TD>
    </TR>
    <TR>
        <TD>Phone</TD>
        <TD><CFINPUT TYPE=TEXT NAME="Phone" SIZE=8 MAXLENGTH=8></TD>
    </TR>
    <TR>
        <TD>E-mail</TD>
        <TD><CFINPUT TYPE=TEXT NAME="Email" SIZE=20 MAXLENGTH=30></TD>
    </TR>
    <TR>
        <TD></TD>
```

```
        <TD><INPUT TYPE=SUBMIT></TD>
      </TR>
    </TABLE>
  </CFFORM>
```

You can use the REQUIRED attribute to ensure that the required fields are filled in prior to form submission. This attribute can take the value YES or NO. In this case, you will use REQUIRED="YES" in both the Name and Phone fields, as shown in Listing 16.7.

Listing 16.7: cfform2.cfm

```
<CFFORM METHOD="POST" ACTION="submit.cfm">
<TABLE BORDER=0 CELLPADDING=5>
    <TR>
        <TD>Name</TD>
        <TD><CFINPUT TYPE=TEXT NAME="Name" SIZE=30 MAXLENGTH=50 REQUIRED="YES"></
TD>
    </TR>
    <TR>
        <TD>Phone</TD>
        <TD><CFINPUT TYPE=TEXT NAME="Phone" SIZE=8 MAXLENGTH=8 REQUIRED="YES"></
TD>
    </TR>
    <TR>
        <TD>E-mail</TD>
        <TD><CFINPUT TYPE=TEXT NAME="Email" SIZE=20 MAXLENGTH=30></TD>
    </TR>
    <TR>
        <TD></TD>
        <TD><INPUT TYPE=SUBMIT></TD>
    </TR>
  </TABLE>
</CFFORM>
```

When you do this, ColdFusion generates all the JavaScript code needed for form validation:

```
<script LANGUAGE=JAVASCRIPT>

<!--

function _CF_onError(form_object, input_object, object_value, error_message)
    {
  alert(error_message);
        return false;
    }
```

```
function _CF_hasValue(obj, obj_type)
  {
  if (obj_type == "TEXT" || obj_type == "PASSWORD")
  {
     if (obj.value.length == 0)
         return false;
     else
         return true;
     }
  else if (obj_type == "SELECT")
  {
      for (i=0; i < obj.length; i++)
        {
     if (obj.options[i].selected)
       return true;
     }

         return false;
  }
  else if (obj_type == "SINGLE_VALUE_RADIO" || obj_type ==
"SINGLE_VALUE_CHECKBOX")
  {

     if (obj.checked)
        return true;
     else
           return false;
  }
  else if (obj_type == "RADIO" || obj_type == "CHECKBOX")
  {

      for (i=0; i < obj.length; i++)
        {
     if (obj[i].checked)
       return true;
     }

         return false;
  }
  }


function  _CF_checkCFForm_1(_CF_this)

   {

   if  (!_CF_hasValue(_CF_this.Name, "TEXT" ))
```

```
        {

          if  (!_CF_onError(_CF_this, _CF_this.Name, _CF_this.Name.value, "Error in
Name text."))

              {

              return false;

              }

          }


      if  (!_CF_hasValue(_CF_this.Phone, "TEXT" ))

          {

          if  (!_CF_onError(_CF_this, _CF_this.Phone, _CF_this.Phone.value, "Error in
Phone text."))

              {

              return false;

              }

          }


      return true;

          }


  //-->

  </script>

  <FORM NAME="CFForm_1" ACTION="submit.cfm" METHOD=POST onSubmit="return
_CF_checkCFForm_1(this)">
    <TABLE BORDER=0 CELLPADDING=5>
        <TR>
          <TD>Name</TD>
          <TD><INPUT TYPE="TEXT" NAME="Name" SIZE=30 MAXLENGTH= 50></TD>
        </TR>
        <TR>
```

```
        <TD>Phone</TD>
        <TD><INPUT TYPE="TEXT" NAME="Phone" SIZE=8 MAXLENGTH= 8></TD>
    </TR>
    <TR>
        <TD>E-mail</TD>
        <TD><INPUT TYPE="TEXT" NAME="Email" SIZE=20 MAXLENGTH= 30></TD>
    </TR>
    <TR>
        <TD></TD>
        <TD><INPUT TYPE=SUBMIT></TD>
    </TR>
    </TABLE>
</FORM>
```

When this form is used, attempts to submit the form without filling the required fields generates JavaScript alert dialog boxes like the following one.

However, the default message used by the ColdFusion-generated JavaScript functions doesn't provide much useful information. You can adjust this with the MESSAGE attribute. You use this function to specify an alternative error message to the default one provided by ColdFusion:

```
<CFINPUT TYPE=TEXT NAME="Name" SIZE=30 MAXLENGTH=50 REQUIRED="YES" MESSAGE="Please
enter a name.">
```

The REQUIRED and MESSAGE attributes can be used with any of the ColdFusion form field tags.

Ensuring That Text Fields Contain Properly Formatted Data

When using ColdFusion text fields (CFINPUT or CFTEXTINPUT), you can implement client-side validation of the data's format in the fields. This is done using the VALIDATE attribute. This attribute takes one of the following values:

Date   Validates field data as a U.S. date in the format mm/dd/yy.

EuroDate   Validates field data as a European date in the format dd/mm/yyyy.

Time   Validates field data as a time in the format hh:mm:ss.

Float   Validates field data as a floating-point number.

Integer   Validates field data as an integer number.

Telephone   Validates field data as a U.S. phone number in the format XXX-XXX-XXXX or *XXX XXX XXXX*. The area code and the exchange must start with digits between 1 and 9.

Zipcode   Validates field data as a U.S. five-digit or nine-digit ZIP code in the format *XXXXX*, XXXXX-XXXX, or *XXXXX XXXX*.

Creditcard   Validates field data as a credit card number. Blanks or dashes can be included in the number.

Social_security_number   Validates field data as a U.S. Social Security number in the format XXX-XX-XXXX or *XXX XX XXXX*.

Using the VALIDATE attribute implements client-side JavaScript validation just as using REQUIRED does. In fact, it uses the same default message for failure as does REQUIRED, which can be overridden with the MESSAGE attribute.

As an example, consider the Phone field in your form. If you extend your specification to require a full U.S.-style phone number with an area code, you can use ColdFusion to implement format verification by adjusting your CFINPUT tag accordingly:

```
<TD><CFINPUT TYPE=TEXT NAME="Phone" SIZE=12 MAXLENGTH=12 REQUIRED="YES"
VALIDATE="Telephone" MESSAGE="The phone number is either missing or invalid.">
```

Because the same custom message is being used both when the field fails to be filled in and when it contains improperly formatted data, the text of the message has to be written in a way to convey both possible errors. The VALIDATE and REQUIRE validation failures do not have unique error messages.

Enhancing Validation with JavaScript

The ColdFusion validation attributes you have looked at so far have addressed only forcing a field to be required and checking the data provided in text fields. At other times, however, it may be necessary to validate the data provided in other fields. For instance, you may need to check that certain combinations of data in check boxes, radio buttons, select lists, or sliders are provided correctly by the user.

In these instances, you need to do some manual JavaScript programming to implement client-side validation. However, ColdFusion provides two attributes that help enhance the process: ONVALIDATE and ONERROR.

The ONVALIDATE attribute is used with CFINPUT, CFGRID, CFSLIDER, CFTEXTINPUT, and CFTREE to specify the name of a JavaScript function of your own creation to handle input validation. You won't look at the details of writing the JavaScript here but will simply outline the information needed to implement JavaScript validation functions, given knowledge of JavaScript.

The function will be passed three objects: the form object, the field object being validated, and the value of the field object being validated. This means a function can be written that works entirely independently of the form itself because it has all the information it needs available to it.

Therefore, in writing a function for use with ONVALIDATE, you must write the relevant function definition to take into account the three objects being passed to it. An example is the following:

```
Function FieldTest(TheForm,TheField,TheValue) {

    Validation Code Goes Here

}
```

Consider our simple form. What you haven't been able to test using the other validation attributes is the validity of the e-mail address if one is entered. You could use ONVALIDATE to play that role. First, you specify the name of a function to call in the appropriate CFINPUT tag:

```
<TD><CFINPUT TYPE=TEXT NAME="Email" SIZE=20 MAXLENGTH=30 ONVALIDATE="TestEmail"></TD>
```

Next, you write your validation function:

```
<SCRIPT LANGUAGE="JavaScript1.2">
<!--START OF SCRIPT

function TestEmail(TheForm,TheField,TheValue) {

    if (TheValue != "") {
        at = TheValue.indexOf('@',0);
        if (TheValue == -1 || TheValue.indexOf('.',at) == -1) {
            return false;
        }
    }

    return true;

}

// END SCRIPT -->
</SCRIPT>
```

If the e-mail address meets the specification, True is returned; otherwise, False is returned. If False is the result, the default ColdFusion error alert dialog box is displayed.

In addition to supporting a custom function for validation, you can specify a custom function to execute if validation fails. This is done using the ONERROR attribute with the CFGRID, CFINPUT, CFSELECT, CFSLIDER, CFTEXTINPUT, and CFTREE tags.

Functions designed for use with ONERROR work in much the same way as those with ONVALIDATE except that one extra attribute is passed to the function: the error message associated with the error. For instance, if you want a custom function to handle errors generated in our preceding example, you can add the ONERROR attribute to the CFINPUT tag:

```
<TD><CFINPUT TYPE=TEXT NAME="Email" SIZE=20 MAXLENGTH=30 ONVALIDATE="TestEmail"
ONERROR="EmailError"></TD>
```

Then, you write your JavaScript function:

```
<SCRIPT LANGUAGE="JavaScript1.2">
<!--START OF SCRIPT

function EmailError(TheForm,TheField,TheValue,TheError) {

    Custom error handling code
    return false;

}

// END SCRIPT -->
</SCRIPT>
```

The only critical point to note about writing functions to work with the ONERROR attribute is that they should return a False value.

Where Do We Go from Here?

In this chapter, you finished looking at forms and the ways in which ColdFusion enhances them, making them more programmer and user friendly.

Going forward, you will move on to an important topic: the Web Application Framework. ColdFusion offers more than just the capability to develop individual, interactive templates. It also offers the capability to build applications out of collections of templates.

Using the Web Application Framework, these sets of templates can work together in an integrated fashion to develop anything from complete Internet commerce systems, including shopping carts and account management, to a functional guest book system.

In the next chapter, you will look at all the major aspects of the Web Application Framework, including application-level settings and client-state management.

chapter 17

Implementing the ColdFusion Web Application Framework

The ColdFusion Application Framework is a set of ColdFusion templates that enables you to:

- Maintain state by setting variables that can be accessed from any template in your application framework.
- Provide custom error messages. Customized error handling is discussed in more detail in Chapter 18, "Implementing Error Control."
- Enhance the security of an application. Application security is discussed in more detail in Chapter 30, "Application Security."

In this chapter, you will learn how to maintain variable states by setting up and using the features of the ColdFusion Application Framework.

Creating the ColdFusion Application Framework

Until this point, you have coded ColdFusion templates that enable you to query databases, create arrays and lists, validate form input, and pass variables between templates. Yet you have not been able to maintain *state* over a series of templates. Maintaining state enables you to access information set in previous templates without having to pass that information between templates. In past chapters, whenever you wanted to access variables set in a previous template, you had to ensure that they were passed along either through URL or form parameters, or by storing them in a database for later access. Cold-Fusion lets you also store this information in variables that are available to any template within your application. The types of variables that are designed to work with the Cold-Fusion Application Framework are listed in Table 17.1. You will learn more about creating and managing these variables later in this chapter.

TABLE 17.1:   Variable Types

Variable Type	Description
Client	Tied to a single client (or browser) and can persist over multiple sessions
Session	Exists for one client during a single session
Application	Tied to a single application and accessible by multiple clients
Server	Accessible by all clients and applications on a single server

Creating the *Application.cfm* Template

To use the ColdFusion Application Framework, you must first create a single application template in the root directory of your application. This template must be named `Application.cfm` (see Figure 17.1). After the `Application.cfm` template has been created, it will be included at the beginning of every template processed within the application framework.

> **WARNING** If you are using a Unix platform, the name of your application file must be `Application.cfm` (not `application.cfm`) in order for it to be recognized. This is because Unix is a case-sensitive environment.

FIGURE 17.1
Example of the `Applica-tion.cfm` template

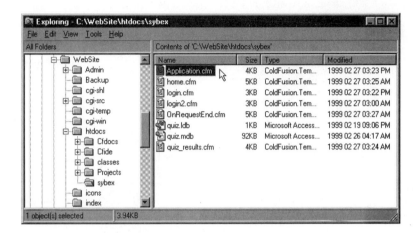

Creating the *OnRequestEnd.cfm* Template

From ColdFusion 4.0.1 you can also create a template that will be processed at the end of every page in your application framework. You can use this template, called `OnRequest-End.cfm`, to create a standard footer for all pages of your application or to execute a set of code after all the processing in the caller template has occurred. This is an optional template and is not required to make the application framework operational. This template must reside in the same directory as the template being processed. If you create this template, it cannot be of zero length, or ColdFusion will produce an error.

> **WARNING** If you are using a Unix platform, the name of your OnRequestEnd file must be `OnRequest-End.cfm` (not `onrequestend.cfm`) in order for it to be recognized. This is because Unix is a case-sensitive environment.

Understanding the Application Directory Structure

The application framework consists of all templates in the specified directory and any subdirectories. It is processed as follows:

1. The user connects to a ColdFusion template.

2. Before the template is processed, ColdFusion checks the directory in which the template resides for an `Application.cfm` template.

3. If no `Application.cfm` is found, ColdFusion looks to the next higher level directory until one is found.

4. If no `Application.cfm` is ever found, then processing of the template takes place as usual, and it is not tied to any ColdFusion application.

5. If `Application.cfm` is found, `Application.cfm` is processed first, and then the template is processed.

6. After the template has been processed, ColdFusion searches the same directory for `OnRequestEnd.cfm`.

7. If no `OnRequestEnd.cfm` is found, nothing else happens (ColdFusion looks only in the current directory for `OnRequestEnd.cfm`).

8. If `OnRequestEnd.cfm` is found in the same directory, then it is processed and included at the end of the template.

WARNING   If ColdFusion encounters an error, **CFABORT** tag, or **CFEXIT** tag, the `OnRequestEnd.cfm` file will not be processed.

The `Application.cfm` template is useful because in it you can create global settings that can then be accessed by all templates in your application directory structure. You can use `OnRequestEnd.cfm` to process a standard footer for every template in your application.

Look at the example in Figure 17.2. When the `index.cfm` template is called, ColdFusion checks whether an `Application.cfm` template is in the `chapter17` directory. Because one is not there, ColdFusion then looks in its parent directory, `sybex`. Because an `Application.cfm` template is in the `sybex` directory, it is processed first, and then the `index.cfm` template is processed.

FIGURE 17.2

The `Application.cfm` template is in the parent directory `sybex`.

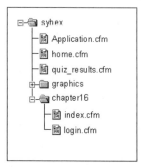

In the example in Figure 17.3, when the `index.cfm` template is called, ColdFusion finds an `Application.cfm` template in the `chapter17` directory. This `Application.cfm` template is processed instead of the one in the `sybex` parent directory.

FIGURE 17.3

Both directories have their own `Application.cfm` templates.

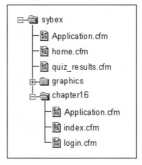

Only one `Application.cfm` template and one `OnRequestEnd.cfm` template is ever processed. Remember this when you are including other files within your template. If you include the `login.cfm` template in the `home.cfm` template by using the CFINCLUDE tag, the only `Application.cfm` file that will be processed is the one in the `sybex` directory (see Figure 17.3). If you want the `Application.cfm` template in the `chapter17` directory to be processed, then you must explicitly include it by using the CFINCLUDE tag.

Understanding Details of the *Application.cfm* Template

Your `Application.cfm` template is where you define the settings for your application. The following list demonstrates various types of functionality you can code into your `Application.cfm` template; you can:

- Enable session, client, and application management, which allows you to use session, client, and application variables
- Set timeouts for the application and any sessions tied to it
- Define the location where you want to store client variables
- Define global settings such as data sources, fonts, colors, etc.
- Authorize access to the application templates by verifying user permissions
- Account for application errors and create customized error pages

To enable session, client, and application management in an `Application.cfm` template, you should use the CFAPPLICATION tag. The following code displays the syntax for the CFAPPLICATION tag and Table 17.2 details the attributes of this tag.

```
<CFAPPLICATION NAME="Name"
CLIENTMANAGEMENT="Yes/No"
```

```
SESSIONMANAGEMENT="Yes/No"
SETCLIENTCOOKIES="Yes/No"
SESSIONTIMEOUT="#CreateTimeSpan(days, hours, minutes, seconds)#"
APPLICATIONTIMEOUT="#CreateTimeSpan(days, hours, minutes, seconds)#"
CLIENTSTORAGE="registry/cookie/name of data source"
SetDomainCookies="Yes/No"
>
```

TABLE 17.2: CFAPPLICATION Tag Attributes

Attribute	Description	Value	Default	Required
NAME	The name of a given application (maximum of 64 characters in length). In version 4.0.1 the name is required in case you have session variables tied to two separate applications.	Name	n/a	yes
SESSIONMANAGEMENT	Enables session variables.	Yes/No	No *	no
SESSIONTIMEOUT	A time limit to specify when a session has expired.	#CreateTime-Span(days, hours, minutes, seconds)#	*	no
CLIENTMANAGEMENT	Enables client variables.	Yes/No	No	no
CLIENTSTORAGE	Specifies where ColdFusion should store client variables.	registry/ cookie/ name of a data source **	registry *	no
SETCLIENTCOOKIES	Specifies whether ColdFusion uses cookies when defining client and session variables.	Yes/No	Yes	no
SETDOMAINCOOKIES	Specifies whether ColdFusion should set CFID and CFTOKEN cookies at the domain level for sharing client variables in a cluster.	Yes/No	No	no
APPLICATIONTIMEOUT	A time limit to specify when the application has expired.	#CreateTime-Span(days, hours, minutes, seconds)#	*	no

* Default specified in the ColdFusion Administrator

** When using clusters you cannot use 'registry' for ClientStorage.

A basic Application.cfm template might look like that in the following code. This code shows how to turn on session management, set timeouts for both the application and a user session, turn on client management, set application and server constants such as standard background color and font face, and test whether a user has logged in. You are not expected to understand the code at this point; later in this chapter you will learn in more detail about the interactions coded in this template.

```
<!--- Application.cfm --->

<!DOCTYPE HTML PUBLIC "-//W3C//DTD HTML 4.0 Transitional//EN">

<!----------------------------------------------------------------
This template enables the application framework and is
included at the beginning of every file within its application
scope.
----------------------------------------------------------------->

<!----------------------------------------------------------------
Set application name; client variables on; session variables on;
allow cookies; session timeout after 20 minutes; application
timeout after 2 days; store client variables in registry
----------------------------------------------------------------->
<CFAPPLICATION NAME="MyApp"
    SESSIONMANAGEMENT="Yes"
    SETCLIENTCOOKIES="Yes"
    SESSIONTIMEOUT="#CreateTimeSpan(0, 0, 20, 0)#"
    APPLICATIONTIMEOUT="#CreateTimeSpan(2, 0, 0, 0)#"
    CLIENTMANAGEMENT="Yes"
    CLIENTSTORAGE="Registry">

<!----------------------------------------------------------------
Set Server constants that can be accessed by any client
----------------------------------------------------------------->
<CFLOCK TIMEOUT="30"
    THROWONTIMEOUT="Yes"
    NAME="server"
    TYPE="Exclusive">
    <CFIF NOT #ISDEFINED("server.season")#>
        <!------------------------------------------------
        The season is currently set to a string, but could
        easily be determined automatically by time of year.
        ------------------------------------------------->
        <CFSET SERVER.SEASON = "Spring Time">
    </CFIF>
</CFLOCK>

<!----------------------------------------------------------------
Set Application constants
----------------------------------------------------------------->
<CFLOCK TIMEOUT="30"
```

```
     THROWONTIMEOUT="Yes"
     NAME="#Application.ApplicationName#"
     TYPE="Exclusive">
     <CFIF NOT #ISDEFINED("Application.Started")#>
        <CFSET APPLICATION.TITLE = "My Quiz Application">
        <CFSET APPLICATION.DB = "quiz">
        <CFSET APPLICATION.EMAIL = "kmotlagh@geocities.com">
        <CFSET APPLICATION.BGCOLOR = "##ffffff">
        <CFSET APPLICATION.FACE = "Arial">
        <CFSET APPLICATION.STARTED = TRUE>
     </CFIF>
</CFLOCK>

<!---------------------------------------------------------------
Test to see if user has logged in
--------------------------------------------------------------->
<CFLOCK TIMEOUT="30"
     THROWONTIMEOUT="Yes"
     NAME="#Session.SessionID#"
     TYPE="ReadOnly">
     <CFIF NOT ISDEFINED("Session.Started")>
        <CFSET LOGIN = "">
     </CFIF>
</CFLOCK>

<CFIF ISDEFINED("Login")>
     <!-------------------------------------------------------
     Tests to see if user is logging in.  Since the
     session.initialized variable has not yet been set, the
     processing of the login2.cfm would be aborted unless the
     following cfif statement is added
     ------------------------------------------------------->
     <CFSET PATH=GETDIRECTORYFROMPATH(#CGI.CF_TEMPLATE_PATH#)>
     <CFIF (CGI.CF_TEMPLATE_PATH IS NOT "#path#login.cfm")
     AND (CGI.CF_TEMPLATE_PATH IS NOT "#path#login2.cfm")>
        <CFINCLUDE TEMPLATE="login.cfm">

        <!-------------------------------------------------
        Aborts processing of any template except login.cfm
        and login2.cfm until user has logged in
        ------------------------------------------------->
        <CFABORT>
     </CFIF>
</CFIF>
```

Working with Application Scope

Now that you know how to create the `Application.cfm` template, you need to learn how to use the variables associated with the ColdFusion Application Framework. These variables are listed in Table 17.1. Each of these variable types has a particular *scope* within the framework of the application. The scope refers to the time and location that a particular variable is available for use. It is important to understand the different scopes of each application variable type in order to know when a variable should be used. If you use the wrong type of variable at the wrong time, you could risk making your application insecure, loading too much data into the server's memory, or losing information that you wanted to store indefinitely. Table 17.1 briefly details the scope of each type of variable. A more in-depth discussion of each variable scope is included in other sections of this chapter.

Using Client Management

Client variables are associated with a single client (or browser) and can persist over multiple sessions. This means that if you set a client variable for a user who has visited your site, that variable will be stored and can be retrieved during the user's next visit (provided they connect using the same client). If Person A and Person B visit your site, each will have access only to the client variables set for their client. Person A would not be able to see Person B's client variables. This restriction is useful because it enables you to track user information over a period of visits.

ColdFusion defines a client through the application name specified in the CFAPPLICATION tag and by setting two cookies: CFID and CFTOKEN.

CFID   An incremented ID for each client that connects to the server

CFTOKEN   A random number used in conjunction with CFID to uniquely identify a particular client

ColdFusion sets these cookies only once (in previous versions they were set at every page request). ColdFusion, by default, also stores these two variables in the registry with any other client variables that have been set. The registry is the default storage mechanism, but cookies or a data source can also be used.

When a user connects to an application with ClientManagement enabled, ColdFusion determines whether the CFID and CFTOKEN cookies exist. If they do, then the associated client variables are stored in the specified storage mechanism (the registry is the default) and are available for use to that client. If not, then ColdFusion sets a new CFID and CFTOKEN for that client in the storage mechanism and with the client (using cookies).

Another client variable, called URLTOKEN, is added to the storage device. This is a combination of the CFID and CFTOKEN variables. URLTOKEN can be used to pass the CFID and CFTOKEN values through URL or form parameters in case cookies have been disabled on the client side.

Examples of using client variables include storing the following:

- User display preferences such as background colors, page layouts, font faces
- User content preferences such as feature stories, stock preferences, favorite links
- Counts of how many times a user has visited and when they visited last
- Items in a shopping cart and past purchases
- Scores for quizzes or games

Because the default storage space for client variables is the registry, it is wise not to store too much information in client variables.

Enabling Client State Management

Client variables are enabled using the CFAPPLICATION tag in the Application.cfm template (see Table 17.2). Because client variables are tied to a particular application, a name must be specified in the CFAPPLICATION tag by using the NAME attribute. The CLIENT-MANAGEMENT attribute must also be set to YES. The location to store all client variables can be specified using the CLIENTSTORAGE attribute. The default storage space is the registry. The optional storage spaces include:

Registry   Variables are stored by default for 90 days.

Cookie   All built-in client variables and any client variables set within an application are stored in the CFGLOBALS cookie on the client side. There are limitations to using cookie for storing your client variables. These limitations are discussed in more detail later in this section. The default storage time for cookies is approximately 38 years.

External data source   An ODBC or native data source can be used to store client variables for a default of 10 days. This data source needs to be set up in the ColdFusion Administrator as described later in this section.

WARNING   If you are using ColdFusion on a cluster, the CLIENTSTORAGE value must be either a data source name or cookie. You cannot use registry as a CLIENTSTORAGE value.

You also have the option of specifying whether to use cookies for storing only your CFID and CFTOKEN variables by using the SETCLIENTCOOKIES attribute. If you choose to prohibit the use of cookies, you must be prepared to pass both the CFID and CFTOKEN variables through URL or form parameters on every template of your application. You would do this by using the URLTOKEN client variable. This is discussed later in the section "Client State Management and Cookies." If these variables are not passed, you risk losing control of client management.

The following code shows the syntax of a CFAPPLICATION tag that has enabled client variables, allowed the use of cookies to store the CFID and CFTOKEN, and specified the storage space as the registry.

```
<CFAPPLICATION NAME="MyApp"
CLIENTMANAGEMENT="Yes"
SETCLIENTCOOKIES="Yes"
CLIENTSTORAGE="registry">
```

Using the ColdFusion Administrator

You can use the ColdFusion Administrator to change the default storage mechanism for your client variables. This change will indicate which storage mechanism is used for each application on the server unless otherwise specified within the Application.cfm template. When you open the ColdFusion Administrator, select the Variables option under the Server section on the left-hand frame (see Figure 17.4).

FIGURE 17.4
Client variable settings in the ColdFusion Administrator

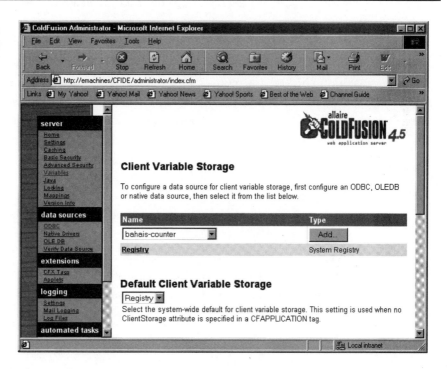

Adding a Client Storage Data Source

In the first section of the ColdFusion Administrator Variables page, called Client Variable Storage, you can add a configured data source. You would add a data source if you want to store your client variables in a database as opposed to the registry or cookies. Advantages of storing client variables in a database include:

- The ability to easily view information related to all clients of an application
- The ability to query the data from this database
- The option to easily port the data from one server to another

Before you can add a data source in this section, you must have already configured your data source in the Data Source section of the ColdFusion Administrator.

> **NOTE** For more information on configuring a data source, refer to Chapter 3, "Getting Data From A Database" or Chapter 35, "ColdFusion Administration."

After you configure your data source, it is available to you under the pull-down Name menu. Select the data source you wish to add for client storage, then select Add. Follow the instructions on the next screen to create the client storage data source.

When a client storage data source is added, two tables are created in the data source database. The first table, CDATA, stores information in the following field names:

cfid Stores a combination of the CFID and CFTOKEN variables (text field that holds a maximum of 20 characters)

app Stores the application name (text field that holds a maximum of 64 characters)

data- Stores a combination of the HITCOUNT, LASTVISIT, and TIMECREATED variables (memo field)

The second table, CGLOBAL, stores additional information in the following field names:

cfid- Stores a combination of the CFID and CFTOKEN variables (text field that holds a maximum of 20 characters)

data- Stores a combination of the HITCOUNT, LASTVISIT, and TIMECREATED variables (memo field)

lvisit- Stores the date and time of a client's last visit (Date/Time field)

You should notice that Registry is already available with a type of System Registry. If you select Registry, you will see a screen (see Figure 17.5) where you can modify the default expiration time period for client variables stored in the registry. The default is 90 days.

> **NOTE** If you need more assistance with client variable storage, please refer to Chapter 35.

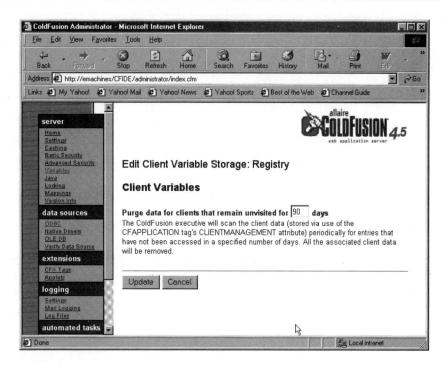

FIGURE 17.5
Registry for Client Variable
Storage

Setting the Default Client Variable Storage

The second section of the Variables screen is for setting the default storage mechanism for client variables. The two options available are *registry* and *cookie*. Registry is the default when ColdFusion is first installed.

If Registry is chosen, then all client variables for any ColdFusion application on your server will be stored in the server registry unless otherwise stated in the application's CFAPPLICATION tag.

WARNING   If you are using ColdFusion on a cluster, the CLIENTSTORAGE value must be either a data source name or cookie. You cannot use registry as a CLIENTSTORAGE value.

If Cookie is chosen, then all client variables for any ColdFusion application on your server will be stored in a client-side cookie called CFGLOBALS (unless otherwise stated in the application's CFAPPLICATION tag). Be careful in choosing this option! Check the warnings about using cookies later in the section "Client State Management and Cookies."

If you want to specify a data source as your client storage mechanism, you must have first added the data source under Client Variable Storage (described in the previous section). Then you can select the data source in the pull-down menu.

Working with Client Variables

Now that you've enabled client management, you are ready to start creating and using client variables. Client variables are set and accessed in basically the same manner as standard variables. The difference, of course, is that client variables are persistent and can be referenced from any template within a ColdFusion application.

NOTE For information on creating and referring to standard variable types, please see Chapter 4, "Creating and Manipulating Variables."

Creating Client Variables

To create a client variable, you must use the CFSET or CFPARAM tags. You must also scope your variable name with the prefix `client`. If you do not scope the variable with `client`, then it will be created as a standard ColdFusion variable and only be accessible to the current template. The following code sets a passed form field equal to the client variable `client.user_name`.

```
<CFPARAM NAME="client.user_name" DEFAULT="#form.user_name#">
```

or

```
<CFSET CLIENT.USER_NAME="#form.user_name#">
```

WARNING Arrays, structures, and query recordsets cannot be stored in client variables. Client variables are also limited to 255 characters.

Referring to Client Variables

Referring to client variables is as simple as creating them. Just follow the standard rules for accessing any variable. Remember that when you refer to a variable within a Cold-Fusion tag, you generally do not need to use pound signs. Here are two examples of referring to the client variable `client.user_name`:

```
<CFIF NOT IsDefined("client.user_name")>
insert code here…
</CFIF>
```

and

```
<CFOUTPUT>#client.user_name#</CFOUTPUT>
```

Although you don't have to use the `client` prefix when referring to the variable, it is good programming practice to do so.

Using Variable Prefixes and Scoping Your Variables

You should get into the habit of scoping your variables by always using variable prefixes. For example, use `client.var1` instead of `var1`. This reduces the processing time that ColdFusion takes to evaluate the variable. If you don't use prefixes, variables will be evaluated in the following order:

1. Regular variables

2. CGI variables

3. File variables

4. URL variables

5. Form variables

6. Cookie variables

7. Client variables

You may notice that application, server, and session variables (discussed in subsequent sections of this chapter) are not included in the preceding list. This is because prefixes for these variables must be specified. Otherwise, ColdFusion will return an error. If you have a form variable called `MyVar` and a client variable by the same name (and you don't specify the prefix), ColdFusion will always return the value of the form variable, because form variables are evaluated first.

Using Built-In Client Variables

You can refer to several built-in client variables in your ColdFusion applications (see Table 17.3). These built-in client variables are stored in the registry by default and are tied to a specific CFID and CFTOKEN.

TABLE 17.3: Built-In Client Variables

Variable Name	Description
Client.CFID	An incremented ID for each client that connects to the server
Client.CFTOKEN	A randomly generated number used to uniquely identify a particular client
Client.URLToken	A combination of **CFID** and **CFTOKEN**–to be passed between templates when cookies are not used
Client.LastVisit	Records the timestamp of the last visit made by a client

TABLE 17.3: Built-In Client Variables *(continued)*

Variable Name	Description
Client.HitCount	The number of page requests tied to a single client (tracked using CFID and CFTOKEN)
Client.TimeCreated	Records the timestamp when CFID and CFTOKEN were first created for a particular client

Retrieving a List of Client Variables

To retrieve a list of all currently set client variables, use the GetClientVariablesList function. This function returns a comma-delimited list of all client variable names except the built-in client variables (see Table 17.3). To display a list of client variable names, use the following code:

```
<CFOUTPUT>
Client variables currently available for use are: #GetClientVariablesList()#
</CFOUTPUT>
```

NOTE   For more information on using the GetClientVariablesList function, please refer to Appendix 2, "ColdFusion Function Reference."

Deleting Client Variables

Although the CLIENTSTORAGE attribute of the CFAPPLICATION tag offers three types of storage options, cookies will be used no matter which option you specify (unless you have set the SETCLIENTCOOKIES attribute to No). Remember that the CFID and CFTOKEN values are still stored as cookies on the client even if the storage option has been set to registry or the name of a data source. This is so that a particular client can be recognized when they return to your application. Therefore, client information is, by default, stored in two places:

Cookies   The CFID and CFTOKEN values are stored in a cookie on the client.

Registry   The built-in client variables (CFID, CFTOKEN, URLTOKEN, LastVisit, HitCount, and TimeCreated) as well as any other client variables are stored in the server registry (unless you have specified a different default storage mechanism).

You can delete client data from the registry and from cookies in several ways. These possibilities are discussed in the following sections.

If you have chosen to store your client data in a data source or as cookies, then you can delete them in the standard way:

Data source   Use CFQUERY to delete records or field values in the client storage data source. See Chapter 10, "Using CFQUERY and SQL to Interact With the Database."

Cookie   Use the CFCOOKIE tag and set the EXPIRES attribute equal to Now. See Chapter 4.

Deleting a Single Client Variable

If you need to delete only a single client variable that you have set, you use the Delete-ClientVariable function.

NOTE

For more information on using the DeleteClientVariable function, please refer to Appendix 2.

DeleteClientVariable takes one argument: the name of the client variable to be deleted. If you know the name of the client variable you wish to delete, you can use the following code. If the client variable you are attempting to delete does not exist, you will not receive an error and your application will continue to work as before.

```
<CFSET deleted = DeleteClientVariable("client.user_name")>
Delete confirmed? <CFOUTPUT>#deleted#</CFOUTPUT>
```

In this code, the variable deleted will return a Yes or No value, depending upon whether client.user_name existed and was successfully deleted.

Deleting All Client Variables

If you want to delete all client variables, you could loop through GetClientVariables-List and delete each client variable in the list as shown in the following code. For this code, you do not have to know the name of each client variable.

WARNING

The following code does not delete the client cookies (CFID, CFTOKEN, and CFGLOBALS), nor does it delete the built-in client variables stored in the registry (CFID, CFTOKEN, URLTOKEN, LastVisit, HitCount, and TimeCreated). It deletes only client variables created within the application framework.

```
<CFLOOP INDEX="x" LIST="#GetClientVariablesList()#">
<CFSET deleted = deleteclientvariable("#x#")>
</CFLOOP>
```

Deleting Client Cookies

If you would like to also delete the CFID, CFTOKEN, and/or CFGLOBALS cookies on the client side, you would use the following code. This code is useful if you no longer want the user to have access to any client variables. The next time the client accesses a page, they will be assigned a new CFID and CFTOKEN unless you have added some login procedure.

```
<CFCOOKIE NAME="cfid" EXPIRES="NOW">
<CFCOOKIE NAME="cftoken" EXPIRES="NOW">
<CFCOOKIE NAME="cfglobals" EXPIRES="NOW">
```

Managing Client State Management and Cookies

Table 17.4 describes several limitations of using cookies to store any client variables.

TABLE 17.4: Cookie Limitations

Limitation	Description
Not all browsers support cookies.	Cookies are supported in current versions of Netscape Communicator and Microsoft Internet Explorer, but are not supported in earlier versions (which are still in use). Other browsers generally don't offer cookie support. This limits their usefulness (as compared with URL parameters) for passing information from page to page within a site in a browser-independent manner.
Users can disable the use of cookies.	This requires you to pass the CFID and CFTOKEN values to every template in your application.
There are limits on the number of cookies that can be set.	A server can only set 20 cookies in a client browser with newer cookies replacing older ones as this limit is crossed. This means that if you have many applications on your server that set cookies, it is quite possible that the cookies set by one application may be overwritten by another application. (Remember that CF can use three cookies to store client variable data for one application: CFID, CFTOKEN, and CFGLOBALS.)
CFID, CFTOKEN, and CFGLOBALS (if ClientStorage has been set to cookie) will be set for each page request.	CFLOCATION cannot be used because a cookie cannot be set on the same page that a CFLOCATION tag is used.
Cookies have a length limit of 4,096 characters (4KB).	This length includes the value, name, and additional information such as the expiration date. Effectively, this means the actual value stored in the cookie needs to be less than 4KB in length.

If, for whatever reason, you decide that you do not want to use cookies to store the CFID, CFTOKEN, and/or CFGLOBALS, then you must pass the CFID and CFTOKEN variables to each template in your application. You also must specify an option other than cookie as the value for CLIENTSTORAGE in your CFAPPLICATION tag.

Passing *CFID* and *CFTOKEN*

To pass the CFID and CFTOKEN variables to each template in your application, you should append the client variable URLTOKEN to any link you are creating. In the following code you can see how URLTOKEN is passed through form fields, through hyperlinks (URLs), and by using JavaScript.

WARNING   When you pass URLTOKEN to each template in your application, both the CFID and CFTOKEN client variables can be viewed in the browser location bar. This means that a user can bookmark the page and later access the client information tied to that CFID and CFTOKEN.

```
<CFOUTPUT>
<!--- An example of passing URLTOKEN through a form --->
<FORM ACTION="quiz_results.cfm?#URLTOKEN#" METHOD="post">
...
</FORM>
</CFOUTPUT>

<CFOUTPUT>
<!--- An example of passing URLTOKEN through the URL --->
<A HREF="quiz_results.cfm?#URLTOKEN#">...</A>

<!--- An example of passing URLTOKEN using JavaScript --->
</CFOUTPUT>

<CFOUTPUT>
<FORM>
<INPUT TYPE="Button"
VALUE="Get New Question!"
onClick="location.href='home.cfm?#URLTOKEN#'">
</FORM>
<CFOUTPUT>
```

CFLOCATION

In Chapter 4 you learned how to work with cookies. The cookie is set by sending a cookie header through the browser. After this header has been received and processed by the server, then the cookie is available for use.

Unfortunately, when using CFLOCATION, a redirection header is sent through the browser. This header cancels out the cookie header and therefore prevents the cookie from being set. As a result, you cannot use CFLOCATION and CFCOOKIE in the same template.

This restriction is important to understand when using client management, because the CFID and CFTOKEN cookies can be set on any page in your application framework. If you were using CFLOCATION, then this would normally cause a problem. Luckily, ColdFusion automatically adds the URLTOKEN client variable to the CFLOCATION header. The only problem is that the CFID and CFTOKEN can then be viewable in the browser's location bar. To prevent this from happening, you can use the CFLOCATION attribute ADDTOKEN. ADD-TOKEN can be set to Yes or No. The syntax is <CFLOCATION url="home.cfm" ADDTOKEN="No">. This will prevent the URLTOKEN from being passed.

WARNING   If you specify NO for the ADDTOKEN attribute, and cookies have been disabled in your application, then this will cause your client variable data to be lost.

Exporting the Client Variable's Registry Entry

If you use the registry to store client data, you may at some point need to move this data from one server to another. If this is the case, you can export the following registry key to a file:

```
HKEY_LOCAL_MACHINE\SOFTWARE\Allaire\ColdFusion\CurrentVersion\Clients
```

You can move your registry key by following these steps:

1. Open the registry (RegEdit command).
2. Find the appropriate key.
3. Select Registry ➤ Export Registry File.
4. Give the key a filename.
5. Move the file to another server.
6. Open the registry on the new server.
7. Select Registry ➤ Import Registry File.
8. Select the file to import.

Using Session Management

Session variables are associated with a single client but persist only during a particular client session. They have a specified timeout period and are stored in the server's RAM (as opposed to the registry, like client variables). The default timeout period (set in the ColdFusion Administrator) is 20 minutes. The timeout clock starts ticking when there is inactivity between the client and the server. Unlike client variables, session variables are intended to be used for short periods of time. After session variables have expired, each time a user returns using the same client, their session variables must be re-established. It is wise to keep the expiration date for session variables to a minimum because they are limited by the server's RAM.

Session variables, like client variables, are defined by the CFID and CFTOKEN cookies, and the application name provided in the CFAPPLICATION tag. Provided that Session-Management has been enabled, ColdFusion stores these two variables as session variables in the server's RAM along with other session variables that may have been set.

When a user connects to an application with SessionManagement enabled, ColdFusion determines whether the CFID and CFTOKEN cookies exist. If they do, then these variables are also set in the server's RAM, and all session variables are available for use to that client. If not, then ColdFusion sets a new CFID and CFTOKEN for that client in both the server's RAM and with the client (using cookies). ColdFusion sets these cookies only once (in previous versions they were set at every page request).

The URLTOKEN variable is also added to the server's RAM as a session variable. It can be used in much the same way as client.URLTOKEN if cookies have been disabled (see the previous section, "Using Client Management").

Starting with ColdFusion 4, the scope of session variables was tied only to the CFID, instead of to both the CFID and CFTOKEN. This is not the intended functionality. This has been fixed in version 4.0.1

Standard uses for session variables include:

- Enforcing user login
- Tracking preferences, scores, and counts that need to be kept only during a single session
- Storing arrays instead of passing them between templates
- Storing calculations based on information stored in client variables
- Storing query recordsets (accessible only by a particular user session), as opposed to running a query multiple times

Enabling Session Variables

Session variables are also enabled using the CFAPPLICATION tag in the Application.cfm template (see Table 17.2). Because session variables are tied to a particular application, a name must be specified in the CFAPPLICATION tag by using the NAME attribute. The SESSIONMANAGEMENT attribute must also be set to Yes. Optionally, you can set the session timeout period using the SESSIONTIMEOUT attribute. If you don't specify a timeout period, the timeout will default to the settings in the ColdFusion Administrator. You also have the option of specifying whether to use cookies by using the SETCLIENTCOOKIES attribute. If you choose to prohibit the use of cookies, you must be prepared to pass both the CFID and CFTOKEN variables through URL or form parameters on every template of your application. If these variables are not passed, you risk losing control of session and client management.

The following code shows the syntax of a CFAPPLICATION tag that has enabled session variables, allowed the use of cookies, and set a session timeout of 20 minutes.

```
<CFAPPLICATION NAME="MyApp"
SESSIONMANAGEMENT="Yes"
SETCLIENTCOOKIES="Yes"
SESSIONTIMEOUT="#CreateTimeSpan(0, 0, 20, 0)#">
```

NOTE The CreateTimeSpan function is discussed in more detail in Appendix 2.

If you are using CF on a cluster, you cannot reliably use session management because session variables are stored in a single server's RAM. Clusters enable clients to connect to multiple servers, so if a client connects to a server that does not have its related CFID and CFTOKEN stored in RAM, then an error will occur.

Using the CF Administrator

You can use the ColdFusion Administrator to enable session variables as well as set their default and maximum timeout values. When you open the ColdFusion Administrator, select the Variables option under the Server section on the left-hand frame (see Figure 17.6).

FIGURE 17.6

Enabling session management in the ColdFusion Administrator

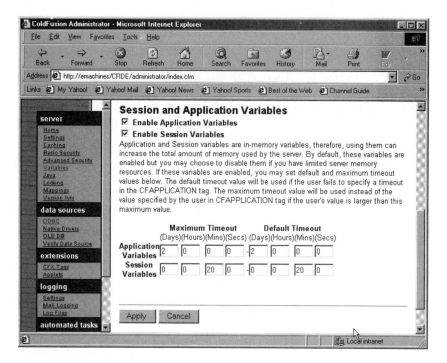

Enabling Session Management

Look at the third section of the ColdFusion Administrator screen, titled Session and Application Variables. This is where you can enable or disable the use of session variables on a server. If session variables are disabled, then session management cannot be used with any application on the server; even if you specify that the SESSIONMANAGE-MENT attribute of a CFAPPLICATION tag is set to Yes, you will still not be able to use session variables. You may choose not to enable session variables to reduce the amount of strain you put on the server's RAM (session variables are stored in the server's RAM).

NOTE   For more information on the Variables section of the ColdFusion Administrator, please refer to Chapter 35.

Setting the Default and Maximum Timeout Values

In the Session and Application Variables section of the ColdFusion Administrator's Variables screen, you can also specify default and maximum timeouts for session variables.

The default value applies to all applications on a particular server. Setting the SESSION-TIMEOUT attribute of the CFAPPLICATION tag in a particular Application.cfm template can overwrite this default.

The maximum value refers to the maximum timeout value allowed for any application on a particular server. ColdFusion will not allow a session timeout period higher than this. Setting a higher session timeout value in a particular application will cause ColdFusion to use the Administrator's maximum timeout value.

Working with Session Variables

If you have enabled SESSIONMANAGEMENT in your Application.cfm template, you are now ready to start creating and using session variables.

WARNING   In the following versions of Internet Explorer, session variables may be lost or work unexpectedly when more than one window is opened: 4, 4.01, 4.01sp1, 4.01sp2, 5.0dp1. For an explanation of this bug, please refer to Microsoft's site at http://support.microsoft.com/support/kb/articles/q196/3/83.asp.

Creating Session Variables

Creating session variables is basically the same as creating client variables, except that session variables must also be locked. Whenever you read or write a session variable, you need to use the CFLOCK tag around it. CFLOCK is discussed in more detail at the end of this chapter.

To create a session variable, you must use the CFSET or CFPARAM tags. You must also scope your variable name with the prefix `session`. The following code sets a passed form field equal to the session variable `session.user_name`:

```
   <CFLOCK TIMEOUT="30" NAME="#Session.SessionID#">
<CFPARAM NAME="session.user_name"
DEFAULT="#form.user_name#">
   </CFLOCK>
```

or

```
   <CFLOCK TIMEOUT="30" NAME="#Session.SessionID#">
<CFSET session.user_name="#form.user_name#">
   </CFLOCK>
```

You can also store arrays and query recordsets in session variables. To store a query recordset in a session variable, follow this code:

```
   <cfquery name="getStates" datasource="application.db">
   select * from states
   </cfquery>
   <CFLOCK TIMEOUT="30" NAME="#Session.SessionID#">
<CFSET session.query_results = getStates >
   </CFLOCK>
```

Storing query results in session variables is useful because it allows you to limit the connections you make to a database, thereby speeding up the process.

Referring to Session Variables

You must use the CFLOCK tag around any block of code containing a reference to a session variable. The CFLOCK should be a ReadOnly lock. For more information on the CFLOCK tag, please refer to the end of this chapter.

Here are two examples of referring to the session variable `session.user_name`:

```
   <CFLOCK TIMEOUT="30"   NAME="#Session.SessionID#" TYPE="ReadOnly">
      <CFIF NOT IsDefined("session.user_name")>
          insert code here…
      </CFIF>
</CFLOCK>
```

and

```
   <CFLOCK TIMEOUT="30"   NAME="#Session.SessionID#" TYPE="ReadOnly">
      <cfoutput>#session.user_name#</cfoutput>
</CFLOCK>
```

Unlike client variables, you must always include the `session` prefix when referring to session variables. ColdFusion does not automatically evaluate session variables.

NOTE Session variables are stored in ColdFusion structures and can be accessed using the structure functions as outlined in Chapter 14, "Working with ColdFusion Data Structures."

Using Built-In Session Variables

There are built-in session variables similar to client variables. Table 17.5 lists the built-in session variables that can be referred to in your applications. These built-in session variables are all stored in the server's RAM, and are tied to a specific CFID and CFTOKEN.

TABLE 17.5: Built-In Session Variables

Variable Name	Description
Session.CFID	An incremented ID for each client that connects to the server.
Session.CFTOKEN	A randomly generated number used to uniquely identify a particular client.
Session.URLToken	A combination of the CFID and CFTOKEN. To be passed between templates when cookies are not used. It appears as CFID=50&CFTOKEN=25239742
Session.SessionID	A variable unique to each session. It is a combination of the application name, the CFID, and CFTOKEN variables. It appears as AppName_50_25239742 (where 50 is the CFID and 25239742 is the CFTOKEN). Use this variable in conjunction with CFLOCK to secure read/write access to your session variables.

Retrieving a List of Session Variables

Because session variables are stored in RAM as opposed to the registry, you access them somewhat differently than you do client variables. To retrieve a list of all currently set session variables, you must loop through the session structure.

NOTE For more information on using structures, please refer to Chapter 14, "Working with ColdFusion Data Structures."

NOTE For more information on looping, please refer to Chapter 13, "Looping."

If you use the following code, you can retrieve an entire list of all session variables, including the built-in session variables described in Table 17.5.

```
<CFLOCK TIMEOUT="30"
NAME="#Session.SessionID#"
TYPE="ReadOnly">
<CFLOOP COLLECTION=#session# ITEM=y>
  <CFOUTPUT>
  Key = #y# (Value = #session[y]#)<BR>
  </CFOUTPUT>
  </CFLOOP>
  </CFLOCK>
```

Deleting Session Variables

Because session variables can be retrieved through a structure, they can also be deleted by using structures. If you know the specific session variable that you want to delete, you would use the `StructDelete` function. If you want to delete all session variables, you can use the `StructClear` function. Both examples are demonstrated in the following code. Remember to surround your code with a CFLOCK tag.

```
<!--- In order to delete a single session variable
     use the StructDelete function --->
<CFLOCK TIMEOUT="30" NAME="#Session.SessionID#" TYPE="Exclusive">
    <CFSET session.test = "foo">
    #session.test#
    <CFSET StructDelete(Session, "test")>
    <CFIF IsDefined("session.test")>
        test exists
    <CFELSE>
        deleted
    </CFIF>
</CFLOCK>

<!--- In order to delete the entire session structure
     use the StructClear function --->
<CFLOCK TIMEOUT="30" NAME="#Session.SessionID#" TYPE="Exclusive">
    <CFSET StructClear(Session)>
</CFLOCK>
```

TIP

The custom tag `CF_SESSION_KILL` by Ben Archibald (http://www.ChangeMedia.com) is a good example of using `StructDelete`. The custom tag can be found in the custom tags folder of the accompanying CD.

Even though session management provides a SESSIONTIMEOUT option, it is sometimes useful to kill a user's session before that timeout period expires. You may want to delete all references to a client session in the following instances:

- When the user clicks a logout button
- When the user closes their browser
- If the user leaves your Web site

`StructDelete` and `StructClear` are useful in deleting these references. The next two scenarios explain different approaches to ending a particular session.

WARNING

In ColdFusion 4.5, clearing all session variables with StructClear is not advised. If you do this, several special session variables such as **CFID** and **CFTOKEN** which are needed to maintain the session will be cleared and can cause problems when you try to set new session variables later in your templates.

Ending a Session When the Browser Is Closed

A session normally times out after the client makes no more connections to the Web server and the SESSIONTIMEOUT, as specified in the CFAPPLICATION tag or in the administrator, expires. However, you can cause a session to time out before the end of that time period provided the user closes their browser.

Because a session is tied to the CFID and CFTOKEN cookies that are normally set on the client side, if these cookies no longer existed, then the user would have to begin a new session. If you want to ensure that these cookies expire when the user closes their browser, then all you have to do is reset the cookies to their current values but with no expiration. If no EXPIRE attribute is set for a cookie, it automatically expires upon the close of the browser and doesn't get written to the client side. By re-creating the CFID and CFTOKEN cookies, you are effectively overwriting the existing ones that are set to expire sometime in the future. See the following code for the code that can be used to reset the CFID and CFTOKEN cookies.

```
<CFLOCK TIMEOUT="30" NAME="#Session.SessionID#" TYPE="Exclusive">
<CFCOOKIE NAME="CFID" VALUE="#session.CFID#">
<CFCOOKIE NAME="CFTOKEN" VALUE="#session.CFTOKEN#">
</CFLOCK>
```

WARNING   If you are using client management, you should know that client variables will also no longer be accessible by the client when resetting cookies to have no expiration date. This is because the CFID and CFTOKEN cookies are used for both client and session variables.

Ending a Session When the User Logs Out

If you provide a logout option for your users, killing the user session becomes simple. When the user logs out, you send them to a ColdFusion template where you can use the StructClear function to kill their session. Of course, this method requires that the user remember to log out.

Managing Session Management and Cookies

Session management relies on the CFID and CFTOKEN values that are normally set as client cookies to keep track of a client's session variables in the server RAM. Please refer to Table 17.4 for a brief overview of the limitations to using cookies.

If upon reviewing Table 17.4 you decide that you do not want to use cookies to store the CFID, CFTOKEN, and/or CFGLOBALS, then you must pass the CFID and CFTOKEN variables to each template in your application.

Passing *CFID* and *CFTOKEN*

To pass the CFID and CFTOKEN variables to each template in your application, you should append the session variable `session.URLToken` to any link you are creating. In the following code you can see that `session.URLTOKEN` is passed through form fields, through hyperlinks (URLs), and by using JavaScript in the same way as `client.URLTOKEN`.

WARNING   When you pass `session.URLTOKEN` to each template in your application, both the CFID and CFTOKEN session variables can be viewed in the browser location bar. This means that a user can bookmark the page and later access the client information tied to that **CFID** and **CFTOKEN**.

```
<CFOUTPUT>
<!--- An example of passing session.URLTOKEN
      through a form --->
<CFLOCK TIMEOUT="30" NAME="#Session.SessionID#" TYPE="ReadOnly">
<FORM
ACTION="quiz_results.cfm?#session.URLTOKEN#"
METHOD="post">
</CFLOCK>
...
</FORM>

<!--- An example of passing session.URLTOKEN
      through the URL --->
<CFLOCK TIMEOUT="30" NAME="#Session.SessionID#" TYPE="ReadOnly">
<A HREF="quiz_results.cfm?#session.URLTOKEN#">...</A>
</CFLOCK>

<!--- An example of passing session.URLTOKEN
      using Javascript --->
<FORM>
<CFLOCK TIMEOUT="30" NAME="#Session.SessionID#"
TYPE="ReadOnly">
<INPUT TYPE="Button" VALUE="Get New Question!"
onClick="location.href='home.cfm?#session.URLTOKEN#'">
</CFLOCK>
</FORM>
</CFOUTPUT>
```

Handling *CFLOCATION*

The handling of CFLOCATION is the same for session variables as it is for client variables. Please refer to the previous section, "Client State Management and Cookies," for more information on CFLOCATION.

Using Application Variables

Application variables are associated with a single application and are accessible by multiple clients. Specifically, they are tied to the application name specified in the CFAPPLICATION tag. To enable application variables, you must add a CFAPPLICATION tag with a NAME attribute to your application.cfm template.

Application variables, like session variables, also have a timeout period. The default timeout period (set in the ColdFusion Administrator) is two days. The timeout clock starts ticking when activity ceases between any client and the application. Application variables also expire if the ColdFusion server has been stopped.

Like session variables, application variables are stored in the server's RAM. Although this provides performance advantages (quick and easy access), it may limit the amount of information you should consider storing in an application variable. The amount of information you can store in application variables will depend on the amount of your server's RAM.

Application variables can be used to store information needed for all clients of a particular application. Some typical reasons for using application variables include:

- Standardizing background colors, fonts, and other visual controls for all clients of a particular application
- Setting standards such as the application title, data sources, and e-mail contacts
- Keeping track of counts such as the number of products ordered, number of visitors, etc.
- Storing arrays that can be accessed by all clients instead of passing them between templates
- Storing query recordsets that can be accessed by all clients, as opposed to running a query multiple times

Enabling Application Variables

Application variables are enabled by using the CFAPPLICATION tag in your Application.cfm template (see Table 17.2). In the CFAPPLICATION tag you must specify a name for your application using the NAME attribute. You also have the option of setting the application timeout period using the APPLICATIONTIMEOUT attribute. If you don't specify a timeout period, the timeout will default to the settings in the ColdFusion Administrator. The following code shows the syntax of a CFAPPLICATION tag that has enabled application variables.

```
<CFAPPLICATION
NAME="MyApp"
APPLICATIONTIMEOUT="#CreateTimeSpan(2, 0, 0, 0)#">
```

If you are using CF on a cluster, you cannot easily use application management because application variables are stored in a single server's RAM. Clusters enable clients to connect to multiple servers, so if a client connects to a server that does not recognize a particular application name, then an error will occur.

Using the CF Administrator

You can use the ColdFusion Administrator to enable application variables as well as set their minimum and maximum timeout values. When you open the ColdFusion Administrator, select the Variables option under the Server section on the left-hand frame (see Figure 17.6).

Enabling Session Management

Look at the third section of the ColdFusion Administrator Variables screen, titled Session and Application Variables. This is where you can enable or disable the use of application variables on a server. If application variables are disabled, then application management cannot be used, even if you specify a CFAPPLICATION tag in an Application.cfm template. You may choose not to enable application variables to reduce the amount of strain you put on the server's RAM (because application variables are stored in the server's RAM).

For more information on the Variables section of the ColdFusion Administrator, please refer to Chapter 35.

Setting the Default and Maximum Timeout Values

In the Session and Application Variables section of the ColdFusion Administrator's Variables screen, you can also specify default and maximum timeouts for application variables.

The default value applies to all applications on a particular server. Setting the APPLICATIONTIMEOUT attribute of the CFAPPLICATION tag in a particular Application.cfm template can overwrite this default.

The maximum value refers to the maximum timeout value allowed for any application on a particular server. This cannot be overwritten or superseded by the APPLICATIONTIMEOUT set in a CFAPPLICATION tag. ColdFusion will not allow an application timeout period higher than the maximum set value. Setting a higher application timeout value in a particular application will cause ColdFusion to use the Administrator's maximum timeout value.

Working with Application Variables

You are ready to start working with application variables once they have been enabled with the CFAPPLICATION tag. In this section you will learn how to create, refer to, retrieve, and delete application variables.

Creating Application Variables

Creating application variables is basically the same as creating session variables, except for the name prefix. Application variables must also be locked. Whenever you read or write an application variable, you need to use the CFLOCK tag around it. CFLOCK is discussed in more detail at the end of this chapter.

Just as with session and client variables, you must use the CFSET or CFPARAM tags to create an application variable. Remember to always scope the variable name with the prefix application. The following code sets a string equal to the application variable application.title.

```
<CFLOCK TIMEOUT="30"
NAME="#Application.ApplicationName#">
  <CFPARAM NAME="application.title"
DEFAULT="My Quiz Application">
  </CFLOCK>
```

or

```
<CFLOCK TIMEOUT="30"
NAME="#Application.ApplicationName#">
  <CFSET Application.title="My Quiz Application">
  </CFLOCK>
```

As with session variables, you can store arrays and query recordsets in application variables. To store a query recordset in an application variable, follow this code:

```
<CFLOCK TIMEOUT="30"
NAME="#Application.ApplicationName#">
  <CFSET application.query_results = Name_of_Query>
  </CFLOCK>
```

Referring to Application Variables

Referring to application variables is done just as with session variables. You must use the CFLOCK tag around any block of code containing a reference to an application variable. The CFLOCK should be a ReadOnly lock. For more information on the CFLOCK tag, please refer to the end of this chapter.

You must also remember to include the application prefix when referring to application variables. ColdFusion does not automatically evaluate application variables when no prefix is specified. Here are two examples of referring to the application variable `application.title`:

```
<CFLOCK TIMEOUT="30"
      NAME="#Session.SessionID#"
      TYPE="ReadOnly">
      <CFIF NOT IsDefined("application.title ")>
            insert code here…
      </CFIF>
</CFLOCK>
```

and

```
<CFLOCK TIMEOUT="30"
      NAME="#Application.ApplicationName#"
      TYPE="ReadOnly">
      <CFOUTPUT>
            <HEAD>
            <TITLE>#Application.Title#</TITLE>
            </HEAD>
      </CFOUTPUT>
</CFLOCK>
```

> **NOTE** Application variables are stored in ColdFusion structures and can be accessed using the structure functions as outlined in Chapter 14, "Working with ColdFusion Data Structures."

Using Built-In Application Variables

There is currently only one built-in application variable that stores the NAME attribute of the application set in the CFAPPLICATION tag. This variable, `Application.ApplicationName`, is used to uniquely identify each application. For this reason, you should make sure that each of your applications has a unique name.

Retrieving a List of Application Variables

Retrieving a list of all application variables is done exactly as with session variables. Because application variables are also stored in a structure, you can access them by looping through the structure name `application`.

> **NOTE** For more information on using structures, please refer to Chapter 14. For more information on looping, please refer to Chapter 13.

If you use the following code, you can retrieve an entire list of all application variables, including the built-in application variable `Application.ApplicationName`.

```
    <CFLOCK TIMEOUT="30"
    NAME="#Application.ApplicationName#"
    TYPE="ReadOnly">
<CFLOOP COLLECTION=#application# ITEM=x>
    <CFOUTPUT>
    Key = #x# (Value = #application[x]#)<BR>
    </CFOUTPUT>
    </CFLOOP>
    </CFLOCK>
```

Deleting the Application Structure

Application variables, like session variables, can be retrieved or deleted by using structures. If you know the specific application variable that you want to delete, you would use the StructDelete function. If you want to delete all application variables, you can use the StructClear function. Both of these examples are demonstrated in the following code. Remember to surround your code with CFLOCK tags.

```
    <!--- In order to delete a single application variable
        use the StructDelete function --->
    <CFLOCK TIMEOUT="30"
    NAME="#Application.ApplicationName#"
    TYPE="Exclusive">
    <CFSET application.title = "My Quiz Application">
    #application.title#
    <CFSET StructDelete(Application, "title")>
    <CFIF IsDefined("application.title")>
    still exists
    <CFELSE>
    deleted
    </CFIF>
    </CFLOCK>

    <!--- In order to delete the entire application structure
        use the StructClear function --->
    <CFLOCK TIMEOUT="30"
    NAME="#Application.ApplicationName#"
    TYPE="Exclusive">
    <CFSET StructClear(Application)>
    </CFLOCK>
```

There are different reasons why you might want to delete application variables. Most notably, you may want to reset application variables to their default values. If you delete application variables, they will be recreated by the Application.cfm file the next time it is accessed, effectively resetting the variables to their default value.

WARNING   In ColdFusion 4.5, clearing all application variables with StructClear is not advised. If you do this, several special application variables which are needed to maintain the application will be cleared and can cause problems when you try to set new application variables later in your templates.

Using Server Variables

Server variables aren't tied to any application; they are tied to a single ColdFusion server and can be accessed by all clients and applications on that server. They are stored in the server's RAM until the server has been stopped. You use server variables when you want to create a variable that can be accessed by any client connecting to your server. These variables are persistent and are lost only if the server is shut down. Therefore, you do not want to store too much data in server variables.

WARNING   If you are using CF on a cluster, you cannot reliably use server variables because they are tied to and stored in a single server's RAM. Clusters enable clients to connect to multiple servers, so each time a client connects to a different server, the server variables will change or may not be available—resulting in an error.

It is important to note that although server variables are stored in RAM (like session and application variables) they cannot be accessed as a structure. So retrieving a list of server variables and deleting server variables cannot be done at this time.

NOTE   Although server variables cannot be deleted, they can be reset. This is an important distinction: Once created, server variables cannot be deleted, so uncontrolled use of server variables isn't wise because they will persist until the server is rebooted.

Creating Server Variables

Server variables must be locked when created, just like session and application variables. Whenever you read or write a server variable, you need to use the CFLOCK tag around it. CFLOCK is discussed in more detail at the end of this chapter.

As with all other variable scopes, you must use the CFSET or CFPARAM tags to create a server variable. You must also preface your variable name with the prefix `server`. The following code sets a string equal to the server variable `server.season`.

```
<CFLOCK TIMEOUT="30"
NAME="#Application.ApplicationName#">
    <CFPARAM NAME="server.season"
DEFAULT="Spring">
</CFLOCK>
```

or

```
<CFLOCK TIMEOUT="30"
NAME="#Application.ApplicationName#">
    <CFSET server.season="Spring">
</CFLOCK>
```

As with session and application variables, you can store arrays and query recordsets in server variables. To store a query recordset in a server variable, follow this code:

```
<CFLOCK TIMEOUT="30"
NAME="#Application.ApplicationName#">
    <CFSET server.query_results = Name_of_Query>
</CFLOCK>
```

Referring to Server Variables

Referring to server variables is done just as with session and application variables. You must use the CFLOCK tag around any block of code containing a reference to a server variable. The CFLOCK should be a ReadOnly lock. For more information on the CFLOCK tag, please refer to the end of this chapter.

You must always remember to include the server prefix when referring to a server variable. ColdFusion does not automatically evaluate server variables when no prefix is specified. Here are two examples of referring to the server variable server.season:

```
<CFLOCK TIMEOUT="30"
        NAME="Server"
        TYPE="ReadOnly">
        <CFIF NOT IsDefined("server.season")>
            insert code here...
        </CFIF>
</CFLOCK>
```

and

```
<CFLOCK TIMEOUT="30"
        NAME="Server"
        TYPE="ReadOnly">
        <CFOUTPUT>
            It is #Server.season# in North America
        </CFOUTPUT>
</CFLOCK>
```

NOTE   Unlike session and application variables, server variables are not stored in ColdFusion structures for security reasons. This means they cannot be accessed using structure functions.

Using Built-In Server Variables

There are several built-in server variables detailing information about ColdFusion and the server:

Server.ColdFusion.ProductName   Name of the ColdFusion product running on the server

Server.ColdFusion.ProductVersion   Version number of ColdFusion product

Server.ColdFusion.ProductLevel   Edition of ColdFusion product (Enterprise, Professional, etc.)

Server.ColdFusion.SerialNumber   Serial number for currently installed version of ColdFusion

Server.OS.Name   Name of operating system running on the server (Windows 95, Windows NT, Solaris, etc.)

Server.OS.AdditionalInformation   Additional information about installed operating system (service packs, updates, etc.)

Server.OS.Version   Version of installed operating system

Server.OS.BuildNumber   Build number of installed operating system

---

WARNING   Server variables are read/write. Be careful about overwriting the built-in variable information.

Using *CFLOCK*

One issue that has not been discussed in this chapter is that of simultaneous read and write access to certain variables with persistent scope. Session, application, and server variables are not protected from simultaneous read/write access. Therefore, you should always use the CFLOCK tag when reading and writing to these variable scopes. If these variables are not protected, or locked, during read/write access, it is possible that several requests, or threads, to read and write to these variables could occur at the same time. This could result in corrupting the data being written or read, or possibly hanging the ColdFusion server.

For example, say you have an application variable application.MyQuery set in your Application.cfm template and it stores a query recordset. Person A logs on at the exact same time as Person B. Both of their clients request the Application.cfm template at the same time and attempt to write the results of a query to application.MyQuery at the same time. Because these variables are not protected, the results cannot be predicted and could be corrupted. To prevent this, use the CFLOCK tag as described in this section.

NOTE   Although session variables are not shared between clients, it is still possible for one client to have multiple threaded access to a session variable. This could occur if frames are used, or if the user decides to reload or refresh the page.

Understanding the *CFLOCK* Tag

The CFLOCK tag has several attributes (see Table 17.6). These attributes are described in detail in the following list:

NAME   Although this attribute is not required, it is highly recommended that you use it. The name should reference the variable scope that you are locking.

For session variables you should use `session.sessionID`.

For application variables you should use `application.applicationName`.

For server variables you should use `server`.

If two CFLOCK tags share the same name, then only one tag can be accessed at a time. If you do not name them in this manner, you could run into read/write access problems.

For example, if `application.test` is set in one template, but no CFLOCK name is specified, ColdFusion will automatically generate a random name to lock the code. But say that in a second template someone is trying to read `application.test` and the lock around that code has no NAME attribute as well. ColdFusion will generate a unique name, but it will not be the same name that locks the write access to `application.test` in the first template. So you could have one user writing to the variable and another user reading the variable at the same time. This can cause the server to hang, or incorrect data to be written to the variable.

TYPE   The two options are `ReadOnly` and `Exclusive`. The default type, if not specified, is `Exclusive`.

An `exclusive` lock should always be used when you are writing data to one of these variables. This lock only allows one request to process at a time. All other requests to read or write must wait until the block of code has been unlocked. The disadvantage to using this lock is that it decreases performance. Because all requests must wait in line, processing of templates slows down.

A `ReadOnly` lock allows more than one request to access the block of code inside the CFLOCK tag. Because requests do not have to wait, this option is faster. But, if an `Exclusive` lock has already locked the code, then the `ReadOnly` lock will have to wait.

TIMEOUT   TIMEOUT is required and specified in seconds. If a CFLOCK block of code is currently locked, this attribute specifies the number of seconds that the next request to the same CFLOCK must wait before the current lock times out.

THROWONTIMEOUT   THROWONTIMEOUT is not required but will default to Yes. Yes means that if the TIMEOUT expires, then CF will produce an error. Using the CFTRY and CFCATCH tags (see Chapter 18) can catch the error. If No is specified, then the template will continue to be processed and the code in the CFLOCK tags will be skipped.

WARNING   CFLOCK names are not shared in a clustered environment.

The syntax for the CFLOCK tag is shown in the following code.

```
<CFLOCK NAME="the_name_of_your_lock"
        TYPE="ReadOnly/Exclusive"
        TIMEOUT="timeout in seconds"
        THROWONTIMEOUT="Yes/No"
SCOPE="Application/Server/Session>

   ...Block of code to be locked
</CFLOCK>
```

TABLE 17.6: Attributes of the CFLOCK Tag

Attribute	Required	Value	Default
NAME	No	For session variables you should use `session` `.sessionID` For application variables you should use `application` `.applicationName` For server variables you should use `server`	Randomly generated name
TYPE	No	ReadOnly/Exclusive	Exclusive
TIMEOUT	Yes	Time in seconds	N/A
THROWONTIMEOUT	No	Yes/No	Yes

Nesting *CFLOCK* Tags

It is important to understand the nesting process of CFLOCK tags while you are using them in your application. If you nest tags inconsistently, serious problems could occur that could cause your server to hang or crash. These problems are sometimes referred to as deadlocks. It is far better to avoid nesting if at all possible.

When nesting your CFLOCK tags, bear in mind that many users can be attempting to access CFLOCK tags of the same name scope at the same time. For example, in one template a user could be accessing an exclusively locked block of code with the name #application.applicationname#, while in another template a different user could be accessing a different exclusively locked block of code by the same name. Because these two locks share the same name, the user who accesses their lock first will have an exclusive lock on it while the second user will have to wait. This is fine and how locking is intended to work.

But what if you have code being accessed by User A in one template and code being accessed by User B in a second template? In the following block of code you have a lock on the application scope followed by a nested lock on the server scope.

```
<CFLOCK TIMEOUT="30"
   THROWONTIMEOUT="No"
   NAME="#Session.SessionID#"
   TYPE="Exclusive">
   <CFSET SESSION.STARTED = TRUE>

   <CFLOCK TIMEOUT="30"
      THROWONTIMEOUT="No"
      NAME="server"
      TYPE="Exclusive">
      <CFIF NOT #ISDEFINED("server.season")#>
         <CFSET SERVER.SEASON = "Spring">
      </CFIF>
   </CFLOCK>
</CFLOCK>
```

In the second block of code that follows, you have the opposite. If User A accesses the first template and locks the session scope at the same time that User B accesses the second template and locks the server scope, then what happens next? Neither user can continue with his or her block of code because in each case someone else has exclusively locked the next block of code.

```
<CFLOCK TIMEOUT="30"
   THROWONTIMEOUT="No"
   NAME="server"
   TYPE="Exclusive">
<CFIF NOT #ISDEFINED("server.season")#>
<CFSET SERVER.SEASON = "Spring">
</CFIF>

   <CFLOCK TIMEOUT="30"
      THROWONTIMEOUT="No"
      NAME="#Session.SessionID#"
      TYPE="Exclusive">
      <CFSET SESSION.STARTED = TRUE>
   </CFLOCK>
</CFLOCK>
```

Therefore, locking must be done in a consistent manner throughout your application. You should always lock the variable scopes in the same order. For example, lock session scopes first, then application, and then server scopes. But do not lock in this order: application, session, and server. At times it can be difficult to do this, so it is strongly advised to avoid nested CFLOCK tags if at all possible. Also, if you use a CFINCLUDE tag inside a CFLOCK tag, you must be especially careful about what locking occurs in the included template.

The following code provides an example of code that appears to be impossible to lock appropriately. In the CFQUERY tag , you have references to both session and application variables. You also reference a session variable in the SQL as well. You cannot very well nest a CFLOCK tag within the first CFQUERY tag, as this is not proper ColdFusion coding and will produce an error. So how do you lock these variables?

```
<CFQUERY NAME="session.get_question"
    DATASOURCE="#Application.DB#"
DBTYPE="ODBC">
    SELECT *
    FROM questions
    WHERE questions.question_id =
#session.question_id#
</CFQUERY>
```

The following code provides the solution. Instead of trying to nest locks within the CFQUERY tag, which would be illegal anyway, the variable Application.DB is set to a non-persistent variable that does not need to be locked. Then in the CFQUERY tag, you only need to lock the session scope and reference the non-persistent variable DB, as opposed to also locking the application scope.

```
<CFLOCK TIMEOUT="30"
    THROWONTIMEOUT="Yes"
    NAME="#Application.ApplicationName#"
    TYPE="READONLY">
    <CFSET DB = Application.DB>
</CFLOCK>

<CFLOCK TIMEOUT="30"
    THROWONTIMEOUT="Yes"
    NAME="#Session.SessionID#"
    TYPE="Exclusive">
<CFQUERY NAME="session.get_question"
        DATASOURCE="#DB#"
DBTYPE="ODBC">
        SELECT *
        FROM questions
        WHERE questions.question_id =
#session.question_id#
    </CFQUERY>
</CFLOCK>
```

CFLOCK in ColdFusion 4.5

In ColdFusion 4.5, you have the option to automatically control variable locking through the ColdFusion Administrator. Using the Variable Locking page of the ColdFusion Administrator (which is discussed in Chapter 35, "ColdFusion Administration"), you can define automatic behavior for server, application and session variables.

For each of these three types of variables, you have three choices:

- No automatic checking or locking: All locking must be done with the CFLOCK tag as outlined above.
- Full checking: Any attempt to read or write the specified type of variable outside a CFLOCK tag will cause an error.
- Automatic read locking: Any attempt to write the specified type of variable outside a CFLOCK tag will cause an error.

In addition, you can force all requests from the same session to occur sequentially, waiting for previous requests to finish, in order to prevent multiple requests from the same session to simultaneously access session variables. To enforce this policy, select the Single Threaded Sessions option on the Variable Locking page of the ColdFusion Administrator.

Using *CFLOCK* in Other Situations

You can also use CFLOCK in the following situations:

- When working with file updates (see Chapter 19, "File Management")
- When invoking a CFX (See Chapter 31, "Building Custom Tags")

Putting It All Together

This section will demonstrate all the application framework features that you have learned about in this chapter. A full application will be described in detail so that you can see how each of these features is supposed to be employed practically. This application is built on the same basic templates that you originally created in Chapter 1, "Creating Your First ColdFusion Template," Chapter 2, "Passing Data Between ColdFusion Templates," and Chapter 3, "Getting Data from a Database." It is a quiz application. The features that have been built into this application by using the application framework are:

- A login procedure that allows entry to authorized users for a single session. After the session has timed out, users must log in again.
- Global settings using application variables (font face, background color, etc.).

- Storage of query results in application and session variables so that connections to the database are minimized, therefore increasing performance.
- Locking of persistent scope variables to ensure proper read/write access.
- Use of the standard footer template, OnRequestEnd.cfm, to calculate total scores for the current user and all users.
- Use of session, application, server, and client variables.

If you would like to use this quiz application, you need to do the following:

1. Move the following templates from the chapter17 directory on the accompanying CD to the sybex folder in your Web server root directory:
   - Application.cfm
   - login.cfm
   - login2.cfm
   - home.cfm
   - quiz_results.cfm
   - OnRequestEnd.cfm

2. Move the database quiz.mdb from the chapter17 directory on the accompanying CD to the sybex folder in your Web server root directory.

3. If you have not already done so, create a data source for the quiz.mdb file in the ColdFusion Administrator. Call this data source **quiz**. (If you need assistance creating a data source, please see Chapter 35.)

4. You may need to stop and start the ColdFusion services in order for the data-source changes to take effect.

5. When your ColdFusion services and Web server are running, open your browser and go to the following URL: http://127.0.0.1/sybex/home.cfm.

6. Make sure that cookies are enabled so that the application will work properly.

7. Use the username **kristin** and the password **motlagh**. The usernames and passwords are stored in the quiz.mdb database.

Application.cfm

The Application.cfm template is always processed at the beginning of any template in the application structure. It is the ideal place to set persistent scope variables and implement a user verification scheme. First look at the template provided in Listing 17.1, and then read the description of its interactions. The comments provided within the template are also useful for understanding the code.

LISTING 17.1: *Application.cfm*

```
<!--- Application.cfm --->
<!DOCTYPE HTML PUBLIC "-//W3C//DTD HTML 4.0 Transitional//EN">

<!------------------------------------------------------------
Set application name; client variables on; session
variables on; allow cookies; session timeout after 20
minutes; Application timeout after 2 days; store client
variables in registry
------------------------------------------------------------>

<CFAPPLICATION NAME="MyApp"
    SESSIONMANAGEMENT="Yes"
    SETCLIENTCOOKIES="Yes"
    SESSIONTIMEOUT="#CreateTimeSpan(0, 0, 20, 0)#"
    APPLICATIONTIMEOUT="#CreateTimeSpan(2, 0, 0, 0)#"
    CLIENTMANAGEMENT="Yes"
    CLIENTSTORAGE="Registry">

<!------------------------------------------------------------
Used to reset application, session, and client variables
for testing purposes. You must remove the comments
surrounding the next set of code variables to clear all
variable scopes, and then replace the comments so the
application will run normally.
------------------------------------------------------------>
<!---
<CFSET STRUCTCLEAR(APPLICATION)>
<CFSET STRUCTCLEAR(SESSION)>
<CFLOOP INDEX="x" LIST="#GetClientVariablesList()#">
    <CFSET DELETED = DELETECLIENTVARIABLE("#x#")>
</CFLOOP>
<CFCOOKIE NAME="cfid" EXPIRES="NOW">
<CFCOOKIE NAME="cftoken" EXPIRES="NOW">
<CFCOOKIE NAME="cfglobals" EXPIRES="NOW">
<CFABORT>
--->

<!------------------------------------------------------------
Set Server constants that can be accessed by any client
------------------------------------------------------------>
<CFLOCK TIMEOUT="30"
    THROWONTIMEOUT="Yes"
    NAME="server"
    TYPE="Exclusive">
    <CFIF NOT #ISDEFINED("server.season")#>
        <!------------------------------------------------------------
        The season is currently set to a string, but could
        easily be determined automatically by time of
year.
        ------------------------------------------------------------>
```

```
            <CFSET SERVER.SEASON = "Spring Time">
        </CFIF>
    </CFLOCK>


    <!--------------------------------------------------------
    Set Application constants
    -------------------------------------------------------->
    <CFLOCK TIMEOUT="30"
        THROWONTIMEOUT="Yes"
        NAME="#Application.ApplicationName#"
        TYPE="Exclusive">
        <CFIF NOT #ISDEFINED("Application.Started")#>
            <CFSET APPLICATION.TITLE = "My Quiz Application">
            <CFSET APPLICATION.DB = "quiz">
            <CFSET APPLICATION.EMAIL =
    "kmotlagh@geocities.com">
            <CFSET APPLICATION.BGCOLOR = "##ffffff">
            <CFSET APPLICATION.FACE = "Arial">
            <CFSET APPLICATION.STARTED = TRUE>
        </CFIF>
    </CFLOCK>


    <!--------------------------------------------------------
    Test to see if user has logged in. If they haven't a
    non-persistent login variable is set. This is so you do
    not have to use a <CFLOCK> tag around the next block of
    code.
    -------------------------------------------------------->
    <CFLOCK TIMEOUT="30"
        THROWONTIMEOUT="Yes"
        NAME="#Session.SessionID#"
        TYPE="ReadOnly">
        <CFIF NOT ISDEFINED("Session.Started")>
            <CFSET LOGIN = "">
        </CFIF>
    </CFLOCK>

    <CFIF ISDEFINED("Login")>
        <!--------------------------------------------------------
        Since the session.started variable has not yet
        been set (it is set when the user successfully logs in
        in the login2.cfm template), the processing of the
        login2.cfm would be aborted unless the following cfif
        statement is added
        -------------------------------------------------------->

        <CFSET
    PATH=GETDIRECTORYFROMPATH(#CGI.CF_TEMPLATE_PATH#)>
```

```
<CFIF (CGI.CF_TEMPLATE_PATH IS NOT "#path#login.cfm")
AND (CGI.CF_TEMPLATE_PATH IS NOT "#path#login2.cfm")>
    <CFINCLUDE TEMPLATE="login.cfm">

    <!-------------------------------------------------
    Aborts processing of any template except login.cfm
    and login2.cfm until user has logged in
    ------------------------------------------------->
    <CFABORT>
  </CFIF>
</CFIF>
```

In this Application.cfm template (Listing 17.1), the following interactions are created:

1. The use of all persistent variable scopes are enabled.

2. Code to delete session and application structures, as well as client variables and cookies, is provided in a commented tag. This is useful only for testing purposes during the development process. If you remove the comments from around this block of code, you can clear out the variable scopes and start fresh. Just remember that unless this code is commented out, the application will not work properly.

3. The only server variable that is set in this application is server.season. It is accessible by every page request to the current server. It is used here as an example of creating a server variable. Ideally, if you were to set the season, you would do it dynamically based on the time of year and location in the world.

4. Standard application variables are set for font faces, background color, administrator e-mail, etc. These variables will be used many times on most pages in the application. If they ever had to be changed, you would need to modify only the Application .cfm template as opposed to every occurrence of where these variables are used.

5. The final block of code is used to determine whether a user has logged in and begun a session. If they had logged in, then session.started would be set and this block of code would be skipped. If they hadn't logged in, then they would be redirected to a login page and all other processing would be aborted. The redirection does not occur if they are already in the login process, because that would result in the user never properly being verified. They would always be redirected to the login page and login2.cfm would never process. The verification occurs at login2.cfm.

If the user has logged in and session.started has been set, then processing of the calling template occurs as usual.

Login.cfm

The user is sent to this template if they have not logged in and `session.started` does not exist. They are prompted to log in and begin a new session (see Figure 17.7). Look at Listing 17.2 and then read the explanation of the interactions in this template.

FIGURE 17.7

Login.cfm

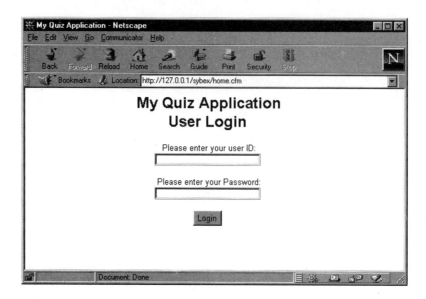

LISTING 17.2: *login.cfm*

```
<!--- login.cfm --->
<!DOCTYPE HTML PUBLIC "-//W3C//DTD HTML 4.0 Transitional//EN">

<!------------------------------------------------------
Use CFLOCK to restrict access to the reading of
application variables in this template to only one user
at a time.
------------------------------------------------------>
<CFLOCK TIMEOUT="30"
    THROWONTIMEOUT="Yes"
    NAME="#Application.ApplicationName#"
    TYPE="ReadOnly">
    <CFSET title = Application.Title>
    <CFSET bgcolor = Application.Bgcolor>
    <CFSET face = Application.Face>
    <CFSET email = Application.Email>
</CFLOCK>
```

```
<CFOUTPUT>
   <HTML>
   <HEAD>
      <TITLE>#title#</TITLE>
   </HEAD>

   <BODY BGCOLOR="#bgcolor#">

   <DIV ALIGN="center">
      <B><FONT FACE="#face#" SIZE="5">
      #title#<br>User Login</FONT></B>

      <FORM ACTION="login2.cfm" METHOD="POST">
         <FONT FACE="#face#" SIZE="2">

<!-----------------------------------------
If client.user_name exists (set in login2.cfm), welcomes them back
------------------------------------------>
         <CFIF ISDEFINED("Client.user_name")>
            <B>Welcome to #title#
            #client.user_name#!</B><P>
            Please login to start a new session.
         </CFIF>

<!-----------------------------------------
Prompts user to enter username and password.
------------------------------------------>

         <P>Please enter your user ID:<BR>
         <INPUT TYPE="Text" NAME="user_id"
SIZE="20">

         <P>Please enter your Password:<BR>
         <INPUT TYPE="password" NAME="password"
         SIZE="20">

         <P>
         <INPUT TYPE="Submit" NAME="Submit"
         VALUE="Login">
      </FORM>
   </DIV>

   </BODY>
   </HTML>
</CFOUTPUT>
```

First, all the application variables that will be used in this template are set to non-persistent variables. Because you need to use CFLOCK around any read or write access of an application variable, it is more efficient to read these variables only once they are in the template, thereby using only one CFLOCK tag. These variables, once reset to non-persistent variables, can be accessed throughout the page without adding additional CFLOCK tags.

Second, the login form is created. You will notice that if `client.user_name` exists, then the user is welcomed back and prompted to start a new session. Although it appears that this client variable may not be very useful, you could use this information to track how many unique visitors there are to your site, even though you still want them to log in each time.

Finally, the Username and Password fields are displayed so that the user can log in. If you are testing this application, you can use the user name **kristin** and the password **motlagh**.

Now these fields will be sent to `login2.cfm` to be verified against a database.

Login2.cfm

Remember that for each of these templates, `Application.cfm` is processed first. Because at this point the user has not been verified and `session.started` has not been initialized, the `Application.cfm` template would normally throw the user back to `login.cfm`. But a statement was added to the `Application.cfm` file that prevented this from happening if the calling template was either `login.cfm` or `login2.cfm`. You can refer back to Listing 17.1 for a more complete description.

Listing 17.3 contains the code for `login2.cfm`.

LISTING 17.3: *login2.cfm*

```
<!--- login2.cfm --->
<!DOCTYPE HTML PUBLIC "-//W3C//DTD HTML 4.0 Transitional//EN">

<!------------------------------------------------------
Use CFLOCK to restrict access to the reading of
application variables in this template to only one user
at a time.
------------------------------------------------------->

<CFLOCK TIMEOUT="30"
    THROWONTIMEOUT="Yes"
    NAME="#Application.ApplicationName#"
    TYPE="ReadOnly">
    <CFSET title = Application.Title>
    <CFSET bgcolor = Application.Bgcolor>
    <CFSET face = Application.Face>
    <CFSET email = Application.Email>
    <CFSET db = Application.DB>
</CFLOCK>
```

```
<!---------------------------------------------------------
Security_check query verifies that form.user_name and
form.password are valid.
------------------------------------------------------>
<CFQUERY NAME="security_check" DATASOURCE="#db#">
SELECT passwords.user_id,
   passwords.password,
   passwords.user_name
FROM    passwords
WHERE passwords.user_id = '#form.user_id#' AND
      passwords.password = '#form.password#'
</CFQUERY>

<!---------------------------------------------------------
If form.user_name and form.password are not valid then
Prompt the user to log in again.
------------------------------------------------------>
<CFIF SECURITY_CHECK.RECORDCOUNT IS 0>
   <CFOUTPUT>
      <HTML>
      <HEAD>
         <TITLE>#title#</TITLE>
      </HEAD>

      <BODY BGCOLOR="#bgcolor#">

      <DIV ALIGN="center">
         <CFINCLUDE TEMPLATE="login.cfm">
         <FONT FACE="#face#" SIZE="2">
         Your User ID and Password are not in our
         database.<BR>Please try again.
         </FONT>
      </DIV>

      </BODY>
      </HTML>

   </CFOUTPUT>
   <CFABORT>

<!---------------------------------------------------------
If the user_name and password are verified, then the
session is started, client.user_name is set, and the user
is redirected to the home.cfm template
------------------------------------------------------>
<CFELSE>

   <CFLOCK TIMEOUT="30"
      THROWONTIMEOUT="Yes"
      NAME="#Session.SessionID#"
```

```
            TYPE="Exclusive">
            <CFSET SESSION.STARTED = TRUE>
        </CFLOCK>

        <CFSET CLIENT.USER_NAME = "#security_check.user_name#">

        <CFLOCATION URL="home.cfm" ADDTOKEN="no">
    </CFIF>
```

First, the application variables are again set to non-persistent variables so that a minimum of CFCLOCK tags are used. Second, the form fields user_name and password that are passed to this template are checked against a database containing valid usernames and passwords.

If the query returns no results, this means that no matching user_name and password combination was found and the user must try to log in again. The login.cfm template is then included in this section of code. Figure 17.8 shows the login screen if the user was not verified.

FIGURE 17.8

Login2.cfm

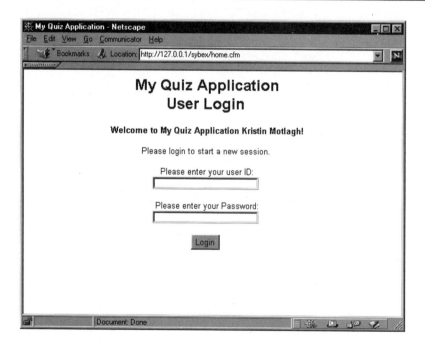

But, if the user is verified, then `session.started` is initialized and the client variable `user_name` is set. Then the user is redirected using a CFLOCATION tag to the `home.cfm` template and they can begin using the quiz application.

Home.cfm

`home.cfm` is a modified version of the template created in Chapters 1, 2, and 3. If you would like to know more about how to create the actual quiz, please refer to those chapters. In this chapter the quiz has been enhanced by using the application framework, and that is what the explanations will focus on.

Figure 17.9 shows the new `home.cfm` template. It is similar to one created in Chapter 3, except for the display of:

- The client username in the welcome message
- The server variable `session.season`
- A score card for the current user and all users

FIGURE 17.9
Home.cfm

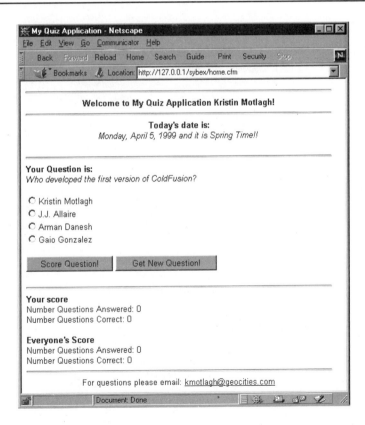

Listing 17.4 contains the code used to generate this template. An explanation of the code follows the listing.

LISTING 17.4: *home.cfm*

```
<!--- home.cfm --->
<!DOCTYPE HTML PUBLIC "-//W3C//DTD HTML 4.0 Transitional//EN">


<!------------------------------------------------------
The following query determines the number of questions
available in the database and stores it in an application
variable.  If this query has been run once, it will not
run again until the application times out or has been
deleted.
------------------------------------------------------->

<CFLOCK TIMEOUT="30"
    THROWONTIMEOUT="Yes"
    NAME="#Application.ApplicationName#"
    TYPE="Exclusive">
    <CFIF NOT ISDEFINED("question_id") AND
        NOT ISDEFINED("application.get_count")>
        <CFQUERY NAME="application.get_count"
            DATASOURCE="#Application.DB#"
            DBTYPE="ODBC">
            SELECT count(questions.question_id) as
            total_questions
            FROM questions
        </CFQUERY>
    </CFIF>
</CFLOCK>


<!------------------------------------------------------
All application variables that need to be accessed in
This template are set to regular page variables, in order
to reduce the number of cflocks used.
------------------------------------------------------->
<CFLOCK TIMEOUT="30"
    THROWONTIMEOUT="Yes"
    NAME="#Application.ApplicationName#"
    TYPE="READONLY">
    <CFSET db = Application.DB>
    <CFSET title = Application.Title>
    <CFSET bgcolor = Application.Bgcolor>
    <CFSET face = Application.Face>
    <CFSET email = Application.Email>
    <CFSET total_questions =
    application.get_count.total_questions>
</CFLOCK>
```

```
<!--------------------------------------------------------
If the variable question_id exists (passed from
quiz_results.cfm), this query returns that question.
Otherwise, a random question is returned. The results are
stored in a session variable that is accessible on
quiz_results.cfm.
--------------------------------------------------------->

<CFLOCK TIMEOUT="30"
   THROWONTIMEOUT="Yes"
   NAME="#Session.SessionID#"
   TYPE="Exclusive">
   <CFQUERY NAME="session.get_question"
   DATASOURCE="#DB#" DBTYPE="ODBC">
      SELECT questions.question_id,
         questions.question,
         questions.answer1,
         questions.answer2,
         questions.answer3,
         questions.answer4,
         questions.correct_answer
      FROM questions
      WHERE questions.question_id =
      <CFIF ISDEFINED("question_id")>
         #question_id#
      <CFELSE>
         #RandRange(1, total_questions)#
      </CFIF>
   </CFQUERY>
</CFLOCK>

<CFOUTPUT>
   <HTML>
   <HEAD>
      <TITLE>#Title#</TITLE>
   </HEAD>

   <BODY BGCOLOR="#bgcolor#">

   <DIV ALIGN="center">
      <FONT FACE="#face#" SIZE="2">
      <HR><B>Welcome to #Title#
      #client.user_name#!<BR></B><HR>

      <B>Today's date is:</B><BR>
      <CFSET TODAY =
DATEFORMAT(NOW(), "dddd, mmmm d, yyyy")>
```

```
<CFLOCK TIMEOUT="30"
    THROWONTIMEOUT="Yes"
    NAME="server"
    TYPE="ReadOnly">
    <I>#today# and it is #server.season#!!</I>
</CFLOCK>

    </FONT>
  </DIV>
</CFOUTPUT>

<!------------------------------------------------------
The following is code that dynamically generates each
quiz question
------------------------------------------------------>
<CFLOCK TIMEOUT="30"
    THROWONTIMEOUT="Yes"
    NAME="#Session.SessionID#"
    TYPE="ReadOnly">
    <CFOUTPUT QUERY="session.get_question">
        <FONT FACE="#Face#" SIZE="2">

        <FORM ACTION="quiz_results.cfm" METHOD="post">

        <P><HR><B>Your Question is:</B>
        <BR><I>#question#</I><P>

        <INPUT TYPE="hidden" NAME="today" VALUE="#today#">

        <INPUT TYPE="radio" NAME="user_answer"
        VALUE="#answer1#">#answer1#<BR>
        <INPUT TYPE="radio" NAME="user_answer"
        VALUE="#answer2#">#answer2#<BR>
        <INPUT TYPE="radio" NAME="user_answer"
        VALUE="#answer3#">#answer3#<BR>
        <INPUT TYPE="radio" NAME="user_answer"
        VALUE="#answer4#">#answer4#<BR>

        <INPUT TYPE="hidden" NAME="user_answer_required"
        VALUE="Please select an answer!">

        <P><INPUT TYPE="Submit" VALUE="Score Question!">
        <INPUT TYPE="Button" VALUE="Get New Question!"
        ONCLICK="location.href='home.cfm'">
        </FORM>

    </CFOUTPUT>
</CFLOCK>
```

The first query determines the total number of questions in the database and stores this value in an application variable. If this query has been run once, it will not be run again until the application structure is cleared, the server is shut down, or the application times out.

Then, all standard application variables are again set to non-persistent variables. In this case the total number of questions is also stored in a non-persistent variable, so that it can be easily used in the next query without having to employ the use of CFLOCK.

The next query is set as a session variable so that the quiz_results.cfm template can access the results without having to run another query. If a question_id exists, then that question and its related data are pulled from the database and stored in session.get_ question. Remember that you can store query recordsets in session variables. Otherwise, a random question is generated.

Then, after the page header information is displayed, the quiz question and its answers are displayed. Because this data is stored in a session variable, a CFLOCK tag must surround the entire block of code.

You will notice that there is no more code in the home.cfm template, but the display shows a score card. The score card and its results are processed in the OnRequestEnd .cfm template. Remember that the OnRequestEnd.cfm template is processed at the end of every application page in the current directory. The OnRequestEnd.cfm template will be explained later in this section.

quiz_results.cfm

When the user answers a question and clicks the Score Question button on the home.cfm template, they are sent to the quiz_results.cfm template. The user_answer is sent as a form field to quiz_results.cfm. The purpose of the quiz_results.cfm template is to evaluate the user's answers and provide feedback. Again, please refer to Chapter 3 for more information on the code used to generate these interactions.

Figure 17.10 shows the response that is displayed when the user selects the incorrect answer. Listing 17.5 shows the code used to generate this interaction.

FIGURE 17.10

Quiz_Results.cfm

```
LISTING 17.5: quiz_results.cfm

<!--- quiz_results.cfm --->
<!DOCTYPE HTML PUBLIC "-//W3C//DTD HTML 4.0 Transitional//EN">


<!-------------------------------------------------------
All application variables that need to be accessed in
This template are set to regular page variables, in order
to reduce the number of cflocks used.
-------------------------------------------------------->
<CFLOCK TIMEOUT="30"
   THROWONTIMEOUT="Yes"
   NAME="#Application.ApplicationName#"
   TYPE="READONLY">
   <CFSET TITLE = APPLICATION.TITLE>
   <CFSET BGCOLOR = APPLICATION.BGCOLOR>
   <CFSET FACE = APPLICATION.FACE>
   <CFSET EMAIL = APPLICATION.EMAIL>
</CFLOCK>

<CFOUTPUT>
   <HTML>
   <HEAD>
      <TITLE>#Title# Results</TITLE>
   </HEAD>
```

```
   <BODY BGCOLOR="#Bgcolor#">

<!-------------------------------------------------------
   If user requests this template directly without
   answering a quiz question, then they are prompted to
   take the quiz.
   ------------------------------------------------------->
   <CFIF NOT ISDEFINED("form.user_answer") OR
      NOT ISDEFINED("form.today")>
      <DIV ALIGN="center">
         <FONT FACE="#Face#" SIZE="2">
         <HR><B>Welcome to #Title#
         #client.user_name#!</B><HR>
         <I><A HREF="home.cfm">Start the
quiz!</A></I>
         </FONT>
      </DIV>

      </BODY>
      </HTML>
      <CFABORT>
   </CFIF>

   <DIV ALIGN="center">
      <FONT FACE="#Face#" SIZE="2">
      <HR><B>Quiz Results!</B><HR>
      <B>Thank you for taking my short quiz!</B><P>
      </FONT>
   </DIV>
</CFOUTPUT>

<!-------------------------------------------------------
The users answers are evaluated against the query results
from the session.get_question query run in the home.cfm
file.  This way, the query does not need to be run twice.
------------------------------------------------------->
<CFLOCK TIMEOUT="30"
   THROWONTIMEOUT="Yes"
   NAME="#Session.SessionID#"
   TYPE="Exclusive">
   <CFOUTPUT QUERY="session.get_question">

      <FONT FACE="#Face#" SIZE="2">

      <!-----------------------------------------------
      Message if user answer is correct
      ----------------------------------------------->
      <CFIF FORM.USER_ANSWER IS CORRECT_ANSWER>
         <B><FONT COLOR="##008000">
Congratulations!!!
         You are correct!</FONT></B><P>
```

```
<!-------------------------------------------------
Message if user answer is not correct
------------------------------------------------->
<CFELSE>
    <B><FONT COLOR="##FF0000">
    I'm sorry, but that is the wrong answer.
    <A
HREF="home.cfm?question_id=#question_id#">
        Please try again.</A>
</FONT></B><P>
    </CFIF>

    <B>The question was:</B> #question#<BR>

    <!-------------------------------------------------
    Additional message if user answer is not correct
    ------------------------------------------------->
    <CFIF FORM.USER_ANSWER IS NOT CORRECT_ANSWER>
        <B>Your answer was:</B> #user_answer#<BR>

    <!-------------------------------------------------
    Additional message if user answer is correct
    ------------------------------------------------->
    <CFELSE>
        <B>The correct answer is:</B>
        #correct_answer#<BR>
    </CFIF>

    <B>You took the quiz on:</B> #today#<P>
    </FONT>
  </CFOUTPUT>
</CFLOCK>

<CFOUTPUT>
    <DIV ALIGN="center">
        <FONT FACE="#Face#" SIZE="2">
        <B><A HREF="home.cfm">Start the quiz
again?</A></B>
    </DIV>
</CFOUTPUT>
```

Again, the first thing that occurs in this template is to set all application variables to non-persistent variables to limit the number of CFLOCK tags used.

The next major block of code determines whether the user_answer form field exists. If the user were to bookmark the page quiz_results.cfm and go directly to it without answering a question, this would normally cause an error. But instead, the template checks whether this form field exists and if it doesn't, the user is prompted to go to the home.cfm template and the rest of the template is aborted. Remember that when a template is aborted, the OnRequestEnd.cfm template is never processed.

Then, the user_answer is evaluated against correct_answer stored in the session .get_question variable. If it is correct, the user is congratulated; otherwise, they are prompted to answer the same question again.

And finally, the OnRequestEnd.cfm template is processed and displays the current score of the user and all other users. OnRequestEnd.cfm is discussed next.

OnRequestEnd.cfm

The final template in this application is the OnRequestEnd.cfm template. This template is executed at the end of each application page in the current directory. It will not be processed if the calling template aborts, exits, or returns an error. Listing 17.6 shows the code that is processed at the end of each template.

LISTING 17.6: *OnRequestEnd.cfm*

```
<!--- OnRequestEnd.cfm --->

<!-------------------------------------------------------
If the application scores (a count of all users scores)
have not been set, this code sets the defaults; CFLOCK is
used to protect the write of application variables.
------------------------------------------------------->

<CFLOCK TIMEOUT="30"
    THROWONTIMEOUT="Yes"
    NAME="#Application.ApplicationName#"
    TYPE="Exclusive">
    <CFPARAM NAME="application.total_questions" DEFAULT=0>
    <CFPARAM NAME="application.number_correct" DEFAULT=0>
</CFLOCK>

<!-------------------------------------------------------
If the session scores (tied to one user session) have not
been set, this code sets the defaults; CFLOCK is used to
protect the write  of session variables.
------------------------------------------------------->
<CFLOCK TIMEOUT="30"
    THROWONTIMEOUT="Yes"
    NAME="#Session.SessionID#"
    TYPE="Exclusive">
    <CFPARAM NAME="session.total_questions" DEFAULT=0>
    <CFPARAM NAME="session.number_correct" DEFAULT=0>
</CFLOCK>
```

```
<!----------------------------------------------------------
If the current template is quiz_results.cfm, and a
question has been answered, the following code will be
executed.
---------------------------------------------------------->
<CFIF GETFILEFROMPATH(#CGI.CF_TEMPLATE_PATH#) IS
"QUIZ_RESULTS.CFM">

    <!--------------------------------------------------------
    1 is added to the application total count.
    -------------------------------------------------------->
    <CFLOCK TIMEOUT="30"
        THROWONTIMEOUT="Yes"
        NAME="#Application.ApplicationName#"
        TYPE="Exclusive">
        <CFSET APPLICATION.TOTAL_QUESTIONS =
        APPLICATION.TOTAL_QUESTIONS + 1>
    </CFLOCK>

    <!--------------------------------------------------------
    1 is added to the session total count; set the session
    variable correct_answer equal to the regular page
    variable correct_answer so that you do not have to use a CFCLOCK tag around the
next tag.
    -------------------------------------------------------->
    <CFLOCK TIMEOUT="30"
        THROWONTIMEOUT="Yes"
        NAME="#Session.SessionID#"
        TYPE="Exclusive">
        <CFSET SESSION.TOTAL_QUESTIONS =
        SESSION.TOTAL_QUESTIONS + 1>
        <CFSET CORRECT_ANSWER =
        SESSION.GET_QUESTION.CORRECT_ANSWER>
    </CFLOCK>

    <!--------------------------------------------------------
    If the user has answered correctly, then 1 is added to
    both the session total correct count and the
    application total correct count.
    -------------------------------------------------------->

    <CFIF FORM.USER_ANSWER IS CORRECT_ANSWER>
        <CFLOCK TIMEOUT="30"
            THROWONTIMEOUT="Yes"
            NAME="#Session.SessionID#"
            TYPE="Exclusive">
            <CFSET SESSION.NUMBER_CORRECT =
            SESSION.NUMBER_CORRECT + 1>
        </CFLOCK>
```

```
        <CFLOCK TIMEOUT="30"
            THROWONTIMEOUT="Yes"
            NAME="#Application.ApplicationName#"
            TYPE="Exclusive">
            <CFSET APPLICATION.NUMBER_CORRECT =
            APPLICATION.NUMBER_CORRECT + 1>
        </CFLOCK>
    </CFIF>
</CFIF>

<!----------------------------------------------------------
Displays the total scores for the user and everyone else.
----------------------------------------------------------->
<CFOUTPUT>
    <HR>
    <FONT FACE="Arial" SIZE="2">
    <CFLOCK TIMEOUT="30"
        THROWONTIMEOUT="Yes"
        NAME="#Session.SessionID#"
        TYPE="ReadOnly">
        <B>Your score</B><BR>
        Number Questions Answered:
        #session.total_questions#<BR>
        Number Questions Correct:
        #session.number_correct#<P>
    </CFLOCK>

    <CFLOCK TIMEOUT="30"
        THROWONTIMEOUT="Yes"
        NAME="#Application.ApplicationName#"
        TYPE="ReadOnly">
        <B>Everyone's Score</B><BR>
        Number Questions Answered:
        #application.total_questions#<BR>
        Number Questions Correct:
        #application.number_correct#

        <DIV ALIGN="center">
            <HR>
            For questions please email:
            <A HREF="mailto:#Application.Email#">
#Email#</A>
        </DIV>
    </CFLOCK>

    </FONT>
</CFOUTPUT>

</BODY>
</HTML>
```

You have seen examples of `OnRequestEnd.cfm` in both `home.cfm` and `quiz_results.cfm` (see Figures 16.9 and 16.10). You did not see the results of `OnRequestEnd.cfm` in the other templates because they were aborted before the processing of `OnRequest-End.cfm` could occur.

In this application example, `OnRequestEnd.cfm` is used to track the total questions answered for the current user and all users, as well as the total correct answers for each. If these values have not been set, then they are set to 0 using the CFPARAM tag.

Next, whenever the user answers a question and goes to the `QuizResults.cfm` template, a count of 1 is added to both the `session.total_questions` and `application.total_questions`. Then, if the user's answer is correct, a count of 1 is also added to both the `session.number_correct` and `application.number_correct` variables.

The difference between the application variables and the session variables is that the application variables store the data of all users accessing the quiz. So in Figure 17.11 you can see that although the current user has answered only one question, someone else has also answered one question, making the `application.total_questions` count 2.

FIGURE 17.11
OnRequestEnd.cfm

In the final block of code these scores are displayed and a standard footer is used.

Reviewing Variable Scope

In this chapter, you have learned how to create true applications in ColdFusion by using the application framework and persistent variable scopes. Table 17.7 presents a review of these variable scopes.

TABLE 17.7: Variable Types

Variable Type	Required Locking	Storage	Timeout Defaults	Description
Client	N/A	Registry/ Cookies/ Data Source	90 days	Tied to a single client (or browser) and can persist over multiple sessions
Session	Yes	Server RAM	20 minutes	Exist for one client during a single session
Application	Yes	Server RAM	2 days	Tied to a single application and accessible by multiple clients
Server	Yes	Server RAM	When server is shut down	Accessible by all clients and applications on a single server

Knowledge Base Articles

The following Knowledge Base articles can be found on Allaire's Web site, `http://www.allaire.com/Support/KnowledgeBase/SearchForm.cfm`. Each article addresses some aspect of working with the application framework and its variable scopes.

Article 288 "Changing Client Variable Timeouts in CF 3"

Article 968 "Using Application Variables to Cache Static Query Results"

Article 8159 "Session Variables Do Not Work after 4 Upgrade"

Article 1152 "Differentiating Application, Session, and Client Variables"

Article 1113 "Speeding Up Deletion of Client Variables"

Where Do We Go from Here?

In the next chapter, you will look at an important aspect of any ColdFusion application: error control. There are many possible sources of errors in ColdFusion applications, including mistakes in your ColdFusion code, invalid data provided by a user, and problems in the configuration or operation of the server.

However, it is unwise to let users to see the standard error messages generated by ColdFusion or to let your applications continue to operate with invalid data from the user that could lead to strange or unexpected results. This is where error control comes into play, providing ways for you to write into your applications actions to take when errors occur. This is loosely tied to the topics discussed in this chapter because some types of error control are implemented in the `Application.cfm` file.

Another topic tied into the application framework is application security. To learn more about securing your applications, please refer to Chapter 30, which discusses limiting access to your applications.

chapter 18

Implementing Error Control

- Handling Errors through the Application Framework

- Working with Customized Exception Handling

In this chapter, you will learn how to customize the error messages that are displayed to your Web site users. Not only will this make it easier for users to decipher returned error messages, but the messages will also fit into the look and feel of your application. The examples in this chapter are built from those you worked with in Chapter 17, "Implementing the ColdFusion Application Framework." Please refer to Chapter 17 if you have questions about the application features of this chapter's examples.

Handling Errors through the Application Framework

In the preceding chapter, you learned about creating ColdFusion applications using the ColdFusion Application Framework. In this section, you will learn how to implement generalized error control using that same application framework and a ColdFusion tag, CFERROR.

ColdFusion allows for two types of generalized error handling within the application framework (more specialized error handling for all situations will be covered in the "Working with Customized Exception Handling" section of this chapter). The types of general errors are validation errors, request errors, and exceptions.

Validation errors occur when a user has improperly submitted a form. Perhaps they didn't fill out required form fields, or the data they entered is not in the correct format. In Chapter 15, "Forms," you learned how to use ColdFusion form tags to account for these user errors. The ColdFusion form tags then generated error messages to the user describing which fields were filled incorrectly or still needed to be filled. The error page that the user viewed, though, was not customized and did not necessarily fit into the look and feel of your ColdFusion application (see Figure 18.1). ColdFusion enables you to create a customized template to display the same validation error information using the CFERROR tag (see Figure 18.2).

NOTE Refer to Chapter 15 for more information on ColdFusion form tags.

Request errors occur during the normal processing of a ColdFusion template. These errors may be due to misspelled variable names, nonexistence of included files, or other template processing problems. Normally, if a variable name is misspelled, you will receive an error like that in Figure 18.3. But when using ColdFusion error handling, you can customize the error messages as in Figure 18.4.

FIGURE 18.1
The standard ColdFusion
validation error page

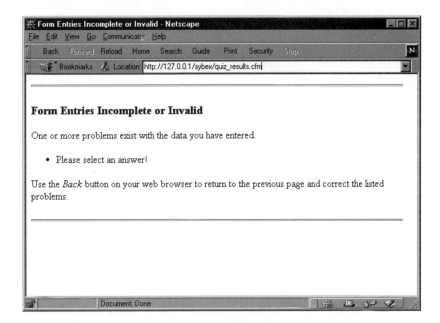

FIGURE 18.2
A customized ColdFusion
validation error page

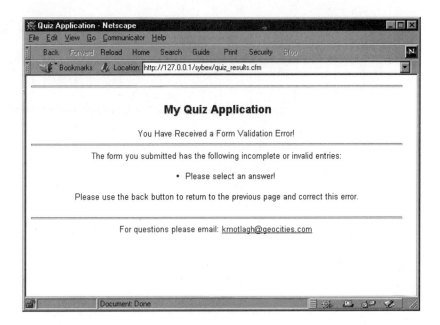

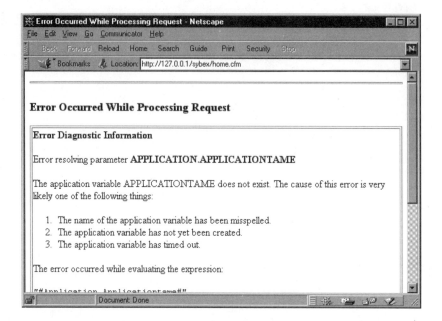

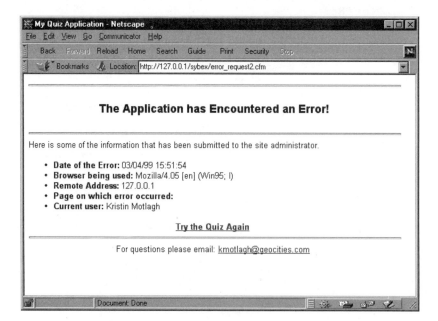

To work with the ColdFusion error-handling mechanism, you need to do two things:

1. Place a CFERROR tag in the template that you would like to have ColdFusion check for errors.

2. Create a customized error template that ColdFusion jumps to whenever an error is encountered.

Understanding the *CFERROR* Tag

The CFERROR tag is placed in a template to catch application errors. As discussed previously, CFERROR is able to catch two types of errors: validation and request. The following code shows the correct syntax for both types of CFERROR tags:

```
<CFERROR TYPE="REQUEST"
    TEMPLATE="error_request.cfm"
    MAILTO="kmotlagh@geocities.com">

<CFERROR TYPE="VALIDATION"
    TEMPLATE="error_validation.cfm"
    MAILTO="kmotlagh@geocities.com">
```

Table 18.1 describes each of the CFERROR attributes in detail.

TABLE 18.1:   CFERROR Attributes

Attribute	Default	Required	Values	Description
TYPE	Request	No	Request	Catches errors that result from the processing of a template.
			Validation	Catches user errors in submitting form data.
			Exception	Catches exceptions such as those created by the **CFTHROW** tag. New in ColdFusion 4.5.
			Monitor	Creates an exception monitor. New in ColdFusion 4.5.
TEMPLATE	N/A	Yes	The name of the error template	The name of the template that will provide the customized error information to the user.
EXCEPTION	N/A	Yes if the type is Ex ception or Monitor	An exception type	Specifies the type of exception to be handled when the type is Exception or Monitor
MAILTO	N/A	No	The e-mail address of the system administrator	This e-mail address can be used to direct error information to a site administrator.

Although the CFERROR tag can be used in any template in which you would like to catch errors, it can also be placed in the Application.cfm template to catch errors throughout your entire application. This is, in most cases, the best solution for error handling.

NOTE To learn more about the ColdFusion Application Framework, please refer to Chapter 17.

Because the Application.cfm template is processed before each template in your application framework, adding your CFERROR tags to this template is useful for catching all errors in your application.

Listing 18.1 shows how a CFERROR tag was added to the Application.cfm template that was used in Chapter 17.

TIP The code in Listing 18.1 is also in a file titled Application18a.cfm in the **chapter18** folder of your CD. If you use the file on the CD, save it to the **sybex** folder in your Web server root directory and rename it Application.cfm.

TIP In Listing 18.1, all bold lines indicate modifications that have been made. This convention is used throughout this chapter.

Listing 18.1: *application18a.cfm*

```
<!--- Application.cfm --->
<!DOCTYPE HTML PUBLIC "-//W3C//DTD HTML 4.0 Transitional//EN">

<!-----------------------------------------------------------
Set application name; client variables on; session variables on;
allow cookies; session timeout after 20 minutes; application
timeout after 2 days; store client variables in registry.
----------------------------------------------------------->
<CFAPPLICATION NAME="MyApp"
   SESSIONMANAGEMENT="Yes"
   SETCLIENTCOOKIES="Yes"
   SESSIONTIMEOUT="#CreateTimeSpan(0, 0, 20, 0)#"
   APPLICATIONTIMEOUT="#CreateTimeSpan(2, 0, 0, 0)#"
   CLIENTMANAGEMENT="Yes"
   CLIENTSTORAGE="Registry">

<!-----------------------------------------------------------
Redirect users to error page if validation error occurs.
----------------------------------------------------------->
```

```
<CFERROR TYPE="VALIDATION"
    TEMPLATE="error_validation.cfm"
    MAILTO="kmotlagh@geocities.com">

<!-------------------------------------------------------------
Used to reset application, session, and client variables for
testing purposes. You must remove the comments to clear all
variable scopes, and then replace the comments so the application
will run normally.
----------------------------------------------------------------->
<!---
<CFSET STRUCTCLEAR(APPLICATION)>
<CFSET STRUCTCLEAR(SESSION)>
<CFLOOP INDEX="x" LIST="#GetClientVariablesList()#">
    <CFSET DELETED = DELETECLIENTVARIABLE("#x#")>
</CFLOOP>
<CFCOOKIE NAME="cfid" EXPIRES="NOW">
<CFCOOKIE NAME="cftoken" EXPIRES="NOW">
<CFCOOKIE NAME="cfglobals" EXPIRES="NOW">
<CFABORT>
--->

<!-------------------------------------------------------------
Set Server constants that can be accessed by any client.
----------------------------------------------------------------->
<CFLOCK TIMEOUT="30"
    THROWONTIMEOUT="Yes"
    NAME="server"
    TYPE="Exclusive">
    <CFIF NOT #ISDEFINED("server.season")#>
        <!-------------------------------------------------
        The season is currently set to a string, but could
        easily be determined automatically by time of year.
        ------------------------------------------------->
        <CFSET SERVER.SEASON = "Spring Time">
    </CFIF>
</CFLOCK>

<!-------------------------------------------------------------
Set Application constants.
----------------------------------------------------------------->
<CFLOCK TIMEOUT="30"
    THROWONTIMEOUT="Yes"
    NAME="#Application.ApplicationName#"
    TYPE="Exclusive">
    <CFIF NOT #ISDEFINED("Application.Started")#>
        <CFSET APPLICATION.TITLE = "My Quiz Application">
        <CFSET APPLICATION.DB = "quiz">
```

```
        <CFSET APPLICATION.EMAIL = "kmotlagh@geocities.com">
        <CFSET APPLICATION.BGCOLOR = "##ffffff">
        <CFSET APPLICATION.FACE = "Arial">
        <CFSET APPLICATION.STARTED = TRUE>
    </CFIF>
</CFLOCK>

<!---------------------------------------------------------------
Test to see if user has logged in. If they haven't, a
non-persistent login variable is set. This is so you do not have
to use a CFLOCK tag around the next block of code.
---------------------------------------------------------------->
<CFLOCK TIMEOUT="30"
    THROWONTIMEOUT="Yes"
    NAME="#Session.SessionID#"
    TYPE="ReadOnly">
    <CFIF NOT ISDEFINED("Session.Started")>
        <CFSET LOGIN = "">
    </CFIF>
</CFLOCK>

<CFIF ISDEFINED("Login")>
    <!-------------------------------------------------
    Since the session.initialized variable has not yet been
    set, the processing of the login2.cfm would be aborted
    unless the following CFIF statement is added.
    ------------------------------------------------->
    <CFSET PATH=GETDIRECTORYFROMPATH(#CGI.CF_TEMPLATE_PATH#)>
    <CFIF (CGI.CF_TEMPLATE_PATH IS NOT "#path#login.cfm")
    AND (CGI.CF_TEMPLATE_PATH IS NOT "#path#login2.cfm")>
        <CFINCLUDE TEMPLATE="login3.cfm">

        <!-------------------------------------------------
        Aborts processing of any template except login.cfm
        and login2.cfm until user has logged in.
        ------------------------------------------------->
        <CFABORT>
    </CFIF>
</CFIF>
```

Creating Error Templates

In the preceding section, you added a CFERROR tag to your `Application.cfm` template. This error tag pointed to a specific template intended to handle validation errors. The only problem is that you have not yet created this template. In this section, you will create error templates for both validation and request errors.

Before you start, you must know several facts about creating error templates:

- ColdFusion provides several error variables that you can access in your templates. These variables are different for validation and request error templates. They are detailed in Tables 18.2 and 18.3.
- You cannot use any ColdFusion code within your error templates except the error variables. This includes CFOUTPUT and CFIF tags, as well as any variables besides the error variables described above. Using other ColdFusion code could potentially create another error in your error template, and then the browser would be in a loop trying to process the errors.
- You can use HTML and JavaScript in your error templates.
- Because ColdFusion processing is limited on ColdFusion error templates, you also cannot encrypt them.

NOTE   In version 4.5 of ColdFusion, the Exception type has been added to the CFERROR tag. Error-handling templates invoked with this type do not face restrictions in the use of ColdFusion code of the type outlined above. This makes them more powerful than using the Request type.

The Validation Error Template

First, create the error template for validation errors. This template will be called error_validation.cfm and should be saved to the sybex folder in your Web server root directory. Because you want to provide useful information to the user about the specific error that has occurred, ColdFusion has provided several built-in validation error variables that you can add to your template (see Table 18.2). Listing 18.2 shows how to create a basic validation error template. You will notice that no other ColdFusion code is used except a reference to an error variable.

TABLE 18.2:   Validation Error Variables

Error Variable	Description
Error.ValidationHeader	Header text (enclosed in H3 tags)
Error.InvalidFields	A list of the errors (unordered)
Error.ValidationFooter	Footer text
Error.MailTo	The e-mail address specified in the CFERROR tag

TIP   The code in Listing 18.2 is also in a file entitled error_validation.cfm in the chapter18 folder of your CD-ROM. If you use the file on the CD-ROM, save it to the sybex folder in your Web server root directory.

Listing 18.2: *error_validation.cfm*

```
<!--- error_validation.cfm --->
<!DOCTYPE HTML PUBLIC "-//W3C//DTD HTML 4.0 Transitional//EN">

<HTML>
<HEAD>
    <TITLE>Quiz Application</TITLE>
</HEAD>

<BODY BGCOLOR="#ffffff">

    <DIV ALIGN="center">
        <FONT FACE="Arial" SIZE="2">
        <HR><H3>My Quiz Application</H3>
        You Have Received a Form Validation Error!
        <HR>
        The form you submitted has the following incomplete
or invalid entries:<P>
        #Error.InvalidFields#<P>
        Please use the back button to return to the previous
page and correct this error.<P>

        <HR>For questions please email:
        <A HREF="mailto:#Error.MailTo#">#Error.MailTo#</A>
        </FONT>

    </DIV>

</BODY>
</HTML>
```

Now that you have added a CFERROR validation tag to your Application.cfm template and have created a validation error template, you can test the results. If you have not already done so, make sure that the following files from the **chapter17** folder on the CD-ROM are in the **sybex** folder in your Web server root directory:

- Application18a.cfm (rename it as Application.cfm)
- error_validation.cfm
- home.cfm
- login.cfm
- login2.cfm
- OnRequestEnd.cfm
- quiz_results.cfm
- quiz.mdb (If you have not already done so, you need to add this Access database as a data source in the ColdFusion Administrator.)

Now go to your browser and open `http://127.0.0.1/sybex/home.cfm`.

You will probably have to log in first (with the username **kristin** and the password **motlagh**). Then you will see a quiz form (see Figure 18.5). Select Score Question! but don't select a quiz answer (see Figure 18.5) and you should see an error template similar to that shown in Figure 18.6.

FIGURE 18.5
Submitting a form with no data

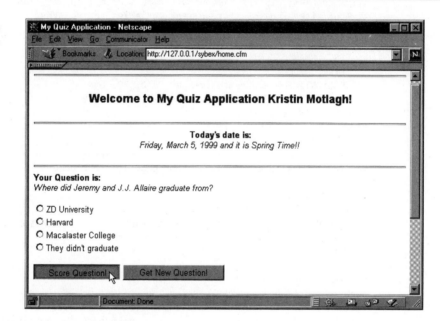

The Request Error Template

Accounting for request errors is similar to accounting for validation errors. You need to add a CFERROR request tag to your `Application.cfm` template (or any template in which you would like to catch errors). Your `Application.cfm` template would then look like that in Listing 18.3.

TIP

The code in Listing 18.3 is also in a file entitled `Application18b.cfm` in the **chapter18** folder of your CD-ROM. If you use the file on the CD-ROM, save it to the **sybex** folder in your Web server root directory and rename it as `Application.cfm`.

Listing 18.3: *application18b.cfm*

```
<!--- Application.cfm --->
<!DOCTYPE HTML PUBLIC "-//W3C//DTD HTML 4.0 Transitional//EN">


<!----------------------------------------------------------------
Set application name; client variables on; session variables on;
allow cookies; session timeout after 20 minutes; application
timeout after 2 days; store client variables in registry.
----------------------------------------------------------------->
<CFAPPLICATION NAME="MyApp"
   SESSIONMANAGEMENT="Yes"
   SETCLIENTCOOKIES="Yes"
   SESSIONTIMEOUT="#CreateTimeSpan(0, 0, 20, 0)#"
   APPLICATIONTIMEOUT="#CreateTimeSpan(2, 0, 0, 0)#"
   CLIENTMANAGEMENT="Yes"
   CLIENTSTORAGE="Registry">


<!----------------------------------------------------------------
Redirect users to appropriate error page if error occurs.
----------------------------------------------------------------->
<CFERROR TYPE="REQUEST"
   TEMPLATE="error_request.cfm"
   MAILTO="kmotlagh@geocities.com"><CFERROR TYPE="VALIDATION"
   TEMPLATE="error_validation.cfm"
   MAILTO="kmotlagh@geocities.com">


<!----------------------------------------------------------------
Used to reset application, session, and client variables for
testing purposes. You must remove the comments to clear all
variable scopes, and then replace the comments so the application
will run normally.
----------------------------------------------------------------->
<!---
<CFSET STRUCTCLEAR(APPLICATION)>
<CFSET STRUCTCLEAR(SESSION)>
<CFLOOP INDEX="x" LIST="#GetClientVariablesList()#">
   <CFSET DELETED = DELETECLIENTVARIABLE("#x#")>
</CFLOOP>
<CFCOOKIE NAME="cfid" EXPIRES="NOW">
<CFCOOKIE NAME="cftoken" EXPIRES="NOW">
<CFCOOKIE NAME="cfglobals" EXPIRES="NOW">
<CFABORT>
--->


<!----------------------------------------------------------------
Set Server constants that can be accessed by any client.
----------------------------------------------------------------->
```

```
<CFLOCK TIMEOUT="30"
   THROWONTIMEOUT="Yes"
   NAME="server"
   TYPE="Exclusive">
   <CFIF NOT #ISDEFINED("server.season")#>
      <!-----------------------------------------------
      The season is currently set to a string, but could
      easily be determined automatically by time of year.
      ------------------------------------------------->
      <CFSET SERVER.SEASON = "Spring Time">
   </CFIF>
</CFLOCK>

<!---------------------------------------------------------------
Set Application constants.
---------------------------------------------------------------->
<CFLOCK TIMEOUT="30"
   THROWONTIMEOUT="Yes"
   NAME="#Application.ApplicationName#"
   TYPE="Exclusive">
   <CFIF NOT #ISDEFINED("Application.Started")#>
      <CFSET APPLICATION.TITLE = "My Quiz Application">
      <CFSET APPLICATION.DB = "quiz">
      <CFSET APPLICATION.EMAIL = "kmotlagh@geocities.com">
      <CFSET APPLICATION.BGCOLOR = "##ffffff">
      <CFSET APPLICATION.FACE = "Arial">
      <CFSET APPLICATION.STARTED = TRUE>
   </CFIF>
</CFLOCK>

<!---------------------------------------------------------------
Test to see if user has logged in. If they haven't, a
non-persistent login variable is set. This is so you do not have
to use a <CFLOCK> tag around the next block of code.
---------------------------------------------------------------->
<CFLOCK TIMEOUT="30"
   THROWONTIMEOUT="Yes"
   NAME="#Session.SessionID#"
   TYPE="ReadOnly">
   <CFIF NOT ISDEFINED("Session.Started")>
      <CFSET LOGIN = "">
   </CFIF>
</CFLOCK>

<CFIF ISDEFINED("Login")>
   <!----------------------------------------------------
   Since the session.initialized variable has not yet been
   set, the processing of the login2.cfm would be aborted
```

```
unless the following cfif statement is added.
---------------------------------------------------->
<CFSET PATH=GETDIRECTORYFROMPATH(#CGI.CF_TEMPLATE_PATH#)>
<CFIF (CGI.CF_TEMPLATE_PATH IS NOT "#path#login.cfm")
AND (CGI.CF_TEMPLATE_PATH IS NOT "#path#login2.cfm")>
    <CFINCLUDE TEMPLATE="login.cfm">

    <!-------------------------------------------------
    Aborts processing of any template except login.cfm
    and login2.cfm until user has logged in.
    -------------------------------------------------->
    <CFABORT>
  </CFIF>
</CFIF>
```

Now, you can create the error template for request errors. This template will be called **error_request.cfm** and should be saved to the **sybex** folder in your Web server root directory. There are built-in error variables for request errors that provide useful information to the user about the specific error that has occurred (see Table 18.3). Listing 18.4 shows how to create a basic request error template. Remember that you cannot use any ColdFusion code other than the error variables provided by CFERROR.

TABLE 18.3:   Request Error Variables

Error Variable	Description
Error.Diagnostics	A full description of the problem that caused the error
Error.Browser	The client browser type and version
Error.DateTime	The date and time that the error occurred
Error.GeneratedContent	The failed request's generated content
Error.HTTPReferer	The URL on which the error occurred
Error.MailTo	The mailto address specified in the CFERROR request tag
Error.QueryString	The query string after the ? in the URL
Error.RemoteAddress	The client's IP address
Error.Template	The template path on which the error occurred

TIP

The code in Listing 18.4 is also in a file titled **error_request18a.cfm** in the **chapter18** folder of your CD-ROM. If you use the file on the CD-ROM, save it to the **sybex** folder in your Web server root directory and rename it **error_request.cfm**.

Listing 18.4: *error_request18a.cfm*

```
<!--- error_request.cfm --->
<!DOCTYPE HTML PUBLIC "-//W3C//DTD HTML 4.0 Transitional//EN">

<HTML>
<HEAD>
    <TITLE>Quiz Application</TITLE>
</HEAD>

<BODY BGCOLOR="#ffffff">

<DIV ALIGN="center">
    <FONT FACE="Arial" SIZE="2">
    <HR>
    <H3>The Application Has Encountered a Request Error!</H3>
    <HR>
</DIV>

<H4>Error Information....</H4>
<UL>
<LI><B>Date and Time:</B> #Error.DateTime#
<LI><B>Browser:</B> #Error.Browser#
<LI><B>Remote Address:</B> #Error.RemoteAddress#
<LI><B>HTTP Referer:</B> #Error.HTTPReferer#
<LI><B>Template:</B> #Error.Template#
<LI><B>Query String:</B> #Error.QueryString#
<LI><B>Diagnostics:</B>
<FORM>
        <TEXTAREA NAME="Diagnostics"
                    COLS="42"
                    ROWS="5"
                    WRAP="VIRTUAL">
#Error.Diagnostics#
</TEXTAREA>
    </FORM>
    </UL>

    Please notify the <A HREF="mailto:#Error.MailTo#">administrator</A> of this error.
Remember to provide all pertinent information.

    <HR>
    <DIV ALIGN="center">
    For questions please email:
    <A HREF="mailto:#Error.MailTo#">#Error.MailTo#</A>
    </DIV>

    </BODY>
    </HTML>
```

To test the results, you need to first create an error. To create a simple error, rename any variable being referenced in your home.cfm template to a variable name that has not yet been created. Now go to your browser and open http://127.0.0.1/sybex/home.cfm.

If your session has timed out, you may need to log in again (using the username **kristin** and the password **motlagh**). You should see an error template like that shown in Figure 18.6.

FIGURE 18.6

A request error template

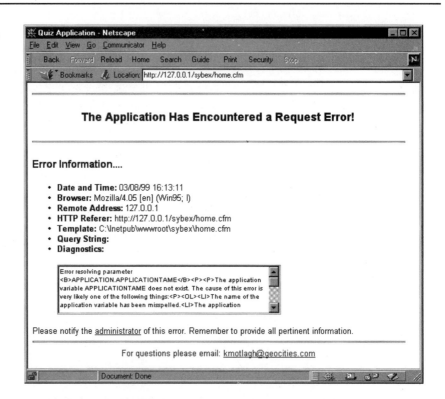

The Exception Error Template

With ColdFusion 4.5, The Exception type was added to the CFERROR tag that allowed the CFERROR tag to be used to trap specific types of errors, or exceptions, and provide a custom error handling template for those errors. Exceptions in the context of the CFCATCH and CFTHROW tags will be discussed later in the section, "Working with Customized Exception Handling." We will cover the specifics of using CFERROR with exceptions then.

Logging Error Messages When Using *CFERROR*

One of the problems with using CFERROR tags, and the resulting error templates, is that you cannot incorporate any ColdFusion code. As a result, you cannot log any of the error information into a database or automatically send an e-mail to the administrator with all the diagnostic information attached.

There is a way to get around this, however. This section will show you how to log request error information to a database by using JavaScript to redirect the browser to a ColdFusion template that can include ColdFusion code.

The procedure to do this is as follows:

1. A request error is encountered, and the user is directed to the request error template, `error_request.cfm`.

2. Because the `Application.cfm` template is run for each page within your application, the CFERROR tags in the `Application.cfm` template are disabled when accessing the `error_request.cfm` template. If they are not disabled, an error loop could potentially occur.

3. The `error_request.cfm` template contains a form with hidden fields and a text area field. These fields store the error variables that will be passed on to the next template, `error_request2.cfm`.

4. `error_request.cfm` has a JavaScript event command when loading the page to automatically submit the form. This means that when `error_request.cfm` is accessed, the form containing the error variables is automatically submitted to `error_request2.cfm`. The CFERROR tags in the `Application.cfm` template are also disabled for `error_request2.cfm`.

5. Because `error_request2.cfm` is not the request error template, you can add ColdFusion code that will log the error variables into a database. These error variables were passed as hidden form fields from the request error template through the URL.

NOTE   All messages, including error messages, are logged to the log files in `c:\cfusion\log` (on most systems). You can always manually refer to these files for a comprehensive list of all errors. This is especially useful where special characters such as quotation marks prevent logging of the complete error messages to a database.

The first step is to modify your `Application.cfm` template to disable error handling if the current template is `error_request.cfm` or `error_request2.cfm` (see Listing 18.5). You can determine the current template path by using the function and argument `GETDIRECTORYFROMPATH(#CGI.CF_TEMPLATE_PATH#)`.

NOTE   To find out more about CGI variables, please refer to Chapter 4.

TIP   The code in Listing 18.5 is also in a file titled `Application18c.cfm` in the **chapter18** folder of your CD-ROM. If you use the file on the CD-ROM, save it to the **sybex** folder in your Web server root directory and rename it `Application.cfm`.

Listing 18.5: *application18c.cfm*

```
<!--- Application.cfm --->
<!DOCTYPE HTML PUBLIC "-//W3C//DTD HTML 4.0 Transitional//EN">

<!--------------------------------------------------------------
Set application name; client variables on; session variables on;
allow cookies; session timeout after 20 minutes; application
timeout after 2 days; store client variables in registry.
--------------------------------------------------------------->
<CFAPPLICATION NAME="MyApp"
    SESSIONMANAGEMENT="Yes"
    SETCLIENTCOOKIES="Yes"
    SESSIONTIMEOUT="#CreateTimeSpan(0, 0, 20, 0)#"
    APPLICATIONTIMEOUT="#CreateTimeSpan(2, 0, 0, 0)#"
    CLIENTMANAGEMENT="Yes"
    CLIENTSTORAGE="Registry">

<!--------------------------------------------------------------
Redirect users to error page if error occurs, unless current template is
error_request2.cfm or error_request.cfm.
--------------------------------------------------------------->
<CFSET PATH=GETDIRECTORYFROMPATH(#CGI.CF_TEMPLATE_PATH#)>
<CFIF (CGI.CF_TEMPLATE_PATH IS NOT "#path#error_request2.cfm")
    AND (CGI.CF_TEMPLATE_PATH IS NOT "#path#error_request.cfm")>

<CFERROR TYPE="REQUEST"
    TEMPLATE="error_request.cfm"
    MAILTO="kmotlagh@geocities.com">
<CFERROR TYPE="VALIDATION"
    TEMPLATE="error_validation.cfm"
    MAILTO="kmotlagh@geocities.com">

</CFIF>

<!--------------------------------------------------------------
Used to reset application, session, and client variables for
testing purposes. You must remove the comments to clear all
```

```
variable scopes, and then replace the comments so the application
will run normally.
------------------------------------------------------------------>
<!---
<CFSET STRUCTCLEAR(APPLICATION)>
<CFSET STRUCTCLEAR(SESSION)>
<CFLOOP INDEX="x" LIST="#GetClientVariablesList()#">
   <CFSET DELETED = DELETECLIENTVARIABLE("#x#")>
</CFLOOP>
<CFCOOKIE NAME="cfid" EXPIRES="NOW">
<CFCOOKIE NAME="cftoken" EXPIRES="NOW">
<CFCOOKIE NAME="cfglobals" EXPIRES="NOW">
<CFABORT>
--->

<!-----------------------------------------------------------------
Set Server constants that can be accessed by any client.
------------------------------------------------------------------>
<CFLOCK TIMEOUT="30"
   THROWONTIMEOUT="Yes"
   NAME="server"
   TYPE="Exclusive">
   <CFIF NOT #ISDEFINED("server.season")#>
      <!--------------------------------------------------
      The season is currently set to a string, but could
      easily be determined automatically by time of year.
      -------------------------------------------------->
      <CFSET SERVER.SEASON = "Spring Time">
   </CFIF>
</CFLOCK>

<!-----------------------------------------------------------------
Set Application constants.
------------------------------------------------------------------>
<CFLOCK TIMEOUT="30"
   THROWONTIMEOUT="Yes"
   NAME="#Application.ApplicationName#"
   TYPE="Exclusive">
   <CFIF NOT #ISDEFINED("Application.Started")#>
      <CFSET APPLICATION.TITLE = "My Quiz Application">
      <CFSET APPLICATION.DB = "quiz">
      <CFSET APPLICATION.EMAIL = "kmotlagh@geocities.com">
      <CFSET APPLICATION.BGCOLOR = "##ffffff">
      <CFSET APPLICATION.FACE = "Arial">
      <CFSET APPLICATION.STARTED = TRUE>
   </CFIF>
</CFLOCK>
```

```
<!-----------------------------------------------------------
Test to see if user has logged in. If they haven't, a
non-persistent login variable is set. This is so you do not have
to use a CFLOCK tag around the next block of code.
----------------------------------------------------------->
<CFLOCK TIMEOUT="30"
   THROWONTIMEOUT="Yes"
   NAME="#Session.SessionID#"
   TYPE="ReadOnly">
   <CFIF NOT ISDEFINED("Session.Started")>
      <CFSET LOGIN = "">
   </CFIF>
</CFLOCK>

<CFIF ISDEFINED("Login")>
   <!---------------------------------------------------
   Since the session.initialized variable has not yet been
   set, the processing of the login2.cfm would be aborted
   unless the following CFIF statement is added.
   --------------------------------------------------->
   <CFSET PATH=GETDIRECTORYFROMPATH(#CGI.CF_TEMPLATE_PATH#)>
   <CFIF (CGI.CF_TEMPLATE_PATH IS NOT "#path#login.cfm")
   AND (CGI.CF_TEMPLATE_PATH IS NOT "#path#login2.cfm")>
      <CFINCLUDE TEMPLATE="login.cfm">

      <!---------------------------------------------------
      Aborts processing of any template except login.cfm
      and login2.cfm until user has logged in.
      --------------------------------------------------->
      <CFABORT>
   </CFIF>
</CFIF>
```

Next, you need to modify your error_request.cfm template to reflect the changes
shown in Listing 18.6. You will be creating a form and automatically submitting the
results to error_request2.cfm by using JavaScript.

TIP

The code in Listing 18.6 is also in a file titled error_request18b.cfm in the chapter18
folder of your CD-ROM. If you use the file on the CD-ROM, save it to the sybex folder in your
Web server root directory and rename it error_request.cfm.

Listing 18.6: *error_request18b.cfm*

```
<!--- error_request.cfm --->
<!DOCTYPE HTML PUBLIC "-//W3C//DTD HTML 4.0 Transitional//EN">
```

```
<HTML>
<HEAD>
   <TITLE>Quiz Application</TITLE>
</HEAD>

<BODY BGCOLOR="#ffffff" onLoad="document.MyForm.submit()">

<DIV ALIGN="center">
   <FONT FACE="Arial" SIZE="2">
   <HR>
   <H3>The Application Has Encountered a Request Error!</H3>
   <HR>

   <H4>Please wait while the administrator is
   notified....</H4>
   <FORM ACTION="error_request2.cfm"
      METHOD="POST"
      NAME="MyForm">
      <INPUT TYPE="Hidden"
         NAME="ErrorDate"
         VALUE="#Error.DateTime#">
      <INPUT TYPE="Hidden"
         NAME="Browser"
         VALUE="#Error.Browser#">
      <INPUT TYPE="Hidden"
         NAME="RemoteAddress"
         VALUE="#Error.RemoteAddress#">
      <INPUT TYPE="Hidden"
         NAME="HTTPReferer"
         VALUE="#Error.HTTPReferer#">
      <INPUT TYPE="Hidden"
         NAME="Template"
         VALUE="#Error.Template#">
      <INPUT TYPE="Hidden"
         NAME="QueryString"
         VALUE="#Error.QueryString#">
      <INPUT TYPE="Hidden"
         NAME="MailTo"
         VALUE="#Error.MailTo#">
      <TEXTAREA NAME="Diagnostics"
            COLS="42"
            ROWS="1"
            WRAP="VIRTUAL">#Error.Diagnostics#</TEXTAREA>
   </FORM>

   <HR>For questions please email:
   <A HREF="mailto:#Error.MailTo#">#Error.MailTo#</A>
</DIV>

</BODY>
</HTML>
```

Next, you need to create the template, error_request2.cfm. In error_request2.cfm, you will log all the error information into a database table and display only user-pertinent information (see Listing 18.7).

TIP

To log information to a database, you need to make sure that you have copied the quiz.mdb database file from the chapter18 folder on the accompanying CD-ROM to the sybex folder in your Web server root directory. You also need to ensure that a ColdFusion data source has been added for the quiz.mdb file.

TIP

The code in Listing 18.7 is also in a file entitled error_request2.cfm in the chapter18 folder of your CD-ROM. If you use the file on the CD-ROM, save it to the sybex folder in your Web server root directory.

Listing 18.7: *error_request2.cfm*

```
<!--- error_request2.cfm --->
<!DOCTYPE HTML PUBLIC "-//W3C//DTD HTML 4.0 Transitional//EN">


<!--------------------------------------------------------------
All application variables that need to be accessed in this
template are set to regular page variables, in order to reduce
the amount of cflocks used.
-------------------------------------------------------------->
<CFLOCK TIMEOUT="30"
    THROWONTIMEOUT="Yes"
    NAME="#APPLICATION.ApplicationName#"
    TYPE="READONLY">
    <CFSET DB = APPLICATION.DB>
    <CFSET TITLE = APPLICATION.TITLE>
    <CFSET BGCOLOR = APPLICATION.BGCOLOR>
    <CFSET FACE = APPLICATION.FACE>
</CFLOCK>

<CFOUTPUT>
    <HTML>
    <HEAD>
        <TITLE>#title#</TITLE>
    </HEAD>

    <BODY BGCOLOR="#bgcolor#">

    <CFIF NOT ISDEFINED("FORM.Diagnostics") AND
        NOT ISDEFINED("FORM.ErrorDate") AND
```

```
            NOT ISDEFINED("FORM.Browser") AND
            NOT ISDEFINED("FORM.RemoteAddress") AND
            NOT ISDEFINED("FORM.HTTPReferer") AND
            NOT ISDEFINED("FORM.Template") AND
            NOT ISDEFINED("FORM.QueryString") AND
            NOT ISDEFINED("FORM.User_Name")>
            <DIV ALIGN="center">
               <FONT FACE="#Face#" SIZE="2">
               <HR><H3>Welcome to #Title#
               #CLIENT.user_name#!</H3><HR>
               <I><A HREF="home.cfm">Start the quiz!</A></I>
               </FONT>
            </DIV>

            </BODY>
            </HTML>
            <CFABORT>
        </CFIF>
</CFOUTPUT>

<CFTRANSACTION>
    <CFQUERY NAME="add_error"
        DATASOURCE="#db#"
        DBTYPE="ODBC">
        INSERT INTO errors (
            ErrorDate,
            Browser,
            RemoteAddress,
            HTTPReferer,
            Template,
            QueryString,
            User_Name,
            Diagnostics
            )
        VALUES (
            '#FORM.ErrorDate#',
            '#FORM.Browser#',
            '#FORM.RemoteAddress#',
            '#FORM.HTTPReferer#',
            '#FORM.Template#',
            '#FORM.QueryString#',
            '#CLIENT.user_name#',
            '#HTMLCodeFormat(FORM.Diagnostics)#'
            )
    </CFQUERY>
</CFTRANSACTION>

<CFOUTPUT>
```

```
<DIV ALIGN="center">
  <FONT FACE="#face#" SIZE="2">
  <HR>
  <H3>The Application Has Encountered an Error!</H3>
  <HR>
  </FONT>
</DIV>

<FONT FACE="#face#" SIZE="2">
Here is some of the information that has been submitted
to the site administrator. <P>
<UL>
<LI><B>Date of the Error:</B> #FORM.ErrorDate#
<LI><B>Browser being used:</B> #FORM.Browser#
<LI><B>Remote Address:</B> #FORM.RemoteAddress#
<LI><B>Page on which error occurred:</B>
#FORM.HTTPReferer#
<LI><B>Current user:</B> #CLIENT.user_name#
</UL>

<DIV ALIGN="center">
  <B><A HREF="home.cfm">Try the Quiz Again</A></B>
  <HR>For questions please email:
  <A HREF="mailto:#FORM.MailTo#">#FORM.MailTo#</A>
</DIV>
</FONT>

</CFOUTPUT>

</BODY>
</HTML>
<CFABORT>
```

To test this code, create an error by renaming a variable in your home.cfm template to an unassigned variable name. Load home.cfm in your browser using the following URL: http://127.0.0.1/sybex/home.cfm. You should see error_request.cfm pop up briefly and then be redirected to error_request2.cm (see Figure 18.7). If you were to check the database table, the new error information would be logged in the errors table of the quiz.mdb file.

TIP   If you want to e-mail the error information to the administrator, please refer to "Using the CFMAIL Tag" in Chapter 21, "Sending Mail."

WARNING	You must be careful in implementing this type of code because you could easily find yourself in an error loop. If the code you use in `error_request2.cfm` has an error, this sort of error handling will not work properly.

FIGURE 18.7
A redirected request error
template

Working with Customized Exception Handling

Since version 4, ColdFusion has provided a more structured way of handling errors within ColdFusion templates. This new type of error handling enables you to account for specific types of errors within a specific template, without necessarily aborting the processing of the entire template. Remember that with Validation and Request types of the CFERROR tag the processing of the template is aborted and the user is redirected to a custom error page. CFTRY and CFCATCH enable errors to be handled directly within the template throwing the exception. They can also be used with ColdFusion code to provide pages that can be more easily customized. To use this new error-handling code you must learn about the tags listed in Table 18.4.

TABLE 18.4: Exception-Handling Tags

Tag Name	Attributes	Description
CFTRY	N/A	Used to test a block of code for errors. Must be used with one or more CFCATCH tags. If a certain type of error occurs inside a **CFTRY** tag, then ColdFusion looks to see whether there is a corresponding CFCATCH tag of the same type.

TABLE 18.4: Exception-Handling Tags *(continued)*

Tag Name	Attributes	Description
CFCATCH	TYPE	Ten types of errors can be caught by using **CFCATCH**. Inside the CFCATCH tag is where you place HTML and ColdFusion code that will be displayed if a particular **CFCATCH** type error is caught.
CFTHROW	TYPE, MESSAGE, DETAIL, ERRORCODE, EXTENDEDINFO	Used to throw an exception. For example, you can use this tag in testing purposes or you can create an exception based upon certain conditions being met.

Specifically, you must enclose the code you wish to be checked for errors within the CFTRY tags. You can enclose an entire template or just a particular piece of code.

You must also include one or more CFCATCH tags inside the CFTRY tag pair; they should be placed immediately before the end CFTRY tag. The general format should look like the following:

```
<CFTRY>
    ...HTML and CFML code
<CFCATCH>
...code used to handle
exceptions
</CFCATCH>
</CFTRY>
```

The following code shows an example of using CFTRY and CFCATCH to catch a database error. Figure 18.8 shows how this template might look in the browser if an error was caught.

```
<CFTRY>
  <CFTRANSACTION>
    <CFQUERY NAME="add_error"
        DATASOURCE="#db#"
        DBTYPE="ODBC">
        INSERT INTO errors (
            ErrorDate,
            Browser,
            RemoteAddress,
            HTTPReferer,
            Template,
            QueryString,
            User_Tame,
            Diagnostics
            )
        VALUES (
            '#FORM.ErrorDate#',
            '#FORM.Browser#',
            '#FORM.RemoteAddress#',
```

```
            '#FORM.HTTPReferer#',
            '#FORM.Template#',
            '#FORM.QueryString#',
            '#CLIENT.user_name#',
            '#HTMLCodeFormat(FORM.Diagnostics)#'
            )
       </CFQUERY>
    </CFTRANSACTION>

    <CFCATCH TYPE="Database">
    <DIV ALIGN="center">
       <FONT FACE="Arial">
       <HR>
       <H3>There Was a Database Error!</H3>
       <HR>
       </FONT>
    </DIV>

    <FONT FACE="Arial">
    The error information is as follows:<p>
    <CFOUTPUT>
       <B>SQL STATE</B>: #CFCATCH.SQLSTATE#<BR>
       <B>NATIVE ERROR CODE</B>:    #CFCATCH.NATIVEERRORCODE#<BR>
       <B>TYPE</B>: #CFCATCH.TYPE#<BR>
       <B>MESSAGE</B>: #CFCATCH.MESSAGE#<BR>
       <B>TAG CONTEXT</B>:
       <UL>
          <CFLOOP INDEX="a"
          FROM="1"
          TO=#ARRAYLEN(CFCATCH.TAGCONTEXT)#>
             <CFSET CURRENT_TAG_STACK =
#CFCATCH.TAGCONTEXT[A]#>
          <LI><B>#CURRENT_TAG_STACK["ID"]#</B>
          (#CURRENT_TAG_STACK["LINE"]#,
#CURRENT_TAG_STACK["COLUMN"]#)
          #CURRENT_TAG_STACK["TEMPLATE"]#
          </CFLOOP>
       </UL>
       <B>DETAILS</B>:
       <FORM>
          <TEXTAREA COLS=50 ROWS=1 NAME='DETAIL'>
#HTMLEDITFORMAT(CFCATCH.DETAIL)#
</TEXTAREA>
       </FORM>
    </CFOUTPUT>
    </FONT>
    </CFCATCH>

</CFTRY>
```

FIGURE 18.8

Catching a database error

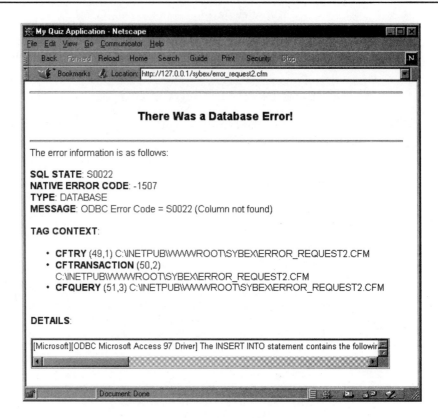

In the preceding code, the CFCATCH tag will catch any database errors that occur within the CFTRY tags, notify the user that an error has occurred, provide specific details through the use of built-in variables (shown in Table 18.5) and then continue with the processing of the template. If any other type of error occurs, a standard ColdFusion error message will be displayed and the processing of the template will be aborted. In the next section you will look at other types of errors that can be caught by using CFTRY and CFCATCH.

Types of Errors

Using CFTRY and CFCATCH, you can handle up to 10 types of errors. The error type is specified in the TYPE attribute of the CFCATCH tag. The syntax is written as follows:

```
<CFCATCH TYPE="type_of_error">
```

These error types are described in the following list:

Application   Default. Catches errors raised with the CFTHROW tag.

Database   Catches errors that are a result of failed database operations or SQL statements, and other ODBC problems.

Template   Catches general errors within an application template such as errors caused by CFINCLUDE, CFMODULE, or CFERROR.

Security   Catches errors related to ColdFusion code working with security.

Object   Catches errors related to ColdFusion code working with objects.

MissingInclude   Catches errors that result from missing included files.

Expression   Catches errors that result from a failing evaluation of an expression.

Lock   Catches errors that result from failing CFLOCK tags, for example, if a CFLOCK tag times out.

Any   Default. This CFCATCH type should be the last CFCATCH tag within a CFTRY tag pair. Catches failed database operations. Catches errors raised with the CFTHROW tag. Catches general errors within an application template, such as errors caused by CFINCLUDE, CFMODULE, or CFERROR. Catches errors that result from missing included files. This type will also catch serious application errors, such as access violations and internal exceptions. If you are not prepared to handle these errors, ColdFusion could become unstable.

Custom_Type   This is a user-specified type. It must match a type name specified in a CFTHROW tag. Catches errors raised with the CFTHROW tag.

If a TYPE attribute is not specified within a CFCATCH tag, then it defaults to Any. Also, CFCATCH tags are evaluated in the order coded on the page. A CFCATCH tag with the type of Any should always be last within a CFTRY tag pair.

Within a CFCATCH tag pair, you can access CFCATCH variables related to a specific CFCATCH TYPE attribute. In the preceding code, you saw how several CFCATCH database variables were used inside the CFCATCH tag. A full list of variables accessible for each CFCATCH TYPE is outlined in Table 18.5.

T A B L E   1 8 . 5 : Exception-Handling Variables*

Applicable Type	Variable Name	Description
Available to all types	CFCATCH.TYPE	Type specified in CFCATCH tag.
	CFCATCH.MESSAGE	Provides diagnostic information or an empty string.
	CFCATCH.DETAIL	CFML interpreter message containing HTML.
	CFCATCH.TAGCONTEXT**	An array of structures that can be used to display the name, position, and path of each tag in the tag stack. For an example, see the previous code that uses CFTRY and CFCATCH to catch a database error.

TABLE 18.5: Exception-Handling Variables* *(continued)*

Applicable Type	Variable Name	Description
Database	CFCATCH.NATIVEERRORCODE	Returns database error code based on database drivers, or –1.
	CFCATCH.SQLSTATE	Returns database error code based on database drivers, or –1.
Expression	CFCATCH.ERRNUMBER	Expression error number.
MissingInclude	CFCATCH.MISSINGFILENAME	Name of missing file.
Lock	CFCATCH.LOCKNAME	Name of lock or **anonymous**.
	CFCATCH.LOCKOPERATION	Operation that failed: **timeout**, **Create Mutex**, or **Unknown**.
Application or *Custom_Type*	CFCATCH.EXTENDEDINFO	Error information pulled from a **CFTHROW** tag by the same **TYPE** name.
Custom_Type	CFCATCH.ERRORCODE	An error code provided in a **CFTHROW** tag by the same **TYPE** name.

* All variables must be specified in uppercase.
** Enable CFML Stack Trace must be checked in the ColdFusion Administrator Debugging settings.

WARNING If the code used inside a **CFCATCH** tag pair causes an error, the error cannot be handled by the **CFTRY** tag immediately enclosing it.

CFTHROW

You can use the CFTHROW tag to create your own exceptions. The exceptions created by a CFTHROW tag can be caught by CFCATCH tags with the TYPE attributes of Application, Any, or your own custom type. The general format should look like this:

```
<CFTRY>
    ...HTML and CFML code<CFTHROW TYPE="custom name">
<CFCATCH TYPE="same as cfthrow name">
...code used to handle
the custom CFTHROW exception
</CFCATCH>
</CFTRY>
```

The syntax for CFTHROW is shown here:

```
<CFTHROW TYPE="application/any/or a custom name"
MESSAGE="any_message"
DETAIL="detailed_description"
ERRORCODE="error_code"
EXTENDEDINFO="any_additional_information">
```

The following list describes each attribute that is used with CFTHROW (all attributes are optional):

TYPE   Application, Any, or a custom name.

MESSAGE   A message you want to display to the user.

DETAIL   ColdFusion provides a detailed description of the error. You can add to this description when using the DETAIL attribute.

ERRORCODE   A specific error code you want to display to the user.

EXTENDEDINFO   Any additional information you wish to specify.

If you specify a type when using the CFTHROW tag, then the corresponding CFCATCH tag must have the same type name. This name can be Application, Any, or a name defined by you. It should not be any of the other default types (such as Database or Lock).

NOTE   From ColdFusion 4.5, it is possible to specify custom exception type names in hierarchical classes such as MyApp.ValidationRules.SpecificException. In the CFCATCH tag, you can specify an exception type as a general group in this hierarchy and trap all exceptions below it in the hierarchy. This way, you can specify any of three types of catch this exception type: MyApp, MyApp.ValidationRules or MyApp.ValidationRules.SpecificException.

TIP   ColdFusion 4.5's hierarchical exception naming and matching scheme is incompatible with previous version of ColdFusion where the exception type name in the CFTHROW and CFCATCH tags must match exactly. If you need to maintain backwards compatibility, you can use the <CFSETTING CATCHEXCEPTIONBYPATTERN="No"> tag in your Application.cfm file to ensure that ColdFusion 4.5 does not behave using the new class hierarchy matching scheme.

The CFTHROW variables available inside the CFCATCH tags are:

- CFCATCH.TYPE
- CFCATCH.MESSAGE
- CFCATCH.DETAIL
- CFCATCH.TAGCONTEXT
- CFCATCH.EXTENDEDINFO
- CFCATCH.ERRORCODE

Refer to Table 18.5, presented earlier, for more details about these variables.

The results might look like those in Figure 18.9. The following code shows an example of how to use CFTHROW with the CFTRY and CFCATCH tags:

```
<CFTRY>
    <CFIF NOT ISDEFINED("test")>
        <CFTHROW MESSAGE="<H3>The Variable 'test' Has Not Been
Defined!</H3>"
            Type="My_Error"
            Detail="ColdFusion Data:"
            ErrorCode="01"
            ExtendedInfo="This is for testing purposes">
    </CFIF>

    <CFCATCH Type="My_Error">
        <CFOUTPUT>
            <DIV ALIGN="center"><HR>
                <FONT FACE="Arial">
                #CFCATCH.MESSAGE#
                </FONT>
                <HR>
</DIV>
            <B>TYPE: </B>#CFCATCH.TYPE#<BR>
            <B>DETAILS: </B>#CFCATCH.DETAIL#<BR>
            <B>ERRORCODE: </B>#CFCATCH.ERRORCODE#<BR>
            <B>EXTENDEDINFO: </B>#CFCATCH.EXTENDEDINFO#<BR>
        </CFOUTPUT>
    </CFCATCH>
</CFTRY>
```

FIGURE 18.9

CFTHROW example

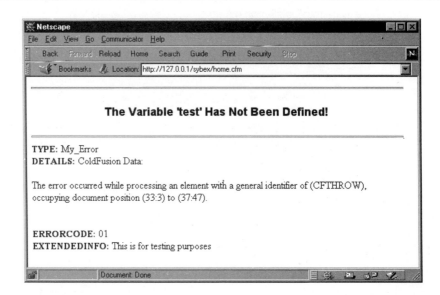

ColdFusion 4.5 introduces the **CFRETHROW** tag, which rethrows the currently active exception. It takes no attributes. This tag is used within a **CFCATCH** block and is often used to rethrow an exception when the error handler cannot handle the thrown error.

Catching Exceptions with *CFERROR*

As mentioned earlier in this chapter, when you reviewed the CFERROR tag from Cold-Fusion 4.5, the CFERROR tag supports the Exception type that allows you to specify an exception-handling template in the event of exceptions. This allows you to create an exception-handling template that you can apply to all templates in an application instead of writing exception-handling code for each template.

In order to understand the significance of this, consider the last example of the CFTHROW tag:

```
<CFTRY>
    <CFIF NOT ISDEFINED("test")>
        <CFTHROW MESSAGE="<H3>The Variable 'test' Has Not Been
Defined!</H3>"
            Type="My_Error"
            Detail="ColdFusion Data:"
            ErrorCode="01"
            ExtendedInfo="This is for testing purposes">
    </CFIF>

    <CFCATCH Type="My_Error">
        <CFOUTPUT>
            <DIV ALIGN="center"><HR>
                <FONT FACE="Arial">
                #CFCATCH.MESSAGE#
                </FONT>
                <HR>
</DIV>
            <B>TYPE: </B>#CFCATCH.TYPE#<BR>
            <B>DETAILS: </B>#CFCATCH.DETAIL#<BR>
            <B>ERRORCODE: </B>#CFCATCH.ERRORCODE#<BR>
            <B>EXTENDEDINFO: </B>#CFCATCH.EXTENDEDINFO#<BR>
        </CFOUTPUT>
        <CFABORT>
    </CFCATCH>
</CFTRY>
```

Here we have used the CFTRY and CFCATCH tags to throw, catch, and handle a custom exception of the type My_Error. If you wanted to catch this type of exception for all templates in your application, you would use the CFERROR tag in your Application.cfm template instead of the CFTRY and CFCATCH tags in each template.

First, you would want to add the following CFERROR tag to your Application.cfm file:

```
<CFERROR TYPE="Exception" EXCEPTION="My_Error" TEMPLATE="myerror.cfm">
```

You can specify CFERROR to catch any exception that could be specified in a CFCATCH tag, as outlined earlier in this chapter.

Next, you need to change the code throwing the error to:

```
<CFIF NOT ISDEFINED("test")>
    <CFTHROW MESSAGE="<H3>The Variable 'test' Has Not Been
Defined!</H3>"
        Type="My_Error"
        Detail="ColdFusion Data:"
        ErrorCode="01"
        ExtendedInfo="This is for testing purposes">
</CFIF>
```

Notice that we have completely eliminated the CFTRY and CFCATCH code. The CFERROR tag in the Application.cfm file will catch the exception generated by the CFTHROW tag. Then the execution of the template will be stopped and the myerror.cfm exception-handling template specified in the CFERROR tag will be executed.

This means that the myerror.cfm template can now include the following code originally used in the CFCATCH block:

```
<HEAD>
    <TITLE>Error found!</TITLE>
</HEAD>
<BODY>
    <CFOUTPUT>
        <DIV ALIGN="center"><HR>
            <FONT FACE="Arial">
            #Error.MESSAGE#
            </FONT>
            <HR>
        </DIV>
        <B>TYPE: </B>#Error.TYPE#<BR>
        <B>DETAILS: </B>#Error.DETAIL#<BR>
        <B>ERRORCODE: </B>#Error.ERRORCODE#<BR>
        <B>EXTENDEDINFO: </B>#Error.EXTENDEDINFO#<BR>
    </CFOUTPUT>
</BODY>
```

The major difference now is that you are using the `Error` structure (as you did in `Request` and `Validation` error templates) to access information about the error. All the CFCATCH variables outlined in Table 18.5 are available in the Error structure, as are all of those outlined in Table 18.6.

T A B L E 1 8 . 6 :   Exception Error Variables

Error Variable	Description
Error.Diagnostics	A full description of the problem that caused the error.
Error.Browser	The client browser type and version.
Error.DateTime	The date and time that the error occurred.
Error.GeneratedContent	The failed request's generated content.
Error.HTTPReferer	The URL on which the error occurred.
Error.MailTo	The `mailto` address specified in the CFERROR request tag.
Error.QueryString	The query string after the ? in the URL.
Error.RemoteAddress	The client's IP address.
Error.Template	The template path on which the error occurred.

Where Do We Go from Here?

In this chapter, you learned how to control errors in your ColdFusion templates and throughout your applications. You learned about general application error control using CFERROR and you learned how to handle more structured errors using CFTRY, CFCATCH, and CFTHROW.

In the next chapter, you will learn how to manage files on your server. Remember the information that you have learned in this chapter and try to apply it to the ColdFusion code you will learn in the following chapters.

chapter 19

File Management

- Understanding the CFFILE Tag

- Uploading Files from a Form

- Manipulating Files on the Server

- Working with Text Files

- Working with Directories

- Addressing Security Concerns

ColdFusion provides facilities for working with files on the server, as well for sending files from the client browser to the server for storage and processing.

For the most part, this work is accomplished with the CFFILE tag. This tag enables you to upload files from the browser through <INPUT TYPE=FILE> form fields; to copy, move, delete, and rename existing files; and to change and read the content of text files.

An additional tag, CFDIRECTORY, allows the creation and renaming of directories on the server as well as the generation of lists of files in a directory.

Understanding the *CFFILE* Tag

Before learning how to use the CFFILE tag in real applications, you need to take a quick look at the general structure of the tag.

The CFFILE tag can take many attributes. However, one attribute is central to how the tag works: the ACTION attribute. Not only does the ACTION attribute determine what will happen, it also determines which other attributes are valid and can even affect the meaning of some attributes.

The CFFILE tag can take eight values for the ACTION attribute:

UPLOAD   Uploads a file from a form to the server

MOVE   Moves a file to a new location

RENAME   Renames a file

COPY   Makes a copy of a file in a new location

DELETE   Deletes a file

READ   Reads the contents of a text file into a variable

WRITE   Writes content to a text file

APPEND   Adds content to a text file

READBINARY   Reads a binary file

In all cases, the files being affected reside on the ColdFusion server. ACTION=UPLOAD is a small exception in that it involves uploading a file from the client system's hard disk to a file on the server.

Throughout this chapter, you will be considering specific cases from the preceding list. In each case, you will review which attributes can be used with the specific action.

Uploading Files from a Form

In Chapter 15, "Forms," we purposely avoided discussion of *upload fields* (<INPUT TYPE=FILE>). In this chapter, we will finally discuss how to use these fields to upload files from a client system to the server.

There are two pieces to the puzzle: the form itself, and the ColdFusion template that receives the file from the form and performs some kind of action on it.

Creating a File Upload Form Field

First, let's review the HTML used to create file *upload form fields*.

A file upload form field is creating using the TYPE=FILE attribute of the INPUT tag. For instance, the following form creates a file upload field:

```
<FORM ACTION="upload.cfm"
 METHOD="POST"
 ENCTYPE="multipart/form-data">
File: <INPUT TYPE="FILE" NAME="MYFile"><BR>
<INPUT TYPE="SUBMIT">
</FORM>
```

This code produces a form that looks like the one in Figure 19.1.

FIGURE 19.1
A file upload field in a form

The FORM tag includes the ENCTYPE attribute set to `multipart/form-data`. This tells the server that the form includes a file upload as part of the data being sent and is an essential part of the FORM tag.

Users can either enter a full path and filename in the field, or can click the Browse button to choose a file from a file dialog box.

After a file is chosen, the path and filename appear in the form field, as shown in Figure 19.2.

FIGURE 19.2
A selected file appears in the form.

When the user submits the form, the file is sent along with the rest of the form data, much in the same way that a file is attached to an e-mail message. The script or application receiving the form also can access the file and perform any relevant action on the file or its contents.

Acting on an Uploaded File

It is at this stage, after a file is uploaded with a form, that a ColdFusion template can act on this file, using the CFFILE tag. As would be expected, the UPLOAD action of the CFFILE tag is used to manipulate the uploaded file.

When ACTION="UPLOAD" is used with the CFFILE tag, six other attributes are available for use, as outlined in the following list:

ACCEPT   Specifies which types of files should be accepted for upload, effectively limiting the range of files that can be uploaded. If used, the value of this field should be a comma-separated list of MIME types, such as `image/jpeg, text/html`.

ATTRIBUTES   Specifies file attributes to be set on an uploaded file. The value of this field is a comma-separated list of attributes from the following list: ReadOnly, Temporary, Archive, Hidden, System, and Normal. If this attribute is not used, then the original attributes of the uploaded file are retained.

DESTINATION   Specifies the directory on the ColdFusion server where the uploaded file should be saved. This is a required attribute. The attribute can also specify a new name for the file.

FILEFIELD   Specifies the name of the form field being used to upload the file. This is a required attribute.

MODE   Specifies the permissions that should be applied to a file when it is saved. This attribute is not applied in the Windows version of ColdFusion. In the Solaris version of ColdFusion, possible values are numerical octal triplets that are valid with the Unix chmod command.

NAMECONFLICT   Specifies how name conflicts between the uploaded file and existing files on the ColdFusion server should be handled. Possible values are ERROR (the file is not saved and an error message is returned), SKIP (the file is not saved and an error is not generated), OVERWRITE (the existing file is overwritten by the uploaded file if the names are the same), and MAKEUNIQUE (a new, unique file name will be created by the ColdFusion server for the uploaded file, and a variable called File.ServerFile will be created containing the name of the uploaded file). ERROR is the default value for this attribute.

Let's consider a simple example. Your form contains a field named UploadFile, which is a file upload field. The file being uploaded in this field should be saved in the directory c:\temp and a new filename should automatically be assigned to the uploaded copy of the file. This is achieved with the following CFFILE tag:

```
<CFFILE ACTION="UPLOAD"
  FILEFIELD="UploadFile"
  DESTINATION="C:\temp"
  NAMECONFLICT="MAKEUNIQUE">
```

The name of the resulting file can be found in the File.ServerFile variable (see Figure 19.3):

```
<CFFILE ACTION="UPLOAD"
  FILEFIELD="UploadFile"
  DESTINATION="C:\temp"
  NAMECONFLICT="MAKEUNIQUE">

<CFOUTPUT>Your file was uploaded and saved as #File.ServerFile#</CFOUTPUT>
```

FIGURE 19.3
Automatically generated
filenames are stored in the
ServerFile variable.

FIGURE 19.3
Automatically generated
filenames are stored in the
ServerFile variable.

Making Sure an Upload Worked

Often, it is necessary to make sure the upload action was successful. Whenever `ACTION="UPLOAD"` is used, a range of variables with the `File.` prefix are created, providing information about the success or failure of a file upload operation. These variables can be used in your template like other variables and parameters.

The available variables are outlined in the following list:

`File.AttemptedServerFile`   Name under which ColdFusion initially tried saving the file.

`File.ClientDirectory`   Directory in which the uploaded file existed on the user's computer system.

`File.ClientFile`   The name of the uploaded file on the user's computer system.

`File.ClientFileExt`   The extension, without the leading dot (for instance, `htm` and not `.htm`), of the uploaded file on the user's computer system.

`File.ClientFileName`   The name, without the extension, of the uploaded file on the user's computer system.

`File.ContentSubType`   MIME subtype of the uploaded file (the part after the slash in the MIME type).

`File.ContentType`   MIME type of the uploaded file.

`File.DateLastAccessed`   Last access date and time of the uploaded file.

File.FileExisted   Specifies whether the uploaded file already existed in the specified directory on the ColdFusion server. Possible values are YES and NO.

File.FileSize   The size of the uploaded file.

File.FileWasAppended   Specifies whether the uploaded file was appended to an existing file on the ColdFusion server. Possible values are YES and NO.

File.FileWasOverwritten   Specifies whether the uploaded file overwrote an existing file on the ColdFusion server. Possible values are YES and NO.

File.FileWasRenamed   Specifies whether the uploaded file was renamed before being saved on the ColdFusion server. Possible values are YES and NO.

File.FileWasSaved   Specifies whether the uploaded file was saved on the ColdFusion server. Possible values are YES and NO.

File.OldFileSize   The size of a file that was overwritten by the uploaded file.

File.ServerDirectory   The directory in which the uploaded file was saved on the ColdFusion server.

File.ServerFile   The filename under which the uploaded file was saved on the ColdFusion server.

File.ServerFileExt   The extension of the filename, without the leading dot (for instance, htm and not .htm), under which the uploaded file was saved on the ColdFusion server.

File.ServerFileName   The filename, without the extension, under which the uploaded file was saved on the ColdFusion server.

File.TimeCreated   The time that the uploaded file was saved on the ColdFusion server.

File.TimeLastModified   The time that the uploaded file was last modified.

Manipulating Files on the Server

After uploading files, the next most common set of operations on files is moving, renaming, copying, and deleting them using the CFFILE tag. Moving, renaming, and copying are handled in essentially the same way, so we will present them together, followed by a look at file deletion using ColdFusion.

Moving, Renaming, and Copying Files

Moving, renaming, and *copying* files are simple operations, using the CFFILE tag. These actions are performed using the ACTION="MOVE", ACTION="RENAME", and ACTION="COPY" attributes, respectively.

In all three cases, the same three additional attributes to the CFFILE tag are available:

SOURCE   Specifies the file (including full path) on which to perform the action. This is a required attribute.

DESTINATION   Specifies the destination file (including full path) when renaming or copying, or the destination directory when moving. Depending on the action being performed, the source file will be moved to the specified directory, renamed to the specified file, or copied to the specified file. This is a required attribute.

ATTRIBUTES   This attribute mirrors the ATTRIBUTES attribute available when using ACTION="UPLOAD". It specifies a comma-delimited list of file attributes that will be applied to the file resulting from a move, rename, or copy action. The comma-delimited list can be chosen from the following list of file attributes: ReadOnly, Temporary, Archive, Hidden, System, and Normal. When this attribute is not used, the original source file's attributes are maintained for the destination file.

Anyone with a modest familiarity with the DOS command prompt or basic Unix file manipulation commands should be able to understand the use of the CFFILE tag to move, rename, or copy files.

Consider the DOS move, rename, and copy commands. In all cases, these commands take two arguments: the first corresponds to the SOURCE attribute in the CFFILE tag, and the second to the DESTINATION attribute in the CFFILE tag.

For instance, the following DOS command:

```
move c:\temp\test.txt d:\newdir
```

performs the same action as the following tag:

```
<CFFILE ACTION="MOVE"
  SOURCE="c:\temp\test.txt"
  DESTINATION="d:\newdir">
```

Similarly, the following command:

```
rename c:\temp\test.txt c:\temp\new.txt
```

maps to:

```
<CFFILE ACTION="RENAME"
  SOURCE="c:\temp\test.txt"
  DESTINATION="c:\temp\new.txt">
```

and the following string:

```
copy c:\temp\test.txt d:\newdir\new.txt
```

has the same effect as:

```
<CFFILE ACTION="COPY"
  SOURCE="c:\temp\test.txt"
  DESTINATION="d:\newdir\new.txt">
```

Deleting Files

Deleting a file using the ACTION="DELETE" attribute of CFFILE is even easier than copying, moving, and deleting because only one required attribute needs to be used.

The FILE attribute is used to specify the filename (with its complete path) of a file to delete from the ColdFusion server. The command would be written as the following:

```
<CFFILE ACTION="DELETE"
 FILE="c:\temp\test.txt">
```

WARNING   Deleting files in templates should be done with great care because there is no second chance. After the tag executes, the file is permanently deleted without so much as a confirmation.

Working with Text Files

The CFFILE tag provides a useful mechanism for working with text files and the text they contain.

Three actions are possible when working with text files: reading, writing, and appending. We will present each in turn.

Reading a Text File

Reading the contents of a text file is done using the ACTION="READ" attribute of the CFFILE tag. With the addition of the following two attributes, it is possible to read the entire contents of a file into a ColdFusion variable:

FILE   Specifies the name of the file (including the path) to be read; this is a required attribute.

VARIABLE   Specifies the name of the variable in which to store the contents of the text file; this is a required attribute.

After the contents of a file are stored in a variable, they can be manipulated like any other string and array data, using the functions discussed in Chapter 14, "Working with ColdFusion Data Structures." The data can also be displayed using the standard CFOUTPUT tag.

The following example reads the contents of the text file c:\temp\test.txt into a variable named TestVar and then displays the contents for the user:

```
<CFFILE ACTION="Read"
 FILE="c:\temp\test.txt"
 VARIABLE="TestVar">

<H1>The contents of test.txt</H1>
<CFOUTPUT># TestVar#</CFOUTPUT>
```

Writing to a File

As would be expected, *writing* to a file is achieved using the `ACTION="WRITE"` attribute of the `CFFILE` tag. When using this action, it is possible to create text files for numerous reasons, including reports, error messages when problems occur in a template, or any other task that benefits from the creation of a text file. Dynamic data can be included in the resulting text file.

When writing to a text file, four other attributes of the `CFFILE` tag are available:

FILE Specifies the name of the file to be created (including the complete path). This is a required attribute.

OUTPUT Specifies the contents of the file to be created. This is a required attribute.

MODE Specifies the permissions that should be applied to a file when it is saved. This attribute is not applied in the Windows version of ColdFusion. In the Solaris version of ColdFusion, possible values are numerical octal triplets that are valid with the Unix `chmod` command.

ATTRIBUTES This attribute mirrors the `ATTRIBUTES` attribute available when using `ACTION="UPLOAD"`. It specifies a comma-delimited list of file attributes that will be applied to the file resulting from a write action. The comma-delimited list can be chosen from the following list of file attributes: `ReadOnly`, `Temporary`, `Archive`, `Hidden`, `System`, and `Normal`. When this attribute is not used, the original source file's attributes are maintained for the destination file.

By way of example, the following tag creates a new text file called `c:\temp\new-test.txt`, and stores dynamic content in it from a form submitted by a user:

```
<CFFILE ACTION="WRITE"
 FILE="c:\temp\newtest.txt"
 OUTPUT="The following form data was submitted
 Name:   #Form.Name#
 E-mail: #Form.Email#">
```

Notice that the value of the `OUTPUT` attribute spans multiple lines. Each line break will be reflected in the resulting text file, and dynamic data (such as `#Form.Email#`) will reflect the value of the parameters. If the user submits the form with the name `Username` and an e-mail address of `user@some.host`, then the resulting text file will look like this:

```
The following data was submitted
Name:   Username
E-mail: user@some.host
```

Appending to a File

Appending to a file, which is achieved using the ACTION="APPEND" attribute of the CFFILE tag, is similar to writing to a text file, except that instead of creating a new file that is initially empty, the output content is added to the end of an existing text file.

This is particularly useful for creating log files for your applications. For instance, your application may want to log each time a user performs a particular action or each time a certain series of events occur. These entries can be accumulated in a single log file, which can then be reviewed at regular intervals to ensure the normal operation of the application.

Appending to a file is similar to writing and makes use of three attributes:

FILE   Specifies the name of the file to be created (including the complete path). This is a required attribute.

OUTPUT   Specifies the contents of the file to be created. This is a required attribute.

ATTRIBUTES   This attribute mirrors the ATTRIBUTES attribute available when using ACTION="UPLOAD". It specifies a comma-delimited list of file attributes that will be applied to the file resulting from a write action. The comma-delimited list can be chosen from the following list of file attributes: ReadOnly, Temporary, Archive, Hidden, System, and Normal. When this attribute is not used, the original source file's attributes are maintained for the destination file.

For instance, the following example appends one line of text to an existing file:

```
<CFFILE ACTION="APPEND"
 FILE="c:\temp\log.txt"
 OUTPUT="Another line of text">
```

Working with Directories

Up to this point, you have considered specifically how to work with files, but not directories. The CFDIRECTORY tag provides the ability to create, delete, rename, and list the contents of directories on the ColdFusion server.

Like the CFFILE tag, the action taken by the CFDIRECTORY tag is controlled by the ACTION attribute, which can take four possible values:

Create   Creates a new directory

Delete   Deletes an existing directory

List   Lists the contents of an existing directory

Rename   Renames an existing directory

Creating a Directory

Directories can be created using the ACTION="Create" attribute and the DIRECTORY attribute, which specifies the full path and name of the directory to create. An optional MODE attribute specifies the mode permissions for the directory when using ColdFusion on Solaris, and takes octal triplets like those used in the Unix chmod command.

For instance, to create a new directory called c:\newdir, you could use the following tag:

```
<CFDIRECTORY ACTION="Create"
 DIRECTORY="c:\newdir">
```

Deleting a Directory

Deleting a directory combines the same DIRECTORY attribute used in creating a directory with ACTION="Delete":

```
<CFDIRECTORY ACTION="Delete"
 DIRECTORY="c:\newdir">
```

WARNING   As is true when deleting files with the CFFILE tag, deleting directories with the CFDIRECTORY tag offers no safety mechanism. Once executed, the directory is deleted forever.

Renaming a Directory

When renaming a directory using ACTION="Rename", two additional attributes are used:

DIRECTORY   Specifies the name and path of the directory to be renamed

NEWDIRECTORY   Specifies the new name and path for the directory

The commands for these attributes would be written as follows:

```
<CFDIRECTORY ACTION="Rename"
 DIRECTORY="c:\newdir" NEWDIRECTORY="c:\newdirrenamed">
```

Listing the Contents of a Directory

The ACTION="List" attribute enables the contents of a directory to be listed in the form of a query result set with five or six columns. The query result set can be used in the same way as any other query, including those created using CFQUERY. The columns are described in the following list:

Attributes   Any attributes applied to a file

DateLastModified   The date on which the file or directory was last modified

Mode   The octal triplet representing the permissions for a file (available only on Solaris servers)

Name   The name of the directory entry

Size   The size of the directory entry

Type   Type of entry (F for a file or D for a directory)

The CFDIRECTORY tag itself can take the following attributes:

DIRECTORY   The name and path of the directory of which to list the contents. This is a required attribute.

NAME   The name of the query result set. This is a required attribute.

FILTER   An optional value specifying a file extension filter to apply to the returned names. For instance, specifying *.txt causes only files with the TXT extension to be included in the results.

SORT   An optional attribute to specify how to sort the returned list of files and directories. This attribute is a comma-separated list of columns from the query output that serve as sort keys. For instance, sorting by name and then by size can be done with SORT="Name,Size". By default, each column is sorted in ascending order, but this can be controlled with ASC for ascending order and DESC for descending order: SORT="Name DESC, Size ASC".

Using the information returned from a list query, you could quickly write a template to display the contents of a directory as a Web page. For instance, Listing 19.1 displays the contents of the c:\temp directory on a ColdFusion server.

Listing 19.1: `cfdirectory.cfm`

```
<HTML>
    <HEAD>
        <TITLE>Displaying a Directory</TITLE>
    </HEAD>
    <BODY>
        <H1>c:\temp</H1>
        <CFDIRECTORY ACTION="List"
         DIRECTORY="c:\temp"
         NAME="listing"
         SORT="Name ASC">
        <TABLE BORDER=0 WIDTH=100%>
        <TR>
        <TD WIDTH=25%><STRONG>Date</STRONG></TD>
        <TD WIDTH=25%><STRONG>Size</STRONG></TD>
        <TD><STRONG>Name</STRONG></TD>
        </TR>
        <CFOUTPUT QUERY="listing">
            <TR>
            <TD>#DateLastModified#</TD>
```

```
                <TD>#Size#</TD>
                <TD>#Name#</TD>
                </TR>
            </CFOUTPUT>
            </TABLE>
        </BODY>
    </HTML>
```

This produces results like those in Figure 19.4.

FIGURE 19.4
A directory listing

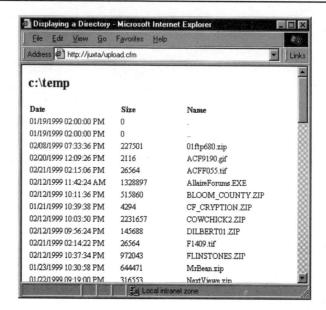

Addressing Security Concerns

The CFFILE and CFDIRECTORY tags present something of a security concern. Because these tags can manipulate files and directories outside of the Web directory tree and can delete files without confirmation, they need to be used with extreme care. The CFFILE tag particularly requires careful scrutiny because it can also be used to upload files onto the server, which could then later be used with malicious intent.

On most sites, the number of people who can create Web content and ColdFusion templates on the server is tightly controlled. In these circumstances, these tags can be used with relative security.

However, some sites allow a wide range of users to create Web content and upload it, usually to personal directories, on the server. In these circumstances, it would be useful to disable dangerous tags such as CFFILE and CFDIRECTORY.

These tags, and other tags of concern, can be disabled on the Basic Security page of the ColdFusion Administrator. The ColdFusion Administrator is discussed in detail in Chapter 35, "ColdFusion Administration." Refer to that chapter for details of disabling and enabling these tags.

Where Do We Go from Here?

The next chapter looks at using ColdFusion Studio to develop ColdFusion-based applications. ColdFusion Studio is a complete development environment for ColdFusion that provides wizards for building complete ColdFusion tags, a query builder for database interaction, syntax validation, and automatic formatting.

ColdFusion Studio also offers the necessary tools to work with ColdFusion Server's remote development services for direct editing of files on a server.

chapter 20

ColdFusion Studio

- Understanding the Studio Interface

- Using Code Development Tools

- Using Correction Tools

- Using Maintenance and Organizational Tools

- Understanding Studio Extensions

In the previous chapters, you learned about ColdFusion and how to create ColdFusion templates. In this chapter, we will show you how to increase your programming productivity by using and customizing ColdFusion Studio.

Studio is an indispensable tool for the ColdFusion developer and is designed to complement your ColdFusion programming needs. This chapter will not discuss all aspects of Studio in great depth, but by the end of it you will be able to increase your productivity by customizing the interface and using the maintenance and organizational tools.

Some of the Studio features that will help your productivity are:

- Customizable keyboard shortcuts to speed up use of ColdFusion Studio
- The integrated DreamWeaver program for a WYSIWYG editor
- The HTML and CFML code Validator and Tag Inspector
- The capability to view your database tables, columns, and records
- A drag-and-drop interface for creating SQL statements
- The Tag Chooser, which makes it easy to access HTML and CFML tags
- The Expression Builder, which provides access to functions and operators for creating expressions
- The capability to use both internal and external browsers to view your Web pages
- Easy upload capabilities and the capability to organize your Web applications using Projects
- Find, Extended Find, Replace, and Extended Replace features, along with Regular Expression capabilities, to more easily update and maintain your Web applications
- The capability to save and reuse tag snippets
- Built-in debugging capabilities to easily isolate and step through your applications
- The Site View tab, which makes it possible to see how the templates in your sites are connected
- Link Verifier to verify your external and internal hyperlinks
- The capability to integrate third-party version source control applications with Studio for your team projects

Understanding the Studio Interface

When first looking at the Studio interface, it is easy to become overwhelmed by all the tabs and buttons. For some, the interface is so overwhelming that they do not take the time to understand all the customizable options. Using Studio isn't always intuitive, either, and some of the more powerful tools aren't displayed prominently so you may not even be aware that they are available to you. This section will describe the Studio interface and familiarize you with it so that you can begin your exploration of this wonderful development environment.

This section includes information on:

- Title bar
- Menu bar
- Toolbars
- Quickbar
- Resource tab
- Little bar
- Work area
- Document tab
- Status bar

Figure 20.1 points out all the major interface features of ColdFusion Studio.

FIGURE 20.1
ColdFusion Studio interface

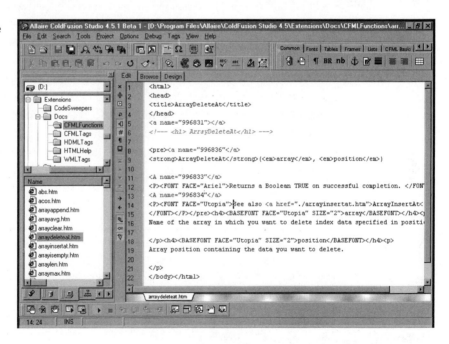

The following list describes the features of the Studio interface. This is just a quick overview of the features. We will be reviewing most of these items in more detail later in this chapter.

Title bar Displays the name of the application, the current active document, and the application's Minimize, Maximize/Restore, and Close buttons.

Menu bar Contains the options for File menu, Edit menu, Search menu, Tools menu, Projects menu, Options menu, Debug menu, Tags menu, View menu, and Help menu. All commands and options available in Studio can be found in one of these menu lists.

Toolbars Five toolbars are visible by default in Studio—Standard toolbar, View toolbar, Edit toolbar, Tools toolbar, and Debugging toolbar.

Quickbar EA type of toolbar with eight default tabs—Common tab, Fonts tab, Tables tab, Frames tab, Lists tab, CFML Basics tab, CFML Advanced tab, and CFFORM tab.

Resource tab The Resource tab contains eight tabs—Local Files tab, Remote Files tab, Database tab, Projects tab, Site View tab, Snippets tab, Help tab, and Tag Inspector tab.

Editor toolbar The Little bar is located between the Resource tab and the Editing toolbar. It has buttons for common and helpful editing tools such as Word Wrap, Show Gutter, Tag Insight, and Tag Validation.

Work area The work area consists of three panes—the Edit Pane, the Browse Pane, and the Design Pane.

Document tab Every open document in Studio gets its own named document tab. Click each tab to access the associated template.

Status bar The status bar is useful for debugging purposes. The far left area of the status bar displays the current line and position of the cursor, and the middle and right areas of the status bar display validation information as well as the absolute path of the file.

NOTE Some self-explanatory or common Windows interface features in the preceding list are not discussed in further detail in the following sections. For example, we will not discuss the menu bar in detail. Please be aware that all the features and tools in this chapter can also be located by navigating the Studio menus.

Toolbars and the Quickbar

Twenty-two pre-made toolbars are immediately available to you in the Studio environment. You can right-click anywhere on a visible toolbar or Quickbar to see a list of them. To activate one, all you have to do is select it from the shortcut list. From there, you can drag it around by its blue title bar and place it anywhere you want as a floating toolbar. You can also drop it on top of the Quickbar to add it as a tab to that feature, or dock it somewhere else on the Studio interface.

TIP   You can quickly and easily find out what a toolbar button does. Simply rest your mouse pointer over the toolbar button and a button hint will appear.

Quickbars and toolbars offer similar functionality in that they are organized groups of buttons that are all related in some function. The only difference is where you place them. For instance, if the Edit toolbar (which holds the buttons for opening, saving, and creating new documents) is undocked from its location and dragged and dropped onto the Quickbar, it then becomes a Quickbar tab.

Toolbars and Quickbars are completely customizable—to the point that you can create your own! Take the following steps to create a toolbar, define toolbar buttons, and add it all to the Quickbar feature:

1. Right-click a toolbar or the Quickbar and choose Customize from the shortcut menu. Figure 20.2 shows the Customize dialog box that is then displayed.

FIGURE 20.2
The toolbar's Customize dialog box

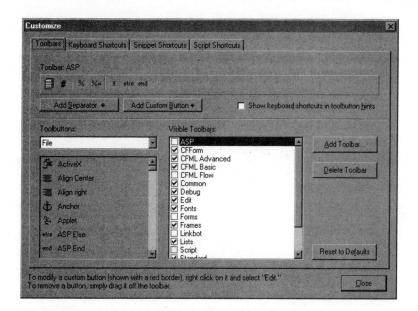

2. Click the Add Toolbar button and type your name when prompted for the new toolbar name. Then press the OK button.

3. Your new toolbar should appear in the Toolbars list. Click it to select it and make sure that you also click the check box to activate it. A blank toolbar, titled with your name, should appear at the top of the dialog box.

4. Now click the Add Custom Button button.

5. In the Custom Toolbutton dialog box that appears, leave Insert Custom Start and End Tags into the Current Document selected. In the Start Tag text box, type **#**. In the End Tag text box, also type **#**. Type **##** in the Caption text box, type **Variable #** **Signs** in the Button Hint, and then press the OK button. You should have a new button on your toolbar with a caption of ##.

6. You can also add buttons to your toolbar by dragging them from the Toolbuttons list. Scroll down the list of tool buttons, drag the CFOUTPUT tag from the list, and drop it onto your new toolbar.

7. Press the Close button on the Customize dialog box. Your new toolbar should appear somewhere on your screen.

> **WARNING**   Sometimes your toolbar will appear in strange places where it is not easy to spot. Look around carefully if you don't see it. It's sometimes camouflaged by other toolbars.

8. Your new toolbar should function just like any of the other pre-made toolbars in Studio. You can dock and undock it from a toolbar area or place it in the Quickbar. Drag your new toolbar and drop it on top of the Quickbar. It will be added to the end of the Quickbar list.

9. To put your new toolbar first in the list of Quickbar toolbars, right-click anywhere on the Quickbar and select Organize Quickbar from the shortcut menu. The Organize Quickbar dialog box appears that enables you to move your new toolbar to the first location on the Quickbar.

> **TIP**   Try out the new ## button that you created. Type a variable name, highlight it, and then click the ## button. The two # signs will surround your variable name. Also note that if you hold your mouse over the ## button, the button hint you entered, Variable # Signs, will appear.

Resource Tab

The Resource tab is absolutely indispensable in Studio. It consists of eight tabs that enable you to:

- Manage your files locally and remotely

- Manage your databases and SQL queries
- View your document links
- Organize and create reusable bits of code
- Access Help information
- Work interactively with HTML and CFML tags

Table 20.1 discusses the function of each tab in the Resource tab.

TABLE 20.1: Tab Icons from the Resource Tab

Tab Icon	Name	Description
	Files	The Local Files tab is split into a drop-down box and two panes. The drop-down box enables you to access the drives on your machine. The pane immediately below the drop-down box enables you to access your folder structure for the drive you selected. The bottom pane lists all the files in your selected folder and enables you to open the files by double-clicking them.
	Database	The Database tab enables you to use an RDS server to view databases registered as system data sources on the CF server. The drop-down menu at the top of the tab enables you to choose the RDS server, and the pane that takes up the rest of the tab enables you to view all the data sources on that ColdFusion server.
	Projects	The Projects tab enables you to store your files in Projects for easier organization of applications. Using this tab, you can easily create new projects, open existing projects, and upload projects to the appropriate FTP sites. You can also better manage the integrity of your files by integrating a third-party source control program with Projects. The drop-down box at the top of the tab enables you to open your project, and the pane immediately below it shows your folder system. The bottom pane lists all the files you have in the selected folder.
	Site View	After opening a local or remote document, you can see how it is linked to other documents by using the Site View tab.
	Snippets	Use the Snippets tab to create reusable snippets of code that you can use locally on your machine or share with other developers. You can place your snippets into folders for organizational purposes.
	Help	The Help tab features options that enable you to search for topics, read the documentation like a book, and even bookmark Help topics of interest.
	Tag Inspector	The Tag Inspector tab grants you easy access to all the tags used in your active document while also allowing you to edit and modify them using property sheets. The tab is divided into three sections. The top drop-down box enables you to select what tags you would like to view. The pane immediately below the drop-down box enables you to view all the tags used in your document, and the bottom pane presents the property sheet for modification.

TIP You can resize the Resource tab by holding the mouse over its right border, waiting for the double-headed arrow to appear, and then clicking and dragging the border to its new location. You can also reclaim more screen real estate for your work area by pressing F9 on the keyboard or the Resource Tab button on the View toolbar to toggle the Resource tab on and off.

Files Tab

The Local Files tab is self-explanatory. After you've selected the drive and the folder from which you want to view files, just double-click the files to open them in the work area.

TIP Try clicking and dragging files from the Local Files tab onto the work area. You may be surprised by what you find. For instance, highlighting text and then dragging a file onto that text will automatically create an anchor tag for you with the appropriate relative path to that file. Dragging an image onto the work area from the Local Files tab will create an HTML image tag—also with the appropriate relative path to the image. Likewise, dragging a CSS file will have a similar effect—it will create an HTML link tag to that style sheet. Right-click often in Studio. If you right-click a filename and then choose File ➢ Copy from the shortcut menu, you will be presented with a dialog box that enables you to copy the file to a new location.

However, there are some document tab indicators that you should be aware of after you open files in Studio. Saved documents show only the document name in the document tab. Files that have not been saved have an additional X on them, and files that are read-only have an additional red dot on them. Figure 20.3 illustrates these indicators.

FIGURE 20.3
Toolbars and the Quickbar

TIP You can open a file from the Web by choosing File ➢ Open from the Web.

Remote Files

You can access remote files in two ways: You can use FTP to create, open, modify, and save files on a remote server, or you can use RDS to connect to a ColdFusion server to access files and databases through HTTP. To access files through FTP or RDS, select

Allaire FTP & RDS from the list of file sources in the Files tab. You can easily add an FTP or an RDS server by right-clicking in the upper pane of the tab and choosing the appropriate option from the shortcut menu. You will be presented with a relevant dialog box asking for pertinent information to add the server. Follow the prompts in the dialog box to add the server.

TIP

For step-by-step instructions on how to install an FTP or RDS server, use the Help tab to search for remote files.

After you've added the server and connected to it, you can access the folders and files by using the same methods you used in the Local Files tab.

NOTE

You can easily spot an open remote file by the green dot next to its name in the document tab.

TIP

Remember that when you save files you've opened in the Remote Files tab, you're saving them to the remote server, not locally.

You can easily save files to the server by following these simple steps:

1. Open the file in your work area.
2. Choose File➤Save Remote Copy.
3. Select the server, drive, and directory into which you want to save your file, enter the filename, and then press the Save button.

Database Tab

To view databases on a ColdFusion server, you have to configure an RDS server by using the Remote Files tab or by selecting Add RDS Server from the drop-down box at the top of the Database tab. After the RDS server is configured, you must select it from the drop-down box to view all the databases registered as system data sources on the server.

NOTE

All databases, even those on your local machine, are viewed as if they are remote. You must create an RDS server for `localhost` and configure it to your local ColdFusion Application Server in order to view databases on your local machine.

Depending on the configuration of your data source, you may have to provide a login and password before you are allowed to view the database information.

Figure 20.4 shows a database and its tables and columns in the Database tab. Note that each column name is followed by its data type and field length.

FIGURE 20.4

A data source viewed from the Database tab

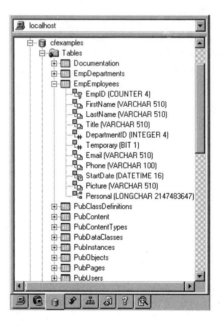

A nice feature of the Database tab is that you can use it to view the records in your database tables. All you have to do is double-click the table name and a separate window will appear with your records.

The real power of the Database tab is that it enables you to easily manipulate your tables and columns by giving you easy access to the SQL Query Builder. Follow the steps below to open the Query Builder and create a SQL SELECT statement:

1. Right-click one of the tables that you want to use in your SELECT statement and choose New Query from the shortcut menu. The Query Builder should appear with the appropriate table open.

2. Right-click anywhere in the Table pane and select Add Table, and then choose the table you would like to add to the query. That table should also appear in the Table pane and the table name will be added to the FROM clause of your SQL statement in the SQL pane.

3. Selecting columns for use in your SQL statement is also easy. Just double-click the column name and it will be added to the Properties pane and the SELECT statement in the SQL pane.

TIP   As you click in the grid of the Properties pane, you will be presented with drop-down lists from which you can select filtering criteria for your column.

WARNING   Deleting columns and filter criteria from your SQL statement can be tricky because you can't modify the query in the SQL pane. To delete this information from the SQL statement, you must delete it from the Properties pane. Just highlight the information you want to delete and press the Delete key on your keyboard. Then you have to click somewhere outside that cell but *inside* the Properties pane to confirm your deletion.

---

4. Creating joins in the Query Builder is also a snap. After you have the two tables open that you would like to join, all you have to do is click the field you would like to join in one table and drag it and drop it onto the corresponding field in the other table. As you do that, you will see the join statement added in the SQL pane.

TIP   To delete a join, right-click the box on the join line in the Table pane and choose Remove Join from the shortcut menu.

TIP   You can create left and right joins by clicking the box on the join line in the Table pane and choosing the appropriate option from the shortcut menu.

---

5. After your SQL statement is complete, you can run the query to test it by clicking the Run Query button on the Query toolbar.

6. When you are ready to save your query, click the Close Query Builder button on the Query toolbar. You will be prompted to save the query and name it. Give it a name but do not insert it into your template. You will be returned to the Studio interface.

7. You will now see your new query listed under the Queries folder in your data source listing.

8. To use your query in your ColdFusion template, simple click it in the Database tab and drag it to the appropriate area of your template in the Edit pane of your work area and drop it. The SQL statement will be inserted in your template with the appropriate CFQUERY tags surrounding it.

TIP   Remember to always try clicking and dragging items from your Resource tabs. You may be surprised by what you get. In the case of database tables and columns, you can drag the names into your Edit pane for use in your ColdFusion templates. This is useful because it avoids the misspellings that often occur when you type column and table names.

WARNING   Although the Query Builder is great for quickly creating SQL **SELECT** statements, we advise that you don't use it to create **INSERT** or **UPDATE** statements because doing so can mangle your code. The Query Builder in MS Access is a more powerful tool for creating **INSERT** and **UPDATE** statements.

Projects Tab

Studio projects are a wonderful way to keep your team projects and even your individual projects organized. You can also perform maintenance functions such as global search-and-replaces and link verification on all the files in your projects because project files are viewed as a unit by Studio. After you have created a Studio project, you can easily FTP it to the server—Studio is even smart enough to upload only those files that have changed since the last time you uploaded the project.

Take the following steps to create a Studio project:

1. Click the New Project button at the top of the Projects tab. The New Projects dialog box will appear.

2. Type a name for your project and then locate it on your local machine. Press the OK button when you are done.

WARNING   Don't use spaces in the names of folders and files in Projects. Some servers have problems with recognizing these names. Make sure that Include Sub-Folders is checked if you want to include all the sub-folders as part of your project.

---

3. The project appears in the Projects tab with folders listed in the top pane and files listed in the bottom pane.

4. When you are ready to upload your files to your server, click the Upload Project button on the Projects tab toolbar. Choose the server and location to which you want to upload your file and be sure to select all the appropriate check boxes in the dialog box.

NOTE   For specific information on adding source control to your projects, use the Help tab and search for Adding Source Control for Development Projects. Unlike many other online Help files in programs, the Help files in Studio are actually helpful and pretty complete.

Site View Tab

The Site View tab does not require much introduction. It enables you to view all the files that are linked to your currently open document. See Figure 20.5.

FIGURE 20.5
The Site View tab

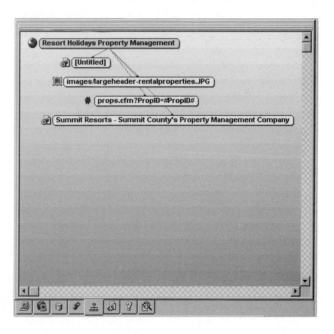

TIP   Click each of the links once to locate the reference in the corresponding code in the work area's Edit pane. Double-click pages to expand the site view further and to see the links associated with that page.

Snippets Tab

In a previous section we discussed how to create new tool buttons with beginning and end tags in Studio. Snippets also enable you to create reusable code, but on a larger scale and with more functionality because you can create keyboard shortcuts to call on the reusable code. Take the following steps to add a snippet to Studio:

1. Tag snippets are organized into folders, so the first step is to add a folder to the Snippet tab by right-clicking in the tab and selecting Create Folder from the shortcut menu. Name the folder **Common HTML**.

2. Right-click the Common HTML folder and select Add Snippet from the shortcut menu. The Snippet dialog box will appear.

3. In the Snippet dialog box, type **Email Link** in the description, **<A HREF="mailto:">** in the Start text area, and **</A>** in the End text area. Press the OK button to close the dialog box. Your new snippet should appear in the Common HTML folder of the Snippets tab, as shown in Figure 20.6.

FIGURE 20.6
Your new snippet in the
Snippets tab

4. Next type your e-mail address in a blank document. Highlight it and then double-click the new snippet. Your e-mail address should now be surrounded by the tag snippet <A HREF="mailto:"> in front and </A> in back. All you have to do is add your e-mail address to the HREF and you're set!

5. You can make your snippet even easier to access by assigning it a keyboard short-cut. Choose Options➢Customize from the menu bar and the Customize dialog box should appear. Choose the Snippet Shortcuts tab.

6. Open the folder that contains your snippet and select the snippet. Then click in the unlabeled text box at the bottom of the dialog box that contains the text None.

7. Press Ctrl+Shift+M. When you do so, you should notice that the word *Comment* appears in the lower-left corner of the dialog box. This means that the keyboard shortcut you selected is already assigned to the HTML comment tag.

8. Press Ctrl+Shift+E. This keyboard shortcut is not assigned to any tag by default. Press the Apply button to accept this new keyboard shortcut.

9. Again, in a blank document, type your e-mail address and highlight it. Now press Ctrl+Shift+E. Your tag snippet should appear around the e-mail address as before.

You just experienced how easy it is to create a snippet and customize it by adding a key-board shortcut. Use this feature often because it will noticeably decrease your coding time.

TIP

Notice that the Snippets tab in Figure 20.11 also includes a folder called `Variables` and a number of snippets. Creating snippets and keyboard shortcuts for these often-used commands is helpful. Note that the `QueryName.` snippet is just a placeholder for whichever query name you are working with. You will have to go into this snippet and edit it (right-click the snippet and choose Edit Snippet from the shortcut menu) each time you want to use it, but when you are working with long templates, it's a small price to pay in exchange for the convenience of a keyboard shortcut. Try using Ctrl+Shift+Q for the `QueryName.` snippet keyboard shortcut.

NOTE

You can share snippets with other developers. Use the Help tab and search for Using Code Snippets to locate detailed directions.

Help Tab and Dialog Box Help

Many people steer clear of the Help features in applications because they are difficult to use, incomplete, or the explanations are hard to understand. Studio's Help features, how-ever, are complete and extremely easy to use. Figure 20.7 shows the Help tab interface.

FIGURE 20.7

Help tab interface

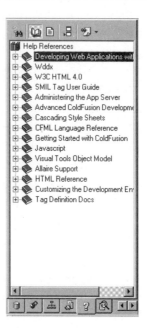

You can locate and read Help files in two ways:

1. Search all files using the search interface

2. Read the Help information using the Reference Tree

Although you might immediately leap to the first method, we recommend that you spend some time looking through the Reference Tree. It's organized by topic into books for easy browsing and even has some detailed information on tangential information such as cascading style sheets and JavaScript.

TIP

If you're working in teams, it can be helpful to write your own Help files and install them on all team-member machines. To do this, create HTML files and save them in the Help subdirectory of the ColdFusion Studio installation directory. (You can additionally create subdirectories in the Help directory for better organization.) If you had the Help files displayed at the time you created the directories and installed the files, press F5 to refresh your screen. After you've done this, you can even search these files.

Context-based Help can also be accessed directly in dialog boxes. Take the following steps to access Help information for a specific function in the Expression Builder dialog box:

1. Select Tools➢Expression Builder from the menu bar and click the Date and Time option of the Functions folder. A list of date/time ColdFusion functions will appear in the right pane.

2. Click the DateFormat function in the right pane to select it.

3. Immediately below the right pane and above the Insert and Cancel buttons, you will see two small buttons. Hold your mouse over them and the tooltips will read Show Help In Separate Window and Toggle Embedded Help. Click the Toggle Embedded Help button. Your screen should now look like Figure 20.8.

FIGURE 20.8
Embedded dialog box help

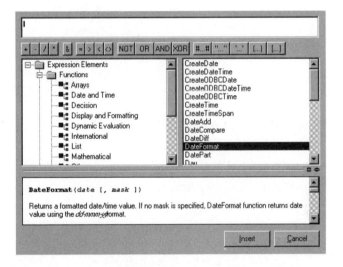

4. Scroll through the new Help dialog box pane. You will notice that the Help information not only covers this function's purpose and syntax, but it also explains how to create the mask for the function.

Tag Inspector Tab

After you have opened a document in Studio, you can use the Tag Inspector to easily pinpoint the location of tags and edit them using the tag property sheets. Figure 20.9 shows the Tag Inspector tab with pointers to important features.

FIGURE 20.9

Tag Inspector tab

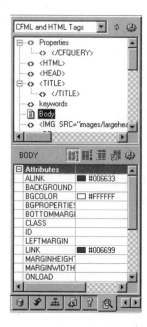

The easiest way to understand what the Tag Inspector is all about is to use it. With this in mind, take the following steps:

1. Open a CFML or HTML document in the Edit pane of your work area.

2. Click the Tag Inspector tab and make sure CFML and HTML Tags is selected from the drop-down box.

3. The top pane displays a tag tree of the CFML and HTML tags you have used in the active document. As you expand the levels of the tree, you will see deeper into the document hierarchy. Click one of the tags in the tag tree. Two things happen. First, the tag that you have clicked in the Tag Inspector top pane is highlighted in the corresponding Edit pane. Second, a tag property sheet appears in the lower pane outlining all the attributes for that tag.

TIP

You can add attributes or change their values by using the tag property sheet.

Little Bar

Although it has a diminutive name, the Little bar has some useful tools. Because most buttons on the bar are self-explanatory (just hold your pointer over the button to see its tooltip), we will highlight only some of the more advanced and useful options.

Show Line Numbers in Gutter

Some developers may not think very much of this option, but it is indispensable for debugging. Because ColdFusion server error messages return a line number for the problem area, it makes life a lot easier for you if you have line numbers in the gutter turned on.

TIP   Remember that the line number and the line position of the cursor are always displayed in the left-most area of the status bar.

Tag Insight

Tag Insight is a tool that you shouldn't even consider turning off. For those of you who like to type your code rather than use tag dialog boxes or wizards, Tag Insight will come in handy. To best understand how to use this tool, take the following steps:

1. Make sure that Tag Insight is turned on in Studio (make sure that it is depressed on the Little bar) and then open a blank document.

2. Start typing **<CFQUERY** and then hit the space bar and wait a second. A drop-down box listing all the attributes for CFQUERY will appear, as shown in Figure 20.10.

FIGURE 20.10
Tag Insight in action

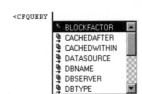

3. Type **N** and then press the Enter key. This will select the NAME attribute from the drop-down box and add it to your tag. Furthermore, it will prepare your attribute to receive a value by adding quotation marks and putting the cursor between the opening and closing quotation marks. The next time you press the space bar and wait, another drop-down list will appear, enabling you to select more attributes for your tag.

Some developers absolutely loathe this feature, and others absolutely love it. Again, like Tag Insight, you have to use it in order to see what it does.

Additional Options for Tag Insight

You do not have to use Tag Insight even if it is activated. If you keep on typing and ignore the drop-down boxes, they will go away. If you've already closed the tag, you can still use Tag Insight. Just put your cursor after the last attribute in the tag and press the spacebar. The Tag Insight dialog box will appear. You can set the time delay for when the Tag Insight boxes appear. Choose Options ➤ Settings from the menu bar and then choose the Tag Help tab in the Settings dialog box. Under the Tag Insight check box, click the Settings button to reveal the Tag Insight Settings dialog box. You can use the slider at the top of this dialog box to change the time delay in seconds. Tag Completion

1. Make sure that Tag Completion is turned on in Studio (make sure that it is depressed on the Little bar) and then open a blank document.

2. Start typing **<CFQUERY** and then type the closing **>** for the tag. After you type the closing > you should see the closing </CFQUERY> tag appear automatically. Tag Completion's job is to close all your tags for you.

WARNING Many developers dislike the Tag Completion feature because they often do not want an end tag to be automatically included. You will see how this can become a problem as you continue to work with Tag Completion. Remember that turning it off is only a mouse-click away on the Little bar.

Automatically Closing Double Quotes, Comments, and Pound Signs

You can also have Studio automatically close double quotes, comments, and # signs by following these steps:

1. Choose Options➤Settings from the menu bar and then choose the Tag Help tab in the Settings dialog box.

2. Under the Tag Completion check box, click the Settings button to reveal the Tag Completion Settings dialog box.

3. Choose the appropriate settings from the check boxes at the bottom of the dialog box.

Tag Validation and the Validate Current Document Button

Tag validation is useful for superficial on-the-fly validation but it does not have much depth. Take the following steps to better understand this point:

1. Make sure that Tag Validation is turned on in Studio (make sure that it is depressed on the Little bar) and then open a blank document.

2. Type **\<FONT WHATEVER="something"\>**. If you have Tag Completion turned on, the end \</FONT\> tag will have appeared as you typed the end bracket of the FONT tag. Note that the red Tag Validation flag also appears in the status bar telling you that the FONT tag is deprecated in HTML 4, as shown in Figure 20.11.

FIGURE 20.11

Tag validation in action

3. The most important thing to note, however, is that tag validation did not pick up that WHATEVER="something" is not a real FONT attribute. To truly validate a tag you must use the Validate Current Document button on the Tools toolbar. Click this button. A validation window will appear, as shown in Figure 20.12. Note that this validation method did pick up the bogus tag attribute.

FIGURE 20.12

More thorough validation

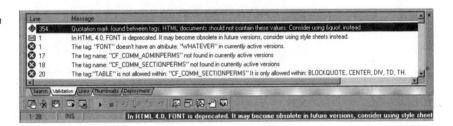

Work Area

The Studio work area consists of three separate, but interrelated, panes— the Edit pane, the Browse pane, and the Design pane. Each pane enables you to view the active document in different views. The Edit pane lets you view and manipulate the template code. The Browse pane acts like a browser and renders your page using an internal version of Internet Explorer. The Design pane lets you view your page in a WYSIWYG editor.

Edit Pane

The Edit pane is one of the most well designed features of Studio. We've already discussed some tools that are available from the Edit pane, such as Tag Insight, Tag Completion, and gutter numbering. Now we will discuss some specific features of the Edit pane, such as color coding and accessing tag editors.

TIP

Before you begin working with Studio, you should make sure that you can undo changes after you've saved a file. To do this, select Options ➤ Settings from the menu bar and choose the Edit tab in the Settings dialog box. Make sure that the last check box, Allow Undo after Save, is checked. This option should be the default but isn't.

As you work with code in Studio's Edit pane, you will notice that tags, attributes, and values are color-coded differently, as shown in Figure 20.13.

FIGURE 20.13

Color coding in the Edit pane

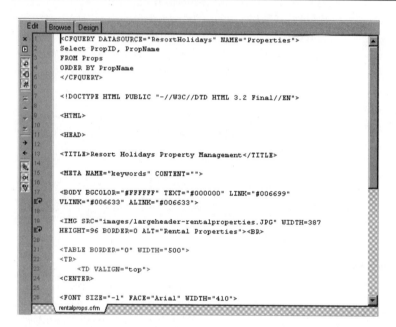

By default, CFML tags and attributes are coded in red with attribute values coded in bright blue. Likewise, HTML tags and attributes are coded in either dark blue, purple, or green with attribute values coded in bright blue. This color-coding scheme enables you to easily separate code from text and is helpful during debugging.

TIP

You can view or modify the color coding settings by choosing Options ➤ Settings from the menu bar and selecting the Color Coding tab in the Settings dialog box. Click a scheme name from the list and then press the Edit Scheme button to modify the scheme.

Earlier in this chapter you were introduced to the Quickbar and toolbars that enabled you to add tags to your templates by clicking a toolbar button to open the Tag Editor for the appropriate tag. You can also access the Tag Editor dialog boxes after the tags have been created by right-clicking the tag in question and choosing Edit Tag from the shortcut menu. Make your changes and press the OK button. Your tag will be updated with your new information.

TIP Remember to right-click often in the Edit pane. The useful features you find in the shortcut menu may surprise you. Use the keyboard shortcuts Ctrl+Tab and Shift+Ctrl+Tab to move backward and forward between open documents.

Browse Pane

The Browse pane is essentially Internet Explorer built into the Studio interface. Although this is a useful tool, you have to configure it before using it. Take the following steps to do this:

TIP You can also view your templates in an external browser by clicking the View External Browser List option on the View toolbar and selecting the browser of your choice from it.

1. Choose Options ➤ Settings from the menu bar and select the Browse page.
2. Click the Development Mappings button to open the Remote Development Settings dialog box.
3. Choose the ColdFusion server you would like to use from the drop-down box at the top of the dialog box.
4. Click the open folder button next to the Studio Path text box to browse the server and select the directory that you wish to browse. Click the OK button when you are through. You should note that the CF Server Path and the Browser Path are automatically filled in for you, as shown in Figure 20.14. At times, ColdFusion Studio will not guess the paths correctly and you will need to correct the automatic selections.

FIGURE 20.14

Adding a development
mapping

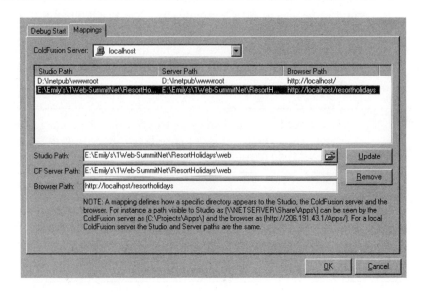

WARNING There is a note at the bottom of the Remote Development Settings dialog box. Read it carefully because you may have to configure the settings a little differently based on your ColdFusion server and Web server configurations. For instance, note that the browser path in Figure 20.19 is mapped to the specific virtual directory on the local host.

5. Click the Apply button to accept this new mapping and then click the OK button twice to exit the dialog boxes.

WARNING Remember to press the Apply button. If you don't, your browse feature will not work.

6. Now try to view your file in the Browse pane. If you have mapped your current directory correctly, you will be able to view your ColdFusion templates (error messages and all!) in the Browse pane, as shown in Figure 20.15.

FIGURE 20.15
Viewing templates in the Browse pane

TIP
Using the internal Browse pane can easily get annoying when you are trying to debug a drill-down interface. When you do this internally, you constantly have to select the first page of the drill-down interface and click through it until you get to the point that you want to evaluate. It is often easier to use an external browser when you are dealing with these types of applications so that you only have to hit the Refresh button in the browser to view your changes.

WARNING
Remember that you should always view your Web applications in multiple browsers to ensure that they look right in the major ones.

Design Pane

The Design pane is a problematic tool in the Studio environment. It uses the same Microsoft engine that is used in FrontPage, which is known to do strange things to templates. The worst thing it does is strip out non-HTML codes from your pages! However, it is a WYSIWYG environment that enables you to easily create HTML pages.

The Design pane does come disabled by default in Studio 4.01, but if you want to enable or disable it manually, you can do so by selecting Options➤Settings from the menu bar and selecting the appropriate check boxes in the Design tab.

WARNING   We highly recommend that you steer clear of the Design pane and use the closely integrated DreamWeaver WYSIWYG editor instead. DreamWeaver comes on your Studio installation CD-ROM, and after you install it, a button on your Little bar will enable you to easily access its interface.

Using Coding Development Tools

Most of the features discussed in the "Using the Studio Interface" section are considered coding development tools; a few other tools are accessible only from the menu bar and not from the rest of the Studio graphical interface. In this section we will discuss those tools—the Tag Chooser, the Expression Builder, and Studio templates and wizards.

Tag Chooser

The Tag Chooser is a dialog box that gives you access to HTML, CFML, and other tags in a nicely organized fashion. Figure 20.16 shows the Tag Chooser interface, which can be accessed by choosing Tools ➤ Tag Chooser from the menu bar. The right pane of the Tag Chooser enables you to select the language and category of tags you want to view, and the left pane enables you to select a specific tag for use in your active document.

FIGURE 20.16
The Tag Chooser interface

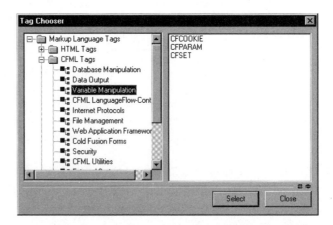

Double-click the tag in the left pane to activate the Tag Editor dialog box for that tag.

Expression Builder

The Expression Builder is similar in concept to the Tag Chooser except it deals with Cold-Fusion functions, not language tags, and is a little more sophisticated. The Expression Builder is a dialog box that gives you access to ColdFusion functions in a well-organized folder system, as shown in Figure 20.17. You can open the Expression Builder by choosing Tools➤Expression Builder from the menu bar.

FIGURE 20.17
The Expression Builder
interface

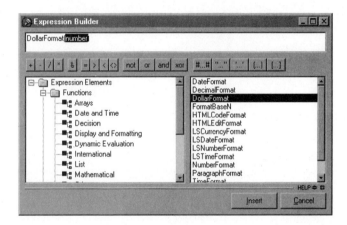

The Expression Builder has three panes. The top pane enables you to build an expression using the ColdFusion functions and the arithmetic operators and other items in the toolbar, and the lower two panes enable you to choose ColdFusion functions.

Remember to use the Expression Builder dialog box Help options that are located directly above the Insert and Cancel buttons. If you click a particular function name in the right pane and then choose the dialog box Help, you will be presented with specifics on how to use the particular function.

Studio Templates and Wizards

When you click the New button on the Standard toolbar or press the keyboard shortcut Ctrl+N, you are telling ColdFusion to create a new template for you based on its default template, as shown in Figure 20.18.

FIGURE 20.18
The default template

You can create your own default template for use in Studio or modify the existing template to fit your needs. The default template is set in the Locations tab of the Settings dialog box, which you can activate by choosing Options ➢ Settings from the menu bar.

Notice that in the default template, all the tags are lowercase. Some developers prefer to have all their tags in uppercase. You can rectify this problem by either modifying the default template, or by choosing Edit ➢ Convert Tag Case from the menu bar. If you would like to ensure that all tags inserted by Studio are in uppercase, choose Options ➢ Settings from the menu bar and make sure that the Lowercase All Inserted Tags check box is unchecked in the HTML tab of the Settings dialog box.

You can also access other templates and wizards in Studio by selecting File ➢ New from the menu bar and selecting the template or wizard from the New Document dialog box, as shown in Figure 20.19.

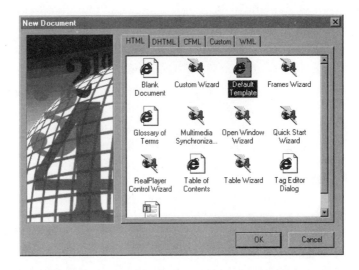

FIGURE 20.19
The New Document
dialog box

The template and wizard names in the dialog box are self-explanatory so we will not discuss them in detail. However, take a little time to play with each of the templates and wizards to see how they can increase your productivity.

Using Correction Tools

Creating ColdFusion applications doesn't stop with inserting tags and functions. You will most likely spend a good portion of your time debugging your code, validating it, and checking it for other problems such as spelling and broken links. In this section we will discuss some tools that will assist you in these tasks.

Debugger

ColdFusion Studio provides an interactive debugger that can be used to:

- Set breakpoints and watches
- Evaluate variables and expressions
- Step through lines of code
- Investigate the code stack
- Monitor recordsets
- Observe variables in all scopes

Because we have limited space and the Studio Help files are so thorough, we will direct you to the proper place in the Help files to find detailed information about the debugging tool:

1. Click the Help tab in your Resource tab and make sure that the Help Reference Tree is selected in the toolbar at the top of the tab.

2. Open the *Developing Web Applications with ColdFusion* book and read Chapter 7, "Debugging and Troubleshooting."

3. Double-click the Using the Interactive Debugger in ColdFusion Studio page to begin your exploration of this feature.

Validation

See the "Tag Validation and the Validate Current Document Button" section of this chapter for information on validation techniques in Studio.

Spelling and Grammar Checker

Anyone who has used a word-processing computer program is probably familiar with the Spelling and Grammar checking options available to them in those programs. Studio also gives you access to these tools; select either option from the Tools toolbar.

Verify Links

One of the most annoying things about surfing the Web is coming upon broken links. Furthermore, having broken links on your Web site is embarrassing and unprofessional. Studio provides you with a Verify Link checker that can help you avoid these common but painful pitfalls. Take the following steps to verify the links on your Web site.

WARNING   Relative links are easy to verify and don't require you to be connected to the Internet. However, if you have links to full URLs and other Web sites, you will need to be connected to the Internet for your site to be properly checked.

---

1. Open the document for which you would like to verify links.

2. Click the Verify Links button on the Tools toolbar. A window appears above the Studio status bar and the Debugging toolbar that lists all the links in the active document, as shown in Figure 20.20.

FIGURE 20.20
Verifying links

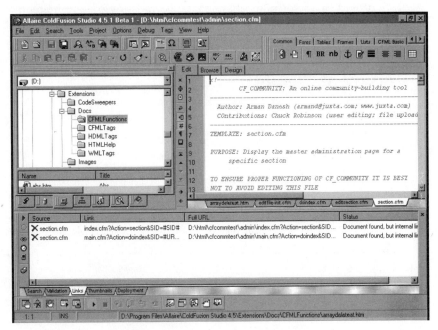

3. Click the Start Link Verification icon on the new window to begin the link verification process. If the link is verified, you will see a green check next to the link. If it does not pass, you will see a red X.

Using Maintenance and Organizational Tools

Early in this chapter we discussed Projects, Version Control, and Remote Development—all Studio tools that are intended to help you with the maintenance and organization of your applications. In this section, we will further that discussion by considering search-and-replace functionality and document weight.

Extended Search and Replace

The tools in the Search menu bar are helpful with site maintenance, but the Extended Search and Replace function is definitely the king of the group. Using this function, you can easily search and replace not only items on one page of your application, but items on every page of your project or site because Extended Search and Replace will recursively search through all the directories you indicate and make the appropriate changes.

In addition, Extended Search and Replace allows the use of Regular Expressions, which provide a powerful mechanism for performing pattern matching in your searches.

To use Extended Search and Replace, select Search➢Extended Replace from the menu bar and then follow the prompts in the dialog box.

Document Weight

The term *document weight* refers to how long it takes for a page and all its associated files to download. Studio has a feature that will calculate the download time based on different modem speeds. To use it, follow these steps:

1. Open a file in Studio.

2. Select Tools➢Document Weight from the menu bar. You will be presented with a dialog box similar to Figure 20.21. Notice that the top pane lists all the files that are being downloaded, and the bottom pane gives you the file sizes for all the files and the estimated download times over different modem speeds.

FIGURE 20.21

Document weight

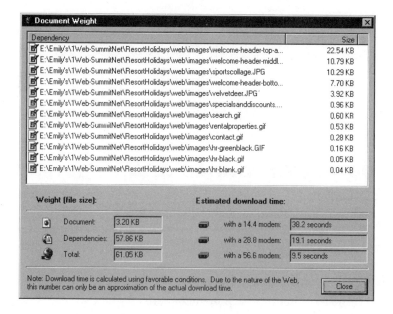

Studio Extensions

Custom tags are arguably the most powerful feature of ColdFusion Application Server, so it is only appropriate that Studio allow customization of its own interface to accommodate them—and so it does. In our earlier discussion of the Help tab, we mentioned that Studio enables developers to create their own Help files and add them to the Help tab in the Reference Tree and the Search interface. Studio goes even further, enabling you to also create your own Tag Editors, customize the Tag Chooser and Expression Builder, and even build your own wizards.

This topic is covered extensively in the Studio Help files. You can access those files by clicking the Help tab and choosing the *Customizing the Development Environment* book.

TIP   You can also further customize your Studio development environment by creating scripts that manipulate it. Read more about the Visual Tools Object Model (VTOM) by selecting that book from the Help tab.

Where Do We Go from Here?

The next chapter looks at how to send e-mail using ColdFusion tags. This powerful feature of ColdFusion enables the creation of e-mail messages from within ColdFusion templates. This ability can be used for numerous purposes including regular database reports, confirmation messages when users submit special forms, and notifications sent to administrators or Web masters when certain problems or activities occur. Sending e-mail is done with the CFMAIL tag, which is the focus of the next chapter.

PART III

Working the Internet with ColdFusion

Learn to:

- Send e-mail

- Read e-mail

- Use the HTTP protocol

- Access FTP servers

- Work with LDAP servers

Sending Mail

In this chapter, you are going to begin the process of looking at how ColdFusion can be used to interact with various Internet protocols including e-mail, File Transfer Protocol (FTP), and the World Wide Web.

In this chapter we will start with a discussion of the Simple Mail Transfer Protocol (SMTP), which can be used by ColdFusion for sending e-mail messages on a local intranet or Internet. First, you will learn how to configure ColdFusion to use your SMTP server for sending e-mail. Then, you will learn about the CFMAIL tag, which is the key to sending e-mail from ColdFusion.

Preparing ColdFusion to Send E-Mail

To prepare to send e-mail with ColdFusion, you first need to tell ColdFusion where it can find your SMTP server. To do this, you will need to identify the host name or numerical IP address of your mail server.

If you aren't sure of where to find this information, the following guidelines can help:

- If you are developing your Web site on a corporate intranet, then your organization probably already has an internal mail server running that supports SMTP. Consult your network administrator to determine the host name or address of the SMTP server for your intranet. Some organizations may have mail systems that do not support SMTP. In this case, you will need to arrange with your network administrator to install the necessary software so that your corporate e-mail system supports SMTP.

- If you are developing your Web site for the Internet and your organization has a leased line to the Internet, then your organization probably has an SMTP server that is used for receiving and sending e-mail to and from the Internet. In this case, your network administrator can provide you with the host name of the server.

- If you are developing your Web site for the Internet and the site will be hosted at your Internet Service Provider's location, then you will want to use your ISP's SMTP server for sending e-mail. Consult your ISP's support staff to determine the host name of the appropriate server.

With this information in hand, you need to open the ColdFusion Administrator Web page and select the Mail tab to configure the SMTP server. As you can see in Figure 21.1, the mail configuration screen of the ColdFusion Administrator is quite simple. It contains only three fields:

Mail Server   The host name or IP address of your SMTP server.

Server Port   The TCP/IP port used to connect to the server. The default value of 25 is the correct port for the vast majority of SMTP servers, especially those connected to the Internet. Only in special cases should you change this number; your network administrator or ISP can tell you if a nonstandard port is being used.

Connection Timeout   This field specifies the number of seconds ColdFusion should wait before giving up when attempting to connect to the SMTP server. With a reliable connection to your mail server, the default value of 60 seconds should be fine. If your mail server is not reliable and you find that your connections frequently time out, try increasing this value to 120 seconds or even more.

FIGURE 21.1
The Mail configuration screen

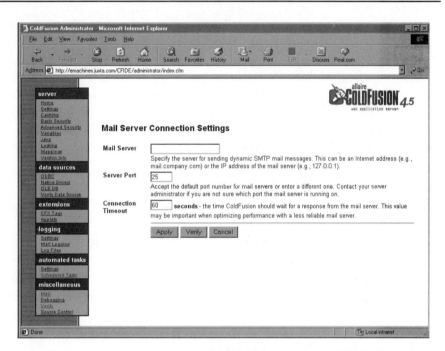

After you have entered the necessary values (at the very least, you need to provide the Mail Server value even if you don't want to change the other two values from their defaults), click the Apply button. The screen will redraw with the correct values filled in.

After you have committed your changes with the Apply button, you should test your mail server connection by using the Verify button. This will cause ColdFusion to check whether it can connect to your SMTP server with the port setting you have specified. If the connection is successful, ColdFusion will inform you with the screen shown in Figure 21.2. Otherwise, you will see an error screen with a brief description of the problem. Common errors include:

Name of host cannot be resolved to address   You have probably typed the host name incorrectly. Double-check the host name and try again.

Remote host is not available (check host part of address) ColdFusion has failed to connect to the server you have specified. Possible causes include an incorrect IP address for the server, a connection timeout value that is too short, or physical problems with the SMTP server itself (it could be off or disconnected from the network, for instance).

FIGURE 21.2
If you have provided the correct mail configuration, then ColdFusion will verify the connection.

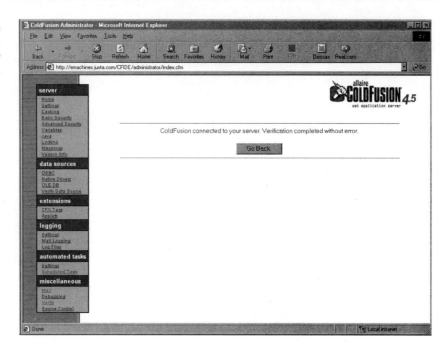

Using the *CFMAIL* Tag

The CFMAIL tag is the key to sending mail in ColdFusion.

The basic mechanism is this: The structure of the e-mail (such the recipient list, the subject line, and sender) are specified as attributes to the CFMAIL tag. The content of the message is placed between opening and closing CFMAIL tags.

The critical attributes used in the CFMAIL tag are:

TO Specifies the e-mail address (or addresses) of the recipients

FROM Specifies the content of the From line of the message

SUBJECT Specifies the Subject line of the e-mail

Let's consider a simple example:

```
<CFMAIL    TO="someone@some.domain"
```

```
       FROM="thesender@another.domain"
       SUBJECT="A Sample ColdFusion E-mail">

This is my test message

</CFMAIL>
```

In this small example, you use the three attribute values just discussed to cause Cold-Fusion to send an e-mail to `someone@some.domain`, with a From address of `the-sender@another.domain` and a Subject line that reads `A Sample ColdFusion E-mail`. The body of the message contains one line: `This is my test message`.

The resulting e-mail message would look something like this:

```
From: thesender@another.domain
To: someone@some.domain
Subject: A Sample ColdFusion E-mail

This is my test message
```

Of course, if this were all that the CFMAIL tag could do, it wouldn't be very useful in the context of ColdFusion. The CFMAIL tag provides much more, including the capability to specify recipients who will receive a copy, the message type, and MIME attachments, as well as the ability to work interactively with database query results in much the same way that the CFOUTPUT tag does.

Using Additional Message Structure Attributes

In addition to the three attributes we have already discussed, the CFMAIL tag also can take the following attributes, which further define the structure of the outgoing message:

CC   Specifies the recipients of a copy of the message (which becomes the CC line in the outgoing message)

BCC   Specifies the recipients of a blind copy of the message (which becomes the BCC line in the outgoing message); recipients of a blind copy are not listed in the message header so the intended recipients are unaware that they have received the message.

TYPE   Specifies the content type of the message. By default, all outgoing messages are assumed to be plain text messages. You can use the TYPE attribute to specify a single alternate type, HTML. HTML messages can be read by HTML-enabled mail programs such as Microsoft Outlook or Netscape Communicator.

MIMEATTACH   Specifies the path and filename of a file to be attached to the outgoing e-mail message as a MIME attachment. MIME attachments are the standard type of attachment and are supported by all leading mail client packages.

SERVER   Specifies an alternate SMTP mail server. By default, the mail server specified in the ColdFusion Administrator (as described earlier in this chapter) is used for sending outgoing messages.

PORT   Specifies an alternate TCP/IP port to use when connecting to the SMTP mail server. By default, the port specified in the ColdFusion Administrator is used.

TIMEOUT   Specifies an alternate connection timeout in seconds to use when connecting to the SMTP mail server. By default, the timeout specified in the ColdFusion Administrator is used.

MAILERID   Specifies a mailer ID that appears in the X-Mailer line of the message header. ColdFusion's default is ColdFusion Application Server. Generally, you will not need to provide an alternate value.

The *TYPE* Attribute

Using the TYPE attribute, you can create HTML e-mail messages that will be formatted correctly by e-mail client software that supports HTML messages. Examples of such software include Microsoft Outlook, Outlook Express, Netscape Communicator, and Netscape Navigator 3.

To do this, you need to add TYPE="HTML" to your CFMAIL tag. Then you can create a message containing HTML tags:

```
<CFMAIL    TO="someone@some.domain"
        FROM="thesender@another.domain"
        SUBJECT="A Sample ColdFusion E-mail"
TYPE="HTML">

<H1>An HTML message</H1>

<HR>

This is my test message

</CFMAIL>
```

The result is a message that looks like the one displayed in Figure 21.3 (Microsoft Outlook is being used here to display the message).

FIGURE 21.3
An HTML e-mail message

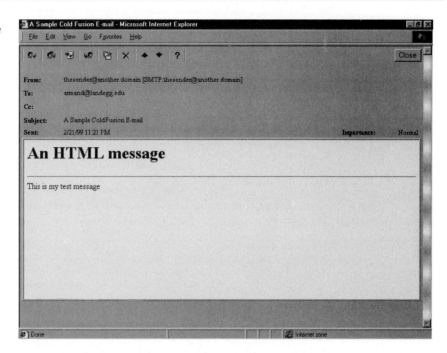

The *MIMEATTACH* Attribute

With the MIMEATTACH attribute, you can attach any type of file to your e-mail including, but not limited to, HTML files, Microsoft Word files, and image files.

To do this, the MIMEATTACH attribute is used to specify the path and filename of the file you want to attach, and then ColdFusion does the rest of the work. For instance, to attach a Microsoft Word document to a message, you would use a CFMAIL tag similar to the one in the following example:

```
<CFMAIL    TO="someone@some.domain"
      FROM="thesender@another.domain"
      SUBJECT="A Sample ColdFusion E-mail"
MIMEATTACH="c:\temp\test.doc">

This is my test message. I have attached a Microsoft Word file.

</CFMAIL>
```

Working with Dynamic Data

You can use dynamic data with the CFMAIL tag in several ways, including:

- Generating e-mail from the contents of a form
- Generating message content from the results of a query (from a database table, for example)
- Generating recipient lists from the results of a query

Generating E-Mail from the Contents of a Form

As with most everything in ColdFusion, you can use the contents of variables, including those that are the result of data submitted in a form, to specify values for tag attributes.

For instance, consider a simple example in which a Web site enables users to send a quick, standardized greeting to a friend by e-mail. The Web site could use a form similar to Listing 21.1.

Listing 21.1: *greeting.cfm*

```
<HTML>
   <HTML>
   <TITLE>Send a Greeting</TITLE>
   </HTML>
   <BODY>
      <H1>Send a Greeting</H1>
      <HR>
      <P>Use the following form to send a greeting to a
      friend by e-mail</P>
      <FORM METHOD=POST ACTION="sendgreeting.cfm">
         Your Friend's E-mail Address: <INPUT TYPE="text" NAME="to" SIZE=20><BR>
         Your Name: <INPUT TYPE="text" NAME="name" SIZE=20><BR>
         <INPUT TYPE=SUBMIT VALUE="Send">
      </FORM>
   </BODY>
</HTML>
```

This code produces a form like the one in Figure 21.4.

FIGURE 21.4

Preparing to send a
greeting

When the user submits this form, it submitted to the ColdFusion template
sendgreeting.cfm, which is shown here:

```
<HTML>
    <HEAD>
        <TITLE>Sending Your Greeting</TITLE>
    </HEAD>
    <BODY>
        <CFMAIL    TO="#Form.to#"
               FROM="address@some.host"
               SUBJECT="A Greeting">
        Hi!

        This is a quick, computer-generated greeting sent to
        You courtesy of #Form.name# and the CFMAIL tag.
        </CFMAIL>
        <H1>Message Sent</H1>
        <CFOUTPUT>
            <P>Your message to #Form.to# has been sent </P>
        </CFOUTPUT>
    </BODY>
</HTML>
```

What has happened here is that the contents of the to field in the form are used to address the message, and the contents of the name field are used to personalize the message.

Of course, our `sendgreeting.cfm` template has a fundamental problem: What happens if no e-mail address is specified? You need to add some error handling to account for this possibility, as shown in Listing 21.2.

Listing 21.2: *sendgreeting.cfm*

```
<HTML>
    <HEAD>
        <TITLE>Sending Your Greeting</TITLE>
    </HEAD>
    <BODY>
        <CFIF Form.to is not "">
        <CFMAIL    TO="#Form.to#"
                   FROM="address@some.host"
                   SUBJECT="A Greeting">
        Hi!

            This is a quick, computer-generated greeting sent to
            You courtesy of #Form.name# and the CFMAIL tag.
            </CFMAIL>
            <H1>Message Sent</H1>
            <CFOUTPUT>
                <P>Your message to #Form.to# has been sent </P>
            </CFOUTPUT>
        <CFELSE>
            <H1>Oops ...</H1>
            <P>You need to provide an E-mail address for
            the recipient. Hit the Back button to return to
            the form and provide one. Thanks.</P>
        </CFIF>
    </BODY>
</HTML>
```

Now, if the user forgets to provide an e-mail address, they will be presented with an error message like the one in Figure 21.5, and no attempt will be made to send an e-mail.

FIGURE 21.5
It is important to check
for errors before sending
an e-mail.

Let's take this use of forms one step further and see how CFMAIL can be used to quickly set up a contact form that gets submitted by e-mail to a predetermined address. Consider the standard contact form shown in Listing 21.3.

Listing 21.3: *contact.cfm*

```
<HTML>
   <HEAD>
      <TITLE>Contact Us</TITLE>
   </HEAD>
   <BODY>
      <H1>Contact Us</H1>
      <HR>
      <FORM METHOD=POST ACTION=submitcontact.cfm>
      <TABLE BORDER=0>
      <TR>
         <TD>First Name:</TD>
         <TD><INPUT TYPE="text" NAME="firstname" SIZE=20></TD>
      </TR>
      <TR>
         <TD>Last Name:</TD>
         <TD><INPUT TYPE="text" NAME="lastname" SIZE=20></TD>
      </TR>
      <TR>
```

```
            <TD>Address:</TD>
            <TD><INPUT TYPE="text" NAME="address" SIZE=20></TD>
         </TR>
         <TR>
            <TD>City:</TD>
            <TD><INPUT TYPE="text" NAME="city" SIZE=20></TD>
         </TR>
         <TR>
            <TD>State:</TD>
            <TD><INPUT TYPE="text" NAME="state" SIZE=20></TD>
         </TR>
         <TR>
            <TD>Post Code:</TD>
            <TD><INPUT TYPE="text" NAME="postcode" SIZE=20></TD>
         </TR>
         <TR>
            <TD>Country:</TD>
            <TD><INPUT TYPE="text" NAME="country" SIZE=20></TD>
         </TR>
         <TR>
            <TD>Phone:</TD>
            <TD><INPUT TYPE="text" NAME="phone" SIZE=20></TD>
         </TR>
         <TR>
            <TD>Fax:</TD>
            <TD><INPUT TYPE="text" NAME="fax" SIZE=20></TD>
         </TR>
         <TR>
            <TD>E-mail:</TD>
            <TD><INPUT TYPE="text" NAME="email" SIZE=20></TD>
         </TR>
         <TR>
            <TD>Comments:</TD>
            <TD><TEXTAREA NAME="comments" ROWS=10 COLS=30></TEXTAREA></TD>
         </TR>
         <TR>
            <TD> </TD>
            <TD><INPUT TYPE="submit"></TD>
         </TR>
         </TABLE>
         </FORM>
      </BODY>
   </HTML>
```

So far, this looks like a fairly generic contact form. With ColdFusion, though, you can easily create the submitcontact.cfm template that will process the contents of the form, generate a contact e-mail to the appropriate recipient, and inform the Web user that the form has been submitted (see Listing 21.4).

Listing 21.4: *submitcontact.cfm*

```
<HTML>
   <HEAD>
      <TITLE>Thanks</TITLE>
   </HEAD>
   <BODY>
   <CFMAIL    FROM="#Form.email#"
         TO="me@my.domain"
         SUBJECT="Automated Contact Form Submission">
   Hi! My name is #Form.firstname# #Form.lastname# and
   I used your online contact form to send you the following
   Comments:

   #Form.comments#

   You can reach me at:

   Address:    #Form.address#
         #Form.city#, #Form.state#
         #Form.postcode#
         #Form.country#

   Telephone:    #Form.phone#
   Fax:        #Form.fax#
   E-mail:    #Form.email#
   </CFMAIL>
   <H1>Thanks!</H1>
   <HR>
   Your form has been successfully submitted. Someone will be contacting you
shortly.
   </BODY>
</HTML>
```

Here you have used ColdFusion to easily create a template that not only sends the contents of the form as a formatted e-mail, but also informs the Web user that their form has been submitted. This code is easier to generate than a similar CGI-BIN form to a mail handler written in a language such as Perl or C and is more effective than the less elegant approach of using mailto:me@my.domain as the value of the FORM tag's ACTION attribute. In the latter case, the form gets submitted in an unformatted style to the e-mail address, and the user receives no confirmation that the message has been sent.

Generating Message Content from a Query

As you did with the CFOUTPUT tag, you can use the results of a query to generate dynamic output for a mail message.

Consider a theoretical example: You have a data source named GuestData that contains a single table called Contacts, which is a list of contact names and e-mail addresses received from a guest book on your Web site. You want to create an e-mail–based report of all the e-mail addresses in this table. You could use ColdFusion to create the following template:

```
<HTML>
    <HEAD>
        <TITLE>Contact Report</TITLE>
    </HEAD>
    <BODY>
        <CFQUERY NAME="Contacts" DATASOURCE="GuestData">
            Select * from Contacts order by Email
        </CFQUERY>
        <CFMAIL    TO="me@my.domain"
                FROM="me@mydomain"
                SUBJECT="Contact List Report"
                QUERY="Contacts">
        Here is the current list of contacts in the guest book:

        <CFOUTPUT>
        #Email# -- #Name#
        </CFOUTPUT>
        </CFMAIL>
        <H1>Done!</H1>
        <P>The Report has been sent to me@my.domain.</P>
    </BODY>
</HTML>
```

This template will produce an e-mail message whose body looks like the following:

```
Someone@some.where -- Some Person
Anotherone@else.where -- Another Person
Yetanother@who.else - Yet Another Person
Etc.
```

In this example, you have used the QUERY attribute to specify which query results are accessible to the CFMAIL tag and then used the CFOUTPUT tag in the body of the message to iterate through all the rows of the query result and display the relevant information.

Generating Recipient Lists from a Query

This is where dynamic data becomes extremely useful with the CFMAIL tag. Let's consider the guest-book list but assume that this time you want to send a form message to each person on the list.

Again you use the QUERY attribute of the CFMAIL tag, but you use your dynamic data in a slightly different way:

```
<HTML>
    <HEAD>
        <TITLE>Contact Report</TITLE>
    </HEAD>
    <BODY>
        <CFQUERY NAME="Contacts" DATASOURCE="GuestData">
            Select * from Contacts order by Email
        </CFQUERY>
        <CFMAIL    TO="#Email#"
                FROM="me@mydomain"
                SUBJECT="Thanks!"
                QUERY="Contacts">
        This is just a quick message to everyone who has
        used the guest book. Thanks and I hope to see you
        again soon at my site!
        </CFMAIL>
        <H1>Done!</H1>
        <P>The E-mails have been sent.</P>
    </BODY>
</HTML>
```

In this example, you use the column Email from your query result to generate an e-mail to each individual in the Contacts table. For each row of your table, separate e-mail will be addressed to the e-mail addresses stored in the Email field.

You can take this even further by personalizing each outgoing message. Consider the following CFMAIL segment, which builds on the preceding example:

```
<CFMAIL    TO="#Email#"
        FROM="me@mydomain"
        SUBJECT="Thanks!"
        QUERY="Contacts">

Dear #Name#,

This is just a quick message to everyone who has
used the Guest book. Thanks and I hope to see you
again soon at my site!
</CFMAIL>
```

Now what's happening is only slightly more complex. Not only is each row of the query result used to create a separate message to a different contact, but for each message, the Name field of the row is used to personalize the text of the message. Let's look at an example. Say you have two rows in your query result, as shown in the following Table 21.1.

TABLE 21.1: Your Query Results

Email	Name
Someone@some.domain	Some One
Another@another.domain	Someone Else

In this case, two e-mails will be generated. The first, to Someone@some.domain, will be personally addressed to Some One and the second, to Another@another.domain, will be personally addressed to Someone Else.

At this point you should note three other attributes of the CFMAIL tag that can be used with the QUERY attribute:

MAXROWS   Specifies the maximum number of query rows to process. For instance, in the preceding example of sending a message to multiple people from a query result, if the result contained 10 rows but MAXROWS was set to 5, e-mail would be generated for only the recipients represented by the first five rows of the query result.

STARTROW   Specifies the first row to process in a query result. Again, in our last example, if the result contained 10 rows but STARTROW was set to 6, e-mail would be generated only for the recipients represented by rows 6 through 10.

GROUP   Specifies the column name on which to perform grouping. For example, if you specify Email as your group column and the same e-mail address is repeated in two rows, then only one e-mail will be generated for this address, effectively grouping multiple rows with the same e-mail address into one result.

GROUPCASESENSITIVE   Specifies whether grouping with the GROUP attribute should be case sensitive. This attribute takes TRUE or FALSE as its value and TRUE is the default value. This attribute behaves in the same way as it does for the CFOUTPUT tag discussed in Chapter 12, "Grouping, Nesting, and Formatting Outputs."

Using the *CFMAILPARAM* Tag

The CFMAILPARAM tag, new in ColdFusion 4.5, can be used between the opening and closing <CFMAIL> and </CFMAIL> tags. This tag can be used for two purposes:

- Attaching more than one file as an alternative to the MIMEATTACH attribute of the CFMAIL tag.
- Adding message headers to your outgoing e-mail.

To add a mail message using the CFMAILPARAM tag, use the FILE attribute to specify the file's path and name:

```
<CFMAIL   TO="me@my.domain"
     FROM="me@mydomain"
     SUBJECT="Attachment test">
     <CFMAILPARAM FILE="C:\some\file.txt">
     This message has an attachment.
</CFMAIL>
```

You can use multiple CFMAILPARAM tags to attach multiple files:

```
<CFMAIL   TO="me@my.domain"
     FROM="me@mydomain"
     SUBJECT="Attachment test">
     <CFMAILPARAM FILE="C:\some\file.txt">
     <CFMAILPARAM FILE="C:\some\otherfile.txt">
     This message has two attachments.
</CFMAIL>
```

To add headers to your mail message, use the NAME and VALUE attributes of the CFMAILPARAM tag. For instance, to add a Reply-To header set to the address me@otherdomain to a message, use the CFMAILPARAM tag as follows:

```
<CFMAILPARAM NAME="Reply-To" VALUE=me@otherdomanin
```

You can combine CFMAILPARAM tags by attaching files with those setting headers in the same message:

```
<CFMAIL   TO="me@my.domain"
     FROM="me@mydomain"
     SUBJECT="Attachment test">
     <CFMAILPARAM NAME="Reply-To" VALUE=me@otherdomanin
     <CFMAILPARAM FILE="C:\some\file.txt">
     <CFMAILPARAM FILE="C:\some\otherfile.txt">
     This message has two attachments.
</CFMAIL>
```

Where Do We Go from Here?

In this chapter, you have learned how to use ColdFusion to take advantage of one half of the e-mail puzzle: sending e-mail using SMTP and the CFMAIL tag.

In the next chapter, you will look at the other half of the puzzle: reading incoming e-mail from a POP server by using the CFPOP tag. This tag provides a means by which Web-based e-mail applications can be quickly developed and used for numerous other purposes, including generating searchable e-mail inboxes on POP servers.

After learning the mechanics of the CFPOP tag, you will combine that knowledge with the information you have learned in this chapter to put together a full-blown, Web-based, e-mail application.

chapter 22

Reading Mail

- Using the CFPOP tag

- Handling Attachments

- Using Other Attributes

- Building a Web-Based E-Mail System

Now that you know how to send e-mail using ColdFusion, you will look at the other side of e-mail: reading e-mail from a Post Office Protocol (POP) server.

POP mail servers are a common type of service offered by Internet Service Providers for users to access their inboxes. Even if corporate e-mail systems rely on other technology to deliver mail to their users, POP is often provided as an alternate means for accessing the contents of inboxes.

POP mail servers can be accessed using all of today's common e-mail software, including Netscape Communicator, Microsoft Outlook Express, Eudora, and Pegasus Mail.

In this chapter, you will look at how you can use the CFPOP tag to access the contents of a user's inbox, and then make those contents accessible through a Web page.

After learning the basics of the tag, you will combine this knowledge with what you learned in the preceding chapter about the CFMAIL tag to create a Web-based e-mail system that enables users to access their inboxes through a standard Web browser.

Using the *CFPOP* Tag

The CFPOP tag provides all the functionality needed to access the contents of an inbox on a POP server. This functionality includes the ability to:

- Obtain a complete or partial list of message headers
- Obtain the header and contents of one or more messages
- Download and save attachments from messages

The first step in using the CFPOP tag is to understand the information needed to access a POP server. The following attributes are necessary in order to use the CFPOP tag successfully:

SERVER   Specifies the host name or IP address of the POP server. Without the complete host name (such as `mail.domain.name`) or a complete IP address for the host (such as `10.10.10.10` {I would use a more clear IP adddress I find that the 10.10.10.10 type addresses are easier for readers without networking backgrounds. AED}), it is impossible to connect to a POP server.

USERNAME   Specifies the mail username for the inbox being accessed. This may be different from the username they use to log into their workstation in a corporate environment or the username they use to establish a dial-up connection with their Internet provider. Using the CFPOP tag, you can access a single user's inbox. To access multiple users' inboxes, you need to use the CFPOP tag once for each user. The ColdFusion documentation for the CFPOP tag refers to the ability to create an anonymous POP connection; although this is possible, few, if any, POP servers you will work with will allow you to use an anonymous connection to achieve any practical results. Therefore, you will want to connect to a POP server as a specific user.

PASSWORD   Specifies the password for the mail username indicated by the USER-NAME attribute.

For example, to access the inbox of `user1` on the mail server `mail.domain.name` by using the password `pass1`, you would use the following basic attributes to the CFPOP tag:

```
<CFPOP SERVER="mail.domain.name" USERNAME="user1" PASSWORD="pass1">
```

In addition to specifying the server and user information for the inbox, it is important to specify the action to perform after you are connected to the server. You do this by using the `ACTION` attribute, which takes three possible values:

GetHeaderOnly   Retrieves a partial or complete list of message headers without the content of the messages.

GetAll   Retrieves the header and content of one or more messages (optionally including attachments, as you will see later in the "Handling Attachments" section).

Delete   Deletes one or more messages from the inbox on the POP server.

Accessing a List of Messages in an Inbox

The default action, if none is specified, is for the CFPOP tag to retrieve a list of message headers from the inbox.

For instance, consider the following tag:

```
<CFPOP SERVER="mail.domain.name" USERNAME="user1" PASSWORD="pass1"
ACTION="GetHeaderOnly">
```

This causes ColdFusion to connect to the POP server `mail.domain.name`, log in as `user1` with the password `pass1`, and retrieve the message headers for all the messages stored in the user's inbox.

Of course, after this information is retrieved, it begs the question: What can you do with it now?

As with the results of the CFQUERY tag, the CFPOP tag requires that the retrieved data be named using the `NAME` attribute. Once named, the data can be manipulated and displayed using the CFOUTPUT and CFLOOP tags just as you did in Chapter 3, "Getting Data from a Database."

Therefore, to make your tag complete, you need to add the NAME attribute:

```
<CFPOP SERVER="mail.domain.name" USERNAME="user1" PASSWORD="pass1"
ACTION="GetHeaderOnly" NAME="mail">
```

After you have named the results, you can access all the data in the result set through common tags such as CFOUPUT or CFLOOP.

As you will recall from our discussion of the results of database queries in Chapter 3, result sets consist of multiple rows of multiple columns (or fields) where each row represents a single result set. Data is returned by the CFPOP tag in much the same way: Each row represents a message and each column represents a field in the header of the message (when using the GetHeaderOnly action).

The following header fields are made available in the result set when using the GetHeaderOnly action:

DATE   The date of the message as a date object

FROM   The contents of the message's From line

MESSAGENUMBER   The number of the message in the inbox

REPLYTO   The contents of the message's ReplyTo line

SUBJECT   The contents of the message's Subject line

CC   The contents of the message's Cc line

TO   The contents of the message's To line

HEADER   The complete contents of the message's header in a single field

In addition, the RecordCount variable can be used to ascertain the number of messages in the result set, just as it was used for the results of database queries.

Listing 22.1 shows how this can be put together in a small example—displaying the contents of an inbox as a Web page.

Listing 22.1: *cfpop.cfm*

```
<HTML>
    <HEAD>
        <TITLE>CFPOP Example: A Complete Message</TITLE>
    </HEAD>
    <BODY>
        <H1>INBOX CONTENTS</H1>
        <HR>
        User: user1
        <HR>
        <CFPOP SERVER="mail.domain.name" USERNAME="user1" PASSWORD="pass1"
ACTION="GetHeaderOnly" NAME="mail">
        <CFOUTPUT>
            Total Messages: #mail.RecordCount#
        </CFOUTPUT>
        <TABLE BORDER=0 CELLPADDING=3>
        <TR VALIGN=TOP>
```

```
        <TD WIDTH=10%><STRONG>#</STRONG></TD>
        <TD WIDTH=30%><STRONG>Subject</STRONG></TD>
        <TD WIDTH=20%><STRONG>From</STRONG></TD>
        <TD WIDTH=20%><STRONG>Date</STRONG></TD>
    </TR>
    <CFOUTPUT QUERY="mail">
        <TR VALIGN=TOP>
            <TD>#mail.MESSAGENUMBER#</TD>
            <TD>#mail.SUBJECT#</TD>
            <TD>#mail.FROM#</TD>
            <TD>#mail.DATE#</TD>
        </TR>
    </CFOUTPUT>
    </TABLE>
  </BODY>
</HTML>
```

This code produces results similar to Figure 22.1.

FIGURE 22.1

Displaying the contents of an inbox using CFPOP

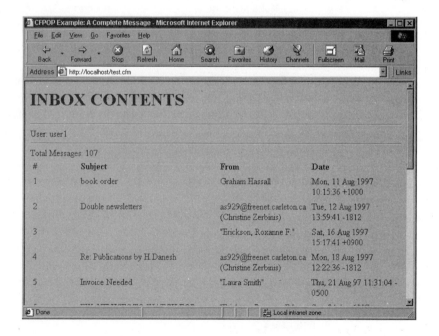

Displaying a Specific Message

In addition to displaying a list of messages in an inbox, it is useful to display the complete contents of a specific message. To do so, you want to use the GetAll value for the ACTION attribute of the CFPOP tag.

Consider our previous example, in which the list of the contents of an inbox was displayed. In this example, the following CFPOP tag was used:

```
<CFPOP SERVER="mail.domain.name" USERNAME="user1" PASSWORD="pass1"
ACTION="GetHeaderOnly" NAME="mail">
```

Now, what changes need to be made to retrieve the entire contents of the second message in the inbox? First, the ACTION attribute should become ACTION="GetAll". Second, you need to use yet another attribute of the CFPOP tag: MESSAGENUMBER. With this attribute you can specify that you want to retrieve the second message by using MESSAGENUMBER=2.

NOTE   The MESSAGENUMBER attribute can take more than one message as its value. This is done by providing a comma-separated list as a value. For instance, to retrieve messages 2, 3, and 5, you could use MESSAGENUMBER="2,3,5".

In addition to the header fields that are returned with a CFPOP query when ACTION is set to GetHeaderOnly, an additional field containing the body (contents) of a message is returned when ACTION is set to GetAll. This field is named BODY.

Put all together, a page designed to display the contents of the second message in the preceding inbox example would look like Listing 22.2.

Listing 22.2: *cfpop2.cfm*

```
<HTML>
   <HEAD>
      <TITLE>CFPOP Example: An Inbox</TITLE>
   </HEAD>
   <BODY>
      <H1>MESSAGE NUMBER 2</H1>
      <HR>
      User: user1
      <HR>
      <CFPOP SERVER="mail.domain.name" USERNAME="user1" PASSWORD="pass1"
ACTION="GetAll" MESSAGENUMBER=2 NAME="mail">
      <CFOUTPUT QUERY="mail">
         Message Number: #mail.MESSAGENUMBER#<BR>
         From: #mail.FROM#<BR>
         Subject: #mail.SUBJECT#<BR>
```

```
        Date: #mail.DATE#<HR>
        #mail.BODY#
    </CFOUTPUT>
  </BODY>
</HTML>
```

This code should produce results similar to those in Figure 22.2 by using CFPOP to connect to the server and retrieve the entire message (ACTION="GetAll") for the second message (MESSAGENUMBER=2). The retrieved message is placed in the mail query variable, which is then used to output the message.

FIGURE 22.2
Displaying a complete message

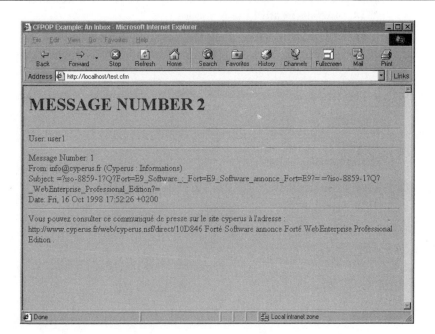

Handling Attachments

Today's e-mails are often much more complex than the simple text messages used in the previous examples. Particularly, e-mails today may contain attachments.

Luckily, the CFPOP tag can also be used to handle MIME attachments—the standard for mail attachments—with relative ease. This is done by using the ATTACHMENTPATH attribute. This attribute specifies a path where the attachments for a message can be saved.

For instance, in the preceding example of displaying message 2, you could adjust the CFPOP tag to be the following:

```
<CFPOP SERVER="mail.domain.name" USERNAME="user1" PASSWORD="pass1" ACTION="GetAll"
MESSAGENUMBER=2 ATTACHMENTPATH="c:\temp" NAME="mail">
```

This adjustment now indicates that any attachments should be downloaded with the message and saved in the directory c:\temp.

Of course, this change isn't much good if the files are saved, but the user has no way of knowing the names of the files or of retrieving them through their Web browser. The answer lies in two additional fields that are provided in the query result when the ATTACHMENTPATH attribute is used:

ATTACHMENTS   A tab-separated list of the original names of all attachments

ATTACHMENTFILES   A comma-separated list of the temporary filenames used to save the files in the ATTACHMENTPATH directory

These two fields are useful because they enable users to download attachments after reading a message. Consider the sample CFPOP tag in the preceding example. If c:\temp is accessible on the Web site in question as /temp, then attachments can be downloaded by providing links to /temp/<attachmentfilename>.

Because it is possible to loop over comma-separated lists, providing a clickable list of links to attachments becomes a simple task:

```
Attachments:
<UL>
<CFLOOP INDEX="ListElement" LIST="#mail.ATTACHMENTFILES">
    <CFOUTPUT><LI><A
HREF="/temp/#ListElement#">#ListElement#</A></CFOUTPUT>
</CFLOOP>
</UL>
```

There is only one point of concern regarding downloading attachments. A simple, automated way does not exist to remove the attachments that have been downloaded to the Web server once a user is finished with them. Instead, the CFFILE tag must be used to delete the attachments. For instance, you could combine CFLOOP with CFFILE to delete all the downloaded attachments from this example:

```
<CFLOOP INDEX="ListElement" LIST="#mail.ATTACHMENTFILES">
    <CFFILE ACTION="Delete" FILE="c:\temp\#ListElement#">
</CFLOOP>
```

NOTE   Normally, ColdFusion does not take steps to ensure that filenames generated for attachments are unique. In version 4.5, ColdFusion added the GENERATEUNIQUEFILENAMES attribute of the CFPOP tag. The possible values of the attribute are YES or NO; the default value is NO. When set to YES, ColdFusion will ensure that attachments are assigned unique file names.

Using Other Attributes

Some other attributes of the CFPOP tag are important to be aware of, even if you may only rarely have cause to use them. These are outlined in the following list:

TIMEOUT   Specifies the length of time to wait for the server to return the requested data before giving up. The default is 60 seconds, but for poor connections or slow servers, it may be necessary to increase this value.

MAXROWS   Specifies the maximum number of messages to return in a single CFPOP query. This can be useful, for instance, if a user has a large inbox and only a specified number of messages should be retrieved at once.

STARTROW   Specifies the first message to start retrieving. Used in combination with MAXROWS, it is possible to, for instance, display an inbox 100 messages at a time. Also, MAXROWS and STARTROW can be combined to have the same effect as MESSAGENUMBER. For instance, STARTROW=10 MAXROWS=1 retrieves the same message as MESSAGENUM-BER=10.

Building a Web-Based E-Mail System

Now it is time to put together a complete e-mail client application. This client is designed to provide a generic interface by which a Web user can access their mail on any Internet-connected POP mail server. That is, anyone with a POP mailbox can provide their username, password, and mail server name and then view their inbox, read messages, and send messages.

First let's look at the necessary pieces of the puzzle. Our application consists of six ColdFusion templates, as outlined in the following list:

index.cfm   Provides a form in which the user can provide their username, password, server name, and e-mail address for their mail account

inbox.cfm   Displays the inbox for the user

readmessage.cfm   Displays a specific complete message

compose.cfm   Used to compose messages (including replies and forwarded messages)

send.cfm   Sends a composed message and returns the user to their inbox

delete.cfm   Deletes a specified message and returns the user to their inbox

Taken together, these six files provide the following functionality:

- Viewing an inbox
- Reading messages
- Replying to messages
- Forwarding messages
- Deleting messages
- Composing new messages

To analyze the way in which this e-mail client works, you will look at each of these files in turn.

index.cfm

The index.cfm file is where the application begins. This template is presented to the user the first time they access the application. It simply displays a form asking the user for the following information:

Username   The username for the mail account being accessed.

Password   The password for the mail account being accessed.

Server name   The host name of the POP server on which the mail account is located.

E-mail address   The user's e-mail address. This is used to construct From lines on all outgoing messages the user composes.

When the user submits the form, the information is sent to the inbox.cfm template. The result is a template file shown in Listing 22.3.

Listing 22.3: *index.cfm*

```
<HTML>

    <HEAD><TITLE>Read Mail</TITLE></HEAD>

    <BODY>
    <DIV ALIGN=CENTER>

        <H1>Read Mail</H1>

        <FORM METHOD=post ACTION=inbox.cfm>
```

```
<TABLE ALIGN=CENTER BORDER=0>

    <TR><TD>
    Username:
    </TD>
    <TD>
    <INPUT TYPE=text SIZE=10 NAME=user>
    </TD></TR>

    <TR><TD>
    Password:
    </TD>
    <TD>
    <INPUT TYPE=password SIZE=10 NAME=password>
    </TD></TR>

    <TR><TD>
    Server:
    </TD>
    <TD>
    <INPUT TYPE=text SIZE=10 NAME=server>
    </TD></TR>

    <TR><TD>
    E-mail Address:
    </TD>
    <TD>
    <INPUT TYPE=text SIZE=10 NAME=email>
    </TD></TR>

    <TR><TD COLSPAN=2 ALIGN=CENTER>
    <INPUT TYPE=submit VALUE="Read Mail">
    </TD></TR>

  </TABLE>
  </FORM>

</DIV>
</BODY>

</HTML>
```

This template creates a simple form like the one shown in Figure 22.3.

FIGURE 22.3
The mail client login form

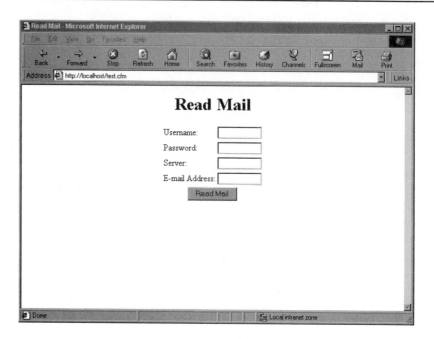

Technically, there is little to note in this template beyond the names of the form fields (which, logically, are named user, password, server, and email) and the fact that the data is submitted to the template inbox.cfm.

inbox.cfm

The inbox template is where the real work begins, and it is here that the process gets a little more complicated. The goal is to connect to the specified server, open the specified inbox, and retrieve all message headers.

These headers then need to be displayed in reverse chronological order, and links need to be provided to enable the user to compose a new message, delete any specific message, read any specific message, and forward or reply to any specific message.

This is done with the template in Listing 22.4 (the lines have been numbered for ease of reference).

Listing 22.4: *inbox.cfm*

```
<HTML>

    <HEAD><TITLE>Read Mail: Inbox</TITLE></HEAD>

    <BODY>
```

```
    <CFIF IsDefined("Form.server")>
        <CFSET user = Form.user>
        <CFSET password = Form.password>
        <CFSET server= Form.server>
        <CFSET email= Form.email>
    <CFELSE>
    <CFSET user = URL.user>
    <CFSET password = URL.password>
    <CFSET server= URL.server>
    <CFSET email= URL.email>
    </CFIF>

    <CFSET
token="user=#user#&password=#password#&server=#server#&email=#email#">

    <DIV ALIGN=CENTER>

    <CFOUTPUT>
        <H1>Inbox for <U>#user#</U> on <U>#server#</U></H1>
    </CFOUTPUT>

    <CFPOP SERVER="#server#" USERNAME="#user#"
    PASSWORD="#password#" ACTION="GetHeaderOnly"
    NAME="inbox">

    <CFOUTPUT>
        <H4>You have #inbox.RecordCount# messages in
        your Inbox</H4>
    </CFOUTPUT>

    <FONT FACE=Arial,Helvetica SIZE=2>
    [<CFOUTPUT><A HREF="compose.cfm?#token#&action=Compose">COMPOSE</a></CFOUTPUT>]
    </FONT>

    <TABLE BORDER=0 CELLPADDING=3 ALIGN=CENTER>

    <TR VALIGN=TOP>

    <TD WIDTH=20%>
    </TD>

    <TD BGCOLOR="#020A33" WIDTH=30%>
    <FONT COLOR="yellow" FACE=Arial,Helvetica
    SIZE=2>SUBJECT</FONT>
    </TD>

    <TD BGCOLOR="#020A33" WIDTH=30%>
    <FONT COLOR="yellow" FACE=Arial,Helvetica
    SIZE=2>FROM</FONT>
    </TD>
```

```
<TD BGCOLOR="#020A33" WIDTH=20%>
<FONT COLOR="yellow" FACE=Arial,Helvetica
SIZE=2>DATE</FONT>
</TD>
</TR>

<CFLOOP INDEX=message
FROM="#inbox.RecordCount#" TO="1" STEP=-1>
   <TR VALIGN=TOP>

   <TD BGCOLOR="lightsteelblue">
   <FONT FACE=Arial,Helvetica SIZE=2>
   <CFOUTPUT>
   <NOBR><A HREF="compose.cfm?#token#&message=#message#&action=Reply">r</A>
   <A HREF="compose.cfm?#token#&message=#message#&action=Forward">f</A>
   <A HREF="delete.cfm?#token#&message=#message#">d</A></NOBR>
   </CFOUTPUT>
   </FONT>
   </TD>

   <CFOUTPUT QUERY=inbox STARTROW=#message#
   MAXROWS=1>

   <TD BGCOLOR="lightsteelblue">
   <NOBR><FONT FACE=Arial,Helvetica SIZE=2>
   <CFIF LEN(#inbox.SUBJECT#) greater than
   0>
      <CFIF Len(#inbox.SUBJECT#) greater
      than 27>
         <A HREF="readmessage.cfm?#token#&message=#inbox.MESSAGENUMBER#">
         #Left(inbox.SUBJECT,25)# ...
         </A>
      <CFELSE>
         <A HREF="readmessage.cfm?#token#&message=#inbox.MESSAGENUMBER#">
         #inbox.SUBJECT#</A>
       </CFIF>
   <CFELSE>
      <A HREF="readmessage.cfm?#token#&message=#inbox.MESSAGENUMBER#">
       NO SUBJECT</A>
   </CFIF>
   </FONT></NOBR>
   </TD>

   <TD BGCOLOR="lightsteelblue">
   <NOBR><FONT FACE=Arial,Helvetica SIZE=2>
   <CFIF Len(#inbox.FROM#) greater than 20>
      #Left(inbox.FROM,18)# ...
   <CFELSE>
      #inbox.FROM#
   </CFIF>
   </FONT></NOBR>
   </TD>
```

```
<TD BGCOLOR="lightsteelblue">
<FONT FACE=Arial,Helvetica SIZE=2>
#inbox.DATE#
</FONT>
</TD>

</CFOUTPUT>

</TR>
</CFLOOP>

</TABLE>

</DIV>

</BODY>

</HTML>
```

At first this may seem daunting, but in reality it is quite a simple template that happens to need a lot of code. The end result is an inbox that looks like the one shown in Figure 22.4.

FIGURE 22.4
An inbox displayed by using ColdFusion

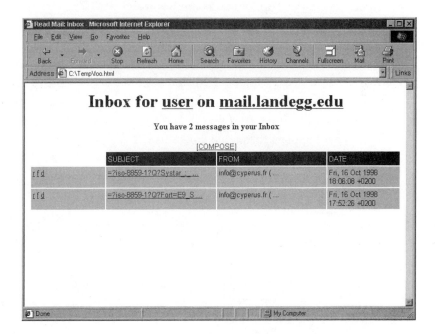

The template can easily be divided into three distinct components where the work is being done. You will look at each of these in turn.

Lines 4 to 16

This section has the job of setting some variables that will be needed throughout the rest of the template file.

Setting the variables starts with the CFIF clause (lines 4 to 14). This clause determines whether the input data (username, password, and so on) is being provided from a form (in other words, from the index.cfm template) or as URL parameters.

You set these variables so that once the user has logged in, the four pieces of information provided are passed through the rest of the application by the use of URL parameters. You pass along these variables from page to page by setting variables purely for ease of programming. Several other options exist to achieve the same result, including the following:

- Using cookies
- Using client variables
- Using hidden form fields

However, the purpose of this example is mail-related programming, so the programmatically simplest option has been chosen.

The CFIF clause is used to check whether any form data exists (by checking for the existence of one of the form fields). If the form data exists, then it is assigned to the variables user, password, server, and email. If the form data doesn't exist, then the information is extracted from the URL and is stored in the same variables.

The final step in this segment of code is to create a token (line 16). The token is used to create the portion of a URL that would be used to pass these four pieces of information to another template through a link. This URL segment is stored in the variable token, which can then be used to quickly build all URLs for links throughout the rest of the template.

Lines 20 to 22

This segment of the template consists of the CFPOP tag, which retrieves all the message headers. Although it is a small section of the template, it is the second major piece of programming logic in the template.

In the CFPOP tag, three of the four variables created earlier (user, password, and server) are used to open the user's inbox and access the list of headers.

Lines 48 to 103

Although this segment is the longest of the three by far, in terms of the logic of the program, it is a single unit. In this segment, each header is displayed as a single row of a table to create the inbox you saw earlier in Figure 22.4.

This entire section consists of a single CFLOOP clause, which is used to iterate over each row in the query result. It is important to notice that the FROM and TO attributes are used to loop backward from the last row to the first in order to display the messages in reverse chronological order. You use inbox.RecordCount to specify the last row in the query result.

Next, each of the four columns of the row is output in turn. The first (lines 51 to 59) consist of three single-letter links that provide the capability to reply to, forward, or delete the specified message. Notice how the links are built: They include the value of the token variable, plus a parameter providing the number of the message that is to be affected. In the case of the Reply To and Forward options, the links are to the compose.cfm template, and an action attribute is set. As you will see later when you look at the compose.cfm template, this action determines the initial appearance of the message composition form.

The three columns are all processed inside a single CFOUTPUT clause. This CFOUTPUT section is used to provide access to the fields in the row specified by each iteration of the loop. The CFLOOP tag itself is not providing access to the fields in the row, but simply providing a counter pointing to the appropriate row. The STARTROW attribute of the CFOUTPUT tag specifies which row is currently being worked with, and MAXROWS=1 ensures that only one row at a time is processed by the CFOUTPUT tag.

In the second column of the row, the subject is displayed (Lines 62 to 80). The subject is used as a link so that the user can click the Subject line to read a specific message.

However, displaying the subject requires a bit of thinking. First, what happens if the Subject line is blank? How can the necessary link be displayed? Second, what happens with an extremely long Subject line? This can make the layout of the table unattractive and difficult to use.

This problem is addressed by the following logic, which is represented by the embedded CFIF clauses in lines 63 through 78:

1. Check whether the Subject line is blank. If it is not blank, proceed to the next step; otherwise, display the Subject line as NO SUBJECT.

2. Because the Subject line is not blank, it can be displayed. Therefore, check the length of the Subject line. If it is longer than 27 characters, then display the first 25 characters of the Subject line followed by an ellipsis; otherwise, display the complete Subject line.

The choice of 27 characters as the cutoff length for shortening a Subject line is purely arbitrary and can be adjusted by the dictates of a specific design.

Each Subject line is displayed as a link to the `readmessage.cfm` template, and the token and message number are passed to this template so that it can retrieve and display the appropriate message.

Displaying the next column, the message's From line, is a little bit simpler (lines 81 to 89). The only decision that needs to be made here is regarding the length of the From line, because, as with the Subject line, it is possible to have an extremely long From line. Here, you use the arbitrary cutoff of 18 characters to decide when to cut short the From line.

Notice that no provisions are being made for blank From lines. This is because the From line is not being used as a link and, therefore, a blank From line does not affect the functionality of the application.

Finally, the last column is displayed (lines 90 to 100). This column is used to display the date of the message.

readmessage.cfm

The next template you will look at is the `readmessage.cfm` template, because this is the logical second stop for most users: After they view their inbox, they will generally attempt to read their new messages.

This template simply retrieves the contents of a specified message and displays it along with a menu, as shown in Listing 22.5.

Listing 22.5: *readmessage.cfm*

```
<HTML>

    <HEAD><TITLE>Read Mail: Read Message</TITLE></HEAD>

    <BODY>

        <CFSET
token="user=#URL.user#&password=#URL.password#&server=#URL.server#&email=#URL.email#">

        <DIV ALIGN=CENTER>

        <CFOUTPUT>
            <H1><U>#URL.user#</U></H1>
        </CFOUTPUT>
```

```
          <CFPOP SERVER="#URL.server#"USERNAME="#URL.user#"
PASSWORD="#URL.password#"
     ACTION="GetAll" NAME="inbox" MESSAGENUMBER="#URL.message#">

     <CFOUTPUT>
        <H4>MESSAGE NUMBER #URL.message#</H4>
     </CFOUTPUT>

     <FONT FACE=Arial,Helvetica SIZE=2>[<CFOUTPUT>
     <A HREF="inbox.cfm?#token#">INBOX</A> |
     <A HREF="compose.cfm?#token#&action=Compose">COMPOSE</A> |
     <A HREF="compose.cfm?#token#&message=#URL.message#&action=Reply">REPLY</A> |
     <A HREF="compose.cfm?#token#&message=#URL.message#&action=Forward">FORWARD</
A> |
     <A HREF="delete.cfm?#token#&message=#URL.message#">DELETE</A>
     </CFOUTPUT>]</FONT>

     </DIV>

     <BR><BR>

     <DIV ALIGN=LEFT>

     <CFOUTPUT QUERY=inbox MAXROWS=1>
        <STRONG>SUBJECT: #inbox.SUBJECT#</STRONG>
        <HR>
        <PRE>
        FROM: #inbox.FROM#
        DATE: #inbox.DATE#
        TO:   #inbox.TO#
        CC:   #inbox.CC#</PRE>
        <HR>
        <PRE>#inbox.BODY#</PRE>
     </CFOUTPUT>

     </DIV>
   </BODY>

   </HTML>
```

Immediately, you will notice how much shorter this template is compared to the
inbox.cfm template. That is because far fewer decisions need to be made to display a
single message than were needed to display a neatly formatted, functional inbox.
Nonetheless, there are still four main parts to this template, as outlined in the following sections.

The readmessage.cfm template displays a message, as shown in Figure 22.5.

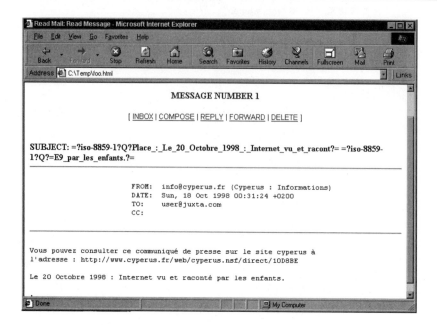

FIGURE 22.5
Reading a message

Line 4

In Line 4, you set your token again, just as you did in the inbox.cfm template. However, unlike the inbox.cfm template, there is no ambiguity about where your information is coming from: It is being passed in the URL. Therefore, you can proceed to build the token directly from the URL parameters without first assigning those values to other variables. Indeed, throughout this template and the compose.cfm template, the URL parameters are accessed directly.

Lines 9 to 10

This is where the CFPOP tag is used to retrieve the message. Notice the use of the GetAll value for the ACTION attribute and the use of the MESSAGENUMBER attribute to specify the message to be retrieved.

Lines 14 to 20

This section of the template displays the menu that appears above the message in Figure 22.5.

This menu provides access to all the major functions, including composing, replying, forwarding, and deleting, as well as a quick way to return to the inbox. All of these are formed of links that include the token and, where needed, the message number and an action.

Lines 24 to 34

In this final section of the template file, the message itself is displayed. This section makes simple use of the CFOUTPUT tag to display the results of the single row returned by the CFPOP query.

compose.cfm

The last main template is the compose.cfm template. This template provides three functions:

- Composing new messages
- Replying to messages
- Forwarding messages

These three functions can all be performed by the same template file because replying and forwarding are special cases of composing: The composition form needs to include preset recipients or body text when a user replies or forwards. After that preset data is in the message composition form, then everything works in the same way as composing a new message.

With this in mind, the compose.cfm looks like Listing 22.6.

> **Listing 22.6:** *compose.cfm*

```
<HTML>

    <HEAD><TITLE>Read Mail: Compose Message</TITLE></HEAD>

    <BODY>

        <CFSET
token="user=#URL.user#&password=#URL.password#&server=#URL.server#&email=#URL.email#">

        <CFSET To = "">
        <CFSET Cc = "">
        <CFSET Subject = "">
        <CFSET Body = "">

        <CFSET SingleNewline = Chr(13) & Chr(10)>
        <CFSET DoubleNewline = SingleNewline & SingleNewline

        <CFIF #URL.action# is "Forward" or #URL.action# is "Reply">

            <CFPOP SERVER="#URL.server#" USERNAME="#URL.user#"
PASSWORD="#URL.password#"
            ACTION="GetAll"    NAME="message" MESSAGENUMBER="#URL.message#">
```

```
    <CFIF #URL.action# is "Forward">
        <CFSET Subject = "[FWD] #message.SUBJECT#">
        <CFSET Body = #DoubleNewline# & "Forwarded Message" & #SingleNewline# &
        "-----------------" & #DoubleNewline# & "#message.BODY#">
    <CFELSE>
        <CFSET To = "#message.FROM#">
        <CFSET Cc = "#message.CC#">
        <CFSET Subject = "[REPLY] #message.SUBJECT#">
        <CFSET Body = #DoubleNewline# & "Original Message" & #SingleNewline# &
        "----------------" & #DoubleNewline# & "#message.BODY#">
    </CFIF>
</CFIF>

 <DIV ALIGN=CENTER>

<H1>Compose Message</H1>

</DIV><P>

<DIV ALIGN=LEFT>

<CFOUTPUT>
    <FORM METHOD=post ACTION="send.cfm?#token#">
</CFOUTPUT>

<TABLE BORDER=0 CELLSPACING=5>

<TR>
<TD ALIGN=RIGHT>TO:</TD>
<TD>
<CFOUTPUT><INPUT TYPE=text SIZE=30 NAME=To VALUE="#To#"></CFOUTPUT>
</TD>
</TR>

<TR>
<TD ALIGN=RIGHT>CC:</TD>
<TD>
<CFOUTPUT><INPUT TYPE=text SIZE=30 NAME=Cc VALUE="#Cc#"></CFOUTPUT>
</TD>
</TR>

<TR>
<TD ALIGN=RIGHT>SUBJECT:</TD>
<TD>
<CFOUTPUT><INPUT TYPE=text SIZE=40 NAME=Subject
VALUE="#Subject#"></CFOUTPUT>
</TD>
</TR>

</TABLE>
```

```
<HR>

<TEXTAREA COLS=50 ROWS=15 NAME=Body WRAP=HARD>
<CFOUTPUT>#Body#</CFOUTPUT>
</TEXTAREA>

<HR>

<INPUT TYPE=Submit VALUE="Send">

</FORM>

</DIV>
</BODY>

</HTML>
```

Other than setting the token at the start of the template, this file has only two main parts, which are explained in the following sections. A sample message composition form is shown in Figure 22.6.

FIGURE 22.6
Composing a message

Lines 5 to 25

In this section, all the work is done to handle replies and forwarded messages. First, the assumption is made that the user has asked to compose a new message.

In lines 5 to 8, four variables are set, representing the initial contents of the To, Cc, Subject, and Body fields in the message composition form. After this is done, the template needs to check whether the user actually wants to reply to or forward a message.

The flow of the logic (lines 11 to 25) is as follows, and takes place in a series of embedded CFIF clauses:

1. Check whether the user is forwarding or replying to a message. If so, proceed to the next step; otherwise, skip to the next segment of code.

2. Retrieve the entire contents of the message in question by using the CFPOP tag (lines 12 and 13).

3. Check whether the user is forwarding the message. If so, preset the value of the Body field to contain the message and create an appropriate Subject line. Otherwise, the user is replying, and the To, Cc, Subject, and Body fields should all be preset with the appropriate information from the original message being replied to.

Lines 30 to 61

In this section of the template, the actual message composition form is displayed. There are only a few small points to note here:

- The token is appended to the URL used in the ACTION attribute of the FORM tag. This ensures that the necessary information is passed along to the send.cfm template, which will send the message.

- The four variables you created in the previous section of the form are used to preset the values of the four form fields.

send.cfm

When a user finishes composing a message and submits the form presented with the compose.cfm template, the contents of the form are posted to the send.cfm template, as shown in Listing 22.7.

Listing 22.7: *send.cfm*

```
<CFSET
token="user=#URL.user#&password=#URL.password#&server=#URL.server#&email=#URL.email
#&RequestTimeout=500">

<CFMAIL FROM="#URL.email#" TO="#Form.To#" CC="#Form.Cc#"
SUBJECT="#Form.Subject#">
#Form.Body#
</CFMAIL>

<CFLOCATION URL="inbox.cfm?#token#">
```

Only three steps are performed in this template:

1. A token is created, as in all other templates.

2. The message is sent using the CFMAIL tag. Chapter 21, "Sending Mail," covered the details of using the CFMAIL tag; please refer to this chapter if you need to refresh your memory.

3. The CFLOCATION tag is used to return the user to the inbox.cfm template, and the token is passed on the URL to ensure that the user's data continues to propagate through the application.

delete.cfm

The final template to look at is the delete.cfm template, which is invoked when the user clicks the Delete link for a message in either the inbox, or when the user reads a message (see Listing 22.8).

Listing 22.8: *delete.cfm*

```
<CFSET
token="user=#URL.user#&password=#URL.password#&server=#URL.server#&email=#URL.email
#&RequestTimeout=500">

<CFPOP SERVER="#URL.Server#" USERNAME="#URL.user#" PASSWORD="#URL.password#"
ACTION="Delete" NAME="message" MESSAGENUMBER="#URL.message#">

<CFLOCATION URL="inbox.cfm?#token#">
```

As with the send.cfm template, the logic is straightforward:

1. Build a token.

2. Delete the message using the Delete value for the ACTION attribute of the CFPOP tag.

3. Return the user to the inbox.

Shortcomings of the Application

The application you have just built has considerable functionality. Nonetheless, several shortcomings exist because of the limitations of length and complexity imposed by presenting the information in a book. These include the following:

No error handling   If the user enters the wrong username, password, or server name, the inbox will fail to display, and instead the, user will see a ColdFusion error.

No security   The user's password is passed between templates as a URL parameter and in plain text. If used on the Internet, this application exposes the user's password to theft.

No attachment handling   The application fails to inform users if messages have attachments and, if they do, to provide a method for retrieving the attachments.

No blind copies   The application fails to provide a method to create blind carbon copies (bcc) of outgoing messages. This is a shortcoming of the CFMAIL tag.

No safety net   When a user clicks a link to delete a message, the message is deleted. There is no second chance for the user to confirm or reject the decisions to delete the message.

Even with these shortcomings, learning how this application works provides a solid grounding in the e-mail functionality of ColdFusion. If you want to expand the scope of your e-mail–related skills, try addressing some of the shortcomings in the preceding list.

Where Do We Go from Here?

In the next chapter, you will look at another major Internet protocol: Hypertext Transfer Protocol. By using CFHTTP to access the HTTP, you can use ColdFusion to retrieve URLs from the World Wide Web, and then work with the resulting content in ColdFusion.

You can also use CFHTTP to post information to URLs (for instance, automatically submitting information to forms without user intervention).

In addition to the CFHTTP tag, you will look at the CFHTTPPARAM tag, which is used to specify parameters used when posting with the CFHTTP tag.

chapter 23

Using the HTTP Protocol

- Understanding the CFHTTP Tag

- Using the CFHTTP and CFHTTPPARAM Tags

- Creating a Local Shareware Archive

In this chapter, you will learn how ColdFusion can be used to access data on Web servers using the CFHTTP tag. With this tag you can retrieve files from Web servers, store them on the server's hard disk, and display them in the user's browser.

In addition, it is possible to put together queries to be posted to a Web server for processing or storage.

Although this seems like an obscure use of ColdFusion—using a Web application written in ColdFusion to access another Web server—there are many applications of this tag. To highlight this, you will develop a simple application: a system that organizations can use to minimize downloading software from the Internet. Users who want to download software from the Internet start the download from a special page that actually downloads the file and saves it and then enables the user to download the file. In the future, all other users simply receive the local copy of the file.

Understanding the *CFHTTP* Tag

Before diving into the technicalities of the CFHTTP tag, you first need to consider the major types of actions that can be performed with the tag. The CFHTTP tag can be used for four main tasks:

- Retrieving pages from a Web server for local storing or rendering to the user's browser
- Converting delimited text files into usable queries
- Uploading MIME file types to a Web server
- Sending data to a server for processing

Let's look at each of these in turn and consider their applications.

Retrieving Pages from a Web Server

This is probably the most mystifying use of all. The template file in which the CFHTTP tag is processed is a Web page, so why would you want to retrieve one as part of a template? After all, it is possible to redirect a user's browser to a page with the CFLOCATION tag.

The heart of the matter lies in the role played by the CFHTTP tag. The CFLOCATION tag simply sends the user to a new URL, and the template containing the tag ceases processing. In contrast, the CFHTTP tag can be used to access a URL and receive the resulting data, but the template can then continue processing, including manipulating the data received from the Web server.

This is an important distinction. When retrieving pages, several important things can happen:

- The contents of the pages are stored in variables. The content of these variables can then be displayed as part of a template's output by using the CFOUTPUT tag.

- The contents of retrieved pages can be saved to files on the ColdFusion server for later access and manipulation.
- MIME types can be specified when retrieving files, enabling binary files to be retrieved and then processed as needed.

These capabilities can be used in several ways, including:

Creating intelligent agents   An application can be created in which users can specify pages they are interested in. Then, a scheduled template can automatically download those pages on a regular basis and save them on the server to improve access times to those pages for users.

Mirroring files   If your applications rely on files generated on other servers, it is possible to download those files to the ColdFusion server on a regular basis to ensure the current version is always available for processing by your templates.

Converting Delimited Text Files into Queries

A common file format is the delimited ASCII text file. Files of this type contain multiple rows of fields with each field separated by a specified delimiter (often a comma or a tab character). These files are usually structured as follows:

- Each record is on a separate line with a carriage return marking the end of the record.
- Each record contains the same number of characters.
- The first line of the file usually contains the names of the fields in each record separated by the delimiter (as opposed to the actual contents of a record).

This format creates what is essentially a simple database. It is so useful for transmitting this type of tabular data between applications that it is often used as the interchange file format between databases, spreadsheets, and other applications that handle this type of structured data.

Because it is such a common format, data stored in these types of files often can be used by ColdFusion templates as query data. For example, if you have a database server that regularly generates a report in delimited text format, you can use the CFHTTP tag to retrieve the file, break it down by record and field, and then provide the result in a query that can then be processed like all other queries (for instance, by using the CFOUTPUT and CFLOOP tags).

Uploading Binary Files

As you learned in Chapter 18, "File Management," you can use ColdFusion to process and store files that are uploaded from a form by using a file upload field.

However, it can be useful to upload files to a Web server without requiring the user interaction that is essential in the form-based method. Let's consider an example: An organization has an application that runs on an internal Web server sitting behind the company's firewall. One of the actions that this application performs is to generate a set of HTML files based on the current state of data in a database.

These files, however, must be accessible to the general public. There are several ways you can achieve this without the CFHTTP tag, but each has drawbacks:

- Allow outside users access through the firewall to the server running the application, effectively negating the role of the firewall in securing the internal network.
- Manually copy the files to a public Web server that sits outside the firewall. However, if the files are needed frequently or the number of files is large, this can be a tedious and even difficult process.
- Automate the copying of the files with scripts that run on a regular basis. This poses two problems, however. First, depending on the scripting language used, writing the script can prove difficult. Second, if the application does not generate the HTML files on a set schedule, but rather in response to certain actions, a delay can occur before the scheduled script runs to copy the files to the public Web server.

The CFHTTP tag, then, could be used to allow the files to be uploaded to the public Web server right after the ColdFusion application finishes creating them. This minimizes the need for human involvement and ensures that there are no scheduling conflicts or issues in the operation.

Sending Data to a Server for Processing

Because Web servers are often used to host data processing applications—in the form of CGI scripts or ColdFusion templates, for example—another use of the CFHTTP tag is to access these applications and at the same time provide the necessary data for them to perform their assigned tasks.

By combining the CFHTTP tag with the CFHTTPPARAM tag, you can define data to be sent to the server (the role of the CFHTTPPARAM tag) including cookies, form data, and CGI, URL, and file variables, and then have them all sent to the specified Web-server-based application with the CFHTTP tag.

Using the *CFHTTP* and *CFHTTPPARAM* Tags

The first step in understanding the CFHTTP tag is to take a quick look at its attributes. Technically speaking, the tag is quite simple with a manageable number of attributes, but this simplicity belies the range of roles that the tag can play.

The following list outlines the attributes of the CFHTTP tag:

URL   Specifies the URL of the file being accessed.

PORT   Specifies the port to be used in accessing the server.

METHOD   Specifies the method used to access the server. Possible methods are GET and POST.

USERNAME   Specifies the username to use if the server requires authentication.

PASSWORD   Specifies the password to use if the server requires authentication.

NAME   Specifies the name to assign to a query if the CFHTTP tag is being used to convert a delimited text file into a query.

COLUMNS   Specifies a comma-separated list of names to assign to columns when converting a text file to a query. These names override those specified in the first row of the file.

PATH   Specifies the directory in which a downloaded file should be stored.

FILE   Specifies the filename to which downloaded data should be saved on the Cold-Fusion server.

DELIMITER   Specifies the pattern of characters to use as a delimiter between fields in a text file being converted to a query.

TEXTQUALIFIER   Specifies the character used to mark the start and end of a column when the column contains the delimiter character.

RESOLVEURL   Indicates that all URLs in the downloaded file should be converted from relative URLs to absolute URLs to avoid bad links.

PROXYSERVER   Specifies the proxy server to use when accessing the World Wide Web.

PROXYPORT   Specifies the port to use when accessing the World Wide Web through a proxy server.

USERAGENT   Specifies the user agent to provide to the server in order to mimic a specific browser.

THROWONERROR   Specifies if the tag should throw an exception to be caught with the CFTRY and CFCATCH tags when an error occurs. Possible values are YES and NO.

REDIRECT   Specifies the action to take if the CFHTTP tag fails. If set to YES, CFHTTP follows any redirection provided by the server. If set to NO and THROWONERROR is YES, then an exception is thrown.

TIMEOUT   Specifies the time to wait in seconds for a response from a server before assuming the connection has failed.

The Difference between *GET* and *POST*

Let's start with a look at the METHOD attribute. This is the central key to how the CFHTTP tag operates. Using the METHOD attribute, one of two methods can be specified: GET or POST.

The GET method is a one-way method. It is used to retrieve files (both text and binary files) from a server based on a specified URL. That's all, really. Other than information encoded into the URL and the username and password provided for authentication if needed, no information is provided to the Web server for processing or manipulation.

By contrast, the POST method is a two-way interaction in which the CFHTTP tag provides information of different types to the server to be processed by a CGI script, Cold-Fusion template, or other application. The application, in turn, can return data based on the processing it performed.

Using a Basic *GET* Operation

At its most basic, you can use the GET method to retrieve a URL, store the content of the retrieved file in a variable, and then display or manipulate that variable as desired.

For instance, consider the Landegg Academy home page at www.landegg.edu/ shown in Figure 23.1.

FIGURE 23.1
The Landegg Academy
home page

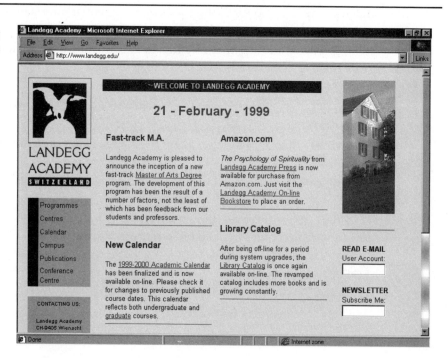

You can retrieve this page by using the following CFHTTP tag:

```
<CFHTTP METHOD=GET
  URL="http://www.landegg.edu/">
```

When you do this, the resulting data is stored by default in the variable CFHTTP.File-Content. You can then use this variable in the rest of your template. For instance, to download the Landegg Academy home page and display it, you would use the following ColdFusion code:

```
<CFHTTP METHOD=GET
  URL="http://www.landegg.edu/">
<CFOUTPUT>#CFHTTP.FileContent#</CFOUTPUT>
```

This produces results like those in Figure 23.2.

FIGURE 23.2
Displaying the Landegg Academy home page by using CFHTTP

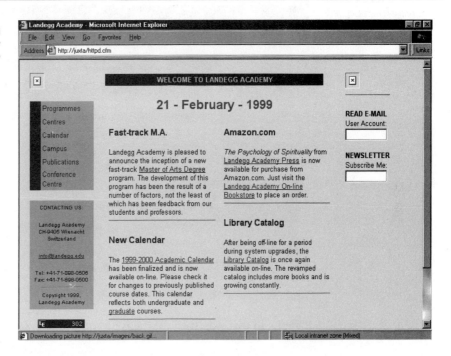

The first thing you probably noticed here is that none of the graphics appear correctly; they all appear to be broken links. This is because of the difference between relative and absolute URLs. Most Web pages encode the paths for images, links, and so on in terms of relative URLs. However, once the HTML code for a Web page is downloaded to the CFHTTP.FileContent variable and this code is then displayed using the CFOUTPUT tag, the relative paths in the code point to locations on the ColdFusion server and not on the original Web server where the file came from.

To solve this problem, you need to be able to tell the CFHTTP tag to convert all these relative links to absolute ones while it downloads the data. This is achieved with the RESOLVEURL attribute. By default, the value of RESOLVEURL is NO. But, set to YES, it causes all relative paths to be converted to absolute ones, resulting in the correct display of the HTML code as shown in Figure 23.3.

```
<CFHTTP METHOD=GET
 URL="http://www.landegg.edu/"
 RESOLVEURL="YES">
<CFOUTPUT>#CFHTTP.FileContent#</CFOUTPUT>
```

FIGURE 23.3
Using the RESOLVEURL attribute

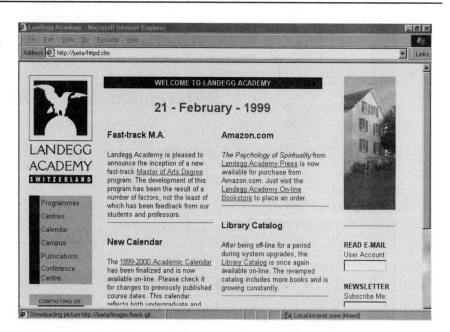

Using RESOLVEURL in this way fixes all the types of URLs, links, and paths shown in the following list:

- Images using IMG SRC
- Links using A HREF
- Forms using FORM ACTION
- Applet references using APPLET CODE
- Script source files using SCRIPT SRC
- Embedded objects using EMBED SRC

- Embedded plug-ins using EMBED PLUGINSPACE
- Background graphics using BODY BACKGROUND
- Frames in a frameset using FRAME SRC
- Background sounds using BGSOUND SRC
- Objects using OBJECT DATA, OBJECT CLASSID, OBJECT CODEBASE, or OBJECT USEMAP

In this way, all graphics, applets, and embedded objects will display correctly; all links will function as they did in the original page; and frame-based sites can be accessed successfully.

Providing a Username and Password

Some sites password protect some or all of their pages by using basic authentication. Under basic authentication, the browser normally displays a password prompt in a dialog box like the one in Figure 23.4.

FIGURE 23.4
Microsoft Internet Explorer's authentication dialog box

To use CFHTTP to access pages protected in this fashion, you can use the USERNAME and PASSWORD attributes. These attributes cause CFHTTP to respond to basic authentication and supply the specified login data to the server.

You have two choices in doing this. One approach is to hard-code a username or password into your template file where appropriate. For instance, the following code:

```
<CFHTTP METHOD=GET
  URL="http://www.landegg.edu/"
  RESOLVEURL="YES"
  USERNAME="user1"
  PASSWORD="pass1">
<CFOUTPUT>#CFHTTP.FileContent#</CFOUTPUT>
```

specifies the username and password to use if the Landegg Academy home page were password protected.

Alternately, you can provide a dynamic username and password that can come from a query result, can be submitted by the user in a form, or can even be obtained from a file stored on the ColdFusion server. For instance, if you have a query result named USER with two fields, `username` and `password`, then you could use the following CFHTTP tag to pass along the `username` and `password` fields to the server:

```
<CFHTTP METHOD=GET
  URL="http://www.landegg.edu/"
  RESOLVEURL="YES"
  USERNAME="#USER.username#"
  PASSWORD="#USER.password#">
```

Saving to a File Using the *GET* Method

The PATH and FILE attributes provide a mechanism for saving the contents of a downloaded URL to a file on the ColdFusion server. For instance, to save the HTML file resulting from downloading the Landegg Academy Web page to a file at `c:\html\landegg.html`, you could use the following CFHTTP tag:

```
<CFHTTP METHOD=GET
  URL="http://www.landegg.edu/"
  PATH="c:\html"
  FILE="landegg.html">
```

When the CFHTTP tag is used in this way, the downloaded contents are not available in the `CFHTTP.FileContent` variable. Attempting to access this variable as in the following code segment will generate an error message like the one shown in Figure 23.5.

```
<CFHTTP METHOD=GET
  URL="http://www.landegg.edu/"
  PATH="c:\html"
  FILE="landegg.html">
<CFOUTPUT>#CFHTTP.FileContent#</CFOUTPUT>
```

FIGURE 23.5
The CFHTTP.File-
Content variable is
unavailable if you down-
load a URL to a file.

A CFHttp.Filecontent variable is not created if a file path is specified.

NOTE

When the PATH and FILE attributes are used, the RESOLVEURL attribute is ignored even if it is present. This means that any content downloaded to a file in this manner will contain relative URL references as opposed to absolute ones.

Saving Binary Files

Just as you can save plain text and HTML downloaded from a Web server to files on the ColdFusion server, so can you save binary files. When you do this, the MIME type of the file is stored in the CFHTTP.MimeType variable. For instance, if you download a ZIP file with the following tag:

```
<CFHTTP METHOD=GET
URL="http://www.landegg.edu/test.zip"
PATH="c:\html"
FILE="landegg.zip
```

then CFHTTP.MimeType would contain the string application/zip.

Converting a Text File into a Query

Another use of the GET method is to retrieve a delimited text file of the type described earlier in this chapter and convert it into a query.

Let's start with a sample delimited text file:

```
firstname,lastname,gender
Arman,Danesh,Male
Kristin,Motlagh,Female
Michael,Dinowitz,Male
```

This file uses commas as the delimiters and contains three records with three fields or columns (`firstname`, `lastname`, `gender`).

If this file is stored on a Web server at `localhost/file.txt`, then you can download this file, as you have learned before, by using the following:

```
<CFHTTP METHOD=GET
  URL="http://localhost/file.txt">
```

However, all this does is place the entire contents of the file, unprocessed in any useful way, into the `CFHTTP.FileContent` variable.

To convert this file into a query, you will use the `NAME`, `DELIMITER`, and `TEXTQUALIFIER` attributes:

```
<CFHTTP METHOD=GET
  URL="http://localhost/file.txt"
  NAME="people"
  DELIMITER=","
  TEXTQUALIFIER="">
```

Here you specify the following:

- The resulting query is called `people`.
- The delimiter is a comma.
- No text qualifier is specified. Therefore, the delimiter cannot appear within a field.

Knowing this, you can proceed to use the query in your template. For instance, the following template would download the preceding file and display it in a table:

```
<CFHTTP METHOD=GET
  URL="http://localhost/file.txt"
  NAME="people"
  DELIMITER=","
  TEXTQUALIFIER="">

<TABLE BORDER=1 CELLPADDING=3>
<CFOUTPUT QUERY="people">
<TR VALIGN=TOP>
<TD>#lastname#, #firstname#</TD>
<TD>#gender#</TD>
</TR>
</CFOUTPUT>
</TABLE>
```

The results look like Figure 23.6.

FIGURE 23.6
Delimited text files can be
converted into queries.

If you need to use a text qualifier, the process changes slightly. For instance, if you add a fourth record that contains a comma in the `firstname` field, you now need to use a text qualifier. Two steps are required: First, each field in the text file needs to be enclosed in the qualifier. Second, you need to specify the qualifier in the TEXTQUALIFIER attribute.

The result is a delimited text file like this:

```
"firstname","lastname","gender"
"Arman","Danesh","Male"
"Kristin","Motlagh","Female"
"Michael","Dinowitz","Male"
"Jo,Ann","Smith","Female"
```

and a template like this:

```
<CFHTTP METHOD=GET
 URL="http://localhost/file.txt"
 NAME="people"
 DELIMITER=","
 TEXTQUALIFIER="""">

<TABLE BORDER=1 CELLPADDING=3>
<CFOUTPUT QUERY="people">
<TR VALIGN=TOP>
<TD>#lastname#, #firstname#</TD>
<TD>#gender#</TD>
</TR>
</CFOUTPUT>
</TABLE>
```

Notice that you have used a double quote as a qualifier and that in the TEXTQUALIFIER attribute you have had to escape the double quote.

Posting Data to a Server

The final method you are going to look at is how to use the POST method to send data to a server for processing. Using the POST method, you can send the following types of data to the server:

URL   The server will receive the data as if it were appended to the URL using the standard variable1=data2&variable2=data2 syntax.

FormField   The server will receive the data as if it were entered in a named form field by a user and then submitted using the POST method of the FORM tag.

Cookie   The server will receive the data as if the browser had returned cookie data to the server for the requested document.

CGI   The server will receive the data and make it available as a standard CGI environment variable. This can be used to set CGI environment variables such as USERID.

File   The server will receive the data as an uploaded file that can then be saved to disk, for instance with the CFFILE tag.

To upload these types of data to the server, you need to use the CFHTTPPARAM tag.

Using the *CFHTTPPARAM* Tag

The CFHTTPPARAM tag is used to specify name-value pairs for any of the data types outlined in the preceding list. It takes on four attributes:

NAME   The variable name associated with the data being sent to the server

TYPE   The type of data being sent to the server based on the preceding list

VALUE   The data being sent to the server (with TYPE="File", this attribute is not required)

FILE   Specifies the file to upload when using TYPE="File"

Consider the following five CFHTTPPARAM tags:

```
<CFHTTPPARAM TYPE="URL"
  NAME="URLvar"
  VALUE="URLdata">

<CFHTTPPARAM TYPE="FormField"
  NAME="Formvar"
  VALUE="Formdata">

<CFHTTPPARAM TYPE="Cookie"
  NAME="Cookievar"
  VALUE="Cookiedata">
```

```
<CFHTTPPARAM TYPE="CGI"
 NAME="CGIvar"
 VALUE="CGIdata">

<CFHTTPPARAM TYPE="File"
 NAME="Filevar"
 FILE="c:\temp\foo.txt">
```

These five tags upload the following data, respectively:

- A URL variable named URLvar with the value URLdata
- A FormField named Formvar with the value Formdata
- A Cookie named Cookievar with the value Cookiedata
- A CGI variable named CGIvar with the data CGIdata
- A File field named Filevar containing the contents of the file c:\temp\foo.txt

To use these CFHTTPPARAM tags with CFHTTP to upload the data to a URL, you need to use the following construct:

```
<CFHTTP METHOD="POST"
 URL="http://localhost/testpost.cfm">

<CFHTTPPARAM TYPE="URL"
 NAME="URLvar"
 VALUE= "Formdata">

<CFHTTPPARAM TYPE="FormField"
 NAME="Formvar"
 VALUE="Formdata">

<CFHTTPPARAM TYPE="Cookie"
 NAME="Cookievar"
 VALUE="Cookiedata">

<CFHTTPPARAM TYPE="CGI"
 NAME="CGIvar"
 VALUE="CGIdata">

<CFHTTPPARAM TYPE="File"
 NAME="Filevar"
 FILE="c:\temp\foo.txt">

</CFHTTP>
```

Notice that you use METHOD="POST" in the CFHTTP tag and that the CFHTTPPARAM tags are enclosed within opening and closing CFHTTP tags (the closing tag wasn't needed when you used METHOD="GET").

Given this, if you submit this data to another ColdFusion template, then the first four pieces of data being sent could be accessed in that template as:

- URL.URLvar
- Form.Formvar
- Cookie.Cookievar
- CGI.CGIvar

and the file could be accessed using the CFFILE tag:

```
<CFFILE DESTINATION="c:\temp\newfoo.txt"
  NAMECONFLICT="Overwrite"
  FILEFIELD="Filevar"
  ACTION="Upload"
  ATTRIBUTES="Normal">
```

Creating a Local Shareware Archive

Up to this point in the chapter, you have looking at the CFHTTP tag from a mostly theoretical perspective. You haven't really considered how to apply the tag to a practical application.

To close out the chapter, you are going to develop a simple but useful application that depends on the CFHTTP tag to succeed.

Consider the following goal: An organization wishes to allow staff members who have downloaded useful shareware applications to recommend the applications to other staff members through the corporate intranet. At the same time, however, if 200 employees were all to try to download a large piece of shareware in a short span of time, it could easily saturate the limited bandwidth that is available.

As a solution, the organization wants to allow users to recommend shareware through the intranet, but when they do, the file should be downloaded and stored locally so that subsequent users can download the file from the local intranet instead of the Internet.

This can be achieved through the use of two template files and a simple database with a single table.

The database with its table called files would contain the fields outlined in Table 23.1.

TABLE 23.1: Fields in the files Table

Field name	Data type	Description
Id	Number	Primary key for the table (auto-incrementing field)
Name	Text	Name of person recommending the software
Package	Text	Name of the application
URL	Text	URL of the original file

This table can be created in any database that ColdFusion can access, and then the database containing the table should be accessible as the data source `shareware` for the purposes of our templates outlined in the following sections.

Two templates are involved in the application: the submission form and software list (`main.cfm`) and the submission processing form (`submit.cfm`).

The role of `main.cfm` is twofold: It should display a form asking the user to recommend a piece of software and below that display a list of all recommended software with a link for each so that they can be downloaded off the server.

The `submit.cfm` template should accept the form submission, download the specified file, save it to a preset location, and then create an appropriate record in the database.

To make things simple, you will save all downloaded files to the location `c:\html\shareware` and assume that this is accessible via the corporate intranet site at `http://intranet.host.name/shareware`. The name of the file will simply be the Id number from the relevant record in the database.

The *main.cfm* File

The `main.cfm` file is where the bulk of the work takes place. Listing 23.1 is a code listing for the template.

Listing 23.1: main.cfm

```
<CFQUERY NAME="files" DATASOURCE="shareware">
    SELECT * from files ORDER BY Package
</CFQUERY>

<CFSET URLbase="http://intranet.host.name/shareware">

<HTML>
    <HEAD>
        <TITLE>Available Shareware</TITLE>
    </HEAD>

    <BODY>

        <DIV ALIGN=CENTER>
            <H1>Shareware on the Intranet</H1>
        </DIV>

        <HR>

        <EM>If the file you want is not listed below,
feel free to add a file to the recommendation
list using this form</EM><P>
```

```
<FORM METHOD="POST" ACTION="submit.cfm">
<TABLE BORDER=0 CELLPADDING=3>

<TR><TD>Your name:</TD>
<TD><INPUT TYPE="TEXT" NAME="Name"></TD></TR>

<TR><TD>Package name:</TD>
<TD><INPUT TYPE="TEXT" NAME="Package"></TD></TR>

<TR><TD>URL:</TD>
<TD><INPUT TYPE="TEXT" NAME="URL"></TD></TR>

<TR><TD></TD>
<TD><INPUT TYPE="SUBMIT"></TD></TR>

</TABLE>
</FORM>

<HR>

<UL>
<CFOUTPUT QUERY="files">
<LI><STRONG>
<A HREF="#URLbase#/#Id#">#Package#</A>
</STRONG><BR>
Recommended By #Name# (Original URL: #URL#)<BR>
</CFOUTPUT>

</BODY>

</HTML>
```

The logic of the file is straightforward. You start by using CFQUERY to obtain a list of all packages in the database in alphabetical order by package name and store this in a query called `files`.

Next, you set a variable called URLbase that you can use later to build the URLs for the links to each file.

After this initial preparation, the title, instructions, and form are displayed, and then CFOUTPUT is used to produce a bulleted list with one bullet for each package in the query `files`. Here, the URL is built out of a combination of the URLbase variable and the record number for the package being displayed.

The result is a Web page that looks like the one in Figure 23.7.

FIGURE 23.7
The main.cfm template produces this Web page.

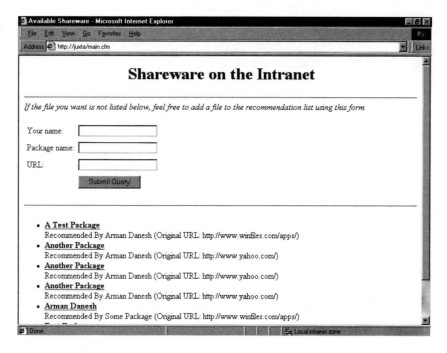

The *submit.cfm* File

When the user submits the form, the data is passed to the submit.cfm template where the work of downloading and storing the file and the related database record is done. The source code for the file looks like Listing 23.2.

Listing 23.2: submit.cfm

```
<CFQUERY NAME="NewRecord" DATASOURCE="shareware">
    INSERT INTO files
    (Name,Package,URL)
    VALUES
    ('#Form.Name#','#Form.Package#','#Form.URL#')
</CFQUERY>

<CFQUERY NAME="TheRecord" DATASOURCE="shareware">
    SELECT * FROM files
    WHERE   Name='#Form.Name#' and
        Package='#Form.Package#' and
        URL='#Form.URL#'
</CFQUERY>

<CFSET ThisFile = #TheRecord.Id#>
```

```
<CFHTTP METHOD="GET"
    URL="#Form.URL#"
    PATH="c:\html\shareware"
    FILE="#ThisFile#"

<CFLOCATION URL="main.cfm">
```

The steps taken here are relatively straightforward. Five tags represent five distinct actions:

1. The data from the form is inserted as a new record in the `files` table in the database using an `insert` query.

2. CFQUERY is used to retrieve the newly created record.

3. CFSET is used to assign the Id number of the newly created record to a variable.

4. The suggested file is downloaded from the specified URL using CFHTTP and is stored in a file whose name is the Id number from the relevant database record.

5. The user is redirected back to the main page using CFLOCATION where the list will now reflect the newly added package.

Shortcomings of the Application

Although this example shows a practical application of the CFHTTP tag, it has some shortcomings as an application that could immediately be deployed on an intranet, including:

- No authorization to ensure that only valid users can recommend files
- No duplicates checking to ensure that no duplicate files are added to the database
- No error checking to ensure that the file was downloaded and saved correctly

As an exercise in applying ColdFusion, you might want to try to address some or all of these issues to create a robust application that can be confidently deployed on a live intranet.

Where Do We Go from Here?

In the next chapter, you will learn about the CFFTP tag, which in many ways complements the CFHTTP tag. Whereas you used the CFHTTP tag to interact with Web servers, you will use the CFFTP tag to work with FTP servers, including uploading and downloading files as well as manipulating files and directories that are already on the server.

chapter 24

Accessing FTP Servers

- Connecting to FTP Servers

- Manipulating Files and Directories on the Server

In many ways, the CFFTP tag is a close relative of the CFHTTP tag that you learned about in the preceding chapter. Whereas the CFHTTP tag enables you to use the Hypertext Transfer Protocol (HTTP) to access Web servers, CFFTP enables you to use the File Transfer Protocol (FTP) to access FTP servers.

Many Web users don't realize that much of the data they are accessing is being served to the Internet by FTP servers as opposed to Web servers. This fact is almost hidden, because it is so easy for a Web page to contain a link to a file on an FTP server, that the user never needs to know the difference. Sites that offer large numbers of files, such as software archives or document repositories, often rely on FTP to make those documents available. After all, FTP was designed for the task, and, in some ways, is still better suited to it than HTTP.

In this chapter, you will learn how to connect to FTP servers, then proceed to upload and download files, and to perform other tasks on the files and directories that are on the server.

Connecting to FTP Servers

Using an FTP server with the CFFTP tag requires two main steps:

1. Connecting to the server.
2. Performing file and directory operations once connected.

Distinguishing between these two roles of the CFFTP tag is achieved with the ACTION attribute. This attribute takes two possible values when dealing with establishing or ending connections:

- Open
- Close

Other attributes that are used after a connection is established are discussed later in the section titled "Manipulating Files and Directories on the Server."

At its simplest, connecting to an FTP server requires three attributes of the CFFTP tag:

- USERNAME
- PASSWORD
- SERVER

For example, to connect to the server ftp.some.domain as user1 using the password pass1, you could use the following tag:

```
<CFFTP ACTION="Open"
 SERVER="ftp.some.domain"
 USERNAME="user1"
 PASSWORD="pass1">
```

However, this approach doesn't address some fundamental issues, including using a proxy server, establishing a passive connection, connecting as an anonymous user, handling special cases such as poor connections, and handling errors.

Connecting through a Proxy Server

If you are behind a firewall and need to connect to a remote FTP server through a proxy server, you can use the PROXYSERVER attribute of the CFFTP tag. This attribute takes the hostname or IP address of your proxy server as a value. For instance, to establish a connection to ftp.some.domain as the user user1 with password pass1 using the proxy server proxy.my.domain, use the following CFFTP tag:

```
<CFFTP ACTION="Open"
 SERVER="ftp.some.domain"
 USERNAME="user1"
 PASSWORD="pass1"
 PROXYSERVER="proxy.my.domain">
```

Establishing a Passive Connection

Some FTP servers require that they be accessed using a passive connection. If you need to establish a passive connection, use the PASSIVE attribute of the CFFTP tag. Possible values are YES and NO; the default value is NO. Set the attribute to YES to establish a passive connection:

```
<CFFTP ACTION="Open"
 SERVER="ftp.some.domain"
 USERNAME="user1"
 PASSWORD="pass1"
 PASSIVE="YES">
```

Making Anonymous FTP Connections

If an FTP server allows anonymous connections for the purpose of downloading files, then the general rule is that the user making the connection must provide the username anonymous (most servers also accept ftp as an alternative), and their e-mail address as a password. For instance, the following lines:

```
<CFFTP ACTION="Open"
 SERVER="ftp.some.domain"
 USERNAME="anonymous"
 PASSWORD="user1@somewhere.com">
```

establish an anonymous connection to ftp.some.domain.

Handling Special Cases

There are two main types of special cases that you may face when making connections:

- Handling poor-quality network connections
- Connecting to servers that use nontraditional ports for FTP access

Handling Poor-Quality Connections

The CFFTP tag provides two attributes that can be used to compensate for poor-quality network connections:

TIMEOUT Specifies the number of seconds to wait for a connection (or operation) to complete before timing out (or giving up). By default, the timeout is set to 30 seconds.

RETRYCOUNT Specifies the number of times a connection (or operation) should be retried if it fails. By default, this is set to one retry.

Generally, if you have a poor-quality connection to a specific FTP server, it is useful to use these two attributes in the following ways:

- Try setting the TIMEOUT value to several minutes instead of the default 30 seconds. Setting it to 300 seconds, for instance, should be sufficient for all but the worst connections; if a connection or operation requires a TIMEOUT value greater than 300 seconds, then the performance of that connection will probably be so poor as to render the connection practically useless.
- Try setting the RETRYCOUNT slightly higher; for instance, to 2 or 3 instead of the default 1. If you find you need a higher value, you probably have a more fundamental problem that needs to be addressed, such as FTP server configuration.

Connecting to Servers That Use Nontraditional Ports

All Internet protocols, including FTP, use default ports to establish connections between two machines. In the case of the FTP, this port is port 21.

However, in some cases, an FTP server will be configured to use a different port from the default to establish connections. This is often done for security reasons to protect the FTP server from attacks from the Internet. At other times, multiple FTP servers may be running on one machine, and each will use its own unique port.

If you need to connect to a server using a nontraditional port, you need to add the PORT attribute to your CFFTP tag. For instance, to connect to a server running on port 8000, simply use PORT=8000 in your CFFTP tag.

Handling Errors

As with any other type of network service, there are many ways in which an attempt to use the service can fail. These can range from server failure or misconfiguration to poor or nonexistent network connections to an incorrect username or password.

The CFFTP tag provides mechanisms for catching and reacting to these errors. The STOPONERROR attribute enables errors to be handled in two ways:

- When the attribute is set to YES, processing stops when an error condition is encountered, and the ColdFusion server displays a relevant error message, like the one in Figure 24.1.
- When the attribute is set to NO, processing continues and information about the error is placed into three variables, which can then be analyzed and reacted to by the code in a ColdFusion template.

FIGURE 24.1
An FTP error when
STOPONERROR is set
to YES

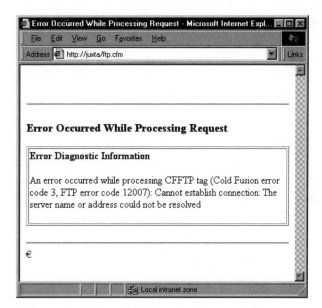

Handling Errors in Your Template

If you opt to set STOPONERROR to NO, then you will be provided with the following variables that can be used to check whether an error has occurred and, if necessary, to react to the error:

CFFTP.Succeeded   Indicates whether the CFFTP tag completed the requested task successfully. Possible values are YES or NO.

CFFTP.ErrorText   Provides a text message describing the error.

CFFTP.ErrorCode   Provides a numerical error code, as shown in Table 24.1.

TABLE 24.1:   CFFTP Error Codes

Code	Meaning
0	Operation succeeded
1	System error (OS or FTP protocol error)
2	An Internet session could not be established
3	FTP session could not be opened
4	File transfer mode not recognized
5	Search connection could not be established
6	Invoked operation valid only during a search
7	Invalid timeout value
8	Invalid port number
9	Not enough memory to allocate system resources
10	Cannot read contents of local file
11	Cannot write to local file
12	Cannot open remote file for reading
13	Cannot read remote file
14	Cannot open local file for writing
15	Cannot write to remote file
16	Unknown error
17	Reserved
18	File already exists
19	Reserved
20	Reserved
21	Invalid retry count specified

By simply applying these variables, you can react to errors as necessary without confronting the user with ColdFusion error messages.

Consider the following code segment:

```
<CFFTP ACTION="Open"
 SERVER="ftp.some.domain"
 USERNAME="user1"
 PASSWORD="pass1"
 STOPONERROR="no">

<CFIF CFFTP.Succeeded is "No">
    <!---Code to process if the FTP
         attempt fails goes here-➡
<CFELSE>
    <!---Code to process if the FTP
         attempt succeeds goes here-➡
</CFIF>
```

Here you see how the CFFTP.Succeeded variable can be used to handle FTP-related errors in a simple way. By placing the appropriate code where indicated by the comments, it is possible to display the error message as desired, or to programmatically react to the error message. In the following example, the error message is displayed for the user by using the CFFTP.ErrorText variable:

```
<CFFTP ACTION="Open"
 SERVER="ftp.some.domain"
 USERNAME="user1"
 PASSWORD="pass1"
 STOPONERROR="no">

<CFIF CFFTP.Succeeded is "No">
    <H1>Error Has Occurred</H1>
    Your attempt to connect to an FTP server has failed with the following
    error message:
    <UL>
    <LI><CFOUTPUT>#CFFTP.ErrorText#</CFOUTPUT>
    </UL>
<CFELSE>
    <!---Code to process if the FTP
         attempt succeeds goes here-➡
</CFIF>
```

When an error occurs, this code produces results like those in Figure 24.2.

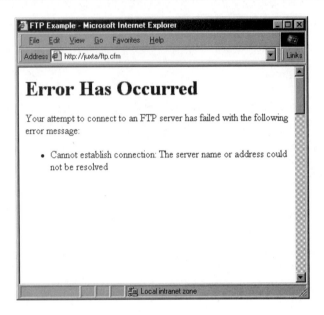

FIGURE 24.2

Displaying an error message by using ColdFusion

Maintaining Your Connections

So far, you have looked at how to establish a connection to an FTP server, but have not considered a larger issue: How to keep that connection open so that multiple file and directory operations can be performed.

By default, the CFFTP tag will establish the connection requested and then promptly disconnect it. This makes the act of opening a connection rather pointless. But you can resolve this problem by caching connections. A cached connection is kept open and assigned a name, so that subsequent operations, including the file and directory operations you will learn about later in this chapter, can make use of the open connection.

To cache a connection when initially accessing an FTP server, add the CONNECTION attribute to the CFFTP tag. In the previous example in which you established an anonymous FTP connection, you could cache it using the following tag:

```
<CFFTP ACTION="Open"
  SERVER="ftp.some.domain"
  USERNAME="anonymous"
  PASSWORD="user1@somewhere.com"
  CONNECTION="FtpConnection">
```

Once established with the CONNECTION attribute in this way, future CFFTP tags in the same template can use the connection name FtpConnection to access the specified server, as you will see later in the "Using the ACTION Attribute" section of this chapter.

Manipulating Files and Directories on the Server

When attempting file and directory operations using the CFFTP tag, a far richer set of attributes is available for use. These attributes are outlined in the following list:

ACTION   Specifies the action to perform.

USERNAME   Specifies the username to use in connecting to the server if the connection is not cached.

PASSWORD   Specifies the password to use in connecting to the server if the connection is not cached.

NAME   Specifies the query name for the results of a directory listing (ACTION="ListDir").

SERVER   Specifies the server to connect to if the connection is not cached.

TIMEOUT   Specifies the timeout value in seconds to use when attempting the operation. The default is 30 seconds.

PORT   Specifies the port to use for the operation. The default is port 21 for FTP operations.

CONNECTION   Specifies the name of the FTP connection. This is used to access an existing cached connection or to cache a new connection.

ASCIIEXTENSIONLIST   A list of file extensions, separated by semicolons, which will automatically be downloaded using ASCII mode (as opposed to binary mode) when TRANSERMODE="Autodetect". By default, the list is txt;htm;html;cfm;cfml;shtm;shtml;css;asp;asa.

TRANSFERMODE   Specifies the transfer mode to use for moving files between the FTP server and client (or vice versa). Possible values are ASCII, Binary, or Autodetect (see ASCIIEXTENSIONLIST). The default is Autodetect.

AGENTNAME   The name of the application or entity conducting a file transfer.

FAILIFEXISTS   Indicates whether the ACTION="GetFile" operation should fail if a local file already exists with the specified local filename for the transfer. Possible values are YES and NO, and the default value is YES.

DIRECTORY   Specifies the directory to perform an action on, and is required for ACTION="ChangeDir", ACTION="CreateDir", ACTION="ListDir", and ACTION="ExistsDir".

LOCALFILE   Specifies the name of the file on the local system. Required for ACTION="GetFile" and ACTION="PutFile".

REMOTEFILE   Specifies the name of the file on the FTP server. Required for ACTION="GetFile", ACTION="PutFile", and ACTION="ExistsFile".

ATTRIBUTES   Specifies a list of attributes, separated by commas, to apply to local files when ACTION="GetFile" is used. Possible attributes are ReadOnly, Hidden, System, Archive, Directory, Compressed, Temporary, Normal. The default value is Normal.

ITEM   Specifies the file or directory on which to perform an operation. Required for ACTION="Exists" and ACTION="Remove".

EXISTING   Specifies the current name of a file or directory on the FTP server. Required for ACTION="Rename".

NEW   Specifies the new name for a file or directory on the FTP server. Required for ACTION="Rename".

RETRYCOUNT   Specifies the number of retries for an operation before giving up. The default value is 1.

STOPONERROR   Specifies how to handle error conditions for an operation. See the "Handling Errors" section earlier in this chapter.

Although this list of attributes seems daunting, it really isn't bad. You will start by taking a look at the ACTION attribute, and then will consider the major actions most commonly used when working with an FTP server:

- Getting a file
- Putting a file
- Getting a directory listing
- Changing directories

Using the *ACTION* Attribute

The ACTION attribute is the centerpiece of any CFFTP file or directory operation. Possible file and directory operations are specified by the values of this attribute, as outlined in Table 24.2.

TABLE 24.2:   Possible values for the ACTION attributes

VALUE	RESULTING ACTION
ChangeDir	Changes directory on the FTP server. Use the DIRECTORY attribute to specify the directory to change to.
CreateDir	Creates a new directory on the FTP server. Use the DIRECTORY attribute to specify the directory to create.
ListDir	Obtains a list of the contents of a directory on the FTP server. The resulting list is stored in the query specified with the NAME attribute. Use the DIRECTORY attribute to specify which directory to list the contents of.

TABLE 24.2: Possible values for the ACTION attributes *(continued)*

VALUE	RESULTING ACTION
GetFile	Copies a file from the remote FTP server to the local ColdFusion server. Use the REMOTE-FILE attribute to specify the file to copy, and the LOCALFILE attribute to specify the name of the new copy of the file on the local system.
PutFile	Copies a file from the local ColdFusion server to the remote FTP server. Use the LOCAL-FILE attribute to specify the file to copy, and the REMOTEFILE attribute to specify the name of the new copy of the file on the remote server.
Rename	Renames a file on the FTP server. Use the EXISTING attribute to specify the file to rename, and the NEW attribute to specify the new name of the file.
Remove	Deletes a file on the FTP server. Use the ITEM attribute to specify the file to delete.
GetCurrentDir	Returns the name of the path and name of the current directory in the variable CFFT-PResult.ReturnValue.
GetCurrentURL	Returns the current URL on the FTP server in the variable CFFTPResult.ReturnValue.
ExistsDir	Returns YES or NO in the variable CFFTPResult.ReturnValue to indicate whether the directory specified with the DIRECTORY attribute exists on the FTP server.
ExistsFile	Returns YES or NO in the variable CFFTPResult.ReturnValue to indicate whether the file specified with the REMOTEFILE attribute exists on the FTP server.
Exists	Returns YES or NO in the variable CFFTPResult.ReturnValue to indicate whether the file or directory specified with the ITEM attribute exists on the FTP server.

Some of these actions dictate that certain corresponding attributes must be used in the CFFTP tag, as outlined in Table 24.3.

TABLE 24.3: Attributes Required with Actions

If the ACTION is ...	Then the following attributes are required
ChangeDir	DIRECTORY
CreateDir	DIRECTORY
ListDir	DIRECTORY, NAME
GetFile	LOCALFILE, REMOTEFILE
PutFile	LOCALFILE, REMOTEFILE
Rename	EXISTING, NEW
Remove	ITEM
ExistsDir	DIRECTORY
ExistsFile	REMOTEFILE
Exists	ITEM

When specifying any of the actions outlined in Table 24.3, if you have an already cached, open connection, then the SERVER, USERNAME, and PASSWORD attributes are not required—only the CONNECTION attribute is required. For instance, with the cached connection called FtpConnection used earlier in this chapter, you could get the current directory with

```
<CFFTP CONNECTION="FtpConnection"
 ACTION="GetCurrentDir">
```

If the cached connection is not available, then adding SERVER, USERNAME, and PASS-WORD to the tag would enable a connection to the server to be established to perform the GetCurrentDir action.

In all the following examples in this chapter, it is assumed that a cached connection called FtpConnection exists, and that it should be used for all the operations.

Getting a File

Downloading a file from the current directory of the remote server to the local ColdFusion server involves using ACTION="GetFile". To do this, you need to specify two attributes: LOCALFILE and REMOTEFILE.

For instance, to download the file foo.txt from the current directory on the FTP server to the c:\temp directory on the local ColdFusion server, you could use

```
<CFFTP CONNECTION="FtpConnection"
 ACTION="GetFile"
 REMOTEFILE="foo.txt"
 LOCALFILE="c:\temp\foo.txt">
```

If, in the process of downloading the file you want the new copy on the ColdFusion server to have the name newfoo.txt, you can change the value of the LOCALFILE attribute:

```
<CFFTP CONNECTION="FtpConnection"
 ACTION="GetFile"
 REMOTEFILE="foo.txt"
 LOCALFILE="c:\temp\newfoo.txt">
```

Putting a File

Putting a file is the reverse process of getting a file: It uploads a file from the local Cold-Fusion server to the remote FTP server, and uses the LOCALFILE and REMOTEFILE attributes to specify the necessary information.

For instance, to upload the file c:\temp\foo.txt on the local system to the current directory on the remote FTP server, you would use the following tag:

```
<CFFTP CONNECTION="FtpConnection"
 ACTION="PutFile"
 REMOTEFILE="foo.txt"
 LOCALFILE="c:\temp\foo.txt">
```

Similarly, if you want the resulting file on the remote FTP server to have the name newfoo.txt, you simply change the value of the REMOTEFILE attribute:

```
<CFFTP CONNECTION="FtpConnection"
 ACTION="PutFile"
 REMOTEFILE="newfoo.txt"
 LOCALFILE="c:\temp\foo.txt">
```

Getting a Directory Listing

In working with the files on an FTP server, you often need to download a directory listing of files on the server to present in a ColdFusion template. You achieve this by using the ACTION="ListDir" attribute, combined with the NAME and DIRECTORY attributes.

For instance, the following tag downloads the content of the top-level directory of the FTP server and stores the results in the query named DirList:

```
<CFFTP CONNECTION="FtpConnection"
 ACTION="ListDir"
 DIRECTORY="/*"
 NAME="DirList">
```

The resulting query contains the columns described in the following list:

Name   Filename of the element specified by the current row of the query

Path   File path of the current row of the query (without a drive specified)

URL   Full URL of the element specified by the current row of the query

Length   File size of the element specified by the current row of the query

LastModified   Modification date of the element specified by the current row of the query

Attributes   File attributes of the element specified by the current row of the query

IsDirectory   A Boolean value indicating whether the element specified by the current row of the query is a directory (a True value) or a file (a False value)

Mode   Octal string representing UNIX permissions

Using this information, you can display the contents of a directory you have listed:

```
<CFFTP CONNECTION="FtpConnection"
 ACTION="ListDir"
 DIRECTORY="/*"
 NAME="DirList">

<TABLE BORDER=0 CELLSPACING=3>
<TR VALIGN=TOP>
 <TD><STRONG>PATH/NAME</STRONG></TD>
 <TD><STRONG>SIZE</STRONG></TD>
 <TD><STRONG>Last Modified</TD>
</TR>
```

```
<CFOUTPUT QUERY="DirList">
<TR VALIGN=TOP>
 <TD>
  #Path#/#Name#<CFIF IsDirectory>/</CFIF>
 </TD>
 <TD>#Length#</TD>
 <TD>#DateFormat(LastModified)#</TD>
</TR>
</CFOUTPUT>

</TABLE>
```

This code produces results like those in Figure 24.3.

FIGURE 24.3
Displaying a directory
listing

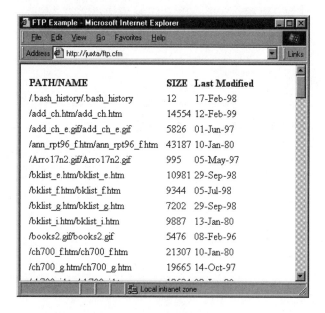

Notice the use of a test on the Boolean IsDirectory value to determine whether an element is a directory, and whether it is to put a / after the name (a typical Unix and FTP convention for specifying directories). You can take this a step further, and make all files clickable so that users can download the files. This can be done with the URL value:

```
<CFFTP CONNECTION="FtpConnection"
 ACTION="ListDir"
 DIRECTORY="/*"
 NAME="DirList">
```

```
<TABLE BORDER=0 CELLSPACING=3>
<TR VALIGN=TOP>
 <TD><STRONG>PATH/NAME</STRONG></TD>
 <TD><STRONG>SIZE</STRONG></TD>
 <TD><STRONG>Last Modified</TD>
</TR>

<CFOUTPUT QUERY="DirList">
<TR VALIGN=TOP>
 <TD>
  <CFIF IsDirectory>
   #Name#/
  <CFELSE>
   <A HREF="#URL#">#Name#</A>
  </CFIF> </TD>
 <TD>#Length#</TD>
 <TD>#DateFormat(LastModified)#</TD>
</TR>
</CFOUTPUT>

</TABLE>
```

This code produces results like those in Figure 24.4.

FIGURE 24.4
Turning filenames into
clickable links

Changing Directories

Finally, you will look at changing directories, another critical action in being able to navigate an FTP server and upload and download files. You change directories by using `ACTION="ChangeDir"` and the `DIRECTORY` attribute.

For instance, if the current directory has a subdirectory called `pub`, you could change the current directory to the `pub` directory with the following tag:

```
<CFFTP CONNECTION="MyFtp"
  ACTION="ChangeDir"
  DIRECTORY="pub">
```

Also, just as the two-dot (. .) combination indicates the parent directory of the current directory when using the `cd` command in DOS or Unix, it can also be used to change to the parent directory of the current directory when using the `ACTION="ChangeDir"` attribute:

```
<CFFTP CONNECTION="MyFtp"
  ACTION="ChangeDir"
  DIRECTORY="..">
```

Where Do We Go from Here?

In the next chapter, you will look at the last Internet protocol discussed in this section of the book: Lightweight Directory Access Protocol, or LDAP.

LDAP is used to create directory structures for the hierarchical storage of information about people and resources within organizations. Many of the Internet white-pages services that are used on the Web to locate phone numbers and e-mail addresses are based on LDAP servers.

The next chapter won't address the intricacies of setting up your own LDAP server, which can be quite complex. Instead, you will start with an overview of what LDAP is and how it is structured, and then move on to using the CFLDAP server to access public Internet white pages running on an LDAP server.

chapter 25

Working with LDAP Servers

- Understanding LDAP

- Using CFLDAP

- Querying LDAP servers with CFLDAP

The final Internet protocol tag that you need to look at is CFLDAP. This tag is used to interact with servers running *the Lightweight Directory Access Protocol*, also known as LDAP.

LDAP is emerging as the standard for storing and disseminating structured directories of information, such as information about corporate employees or information about the nodes on a computer network. Common applications include Internet white-pages systems and corporate-employee and user-account management systems.

In this chapter, you will learn what LDAP is and then take a quick look at the CFLDAP tag and how it can be used. Finally, you will create a concrete example in which to develop a template for issuing a query to an LDAP server and displaying the results.

Understanding LDAP

LDAP is an Internet protocol for storing and sharing structured directories of information.

As LDAP has grown in popularity and companies such as Netscape have developed commercial-grade, manageable, LDAP-server software, the applications of this protocol have increasingly diversified. LDAP is being used to replace OS-specific user databases and authentication systems and to build employee directories; it also provides a tool for information systems departments to track and manage all hardware and software deployed on a network, and much more.

At the center of LDAP is the directory. Therefore, you need to start by understanding what a directory is.

Understanding Directories

Directories are databases designed to be read far more often then they are updated. Accordingly, LDAP servers are optimized to provide quick response time when faced with high volumes of lookup.

Technically, there is no limitation on the type of information that can be stored in an LDAP directory. The real issue is how data is structured.

Structurally, directories contain entries, and individual entries are collections of attributes. Each entry has a name, referred to as the *distinguished name*, which provides a unique, unambiguous way in which to refer to an entry in the directory.

The information in a directory is arranged in a hierarchical tree. These trees are arranged in a structure reflecting political, geographic, or organizational divisions. In fact, individual organizational directories can be seen as fitting into a larger global directory, parts of which are publicly accessible and parts of which have limited access.

For instance, Figure 25.1 shows a simplified image of a global directory structure. In this example, Sybex may not want its segment of the tree made public, so it runs a private directory server that cannot be accessed from outside the organization whereas

Juxta Publishing takes the reverse approach, making its directory information publicly accessible.

FIGURE 25.1
A simplified directory
structure

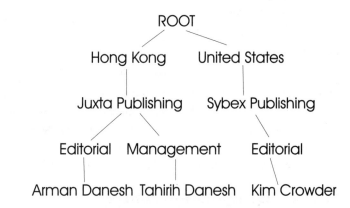

Individual entries in the directory tree are referenced by a distinguished name in the form of an attribute-value pair written as `attribute=value`. At different levels of the hierarchy, different attributes serve as the distinguished name of an entry.

At the country level, the country attribute, referred to by the attribute name `c`, is the entry name and takes the form `c=US` or `c=GB`. Similarly, at the organization level, the organization attribute named `o` is the entry name, as in `o=Juxta Publishing` or `o=Sybex Publishing`. Figure 25.2 shows the simple directory tree you just looked at with the names of the entries identified by their attribute-value pairs.

FIGURE 25.2
Using attribute-value pairs
to name entries

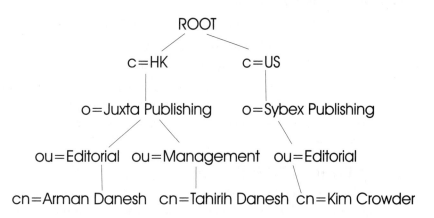

There are numerous attributes in use in directories deployed in organizations around the world, but some common ones found in employee directories and user directories are:

c   Country

st   State/province

l   Locality/city

o   Organization

ou   Organizational unit/department

cn   Common name/full name of a person

For a further overview of LDAP, visit the LDAP page at the University of Michigan at `http://www.umich.edu/~dirsvcs/ldap/`. The University of Michigan has developed the most widely used LDAP implementation and provides references to resources describing LDAP as well as LDAP software and mailing lists.

Building a Distinguished Name

As mentioned earlier, each entry in a directory can be referenced by a unique name known as the distinguished name. This is not simply the entry name we just discussed. After all, there might be a Juxta Publishing in more than one country, which means there is no guarantee that `o=Juxta Publishing` is a unique identifier for the organization.

Instead, the distinguished name of an entry is built by taking the name of the entry in question and adding the names of its ancestors back up to the root, all separated by commas. For instance, in the tree shown in Figure 25.2, the distinguished name of Arman Danesh is: `cn=Arman Danesh, o=Juxta Publishing, c=HK`.

Searching a Directory

The process of searching a directory is as follows:

1. Specify the sub-tree to be searched.

2. Specify a search using an information filter.

For example, suppose you wanted to search the Juxta Publishing sub-tree for an employee named `Arman Danesh`. You would specify `o=Juxta Publishing` as the top of the sub-tree to be searched and indicate that the search should look for entries with `Arman Danesh` in their name.

Using Public LDAP Servers

Several Internet white pages and person directories operate public LDAP servers that can be queried from anywhere on the Internet. The following list is a selection of these directories:

Bigfoot   `ldap.bigfoot.com`

Four11 `ldap.four11.com`

Infospace `ldap.infospace.com`

Later in this chapter, you will work with the Four11 server in an example.

Using *CFLDAP*

The CFLDAP tag is the route through which ColdFusion can interact with LDAP servers. Using the CFLDAP tag, several types of actions are possible. These actions are specified by using values of the `ACTION` attribute, including the following:

Query Searches a directory for information. This is the default action.

Add Adds entries to a directory.

Modify Modifies entries in a directory.

Modifydn Modifies the distinguished name of entries in the directory.

Delete Deletes entries from the directory.

To use any action except the `Query` action requires access to an LDAP server where you have permission to make modifications. For this reason, you will only work through a concrete example of the `Query` action after you finish covering the basics of the CFLDAP tag.

When using the actions, different attributes are required with the CFLDAP tag, as outlined in Table 25.1.

T A B L E   2 5 . 1 : Possible CFLDAP Actions

Action	Required Attributes
Query	NAME, START, ATTRIBUTES
Add	ATTRIBUTES
Modify	DN, ATTRIBUTES
Modifydn	DN, ATTRIBUTES
Delete	DN

In total, the CFLDAP tag can take the following attributes:

SERVER The host name or the IP address of the LDAP server. This is required with all actions.

PORT The port to use in connecting to the LDAP server. The default value is 389.

USERNAME The username to use in connecting to the LDAP server. If none is provided, the default is an anonymous connection.

PASSWORD The password to use in connecting to the LDAP server. This should correspond to any username that is specified.

NAME   The name to associate with the query result set when using the Query action.

TIMEOUT   The maximum timeout in seconds when waiting for an LDAP server to process an action. The default value is 60 seconds.

MAXROWS   The maximum number of entries to be returned when using the Query action. The default is no maximum.

START   The distinguished name of the entry at the top of the sub-tree being searched when using the Query action.

SCOPE   The scope of the search when using the Query action. Possible scopes are ONELEVEL (searches all entries one level below the entry specified with the START attribute), BASE (searches only the entry specified with the START attribute), or SUBTREE (searches all entries in the sub-tree starting with the entry specified with the START attribute). The default scope is ONELEVEL.

ATTRIBUTES   A comma-separated list of attributes to be returned when using the Query action. Indicates a semicolon-separated list of attributes to be updated with the Add, Modifydn, and Modify actions.

FILTER   The search criteria when using the Query action. The filter should take the form attribute=value. The * symbol can be used as a wildcard character. For instance, to search for all employees named Arman Danesh, use cn=Arman Danesh. By default, the filter is objectclass=*.

FILTERFILE   A string indicating a file and section of that file containing LDAP filter strings specifications. The value of the parameter is filename, sectioname.

SORT   Indicates a list of one or more attributes to use in sorting the query results. If you specify a list of more than one attribute name, separate the attributes with commas.

SORTCONTROL   The sort order for query result sets when using the Query action. Possible values are ASC for an ascending sort, DESC for a descending sort, and NOCASE for a case-insensitive sort. You can combine these values (for instance using both ASC and NOCASE for a case-insensitive, ascending sort).

STARTROW   Indicates which row from the LDAP query result should be treated as the first row of the ColdFusion query result set.

DN   The distinguished name of the entry to alter when using the Add, Modify, Modifydn, or Delete actions.

REFERRAL   Indicates the number of hops allowed when an LDAP query is being referred to other servers.

REBIND   Indicates if the original authentication credentials should be used to authenticate when following a referral. Possible values are YES and NO.

MODIFYTYPE   Indicates the action to perform with an attribute and a multi-value list of attributes. Possible values are Add (append the attribute to the list), Delete (delete the attribute from the list), Replace (replace an attribute in the list). Replace is the default value.

SEPARATOR   Indicates the character used to separate attributes in multi-attribute lists.

SECURE   Identifies the type of security to use if connecting to an LDAP server on a secure connection. Two types of security are possible, CFSSL_BASIC or CFSSL_CLIENT_AUTH. The value of this attribute takes one of two forms: CFSSL_BASIC, certificate_database or CFSSL_CLIENT_AUTH,certificate_database, certificate_name,key_database,key_password.

Querying LDAP Servers with *CFLDAP*

Now that you have reviewed the basics of the CFLDAP tag, let's build a simple application to allow searches of the Bigfoot directory by name. For all matches, the name, state, country, organization, and e-mail address should be displayed.

First, you need a form in which users can specify the name they are searching for:

```
<FORM METHOD=POST ACTION="submit.cfm">
Name to search for:
<INPUT TYPE="TEXT" NAME="Name">
<INPUT TYPE="SUBMIT">
</FORM>
```

Next, you need to build a simple template that queries the Bigfoot server based on the information provided by the user:

```
<CFLDAP SERVER="ldap.four11.com"
ACTION="QUERY"
NAME="Results"
START="c=*"
ATTRIBUTES="cn,o,st,c,sn"
FILTER="cn=#Form.Name#">

<CFOUTPUT QUERY="Results">
#cn#
(<CFIF st is not "">#st#, </CFIF>#c#)
<CFIF o is not "">Organization: #o#</CFIF><BR>
</CFOUTPUT> {!!!!!!!!!
```

What happens here is really quite simple. The CFLDAP tag is built to specify the Four11 server and the Query action. The START attribute indicates that you are searching for any country. You select the attributes you want from the directory with the ATTRIBUTES attribute. Finally, the FILTER attribute specifies that you are looking for a name that matches the name specified by the user in the form.

The CFOUTPUT block displays the name of the person, the state if it is available, the country and, finally, the organization where available.

For instance, if you search for entries that match the name Danesh, you get results like those in Figure 25.3.

FIGURE 25.3
Searching the Four11 directory by using ColdFusion

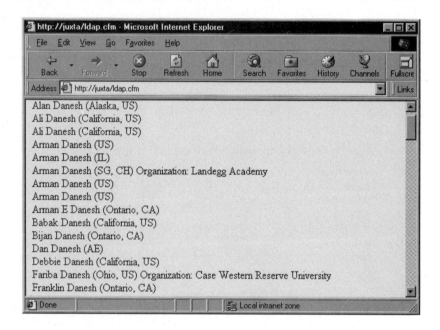

Where Do We Go from Here?

This chapter wraps up our look at the use of ColdFusion to interact with Internet services including mail, HTTP, FTP, and LDAP.

The next section of the book looks at a variety of advanced subjects including dynamic expressions, ColdFusion scripting, scheduling events, creating a search engine, security, and ColdFusion administration. We start this section with a look at evaluating dynamic expressions. Dynamic expression evaluation is a technique that enables expressions to be built dynamically by using string values, expressions, and operations. In this way, the exact nature of an expression can be created programmatically as a template is being processed.

PART IV

Advanced Concepts

Learn to:

- ■ Evaluate dynamic expressions

- ■ Use scripts in ColdFusion

- ■ Schedule events

- ■ Implement a search engine

- ■ Enhance application security

- ■ Build custom tags

- ■ Include external objects

- ■ Use WDDX

- ■ Use the CFREGISTRY tag

chapter 26

Evaluating Dynamic Expressions

- Understanding Dynamic Expressions

- Working with Dynamic Expressions

In this chapter, you will learn about *dynamic expressions*. Dynamic expressions provide a way to extend the functionality of basic ColdFusion expressions. Basic ColdFusion expressions are dynamic only insofar as their values can be determined at the time of execution by the value of variables. Dynamic expressions take this level of abstraction one level further, allowing the expression itself to be determined at the time of execution based on the value of variables.

You will learn the mechanics of building dynamic expressions and then will look at the application of dynamic expression using four functions:

- Evaluate
- DE
- SetVariable
- IIf

Understanding Dynamic Expressions

In Chapter 6, "Writing Expressions," you learned how to build and use ColdFusion expressions. Expressions are powerful in their own right, allowing for a degree of abstraction in your ColdFusion templates. For instance, you can use the expression

```
#Form.Number# + 1
```

to add 1 to the value submitted by the user in the form. The expression itself has no value at the time the code is written, but instead evaluates to a different value each time the code is executed, depending on the value entered by the user. Dynamic expressions offer the capability to carry this abstraction one level further.

Let's consider a simple example. Look at the following variable assignments:

```
<CFSET Num1=1>
<CFSET Num2=2>
<CFSET Num3=3>
```

How would you increment one of these three values by 1 and assign it to another variable where the user can specify which value to increment by submitting a number through a form?

At first glance, you could achieve this by using a CFIF construct or a CFSWITCH/ CFCASE construct:

```
<CFSWITCH EXPRESSION="#Form.Number#">
    <CFCASE VALUE="1">
        <CFSET NewNum = Num1 + 1>
    </CFCASE>
```

```
    <CFCASE VALUE="2">
        <CFSET NewNum = Num2 + 1>
    </CFCASE>
    <CFCASE VALUE="3">
        <CFSET NewNum = Num3 + 1>
    </CFCASE>
</CFSWITCH>
```

Although this example works, it is far from concise or elegant. In addition, if the number of possible variables you are working with is large, then you have a lot of coding to do to make things work. For instance, if you have 100 variables, num1 through num100, you would need to write 100 CFCASE blocks.

This is where dynamic expressions come in. The idea here is to create a string that, when evaluated, is the expression you need to increment the desired variable. For instance, the following expression

```
"Num#Form.Number# + 1"
```

is a simple string. If the user submits the number 3, then this string evaluates to

```
Num3 + 1
```

If you then, in turn, are able to evaluate this new expression, you can effectively add 1 to the desired value without having to use multiple conditions.

This is what dynamic expressions are all about: evaluating a string expression to get another expression, which can in turn be evaluated.

Dynamic Expressions and Strings

To build dynamic expressions, you first need to consider some dynamics of strings. Dynamic expressions are built out of string expressions. String expressions are nothing more than regular ColdFusion expressions inside a string (in other words, inside quotation marks).

For instance, consider the simple expression 1+2. This can be converted into a string expression by surrounding it by quotes: "1+2". This is a subtle difference but an important one. Consider the following ColdFusion code:

```
<CFSET Value1 = 1 + 2>
<CFSET Value2 = "1 + 2">
<CFOUTPUT>
    Value1: #Value1#
    <BR>
    Value2: #Value2#
</CFOUTPUT>
```

This produces the following results:

```
Value1: 3
Value2: 1 + 2
```

Why should the two results be different? In the first CFSET tag, the expression 1 + 2 is evaluated (resulting in 3) and is assigned to Value1. But, in the second example the expression "1 + 2" evaluates to a string (the string 1 + 2) which is assigned to Value2. The arithmetic expression 1 + 2 within the string is not evaluated here; the string expression is the only expression that is evaluated.

By way of example, recall the simple CFSWITCH code used earlier in this chapter:

```
<CFSWITCH EXPRESSION="#Form.Number#">
    <CFCASE VALUE="1">
        <CFSET NewNum = Num1 + 1>
    </CFCASE>
    <CFCASE VALUE="2">
        <CFSET NewNum = Num2 + 1>
    </CFCASE>
    <CFCASE VALUE="3">
        <CFSET NewNum = Num3 + 1>
    </CFCASE>
</CFSWITCH>
```

We could obtain the value of NewNum in a simpler matter if we could create a string containing "Num#Form.Number# + 1" which will be "Num1 + 1", "Num2 + 1" or "Num3 + 1" depending on the value of Form.Number and then simply evaluate the string as an arithmetic expression. This is exactly what dynamic expressions can do:

```
<CFSET Expression = "Num#Form.Number# + 1">
<CFSET NewNum = Evaluate(Expression)>
```

Dynamic expressions are all about evaluating this inner expression within the string expression. However, some complexities are introduced when you attempt to take a standard ColdFusion expression and embed it into a string (in other words, put it inside quotation marks). These complexities arise out of the need to escape certain characters. We discussed escaping in general in Chapter 6 but here you need to review escaping and how it works.

Consider the following standard ColdFusion expression:

```
"Hello " & "there"
```

If you want to put this expression inside quotation marks to convert it to a string expression as you did with 1 + 2 earlier, you might want to try using

```
""Hello " & "there""
```

But, as you learned in Chapter 6, to include a double quote mark inside a string that is enclosed in double quotes, you need to escape the quote marks inside the string. This means repeating each double quote inside the string:

```
"""Hello "" & ""there """
```

Inside the string, you have four pairs of escaped double-quote marks (underlined so that they are easy to identify). Each of these represents one of the double quotes in the original expression.

You can improve readability slightly by alternating single and double quotation marks. There is no reason a string can't be enclosed in single quotation marks. If a string is enclosed in single quote marks, then double quote marks can be used inside the string without being escaped; in this case, single quotes would need escaping. Therefore, you can eliminate the pairs of double quotes by escaping your expression in single quotes:

```
'"Hello " & "there"'
```

Table 26.1 provides some examples of the way in which different string expressions can be converted into dynamic expressions (by being put inside quotes).

T A B L E   2 6 . 1 :   Quoting Expressions

Original Expression Text	Converted String Expression
`"This is a double quote ""`	`"""This is a double quote """""`
`'This is a single quote ''`	`'''This is a single quote '''''`
`'This is a double quote "'`	`'''This is a double quote "'''`
`"This is a single quote'"`	`"""This is a single quote'"""`

In the first example, the original expression has double quotes to surround the expression and includes a third double quote inside the string. In the converted string expression, all double quotes are escaped and an additional pair of double quotes must surround the whole expression. The original expression text has three double quotes and the string expression equivalent has eight double quotes

The same is true for the second example. All the single quotes must be escaped and an additional pair of single quotes must surround the entire expression. You start with three single quotes and end up with eight single quotes.

The third example is quite different; it has a mixture of double and single quotes. As a rule, you escape the quotes within the original, which are the same type of quotes used to enclose it when converting it to a dynamic expression. Therefore, for this example, if the surrounding quote is a single quote, you escape all single quotes.

The last example is similar to the third one. The only difference is that the surrounding quotes are double quotes. So, all double quotes in the expression must be escaped.

Working with Dynamic Expressions

You now understand the dynamics of building a dynamic expression: taking a standard ColdFusion expression and converting it into a string expression by following the necessary rules of escaping quote marks within the expression. However, you still don't know how to evaluate these dynamic expressions. The simplest way to evaluate a dynamic expression is by using the Evaluate function. The Evaluate function enables you to carry evaluation of a dynamic expression out to its completion.

Let's start with our simple 1 + 2 expression. When converted to a string, you have "1 + 2". In the following code, you assign the string expression to a variable and then evaluate it using the Evaluate function:

```
<CFSET Expression = "1 + 2">
<CFOUTPUT>#Evaluate(Expression)#</CFOUTPUT>
```

The result is that 3 is output: The arithmetic expression contained within the string expression has been evaluated by the Evaluate function.

Of course, this doesn't seem to offer much in the way of additional functionality. After all, you could simply have assigned 1 + 2 to a variable and output the results:

```
<CFSET Result = 1 + 2>
<CFOUTPUT>#Result#</CFOUTPUT>
```

Consider the following example, however:

```
<CFSET Expression = "1 + Increment">
<CFSET Increment = 2>
<CFOUTPUT>#Evaluate(Expression)#</CFOUTPUT>
```

Here, as well, the output is 3. In this case, the string expression is 1 + Increment and, because Increment is set to 2, the result of evaluating the string expression with Evaluate is 3.

The power here is that you can reuse this string expression with different values of Increment in the same template:

```
<CFSET Expression = "1 + Increment">

<CFSET Increment = 2>
```

```
<CFOUTPUT>1 + #Increment# = #Evaluate(Expression)#<BR></CFOUTPUT>

<CFSET Increment = 4>
<CFOUTPUT>1 + #Increment# = #Evaluate(Expression)#<BR></CFOUTPUT>
```

The output would be

```
1 + 2 = 3
1 + 4 = 5
```

Each time you use `Evaluate`, the arithmetic expression in the string `Expression` is dynamically evaluated based on the value of `Increment`.

There is a caveat here, though. You need to take care in using pound signs inside string expressions.

For instance, consider the following example:

```
<CFSET Increment = 2>
<CFSET Expression = "1 + #Increment#">
<CFSET Increment = 4>
<CFOUTPUT>#Evaluate(Expression)#</CFOUTPUT>
```

Based on the previous discussion, you might first think that the resulting output would be 5. However, a subtle and important difference exists between the string expression in this example and the one in the previous examples.

In this case, when you assign a string value to `Expression`, you use pound signs around `Increment` inside the string expression. By doing this, you cause the value of `Increment` to be included in the string rather than the variable name. Therefore the string `"1 + 2"` (rather than `"1 + Increment"`) is stored in `Expression`. Therefore, regardless of the value of `Increment` later in the template, using `Evaluate(Expression)` will always result in 3. This highlights the subtle difference between the dynamic expression `"1 + Increment"` and the expression `"1 + #Increment#"`, which is evaluated one time, after which the value can never change.

Other Dynamic Expression Functions

You can use three other functions in working with dynamic expressions:

- `DE`
- `SetVariable`
- `IIf`

We will consider these briefly.

Using the *DE* Function

The DE function is known as the delay evaluation function. According to the ColdFusion documentation, the DE function returns a string expression with quotes wrapped around it and the necessary quotes within the string escaped. This can be used, in conjunction with `Evaluate` or `IIf` (covered later in this chapter), to prevent evaluation of the resulting string expression. Table 26.2 shows the distinction between using `Evaluate` with and without the DE function.

T A B L E 2 6 . 2 : The DE Function and the Evaluate Function

To get	Use
The value of the variable G	Evaluate("G")
The string G	Evaluate(DE("G"))

The advantage of this function may seem limited in this context. However, it does provide one advantage: It does the work of enclosing an expression in quotation marks and performing the necessary escaping. Therefore, the assignment

```
<CFSET Expression = "'Some ""double"" quotes'">
```

is functionally the same as

```
<CFSET Value = 'Some "double" quotes'>
<CFSET Expression = DE(Value)>
```

This proves useful because it enables you to avoid the often confusing task of enclosing your expressions in quotes and handling all the escaping that it entails.

Using the *SetVariable* Function

The `SetVariable` function enables you to assign values to variables whose names are dynamically determined. For instance, if the name of the variable that you wanted to assign a value to is stored in another variable, you could use `SetVariable` to achieve the task:

```
<CFSET VariableToSet = "SomeVariable">
<CFSET Value = 2>
<CFSET Result = SetVariable(VariableToSet,Value) >
```

Here, the value 2 is assigned to the variable `SomeVariable`. The value of `VariableToSet` and `Value` remain unchanged. In addition, the value that was just set (in this case 2) is returned by the `SetVariable` function, and you assign it to the variable `Result`.

By way of further example, consider the following loop where the dynamically generated variable is set to the `Counter` value:

```
<CFLOOP INDEX="Counter" FROM=1 TO=3>
```

```
    <CFSET Result = SetVariable("num#Counter#",Counter)>
</CFLOOP>
```

This produces the same results as the following CFSET tags used earlier in this chapter:

```
<CFSET Num1=1>
<CFSET Num2=2>
<CFSET Num3=3>
```

Using the *IIf* Function

The IIf function is used to achieve the functional equivalent of:

```
<CFIF condition>
    <CFSET Result = Evaluate(Expression1)>
<CFELSE>
    <CFSET Result = Evaluate(Expression2)>
</CFIF>
```

The comparable IIf function would be:

```
<CFSET Result = IIf(condition,Expression1,Expression2)>
```

Let's consider a simple example, preventing a division by zero:

```
<CFSET Expression1 = "Error">
<CFSET Expression2 = "x/y">
<CFSET Result = IIf(y is 0, DE(Expression1), Expression2)>
```

Based on the value of y, either x/y will be evaluated or "Error" will be returned (when y is 0). Notice the use of the DE function for Expression1. If you don't use DE and y is 0, then an attempt will be made to execute Evaluate(Expression1), which is the same as Evaluate("Error"). This will cause ColdFusion to attempt to evaluate Error as a variable. But, you haven't created a variable called Error. You want the string "Error" as the result. So, you use Evaluate(DE("Error")) to return the string "Error". Hence, the use of DE(Expression1) in the IIf function.

Where Do We Go from Here?

In the next chapter, you will look at ColdFusion scripting. ColdFusion scripting was a new addition to ColdFusion with the release of version 4. It provides an alternative syntax for the basic programming constructs such as loops and conditional statements.

Although ColdFusion's tag-based programming constructs are powerful, they can seem counter-intuitive and a little cumbersome for developers with programming experience. ColdFusion scripting offers a way to write server-based scripts using a programming style and syntax that will seem more familiar to many experienced programmers.

chapter 27

ColdFusion Scripting

- Scripting vs. Tag-Based Code

- The Basics of ColdFusion Scripting

Developers who are familiar with other scripting environments for Web application development, including JavaScript and Active Server Pages, often initially think that ColdFusion doesn't offer a full-scale scripting environment.

This reaction comes from ColdFusion being tag-oriented whereas more traditional scripting environments are command, function, and expression based.

However, this focus on tags as the mechanism for all activity in ColdFusion belies the real power of the language. ColdFusion contains almost every major programming construct expected by Web application developers; they are just cloaked in the guise of tags.

Allaire, with version 4 of ColdFusion, is acknowledging that many developers are more comfortable with the style of programming used in JavaScript and other scripting environments. They have introduced a new ColdFusion scripting language that can be used to replace many of the tasks commonly performed with tags.

In this chapter you will review scripting with the ColdFusion scripting language and learn how to use scripts in place of many common ColdFusion tags.

Scripting versus Tag-Based Code

The goal of the ColdFusion scripting language is to make parts of ColdFusion functionality available in script-style syntax that developers may already be comfortable with.

This is not to say that everything done with ColdFusion's tag-based syntax can be achieved through scripts. Rather, any parts of ColdFusion that are truly programmatic (controlling flow, working with expressions, working with functions, and assigning variables) can be written in script syntax form.

For instance, consider the following program code:

```
<CFIF Value is 1>

    <CFSET Result = "One">
<CFELSE>
    <CFSET Result = "None">
</CFIF>
```

In ColdFusion script syntax, the same code would be as follows:

```
<CFSCRIPT>
    if (value is 1)
        Result = "One";
    else
        Result = "None";
</CFSCRIPT>
```

Functionally these are the same. The choice of which approach to take depends on the preference of the developer.

The difference is even more pronounced when it comes to looping constructs. Although you can simulate all popular types of loops in programming languages such as JavaScript and C by using the CFLOOP tag, the syntax of the tag itself does not make the purposes of the loop as readily apparent as they are in the scripting syntax.

For instance, the loop

```
<CFLOOP INDEX="Value" FROM=1 TO=5>
```

becomes

```
for (Value=1; Value less than 6; Value = Value + 1)
```

The latter is simply much clearer for an experienced developer coming from the world of traditional programming.

The Basics of ColdFusion Scripting

The ColdFusion scripting language is really an incremental addition to the ColdFusion environment. It simply serves as a method for bringing familiar JavaScript-style syntax and programming constructs into the ColdFusion environment. This doesn't mean that ColdFusion scripting is a subset of JavaScript, but rather it is designed to be familiar to users of these conventional scripting languages.

The ColdFusion scripting language offers eight script-style statements to the ColdFusion vocabulary:

- If-Else
- While
- Do-While
- For
- Break
- Continue
- For-In
- Switch-Case

Within the ColdFusion scripting environment, no tags are used. Instead, these eight statements can be used in combination with valid ColdFusion expressions (see Chapter 6, "Writing Expressions"), ColdFusion variables (see Chapter 4, "Creating and Manipulating Variables"), and ColdFusion functions (see Chapter 5, "Functions").

To effectively use ColdFusion scripting, you need to learn the eight statements as well as some basic conventions of syntax.

Understanding Basic Syntax

At the center of ColdFusion scripting are statements. In its most basic form, a statement is a single line ended by a semicolon. Line breaks are irrelevant. Consider the following simple assignment statement that assigns the string This is a test to the variable Test:

```
Test = "This is a test";
```

Because the semicolon delineates the end of the statement, it is possible to use line breaks anywhere. For instance, the following statement is exactly the same as the preceding one:

```
Test
=
"This is a test";
```

Multiple statements can also be combined in a series to be treated as a single statement. You create the combination by surrounding the series of statements in curly braces:

```
{ Test = "This is a test"; AnotherTest = "This is another test"; }
```

This preceding example is a compound statement built out of two other statements. Typically, these compound statements are rewritten so that each individual statement is on its own line:

```
{
    Test = "This is a test";
    AnotherTest = "This is another test";
}
```

In addition, more complex statement structures can be built out of other statements. You can build these complex structures by using the eight statement constructs outlined earlier. For instance, the If-Else construct takes the form:

```
If (expression)
    Statement
Else
    Statement
```

In this case, the statements in question can be simple or compound statements. For instance, the following case uses one simple statement and one compound statement:

```
If (Test is "")
    Test = "This is a test";
Else {
    Test = "This is a test";
    AnotherTest = "This is another test";
}
```

Using *If-Else* Constructs

You have already seen the basic form of the `If-Else` statement, but let's review it:

```
If (expression)
    Statement
Else
    Statement
```

This corresponds to the combination of the CFIF and CFELSE tags that take the following form:

```
<CFIF expression>
    Code
<CFELSE>
    Code
</CFIF>
```

Like the tag-based `If` construct, the scripted statement does not require the second `Else` portion. A simple `If` statement is possible:

```
If (expression)
    Statement
```

Using *For* Loops

`For` loops correspond to the CFLOOP tag when using the FROM and TO attributes. If you need to refresh your memory about the CFLOOP tag, refer to Chapter 12, "Looping." Many of the scripting statements are loops, and the concepts discussed in Chapter 12 will help you understand how the scripted loops work.

The syntax of the `For` statement is similar to that used in JavaScript (in contrast, CFLOOP is more familiar to Basic programmers:

```
For (initial expression; test expression; increment expression)
```

To understand how this works, let's look at the relationship between a CFLOOP tag and its corresponding script-based form. Consider the following tag:

```
<CFLOOP INDEX="X" FROM=1 TO=9>
```

This translates into

```
For (X=1; X LT 10; X = X + 1)
```

Therefore, the value of INDEX is the variable used in all three expressions of the scripted loop. The initial expression defines the initial starting value for the index variable. The test expression indicates the expression that must be true for the loop to continue. Finally, the increment expression indicates the change to make to the index variable with each iteration through the loop.

Therefore, you can adjust the size of the increment through the loop by adjusting the increment expression. For instance, if you want to achieve the same result as using STEP=2 in the CFLOOP tag, you simply use X = X + 2 as the increment expression.

In a For loop, the three expressions can be empty. For instance, the loop

```
For ( ; ; )
    Statement;
```

will repeat endlessly unless part of the statement block of the loop causes the loop to end. You can end the loop by using the Break statement that you will look at later in this chapter.

Using *For-In* Loops

A variation on the standard For loop is the For-In loop. The For-In loop is used for looping over a COM collection (see Chapter 30, "Including External Objects") or a structure (see Chapter 13, "Working with ColdFusion Data Structures"). Recall the use of CFLOOP to loop through a structure:

```
<CFSET Employees = StructNew()>
<CFSET result = StructInsert(Employees,"Employee1","Department1")>
<CFSET result = StructInsert(Employees,"Employee2","Department2")>
<CFLOOP COLLECTION="Employees" ITEM="Person">
    Code
</CFLOOP>
```

This corresponds to the following structure in script syntax:

```
Employees = StructNew();
Result = StructInsert(Employees,"Employee1","Department1");
Result = StructInsert(Employees,"Employee2","Department2");
For (Person in Employees)
    Statement;
```

In the preceding loop, during each iteration, the Person variable will be assigned the key for each succeeding entry in the structure.

Using *While* Loops

You can use the CFLOOP tag to create a so-called conditional loop by using the CONDI-TION tag in the following form:

```
<CFLOOP CONDITION="expression">
    Code
</CFLOOP>
```

In ColdFusion scripting, this corresponds exactly to the `While` loop:

```
While (expression)
    Statement;
```

Written in plain English, these loops translate to: "As long as the *expression* is true, continue executing the *statement*." This means that the `statement` will never execute if the `expression` is false when the `While` statement is first encountered.

Using *Do-While* Loops

`Do-While` loops do not have a direct correlation in the CFLOOP tag syntax. Rather, they are a slight variation on the regular `While` loop. In many programming languages, `Do-While` loops are known as `Repeat-Until` loops.

The main difference between the `Do-While` and the `While` loop is that the condition is moved to the end of the loop:

```
Do
    Statement;
While (expression)
```

Translated into plain English, this becomes: "Continue to execute the *statement* until the *expression* is false." This is subtly different from the definition of the `While` loop but it is an important difference: Because the `Do-While` loop tests the expression at the end of the loop, even if the *expression* is false when the loop is first encountered, the statement will execute at least once.

Using *Break* and *Continue*

Sometimes, it is necessary to prematurely end a loop. This can be done with the `Break` statement. Used in the statement block of a loop, it causes the loop to end regardless of the value of the index variable or the condition that normally regulates the flow of the loop.

The `Continue` statement is similar to `Break`. The `Continue` statement, when used in the statement block of a loop, causes the current iteration of the loop to end at the `Continue` statement and the loop to move on to its next iteration.

Using *Switch-Case*

The final script statement to consider is the `Switch-Case` statement. This corresponds to the use of CFSWITCH and CFCASE. The syntax of the `Switch-Case` statement is:

```
Switch (expression) {
    Case value: {
        Statement;
        Break;
```

```
    }
    Case value: {
       Statement;
       Break;
    }
          .


    .


    .



    default: {
       Statement;
       Break;
    }
}
```

Here, each `Case` component of the switch statement ends with a `Break` statement.

Commenting Your Code

Just as with HTML and regular tag-based ColdFusion code, it is a good idea to add comments to your code. Comments are segments of code that are not executed and can contain descriptive statements regarding the logic and purposes of your program code.

ColdFusion scripting supports two types of comments that use the same syntax as JavaScript comments.

One-line comments start with two slashes (//) and continue to the end of the line:

```
// This is a comment
```

Comments do not need to start at the beginning of the line. Instead, they can start after program code on the line:

```
Statement; // This is a comment
```

This type of one-line comment is useful for placing short descriptions of code on the same line as the code itself. For instance, if you are assigning a value to a new variable, you can use a one-line comment to quickly describe the variable:

```
Result = StructInsert(Employees,"Employee1","Department1"); // Result contains the
success status of the insertion
```

One-line comments are also useful for quickly commenting out a single line of code when debugging your scripts.

In addition to these single-line comments, ColdFusion scripts support JavaScript-style multi-line comments. Multi-line comments start with a slash followed by an asterisk (/*) and continue until the first occurrence of an asterisk followed by a slash (*/). This is similar in concept to regular ColdFusion tag comments, which start with <!--- and continue until the first occurrence of --->.

For instance, the following is a multi-line comment:

```
/* This is a multi-line
comment */
```

If any ColdFusion script statements are included between the /* and */, then they are treated as part of the comment:

```
/* The following statement does not execute:
    Statement;
It is part of a comment. */
```

Integrating Scripts in a Template

The values created within a ColdFusion script are accessible within a template, just as are values created with CFSET.

For instance, in the following template, the variable created within the script block is later accessible within the CFOUTPUT tag:

```
<CFSCRIPT>
    myText = "Hello";
</CFSCRIPT>

<CFOUTPUT>
    #myText#
</CFOUTPUT>
```

The most important issue with scripts is that no direct way exists to generate output to the browser. However, the WriteOutput function can generate output to the browser. This function takes a string as a value. Therefore, the preceding code segment can all be executed from within a script:

```
<CFSCRIPT>
    myText= "Hello";
    WriteOutput(myText);
</CFSCRIPT>
```

NOTE   Outside of scripts, the values of variables are accessed using the #VariableName# syntax. Within scripts, values of variables are directly accessed by their names without the pound signs.

Where Do We Go from Here?

Up to this point in the book, you have worked with templates that require a user to request them with their browser for them to execute. However, many features of Cold-Fusion would be more useful if they could automatically be executed on a schedule. For instance, a template could be written that doesn't generate any HTML output for a browser but that rather executes a query and generates an e-mail report based on the query results.

Fortunately, ColdFusion offers a scheduling feature that enables templates to be scheduled for automatic execution. In the next chapter you will learn to use the ColdFusion scheduling capability, both through the ColdFusion Administrator and by using the CFSCHEDULE tag. You will also learn about the special aspects of developing templates for automatic execution.

chapter 28

Scheduling Events

- Scheduling ColdFusion Templates

- Managing and Logging Scheduled Events

So far in this book, you have seen the power of ColdFusion in producing sophisticated Web-based applications that can draw on multiple sources of data, including relational databases, e-mail, Web and FTP servers, and local files on the ColdFusion server. However, in all cases, these Web applications and ColdFusion templates have required that a user with a Web browser explicitly request a template file from the server for it to be executed.

In this chapter, you will see that ColdFusion provides a scheduling mechanism that enables you to create batch-like ColdFusion templates that run at prescheduled times and do not require a user to explicitly request a template with their browser. You can use these scheduled events to create static Web pages out of dynamic data sources, reducing the time that it takes to serve pages to end users. You can also use them to generate e-mail-based reports based on dynamic data sources and to maintain up-to-date indexes for the Verity search engine (See Chapter 29, "Implementing a Search Engine").

You will also learn to schedule events by using the ColdFusion Administrator and the CFSCHEDULE tag. And you will learn about saving scheduled-event output to files to serve as static Web pages, and about the finer points of scheduled-event management and logging.

Scheduling ColdFusion Templates

At its most basic, scheduling a ColdFusion event is simple. You need to provide three pieces of information when scheduling an event:

The dates and times for execution of the event

The URL of the ColdFusion template to be executed

A name for the task so that it can be referred to later

You can specify this information when creating an event by using the ColdFusion Administrator or the CFSCHEDULE tag. You will look at each in turn.

Scheduling an Event with the ColdFusion Administrator

To schedule an event with the ColdFusion Administrator, open the ColdFusion Administrator and select the Scheduled Tasks page. This page should look like the one in Figure 28.1.

FIGURE 28.1

The Scheduled Tasks page

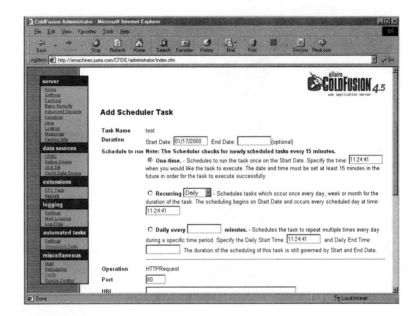

The Scheduled Tasks page provides a simple form that can be used to start the process of scheduling an event followed by a list of scheduled events, if there are any. To create a new scheduled event, start by assigning a name to the event in the Task Name field and clicking the Add New Task button. This should bring up the Add Scheduler Task page, like the one in Figure 28.2.

The Add Scheduler Task page has three main sections for specifying the following information:

- When to execute the task, and how often
- The URL to execute and relevant information, such as username and password for the URL
- Information about how to save the output to a static file on the server (which we will discuss later in the chapter)

FIGURE 28.2
Adding a new task

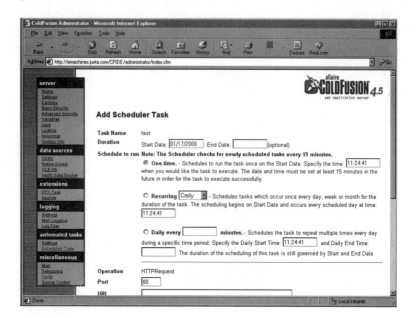

Specifying the Time and Date for a Scheduled Event

As shown in Figure 28.3, the following information needs to be specified when scheduling the time and date for an event:

- The dates during which the event should be executed. This is specified in the Duration section with a start and end date. The start date is required but the end date is optional. Without an end date, the event will execute based on the additional rules specified.
- The frequency with which the event should be executed. The options are:

One-Time   By specifying a time, the event will occur once on the start date at the time specified.

Recurring   By specifying Daily, Weekly, or Monthly, the event will first execute at the specified time on the start date and then at the same time on a daily, weekly, or monthly basis until the end date, if specified, is reached.

Daily Every *X* Minutes   This option enables an event to be scheduled to run at a set interval in minutes between a start time, and end time and to do this every day between the start date and the end date, if specified.

FIGURE 28.3
Specifying the time and
date of an event

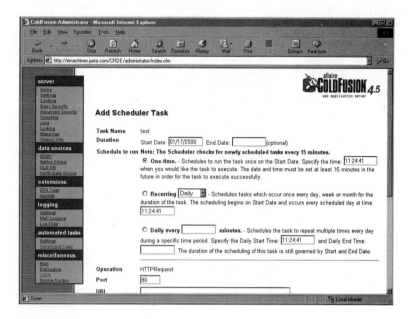

Consider the examples outlined in Table 28.1.

TABLE 28.1:   Examples of Scheduling Tasks

Required Date and Time of the Event	Steps Needed to Schedule the Event
Once only on the 20th of December 1999 at 11:30 A.M.	Set the start date to **12/20/99**. Then select the One-Time option and set the time to **11:30:00**.
Every week on Tuesdays at 2:30 P.M., starting on Tuesday, October 4, 1999, and continuing indefinitely.	Set the start date to **10/4/99** and leave the end date entry blank. Then select the Recurring option, specify Weekly, and set the time to **14:30:00**.
Every hour at 15 minutes past the hour between 9:15 A.M. and 7:15 P.M. for the three-day period from the 6th to the 9th of June 1999.	Set the start date to **06/06/99** and the end date to **06/09/99**. Then select the Daily Every X Minutes option and specify 60 minutes as the interval; set the start time to **9:15:00** and the end time to **19:15:00**.

Specifying the URL to Execute

The second section of the new task page is shown in Figure 28.4. Here you specify the URL to execute at the time specified in the preceding section, and how to execute it.

FIGURE 28.4
Specifying the URL to
execute

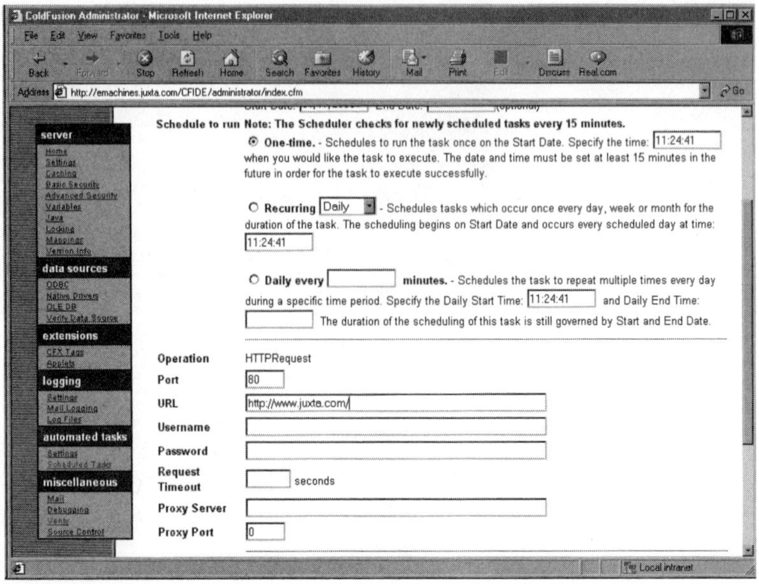

This section contains five fields that can be filled out as follows:

URL   The full URL of the page to execute at the specified times. At a minimum, this field needs to be filled out in this section.

Username   If the specified URL requires a username and password to access it, provide the username here.

Password   If the specified URL requires a username and password to access it, provide the password here.

Request Timeout   Specifies the number of seconds to wait for a page to execute before assuming the connection has failed. The default is 30 seconds, but if you are requesting a page from a busy server or across a poor network connection, you may want to increase this value to the equivalent of several minutes (such as 200 seconds).

Proxy Server   If your ColdFusion server sits behind a corporate firewall, but the URL you are specifying is on a server outside the firewall, then you need to provide the URL for your corporate proxy server (including the host name and port number in the format `proxy.host.name:port`) in this field.

Saving Output to a File

In the final section of the new task page, shown in Figure 28.5, you can specify that the output generated by a scheduled page should be saved to a file.

FIGURE 28.5
Specifying an output file

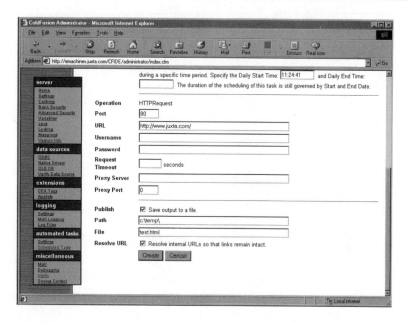

Saving the output of a scheduled task to a file is a good idea for several reasons, including:

Improving performance   If you have pages that are generated from large query result sets, especially against a slow-changing database, it will probably be more efficient to generate static versions of pages on a regular basis, such as daily, rather than letting queries run every time a user requests one of the pages.

Logging of activity   If you output the results of scheduled jobs to static files, you can keep a directory of results of all your scheduled jobs, which can be viewed from a single location by using a Web browser.

Four fields are available when specifying the output file for a scheduled task. The first field, labeled Publish, is a check box. When checked, it indicates that the output should be saved to a file, based on the settings in the three other fields.

WARNING   If the Publish check box is not checked, the output is not saved, regardless of the contents of the other fields in this section.

If output is being saved to a file, then the remaining three fields specify how that should be done:

Path   Specifies the directory in which the output file should be saved. This can be specified as an absolute path on the local system where the ColdFusion server is running (such as c:\data\logs on a Windows system) or as a network accessible directory (\\hostname\sharename on a Windows network).

File   Specifies the filename that the output should be saved to. Combined with the path, this fully identifies the name and location where the output will be saved.

Resolve URL   Indicates, when selected, that any relative URLs in the output should be converted to absolute URLs so that there will be no broken links in the output. This option is especially useful when you are generating static content from scheduled dynamic pages that sit on a different server or in a different directory than the resulting static output files.

Adding the Event

After a task has been fully specified, you can add it by clicking the Create button at the bottom of the page (see Figure 28.5). Next to the Create button is the Cancel button, which causes ColdFusion to discard the information in the form and return to the Scheduled Tasks page.

Scheduling an Event with the *CFSCHEDULE* Tag

Using the CFSCHEDULE tag, you can schedule events as you did through the ColdFusion Administrator as well as perform management tasks such as deleting scheduled jobs. These management tasks are discussed later in the section "Managing and Logging Scheduled Events."

The role that the CFSCHEDULE tag will play is determined by the value of the ACTION attribute:

Update   Creates a new task or changes the settings of an existing task.

Delete   Deletes an existing task.

Run   Executes an existing task.

In this section, you will look at how to use CFSCHEDULE with ACTION=Update. The possible attributes of the CFSCHEDULE tag when ACTION=Update is used are outlined in the following list. All the attributes correspond to information provided when creating a task by using the ColdFusion Administrator.

TASK   Name of the task being updated.

OPERATION   Type of operation to perform when executing this task; currently, the only possible value is HTTPRequest, and this value should be specified.

FILE   Filename in which to store the output of the task if PUBLISH=Yes is set.

PATH   Path of the directory where the output of the task should be stored if PUBLISH=Yes is set.

STARTDATE   The date when the scheduled task should start.

STARTTIME   The time when the scheduled task should start.

URL   The URL to be executed.

PUBLISH   Indicates whether the output of the task should be saved to a file. Possible values are Yes and No (optional).

ENDDATE   The date when the scheduled task should end (optional).

ENDTIME   The time when the scheduled task should end (optional).

INTERVAL   Specifies how often a task should be repeated. Possible values are Daily, Weekly, Monthly, and Execute. Alternately, an interval can be specified numerically in seconds. The default interval is one hour. The minimum interval is one minute.

REQUESTTIMEOUT   Specifies how long to wait for a task to finish executing before giving up (optional).

USERNAME   Specifies the username if the URL requires a username and password (optional).

PASSWORD   Specifies the password if the URL requires a username and password (optional).

PROXYSERVER   Specifies the host name or IP address of a proxy server if accessing a URL outside a firewall (optional).

RESOLVEURL   Indicates whether links in an output file should be converted to absolute URLs. Possible values are Yes or No (optional).

To better understand how the CFSCHEDULE tag can be applied, consider this example: Imagine that an organization has three database reports (called Report 1, Report 2, and Report 3) that employees use in their work. The organization wants to create a Web page that employees can use to schedule the reports to run overnight so they are available in the morning when they need them. To build this application, you first need to define a few guidelines:

When a user runs a report, they want the output stored in their home directory. Home directories are located at \\homedirserver\username.

The Web site is password protected so that only valid users can schedule the reports. This prevents you from having to deal with authentication in your templates.

The reports are templates with the URLs: http://cold.fusion.server/reports/report1.cfm, http://cold.fusion.server/reports/report2.cfm, and http://cold.fusion.server/reports/report3.cfm.

The reports should be scheduled to run at 11:00 P.M. on the day they are requested.

Given these assumptions, the application will consist of two pages:

form.cfm   Presents a form on which the user can request that a report be scheduled

schedule.cfm   Schedules the job as specified by the user, and then displays a confirmation notice for the user

Listing 28.1 shows the source code for form.html.

⤳ **LISTING 28.1:** *form.cfm*

```
<HTML>
    <HEAD>
        <TITLE>Schedule a Report</TITLE>
    </HEAD>
    <BODY>
        <H1>Schedule a Report</H1>
        <HR>
        <FORM METHOD="POST" ACTION="schedule.cfm">
            Select a report:
            <SELECT NAME="report">
            <OPTION VALUE="report1">Report 1
            <OPTION VALUE="report2">Report 2
            <OPTION VALUE="report3">Report 3
            </SELECT>
            <BR>
            Username:
            <INPUT TYPE="TEXT" SIZE="10" NAME="username">
            <BR>
            <INPUT TYPE="SUBMIT" VALUE="Schedule Report">
        </FORM>
    </BODY>
</HTML>
```

This code produces a form like the one in Figure 28.6.

FIGURE 28.6
The scheduling form

The structure of this file is fairly simple; it contains only straightforward HTML. The form has two fields: a select list to choose the report and a text field to specify the username of the user requesting the report. This provides all the information you need to schedule the task.

Listing 28.2 provides the source code for `schedule.cfm`.

LISTING 28.2: *schedule.cfm*

```
<HTML>
    <HEAD>
        <TITLE>Job Scheduled</TITLE>
    </HEAD>
    <BODY>
        <CFSCHEDULE ACTION="Update"
        TASK="#Form.username#-#Form.report#"
        OPERATION="HTTPRequest"
  URL="http://cold.fusion.server/reports/#Form.report#.cfm"
        FILE="#Form.report#-results"
        PATH="\\homedirserver\#Form.username#\"
        PUBLISH="Yes"
  STARTDATE="#dateformat(now(),'mm/dd/yy')#"
        STARTTIME="23:00"
        ENDDATE="#dateformat(now(),'mm/dd/yy')#"          ENDTIME=""
        INTERVAL="Daily">
        <H1>Job Scheduled</H1>
        <HR>
        <CFOUTPUT>
        The report #Form.report#.cfm has been scheduled to
        run tonight at 11:00 p.m. for #Form.username#.
        </CFOUTPUT>
        <P>
        Click <A HREF="form.html">here</A> to schedule
        another report.
    </BODY>
</HTML>
```

This template would produce results like those in Figure 28.7.

FIGURE 28.7
A confirmation notice

Again, the code in this template is fairly simple. The only ColdFusion tag used is the CFSCHEDULE tag. The important attributes are:

TASK   The name of the task is built out of a combination of the username and the selected report to make tasks easy to identify.

URL   The URL is built from the value of Form.report.

FILE   The filename is derived from the report name so the user can find it easily the next day.

PATH   The path is derived from the value of Form.username.

STARTDATE and ENDDATE   You use the Now() function to obtain the current date and then Month(), Day(), and Year() to return the numerical values for the current date. The start date and end date are set the same so that the event occurs only on that day.

INTERVAL   The value is set to Daily to make it occur once, only on the start date.

Managing and Logging Scheduled Events

In addition to being able to schedule events, you can also accomplish the following management tasks by using the ColdFusion Administrator:

- Editing an existing scheduled event
- Deleting an existing scheduled event
- Controlling the refresh interval

Editing an Existing Scheduled Event

The ColdFusion Administrator provides the means to view or change the settings of any previously scheduled event. This is accomplished via the Scheduled Tasks page of the Administrator.

As Figure 28.8 shows, scheduled events appear in a list on the Scheduled Tasks page. The name of each event is a link. Clicking the link opens the Edit Scheduler Task page, which has all the same fields as the Add Scheduler Task page. As shown in Figure 28.9, the Edit Scheduler Task page has all the fields preset with the settings for the selected task.

FIGURE 28.8
The Scheduled Tasks page

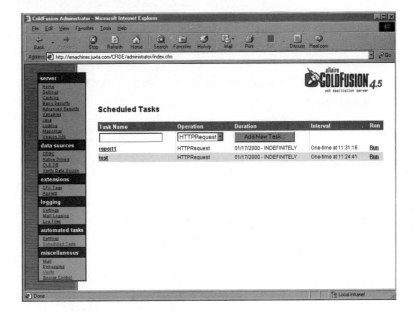

FIGURE 28.9
Editing a scheduled task

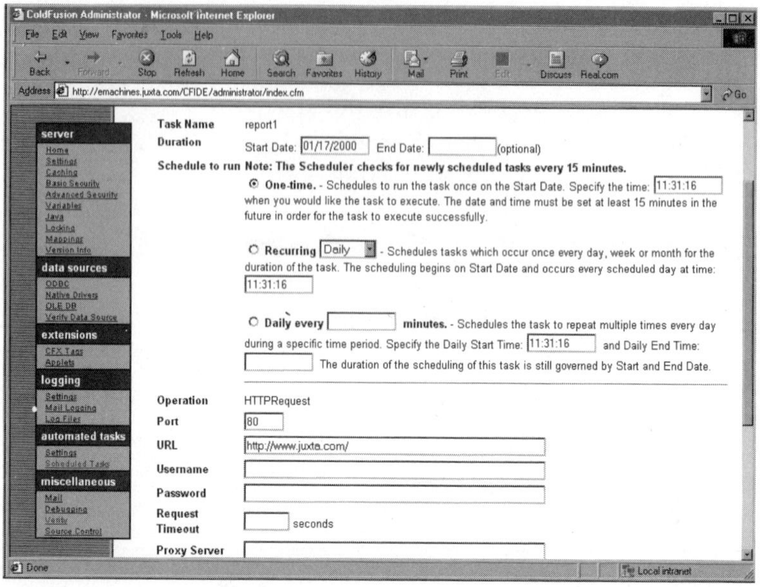

After changing settings as needed, the changes can be saved by clicking the Update button at the bottom of the page.

Deleting an Existing Scheduled Event

To delete a scheduled event, click its link on the Scheduled Tasks page. This brings up the Edit Scheduler Task page (shown earlier in Figure 28.9). Click the Delete button at the bottom of the page to delete the task.

> There is no confirmation when deleting a scheduled event, so be sure that you have selected the correct task before deleting it.

Running an Existing Scheduled Event

You can run an existing scheduled event manually at any time by clicking the Run link in the event's entry on the Scheduled Tasks page. ColdFusion will run the task and will generate its output to a log file or by mail as specified in the event's settings. No confirmation of the success of the task will be displayed in the ColdFusion Administrator.

Controlling the Refresh Interval

When a new task is scheduled, it is added to the list of scheduled tasks—but the scheduler that executes scheduled tasks is not aware of the new task. The scheduler checks the list for new tasks on a regularly scheduled basis, and only from that time on is it aware of a task, and can execute it as scheduled.

What happens if you schedule a task to execute before the scheduler next polls the list for new tasks? The task will fail to execute. By default, the scheduler refreshes its list of active tasks at an interval of 15 minutes. If this interval is too large or too small for the needs of a particular server, it can be changed on the Scheduler Setting page of the ColdFusion Administrator.

Here there is only one value to set: the interval in minutes between each successive check for new tasks by the scheduler. Changing this value to a low setting (such as every one or two minutes) when the list of tasks is large could impose an unnecessary load on a busy ColdFusion server. For most purposes, the default 15-minute interval should prove sufficient.

Where Do We Go from Here?

In the next chapter, you will move on to another advanced topic that ColdFusion helps make simple: implementing a search engine. Most large Web sites offer a search facility in which users can search by keywords (and sometimes even with plain English questions) to find just the right page within a site. ColdFusion integrates the Verity search engine into the ColdFusion server, making it possible to create fast, easy-to-manage search engines for even the largest Web sites. In the next chapter, you will learn how to set up, implement, and maintain a search engine by using ColdFusion and the Verity search engine.

chapter 29

Implementing a Search Engine

- Creating Collections

- Indexing Data

- Creating a Search Interface

One of the most common features of today's large Web sites is a search engine. Through a search engine, users can search for specific documents within a large number of documents on a Web site, effectively finding the proverbial needle in the haystack.

ColdFusion Server leverages the power of Verity's Search 97 indexing engine to provide efficient, easy-to-use search capabilities integrated into the ColdFusion environment. With this facility, you can achieve many results, including:

- Searching HTML documents on a Web site
- Searching the results of queries executed by tags such as CFQUERY and CFPOP
- Searching collections of binary documents such as Microsoft Word documents or Adobe Acrobat files

In this chapter, you will look at the three steps required to create a searchable set of data: defining a collection, indexing the data, and searching the index.

Creating Collections

At the heart of any search system using ColdFusion and Verity is the collection. A *collection* is a set of information that can be indexed and searched as a set. A collection can be used to group types of information such as the following:

- All the HTML files in a Web site
- Files in specific directories to create subject or section-specific search capabilities
- Sets of binary files including the most popular word processor and spreadsheet formats
- Data returned by any standard ColdFusion query

To implement any search engine in ColdFusion, you first need to create a collection. You can do this in two ways: through the ColdFusion Administrator or by using the CFCOLLECTION tag.

Creating Collections by Using the ColdFusion Administrator

The Verity page of the ColdFusion Administrator, shown in Figure 29.1, is where collections are created and managed. This page presents a list of existing collections (the ColdFusion documentation will appear as a default collection if you installed it when you installed ColdFusion Server) followed by a form for creating new collections.

Using this form, you have two options:

- Creating a new collection
- Mapping an existing Verity collection into the ColdFusion environment

This latter option is important because Verity collections can be created using standard Verity tools and there needs to be a way to make ColdFusion aware of these collections so that they can be used in templates.

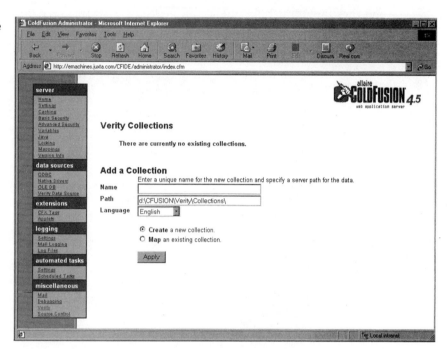

FIGURE 29.1
The Verity Collections page

We will focus on creating and implementing collections via ColdFusion rather than importing existing Verity collections because the latter requires more knowledge of the Verity environment than is necessary to effectively use ColdFusion to create a search engine. To learn how to import existing Verity collections, refer to the *Developing Web Applications with ColdFusion* section of the online documentation.

To create a new collection with the ColdFusion Administrator, you need to provide the following information:

Name   All collections are named so that they can be accessed later in ColdFusion templates.

Path   The location where files related to the collection will be stored (it is best to accept the default—the `Verity\Collections` subdirectory of your ColdFusion directory).

Language   By default, all collections are for English-language data; if you have bought the International Language Search Pack (available from Allaire), then you will be able to select from other European languages for a collection, including French, German, Italian, Portuguese, and Spanish.

After you provide this information, make sure that Create a New Collection is selected and click the Apply button. The new collection will appear at the top of the Verity Collections page, as shown in Figure 29.2.

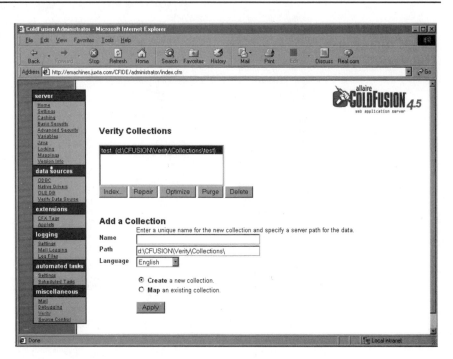

After a collection is created, several administrative tools are then available, as outlined in the following list:

Index   Creates an index of data for the collection. This process is outlined in the "Indexing Data" section of this chapter.

Repair   Repairs a corrupted collection. This is a non-destructive process that may take some time to complete for larger collections.

Optimize   Optimizes a collection. As the amount of data being indexed in a collection grows, it is a good idea to optimize it so that searches can be as efficient as possible.

Purge   Purges all indexes from a collection. This effectively empties the collection of all indexed data and returns it to the state it was in when it was created.

Delete   Deletes a collection. Once deleted, the collection as well as its indexes are inaccessible and the collection will need to be re-created to be used again.

The last four options are simple to use:

1. Select the desired collection.
2. Click the relevant button below the collection list.
3. Click OK in the confirmation dialog box that appears to execute the action or click Cancel to cancel the request.

Using the Index function requires a bit more care and is discussed in the "Indexing Data" section.

Creating Collections with the *CFCOLLECTION* Tag

Using the CFCOLLECTION tag, you can create collections in your ColdFusion templates without having to access the ColdFusion Administrator. This is useful for several reasons, the most notable of which is enabling content creators on your Web site to create collections and search engines without providing them access to the ColdFusion Administrator (which would be an unnecessary security risk).

The CFCOLLECTION tag takes the following four attributes:

ACTION   Indicates which action to perform. Possible actions are Create, Repair, Optimize, Delete, and Map.

COLLECTION   The name of the collection to be created or worked with.

PATH   The path to the directory where the collection should store its files. This is required when using ACTION=Create.

LANGUAGE   The language in which to create a collection when ACTION=Create is used. The default language value is English and the attribute is optional.

Using the CFCOLLECTION tag to repair, optimize, or delete a collection is simple, requiring only the ACTION attribute and the COLLECTION attribute.

To create a collection, though, requires at least three attributes: ACTION, COLLECTION, and PATH. For instance, to create the same collection as was created using the ColdFusion Administrator earlier in this chapter, the following tag should be used:

```
<CFCOLLECTION ACTION="Create"
 COLLECTION="test"
 PATH="d:\cfusion\verity\collections">
```

Indexing Data

Once a collection exists, you can index data for that collection, and this is where things get interesting. After all, having defined a collection, it still remains inert and of little use because it is not associated with any data. The indexing process does this.

Indexing can be done through the ColdFusion Administrator or by using the CFINDEX tag. The processes are not identical, however, and meet different needs. Indexing with the ColdFusion Administrator can be used to index only documents (HTML files or other binary files) and is best suited to collections whose data won't be updated frequently nor require re-indexing. The CFINDEX tag, on the other hand, allows the indexing of query results as well as document files and is well suited to collections that will be updated frequently or that users must update and re-index. You will look at indexing documents first followed by indexing query results.

Indexing Document Files

The easiest way to index a set of document files is through the ColdFusion Administrator. To do this, open the Verity page in the Administrator, select the collection to index from the list at the top of the page, and click the Index button. This will open a page like the one in Figure 29.3.

FIGURE 29.3
Indexing a collection

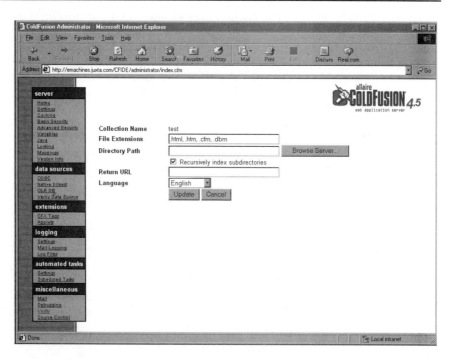

On this page, you can specify the following information:

File Extensions   Enter the extensions, separated by commas, of all file types to be included in the index. The default includes all HTML and ColdFusion template files, but this can be changed to include any file type supported by the Verity system, including:

- HTML
- ColdFusion templates
- Plain text
- Adobe Acrobat
- Adobe FrameMaker MIF Format
- Applix Words
- Corel WordPerfect for Windows and Macintosh
- Lotus AMI Pro
- Lotus Word Pro
- Rich Text Format
- Microsoft Word for Windows, Macintosh, and DOS
- Microsoft Write
- Microsoft Works
- XYWrite
- Corel QuattroPro
- Lotus 1-2-3 for DOS, Windows, and OS/2
- Microsoft Excel
- Corel Presentations
- Lotus Freelance
- Microsoft PowerPoint

Directory Path   Indicate the top-level directory to index. To find a directory, click the Browse Server button to open a Select Directory on the Server window like the one in Figure 29.4, find the desired directory, and click OK. By default, the Recursively Index Subdirectories box is checked. This causes all files matching the specified extensions in the directory and its subdirectories to be indexed. To index only the files in the directory, unselect this option.

Return URL   If the files you are indexing are accessible via a URL, this can be specified using this field. Consider an example: The directory `d:\html` is being indexed. This directory is accessible under the URL `http://some.host/`. By providing `http://some.host/` as the Return URL value, it is possible to quickly build links to found files when searching the index.

Language   English is the default language. If the International Languages Search Pack is installed, another language can be chosen.

FIGURE 29.4
The directory index window

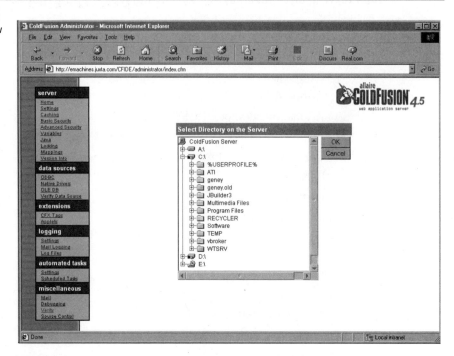

After this information is provided, simply click the Update button to cause the specified files to be indexed. Depending on the number of files being indexed and the speed of the server, this process can take some time. After the process is completed, the Verity Collections page will be displayed. After an index for a collection has been created, it can be updated whenever the content of the collection changes (documents are added, deleted, or edited), by selecting the index and repeating the process.

Using *CFINDEX* to Index a Collection

As an alternative, you can use the CFINDEX tag to create an index of document files. To do this, the following attributes should be used:

COLLECTION   Specifies the name of the collection being indexed.

ACTION   Specifies the action to take. Possible values are Update, Delete, Purge, Refresh, and Optimize. Update updates an index whereas Refresh clears an index and re-creates it. The latter is usually used when indexing for the first time.

TYPE   Specifies the type of index being created. Possible values are File to index a specific file, Path to index a set of files in a specific directory that are of the types specified in the EXTENSIONS attribute, and Custom to index query results (as will be discussed later in this chapter).

KEY   When indexing a specific file, this attribute specifies the filename. When indexing a directory of files, this attribute specifies the path.

EXTENSIONS   Specifies a comma-separated list of file extensions to index when using TYPE=Path.

RECURSE   Indicates whether subdirectories should be indexed when using TYPE=Path. Possible values are Yes and No.

EXTERNAL   Indicates whether the collection was created outside of the ColdFusion environment using Verity's native indexing tools. Possible values are Yes and No.

Optionally, you may need to specify an index language using the LANGUAGE attribute and a return URL using the URLPATH attribute. For instance, the following tag creates an index for the collection test, indexes all HTML and ColdFusion documents in the d:\html directory and its subdirectories, and uses the return URL of http:// some.host/ for access to those files as URLs:

```
<CFINDEX COLLECTION="test"
 ACTION="Refresh"
 TYPE="Path"
 KEY="d:\html"
 URLPATH="http://some.host/"
 EXTENSIONS=".html,.htm,.cfm"
 RECURSE="Yes">
```

This tag can be used anytime the index needs to be re-created because the indexed data has changed.

Indexing Query Results

A powerful use of the Verity search system in ColdFusion is to index the results of queries. At first, this may seem redundant. After all, queries—especially those against databases using the CFQUERY tag—are searches of the contents of a specific data source. However, databases are optimized to retrieve records based on keys and on exact matches for the contents of fields. Searches that attempt to retrieve records with specific text fields containing one or more words are inefficient. Verity indexes, on the other hand, are optimized for this type of text-based search and retrieval.

By indexing the results of a query, these searches can be performed quickly and efficiently against the Verity index, and after the required record is found, it can be retrieved in full from the database by using an efficient query against a primary key or other specific record identifier.

Consider as an example a database table of people's names and addresses. One field is a large text field for making notes about the people in the database. Although finding a specific person by their first name, last name, or country of residence is easy enough, attempting to find all the records containing references to a specific word in the notes field is inefficient. The Verity search engine is better suited to the task.

To index the results of a query, you first need to execute a query that retrieves the required data from the table. For instance, in the preceding example, the query might look like

```
<CFQUERY NAME="People" DATASOURCE="SampleData">
    Select Person_ID, Name, Notes from People
</CFQUERY>
```

where `People` is the table name, `Person_ID` is the primary key, and `Notes` is the field to be indexed. The name is included so that when a search is conducted, the information is available to display in the results without retrieving from the database again.

To index the data, you use the `CFINDEX` tag. There is no way to index database or other query results by using the ColdFusion Administrator. These attributes should be used when indexing a query:

COLLECTION   Should be set to the name of the collection being indexed.

ACTION   Should be set to `Update`

TYPE   Should be set to `Custom`

BODY   Should contain a list of column names to index, separated by commas

KEY   Should contain the name of the column containing the primary key for the result set

TITLE   Should contain the column name containing the title for each record

QUERY   Should contain the name of the query to be indexed

For example, to index the preceding query example, the following `CFINDEX` tag could be used:

```
<CFINDEX COLLECTION="collectionname"
 ACTION="Update"
 TYPE="Custom"
 BPDY="Notes"
 KEY="Person_ID"
 TITLE="Name"
 QUERY="People">
```

Notice the use of `TITLE="Name"` to indicate that, when searching, the title of each item returned will be indicated by the content of the `Name` column.

Creating a Search Interface

After an index is created, you can create a search interface. Searching is done using the CFSEARCH tag, which executes a search against a Verity collection. The tag returns the result as a typical ColdFusion result set that can then be worked with by using standard tags such as CFOUTPUT and CFLOOP. You can use the CFSEARCH tag to search collections containing indexes of documents or indexes of query results.

Searching an Index of Documents

To use the CFSEARCH tag to search an index of documents, you need to use the following attributes:

NAME   Name of the search query for later reference to the results.

COLLECTION   Name of the collection to be searched. Multiple collections can be searched by providing the names as a comma-separated list.

TYPE   Specifies the type criteria to use in the search. Possible values are Simple and Explicit. These will be discussed later in the section "Building a Search Query."

CRITERIA   Specifies the search expression.

MAXROWS   Specifies the maximum number of results to return. This is useful when returning the results in groups (for instance, 10 results at a time). The default is to return all results. This is an optional field.

STARTROW   Specifies the first row to be returned. This is useful in conjunction with MAXROWS when returning results in smaller groups. The default is row 1. This is an optional field.

By way of example, consider the following CFSEARCH tag:

```
<CFSEARCH NAME="results"
  COLLECTION="collectionname"
  TYPE="Simple"
  CRITERIA="Test">
```

This tag searches the collection collectionname for the word Test and returns the results in the result set results.

Using the Results

Just what is returned in a result set by the CFSEARCH tag? For each item (file or query result row) found to match the criteria, the following four columns are returned:

URL   The full URL path for the collection (including the return URL value if one was defined when creating the index). This will be an empty string for indexes of query results.

KEY   The contents of the KEY attribute specified when defining the index. In the case of an index of documents, this will contain the full local path to the file on the server (such as d:\html\file.html). In the case of an index of a query result set, this will contain the value of the column specified with the KEY attribute of the CFINDEX tag.

TITLE The contents of the TITLE attribute specified when creating the index. In the case of an index of documents, this will contain the document title obtained from the document itself (for instance, the text between <TITLE> and </TITLE> in an HTML file). In the case of an index of a query result set, this will contain the value of the column specified with the TITLE attribute of the CFINDEX tag.

SCORE A score indicating how relevant the document is to the search criteria.

For example, the following template searches a collection for the word Test and displays the results in a table:

```
<CFSEARCH NAME="results"
 COLLECTION="collectionname"
 TYPE="Simple"
 CRITERIA="Test">

<TABLE BORDER=0 CELLPADDING=3>
<TR>
    <TD>SCORE</TD>
    <TD>TITLE</TD>
</TR>
<CFOUTPUT QUERY="results">
    <TR>
        <TD>#SCORE#</TD>
        <TD>#TITLE#</TD>
    </TR>
</CFOUTPUT>
</TABLE>
```

This produces results similar to those in Figure 29.5.

By simply adding the use of the URL column in the results, you can make each title a link to the document itself:

```
<CFSEARCH NAME="results"
 COLLECTION="collectionname"
 TYPE="Simple"
 CRITERIA="Test">

<TABLE BORDER=0 CELLPADDING=3>
<TR>
    <TD>SCORE</TD>
    <TD>TITLE</TD>
</TR>
<CFOUTPUT QUERY="results">
    <TR>
        <TD>#SCORE#</TD>
        <TD><A HREF="#URL#">#TITLE#</A></TD>
    </TR>
</CFOUTPUT>
</TABLE>
```

This produces results like those in Figure 29.6.

FIGURE 29.5
Displaying the results of a
search

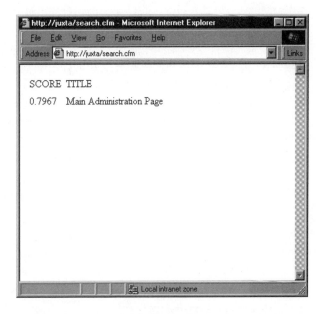

FIGURE 29.6
The results with a title as
a link

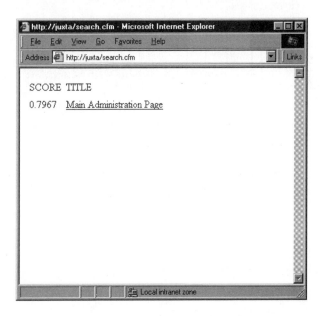

Understanding the Verity Query Syntax

Using the Verity search engine allows for much more complicated searches than the simple ones seen in this chapter. Query expressions for searches can be built out of a rich set of operators.

A distinction exists between simple and explicit queries as specified by the TYPE attribute of the CFSEARCH tag. Syntactically, simple queries are just that: simple. Simple queries accept comma-delimited lists of strings and wildcard characters. Simple queries search for whole words, so a search for `sea` will find only those results containing the word `sea` and not other words such as `search`. Simple searches do provide wildcards, so you can search for `sea*` and retrieve results containing `search` as well.

Nonetheless, simple queries do exhibit stemming properties. That is, a search for `sea` will find words derived from the word `sea` such as `seas` (as opposed to `search`, which contains the string `sea` but is not derived from the word `sea`).

By providing a list of strings separated by commas, the comma is taken to imply logical OR. That is, a search for `sea, ocean` will find all results with either the word `sea` or the word `ocean` or both. Without commas, a series of words is treated as a phrase, so searching for `sea ocean` will find all results with the exact phrase `sea ocean` in them.

In addition, simple queries allow for the use of the basic Boolean operators AND, OR, and NOT in a query. For instance,

```
sea AND ocean
```

finds all results in a collection containing both `sea` and `ocean`, whereas

```
sea NOT ocean
```

finds all results containing `sea` but not `ocean`.

Order of precedence applies when using Boolean operators; AND operators take precedence over OR operators. Therefore, in the expression

```
sea OR ocean AND lake
```

the expression `ocean AND lake` is evaluated first, and the result is then paired with `sea` to be evaluated in the remaining expression.

Using parentheses can override the order of precedence so that

```
(sea OR ocean) AND lake
```

causes `sea OR ocean` to be evaluated first.

Using Wildcards

ColdFusion provides the following wildcard operators for use in queries:

?   Matches any single alphanumeric character

*   Matches zero or more alphanumeric characters

[]   Matches one of the characters contained between the brackets

{}   Matches all the patterns, separated by commas, contained in the curly brackets

^   When used inside square brackets, indicates that a match should be made for any character not contained in the brackets

-   When used inside square brackets, indicates a range of characters

For example, consider the following patterns and their matches, outlined in Table 29.1.

TABLE 29.1:   Using Pattern Matching

Pattern	Match
sea?	Matches seas and seat but not sea
sea*	Matches seas and seat but also sea, search, seam, and any other combination starting with sea
sea[st]	Matches seas and seat but not seam, sea, or search
sea{m,rch}	Matches seam and search but not seat, seas or sea
sea[^st]	Matches seam and seal but not seas or seat
sea[a-z]	Matches every possible combination of sea followed by a single letter including seas, seat, seam, and seal

Using Explicit Queries

Explicit queries are far more complex because each element of the query has to be explicitly stated. For instance, stemming is not done by default, and logical OR is not automatically implied by a comma. Explicit queries are extremely powerful in the hands of a user who understands the principles of building fine-tuned, effective query expressions.

Generally, however, a search engine on an average Web site will not need to offer this type of fine-grained search capability. If it does, the developer of the search engine does not need to master the intricacies of the search syntax, but rather can direct users to help based on Allaire's documentation of the subject. For that reason, we will just glance at the major features of explicit queries. Details of the syntax can be found in the Allaire documentation in *Developing Web Applications with ColdFusion* in Chapter 11, "Indexing and Searching Data."

The major features of explicit queries are as follows:

- Words are not stemmed. A search for sea matches only the word sea.
- Special characters including commas, brackets, parentheses, and single quotation marks have special meanings. To search for those characters, you must use a backslash to escape them. The backslash itself must be escaped, so \\ must be used to search for a backslash.

- All operators except the three Boolean operators must be surrounded by left and right angle brackets (<>). Similarly, to search for the words AND, OR, or NOT, they must be surrounded by double quotes or they will be treated as operators.

Searching an Indexed Query Result

The principles behind searching a query set are the same as those applied when searching an index of documents. Keep in mind the following differences about the data stored in the columns of the search result:

- The URL field is always empty. The data in the query result has nothing to do with URLs. If you want to create a clickable URL so that users can view the complete record found in a search, you need to build a URL from the data stored in the other fields of the search results.
- The KEY column contains the contents of the column name specified in the KEY attribute of the CFINDEX tag when creating the index. Generally, this is used for the primary key of the table being indexed, and the primary key of each record returned by the search is contained in this column.
- The TITLE column contains the contents of the column name specified in the TITLE attribute of the CFINDEX tag when creating the index.

Building a Complete Search System

To apply all this, the next step is to build a complete search system. This system will search the collection named collectionname. For the sake of simplicity, this collection is an index of documents.

The following template file performs two tasks: It presents a search form and, if it receives search criteria from a form, it also executes a search and displays the results:

```
<HTML>
    <HEAD>
        <TITLE>Search</TITLE>
    </HEAD>
    <BODY>
        <H1>Search the site</H1>
        <HR>
        <FORM METHOD=POST ACTION="search.cfm">
            Query:
            <INPUT TYPE=TEXT NAME=CRITERIA SIZE=30>
            <INPUT TYPE=SUBMIT VALUE=SEARCH>
        </FORM>
        <HR>
        <CFIF IsDefined("Form.CRITERIA")>
<CFSEARCH NAME="test" COLLECTION="test"
 CRITERIA="#Form.CRITERIA#">
<TABLE BORDER=0 CELLPADDING=3>
<TR>
```

```
      <TD>SCORE</TD>
      <TD>TITLE</TD>
</TR>
<CFOUTPUT QUERY="test">
<TR>
<TD>#SCORE#</TD>
<TD><A HREF="#URL#">#TITLE#</A></TD>
</TR>
</CFOUTPUT>
</TABLE>
      <CFELSE>
          <STRONG>No Search has been Executed</STRONG>
      </CFIF>
   </BODY>
</HTML>
```

The logic of this template is fairly simple:

- A search form is always displayed. The search form's ACTION attribute points back to the same template. In other words, each time Submit is clicked, the data in the form is submitted back to the same template.
- The CFIF tag uses the ParameterExists function to see whether Form.CRITERIA exists. If this is the first time the template is being accessed, then the variable won't exist and no search is executed or results displayed, as in Figure 29.7. If, on the other hand, the form is submitted, then Form.CRITERIA will exist when the template is accessed and a search will be executed and the results displayed, as in Figure 29.8.

FIGURE 29.7
The first time the template is accessed no search is executed.

FIGURE 29.8
Executing a search and displaying the results

Where Do We Go from Here?

The next chapter addresses a fundamental concern in many interactive applications: security. In applications that interactively access data, you often need to ensure that only authorized users have access to the applications and that they can perform only the tasks for which they have permission. In the next chapter, you will consider issues of application security and how they are addressed in ColdFusion, including issues related to user security, server sandbox security, and administrator security.

chapter 30

Application Security

- Understanding Security

- Using Advanced Security

- Using CFAUTHENTICATE

- Using CFIMPERSONATE

- Using Server Sandbox Security

Security is an extremely important and vast topic. Anytime you place a computer containing information into any form of public place (including in an unlocked room or on a computer network), issues of security arise. These issues center around several questions:

- How can you control who can access your machine?
- How can you control what content is being accessed on your machine?
- How can you control who can access what content on your machine?
- How can you ensure that violations of your security scheme are not likely to occur?

In the context of ColdFusion, the second and third questions can be addressed.

In this ColdFusion environment, several layers of security exist:

- Remote development services security
- User security
- Server sandbox security
- Administrator security

These play different roles in helping to secure, and keep secure, the content on a Cold-Fusion server. In this chapter we will present an overview of some of the relevant security issues and tell you how to protect your network and servers. We will then discuss in detail those aspects that make up ColdFusion advanced security: user security and server sandbox security. Remote development services security and administrator security are discussed in Chapter 35, "ColdFusion Administration."

Understanding Security

There are many aspects to security when developing Web-based applications for Internet or intranet use. These include the following:

- Preventing unauthorized physical access to the computer
- Preventing easy breaking of user passwords
- Preventing unwanted users from accessing the network
- Preventing unwanted users from accessing certain information on a server

Preventing Unauthorized Physical Access to the Computer

The first line of defense in any robust security scheme for an Internet or intranet Web site or application is to ensure that the computer or computers acting as servers for the site are physically secure. This is a fundamental step: Of what use are sophisticated security systems using public key encryption or proxy firewalls if any unauthorized, and possibly ill-intentioned, individual can walk up to a server and attempt to disrupt its operation or corrupt its data?

This may seem to be a minor issue because you can leave the console logged out and any unauthorized person would need to know the root or administrator password to gain access to the system. Unfortunately, protecting the system isn't so simple. By allowing unauthorized physical access to a computer, you do the following:

- Leave the computer susceptible to attempts to hack into the system
- Make it theoretically possible for someone to bypass operating-system security—for instance, by booting from a floppy disk
- Make it possible for an individual to disrupt services by simply powering down the server
- Risk the possible theft of the server, which can be more disastrous than unauthorized network access to the server

All this means that the first step in planning a robust security policy is to ensure the physical security of your servers:

- Keep them in a controlled (preferably locked) space; if possible.
- Physically secure the server to a wall or floor.
- Prevent access to removable media drives such as floppy drives by using locks or other security mechanisms.
- Prevent easy access to the power switches and power outlets to keep intruders from easily turning off the servers.
- Lock the case so that internal access to the hard drives is not possible.

Preventing Easy Breaking of User Passwords

Even if a machine is physically secure, it is still a good idea to ensure that the user accounts and their associated passwords on the servers in question do not provide an easy avenue to break into the machine should someone gain unauthorized physical access. You can take several steps to ensure that passwords provide at least a challenge to the intent hacker:

- Ensure that passwords are sufficiently complex by combining letters, numbers, and other non-word characters into passwords that are not words in any dictionaries. This is essential for your root or administrator password. It is usually a good idea for passwords to be at least 8 characters in length.
- Change passwords frequently and force any users to do so too.
- Don't create unnecessary user accounts. The more accounts that exist on the server, the more chances you will have a weak password that can be stolen or otherwise compromised.

- Never share passwords. This is especially true of the root password. Even if a user is authorized to use the system, make them use their own password, but don't provide them another user's password. This makes it easier to take action in case an authorized user needs to be denied access to the server.

Preventing Unwanted Users from Accessing the Network

The next line of defense should address the security of the network. After all, the whole point of Internet or intranet Web applications is to make information accessible in a networked environment, whether it is a limited corporate network or the public Internet.

Consider an example: Say you have a corporate intranet with a Web application for use inside the corporate network. At the same time, your corporate network is connected to the Internet so that users have Internet access and so that the company can send and receive e-mail. However, you do not want to allow the public to access the internal Web application from the Internet; this would constitute a gross security breach.

To prevent this type of undesirable access to the internal corporate network, you need to implement some form of firewall. A *firewall* refers to any hardware or software solution designed to prevent unwanted incoming access to a network while allowing sufficient outgoing access to external networks for users on the internal network.

Keeping a network secure is complex and requires detailed knowledge of network security. At the basis of network security is your Internet gateway. Your network needs to be connected to the Internet through a gateway that moves data on and off the internal network as needed. This gateway could be a hardware router, a PC connected to the Internet with an ISDN router, or even a simple PC with a 28.8Kbps modem.

In any case, implementing security at the level of this gateway device is usually possible. There are two main ways to do this:

- Using a packet-filtering firewall
- Using a proxy firewall

Using a Packet-Filtering Firewall

Packet filtering is commonly found on hardware routers, and most software-based firewall and routing solutions also make this possible. With packet-filtering, the gateway determines whether packets of network information originating on the Internet should be allowed into the internal network. This is done by examining the originating IP address, the destination IP address, and the port of the connection and comparing these to a list of allowed and forbidden connections. If allowed, the connection is established, but if the attempted connection is forbidden, the packet of information essentially disappears (or is "dropped on the floor" as some say). With packet filtering, you can limit connections on the basis of where they originate, where they are destined for, or the TCP/IP port they are made on (or any combination of these three).

Using a Proxy Firewall

A proxy firewall takes a different approach to the job of securing the internal private network. Under this technique, no direct connections are allowed between the Internet and the internal network. Internal machines connecting to the Internet hand the request to the firewall, which makes the request on their behalf and then returns the results to the internal machine that originated the request. In other words, the proxy firewall acts as a relay for all connections. By the same token, no direct incoming connections exist and only allowed connections are relayed by the proxy firewall.

This may sound similar to a typical packet-filtering firewall, but it's not. With a packet-filtering firewall, machines on the internal network are visible to the Internet even if most types of connections are not allowed by the firewall. With a proxy firewall, the internal network is invisible to the Internet and only the firewall is visible. This adds an extra layer of security because there is no avenue for a potential attacker to determine what machines are on the internal network and their respective IP addresses.

NOTE   For more general information on security planning, please refer to *Mastering Network Security* by Chris Brenton (Sybex).

Preventing Unwanted Users from Accessing Certain Information on a Server

This is the level of security that ColdFusion addresses with its security features and that you will look at more closely in this chapter. In preventing unwanted users from accessing information on a server, you are dealing with issues of authorization and authentication: How do you specify who can access what information? How do you limit access to those users? How do you authenticate that users are who they say they are?

Usually, this type of access control happens at several levels:

Operating system   You generally control access to individual files and directories through security mechanisms that are built into the operating system.

Information service   Individual information services such as Web servers, database servers, and mail servers generally have their own systems for access control.

Custom applications   Custom-built applications often implement their own security systems for access control.

Common to all these access-control environments are two main pieces of the access-control puzzle:

- A directory of users and the information required to authorize and authenticate them (such as usernames and passwords or certificates)
- A list of resources and associated restrictions

In the ColdFusion environment, several types of access control can be implemented:

Remote development services security   This type of security allows control of developer access to the server through the ColdFusion Studio development environment. This access is controlled through a password specified on the Basic Security page of the ColdFusion Administrator as discussed in Chapter 35.

User security   With user security, developers implement security control in their application pages to create runtime access-control systems. We will discuss user security in this chapter.

Server sandbox security   With server sandbox security, security is specified on a per-directory level on a ColdFusion Server (Enterprise edition only) and managed by the administrator of the server. We will discuss server sandbox security in this chapter.

Administrator security   You can secure individual administrative tasks by using administrator security. Full details of this method can be found in the *Administering ColdFusion Server* section of the ColdFusion online documentation.

Using Advanced Security

User security and server sandbox security are managed through the Advanced Server Security page of the ColdFusion Administrator, shown in Figure 30.1.

FIGURE 30.1
The Advanced Server Secu-
rity administration page

FIGURE 30.1
The Advanced Server Secu-
rity administration page

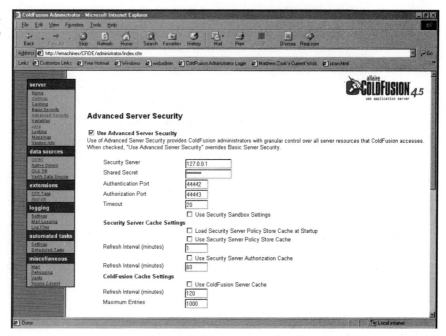

Through advanced security, you define features that, when combined, provide for a complete security system.

Specifying a Security Server

First, you need to specify the server that will act as the security server for your environment. If you are running a single ColdFusion server, then this will always be your ColdFusion server. If, however, you are running multiple ColdFusion servers in a cluster, you can specify one server as the security server for all your ColdFusion systems and then define all the security information in one place.

To specify the security server, open the ColdFusion Administrator's Advanced Server Security page. On this page, you need to:

1. Make sure the Use Advanced Server Security box is checked. Without this, none of the security features you are looking at in this chapter will work.

2. Type the IP address or host name of your security server in the Security Server field. If you are running only one ColdFusion server, then this should be **127.0.0.1** or **localhost**.

3. ColdFusion uses an encryption scheme for validating security actions. This scheme relies on a shared secret that becomes part of the key for encryption. By default, all

new ColdFusion installations have the same key, so it is important to set a new value in the Shared Secret field as soon as you decide to enable advanced security.

4. Click the Apply button at the bottom of the page to commit your changes.

Specifying a User Directory

Throughout the rest of this chapter, you will use a simple security example that you can work through as you proceed. For instance, consider the following template:

```
<CFQUERY NAME="employees" DATASOURCE="EmployeeList">
   SELECT * FROM Employees
</CFQUERY>

<CFOUTPUT>There are #employees.RecordCount# employees.</CFOUTPUT>
<HR>
<CFOUTPUT QUERY="employees">
#LastName#, #FirstName#<BR>
</CFOUTPUT
```

This is a simple template, but consider what would happen if the following rules applied:

- Only authorized users can view the list of names.
- Any valid user can view the number of employees.
- No one else can access any part of the template.

It is this security scenario that you will work through in this chapter.

The first step to implementing this security plan is to specify the user directory to use when authenticating users. ColdFusion supports two types of user directories: LDAP servers and, in the case of the Windows NT version of ColdFusion, Windows NT domain databases. User directories provide ColdFusion access to lists of users and groups of users that can be used to specify access permissions to specific resources.

To define a user directory, click the User Directories button at the bottom of the Advanced Server Security page. This leads to the page titled Registered User Directories for Security Server "CFSM," which provides a list of existing user directories and a small form to initiate the process of creating a new directory (see Figure 30.2).

FIGURE 30.2

The main user directories page

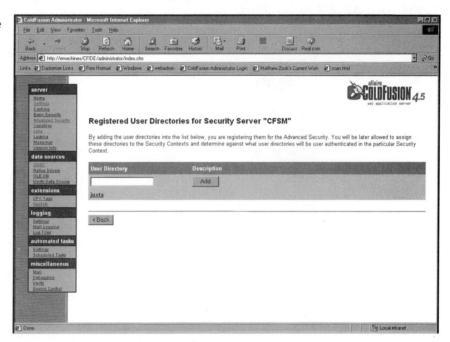

To create a directory, first provide a name for the directory in the User Directory text field. You will use this name in defining your ColdFusion security scheme, but it doesn't need to be directly related to the directory server that it will be used to refer to. Use a name that is meaningful and easy to remember. In this example, use **UserList**. After you have filled in the field with a name, click the Add button to open the New User Directory screen shown in Figure 30.3.

FIGURE 30.3
The New User Directory
screen

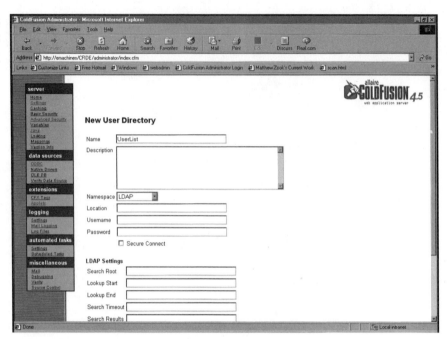

FIGURE 30.3
The New User Directory screen

In this screen, you can provide a more detailed description of the user directory and then define the directory itself. The process depends on whether you want to define a Windows NT or a LDAP directory. Both situations are described in the following sections.

Creating a Windows NT User Directory

Specifying a Windows NT user directory is the easier task of the two. To do this, you need to choose Windows NT in the Namespace field and then provide the Windows network name of your ColdFusion server in the Server field. Finally, click the Apply button at the bottom of the page.

Creating an LDAP User Directory

Defining an LDAP user directory requires somewhat more work:

1. Select LDAP in the Namespace field.

2. Specify the name of the LDAP server in the Server field.

3. Enter the distinguished name and password to use when connecting to the server in the Username and Password fields.

Optionally, you can enter the node from which to start searches, specify the start and of search strings in Lookup Start and Lookup End, define a timeout limit for searches, indicate the maximum number of records to return in searches, and define the search scope as either Subtree or One Level. The choice of these options will depend on the configuration of the LDAP server you are using. You should consult the administrator of the server to determine the correct settings for these options. You may not need to provide any new data or change default settings for these fields.

Defining a Security Context

After you have created a user directory, you need to define a security context. The *security context* is a related, cohesive group of resources and their security information. The security context is an umbrella under which you can create a security scheme. On any one server you can have as many contexts as you need to define the security schemes you plan to use.

For our example, you will create a single security scheme: EmployeeList. This name is chosen to indicate that you are creating a context to define security for your employee list application.

To create this context, click the Security Contexts button at the bottom of the Advanced Server Security page. You will be presented with a screen displaying a list of existing contexts and a form to start the creation of a new one. Type the name of the new context in the field provided and click the Add button. This causes the New Security Context page shown in Figure 30.4. to be displayed.

On this page, you first provide a description of the context. Next, you need to indicate the types of resources that will be secured with the context. These include applications, individual CFML tags, components, custom tags, data sources, individual files, and user objects (arbitrary user-defined objects that can be used to secure many parts of your applications). Because you want to secure some arbitrary section of code, select UserObject. It is advisable to select only those resources that you intend to secure in order to ensure the best performance for your security system.

From version 4.5 of ColdFusion, you can also specify that all resources should be protected by default unless you specifically allow for access to a particular resource for one or more users or groups. The default behavior, which is backward compatible to version 4 of ColdFusion, is to allow access until a rule protecting it is created. Generally, you will only want to protect all resources while implementing your security framework and then turn off this option once a complete security system is designed and implemented.

FIGURE 30.4

The New Security
Context page

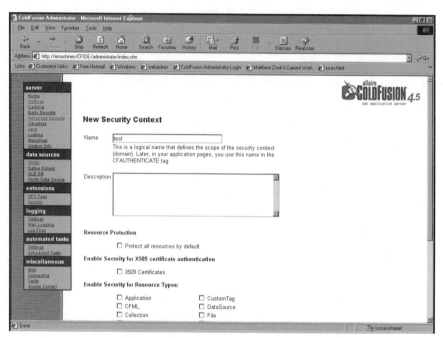

Associating User Directories with Security Contexts

After you add your new context, you will be presented the New Security Context page for editing the context. You use the User Directories button at the bottom of this page to associate specific user directories with the context. When authenticating users within the context, only the selected directories will be used. As you click the User Directories button, you will be presented with a screen where you can specify any available directory as one available to the security context. You will want to choose UserList as being available for your security context.

Defining Security Rules

The next step in setting up a security scheme is to define rules. Rules define what actions are allowed on a specific resource. To define rules, you click the Rules button at the bottom of the Security Context page. This leads to a screen where you can specify a rule name and choose a resource type. The list of resource types will depend on those you checked as being secured by your security context.

You will be creating a rule to control access to the code for displaying the list of users, so you will use **ListDisplay** as the name. You select UserObject for the type of resource, corresponding to the type of resource that you indicated you were securing when you created the context. Finally, you click the Add button.

On the New Resource Rule screen, you can provide a description and then information specific to the type of resource you are securing. For instance, when securing an application, you have to provide the application name. When securing CFML, you need to specify the tag you wish to secure.

In the case of the UserObject, you need to provide a name for the object. You could use **ListDisplayCode**, for instance. You also need to provide the type of action you are securing. If you don't indicate one, the default setting will be Execute, which is suitable for most user objects.

Creating Security Policies

After you define the rules, you need to create policies. Policies play the role of relating users or groups of users with those policies. By doing this, you are indicating which users are allowed to access the resource secured by a rule. If a rule is not associated with users through a policy, then no one can access the specified resource.

To add a policy, click the Policies button at the bottom of the Security Context page, provide a name for the policy, and click Add. In our case, you need a policy to indicate who can access your rule. You can call this **ListDisplayAllowed**. This leads to the New Security Policy screen where you can provide a description of the policy and click the Add button. After the policy is added, it will be appear in a list of existing policies for the security context, as shown in Figure 30.5.

Clicking the name of the policy in the list leads to the Edit Security Policy screen, where you can edit the policy. You do this by first associating one or more rules with the policy (click the Rules button to do this) and one or more users or user groups with the policy (click the Users button to do this).

FIGURE 30.5
Existing policies

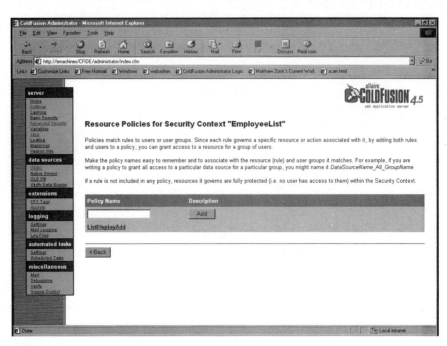

Authentication and Authorization with *CFAUTHENTICATE*

After you have defined a security context and its related rules and policies, you then use the CFAUTHENTICATE tag along with the IsAuthenticated and IsAuthorized functions to implement a security scheme for your applications. The process works like this:

1. CFAUTHENTICATE is used to check a user's username and password against a given security context.

2. IsAuthenticated can then be used to check whether the authentication succeeded. That is, it checks whether the username and password combination was valid.

3. IsAuthorized can then be used to check whether a given authenticated user has permission to access a given resource.

Using *CFAUTHENTICATE*

The CFAUTHENTICATE tag is used to check a username and password combination against a given security context. Once checked, IsAuthenticated and IsAuthorized tell you the results. This tag takes the following attributes:

SECURITYCONTEXT   The name of the security context against which you are authenticating a user.

USERNAME   The username to be authenticated.

PASSWORD   The password to be authenticated.

SETCOOKIE   Indicates whether a cookie should be set to carry the authentication information from page to page. If you don't set a cookie, then each page of a secured application needs to be used on each page of your application. Possible values are Yes and No. By default, the value is Yes.

THROWONFAILURE   Indicates whether authentication failure should throw an exception of type Security to be used by CFCATCH. Possible values are Yes and No. By default, the value is Yes.

You need to note a couple of things about using the CFAUTHENTICATE tag:

- Authentication is the process of checking the username-password combination against all users in the directories associated with a given security context. It does not check permission to access specific resources.
- Authentication needs to be performed on all pages in a secured application. Usually the best place to do this is in the Application.cfm file for the application.

In our example, you would authenticate a username and password by using

```
<CFAUTHENTICATE SECURITYCONTEXT="EmployeeList"
USERNAME="User name goes here"
PASSWORD="Password goes here">
```

Using *IsAuthenticated*

The IsAuthenticated function provides a way to check whether a user is authenticated at any point in your templates. The function takes no parameters and simply tells you the result of the last use of CFAUTHENTICATE by returning True or False. If the value is True, then authentication succeeded and the username and password combination that was tested was valid for the directories associated with the given security context specified in CFAUTHENTICATE.

Using *IsAuthorized*

You use the IsAuthorized tool to secure specific resources based on the access policies you created in your security context. This function takes three arguments: IsAuthorized(ResourceType, ResourceName, Action).

The resource type you specify should match one of those you indicated you are securing in the definition of your security context. Possible values are:

- `Application`
- `CFML`
- `File`
- `DSN`
- `Component`
- `Collection`
- `CustomTag`
- `UserObject`

The resource name value depends on the type of resource being authorized, as shown in Table 30.1.

TABLE 30.1:   The Value of the Resource Name for Different Resource Types

Resource Type	Name Value
Application	The application name
CFML	The tag name
File	The filename
DSN	The data source name
Component	The component name
Collection	The Verity collection name
CustomTag	The custom tag name
UserObject	The object name as specified in the rule definition

Table 30.2 shows that possible values for the action argument are dependent on the type of resource being authorized.

TABLE 30.2:   Possible Actions for Different Resource Types

Resource Type	Possible Actions
Application	ALL, USERCLIENTVARIABLES.
CFML	Valid actions for the specified resources.
FILE	READ, WRITE.
DSN	ALL, CONNECT, SELECT, INSERT, UPDATE, DELETE, SP.
Component	No actions are possible. The argument should not be used.
Collection	DELETE, OPTIMIZE, PURGE, SEARCH, UPDATE.
CustomTag	No actions are possible. The argument should not be used.
UserObject	Actions specified for the object in the rule definition.

Put all together, you could check the authorization of a user to access your employee list example by using the following function:

```
IsAuthorized("UserObject","ListDisplayCode","Execute")
```

Notice that the object name is specified in the rule definition and not the name of the rule. This is the correct name value for a user object.

The function will return `True` if the user is authorized to access the resource as defined in the policies for the security context. Otherwise, `False` is returned.

Putting It All Together

To create your security system, you need to put the two pieces of this puzzle together:

- Authenticating users in an `Application.cfm` file.
- Authorizing users in individual pages of the application.

Authenticating Users

Listing 30.1 shows the `Application.cfm` file for your application.

LISTING 30.1: *application.cfm*

```
<!--- CHECK FOR A USERNAME --->
<CFPARAM name="HaveUsername" default="Yes">

<CFIF IsDefined("Cookie.Username")>
   <CFSET USERNAME=Cookie.Username>
<CFELSE>
   <CFSET USERNAME="">
   <CFIF IsDefined("Form.Username")>
      <CFSET USERNAME=Form.Username>
      <CFCOOKIE NAME="username" VALUE="#Form.Username#">
   <CFELSE>
      <CFSET HaveUsername = "No">
   </CFIF>
</CFIF>

<!--- CHECK FOR A PASSWORD --->
<CFPARAM name="HavePassword" default="Yes">

<CFIF IsDefined("Cookie.Password")>
   <CFSET PASSWORD=Cookie.Password>
<CFELSE>
   <CFSET PASSWORD="">
   <CFIF IsDefined("Form.Password")>
      <CFSET PASSWORD=Form.Password>
      <CFCOOKIE NAME="password" VALUE="#Form.Password#">
```

```
        <CFELSE>
            <CFSET HavePassword = "No">
        </CFIF>
    </CFIF>

    <!--- CHECK AUTHENTICATION STATUS AND IF NOT AUTHENTICATED HANDLE IT --->
    <CFIF NOT IsAuthenticated()>

        <!--- IF WE HAVE A PASSWORD AND USERNAME, TRY AUTHENTICATING --->
        <CFIF HaveUsername and HavePassword>
            <CFTRY>
                <CFAUTHENTICATE
                SECURITYCONTEXT="EmployeeList"
                USERNAME="#USERNAME#"
                PASSWORD="#PASSWORD#"
                SETCOOKIE="Yes">

                <!--- IF AN EXCEPTION IS THROWN, HANDLE IT --->
                <CFCATCH TYPE="Security">
                    <CFCOOKIE NAME="username" VALUE="" EXPIRES="NOW">
                    <CFCOOKIE NAME="password" VALUE="" EXPIRES="NOW">
                    <CFLOCATION URL="index.cfm">
                </CFCATCH>
            </CFTRY>
        </CFIF>

        <!--- OUTPUT A LOGIN FORM --->
        <FORM ACTION="index.cfm" METHOD="POST">
            Username: <INPUT TYPE=text NAME="username"><BR>
            Password: <INPUT TYPE=password NAME="password"><BR>
            <INPUT TYPE=submit VALUE="LOGIN">
        </FORM>

        <CFABORT>

    </CFIF>

    <!--- USER IS AUTHENTICATED, SO WE CONTINUE --->

    <CFAPPLICATION NAME="admin">
```

This may look complicated, but it really isn't. Basically, you make the following assumptions:

- Usernames and passwords will come to the template either from a cookie or, initially, from a form field.

A security issue arises here: If both the username and password are stored in cookies, then they can be stolen from the client machine. Also, the username and password will be transmitted to the server with each page request, increasing the chance that they can be stolen in transit.

- If either a username or password is missing, then a login form needs to be presented.
- If both a username and a password are available and the user is not authenticated, then authentication should be performed and the results checked. If authentication fails, a new login form should be presented.

You start with two blocks of code to see whether a username and a password are available. Both blocks work in the same way. For instance, this is the block of code used to check for the existence of a username:

```
<!--- CHECK FOR A USERNAME --->

<CFPARAM name="HaveUsername" default="Yes">
<CFIF IsDefined("Cookie.Username")>
   <CFSET USERNAME=Cookie.Username>
<CFELSE>
   <CFSET USERNAME="">
   <CFIF IsDefined("Form.Username")>
      <CFSET USERNAME=Form.Username>
      <CFCOOKIE NAME="username" VALUE="#Form.Username#">
   <CFELSE>
      <CFSET HaveUsername = "No">
   </CFIF>
</CFIF>
```

You start by assuming that you have a username by using the HaveUserName variable that you set to Yes. Then, you check for a cookie containing the username, and if it is there, you assign its value to the USERNAME variable for use later. Otherwise, you check whether you have a username provided from a login form and if you do, you assign its value to the USERNAME variable and save the value in a cookie for use in later pages. If neither source of a username is available, you don't have one and you set HaveUserName to No. You use the same logic in checking for a password.

Next, you check whether the user is authenticated. You do this because if the user has already logged in to the application successfully and is simply clicking their way through the application, there is no need to continually re-authenticate them. You can just move on.

Assuming that `IsAuthenticated` returns a `False` value, then you have some work to do. First, you check whether you have both a username and password. If you do, then you perform authentication:

```
<CFTRY>
    <CFAUTHENTICATE
    SECURITYCONTEXT="EmployeeList"
    USERNAME="#USERNAME#"
    PASSWORD="#PASSWORD#"
    SETCOOKIE="Yes">

    <!--- IF AN EXCEPTION IS THROWN, HANDLE IT --->
    <CFCATCH TYPE="Security">
        <CFCOOKIE NAME="username" VALUE="" EXPIRES="NOW">
        <CFCOOKIE NAME="password" VALUE="" EXPIRES="NOW">
        <CFLOCATION URL="index.cfm">
    </CFCATCH>
</CFTRY>
```

Notice that you wrap your attempt at authentication in a CFTRY block so that you can catch a failure and act upon it by using CFCATCH. If authentication fails, you do two things: You empty your cookies so that no username and password are retained, and you reload the template. By clearing the cookies and not passing form variables, you know that when the page reloads the next time, you won't have a username and password, and authentication will not be attempted again but the template will skip this step and move on to the next.

The next step is to display a login form. If you have failed authentication and make it this far through the template, then you know that you need to present a login box. This form is presented and the template aborts with CFABORT so that the page being loaded is not displayed. In this way, the page being requested by the user is displayed only if authentication has succeeded and they get by the CFIF tag where authentication is checked.

Authorizing Users in Individual Pages of the Application

At this point, you are able to do the following:

- If no username or password is available, prompt the user for both with a form.
- If the user is not currently authenticated and you have a username and password, try authentication. If authentication fails, clear the username and password values and start again.
- If authentication succeeds, proceed to display the requested page.

What happens, then, if a user succeeds in authenticating? The requested page is displayed. You need to perform authorization inside individual templates within your application to decide which components to display for the user. In our example template

```
<CFQUERY NAME="employees" DATASOURCE="EmployeeList">
    SELECT * FROM Employees
</CFQUERY>

<CFOUTPUT>There are #employees.RecordCount# employees.</CFOUTPUT>
<HR>
<CFOUTPUT QUERY="employees">
#LastName#, #FirstName#<BR>
</CFOUTPUT
```

you want to display the last part (the employee list) only to users authorized to access it. This is where you get to use the IsAuthorized function:

```
<CFQUERY NAME="employees" DATASOURCE="EmployeeList">
    SELECT * FROM Employees
</CFQUERY>

<CFOUTPUT>There are #employees.RecordCount# employees.</CFOUTPUT>
<HR>
<CFIF ISAuthorized("UserObject","ListDisplayCode","Execute")>
<CFOUTPUT QUERY="employees">
#LastName#, #FirstName#<BR>
</CFOUTPUT
</CFIF>
```

Now, the user list is displayed only when authorization for the resource succeeds.

Using *CFIMPERSONATE*

You can execute a block of code as a specific user using the CFIMPERSONATE tag. To do this, you wrap the code to execute in opening and closing <CFIMPERSONATE> and </CFIMPERSONATE> tags.

The basic form of the CFIMPERSONATE tag is:

```
<CFIMPERSONATE SECURITYCONTEXT="<security context>"
    USERNAME="<username>"
    PASSWORD="<password>"
    TYPE=<impersonation type>">
```

The fields have the following meanings:

- SECURITYCONTEXT: If the TYPE parameter is set to CF, then you should specify the name of a ColdFusion advanced security context in this field. If the TYPE parameter is set to OS, you should specify the name of an NT domain to use for authentication.

- USERNAME: The user name of the user you want to impersonate.
- PASSWORD: The password of the user you want to impersonate.
- TYPE: You can specify two types of impersonating. If you set this field to CF, Cold-Fusion will perform application-level impersonation using the ColdFusion security framework. If you set this field to OS, ColdFusion will use the operating system's security mechanism to control access to files, directories and any other resources protected by the operating system. ColdFusion's security mechanism will not be used. OS type security is only available in Windows NT.

Using Server Sandbox Security

To round out our look at ColdFusion security, you need to consider *server sandbox security*. Server sandbox security takes security contexts, rules, and policies and puts them to a different use than securing individual users and authorizing them to perform specific actions.

Instead, sandbox security is a mechanism by which an administrator can control what individual developers are allowed to do. By way of example, consider an Internet Service Provider that allows their customers to create their own Web sites on the provider's ColdFusion-based Web server. Depending on the user, they should be allowed different levels of permission to use specific tags, data sources, and other resources.

Server sandbox security achieves this by associating specific security contexts with specific directories. Therefore, the ISP in question could create different security contexts with different sets of policies based on the different developers and groups of developers hosting their sites on the server. Then, each developer's Web directory can be associated with a given security context in a sandbox. The developer is limited to using the resources they are granted permission to use in the context and will be denied permission to those for which sandbox is not authorized.

To create a sandbox, first create the desired security context and then perform the following steps:

1. Make sure the Use Security Sandbox Settings check box on the Advanced Security page of the ColdFusion Administrator is checked.
2. Click the Security Sandboxes button on the Advanced Security page.
3. Enter the full path of the directory for which you are creating a sandbox. If you are using Windows, use forward slashes instead of backslashes in the path (in other words, use `c:/html/username` instead of `c:\html\username`).

4. If you are using ColdFusion 4.5, select the type of sandbox from the Type drop-down list. Possible types are: Operating System (protect resources based on a Windows NT domain) or Security Context (protect resources based on permissions in a ColdFusion security context).

5. Click the Add button.

6. Select the name of an existing security context for the sandbox from the Security Context drop-down list if you selected Security Context as your sandbox type in Step 4. Enter a Windows NT domain name in NT Domain field if you selected Operating System as your sandbox type in Step 4.

7. Provide a username and password for the sandbox.

This last step requires some explanation. Instead of requiring a developer to provide a username and password to implement sandbox security, the administrator must indicate the username and password to use in authenticating and authorizing the developer's templates within the sandbox.

This is done with good reason. If no username and password are provided, then no authentication can take place automatically and the developer would have to provide them to authorize their work. In this way, the administrator defines the user to use in authentication and then all work by the developer within the sandbox is authenticated and authorized against the context using the specified username. The developer has no control over the user being used to control their access to resources and hacking can't be attempted on the sandbox through random guessing of passwords.

If you have sandbox security and user security enabled, sandbox security takes precedence.

Where Do We Go from Here?

In the next chapter you will look at how to develop custom tags within ColdFusion. This advanced feature of ColdFusion can greatly enhance application development. Custom tags allow commonly used functionality to be encapsulated within a tag that can then be used anywhere in your templates and applications. For instance, if you have special code to display a menu based on special values, instead of including this code in every template, you can write a custom tag and then use that tag wherever you need the menu to be displayed.

Custom tags are so useful that a growing culture of custom tag distribution and sharing has developed. Custom tags provide an easy way to distribute functionality between developers without requiring developers to understand the intricacies of how tags achieve their results. Hundreds of custom tags are available on the Internet for developers to use in their ColdFusion applications.

chapter 31

Building ColdFusion Custom Tags

- Understanding Custom Tag Basics

- Creating Your First Custom Tag

- Using Advanced Custom Tags

- Using CFX Custom Tags

- Using New ColdFusion 4.0.1 and 4.5 Features

With the introduction of ColdFusion Application Server 3, Allaire added a powerful new feature to the core ColdFusion language: custom tags. This feature has been carried forward to the current version of ColdFusion Server, version 4.5. Custom tags allow developers to create portable and powerful extensions to the language. By building a "black box" architecture, developers are able to create modular, powerful extensions that could be shared not only with other developers on a project but across the Internet as well.

In this chapter, we will discuss the basic architecture of custom tags. You will create a simple custom tag and enhance it into a full-featured, secure ColdFusion custom tag. You will also learn about custom tag enhancements specific to the ColdFusion 4 and 4.5 Server.

Be sure to examine the numerous examples on custom tags on the CD. Many custom tags created by both authors of this book for other developers in the ColdFusion community have been included.

TIP   For even more examples of custom tags, check out the hundreds available (many for free!) at the Allaire Developer's Exchange, `http://www.allaire.com/developer/gallery.cfm`.

Understanding Custom Tag Basics

Two basic aspects of using custom tags need to be understood before considering the details of custom tag development:

- Referencing custom tags
- Scoping custom tags

Referencing Custom Tags

There are two types of custom tags: those developed using the ColdFusion language and those developed using external programming languages such as Visual C++. The latter are generally known as *CFX tags*.

To reference these tags in normal CFML, you use a special notation:

CF_TagName   Tags developed using standard ColdFusion

CFX_TagName   Custom CFX tags written in Visual C++ and similar languages

---

NOTE   An exception to this general pattern arises when `CFMODULE` is used to access custom tags. `CFMODULE` is discussed in depth in Chapter 8, "Including Outside Code."

For instance, a custom tag called `EmailCheck` would be referred to in CFML as `CF_EmailCheck`. This in turn tells the ColdFusion Application Server to look for a file named `EmailCheck.cfm`. Here is an example:

```
<CFSET TEST = Form.EmailAddress>
<CF_EmailCheck Email="#TEST#">
```

Here you see standard CFML (the CFSET) followed by a call to the custom tag. Custom tags take attributes just as most CFML tags do. The only difference is that as the developer of the custom tag, you are left to decide which attributes your tag will use. This will change depending on the particular function of your custom tag.

When you call a custom tag, the server will attempt to find a corresponding CFM file for the tag. It will first check the same directory as the calling template. So, if the CFM file calling the custom tag is in the folder `c:\wwwroot\project1`, the server will first check that folder. If you build a custom tag that is useful for only a particular project, you would typically place the custom tag in the same folder.

The other option is to use the custom tags folder. If you installed ColdFusion on your C drive, this would be the `c:\cfusion\customtags` folder. The advantage of using this folder is that any CFM template on the server can use the tag. If the server cannot find the custom tag in the same directory or in the root custom tags folder, the server will then begin searching any subdirectories under the custom tags folder. It is important to remember that if you have a template with the same name as your custom tag in both the server's custom tags folder and in the same folder as the template that called the tag, the server will give precedence to the file in the same folder.

It is for exactly these reasons that Allaire created the `CFMODULE` tag. Using `CFMODULE` enables you to gain precise control over which custom tag template will be used by the server. The general syntax of `CFMODULE` looks like this:

```
<CFMODULE TEMPLATE="EmailCheck.cfm">
```

This instance of `CFMODULE` tells the server to call `EmailCheck.cfm`. This is the same as this syntax:

```
<CF_EmailCheck>
```

The benefit of using `CFMODULE` is that you know exactly which custom tag is going to be used. The `CFMODULE` tag has other features that help it to be used for including custom tags (see Chapter 8).

Scoping Custom Tags

The second important feature of custom tags is that they exist in their own scope, or environment. Think of this as part of the *black box* nature of custom tags. By this we mean that information is passed to and from custom tags, but data created within the tag does *not* overwrite information outside of the tag. This is important. If not for this feature, a custom tag could accidentally overwrite a variable in the document that called it.

For example, if the calling template has a variable named `Temp` and the custom tag has the code `<CFSET Temp = "MyNewValue">`, the value of TEMP in the calling document would be lost if the calling template and the custom tag did not have separate scopes.

By using a separate scope for custom tags, you can be sure that data will not be corrupted. Hence the *black box* term. Imagine a custom tag as a black box. You send it data. The custom tag does its work. The custom tag then sends the information back to the calling template. You don't know and don't care what happens inside the black box (the custom tag) as long as what you get back is what you want.

Scoping is handled within custom tags by using the `Attributes` and `Caller` prefixes. Any data sent to a custom tag can be referenced within the `Attributes` scope. Using the preceding example, `<CF_EmailCheck Email="#TEST#">`, the variable `Attributes.Test` will be available within the `EmailCheck` custom tag. To send information *from* the custom tag to the calling template, you simply use the `Caller` scope. The following line will set a variable in the calling template: `<CFSET Caller.ValidEmail = "Yes">`. You reference that value in the calling template without the `Caller` scope. Any CFML in the calling template after the use of the custom tag can then refer to the variable as `ValidEmail`, not `Caller.ValidEmail`.

Creating Your First Custom Tag

We have discussed the ways that custom tags are called via templates, so let's jump in now with an example. Pretend that you have a simple application that enables a visitor to enter three numbers. After hitting the Submit button, the visitor then sees the result of multiplying all three numbers. Listing 31.1 shows this application.

LISTING 31.1: *multiplythree.cfm*

```
<!---
   Name    : MultiplyThree
   Purpose : Multiplies three numbers and returns the product.
   Created : February 2, 2000
--->
```

```
<CFPARAM NAME="Form.Number1" DEFAULT=0>
<CFPARAM NAME="Form.Number2" DEFAULT=0>
<CFPARAM NAME="Form.Number3" DEFAULT=0>

<CFIF IsDefined("Form.Fieldnames")>
    <CFSET RESULT = Val(Form.Number1) * Val(Form.Number2) * Val(Form.Number3)>
    <CFOUTPUT>The result of your multiplication of #Val(Form.Number1)#,
#Val(Form.Number2)#, and #Val(Form.Number3)# is #RESULT#</CFOUTPUT>
    <P>
</CFIF>

<FORM ACTION="MultiplyThree.cfm" METHOD="POST">

<CFOUTPUT>
<TABLE BORDER=0>
<TR>
<TD>Number One</TD>
<TD><INPUT TYPE="text" NAME="Number1" SIZE=3 VALUE="#Val(Form.Number1)#"></TD>
</TR>
<TR>
<TD>Number Two</TD>
<TD><INPUT TYPE="text" NAME="Number2" SIZE=3 VALUE="#Val(Form.Number2)#"></TD>
</TR>
<TR>
<TD>Number Three</TD>
<TD><INPUT TYPE="text" NAME="Number3" SIZE=3 VALUE="#Val(Form.Number3)#"></TD>
</TR>
<TR>
<TD COLSPAN=2><INPUT TYPE="Submit" VALUE="Display Result"></TD>
</TR>
</TABLE>
</CFOUTPUT>

</FORM>
```

This application is simple so we won't spend a lot of time discussing it. You have a form that asks the user to enter three numbers, and after the user hits the Submit button, the form calls itself and displays the results. You do a minor bit of error checking by wrapping each of the form variables with the Val command. This ensures that you don't try to multiply a number by a letter.

Let's take this application a step further. Pretend that you work for a company whose sole purpose is to provide multiplication services to its clients. You work 24/7 year-round to take clients' numbers and return the product. It might be useful, then, to create a custom tag that would do some of the grunt work for you. If you could create a custom tag that would do the multiplication, you could then spend more time worrying about the look and feel of the application.

First, you remove the code that does the multiplication (which in this case is one line: `<CFSET RESULT = Val(Form.Number1) * Val(Form.Number2) * Val(Form.Number3)>`) and replace it with a call to a custom tag. See Listing 31.2.

NOTE

In Listing 31.2, you will see the edited code in bold. Code modifications are indicated in bold throughout this chapter.

LISTING 31.2: *multiplythree_2.cfm*

```
<!---
    Name     : MultiplyThree_2
    Purpose  : Multiplies three numbers and returns the product.
    Created  : February 2, 2000
--->

<CFPARAM NAME="Form.Number1" DEFAULT=0>
<CFPARAM NAME="Form.Number2" DEFAULT=0>
<CFPARAM NAME="Form.Number3" DEFAULT=0>

<CFIF IsDefined("Form.Fieldnames")>
    <CF_Multiply NUM1="#Form.Number1#" NUM2="#Form.Number2#" NUM3="#Form.Number3#">
    <CFOUTPUT>The result of your multiplication of #Val(Form.Number1)#,
#Val(Form.Number2)#, and #Val(Form.Number3)# is #RESULT#</CFOUTPUT>
    <P>
</CFIF>

<FORM ACTION=" MultiplyThree_2.cfm" METHOD="POST">

<CFOUTPUT>
<TABLE BORDER=0>
<TR>
<TD>Number One</TD>
<TD><INPUT TYPE="text" NAME="Number1" SIZE=3 VALUE="#Val(Form.Number1)#"></TD>
</TR>
<TR>
<TD>Number Two</TD>
<TD><INPUT TYPE="text" NAME="Number2" SIZE=3 VALUE="#Val(Form.Number2)#"></TD>
</TR>
<TR>
<TD>Number Three</TD>
<TD><INPUT TYPE="text" NAME="Number3" SIZE=3 VALUE="#Val(Form.Number3)#"></TD>
</TR>
<TR>
<TD COLSPAN=2><INPUT TYPE="Submit" VALUE="Display Result"></TD>
</TR>
</TABLE>
</CFOUTPUT>

</FORM>
```

As you can see, you told the server to look for a custom tag called `Multiply.cfm`. Again, the server knows to look for this file because of the use of CF_* syntax. In this case, your code reads:

```
<CF_Multiply NUM1="#Form.Number1#" NUM2="#Form.Number2#" NUM3="#Form.Number3#">
```

How do you name the custom tag, and how do you come up with NUM1, NUM2, and NUM3? Pure, random choice. You can choose not only any name for a custom tag, but also the attributes to send. Of course, it makes sense to name your custom tag after its function. That is why the tag is named `Multiply`. By the same token, it makes sense to give your attributes sensible names. In this case your custom tag is going to take three numbers and multiply them, so you choose NUM1, NUM2, and NUM3 for simplicity's sake. Before you go any further, try running the template as it stands. After you have copied the file from the CD, run it, enter some numbers, and hit the Display Result button. (Be sure you have not copied the file `multiply.cfm` from the CD to your custom tags directory yet.) Notice the error message? It is shown in Figure 31.1.

FIGURE 31.1
ColdFusion error for a missing custom tag

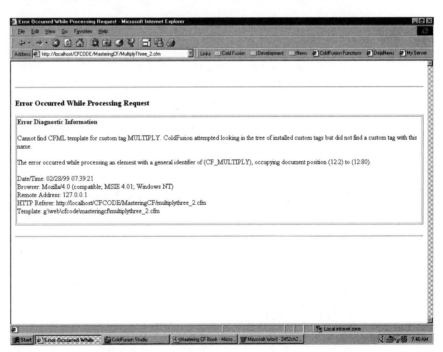

The ColdFusion server gave you an error because you have not created `Multiply.cfm` yet. You should also notice that the error states that the file could not be found in the *tree*

of installed custom tags. This simply reflects that you can store custom tags either in the same directory as the calling template or in the root server's custom tag folder.

Now that you have seen how ColdFusion throws an error for a missing custom tag, you can create your custom tag. Listing 31.3 shows the code of your custom tag.

LISTING 31.3: *multiply.cfm*

```
<!---
    Name     : Multiply
    Purpose : Multiplies three numbers and returns the product.
    Created : February 2, 2000
--->

<!--- Recreate our attributes as local variables --->
<CFSET NUM1 = Val(Attributes.NUM1)>
<CFSET NUM2 = Val(Attributes.NUM2)>
<CFSET NUM3 = Val(Attributes.NUM3)>

<!--- Create the result --->
<CFSET RESULT = NUM1 * NUM2 * NUM3>

<!--- Return the result to the template --->
<CFSET Caller.Result = RESULT>
```

Let's examine this template line by line. You begin by renaming the attributes that were sent to the tag:

```
<CFSET NUM1 = Val(Attributes.NUM1)>
<CFSET NUM2 = Val(Attributes.NUM2)>
<CFSET NUM3 = Val(Attributes.NUM3)>
```

The renaming is completely unnecessary, but you do it to make your code a bit easier to reread. You could just as easily refer to `Attributes.NUM1` in your code, but renaming the variable to `NUM1` means that later you get to type a bit less in your code. As an extra check, you use the `Val` command to ensure that you don't try to multiply non-numeric values.

The next line of code, `<CFSET RESULT = NUM1 * NUM2 * NUM3>`, creates your result. This isn't rocket science; you are basically using the same code you cut out of the original document.

Finally, you use the `Caller` scope to return the value to the calling document. The line `<CFSET Caller.Result = RESULT>` ensures that your calling document can refer to the `Result` variable. You can see the variable being used in this line from Listing 31.2:

```
<CFOUTPUT>The result of your multiplication of #Val(Form.Number1)#,
#Val(Form.Number2)#, and #Val(Form.Number3)# is #RESULT#</CFOUTPUT>
```

Notice how you don't need to use `Caller.Result`, even though that was the name you used in your custom tag. Remember that the custom tag lives in its own scope. When the custom tag set `Caller.Result`, this created a new variable in your program called `Result`.

Run the program again and you will see that the error message has gone away. You will also notice that, functionality-wise, your template acts the same as it did before. But you have created something much more advanced. Now, to share your code with other developers, all you would need to do is copy `multiply.cfm` into the ColdFusion custom tags folder. Even better, if for some reason the laws of mathematics changed so that every multiplication must *also* include a subtraction by 3.14159, you could easily add this new rule to your file. At that point, every application that uses the custom tag would be instantly updated.

Enhancing the *Multiply* Custom Tag

As stated earlier, the custom tag that you created can take any three numbers and multiply them. The tag will then return the result of that multiplication to the template that called it. This is fine by itself but pretty limiting. The `Multiply` custom tag must be sent three, and only three, numbers. If anything more or less is sent, the tag will throw an error.

To create a truly powerful tag, it would be beneficial if your custom tag could take *any* number of attributes. To facilitate this modification, make some basic changes to your custom tag. Instead of sending NUM1, NUM2, and NUM3, send an attribute called NUMBERS. This attribute will be a list of numbers that the tag will multiply. This way, any number of figures may be sent to the tag. You begin by changing your calling document. Listing 31.4 shows the code changes to reflect the new attribute.

LISTING 31.4: *multiplythree_3.cfm*

```
<!---
    Name    : MultiplyThree_3
    Purpose : Multiplies three numbers and returns the product.
    Created : February 2, 2000
--->

<CFPARAM NAME="Form.Number1" DEFAULT=0>
<CFPARAM NAME="Form.Number2" DEFAULT=0>
<CFPARAM NAME="Form.Number3" DEFAULT=0>

<CFIF IsDefined("Form.Fieldnames")>
    <CF_MultiplyNew NUMBERS="#Form.Number1#,#Form.Number2#,#Form.Number3#">
    <CFOUTPUT>The result of your multiplication of #Val(Form.Number1)#,
#Val(Form.Number2)#, and #Val(Form.Number3)# is #RESULT#</CFOUTPUT>
    <P>
</CFIF>
```

```
<FORM ACTION="MultiplyThree_3.cfm" METHOD="POST">

<CFOUTPUT>
<TABLE BORDER=0>
<TR>
<TD>Number One</TD>
<TD><INPUT TYPE="text" NAME="Number1" SIZE=3 VALUE="#Val(Form.Number1)#"></TD>
</TR>
<TR>
<TD>Number Two</TD>
<TD><INPUT TYPE="text" NAME="Number2" SIZE=3 VALUE="#Val(Form.Number2)#"></TD>
</TR>
<TR>
<TD>Number Three</TD>
<TD><INPUT TYPE="text" NAME="Number3" SIZE=3 VALUE="#Val(Form.Number3)#"></TD>
</TR>
<TR>
<TD COLSPAN=2><INPUT TYPE="Submit" VALUE="Display Result"></TD>
</TR>
</TABLE>
</CFOUTPUT>

</FORM>
```

The changed line, `<CF_MultiplyNew NUMBERS="#Form.Number1#,#Form.Number2#,` `#Form.Number3#">`, represents the change you are going to make to your custom tag. As stated previously, you are going to send a list of numbers to your custom tag. In this case, your list is comprised of the three form variables from your application. You will also notice that you are going to use a new custom tag, aptly named `MultiplyNew`. This is simply done so that you can compare the versions. Listing 31.5 shows the new version of your custom tag.

LISTING 31.5: *multiplynew.cfm*

```
<!---
    Name    : MultiplyNew
    Purpose : Multiplies a list of numbers and returns the product.
    Created : February 2, 2000
--->

<!--- Default values --->
<CFPARAM NAME="Attributes.Return" DEFAULT="RESULT">
<CFSET FinalResult = 1>

<!--- Did we send the required attribute? --->
<CFIF NOT IsDefined("Attributes.Numbers")>
    <CFOUTPUT><B>MultiplyNew Error</B> - You must send the Numbers attribute.</
CFOUTPUT>
    <CFABORT>
</CFIF>
```

```
<!--- Did we send a simple value? --->
<CFIF NOT IsSimpleValue(Attributes.Numbers)>
    <CFOUTPUT><B>MultiplyNew Error</B> - The Numbers attribute must be a simple
value.</CFOUTPUT>
    <CFABORT>
</CFIF>

<CFLOOP INDEX="CURR_NUMBER" LIST="#Attributes.Numbers#">
    <CFIF NOT IsNumeric(CURR_NUMBER)>
        <CFOUTPUT><B>MultiplyNew Error</B> - #CURR_NUMBER#, which was sent to the
tag, is not a valid number.</CFOUTPUT>
        <CFABORT>
    </CFIF>
    <CFSET FinalResult = FinalResult * CURR_NUMBER>
</CFLOOP>

<CFSET "Caller.#Attributes.Return#" = FinalResult>
```

This new version of the custom tag has some pretty important enhancements, so we will cover them line by line. You begin by creating a default variable for an attribute. This says, "If the user did not send me an attribute named Return, create one for the user." For every custom tag you work on, the attributes will be divided into three categories:

- Attributes that are not required
- Attributes that are required
- Attributes that, if they are sent to the tag, cause other attributes to be required

In this case, the Return attribute is not required. If the user did not send it, you adopt a default value for the attribute: Result. The purpose of this attribute is simple. In the first version of this tag a variable called Result was automatically created in the calling template. One thing that nice custom tag authors provide for their users is the ability to tell the tag what variable to create. It may be that the user wishes to run the Multiply custom tag on various lists of numbers. For example, imagine the following situation:

```
<CF_MultiplyNew NUMBERS="1,2,3,4,5,6">
<CF_MultiplyNew NUMBERS="10,20,30,40,50,60">
<CF_MultiplyNew NUMBERS="100,200,300,400,500,600">
```

If each instance of CF_MultiplyNew set a variable called Result, you would not be able to compare the three products. Each time, the previous result would be erased. You would see the result of multiplying only the last set of numbers. But, because you have added a new feature that allows you to dynamically set the name of the new variable, you can now use:

```
<CF_MultiplyNew NUMBERS="1,2,3,4,5,6" RETURN="FirstSet">
<CF_MultiplyNew NUMBERS="10,20,30,40,50,60" RETURN="SecondSet">
<CF_MultiplyNew NUMBERS="100,200,300,400,500,600" RETURN="ThirdSet">
```

Each time the custom tag is run, it will use a new value for `Attributes.Return`. This will enable you to access all three variables.

```
<CFOUTPUT>
The result of the first set is #FirstSet#.<BR>
The result of the second set is #SecondSet#.<BR>
The result of the third set is #ThirdSet#.<BR>
</CFOUTPUT>
```

This ability to return results to different variables in the calling template is not something you *have* to do in a custom tag; again, it's just a nice feature to have.

The next line, `<CFSET FinalResult = 1>`, will be used by your tag to keep the current result. As you multiply each set of numbers, you need a way to store the total number. Because every number multiplied by 1 is equal to itself, setting `FinalResult` to 1 has no effect on your result.

The next block of code beginning with `<CFIF NOT IsDefined("Attributes.Numbers")>` and ending with `</CFIF>` makes sure that the calling template sends the `Numbers` attribute. Remember that each custom tag has different kinds of attributes— required, not required, and conditionally required. In this instance, you make `Numbers` a required attribute. If the user does not send the attribute, you display a simple error message and then use the `CFABORT` tag to end execution.

Note that there are two ways of leaving a custom tag: You can use `CFEXIT` or `CFABORT`. If you use `CFEXIT`, the custom tag will stop executing but will not stop the calling template. In this case you use `CFABORT` because you assume that if the calling template has made this mistake, everything else should stop. In other cases, you may need to alternate between using `CFEXIT` and `CFABORT` depending on the nature of particular custom tags and the nature of the errors you are encountering.

After determining that the user has sent all the required attributes (in this case only one), next you need to make sure that the attributes sent are of the correct type. This will change from tag to tag, but in this case, you want to ensure that the `Numbers` attribute is a list. You could use many techniques to achieve this, including the following:

- Check for the comma delimiter by using the `Find` function
- Use the `ListLen` function to make sure you have at least two items

But each of those methods is not *exactly* what you want. In both cases you are assuming that your lists will have at least two elements. But, what if you want your tag to be handle lists with a single element as well? Then neither approach is the perfect solution.

In your custom tag, you haven't done a detailed analysis of the list of numbers being passed to the tag. Instead, you have done a simple test: you check whether the data passed in the Numbers attribute is a simple string (as opposed to a more complex data type such as an array). You do this with the IsSimpleValue function. If there is an error, the CFABORT tag provides the means to halt execution and display an error message.

Next comes the heart of the tag. If you reach this point, you know that you have the proper attribute and that it is a simple string you can treat as a list. You use the following line to loop through the Numbers attribute:

```
<CFLOOP INDEX="CURR_NUMBER" LIST="#Attributes.Numbers#">
```

As you can see, you have told the CFLOOP tag to use Attributes.Number as the list and CURR_NUMBER as the index. The index, CURR_NUMBER, will be set to the current number as you loop through the list. Inside the loop, you do some more simple error checking. For each item in the list, which you can access via the variable CURR_NUMBER, you check to make sure it is a valid number. The following code sample shows that check in action:

```
<CFIF NOT IsNumeric(CURR_NUMBER)>
    <CFOUTPUT><B>MultiplyNew Error</B> - #CURR_NUMBER#, which was sent to the
tag, is not a valid number.</CFOUTPUT>
    <CFABORT>
</CFIF>
```

The IsNumeric function is a quick and simple way to do that. Again, if you encounter a problem with the data, you throw an error message to the user and CFABORT out of the tag. Also note that when you send the error message, you specifically tell the user which item is invalid.

If the current item is a valid number, you simply update your FinalResult variable by multiplying by CURR_NUMBER, as follows:

```
<CFSET FinalResult = FinalResult * CURR_NUMBER>
```

As a side note, if any number in the list is zero, the FinalResult variable will equal zero and will not change. This is the standard rule of multiplication: any value multiplied by zero results in zero (If you want, you could use the ListContains function to search for zero and not even bother with the loop. This would speed things up if you had the possibility of multiplying hundreds of numbers together.)

The final step is to return the result to the calling template. As discussed earlier, the variable that is created in the calling template is dynamic. If the user does not specify a Return attribute, the custom tag will use the name RESULT for the variable. If the user sets the Return attribute, that name will be used instead. The following line shows Cold-Fusion's method of handling dynamic variables:

```
<CFSET "Caller.#Attributes.Return#" = FinalResult>
```

As you can see, to create a dynamic variable in ColdFusion, you can simply wrap the variable name in quotes. In this case, if the user does not set a Return attribute and it defaults to RESULT, you can imagine the previous line as reading <CFSET Caller .RESULT = FinalResult>. Remember that this is not necessary, but it's a nice feature to add to your tag.

Now that you have built your custom tag, you can send any number of figures to the tag. Listing 31.6 is a modification of your previous template. This time you are sending five numbers to the custom tag.

LISTING 31.6: *multiplyfive.cfm*

```
<!---
    Name     : MultiplyFive
    Purpose  : Multiplies five numbers and returns the product.
    Created  : February 10, 2000
--->

<CFPARAM NAME="Form.Number1" DEFAULT=1>
<CFPARAM NAME="Form.Number2" DEFAULT=1>
<CFPARAM NAME="Form.Number3" DEFAULT=1>
<CFPARAM NAME="Form.Number4" DEFAULT=1>
<CFPARAM NAME="Form.Number5" DEFAULT=1>

<CFIF IsDefined("Form.Fieldnames")>
    <CF_MultiplyNew
NUMBERS="#Form.Number1#,#Form.Number2#,#Form.Number3#,#Form.Number4#,#Form.Number5#">
    <CFOUTPUT>The result of your multiplication of #Val(Form.Number1)#,
#Val(Form.Number2)#, #Val(Form.Number3)#, #Val(Form.Number4)#, and
#Val(Form.Number5)# is #RESULT#</CFOUTPUT>
    <P>
</CFIF>

<FORM ACTION="MultiplyFive.cfm" METHOD="POST">

<CFOUTPUT>
<TABLE BORDER=0>
<TR>
<TD>Number One</TD>
<TD><INPUT TYPE="text" NAME="Number1" SIZE=3 VALUE="#Val(Form.Number1)#"></TD>
</TR>
<TR>
<TD>Number Two</TD>
<TD><INPUT TYPE="text" NAME="Number2" SIZE=3 VALUE="#Val(Form.Number2)#"></TD>
</TR>
<TR>
<TD>Number Three</TD>
```

```
<TD><INPUT TYPE="text" NAME="Number3" SIZE=3 VALUE="#Val(Form.Number3)#"></TD>
</TR>
<TR>
<TD>Number Four</TD>
<TD><INPUT TYPE="text" NAME="Number4" SIZE=3 VALUE="#Val(Form.Number4)#"></TD>
</TR>
<TR>
<TD>Number Five</TD>
<TD><INPUT TYPE="text" NAME="Number5" SIZE=3 VALUE="#Val(Form.Number5)#"></TD>
</TR>
<TR>
<TD COLSPAN=2><INPUT TYPE="Submit" VALUE="Display Result"></TD>
</TR>
</TABLE>
</CFOUTPUT>

</FORM>
```

The modifications to your calling template are minor. You simply added extra form fields and CFPARAMs for the form fields. You then passed the new form fields to the MultiplyNew custom tag. This tag easily handled the new numbers and returned the results to the template.

Using Advanced Custom Tags

When ColdFusion Application Server 4 was released, Allaire added new functions and tags to the core language, but, more importantly, they added some interesting new features that directly concern custom tags. These include new ways of calling custom tags, new methods of tag interaction, and other features. We will discuss each of these features in detail.

Using End Tags

The first major enhancement to custom tags is the end tag. Let's take a look to get a better idea of what we mean by *end tag*. Imagine a custom tag that simply inserts a bold tag. Whenever the tag is run, it outputs <B>:

```
<CF_Bold>Text I want bold.
```

To create proper HTML, though, you need to send a </B> to end the bold layout. So let's modify the imaginary tag. Assume that if you send an attribute called Mode, and if it is set to End, the tag will output a </B> tag. Here is how the template may look:

```
<CF_Bold>Text I want to bold.<CF_Bold MODE="End">
```

This works all right but is not very pretty. As you know, HTML uses end tags to mark the end of a particular markup. From version 4, ColdFusion enables you to do the same thing. Imagine the following in your template:

```
<CF_Bold>Text I want to bold.</CF_Bold>
```

This looks just like HTML and is much easier to read. You can code this in ColdFusion 4 or 4.5 due to a new set of variables available to all custom tags. These variables, all prepended with ThisTag, give information about how the tag has been called. The ThisTag variables are:

- ThisTag.ExecutionMode
- ThisTag.HasEndTag
- ThisTag.GeneratedContent
- ThisTag.AssocAttribs

Let's build a real-life example based on a situation more likely to occur when building Web sites. Most Web sites have a site-wide look and feel to them. Perhaps all content is wrapped in a Verdana font that is sized a bit small. Normally you would build all your content in the following way:

```
<FONT FACE="Verdana" SIZE=-1>
The content of our Web site is extremely interesting. You will continue to visit
the site because every time you visit, my advertisers spend more money on me.
</FONT>
```

Even if the content of the site is dynamic, you will probably have something like this in your template:

```
<FONT FACE="Verdana" SIZE=-1>#IntroParagraph#</FONT>
```

As you can well imagine, a potential problem arises if the art department decides that Verdana is just so early '99 and the Web site really needs a Y2K look. Let's then build a custom tag that will handle the markup. You can then easily change the look of the site with little to no work on your part every time the art department throws a fit. Listing 31.7 shows the source code of your new custom tag, CF_Markup.

LISTING 31.7: *markup.cfm*

```
<!---
    Name    : Markup
    Purpose : Wraps content with markup.
    Created : February 10, 2000
--->

<CFSWITCH EXPRESSION="#ThisTag.ExecutionMode#">
```

```
<CFCASE VALUE="Start">
FONT FACE="Verdana" SIZE=-1>
   </CFCASE>

   <CFCASE VALUE="End">
      </FONT>
   </CFCASE>

</CFSWITCH>
```

Markup is a pretty simple tag. You use the new CFSWITCH tag to divide your tag into two cases: Depending on the value of ThisTag.ExecutionMode, which will *always* be available in ColdFusion 4 and 4.5, you either output the beginning font markup or the end. In Listing 31.8, you see the document that calls this tag.

LISTING 31.8: *markup_test.cfm*

```
<!---
    Name    : Markup_Test
    Purpose : Tests our markup custom tag.
    Created : February 2, 1999
--->

<CF_MarkUp>
The content of our Web site is extremely interesting.
You will continue to visit the site because every time
you visit, my advertisers spend more money on me.
</CF_MarkUp>
```

This template is simple. The CF_MarkUp custom tags wrap your content and insert your font tags. If the art department demands a change to the font of the site, you could do it in seconds. Figure 31.2 shows two browsers. The first is the output as defined by Listing 31.8. The browser on the right, though, shows the effect of modifying <FONT FACE="Verdana" SIZE=-1> in Markup.cfm to <FONT FACE="Arial" SIZE=-1 COLOR= "#ff0000">. In approximately two seconds, you can update the look of your text throughout the site. As you can imagine, this capability is incredibly powerful.

FIGURE 31.2
Text modified with the custom tag, CF_Markup

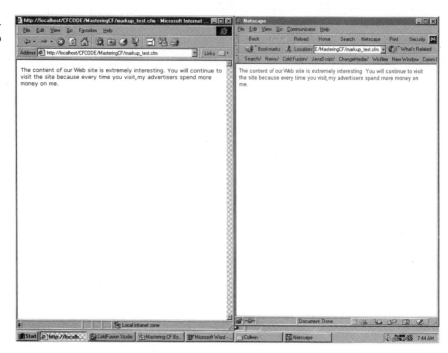

Using *ThisTag.GeneratedContent*

Another new feature of custom tags starting with ColdFusion 4 is the `ThisTag`
`.GeneratedContent` variable. As you might be able to guess, this tag gives you access
to the content that has been generated by the tag. This is useful, therefore, only where
`ThisTag.ExecutionMode` is End. If you think about it, no content has been created
when the tag starts, only when it ends. The same applies to tags without a closing end
tag. This handy feature enables you to make changes to whatever content exists
between the starting and end tags. You can quickly apply this to `Markup.cfm` to create
a simpler version. Listing 31.9 shows `Markup_2.cfm`, a new version of the tag showing
off the use of `ThisTag.GeneratedContent`.

LISTING 31.9: *markup_2.cfm*

```
<!---
    Name    : Markup_2
    Purpose : Wraps content with markup.
    Created : February 10, 2000
--->
```

```
<CFIF ThisTag.ExecutionMode IS "End">
    <CFSET ThisTag.GeneratedContent = "<FONT FACE=""Arial"" SIZE=-1><B>" &
ThisTag.GeneratedContent & "</B></FONT>">
    </CFIF>
```

MarkUp_2 is much simpler then Markup. In this tag, you need only a CFIF statement because you have only one clause. You only care if you are at the end of the tag. Inside the CFIF statement, you simply change the value ThisTag.GeneratedContent, adding a string for your font to the beginning and end of the string. After that is done, you have nothing more to do. To call this tag, replace the call to CF_MarkUp in Listing 31.8 to CF_MarkUp_2. You can also find an example on the CD. (The filename is markup_test_2.cfm.)

Even though this tag is simpler, you may have a slight problem. If the user of the tag forgets to end the tag, their content will never be marked up. This is not horrible, but ColdFusion programmers should do their best to make sure their tags are used correctly. This is a perfect time for the use of another of the ThisTag variables, HasEndTag. In this case, ThisTag.HasEndTag is a Boolean (a True or False value) that lets you know whether an end tag has been included. You can add a simple condition to your tag to add this test for an end tag. Listing 31.10 shows the modification.

LISTING 31.10: *Markup_3.cfm*

```
<!---
    Name    : Markup_3
    Purpose : Wraps content with markup.
    Created : February 10, 2000
--->

<CFIF ThisTag.ExecutionMode IS "Start" AND NOT ThisTag.HasEndTag>
    <CFOUTPUT><B>MarkUp_3 Error:</B> You must call this tag with an end tag as well.
Please be sure to insert a &lt;/CF_MarkUp_3&gt; tag.</CFOUTPUT>
    <CFABORT>
<CFELSEIF ThisTag.ExecutionMode IS "End">
    <CFSET ThisTag.GeneratedContent = "<FONT FACE=""Arial"" SIZE=-1><B>" &
ThisTag.GeneratedContent & "</B></FONT>">
    </CFIF>
```

The first change was to add another clause to your CFIF statement. As you can see, you add a check to see whether you are in the "Start" ExecutionMode and then you add a check to see whether ThisTag.HasEndTag is False. If it is, you output an error message to the user and halt the execution of any more code. The next clause is the same as it was in Markup_2.cfm. But notice the use of CFELSEIF, and not CFELSE. The reason is simple. The first clause does two checks: first, to make sure that ExecutionMode is

"Start", and second to see if you have forgotten the end tag. If this statement as a whole is False, ColdFusion will skip the contents of the clause. But you cannot use a simple CFELSE tag because you could still be in the "Start" ExecutionMode if you did not forget the end tag. Therefore, you use CFELSEIF and make sure you are at the end of your tag. Once again, you can find an example template calling this custom tag on the CD. (The filename is markup_test_3.cfm.)

Using *Intertag* Communication

The last ThisTag variable, AssocAttribs, brings up a whole new feature of custom tags in ColdFusion 4 and later versions. Not only can you use end tags in your development, but you can also wrap custom tags with other custom tags. By itself, this is not a big deal. But, by using AssocAttribs, the CFASSOCIATE tag, and the new ColdFusion functions GetBaseTagList and GetBaseTagData, you can create custom tags that can communicate with other tags that are wrapping them. If you have ever used HTML tables, you have already seen a good example of tags wrapping tags:

```
<TABLE BORDER=1>
    <TR>
    <TD>Data 1</TD>
    <TD>Data 2</TD>
    </TR>
</TABLE>
```

In this example, the TD tags are wrapped by TR tags, which are wrapped by TABLE tags. The TD tags communicate to the TR tags, which in turn communicate to the top-level TABLE tags. The browser uses this combination of tags to create a table.

Since ColdFusion 4, custom tags can now send data to their parent tags, or grab data from their parents, including a list of who their parents are. So, for example, say you had the following code:

```
<CF_GrandPa>
    <CF_Father>
        <CF_Son>
        Info
        </CF_Son>
    </CF_Father>
</CF_GrandPa>
```

The CF_Son tag would not only be able to share its data with CF_Father, but would also be able find out whether it has a Father and GrandPa, and if so, take the data from them.

As you can see already, these new features allow for very complex tag integration. Let's start simply and work with an example that shows child tags sending information to their parents. Listings 31.11, 31.12, and 31.13 contain the code you will be using for the examples.

LISTING 31.11: *tagcommunicationtest.cfm*

```
<!---
    Name     : TagCommunicationTest.cfm
    Purpose  : Tests intertag communication.
    Created  : February 13, 2000
--->

This text exists in the calling document. It is not within a tag.
<P>

<CF_Parent>

    <CF_Child NAME="Luke">
    <CF_Child NAME="Leia">

</CF_Parent>

<CF_Child>
```

LISTING 31.12: *parent.cfm*

```
<!---
    Name     : Parent.cfm
    Purpose  : Tests intertag communication.
    Created  : February 13, 2000
--->

<CFSWITCH EXPRESSION="#ThisTag.ExecutionMode#">

    <CFCASE VALUE="Start">
        <FONT COLOR="#ff0000">This is the beginning of the CF_Parent custom tag.</
FONT>
        <P>
    </CFCASE>

    <CFCASE VALUE="End">
        <FONT COLOR="#ff0000">This is the end of the CF_Parent custom tag.<BR>
        At this point I am going to output information about my children.<BR>
        <CFIF IsDefined("ThisTag.AssocAttribs")>
            <CFOUTPUT>I have a total of #ArrayLen(ThisTag.AssocAttribs)#
children.<P></CFOUTPUT>
            <CFLOOP INDEX="X" FROM=1 TO="#ArrayLen(ThisTag.AssocAttribs)#">
                <CFOUTPUT>
                    Child #X#'s name is #ThisTag.AssocAttribs[X].Name#<BR>
                    Child #X#'s age is #ThisTag.AssocAttribs[X].Age#
                    <P>
                </CFOUTPUT>
```

```
        </CFLOOP>
     <CFELSE>
        I have no children.
     </CFIF>
     </FONT>
     <P>
  </CFCASE>

</CFSWITCH>
```

LISTING 31.13: *child.cfm*

```
<!---
   Name     : Child.cfm
   Purpose : Tests intertag communication.
   Created : February 13, 2000
--->

<CFPARAM NAME="Attributes.Name" DEFAULT="Nameless">
<CFPARAM NAME="Attributes.Age" DEFAULT="#RandRange(1,100)#">

<CFOUTPUT><FONT COLOR="##008800">I am a Child tag and my name is #Attributes.NAME#.
I am #Attributes.AGE# years old.</FONT></CFOUTPUT>

<!--- Check to make sure I have a parent. --->
<CFSET Ancestors = GetBaseTagList()>
<CFIF ListFindNoCase(Ancestors,"CF_Parent")>
   <CFOUTPUT><FONT COLOR="##008800">I have a parent!</FONT><P></CFOUTPUT>
   <CFASSOCIATE BASETAG="CF_PARENT">
<CFELSE>
   <CFOUTPUT><FONT COLOR="##008800">I am an orphan. :(</FONT><P></CFOUTPUT>
</CFIF>
```

We have a lot to talk about here. So, let's start by looking at the output. Figure 31.3 shows the result of running TagCommunicationTest.cfm. To make things a bit easier to read, we used different color outputs to help you see when different tags are in action. A red color lets you know that Parent.cfm is in operation. A green color lets you know that Child.cfm is in action.

Begin by looking at Child.cfm, the innermost tag. You start with two CFPARAM statements. One creates a Name attribute for the child and the other creates a random age. Both these default values can be overwritten if you pass in a Name or Age attribute. In Listing 31.11 you specify a name for the first two times you call Child.cfm and no attributes for the last instance. Your next step is to output some basic information. This is mainly so you can see the tag in action on the Web page.

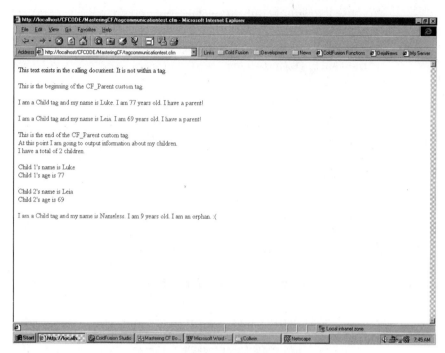

FIGURE 31.3
Using parent and child tags
in a template

The next line, `<CFSET Ancestors = GetBaseTagList()>`, is our first example of tag interaction. The function `GetBaseTagList` returns a list of tags that are wrapping your tag. It is important to remember two facts: First, if the tag is contained with a CFIF tag, the CFIF will show up on the list. Second, the tag itself will show up on the list as well. In this case, this shouldn't bother you. As you can see in the next line, `<CFIF ListFindNo-Case(Ancestors,"CF_Parent")>`, all you need to care about is whether you are wrapped by a tag called `CF_Parent`. If you are, you output a simple message stating so.

The important part is the line *after* the output. The `CFASSOCIATE` tag is what tells Cold-Fusion to associate your data with the parent tag. `CFASSOCIATE` takes two arguments: the name of the base tag to share data with, and `DATACOLLECTION`, which you did not use. In our example you tell ColdFusion to share your data with `CF_PARENT`. By default, `CFASSOCIATE` shares data with parent tags in a structure called `AssocAttribs`. You will see this structure when we talk about `Parent.cfm`. If you wanted to specify a name different from `AssocAttribs`, you would use `DATACOLLECTION` to specify the new name. Why would you use this? Well, imagine if the `CF_PARENT` tag contained both `CF_CHILD` tags and `CF_PET` tags. You would probably want the different tags to create different structures in `CF_PARENT`.

After the CFASSOCIATE tag, all you have left is the other clause of the CFIF statement. You use it to simply output the fact that you are not wrapped within a CF_PARENT tag. You could use it to throw an error condition. This would be useful for custom tags that are not meant to be used alone. For example, if you were building a ColdFusion version of the TABLE, TR, and TD tags, you may want to ensure that TD is never used outside of a TR or TABLE tag.

Now let's take a look at Parent.cfm in Listing 31.12. The tag begins with a CFSWITCH statement. Our custom tag is being used with an end tag, so you want to have a clause for both the beginning (ThisTag.ExecutionMode = "Start") and end (ThisTag.ExecutionMode = "End") of the tag. If the current execution mode is "Start", you simply output a message stating so. Again, this would not usually be necessary. In this case, it provides some visual feedback for the examples.

The next clause is important. In this case, you know you are at the end of the tag. To check whether you have children, you check to see if ThisTag.AssocAttribs has been defined. Remember that in Child.cfm, you used CFASSOCIATE to send data to your parent, and because you did not specify a DATACOLLECTION attribute, by default the server used the name AssocAttribs. If it is defined, then, you know you have children. Now, here comes a tricky part. Pay special attention to these two lines:

```
        <CFOUTPUT>I have a total of #ArrayLen(ThisTag.AssocAttribs)#
children.<P></CFOUTPUT>
        <CFLOOP INDEX="X" FROM=1 TO="#ArrayLen(ThisTag.AssocAttribs)#">
```

Remember when we said that information passed from a tag is saved in AssocAttribs? Well, if you think about it, this could cause a problem if AssocAttribs was a simple structure. In our example, you have two children. If AssocAttribs was only a structure, the second child's information would overwrite the first one's. To get around that, when data is passed from child tags, the server creates AssocAttribs as an *array* of structures. So, you can first check the length of that array to determine how many children you have. Then, you can then loop through each structure by using the CFLOOP command to run from the "1" to "#ArrayLen(ThisTag.AssocAttribs)#". Because you are dealing with an array, to output the information, you need to use both array and structure syntax. Here are the lines to output:

```
            Child #X#'s name is #ThisTag.AssocAttribs[X].Name#<BR>
            Child #X#'s age is #ThisTag.AssocAttribs[X].Age#
```

Notice the reference to ThisTag.AssocAttribs[X] (remember you are in a loop). This ensures that you get the proper array element. Because the value of the array element is a structure, you can use the dot notation to refer to the value of that particular key. You could have also written this as:

```
            Child #X#'s name is #ThisTag.AssocAttribs[X]["Name"]#<BR>
            Child #X#'s age is #ThisTag.AssocAttribs[X]["Age"]#
```

Both examples are valid, but the first one is a bit simpler to read. The CFLOOP displays information about each child, as you saw in Figure 31.3. If for some reason no child tags sent information back to the parent, we output a message stating so. This is present in the ELSE clause of our CFIF that checks to see if ThisTag.AssocAttribs is defined.

That wraps up our discussion of one-way tag communication. As a final note, examine how the child reacts when it is called outside of the parent. The last line of TagCommuni-cationTest.cfm has an example of this. As we said earlier, it may be a good idea for your tag code to prevent such things from happening. The choice is up to you!

Obtaining Information from a Parent Tag

You have examined how a child tag can share information with a parent tag. Let's take things a bit further and have the Child tag grab information from the Parent, again, *if and only if* the Child is being wrapped. By using the GetBaseTagData function, we will show how a child can not only send information to the parent, but also get information from the parent.

Listing 31.14 shows a modified Child.cfm that has the capability to get information from the parent tag. Listing 31.15 is a slight modification to Parent.cfm. You need information for the child to get, so this listing adds a new attribute, FamilyName. Finally, Listing 31.16 shows TagCommunicationTag_2.cfm, a simple modification. You point to the new names of your custom tags and send a FamilyName attribute to the parent.

LISTING 31.14: *child_2.cfm*

```
<!---
    Name     : Child_2.cfm
    Purpose  : Tests intertag communication.
    Created  : February 13, 2000
--->

<CFPARAM NAME="Attributes.Name" DEFAULT="Nameless">
<CFPARAM NAME="Attributes.Age" DEFAULT="#RandRange(1,100)#">

<CFOUTPUT><FONT COLOR="##008800">I am a Child tag and my name is #Attributes.NAME#.
I am #Attributes.AGE# years old.</FONT></CFOUTPUT>

<!--- Check to make sure I have a parent. --->
<CFSET Ancestors = GetBaseTagList()>
<CFIF ListFindNoCase(Ancestors,"CF_Parent_2")>
    <CFSET PARENT_DATA = GetBaseTagData("CF_PARENT_2")>
    <CFOUTPUT><FONT COLOR="##008800">I have a parent!<BR>Our Family Name is
#Parent_Data.FAMILYNAME#.</FONT><P></CFOUTPUT>
    <CFASSOCIATE BASETAG="CF_PARENT_2">
<CFELSE>
    <CFOUTPUT><FONT COLOR="##008800">I am an orphan. :(</FONT><P></CFOUTPUT>
</CFIF>
```

The important change in Listing 31.14 has been bolded. (We did not bold miscellaneous changes to reflect the new version of the code, that is, the _2 changes.) The added line, <CFSET PARENT_DATA = GetBaseTagData("CF_PARENT_2")>, grabs the data from the parent tag that has wrapped you. GetBaseTagData takes two attributes: the name of the tag (in this case, CF_PARENT_2) and a number that reflects what instance of the wrapping tag you want to use. In this case, the second attribute is not used. Let us explain that a bit further. Imagine this scenario:

```
<CF_Parent>
   <CF_Parent>
      <CF_Parent>
         <CF_Child>
      </CF_Parent>
   </CF_Parent>
      </CF_Parent>
```

In this example, the child has multiple parents. If you wanted to get the second CF_Parent (or third) wrapping the inner CF_Child, you could specify so in GetBase-TagData. To get the second level wrapper above you, you would use <CFSET PARENT_DATA = GetBaseTagData("CF_PARENT_2",2)>. This tells you to get the second CF_Parent layer above you. To grab the third layer, you would simply change 2 to 3.

When you called GetBaseTagData, you have the result saved into a structure called PARENT_DATA. At that point, you can access the information just as you would any other structure. The code "Our Family Name is #Parent_Data.FAMILYNAME#" displays the family name that is based on how CF_Parent is called. Now that you've seen the changes to the Child_2 custom tag, let's examine Listing 31.15.

LISTING 31.15: *parent_2.cfm*

```
<!---
   Name    : Parent_2.cfm
   Purpose : Tests intertag communication.
   Created : February 13, 2000
--->

<CFIF IsDefined("Attributes.FamilyName")>
   <CFSET FAMILYNAME = Attributes.FamilyName>
<CFELSE>
   <CFSET FAMILYNAME = "Camden">
</CFIF>

<CFSWITCH EXPRESSION="#ThisTag.ExecutionMode#">

   <CFCASE VALUE="Start">
      <FONT COLOR="#ff0000">
      This is the beginning of the CF_Parent_2 custom tag.<BR>
```

```
            <CFOUTPUT>Our family name is #FAMILYNAME#.</CFOUTPUT>
            </FONT>
            <P>
        </CFCASE>

        <CFCASE VALUE="End">
            <FONT COLOR="#ff0000">This is the end of the CF_Parent_2 custom tag.<BR>
            At this point I am going to output information about my children.<BR>
            <CFIF IsDefined("ThisTag.AssocAttribs")>
                <CFOUTPUT>I have a total of #ArrayLen(ThisTag.AssocAttribs)#
children.<P></CFOUTPUT>
                <CFLOOP INDEX="X" FROM=1 TO="#ArrayLen(ThisTag.AssocAttribs)#">
                    <CFOUTPUT>
                        Child #X#'s name is #ThisTag.AssocAttribs[X].Name#<BR>
                        Child #X#'s age is #ThisTag.AssocAttribs[X].Age#
                        <P>
                    </CFOUTPUT>
                </CFLOOP>
            <CFELSE>
                I have no children.
            </CFIF>
            </FONT>
            <P>
        </CFCASE>

    </CFSWITCH>
```

As before, we have bolded the relevant changes to this tag. In this case, you have a simple attribute check on top of the document. You assign a variable called FAMILYNAME that is equal to the attribute sent in. If you don't have one specified, you use a default family name value. The only other change is also minor. After you output the fact that you are in the beginning of the tag, you output the family name as well. Listing 31.16 shows the calling template using the new names and attributes.

LISTING 31.16: *tagcommunicationtest_2.cfm*

```
<!---
    Name    : TagCommunicationTest_2.cfm
    Purpose : Tests intertag communication.
    Created : February 13, 2000
--->

This text exists in the calling document. It is not within a tag.
<P>

<CF_Parent_2 FAMILYNAME="Skywalker">
```

```
<CF_Child_2 NAME="Luke">
<CF_Child_2 NAME="Leia">

</CF_Parent_2>

<CF_Child_2>
```

Once again, we have bolded only the significant change, which in this case is the passing of `FAMILYNAME="Skywalker"` to the `Parent_2` custom tag. Figure 31.4 shows the output using the new versions of the tags.

FIGURE 31.4
Calling a child tag from outside a parent tag creates orphans.

Using CFX Custom Tags

Because most developers will not create many CFX tags, we will not discuss that process in great detail. We will, however, discuss the tags in general and teach you how to install them on your Web servers.

The best way to think of CFX tags is as powerful, fast, custom tags. The main difference (and the reason for the additional power and speed) is that they are written in a compiled language such as C++, Delphi, or Java. Because they are written in a high-level language, however, it is not as easy to edit and debug them. For every change to a CFX tag, a new version must be compiled and saved to the server. Also, due to implementation differences, you may not be able to install a CFX if your Web site is on an ISP's server. Because they are based on the same set of ideas that custom tags are built on, CFXs can do everything a simple custom tag can do. This includes accepting any number of attributes and returning any set of results. (The only thing CFXs can't do is be used in an end-tag context; that is, you can't use `<CFX_Jedi>...</CFX_Jedi>`.)

Due to their speed, CFX tags can do things you would not want to do in a CFML custom tag. A perfect example of this is `CFX_Spell` by Ben Forta. `CFX_Spell` is a powerful custom tag that can easily and quickly add spell checking to your Web application. Although you could build a spell checker in standard CFML, it would take an extremely long time to look up words in a dictionary. By using C++ as the underlying code, the tag can run much more quickly.

Implementing CFX Tags

CFX tags are typically distributed as DLL files. These are files that your computer will use to execute the custom tag. But before your ColdFusion server can use them, you must register them within the ColdFusion Administrator. After logging into the Administrator with your password, select the CFX Tags menu option. This opens the Registered CFX Tags page, shown in Figure 31.5.

FIGURE 31.5
The Registered CFX
Tags page

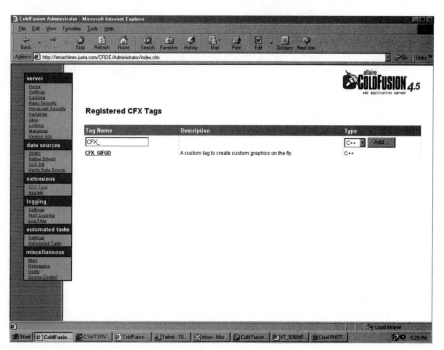

On the Registered CFX Tags page, you will see a list of all registered CFX tags. Each CFX tag has a link to a details page, and you will find an input box to enter the name of a new tag. Let's examine the details of one of the tags, CFX_GIFGD. Figure 31.6 shows the detailed information page for CFX_GIFGD.

FIGURE 31.6
The Edit CFX Tag page

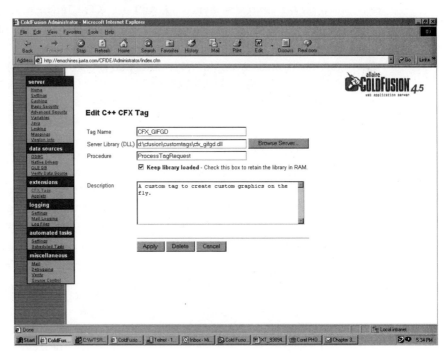

Here you can make some important changes to the tag. First, you can change the name of the tag, but if you do, you need to make sure that every ColdFusion template page that calls this CFX is updated. Second, you can change the location of the DLL file. This field is important because it tells the server where to find the DLL. If this is not set correctly, you will not be able to run the CFX tag.

The next field, Procedure, refers to the particular function within the CFX tag that will be called. This should always be ProcessTagRequest. The Keep Library Loaded setting determines whether the server should keep DLL in RAM. This could increase server performance if you think the CFX tag will be used a lot. The last field is a simple description field. It is there as a reminder in case you forget what a particular CFX tag does.

After you have registered a CFX tag, you can begin using it in your ColdFusion templates. Like standard custom tags, they are called via CFX_Name. For example, to call CFX_GIFDG, you would use:

```
<CFX_GIFGD OPTION1="Blah" OPTION2="Foo">
```

The attributes for a CFX tag will depend on the nature of the CFX tag. Check the documentation that came with the tag to learn the proper way to call them.

Using New ColdFusion 4.0.1 and 4.5 Features

Starting with ColdFusion 4.0.1, the server contains numerous new functions and features. One of the new features is the ATTRIBUTECOLLECTION attribute. You can use this attribute to send dynamic attributes to a custom tag. To implement this feature, you must first create a structure. Each element of the structure should be a name-value pair. For example:

```
<CFSET EXTRA_ATTRIBUTES = StructNew()>
<CFSET EXTRA_ATTRIBUTES.Age = 25>
<CFSET EXTRA_ATTRIBUTES.Sex = "Male">
<CFSET EXTRA_ATTRIBUTES.Job = "Jedi">
<CF_CreatePerson USERNAME="morpheus" ATTRIBUTECOLLECTION="#EXTRA_ATTRIBUTES#">
```

This is the same as:

```
<CF_CreatePerson USERNAME="morpheus" AGE=25 SEX="Male" JOB="Jedi">
```

You can also do the same with CFMODULE:

```
<CFMODULE TEMPLATE="createperson.cfm" USERNAME="morpheus"
ATTRIBUTECOLLECTION="#EXTRA_ATTRIBUTES#">
```

Within the custom tag, attributes passed via ATTRIBUTECOLLECTION are accessed the same as any standard attribute.

This new feature is useful if the arguments you need to send to a custom tag can change on a case-by-base basis. Using ATTRIBUTECOLLECTION and CFIF statements, you can dynamically create the attributes your tag needs depending on the situation.

WARNING   Don't forget! If you specify an attribute name within the ATTRIBUTECOLLECTION structure that *also* exists as an explicit attribute, the explicit value will take precedence over the one specified in the structure.

Because of this new feature, bear in mind that you now cannot use ATTRIBUTECOLLEC-TION as an attribute name for any other purpose aside from passing in a structure.

Where Do We Go from Here?

In the next chapter, you will look at ways to extend ColdFusion to use external objects. Specifically, you will consider the use of Component Object Model (COM) objects. In the Windows environment, COM objects provide an interface that programs can use to provide services to other programs, and through this environment ColdFusion templates can access a wide variety of capabilities not built into the ColdFusion environment.

chapter 32

Including External Objects

- Understanding the Types of External Objects

- Installing and Using COM Objects

- Installing and Using Java Objects

- Executing External Applications

Few people can look at ColdFusion's built-in functions and features and say, "Is that all?" However, power users will be happy to note that ColdFusion is extensible with a wide variety of tools and can even use pre-built components intended for other development environments, such as Microsoft's Active Server Pages or Visual Basic. Many capabilities that are not built into ColdFusion (such as Network News Transfer Protocol, image processing, faxing, and more) can be obtained at a relatively low cost from third-party components that are already available.

In this chapter we will discuss the types of external objects that ColdFusion can harness and provide details on using Component Object Model (COM) objects with Cold-Fusion. We will also discuss how to convert sample code that may come with a COM object into CFML.

In addition, we will look at a new feature of ColdFusion 4.5: the ability to execute external system programs using the CFEXECUTE tag.

Understanding the Types of External Objects

The four main types of external objects usable from ColdFusion are CFX tags, COM objects, Java objects and Common Object Request Broker Architecture (CORBA) objects.

CFX tags are written in C++ Java or Delphi using the ColdFusion Application Programming Interface (CFAPI). They enable you to move complicated logic into a compiled dynamic-link library (DLL) for better performance, and to access functionality not available within the CFML environment. CFX tags, after they are registered in the Cold-Fusion Administrator, can be used like any other ColdFusion tag. Chapter 31, "Building ColdFusion Custom Tags," has a more in-depth discussion of CFX tags.

CORBA objects are supported only in the Enterprise edition of ColdFusion Server. Similar to COM, the Common Object Request Broker Architecture is a specification for software objects to communicate with one another. CORBA is most prevalent on Unix systems, and hence will become a larger part of mainstream ColdFusion development as Allaire releases versions of ColdFusion for more Unix-based operating systems. CORBA objects can be used in ColdFusion via the CFOBJECT tag. A detailed discussion of CORBA usage in ColdFusion is beyond the scope of this book, but you can find more information on CORBA at the Object Management Group's Web site at www.omg.org.

Using an embedded Java Virtual Machine, any Java class on the class path specified by the ColdFusion Administrator can be loaded in a ColdFusion template as an external object. Java classes have the benefit of being cross-platform at the expense of the speed of compiled native code such as COM objects and C++-based CFX tags. However, a wide variety of Java classes is available on the Internet to satisfy most needs. At this time, only ColdFusion 4.5 and above for Windows NT and 2000, supports the use of external Java objects.

COM objects, like CFX tags, are pre-compiled for better performance and provide access to functionality unavailable inside ColdFusion. Unlike CFX tags, a great variety of COM objects created by third-party vendors is already available. The Component Object Model is Microsoft's standard for an interface that programs can use to provide services to one another without having to understand each other's internal structure or even be written in the same language. COM objects can be written in any number of languages, including Visual Basic, C++, Delphi, and Java. COM objects are also frequently used in Microsoft's Active Server Pages—a server-side scripting environment for Web pages similar to ColdFusion. One of the best things about Active Server Pages, as far as ColdFusion developers are concerned, is that ASP's relative lack of built-in functionality has engendered a burgeoning Web-related component industry to provide that missing functionality. Of course, with ColdFusion's COM support, you can take advantage of many of these objects in your ColdFusion applications.

Alternatives to CFX Tags

If you need functionality not provided in ColdFusion, before writing a CFX tag, it may be worthwhile to check ASP- and Visual Basic–related Web sites for a pre-built component that will do the job. Some good places to start looking include:

- www.15seconds.com
- www.activeserverpages.com
- www.ASPZone.com
- www.serverobjects.com

Installing and Using COM Objects

Most third-party COM objects come with installation instructions, but the same basic steps apply to nearly all of them:

1. Place the files for the object into a directory with the appropriate NT permissions.
2. Register the component by using regsvr32.exe.
3. Check the threading model.

Start by placing the file or files associated with the object into a directory you have chosen. These files are usually DLL or OCX files, but will occasionally be of another type, such as EXE. The directory the files are placed in is unimportant (unless the installation instructions for the object specify otherwise), except that anonymous users to your Web site need permission to execute the objects. For Microsoft Internet Information Server, this means that the NT account IUSR_*MachineName* must have read access to the file. Some developers like to have a central location for all components; others simply place them in the \WINNT\SYSTEM32 directory.

Next, it's time to register the component so that the operating system and ColdFusion know where to find it. Unless the instructions that came with the component specify differently, this is accomplished with regsvr32.exe. Simply open a command prompt, change to the directory where you have placed the files for this component, and type **regsvr32.exe filename**. You should receive a message that the component was successfully registered. If an error occurs, it's probably time to contact the component maker for support.

Most of the time you will not have to worry about the component's threading model; however, if ColdFusion seems to lock up on calling the component, the threading model is the first thing to check. To do this, you need Microsoft's OLE/COM Object Viewer. If you do not already have OLEView, as it is commonly known, the first step is to download it from www.microsoft.com/com/resource/oleview.asp.

You can use OLEView to view information about all the COM objects installed on your system. That's a lot of components in most cases, so it may take a little browsing before you find the one you're after. Once you have, select it and choose the Implementation tab in the main window. Look for the Threading Model list box. Possible values for the list box are Apartment, Both, Free, and None. If the current value is None, set it to Apartment; otherwise, try Apartment or Free. It may take some experimentation before you find the threading model for this component that works with ColdFusion. Note that you may need to restart ColdFusion or reboot the server after each threading-model change.

Using COM Objects with ColdFusion

Before you can start using your installed component in ColdFusion, you must create a reference to the object. This is done with the CFOBJECT tag. All you need to know about the object at this point is its program ID, or PROGID. This is generally included in the component's documentation but can also be found on the Registry tab in OLEView, or by searching for the filename in RegEdit. To pick a simple example, we'll use the ASPCrypt component. Since version 4.0, ColdFusion Server has included the built-in Encrypt and Decrypt functions that provide similar functionality to ASPCrypt, but this example makes it easy to understand the process involved in using COM Objects in ColdFusion.

ASPCrypt is a free component written for ASP. It duplicates exactly the functionality of the Unix Crypt() function. It performs one-way encryption and is useful for passwords stored in a database (you encrypt the password that the user types in, and compare it to the encrypted copy of their password stored in the database). You can download ASPCrypt from `http://www.serverobjects.com/products.htm#Aspcrypt`.

One difficulty that ColdFusion developers may encounter when using COM objects is that seldom will any of the sample code be written in CFML. The most common languages for any sample code included with a commercial component are ASP/VBScript and Visual Basic. As such, a certain amount of translation must be done on the part of the ColdFusion developer. Fortunately this is relatively simple, and once learned, will be almost identical for any component you choose to utilize.

Any language that utilizes COM objects must first create a reference to the object. In ASP sample code, the object creation might look like this:

```
Set objCrypt = Server.CreateObject("AspCrypt.Crypt")
```

The ColdFusion equivalent of this line, using CFOBJECT, is

```
<CFOBJECT TYPE="COM"
          NAME="objCrypt"
          CLASS="AspCrypt.Crypt"
          ACTION="Create">
```

The important thing to remember about CFOBJECT is that unlike most other ColdFusion tags, you need not include this tag in every place you wish to use the object it refers to. CFOBJECT creates a reference to an object that can be used any number of times throughout the remainder of the same template. In the case of ASPCrypt, if you wanted to loop through an array of strings and encrypt each string in the array, it would be counterproductive to include the CFOBJECT tag inside your loop. Doing so would re-create the object each time through the loop and potentially place a significant strain on the server. Instead, you would use CFOBJECT to create a reference to ASPCrypt outside of the loop and then use the object each time through the loop.

Starting with ColdFusion 4.5, you can optionally use the CreateObject function to create a COM object in a ColdFusion template. For instance, instead of the CFOBJECT tag we just used to create the objCrypt object, you could use the following tag:

```
<CFSET objCrypt = CreateObject("COM","AspCrypt.Crypt")>
```

You can also use the function inside a CFSCRIPT block:

```
<CFSCRIPT>
   objCrypt = CreateObject("COM","AspCrypt.Crypt");
</CFSCRIPT>
```

To use a COM object, you need to know about its properties and methods. A *property* is a variable internal to the COM object, whereas a *method* is a function of the COM object (in fact, this is exactly how ColdFusion treats them). Most objects come with documentation on properties and methods, but if you need to use an undocumented component, the View Type Information feature of OLEView can give you basic information on an object's properties and methods.

Often the simplest way to learn how to use a new object is to examine and modify the sample code that comes with it. Unfortunately, as we said earlier, chances are the sample code will not be in CFML. The task, then, becomes translation of the sample code to something that ColdFusion will accept. Sample code for ASPCrypt might look something like this:

```
<%
   Set objCrypt = Server.CreateObject("AspCrypt.Crypt")

   strSalt = "JM"
   strValue = "Widgets"

   Response.Write "The encrypted value is " &_
   objCrypt.Crypt(strSalt, strValue)

   Set objCrypt = Nothing
%>
```

How does this look when translated to standard CFML?

```
<CFOBJECT TYPE="COM"
          NAME="objCrypt"
          CLASS="AspCrypt.Crypt"
          ACTION="Create">

<CFSET strSalt = "JM">
<CFSET strValue = "Widgets">
<CFSET strEncrypted = objCrypt.Crypt(strSalt, strValue)>
<CFOUTPUT>The encrypted value is #strEncrypted#</CFOUTPUT>
```

An object's property is generally set with the CFSET tag, in the format <CFSET object.property = value>. Methods can be called in the same way, except that all methods must be followed by parentheses (even if the method takes no arguments) so that ColdFusion can tell them apart from a property.

Those of you who have already used COM objects in ColdFusion versions prior to version 4 know that it can quickly become cumbersome (at best) to use the CFSET syntax with a component that has many properties. If you know what we're talking about, ColdFusion 4's new CFSCRIPT tag (see Chapter 27, "ColdFusion Scripting") will quickly become your new best friend. Here's the same sample used in the preceding code, only this time using CFSCRIPT syntax:

```
<CFOBJECT TYPE="COM"
          NAME="objCrypt"
          CLASS="AspCrypt.Crypt"
          ACTION="Create">
```

```
<CFSCRIPT>
  strSalt = "JM";
  strValue = "Widgets";

  WriteOutput("The encrypted value is " &
  objCrypt.Crypt(strSalt, strValue));
</CFSCRIPT>
```

Notice the similarity of this listing to the original ASP sample code. This similarity greatly reduces the time required to convert a complex example to CFML. It's also easy to see how not having to use the CFSET tag every time you want to set a property or call a method can speed up your development time (not to mention reduce the chances of CFML-induced carpal tunnel syndrome).

Looping Over Collections

Some COM objects will return a set of related values as a single group, called a collection, rather than a series of individual values. To access or display these values, Allaire added the COLLECTION attribute to the CFLOOP tag. Here's how it's used:

```
<CFOBJECT TYPE="COM"
          NAME="objFileSys"
          CLASS="Scripting.FileSystemObject"
          ACTION="Create">

<CFSCRIPT>
  objFolder = objFileSys.GetFolder(GetDirectoryFromPath(GetTemplatePath()));
  objFiles = objFolder.Files;
</CFSCRIPT>

<CFLOOP COLLECTION="#objFiles#" ITEM="objFile">
   <CFOUTPUT>#objFile.Name#<BR></CFOUTPUT>
</CFLOOP>
```

Installing and Using Java Objects

Using the CFOBJECT tag or the CreateObject function you can load and use Java classes or Enterprise Java Beans in your ColdFusion templates. To do so, you first need to specify your Java class path using the ColdFusion Administrator. Your Java class path, which points to all directories containing Java class and the Java Beans that you want use in ColdFusion, should be specified in the Class Path field of the Java page of the ColdFusion Administrator as outlined in Chapter 35, "ColdFusion Administration." The path should be a series of directories separated by semi-colons.

Once the path is in place, you can place any Java Beans or classes you need to use in ColdFusion in one of the directories on the path you specified in order to be able to access them from your templates.

Using Java Objects with ColdFusion

Before you can start using a Java class or Bean in ColdFusion, you must create a reference to the object. This is done with the CFOBJECT tag. All you need to know about the object at this point is the name of class or the Java Bean. For instance, if you have a class named MyClass on the class path you specified in the ColdFusion Administrator, you can create a reference to the class with the CFOBJECT tag:

```
<CFOBJECT TYPE="Java"
          NAME="MyJava"
          CLASS="MyClass"
          ACTION="Create">
```

This creates a reference to MyClass named MyJava. You can then access the methods and properties of MyClass using this reference in ColdFusion:

```
<CFSET result = MyJava.init("test value")>
```

NOTE   Keep in mind that each Java class or Java Bean will have different properties and methods for interacting with it, and you should consult the documentation in order to learn how to use the class.

Starting with ColdFusion 4.5, you can optionally use the CreateObject function to create a Java object reference in a ColdFusion template. For instance, instead of the CFOBJECT tag we just used to create the objCrypt object, you could use the following tag:

```
<CFSET MyJava = CreateObject("Java","MyCrypt")>
```

Executing External Applications

Starting with ColdFusion 4.5, you can execute any process on the server machine in the same way that you can by issuing a command at the command prompt. To do this, you use the CFEXECUTE tag.

The CFEXECUTE tag takes the following basic form:

```
<CFEXECUTE NAME="<program to execute>"
    ARGUMENTS="<command arguments>"
    OUTPUTFILE="<output file>"
    TIMEOUT="<timeout in seconds>">
```

The NAME parameter is required. You need to specify the complete path to the command you want to execute, including any extensions such as .exe in Windows. The remaining parameters, that follow, are optional:

- ARGUMENTS: Specifies the arguments to pass to the command.
- OUTPUTFILE: Indicates the file where any output from the command should be stored. If you do not specify a file, any output will be included in the page generated by your ColdFusion template.
- TIMEOUT: Indicates in seconds how long ColdFusion will wait for the process to generate output. If you specify a value of 0, your template will invoke the specified command and then not wait for output, but proceed to execute the rest of the template. If you are not redirecting output to a file and you do not specify a timeout, then output will not be available in your template.

By way of example, if you want to include the Ethernet statistics output of the netstat command in Windows NT in your template, you would need to include the following tag block :

```
<CFEXECUTE NAME="C:\WinNT\System32\netstat.exe"
    ARGUMENTS="-e"
    TIMEOUT="1">
</CFEXECUTE>
```

Because the netstat.exe-e command returns output quite quickly, a timeout of one second is generally sufficient.

Where Do We Go from Here?

Now that you've got a basic understanding of how COM objects can be used in ColdFusion, you may want to see what pre-built components are out there. The Web sites listed earlier in the chapter are good places to start. In addition to component listings, these sites will provide links to other related repositories. Pick a component that you like and try it out. Maybe you'll want to write your own CFML custom tag to encapsulate the COM object's functionality in a more familiar tag-based syntax for other developers. If you're a VB programmer, ColdFusion's COM support provides an easy way to extend ColdFusion's functionality with your own custom components.

In the next chapter, you'll examine Web Distributed Data Exchange (WDDX), an exciting new technology introduced with ColdFusion 4 that has the potential to revolutionize the way that Web sites interact with one another, as well as to enhance the user's experience with your application.

chapter 33

WDDX

- Understanding WDDX

- Using WDDX with ColdFusion

- Using WDDX with ColdFusion and JavaScript

Web Distributed Data Exchange, or WDDX, is an open, standards-based XML technology introduced by Allaire for the easy transfer of complex data structures between disparate systems. It requires relatively little developer time on either end to implement and enables the creation of richly interactive applications that pull data from many sources. This chapter will introduce the basic concepts behind WDDX, discuss potential applications of this technology, and dissect examples of WDDX in action.

Understanding WDDX

WDDX is a dialect of Extensible Markup Language (XML). If you've been involved in software development at all in the past year, chances are you've heard of XML over and over with little in the way of practical examples.

At its most basic, XML is an extremely flexible markup language in which you get to define your own tags. Chemists have already agreed on a set of XML tags, known as Chemical Markup Language (CML), for marking up chemical formulas. Similar developments are underway for industries such as finance and insurance. All of these industry-specific markup languages provide ways to define data structures common to that industry, such as a financial transaction, an insurance claim, and the like.

NOTE   For more information on XML, please refer to *XML In Record Time* by Natanya Pitts (Sybex).

Where does WDDX fit in? WDDX is not aimed at a particular industry or type of data. Instead, it is a generic way of describing data structures that are common to programming languages. It allows a text-based and platform-neutral representation of not only simple data types such as numbers, strings, and dates, but more complex data types such as arrays, recordsets, and structures (or associative arrays, or collections, or dictionary objects, or whatever they're called in your language of choice).

If we had to choose one word to describe WDDX, it would be *pragmatic*. WDDX was created by people who needed a working solution, now. That's exactly what they got. WDDX is practical, does what it's designed to do, and works well now. Unless WDDX becomes the standard, it may eventually be made obsolete by an official standard in XML-based data interchange. Such a standard is probably a year of arguing away, and even when (and if) a standard is finalized, that will not cause WDDX to cease working. The version stamp built into WDDX will allow future versions to be compatible with such a standard. All that existing applications would require would be to update WDDX parsers.

The Purpose of WDDX

Now that you've got a fair idea of what WDDX consists of, the next question is: What is WDDX good for? The answer: Plenty!

Consider the following scenario: Your business partner has data on a client's Microsoft Active Server Pages–based Web site that you need to retrieve on a regular basis and incorporate into your company's ColdFusion-based intranet. At the same time, you need to make available to another business partner a subset of your intranet's data, consisting of some data from your business partner and some from you. The catch? This partner uses Perl.

Sound like a nightmare? Not really. WDDX modules already exist for COM/ASP and Perl. This means that the first business partner can write an ASP template that selects the appropriate data from their local database and then uses the WDDX COM object to convert their ADO recordset to WDDX and output it to the browser. Back in your ColdFusion-based intranet, you can use CFSCHEDULE to run a template that retrieves the partner's WDDX page with CFHTTP, parse it into a native ColdFusion recordset, and integrate it with your existing data. Making your data available to the second partner is even easier. Simply create a template that selects the data for this partner, and use CFWDDX to convert your ColdFusion recordset into a WDDX packet that is output to the browser. Your partner needs only to retrieve this page and use the existing Perl module for WDDX to convert it into a recordset useful in that environment.

In just a few easy steps, you've transferred complex data structures between different programming environments, running on different operating systems, in different parts of the country (or the world). There's even a name for this sort of distributed application—*Web syndication*. The idea is that as WDDX catches on, popular data repositories on the Web (weather, stock prices, the post office, etc.) will make their data available through a WDDX interface, so that programmers can integrate the data into their own custom applications with a minimum of forehead beating. As you'll see later, Allaire has already done this with the successor to their popular Tag Gallery, the Developer's Exchange. Another important benefit of WDDX in this situation is that none of the developers need to know the first thing about manually coding in XML. They don't have to invent tags, understand the XML Document Object Model, or validate against a Document Type Definition (DTD).

It may have occurred to you that one of the first requirements for jumping on the WDDX bandwagon is support in your programming environment for WDDX. Fortunately, support is widespread and growing almost daily. To take a page from the official WDDX FAQ, available at `http://www.wddx.org`:

"Currently, the WDDX SDK provides modules for JavaScript 1.*x*, ColdFusion 4, COM, Perl, and Java. Note that with the COM module WDDX can be used from within Active

Server Pages, Visual Basic, Delphi, Java, PowerBuilder, and C++. Allaire does not currently indicate they have plans to implement modules for other languages, but using the SDK, any developer will be able to build a module for any language platform that can support the core WDDX data types. Projects are reportedly underway to support WDDX with Python and PHP."

Does all this mean that you need to be working on a complicated distributed application to take advantage of WDDX? Not at all. Consider another scenario: Imagine that you need to write a small application in ColdFusion that requires a structured data store, but you don't want to tie yourself to a particular database. If you've got data in an existing relational database, simply select it with CFQUERY, convert it to WDDX with CFWDDX, and save it to a text file with CFFILE. If there's no pre-existing data, you can create your recordset on the fly before saving it as WDDX. More on this later.

A more realistic example might be this: You're working with a client who will not allow you to modify their pre-existing database, yet they want you to store additional data in the one they have. If there's a long text field, you can simply create a structure that contains the new data, and store that as a WDDX packet in the pre-existing text field. You could take this further in a new database and store all the data that does not need to be searched in a single field as WDDX, so that only one field need be retrieved when displaying the record details.

Using WDDX with ColdFusion

Let's examine some of these great-sounding ideas in terms of actual code. If you've been doing ColdFusion development for long, chances are you've visited Allaire's Developer's Exchange (http://www.allaire.com/developer/gallery.cfm). At the Developer's Exchange, ColdFusion developers can find custom tags and other CF-related utilities written by enthusiasts like themselves. True to its philosophy, Allaire has already created a WDDX interface to the data behind the Developer's Exchange. No official documentation exists on how to use this interface, but with a bit of experimentation, it's possible to provide your own interface to the Developer's Exchange, within the context of your own application.

To that end, let's examine a template that provides a simple interface to the live data coming from Allaire's Web site. The first step is to look at the raw data you're getting back so that you know what you're dealing with. The WDDX interface can be reached at http://www.allaire.com/developer/gallery/remote.cfm.

This template takes two URL parameters (that we know of). The first parameter, ID, specifies the ObjectID of the object you want to retrieve. In Developer's Exchange parlance, an object can be either one item (for example, a custom tag) or a category that contains a list of items. The second URL parameter is useful only for the item list and is called tags. The tags variable is passed directly to the MAXROWS parameter of a CFQUERY on Allaire's side. If you do not specify a tags variable, it defaults to a maximum of five records in any list returned.

Here's what the WDDX code for one particular object looks like:

```
<WDDXPACKET VERSION='1.0'><HEADER></HEADER><DATA><STRUCT><VAR
NAME='CF_VERSION'><STRING>4.5</STRING></VAR><VAR NAME='STATUS'><STRING>1</STRING></
VAR><VAR NAME='PAYMENT_TYPE'><STRING>Freeware</STRING></VAR><VAR
NAME='MODIFIED'><STRING>1999-02-08 12:33:36</STRING></VAR><VAR
NAME='ENCRYPTED'><STRING>No</STRING></VAR><VAR NAME='LICENSE_URL'><STRING> </
STRING></VAR><VAR NAME='EXAMPLE'><STRING> </STRING></VAR><VAR
NAME='DESCRIPTION'><STRING>This tag takes a string, and turns any URL's or e-mail
addresses within that string into HTML links.</STRING></VAR><VAR
NAME='PRICE'><STRING>0</STRING></VAR><VAR NAME='STUDIO_SUPPORT'><STRING>No</STRING></
VAR><VAR NAME='FILE_NAME'><STRING>ACF768.zip</STRING></VAR><VAR
NAME='TYPEID'><STRING>29</STRING></VAR><VAR NAME='OBJECTID'><STRING>8718</STRING></
VAR><VAR NAME='COMPANY'><STRING>Creative Internet Solutions</STRING></VAR><VAR
NAME='BROWSER_VERSION'><STRING> </STRING></VAR><VAR
NAME='EMAIL'><STRING>jmueller@creativeis.com</STRING></VAR><VAR
NAME='COOL_TAGS'><STRING>0</STRING></VAR><VAR NAME='URL'><STRING>http://
www.creativeis.com</STRING></VAR><VAR NAME='AUTHOR'><STRING>Joel Mueller</STRING></
VAR><VAR NAME='PARENT'><STRING>6804,6808</STRING></VAR><VAR
NAME='NAME'><STRING>URLFormat 2.0</STRING></VAR><VAR
NAME='TAG_TYPE'><STRING>Freeware</STRING></VAR><VAR NAME='DOWNLOAD_URL'><STRING> </
STRING></VAR><VAR NAME='DATE'><STRING>1999-02-02 13:15:52</STRING></VAR></STRUCT></
DATA></WDDXPACKET>
```

Without going into detail on the structure of a WDDX packet, you can see that this packet contains a structure (by the STRUCT tag), and that the structure contains a series of name-value pairs with information on the custom tag you requested. The item list consists of a recordset, with each row in the recordset containing its own WDDX packet that looks just like this one. That's right; you can nest WDDX packets inside of WDDX packets.

Before you can browse the entire exchange, you need a starting point. A quick trip to the HTML version of the Exchange reveals four main categories, each with its own object ID. Add some elementary HTML and you've got a page that displays these categories as self-referential links (the page links to itself) passing the object ID on the URL.

```
<B>Select Category</B>
<UL>
    <LI> <A HREF="exchange_browse.cfm?ID=6809">Applications</A>
```

```
    <LI> <A HREF="exchange_browse.cfm?ID=6800">Custom Tags</A>
    <LI> <A HREF="exchange_browse.cfm?ID=6781">Visual Tools</A>
    <LI> <A HREF="exchange_browse.cfm?ID=6792">Web Content</A>
</UL>
```

After you've got an ID, you need to retrieve the WDDX packet and parse it locally:

```
<CFIF IsDefined("URL.ID")>
    <CFTRY>
        <CFHTTP URL="http://www.allaire.com/developer/gallery/
remote.cfm?ID=#URL.ID#&tags=80"
            METHOD="GET"
            RESOLVEURL="false">
        <CFWDDX ACTION="WDDX2CFML"
            INPUT="#CFHTTP.FileContent#"
            OUTPUT="objWDDX">
        <CFCATCH TYPE="Any">
            <CFABORT SHOWERROR="<B>An error occurred </B><P>Try reducing the number of
tags retrieved in CFHTTP, or adding a RequestTimeOut parameter to the URL.</P>">
        </CFCATCH>
    </CFTRY>
</CFIF>
```

Here, the real world intrudes on our example. Because you're downloading data from a remote server, and because of the unreliable nature of the Internet, the possibility exists that your request will time out before you've downloaded the entire list of several hundred custom tags. For this reason, you can use the tags URL parameter to specify a maximum of 80 records returned. Because the server might still be down, use the CFTRY and CFCATCH tags to handle these potential errors. Also, there is a problem with the current implementation of this WDDX interface: There does not seem to be a way to specify a starting row to the remote.cfm template. Because you cannot download the entire list at once and still achieve acceptable response times, you can't ever see the entire list of custom tags. This is an unpublished interface, likely still undergoing revisions, so there may be a way to specify a starting record (or will be soon), but in any case, this is something to keep in mind when designing your implementations.

Now that you know all the problems you're dealing with in this block of code, what are you actually doing here? First, you're using CFHTTP to retrieve remote.cfm, passing the ObjectID you would like on the URL. Second, you're passing the results of the CFHTTP tag to CFWDDX, with the command to convert from WDDX to CFML, and putting the resulting object into the objStruct variable. The next step is to display the data you have. Remember, there are two types of data: an individual item (encoded as a structure) and a list of items (encoded as a recordset containing WDDX packets). A call to the IsStruct function will tell you which type you're dealing with. First, the list of items:

```
<CFIF Not IsStruct(objWDDX)>
    <!--- Loop through recordset and display all object names --->
```

```
<B>Select an item:</B>
<UL>
<CFOUTPUT QUERY="objWDDX">
    <CFWDDX ACTION="WDDX2CFML"
            INPUT="#WDDXOBJECT#"
            OUTPUT="objStruct">
    <LI> <A
HREF="exchange_browse.cfm?ID=#objStruct["OBJECTID"]#">#objStruct["NAME"]#</A>
    </CFOUTPUT>
    </UL>

    ...
```

Because each row of the recordset contains a WDDX packet in the WDDXOBJECT field, you must make a call to CFWDDX each time through the loop to convert the current row into a structure that you can use. The remainder of the code is simply writing this data to the browser. If, however, you're original WDDX object is a structure, as follows:

```
<CFELSE>
    <!--- Display item detail --->
    <CFOUTPUT><H3>#objWDDX["NAME"]#</H3></CFOUTPUT>
    <CFLOOP COLLECTION="#objWDDX#" ITEM="value">
        <CFOUTPUT><B>#value#:</B> #objWDDX[value]#<BR></CFOUTPUT>
    </CFLOOP>
</CFIF>
```

You can simply output the value of the structure. This example has minimal formatting applied; in a real application, you could do however much or little formatting is appropriate.

Putting It All Together

Listing 33.1 shows exchange_browse.cfm in its entirety.

Listing 33.1: *exchange_browse.cfm*

```
<CFIF IsDefined("URL.ID")>
    <!---
        The tags parameter is passed directly to a MAXROWS
        parameter in a CFQUERY on the other end.  Here it is
        limited to 80 records to avoid timeouts.  There does
        not seem to be a way to specify a starting
        row to Allaire's remote.cfm template, or we could
        page through the records.
    --->
    <CFTRY>
        <CFHTTP URL="http://www.allaire.com/developer/gallery/
remote.cfm?ID=#URL.ID#&tags=80"
            METHOD="GET"
```

```
                 RESOLVEURL="false">
          <CFWDDX ACTION="WDDX2CFML"
               INPUT="#CFHTTP.FileContent#"
               OUTPUT="objWDDX">
          <CFCATCH TYPE="Any">
               <CFABORT SHOWERROR="<B> An error occurred </B><P>Try reducing the number
of tags retrieved in CFHTTP, or adding a RequestTimeOut parameter to the URL.</P>">
          </CFCATCH>
       </CFTRY>
    </CFIF>

    <!DOCTYPE HTML PUBLIC "-//W3C//DTD HTML 4.0 Transitional//EN">

    <HTML>
    <HEAD>
       <TITLE>Browse Allaire Developer Exchange</TITLE>
    <STYLE TYPE="text/css">
    body {
       font-family : 'Arial', 'Helvetica', 'sans-serif';
       font-size : 10pt;
    }
    </STYLE>
    <SCRIPT LANGUAGE="JavaScript" TYPE="text/javascript">
    <!--
       function toggleSource() {
          var WDDXSource = document.all.WDDXSource;
          WDDXSource.style.visibility = (WDDXSource.style.visibility == "hidden") ?
"visible" : "hidden";
       }
    //-->
    </SCRIPT>
    </HEAD>

    <BODY BGCOLOR="#FFFFFF">

    <CFIF Not IsDefined("URL.ID")>
    <P>This template demonstrates putting your own face on data from another site.  In
this case,
       we're retrieving WDDX data from the <A HREF="http://www.allaire.com/developer/
gallery">Allaire Developer's Exchange</A>, and displaying it within the
       context of our own pages.  If it seems slow, it's because for each request, the CF
Server must
       retrieve data from the Allaire Web site.  For a real application, you might want to
keep a copy
       of the remote data in a local database for better response times to your users.</P>

    <B>Select Category</B>
    <UL>
```

```
    <LI> <A HREF="exchange_browse.cfm?ID=6809">Applications</A>
    <LI> <A HREF="exchange_browse.cfm?ID=6800">Custom Tags</A>
    <LI> <A HREF="exchange_browse.cfm?ID=6781">Visual Tools</A>
    <LI> <A HREF="exchange_browse.cfm?ID=6792">Web Content</A>
  </UL>
  <CFELSE>
    <CFIF Not IsStruct(objWDDX)>
      <!--- Loop through recordset and display all object names --->
      <B>Select an item:</B>
      <UL>
      <CFOUTPUT QUERY="objWDDX">
        <CFWDDX ACTION="WDDX2CFML"
                INPUT="#WDDXOBJECT#"
                OUTPUT="objStruct">
        <LI> <A
HREF="exchange_browse.cfm?ID=#objStruct["OBJECTID"]#">#objStruct["NAME"]#</A>
      </CFOUTPUT>
      </UL>
    <CFELSE>
      <!--- Display item detail --->
      <CFOUTPUT><H3>#objWDDX["NAME"]#</H3></CFOUTPUT>
      <CFLOOP COLLECTION="#objWDDX#" ITEM="value">
        <CFOUTPUT><B>#value#:</B> #objWDDX[value]#<BR></CFOUTPUT>
      </CFLOOP>
    </CFIF>

    <P><SPAN ID="sourceClick" STYLE="font-weight: bold; cursor: hand"
onClick="toggleSource()">Click here to view WDDX source.</SPAN></P>
    <DIV ID="WDDXSource" STYLE="visibility: hidden">
    <CFOUTPUT>#HTMLEditFormat(Trim(CFHTTP.FileContent))#</CFOUTPUT>
    </DIV>
  </CFIF>

  </BODY>
  </HTML>
```

Using WDDX with ColdFusion and JavaScript

Now that you've seen an example of server-to-server communication using WDDX, let's see how WDDX can be used in server-to-browser communication to enhance the user experience. As an added bonus, you'll use WDDX to replace a server-side database that might otherwise have been implemented in MS Access.

We will use a simple example to highlight how to use WDDX with ColdFusion and JavaScript. This example will retrieve and display random quotes from a hidden frame using WDDX, effectively eliminating the need for a database of quotes on the server.

The Setup

This random quotation example uses JavaScript and DHTML to retrieve random quotes from a hidden frame. It requires Internet Explorer 4 or above, but could be written to accommodate Netscape 4 and above with some extra work. At no time is the entire database of more than 1500 quotes downloaded to the browser, but the quotes are updated at a specified interval without ever reloading the current page. The quotes are not in a database, but in a text file that contains a WDDX recordset. This is a relatively simple demonstration of behind-the-scenes data retrieval, yet this technique is potentially useful in a number of areas, including form validation and multi-step wizards utilizing DHMTL.

The Code

This application consists of three templates: `quotes.cfm`, `quote_toolbox.cfm`, and `quotes.cfm`. `Quotes.cfm` is the page that displays the quotes. It contains almost all the JavaScript code required to retrieve the quote from a hidden frame and display it to the user. `Quote_toolbox.cfm` handles all the WDDX parsing, selects a random quote, and outputs it to the browser as a JavaScript object that is read by `quotes.cfm`. Finally, `all_quotes.cfm` displays all the quotes at once, and enables the user to edit, delete, and add new quotes by way of a `CFGRID` Java applet. The quotes themselves are stored in the file `quotes.wddx`, which is included on the CD-ROM.

Let's begin with Listing 33.2, which shows `quote_toolbox.cfm`. Throughout this section, code lines are numbered for reference purposes.

Listing 33.2: *quote_toolbox.cfm*

```
 1: <CFSETTING ENABLECFOUTPUTONLY="Yes" SHOWDEBUGOUTPUT="No">
 2: <CFIF Not IsDefined("Application.Quotes")>
 3:    <!---
 4:        Read WDDX data from a file,
 5:        parse it into a recordset, and cache
 6:        the recordset in an application variable.
 7:
 8:        Be aware that this takes up slightly more
 9:        than 100K of RAM on the server.
10:    --->
11:    <CFLOCK TIMEOUT="5" THROWONTIMEOUT="Yes" NAME="QuotesVar">
12:        <CFFILE ACTION="READ"
13:            FILE="#GetDirectoryFromPath(GetTemplatePath())#quotes.wddx"
14:            VARIABLE="strWDDX">
15:        <CFWDDX ACTION="WDDX2CFML" INPUT="#strWDDX#" OUTPUT="Quotes">
16:        <CFSET Application.Quotes = Quotes>
17:    </CFLOCK>
```

```
18: <CFELSE>
19:    <!---
20:        Copy the cached recordset to a local variable.
21:    --->
22:    <CFSET Quotes = Application.Quotes>
23: </CFIF>

24: <CFSCRIPT>
25:    // seed the random number generator
26:    Randomize(GetTickCount());
27:    // pick a random record and load it into a structure
28:    curRow = RandRange(1, Quotes.RecordCount);
29:    structQuote = StructNew();
30:    StructInsert(structQuote, "Quote", Quotes.Quote[curRow]);
31:    StructInsert(structQuote, "Attribution", Quotes.Attribution[curRow]);
32: </CFSCRIPT>

33: <CFSETTING EnableCFOutputOnly="No">

34: <!DOCTYPE HTML PUBLIC "-//W3C//DTD HTML 4.0 Transitional//EN">

35: <HTML>
36: <HEAD>
37:    <TITLE>Quotes Toolbox</TITLE>
39: <SCRIPT LANGUAGE="JavaScript" TYPE="text/javascript">
40: <!--
41:    window.onLoad = init();

42:    function init() {
43:       // notify parent window that we're done loading
44:       parent.bLoaded = true;
45:    }

46:    // convert CFML structure to JavaScript object
47:    <CFWDDX ACTION="CFML2JS" INPUT="#structQuote#" TOPLEVELVARIABLE="objQuote">
48: //-->
49: </SCRIPT>
50: </HEAD>
51: <BODY>
52: </BODY>
53: </HTML>
```

In the first block of code (lines 2 to 23), you're reading the WDDX recordset from a text file (quotes.wddx), parsing it into a CFML recordset, and storing that recordset in an application variable for future reference.

Note the use of the CFLOCK tag to prevent potential trouble caused by concurrent writes to the Quotes application variable. This technique provides better performance than reading in the text file and parsing it once every page request. It could, however, become impractical with much larger recordsets because of the amount of memory consumed by storing the recordset in an application variable.

The next step is to select a random row from this recordset in lines 24 to 32. First, you seed the random number generator using the always-changing number returned by GetTickCount. Then, using the RandRange function, you select a random row number. Creating a new structure, you insert the quote and attribution from the current row in your recordset into the structure.

Now that you have your quote, you need only output it as a JavaScript object in lines 39 to 49. The init function is a simple means of notifying any scripts running in quotes.cfm that this page is finished loading and the new quote is available for reading. This will be discussed further when you look at quotes.cfm.

One of the lesser-known features of the CFWDDX tag is the capability to convert CFML objects to JavaScript code that, when run in the browser, creates JavaScript objects that behave the same as their CFML equivalents. Although this does not directly use WDDX, it does take advantage of the objects provided in the JavaScript WDDX module, wddx.js. In the following code, you're simply taking the CFML structure created earlier and outputting it as JavaScript code, which looks something like this:

```
objQuote=new Object();
objQuote.attribution="Steven Wright";
objQuote.quote="If you're not part of the solution, you're part of the
precipitate.";
```

Next, consider quotes.cfm, which displays the quotes and loads new ones. The template is shown in Listing 33.3.

Listing 33.3: *quotes.cfm*

```
1: <CFSETTING ENABLECFOUTPUTONLY="No" SHOWDEBUGOUTPUT="No">

2: <!DOCTYPE HTML PUBLIC "-//W3C//DTD HTML 4.0 Transitional//EN">

3: <HTML>
4: <HEAD>
5:    <TITLE>Quotes WDDX Demo</TITLE>
6: <STYLE TYPE="text/css">
7: body {
8:    font-family : 'Arial', 'Helvetica', 'sans-serif';
9:    font-size : 10pt;
10: }
11: .hotkey {
12:    text-decoration: underline;
13: }
```

```
14: </STYLE>
15: <SCRIPT LANGUAGE="JavaScript" TYPE="text/javascript">
16: <!--
17:     // this variable is manipulated
18:     // by the toolbox page to notify
19:     // us when it is finished loading
20:     var bLoaded = false;

21:     var toolboxURL = "quote_toolbox.cfm";
22:     var toolbox;
23:     var quoteRefresh = 20;
24:     var curRefresh = quoteRefresh;

25:     window.onLoad = init();

26:     function init() {
27:         afterLoad("toolbox = document.frames[0]; timeRefresh()");
28:     }

29:     function afterLoad(strCmd) {
30:         // This function will wait until the bLoaded
31:         // variable is true, then execute the specified
32:         // command.
33:         if (!bLoaded) {
34:             window.setTimeout("afterLoad('" + strCmd + "')", 100);
35:         } else {
36:             eval(strCmd);
37:         }
38:     }

39:     function timeRefresh() {
40:         // This function updates the display of the "New Quote" button
41:         // and decrements the counter
42:         var refreshButton = document.all("btnReload");
43:         refreshButton.innerHTML = "<SPAN CLASS=\"hotkey\">N</SPAN>ew Quote in: "
+ curRefresh
44:         if (curRefresh == quoteRefresh) {
45:             getQuote();
46:         }
47:         curRefresh = ((curRefresh - 1 == 0) ? quoteRefresh : curRefresh - 1);
48:         setTimeout("timeRefresh()", 1000);
49:     }

50:     function getQuote() {
52:         // This function reloads the toolbox frame with a unique URL
53:         // to ensure it is not cached.  After the frame is done reloading,
54:         // this function will call the displayQuote() function.
55:         var refreshButton = document.all("btnReload");
```

```
56:          refreshButton.innerHTML = "Refreshing...";
57:          bLoaded = false;
58:          toolbox.location.href = toolboxURL + "?un=" + new Date().getTime();
59:          curRefresh = quoteRefresh - 1;
60:          afterLoad("displayQuote()");
61:      }

62:      function displayQuote() {
63:          // This function will read the current quote from the toolbox frame
64:          // and output it to the page.
65:          var strOutput = new String();
66:          var quoteBox = document.all.quoteBox;
67:          var refreshButton = document.all("btnReload");
68:          strOutput = toolbox.objQuote.quote
69:          if (toolbox.objQuote.attribution.length > 0) {
70:              strOutput += "<BR><DIV ALIGN=\"right\">&#151; " +
toolbox.objQuote.attribution + "</DIV>";
71:          }
72:          quoteBox.style.textAlign = "left";
73:          quoteBox.innerHTML = strOutput;
74:          refreshButton.innerHTML = "<SPAN CLASS=\"hotkey\">N</SPAN>ew Quote";
75:      }
76: //-->
77: </SCRIPT>
78: </HEAD>

79: <BODY BGCOLOR="#FFFFFF">

80: <H3>Quotes WDDX Demo</H3>

81: <P>This page uses JavaScript and DHTML to retrieve random quotes from a hidden
frame.
82: It requires Internet Explorer 4 or above, but could be written to accommodate
Netscape
83: 4 and above with some extra work.  At no time is the entire database of 1500+
84: quotes downloaded to the browser, but the quotes are updated at a specified
interval without
85: ever reloading the current page.  The quotes themselves are not in a database,
but a text file that
86: contains a WDDX recordset.  This is a relatively simple demonstration of
behind-the-scenes
87: data retrieval, yet this technique has the potential to be very useful in a
number of areas, including
88: form validation and multi-step wizards utilizing DHMTL.</P>

89: <H4 ALIGN="center">Current Quote:</H4>
90: <DIV ALIGN="CENTER">
```

```
 91: <DIV ID="quoteBox" STYLE="width: 50%; border-style: solid; border-width: 1px;
padding: 3px; text-align: center;">Loading...</DIV>
 92: </DIV>
 93: <BR>
 94: <DIV ALIGN="center">
 95: <BUTTON ID="btnReload" NAME="btnReload" ACCESSKEY="n" onClick="getQuote()"
STYLE="width:125px"><SPAN CLASS="hotkey">N</SPAN>ew Quote</BUTTON>
 96: </DIV>

 97: <P><A HREF="all_quotes.cfm">Manage Quotes</A></P>

 98: <CFOUTPUT>
 99: <!--- Ensure the toolbox frame is not cached by inserting a unique value on the
URL --->
100: <IFRAME SRC="quote_toolbox.cfm?un=#GetTickCount()#"
101:         NAME="toolbox"
102:         WIDTH="0"
103:         HEIGHT="0"
104:         MARGINWIDTH="0"
105:         MARGINHEIGHT="0"
106:         HSPACE="0"
107:         VSPACE="0"
108:         SCROLLING="no"
109:         FRAMEBORDER="0"
110:         STYLE="visibility: hidden">This demo requires IE 4 and above.</IFRAME>
111: </CFOUTPUT>
112: </BODY>
113: </HTML>
```

First, you create a hidden frame with quote_toolbox.cfm as its source, in Lines 98 to 111. Note that if you were targeting Netscape Navigator with this sample, you would be unable to use the IFRAME tag, but instead would have to make quotes.cfm and quote_toolbox.cfm part of the same frameset.

The remainder of the important code on this page is all client-side JavaScript. First, you set up the global variables and the page initialization in lines 20 to 28. The first variable that you set is the bLoaded variable; you set it equal to false. Whenever the quote_toolbox.cfm page finishes loading, it sets this variable to true so that the scripts on this page know that it's okay to access objects in the toolbox frame. You set a variable with the number of seconds between quote reloads.

The init function uses the afterLoad function in lines 27 to 29 to wait until the toolbox frame has finished loading before it sets up a global reference to this frame and kicks off the display-quote, load-new-quote sequence. The afterLoad command simply checks whether bLoaded is true; if not, it waits 100 milliseconds and calls itself again. If bLoaded is true, afterLoad executes the command passed in as its argument.

The timeRefresh function in lines 39 to 49 updates the display of the New Quote button every second. When the countdown reaches zero, it calls the getQuote function, which is in lines 50 to 61. The getQuote function reloads the toolbox frame with a unique value on the URL to ensure that the page is not cached. It uses the afterLoad function to call displayQuote (lines 62 to 75) after the toolbox frame is fully loaded. The displayQuote function reads the current quote object from the toolbox frame and inserts it into the quoteBox DIV.

The all_quotes.cfm template began life as a quick and dirty way of displaying all the quotes in the database at once so that people could more easily browse through them. As with all potentially interesting and/or challenging techniques, however, it demanded to be made into something more, and eventually ballooned into a full-featured quote management tool. It uses the CFGRID Java applet to display the quotes and to allow adding, editing, and deleting of said quotes.

Let's take a closer look, because this template is the first in this sample to modify the WDDX data, and along the way you'll discover a limitation in the ColdFusion implementation of recordsets, as well as a way to work around this limitation. See Listing 33.4 for the complete template. Explanations of each part will follow. This source code also uses the WDDX file (quotes.wddx) that contains all the quotes. This file is on the CD-ROM.

Listing 33.4: *all_quotes.cfm*

```
1: <CFSETTING ENABLECFOUTPUTONLY="Yes" SHOWDEBUGOUTPUT="No">
2: <CFIF Not IsDefined("Application.Quotes")>
3:     <!---
4:         Read WDDX data from a file,
5:         parse it into a recordset, and cache
6:         the recordset in an application variable.
7:
8:         Be aware that this takes up slightly more
9:         than 100K of RAM on the server.
10:        --->
11:    <CFLOCK TIMEOUT="5" THROWONTIMEOUT="Yes" NAME="QuotesVar">
12:        <CFFILE ACTION="READ"
13:            FILE="#GetDirectoryFromPath(GetTemplatePath())#quotes.wddx"
14:            VARIABLE="strWDDX">
15:        <CFWDDX ACTION="WDDX2CFML" INPUT="#strWDDX#" OUTPUT="Quotes">
16:        <CFSET Application.Quotes = Quotes>
17:    </CFLOCK>
18: <CFELSE>
19:    <!---
20:        Copy the cached recordset to a local variable.
21:        --->
22:    <CFSET Quotes = Application.Quotes>
23: </CFIF>
```

```
24: <CFIF IsDefined("Form.save")>
25: <CFLOCK TIMEOUT="5" THROWONTIMEOUT="Yes" NAME="QuotesVar">
26: <CFSCRIPT>
27:     RedoIDs = false;
28:     deleteList = "";
29:     saveWDDX = false;
30:     if (ArrayLen(Form.QuoteGrid.RowStatus.Action) GT 0) {
31:         for (i=1; i LTE ArrayLen(Form.QuoteGrid.RowStatus.Action); i=i+1) {
32:             switch (Form.QuoteGrid.RowStatus.Action[i]) {
33:                 case "I": {
34:                     // Insert a new row, and make the Quote ID one greater
35:                     // than the previous Quote ID.  Note that this technique
36:                     // should not be used in place of a database in production
37:                     // systems, as concurrent users could quickly make your life
38:                     // very difficult with this scheme.
39:                     QueryAddRow(Quotes);
40:                     QuerySetCell(Quotes, "Quote_ID",
Quotes.Quote_ID[Quotes.RecordCount - 1] + 1);
41:                     QuerySetCell(Quotes, "Quote", Form.QuoteGrid.Quote[i]);
42:                     QuerySetCell(Quotes, "Attribution",
Form.QuoteGrid.Attribution[i]);
43:                     saveWDDX = true;
44:                     break;
45:                 }
46:                 case "U": {
47:                     // The Quote ID is equal to the row number, so we can look up
48:                     // a particular row to modify without scanning the entire
recordset.
49:                     QuerySetCell(Quotes, "Quote", Form.QuoteGrid.Quote[i],
Form.QuoteGrid.Original.Quote_ID[i]);
50:                     QuerySetCell(Quotes, "Attribution",
Form.QuoteGrid.Attribution[i], Form.QuoteGrid.Original.Quote_ID[i]);
51:                     saveWDDX = true;
52:                     break;
53:                 }
54:                 case "D": {
55:                     // CF has no function to delete a row from a recordset.
56:                     // Assemble a list of rows to be deleted, and build a new
57:                     // recordset without them later.
58:                     deleteList = ListAppend(deleteList,
Form.QuoteGrid.Original.Quote_ID[i]);
59:                     RedoIDs = true;
60:                     saveWDDX = true;
61:                     break;
62:                 }
63:             }
64:         }
65:
```

```
66:        if (Len(deleteList) GT 0) {
67:            // build a new recordset without the rows in the delete-list
68:            newQuotes = QueryNew("Quote_ID,Quote,Attribution");
69:            for (i=1; i LTE Quotes.RecordCount; i=i+1) {
70:                if (ListFind(deleteList, Quotes.Quote_ID[i]) EQ 0) {
71:                    QueryAddRow(newQuotes);
72:                    QuerySetCell(newQuotes, "Quote_ID", Quotes.Quote_ID[i]);
73:                    QuerySetCell(newQuotes, "Quote", Quotes.Quote[i]);
74:                    QuerySetCell(newQuotes, "Attribution", Quotes.Attribution[i]);
75:                }
76:            }
77:            Quotes = newQuotes;
78:            newQuotes = "";
79:        }

80:        if (RedoIDs) {
81:            // If we've deleted one or more rows,
82:            // we need to reset all the Quote ID's so
83:            // they once again match their row number.
84:            for (i=1; i LTE Quotes.RecordCount; i=i+1) {
85:                QuerySetCell(Quotes, "Quote_ID", i, i);
86:            }
87:        }
88:        Application.Quotes = Quotes;
89:    }
90: </CFSCRIPT>
91: <CFIF saveWDDX>
92:     <CFWDDX ACTION="CFML2WDDX" INPUT="#Quotes#" OUTPUT="strWDDX">
93:     <CFFILE ACTION="WRITE"
94:         FILE="#GetDirectoryFromPath(GetTemplatePath())#quotes.wddx"
95:         OUTPUT="#strWDDX#"
96:         ADDNEWLINE="No">
97: </CFIF>
98: </CFLOCK>
99: </CFIF>

100: <CFSETTING EnableCFOutputOnly="No">

101: <!DOCTYPE HTML PUBLIC "-//W3C//DTD HTML 4.0 Transitional//EN">

102: <HTML>
103: <HEAD>
104:    <TITLE>All Quotes</TITLE>
105: <STYLE TYPE="text/css">
106: body {
107:     font-family : 'Arial', 'Helvetica', 'sans-serif';
108:     font-size : 10pt;
```

```
109: }
110: </STYLE>
111: </HEAD>

111: <BODY BGCOLOR="#FFFFFF">

112: <H3>Quote Manager</H3>

113: <DIV ALIGN="center">
114: <CFFORM ACTION="all_quotes.cfm" METHOD="POST" ENABLECAB="Yes"
NAME="QuotesForm">
115: <CFGRID NAME="QuoteGrid" HEIGHT="370" WIDTH="600" QUERY="Quotes"
INSERT="Yes" DELETE="Yes" SORT="Yes" FONT="Arial" BOLD="No" ITALIC="No"
APPENDKEY="No" HIGHLIGHTHREF="No" GRIDDATAALIGN="LEFT" GRIDLINES="Yes"
ROWHEADERS="No" ROWHEADERALIGN="LEFT" ROWHEADERITALIC="No" ROWHEADERBOLD="No"
COLHEADERS="Yes" COLHEADERALIGN="LEFT" COLHEADERITALIC="No" COLHEADERBOLD="No"
SELECTMODE="EDIT" PICTUREBAR="Yes">
116:     <CFGRIDCOLUMN NAME="Quote_ID" HEADERALIGN="LEFT" DATAALIGN="LEFT"
BOLD="No" ITALIC="No" SELECT="No" DISPLAY="No" HEADERBOLD="No" HEADERITALIC="No">
117:     <CFGRIDCOLUMN NAME="Quote" HEADERALIGN="LEFT" DATAALIGN="LEFT"
WIDTH="470" BOLD="No" ITALIC="No" SELECT="Yes" DISPLAY="Yes" HEADERBOLD="No"
HEADERITALIC="No">
118:     <CFGRIDCOLUMN NAME="Attribution" HEADERALIGN="LEFT" DATAALIGN="LEFT"
BOLD="No" ITALIC="No" SELECT="Yes" DISPLAY="Yes" HEADERBOLD="No" HEADERITALIC="No">
119: </CFGRID>
120:     <BR>
121:     <INPUT TYPE="submit" NAME="save" VALUE="Save Changes"> <INPUT
TYPE="button" NAME="cancel" VALUE="Back"
onClick="document.location.href='quotes.cfm'">
122: </CFFORM>
123: </DIV>

124: </BODY>
125: </HTML>
```

The first part of this template is the same as quote_toolbox.cfm. If Application
.Quotes does not exist, you read in the WDDX file, parse it, and store the resulting
recordset in your application variable. To be brief, we'll skip to the interesting parts.

Documenting the CFGRID tag is beyond the scope of this chapter. We'll assume you
can find CFGRID documentation elsewhere, and just tell you what is different about this
implementation. The main problem you encounter is that because there is no actual
database behind this tag, not only can you not use the CFGRIDUPDATE tag, but you cannot
even run a manual SQL query that says, "Update the row that has the ID of *x*." You must
modify your in-memory recordset directly, and here's where you run into that limitation
in ColdFusion's recordset functions: You can use the QuerySetCell function to modify

the contents of a particular row in the recordset, provided you know the row number. However, there is no way to look up a particular row by the value of, say, a primary key field without scanning the entire recordset until you find the one you're looking for. You run into a problem that is similar, but worse, when you need to delete a particular row. ColdFusion has no function to delete a row from a recordset. Instead, you must build a new recordset that doesn't contain the rows you want to eliminate, and then replace the original recordset with the new one.

There are two ways to get around these limitations: You can modify the data structure or modify the data content. If you were to rearrange the recordset so that it is no longer a recordset, you've solved nearly all your problems. You set up the data as a structure that has your primary key field as the name, and an array containing all the other data in the row as the value. This contains all the same data, enables you to quickly look up and modify rows based on an ID, and will even enable you to delete a particular row. So what's the problem? CFGRID doesn't know what to do with a structure full of arrays. It understands only recordsets. You can manually fill in a CFGRID by using loops and CFGRIDROW, but you would also have to rewrite the other pages to accommodate this new data structure, and that's a lot of work.

What, then, is the solution? You already know that you can modify a particular row of a recordset if you know its row number. Your first thought might be to simply include Recordset.CurrentRow as one of the hidden fields in the CFGRID tag. Unfortunately, CFGRID doesn't like that, because CurrentRow is a reserved word. You're left with no viable alternative but to make the Quote_ID in the recordset equal to the row number. It's okay to modify the ID in this way because you don't have to reconcile this data with a back-end database at any point (if you were using a database, this whole problem would be a non-issue). In any case, the ID that is returned by CFGRID now correctly maps to the row number for quick and easy editing of existing rows.

Now that you've got insert and edit done, what about delete? There's still no way to delete a row from a recordset. Because CFGRID enables you to delete multiple rows in one operation, you must assemble a list of rows to be deleted, then later create a new recordset that doesn't contain any of the records you don't want. After this is done, you need to loop through the new recordset and reset all the Quote_ID's back to their row number, because the removal of rows will throw this off. After this is done, you've successfully implemented add, edit, and delete functionality for your in-memory recordset. All that's left is to update your application variable and save the modified recordset as WDDX to your text file.

Where Do We Go from Here?

For more information on WDDX, your first source should be `http://www.wddx.org`. There, you will find the WDDX SDK, put together by Team Allaire member Nate Weiss, as well as public discussion forums where you can ask questions or share your ideas.

In the next chapter you will learn about the `CFREGISTRY` tag, which enables your ColdFusion templates to access a configuration stored in the Windows registry, as well as to create its entries in the registry. In this way, your ColdFusion applications, just like regular Windows applications, can leverage the power of the registry as a central repository for configuration information in the Windows environment.

chapter 34

Using the *CFREGISTRY* Tag

- Understanding the Registry

- Using the CFREGISTRY Tag

- Enhancing Security

- Building a Registry Viewer

The *registry* is a fundamental part of the Windows platform. Serving as a configuration database, it is central to the operation of most applications in the Windows environment and the very operating system itself. In this chapter, you will learn how ColdFusion can access and manipulate the contents of the registry by using the CFREGISTRY tag.

You will start by taking a look at what the registry is and how it works. Then, you will study the mechanics of how the CFREGISTRY tag can be used to view and alter the contents of the registry. Finally, you will build an application, a registry viewer that enables a Web browser to be used to view the contents of the registry on the ColdFusion server.

Understanding the Registry

For many users of Windows 95, 98, and NT, the Windows Registry is the source of great mystery. It is viewed as a black hole filled with information so delicate that any tampering with it could cause the complete failure of a PC and the loss of all data it contains.

Although working with the registry requires care, precision, and attention to detail, it shouldn't be seen as a mysterious entity that is best avoided. In fact, the operation of Windows and of almost every application made for the operating system is so closely dependent on the registry that a basic understanding is important for any Windows user. This is especially true if you are considering using the ColdFusion CFREGISTRY tag to view or manipulate the registry on your server.

Using the Registry

The registry is not that complicated. Basically, it is a central database of information and settings used by Windows to start and to launch applications. The registry is used in everything from selecting drivers for devices, managing users, and controlling security settings.

In the old days of Windows 3.1, these processes would have been done using a myriad of INI files: several for Windows and then one or more for each installed application. In today's Windows platforms, this information is consolidated into the registry. The registry has several important facets that were lacking in the old INI-file model:

- A logical (once you understand it), hierarchical organization
- The capability to search the database
- Simple tools for adding and changing values stored in the registry

Normally, you do not need to access the registry in day-to-day operations. Windows keeps key system settings up to date, and software installation programs will create new keys and values as needed.

Understanding the Structure of the Registry

The registry is structured in a hierarchical tree, just as files and directories are on a disk. The registry is built out of *keys* and *values*. A key can contain individual values as well as sub-keys, which in turn can contain values or sub-keys. This structure maps fairly cleanly to the file and directory model: Keys are like directories, whereas values are like files.

NOTE   The ColdFusion documentation and the CFREGISTRY tag refer to keys as *branches* and values as *entries*. We use the terms interchangeably in this chapter.

The Windows registry has six basic root keys under which all other keys are placed. These can be seen as similar to drives or partitions under which directories and files are placed. These keys are:

HKEY_CLASSES_ROOT   Stores object linking and embedding (OLE) information, as well as file type and extension associations, among other information.

HKEY_CURRENT_CONFIG   Stores information about the current hardware setup.

HKEY_CURRENT_USERS   Stores settings about the user currently using the system.

HKEY_DYN_DATA   Stores dynamic information needed while using the system's hardware. For instance, Plug-and-Play configuration information might be stored here, as well as performance data.

HKEY_LOCAL_MACHINE   Stores information about the hardware and software installed on the system. This is commonly where individual applications will store their own keys and values.

HKEY_USERS   Stores an individual user's settings, including Desktop configuration.

The full name of a key or value is specified in much the same way as file paths: by using the backslash character to mark the hierarchy of keys and sub-keys en route to the destination. For instance,

```
HKEY_LOCAL_MACHINE\Software
```

is the complete name of the Software key, which exists as a sub-key of HKEY_LOCAL_MACHINE.

Accessing the Registry

It may seem unusual to want to access the registry from a ColdFusion template. However, this can be useful for several tasks, including:

- Creating Web-based tools to remotely manage some of the settings on a ColdFusion server

- Checking various system settings to determine the appropriate action to take in a template
- Storing the configuration and settings for a complex Web application, just as other applications store their settings in the registry

Using the Registry on Solaris

The Solaris operating system doesn't include a registry like that used in Windows. However, ColdFusion frequently uses the registry, storing settings there, as well as some of the variables created by templates and applications. For this reason, a registry system is included with the Solaris version of ColdFusion. The registry provides the necessary functionality for these parts of ColdFusion to operate. This scaled-down registry (which doesn't contain any Solaris system settings) is available by using the CFREGISTRY tag.

Using the *CFREGISTRY* Tag

The CFREGISTRY tag is fairly straightforward to use, once you understand how the registry works and is structured. This tag provides five major functions:

- Reading all the keys and values and a certain location in the registry hierarchy
- Reading a specific registry value
- Updating an existing value
- Adding a new value or registry key
- Deleting a registry value or key

The value of the ACTION attribute determines which action is performed when using the CFREGISTRY tag. The following list outlines the possible values for the attribute and their effects:

GetAll Reads all keys and values at a certain location

Get Reads a specific value

Set Updates a value or adds a new value or key

Delete Deletes a key or value

ACTION="GetAll"

Using the ACTION="GetAll" attribute causes the CFREGISTRY tag to retrieve all values and keys at a specific location in the registry hierarchy. To obtain the values and keys at a location, you need to use some or all of the following additional attributes:

BRANCH The complete path and name of the location (or branch) to be read. This is a required attribute.

TYPE   Specifies the type of data to return. Possible data types include String (for string values), DWord for DWord values, Key for registry keys, and Any for all keys and values. By default, this attribute is set to String.

NAME   Specifies the name of the query result set through which to return the requested values and keys. This is a required attribute.

SORT   Specifies the query columns on which to sort the returned data. Possible columns to sort on are Entry, Type, and Value. Sorting can be done either in ascending or descending order, and multiple columns can be used as sort keys and can be separated by commas. For example, SORT="Entry ASC, Type DESC" sorts first in ascending order on the Entry column, and then in descending order on the Type column.

The data from this use of the CFREGISTRY tag is returned as a standard query result set, which can then be used like all result sets (including in the CFOUTPUT and CFLOOP tags). The result set contains three columns:

Entry   The name of the value or key.

Type   The type of value. If the value is binary, this column contains the value Unsupported.

Value   Contains the value of the entry. If the entry is a key, then this column contains the empty string. If the entry is a binary value, then this column also contains the empty string.

For instance, consider the following location in the registry:

```
\HKEY_LOCAL_MACHINE\Software\Microsoft\Windows\CurrentVersion
```

In this location (or branch) of the registry, Windows 95 and 98 store critical information about the current Windows installation. Here, you find values defining everything from the registered owner of the software to the default program files directory to the location where Windows stores Desktop wallpaper. This branch also has numerous subkeys specifying information about specific parts of Windows, such as the logon process or the Control Panel folder.

The following tag retrieves all keys and values at this location and returns them in the query result set called Windows. Information is sorted first by the type of entry, and then by the Entry column. It would be written as follows:

```
<CFREGISTRY ACTION="GetAll"
 BRANCH="HKEY_LOCAL_MACHINE\Software\Microsoft\Windows\CurrentVersion"
 TYPE="Any"
 NAME="Windows"
 SORT="Type ASC, Entry ASC">
```

This result set can then be used in a CFOUTPUT tag to produce a table of the values and keys at the specific location:

```
<TABLE BORDER=0 CELLSPACING=3>
<TR>
<TD><STRONG>Entry</STRONG></TD>
<TD><STRONG>Type</STRONG></TD>
<TD><STRONG>Value</STRONG></TD>
</TR>
<CFOUTPUT QUERY="Windows">
<TR>
<TD>#Entry#</TD>
<TD>#Type#</TD>
<TD>#Value#</TD>
</TR>
</CFOUTPUT>
</TABLE>
```

This code produces a result like the one in Figure 34.1.

FIGURE 34.1
Displaying all values and keys at a specific location

ACTION="Get"

Using ACTION="Get", you can retrieve a specific value from the registry in a fine-grained way. You do so by specifying these additional attributes:

BRANCH   The complete path and name of the location (or branch) to be read. This is a required attribute.

ENTRY   The name of the value to be retrieved from the specified branch. This is a required attribute.

TYPE   Specifies the type of data to return. Possible data types include `String` (for string values), `DWord` for DWord values, and `Key` for registry. By default, this attribute is set to `String`.

VARIABLE   The name of the variable in which to store the returned value. This is a required attribute.

For instance, to return the value of the `RegisteredOrganization` entry from the location used earlier when looking at `ACTION="GetAll"`, the following tag could be used:

```
<CFREGISTRY ACTION="Get"
 BRANCH="HKEY_LOCAL_MACHINE\Software\Microsoft\Windows\CurrentVersion"
 ENTRY="RegisteredOrganization"
 Variable="RegOrg">
```

This will store the value in the `RegOrg` variable, which can then be used in a template—for instance, to output the name of the organization:

```
<CFOUTPUT>Registered Organization: #RegOrg#</CFOUTPUT>
```

ACTION="Set"

`ACTION="Set"` is a little more complicated than the previous two actions, simply because it can be employed for two purposes: to update the value of an existing entry, or to create a new entry or key. Regardless of whether it is being used to update or create, the same four additional attributes are available when using `ACTION="Set"`:

BRANCH   The complete path and name of the location (or branch) to be worked with. This is a required attribute.

ENTRY   The name of the value to be updated or the value or key to be created. This is a required attribute.

TYPE   Specifies the type of data to return. Possible data types include `String` (for string values), `DWord` for DWord values, and `Key` for registry. By default, this attribute is set to `String`.

VALUE   The value of an entry being updated or created. If not provided, string values will default to the empty string and DWord values to zero.

Using these attributes enables you to accomplish the following:

- To update an existing value, provide the branch, name, and new value for the existing entry.
- To create a new entry, provide the branch, name, and type of the value and optionally provide an initial value for the entry.

- To create a new key, provide the branch and key names for the new key and specify TYPE="Key".

For instance, to change the value of the RegisteredOrganization entry (used earlier with ACTION="Get") to New Organization, you use the following tag:

```
<CFREGISTRY ACTION="Set"
  BRANCH="HKEY_LOCAL_MACHINE\Software\Microsoft\Windows\CurrentVersion"
  ENTRY="RegisteredOrganization"
  VALUE="New Organization">
```

Similarly, to create a new sub-key in the same branch called NewApp, use the following tag:

```
<CFREGISTRY ACTION="Set"
  BRANCH="HKEY_LOCAL_MACHINE\Software\Microsoft\Windows\CurrentVersion"
  ENTRY="NewApp"
  TYPE="Key">
```

ACTION="Delete"

As would be expected, you can use ACTION="Delete" to delete an existing entry or key in the registry. Only two attributes are used to do this:

BRANCH   The complete path and name of the location (or branch) to be deleted. This is a required attribute.

ENTRY   The name of the value or key to be deleted. This is a required attribute.

WARNING   Remember, altering the contents of the registry, either by using ACTION="Set" or ACTION="Delete", can make your ColdFusion system unstable or unusable. Take special care with ACTION="Delete" because it is easy to delete an important key, and the tag offers no confirmation of your actions.

Enhancing Security

Like other tags such as CFFILE and CFDIRECTORY, the CFREGISTRY tag poses a potential security risk, especially on systems in which users can create their own templates. In this sort of environment, allowing users to use the CFREGISTRY tag means that any user can manipulate and alter the contents of the registry on the ColdFusion server.

When this is an issue, you can use the ColdFusion Administrator to disable the CFREGISTRY tag for all users. To do this, open the Basic Security section of the Administrator, scroll to the bottom of the page, and unselect the Enable CFREGISTRY check box.

Building a Registry Viewer

To put everything you've learned about the registry together, the rest of this chapter will discuss a simple Web-based registry-viewing tool built in ColdFusion that uses the CFREGISTRY tag. This tool provides a way to view the values in a given key, as well as to open sub-keys from that branch. The template that follows works like this:

- A menu of top-level branches (such as HKEY_CURRENT_MACHINE) is always displayed. The user can select a branch and click the View button to view it.
- If a branch is specified in the URL, then that key is displayed.
- If no branch is specified in the URL and the menu of top-level branches has not been used, then no branch is displayed.
- When a branch is displayed, keys are displayed as links so that they can be viewed in turn.

This process is achieved with the template in Listing 34.1.

LISTING 34.1: *registry.cfm*

```
 1: <HTML>

 2:     <HEAD><TITLE>Registry Viewer</TITLE></HEAD>

 3:     <BODY>

 4:         <CFIF IsDefined("URL.Branch")>
 5:             <CFSET Branch=URL.Branch>
 6:         </CFIF>

 7:         <CFIF IsDefined("Form.Branch")>
 8:             <CFSET Branch = Form.Branch>
 9:         </CFIF>

10:         <FORM METHOD=POST ACTION="viewreg.cfm">

11:             Choose a new branch to view:

12:             <SELECT NAME="Branch">
13:                 <OPTION>HKEY_CLASSES_ROOT
14:                 <OPTION>HKEY_LOCAL_MACHINE
15:                 <OPTION>HKEY_USERS
16:                 <OPTION>HKEY_CURRENT_CONFIG
17:                 <OPTION>HKEY_DYN_DATA
18:             </SELECT>

19:             <INPUT TYPE=SUBMIT VALUE=VIEW>

20:         <FORM>
```

```
21:        <HR>

22:        <CFIF IsDefined("Branch")>
23:           <CFREGISTRY ACTION="GetAll"
24:            BRANCH="#Branch#"
25:            TYPE="Any"
26:            NAME="Windows"
27:            SORT="Type ASC, Entry ASC">

28:           <TABLE BORDER=0 CELLSPACING=3>

29:              <TR>

30:                 <TD COLSPAN=3 ALIGN=LEFT BGCOLOR=CYAN>
31:                    <STRONG><CFOUTPUT>Currently Viewing #Branch#</CFOUTPUT></
STRONG>
32:                 </TD>

33:              </TR>

34:              <TR>

35:                 <TD><STRONG>Entry</STRONG></TD>
36:                 <TD><STRONG>Type</STRONG></TD>
37:                 <TD><STRONG>Value</STRONG></TD>

38:              </TR>

39:              <CFOUTPUT QUERY="Windows">

40:                 <TR>

41:                    <TD>
42:                       <CFIF Type is "KEY">
43:                          <A HREF="viewreg.cfm?branch=#branch#\#Entry#">#Entry#</
A>
44:                       <CFELSE>
45:                          #Entry#
46:                       </CFIF>
47:                    </TD>
48:                    <TD>#Type#</TD>
49:                    <TD>#Value#</TD>

50:                 </TR>

51:              </CFOUTPUT>

52:           </TABLE>

53:        <CFELSE>
```

```
54:           <STRONG>No Branch is Currently Being Viewed</STRONG>

55:       </CFIF>

56:     </BODY>

57: </HTML>
```

This template produces results similar to those in Figure 34.2.

FIGURE 34.2
Viewing the registry with a
Web browser

The template is divided into three main sections:

- Initialization
- Root branch menu
- Querying the registry and displaying the results

Initialization

Initialization takes place in Lines 4 through 9 (refer to Listing 34.1). The logic here is fairly simple: If a branch to view is provided in the URL, then it should be assigned to the variable Branch. Similarly, if the root branch menu has been used and submitted, then the key selected should be assigned to the variable Branch. This is performed after checking the URL for a branch, so that use of the menu will always override a URL-provided branch.

Root Branch Menu

To make things easy, the root branch menu, outlined in Lines 10 through 20 (refer to Listing 34.1), is a simple select field in a form. Notice that the action of the form is to submit the form's contents back to itself. In other words, the template displays the form and processes input from the form.

Querying the Registry and Displaying the Results

The bulk of the work is done after the form is displayed, starting with a test to see whether a branch has been specified by using the following:

```
22:        <CFIF IsDefined("Branch")>
```

and continuing to the end of the template.

The purpose of this initial test is to see whether a key has been specified, and the test is performed by checking whether the variable Branch exists. Looking at the template's initialization section, it is clear that only if a branch is specified in the URL or through the root branch menu will this variable exist. This is important because you want to use the CFREGISTRY tag to access a branch only if a key has been specified. If the variable exists, then you query the registry and display a table of results in a manner similar to that shown when we discussed the use of the ACTION="GetAll" attribute earlier in this chapter.

A few points to note:

- The BRANCH attribute of the CFREGISTRY tag is specified as the value of the Branch variable.
- In the CFOUTPUT segment of the template where you are displaying the results of the CFREGISTRY query, you check whether an entry is a key by testing the value of the Type column from the query. If you find a key, then the name of the entry is displayed as a link back to the template, with the branch specified as a combination of the Branch variable and the Entry column from the query.
- The CFELSE segment displays a message if no branch is specified. Users will see this message the first time they open the template.

Where Do We Go from Here?

In the next three chapters, you will dive into some advanced administrative issues, considering everything from the ColdFusion Administrator to troubleshooting and performance optimization techniques. The next chapter provides details of the ColdFusion Administrator, which you have already seen in passing. Now, you will take a closer look at all its features, and how it can be used to keep your ColdFusion installation functioning properly, with a minimum of problems.

chapter 35

ColdFusion Administration

- Using the ColdFusion Administrator

- Troubleshooting Errors

- Managing Log Files

- Performance Tuning

To close your study of ColdFusion, you need to consider the administration of a ColdFusion server. Specifically, you need to understand how to use all aspects of the ColdFusion Administrator, the Web-based administration system for ColdFusion servers.

Administration is more than just using an administrative tool. It also involves troubleshooting errors, managing logs, and tuning performance. In this chapter you will look at all these facets of administration, starting with a walk through all the administrative forms available in the ColdFusion Administrator and then moving on to topics such as performance tuning, including clustering with ClusterCATS.

Using the ColdFusion Administrator

The ColdFusion Administrator is a full-scale, Web-driven administration system for ColdFusion servers. The Administrator provides the capability to control many aspects of the ColdFusion operation, from data sources to extensions to logging to scheduling. Essentially, the only main administrative task not achieved through the Administrator is starting and stopping the server services, which is done through the Services Control Panel applet in Windows NT and 2000 and from the Start menu in Windows 98.

The ColdFusion Administrator is divided into six sections of multiple pages:

- Server
- Data Sources
- Extensions
- Logging
- Automated Tasks
- Miscellaneous

Accessing the ColdFusion Administrator

To access the ColdFusion Administrator, point your Web browser to an address such as the following:

```
http://hostname/CFIDE/Administrator/index.cfm
```

The *hostname* part of the URL should be the IP address or host name of the Web server on which your ColdFusion server is installed. In the case of a local server, you can use localhost of 127.0.0.1 for the *hostname* part of the URL.

This will display the login screen for the ColdFusion Administrator shown in Figure 35.1.

FIGURE 35.1

Logging in to the
ColdFusion Administrator

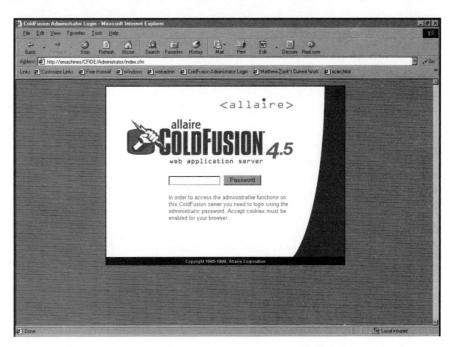

During installation of the ColdFusion server, you specified a password for administration. Provide that password in the field and click the Password button to log in. You should be presented with the first page of the ColdFusion Administrator, the Server Settings page, shown in Figure 35.2.

FIGURE 35.2
After successfully logging in, you will see the Home page of the Administrator.

Server

The Server section of the Administrator is used to set basic settings of the server, including timeouts, cache size, and other general settings, along with basic security, client variable storage, and directory mappings. The screens in the Server section are:

- Home
- Settings
- Cache
- Basic Security
- Advanced Security
- Variables
- Java
- Locking
- Mappings
- Version Info

Settings

The Server Settings screen is used to set several of the following general settings of your ColdFusion server:

Limit Simultaneous Requests to *X*   By limiting the number of requests that can be simultaneously processed, you can improve system performance. At the same time, though, if you get a large number of near-simultaneous requests, many of these requests will need to be queued until other requests finish processing. The default value of five should be suitable for most small Web servers.

Timeout Requests after *X* Seconds   At times requests will take an extremely long time to process and will use server resources for extended periods, effectively limiting the server's performance. By enabling this option, requests that take longer than the number of seconds you specify will be terminated when they cross the threshold. You can override this timeout limit for any particular request by appending `?requesttime-out=<seconds>` to a URL.

Restart at *X* Unresponsive Requests   Sometimes it is possible for the ColdFusion server process to become extremely slow, using up an enormous percentage of the CPU resources on the computer it is running on. This often happens because of problems in third-party components such as ODBC drivers or CFX tags. When this setting is enabled, ColdFusion will track requests to these components that time out, and when the specified number have occurred, will restart the ColdFusion service in an attempt to alleviate problems that develop over time.

Restart when requests terminate abnormaly   Sometimes, requests will suffer an "unexpected exception" error. If too many of these occur, the ColdFusion service should be restarted. When this setting is enabled, ColdFusion will track these errors and if too many occur, will restart the ColdFusion process.

Suppress whitespace by default   Depending on how your ColdFusion templates are formatted, large numbers of spaces, tabs, and carriage returns can occur in sequence leading to larger than necessary files being sent to browsers and making the HTML received by browsers hard to read. When this setting is enabled, ColdFusion will compress these sequences to eliminate unnecessary white space in the final code sent to browsers.

Enforce Strict Attribute Validation   When enabled, the rules by which ColdFusion tags are processed will be stricter than the way standard HTML tags are processed. Normally, both HTML and ColdFusion tags can include irrelevant, extraneous attributes that are not part of the specification for the tag in question. Usually these extra attributes are ignored. When this setting is enabled, however, any ColdFusion tag with extra attributes will generate an error. This setting's goal is to enhance performance as ColdFusion won't have to process and then reject extraneous attributes.

Missing Template Handler   This field specifies a custom template to execute when ColdFusion cannot find a requested template. Consult Chapter 18, "Error Control," for details on handling errors in templates.

Site-wide Error Handler   This field specifies a custom template to execute when an error occurs while processing a request. Consult Chapter 18, "Error Control," for details on handling errors in templates. If this option is enabled and the error-handler document is not present, debugging your application may be nearly impossible.

Caching

The Cache Settings screen is used to set several Cache-related settings of your ColdFusion server:

Template Cache Size   ColdFusion maintains a cache in memory where the most recently processed templates are kept. When a request is received for a template in the cache, it is accessed from the cache rather than accessing the file and reprocessing the template. This can vastly improve performance at the expense of the use of RAM memory. If you have sufficient available memory, consider setting the cache size to the total size of all templates on the server. Then, after they all are processed they will remain in memory and system performance will improve. Keep in mind that if your application handles live data such as from a rapidly changing database or other data source, you won't want to cache in order to ensure that the latest data is used each time a template is requested. Also, take care not to overuse RAM with ColdFusion. You may speed up ColdFusion at the expense of all other services on your system.

Trusted Cache   If templates on your server are not updated between ColdFusion process restarts, then you can force ColdFusion to serve files from the cache without checking files for potential updates by enabling this setting. This will minimize file system overhead and improve performance of the server but also means that you cannot change templates without restarting ColdFusion.

Limit Database Connection Inactive Time   With client-server databases, you can open a connection to the database and then maintain the connection. This can notably improve database performance because each query does not need to open a connection, process the query, and then disconnect. However, maintaining these open connections is done at the expense of making the connection available to other clients. By setting this value to any time greater than zero, ColdFusion will close cached database connections (those that have been kept open) when the connection has been inactive for more than the specified time.

Limit the Maximum Number of Cached Queries   Just as ColdFusion caches processed templates, it can also cache the results of queries. The amount of available cache is specified in terms of the number of queries to cache rather than the amount of

RAM to make available to the cache because of the possibility of widely varying query sizes. When the number of queries is exceeded, the oldest queries are discarded to make way for new ones. Caching of queries requires the use of special attributes in your CFQUERY tags as outlined in Chapter 10, "Using CFQUERY and SQL to Interact with the Database."

WARNING   Caching needs to be handled carefully in ColdFusion. In particular, if data retrieved in queries is likely to change between requests for templates in an application, then it is not a good idea to cache an application. If you do cache templates, then you will return pages based on earlier query results instead of the current data in the data source.

Basic Security

The Basic Security screen lets you set several fundamental security settings for your ColdFusion server. Here you can enable and set the password required for accessing the ColdFusion Administrator as well as the password used by users of ColdFusion Studio for accessing the server. Setting the ColdFusion Administrator password is highly recommended. In addition, you can selectively enable and disable the following tags: CFCONTENT, CFDIRECTORY, CFFILE, CFOBJECT, CFREGISTRY, CFADMIN-SECURITY, and CFEXECUTE. These tags are potential security holes because they provide users on the Web access to data on the server PC outside the scope of the Web server's document root and, in some cases, even allow for the altering of content on the server.

If you restrict access to the tags outlined above, you can still provide limited access to these tags by specifying a directory in the Unsecured tags directory field. Any templates in this directory will not be subject to the tag limitations you have specified.

Advanced Security

The Advanced Security screen is used to configure fine-grained security for your ColdFusion applications. This screen is discussed in detail in Chapter 30, "Application Security."

Variables

As you learned in Chapter 17, "Implementing the ColdFusion Web Application Framework," client variables can be stored in several places, including the registry, cookies, or databases through ODBC or native data sources. On the Client Variable Storage screen, shown in Figure 35.3, you can control these aspects of client variables as well as settings related to application and session variables.

FIGURE 35.3
The Client Variable Storage screen

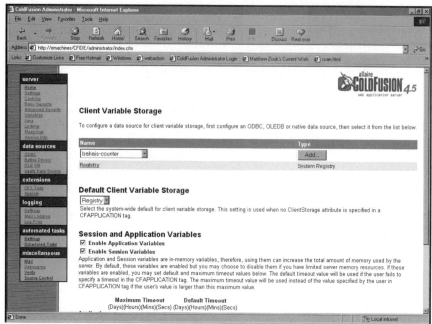

For client variables, you can configure a data source for client variable storage by selecting the data source name from the drop-down list and then clicking the Add button.

You will then be presented with the Create Client Variable Storage screen like the one in Figure 35.4, where you can finish providing information needed to enable the data source. The information asked for on this screen is:

Purge Data for Clients That Remain Unvisited for _X_ Days   Client variables are created for each client that visits. If data for old clients that have not recently visited is not deleted, eventually the size of client variable storage will grow large. By enabling this option and specifying a reasonable delay before purging client variables (this is generally dependent on the nature of your applications), you can keep the size of the client variable store small and efficient.

Disable Global Client Variable Updates   This setting relates to global variables such as HitCount and LastVisit. If you allow updates to be disabled, these variables are updated by ColdFusion only when they are modified or set; otherwise, they are updated for each page request.

Create Client Data sbase Tables   The first time you add data for client storage, ColdFusion will need to create tables for storing the client data. Therefore, only enable this option the first time you add a data source to the client storage list. You can add any number of data sources to the list and then select individual data sources for particular applications by using the CLIENTSTORAGE attribute of the CFAPPLICATION tag in your Application.cfm files.

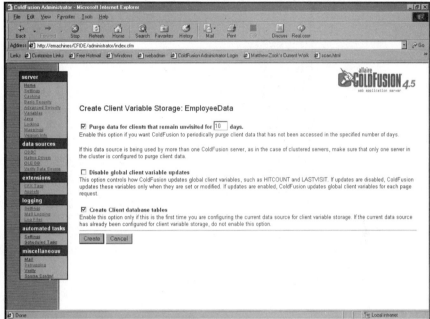

Next, the Client Variable Storage screen allows the selection of a default location for storage of client variables when no alternate location is specified with the CFAPPLICA-TION tag. The possible options for the default location are Cookie for client browser cookies, Registry for the system registry, or any data you added.

Finally, the Client Variable Storage screen allows the selective enabling or disabling of application and session variables and allows the specification of maximum and default timeouts for both types of variables. The default will be used if no timeout is specified in the CFAPPLICATION tag for an application. If a value is specified but it exceeds the maximum timeout, then the maximum timeout will be used.

Java

The Java Settings screen also used to specify Java-related settings so that ColdFusion can work with Java on the server:

Load JVM when starting ColdFusion   If this setting is enabled, ColdFusion will load the Java Virtual Machine when it starts. Otherwise, it will wait until the first request that requires the Virtual Machine before loading it.

Java Virtual Machine Path   This field is used to specify the complete path and filename of the Java Virtual Machine on your system.

Class Path This field is used to specify the class path for your system. ColdFusion uses this path to locate Java classes and Enterprise JavaBeans specified using the CFOBJECT tag or the CreateObject function. The path can be a series of directories separated by semi-colons or a single directory.

Initial Heap Size This field is used to specify the Java Virtual Machine's initial heap size in kilobytes. If you are unsure of what is appropriate for your system, use the default of 1024 kilobytes.

Maximum Heap Size This field is used to specify the maximum heap size for the Java Virtual Machine in kilobytes. If you are unsure what is appropriate for your system, use the default of 16384 kilobytes.

Implementation Options Use this field to specify initialization options for the Java Virtual Machine in the form <name>=<value>; <name>=<value>; <name>=<value>; ....

CFX Jar Path This field specifies the directory containing the ColdFusion cfx.jar file which contains the interfaces necessary to enable Java-based CFXs in ColdFusion 4.5. If ColdFusion is installed in c:\cfusion, this directory will normally be c:\cfusion\java\classes.

Locking

The Variable Locking screen is used to specify how ColdFusion Server 4.5 and above should handle variable locking. Four settings are available on the screen:

Single Threaded Sessions When enabled, requests will be threaded by session ID to ensure that no potential variable locking conflicts can occur by simultaneous requests from the same session.

Server Scope This setting is used to specify how server scope variables should be locked. The possible choices are: No automatic checking or locking (the developer has to ensure that variables are properly locked with the CFLOCK tag), Full checking (Cold-Fusion checks all variables to make sure they are properly locked), Automatic read locking (ColdFusion checks all server variables to make sure they are properly locked when writing and automatically locks variables for reads).

Applications Scope This setting is used to specify how application scope variables should be locked. The possible choices are: No automatic checking or locking (the developer has to ensure that variables are properly locked with the CFLOCK tag), Full checking (ColdFusion checks all variables to make sure they are properly locked), Automatic read locking (ColdFusion checks all server variables to make sure they are properly locked when writing and automatically locks variables for reads).

Session Scope   This setting is used to specify how session scope variables should be locked. The possible choices are: No automatic checking or locking (the developer has to ensure that variables are properly locked with the CFLOCK tag), Full checking (Cold-Fusion checks all variables to make sure they are properly locked), Automatic read locking (ColdFusion checks all server variables to make sure they are properly locked when writing and automatically locks variables for reads).

WARNING   Automatic locking such as Full checking and Automatic read locking can impair performance, especially in applications with a high volume of requests or large numbers of variables.

Mappings

On the Add New Mapping screen, shown in Figure 35.5, you can add directory mappings to ColdFusion just as you can to your Web server.

FIGURE 35.5
The Add New Mapping screen

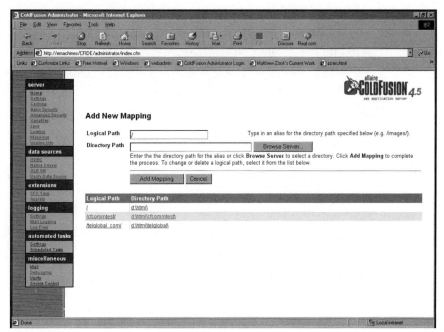

Typically, a Web server or a Web server-based application environment such as Cold-Fusion is configured with a default root directory. When a user accesses the base URL for the server in the form `http://hostname/`, the documents they are provided access to come from this default root directory on the server and below. This default root directory can be anywhere on the system, such as `c:\html`.

At times, there are reasons to store documents and files that need to be accessed via the Web in directories outside the root directory and its subdirectories. This access can be achieved through mappings. For instance, given the preceding example of the root directory, the URL `http://hostname/images/test.gif` would be accessing the file `c:\html\images\test.gif`. However, what if you wanted to store the GIF file in the directory `c:\images`? A Web browser has no way to access this except through mappings. For instance, if you map `/images` to `c:\images`, then the URL `http://hostname/images/test.gif` now points at `c:\images\test.gif`, which is outside the root directory's tree.

Using the ColdFusion Administrator, you need to provide two pieces of information on the Add New Mapping screen to create a mapping:

Logical Path   The path relative to the root URL for the site that you are creating a mapping for. In our example, this would be `/images`.

Directory Path   The absolute system path for which the mapping is being created. In our example, this would be `c:\images`.

At the bottom of the screen is a list of existing mappings. By clicking any mapping (all are displayed as links) you can edit or delete it.

Version Info

The Server Information screen displays current information about your ColdFusion server, as shown in Figure 35.6. This screen is not used to perform any configuration, but instead shows information such as the server version being used, the operating system and version being used, and the serial number of your ColdFusion installation.

FIGURE 35.6
The Server Information
screen

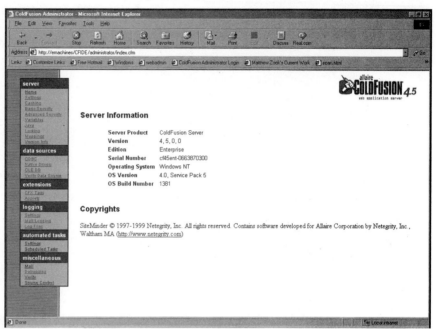

Data Sources

The Data Sources section of the ColdFusion Administrator is used to create and manage a variety of data sources, including ODBC, native, and OLE data sources. It contains four screens:

- ODBC
- Native Drivers
- OLE DB
- Verify Data Source

ODBC

The ODBC Data Sources Available to ColdFusion screen, shown in Figure 35.7, is where you define and manage ODBC data sources such as Microsoft Access and Visual FoxPro databases.

To create a new data source, first type a name for the data source in the field provided and then choose the type of database you will be using for the data source from the drop-down list, as shown in Figure 35.8.

FIGURE 35.7
The ODBC Data Sources
Available to ColdFusion
screen

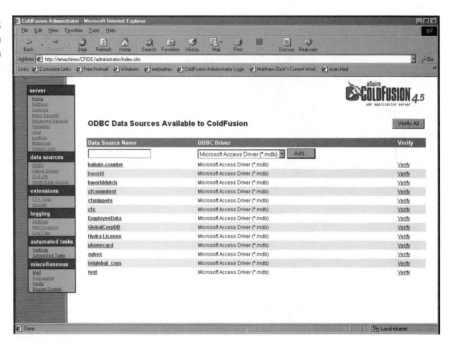

FIGURE 35.8
Choosing a database type
for a new data source

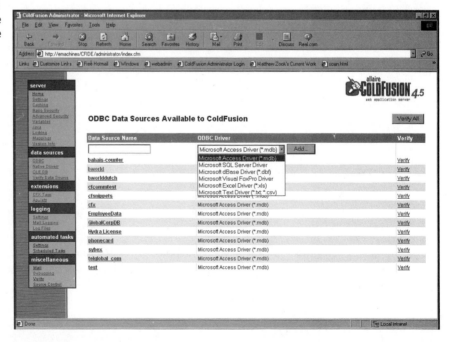

Next, click the Add button. This leads to the Create ODBC Data Source screen shown in Figure 35.9, where you can specify relevant information about the data source.

FIGURE 35.9

The Create ODBC Data Source screen

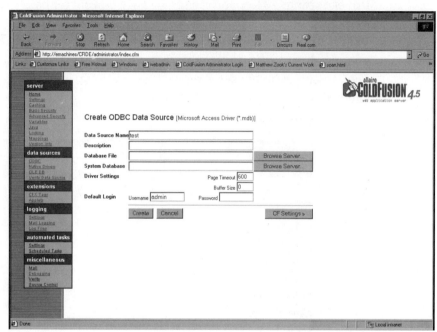

The information that you specify varies from data source type to data source type and is outlined in detail in the ColdFusion online documentation in Chapter 4 of *Administering the ColdFusion Server*.

Because you have worked with Microsoft Access databases throughout this book, you will look at the information to be provided with Microsoft Access data sources:

Data Source Name   The name for the data source. This will reflect the name entered on the ODBC Data Sources Available to ColdFusion screen before clicking the Add button.

Description   A description of the data source.

Database File   The full path and filename of the Access file when creating the data source as a file data source.

System Database   The full path and filename of the Access file when creating the data source as a system data source. System data sources can be accessed by any user on the system and not just the local user. Although the Microsoft Windows ODBC environment makes this distinction, Access sources created through ColdFusion as file data sources are created as system data sources, so the filename can be entered in either the Database File or System Database field.

Driver Settings Here you can set the page timeout for pages querying the database as well as the cache size for pages using the data source.

Default Login If your database requires a username and password, they should be provided here.

The CF Settings button at the right of the screen expands the screen to include several additional settings, as shown in Figure 35.10.

FIGURE 35.10
Extended ODBC settings

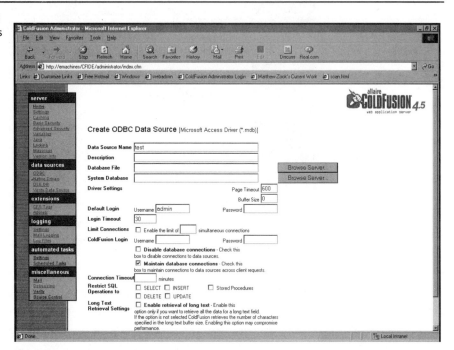

These additional settings enable you to:

- Limit the number of simultaneous connections to the data sources, which improves performance at the expense of having to queue queries for later handling when the number of specified connections are already in use
- Restrict the allowed database operations to specific SQL statements
- Indicate that the connection to the data source should be kept open at least as long as the timeout indicated in the Server Settings screen of the Administrator's Server section

When you have finished specifying the settings for a new data source, simply click the Create button. This will create the data source and return you to the main ODBC screen.

On the main screen, all existing ODBC data sources are listed. To edit or delete an existing data source, simply click the name of the data source. If you want to check whether the data source is configured correctly, click the Verify link associated with the data source you want to test. A screen will be displayed informing you of the test result. For instance, Figure 35.11 shows the successful verification of a data source. When you first define a new data source, the ColdFusion Administrator will automatically attempt to verify it.

FIGURE 35.11
Verifying a data source

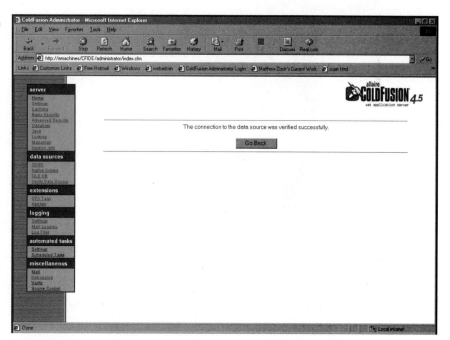

Native Drivers

The Native Drivers screen is used to create data sources using the native drivers for DB2, Informix 7.3, Sybase 11, Oracle 7.3, and Oracle 8 provided with ColdFusion. Creating a native interface data source is much the same as creating an ODBC data source. First, provide a name for the data source, then select a data source type from the drop-down list and click the Add button. This will display the Create Native Interface Data Source screen suited to the data source type that you choose. In our example, you will look at the screen for Sybase 11 data sources. This screen looks much like the screen for creating an ODBC data source. It even can be expanded using the CF Settings button, as shown in Figure 35.12.

FIGURE 35.12
The expanded Create
Native Interface Data
Source screen

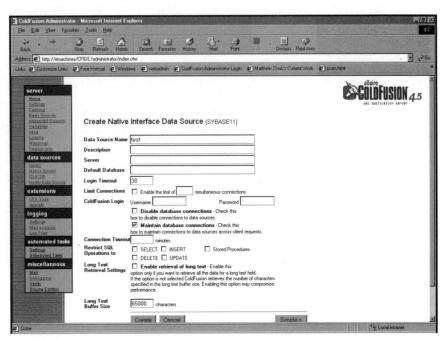

Most of the fields on this screen are similar, or even the same as, those on the screens for creating ODBC data sources. The major difference is that instead of specifying a file for the database, a server and database name are provided.

After you create a new native interface data source, it appears in the list on the main Native Drivers screen and can be updated or deleted by clicking its name. Similarly, the Verify link for each data source can be used to verify the configuration of the data source.

OLE DB

OLE DB data sources are similar in some ways to ODBC data sources in that they are accessed through a standardized interface from clients such as ColdFusion. In the case of OLE DB data sources, these range from Microsoft Exchange and Lotus Notes servers, to data stored in OLE-capable software such as Microsoft Word and Excel, to mainframe-based data.

Generally, the ability to use these data sources depends on OLE DB providers available from third-party developers. To gain access to an existing OLE DB provider from within ColdFusion, you use the OLE DB Data Sources Available to ColdFusion screen shown in Figure 35.13.

FIGURE 35.13
The OLEDB Data Sources
Available to ColdFusion
screen

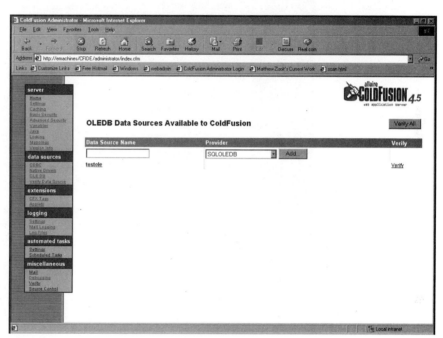

To create an OLEDB data source, provide a name for the data source and the ID of the provider in the appropriate fields and click Add. This will cause the Create OLEDB Interface Data Source screen to be displayed as in Figure 35.14, which shows the fully expanded screen.

FIGURE 35.14
The Create OLEDB Inter-
face Data Source screen

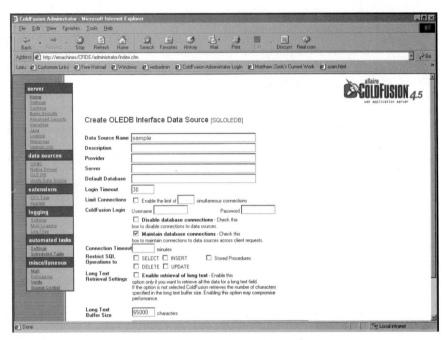

On this form, you need to make sure that the correct Provider and ProviderDSN values are indicated as well as Server name and Default Database, to create a functional
OLEDB data source in ColdFusion.

Verify Data Source

The Verify Data Source screen shown in Figure 35.15 enables you to quickly verify any
existing data source by clicking the name of the data source, or to verify all data sources
by clicking the Verify All button.

Figure 35.16 shows how the results are displayed when verifying all data sources at
one time.

FIGURE 35.15
The Verify Data Source
screen

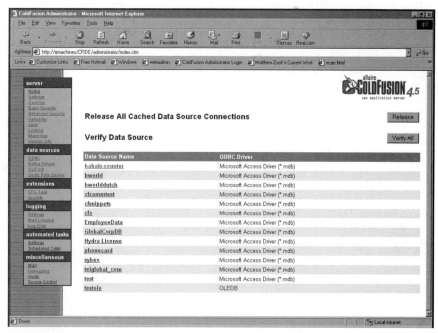

FIGURE 35.16
Verifying all data sources

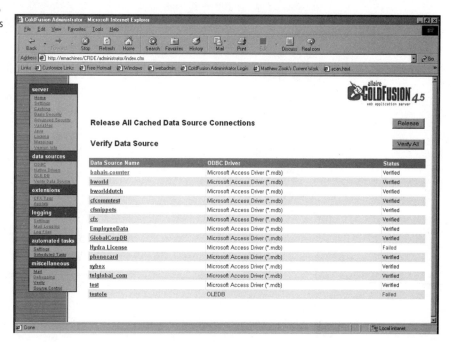

Extensions

The Extensions section of the Administrator is used to increase register extensions to ColdFusion in the form of CFX custom tags (see Chapter 32, "Including External Objects") and Java applets for use with the CFAPPLET tag. This is done through two screens:

- CFX Tags
- Applets

CFX Tags

Unlike custom tags created with ColdFusion, CFX custom tags, which have been developed in a programming language such as Visual C++Delphi, must be registered in the Registered CFX Tags screen of the Administrator for them work. The screen is shown in Figure 35.17.

FIGURE 35.17
The Registered CFX Tags screen

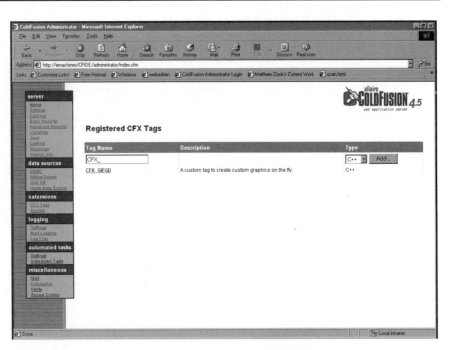

To add a tag, simply provide a name for it in the field; the name should start with CFX_. Then click the Add button. This causes the New CFX Tag screen shown in Figure 35.18 to be displayed.

FIGURE 35.18
The New CFX Tag screen

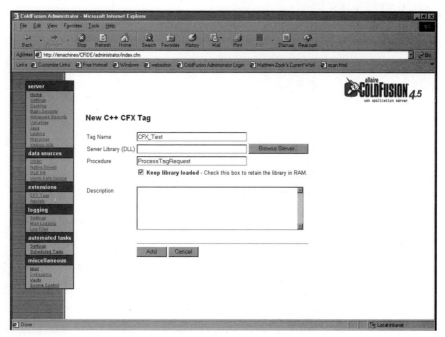

FIGURE 35.18
The New CFX Tag screen

On this screen, you need to provide the name and path of the DLL file (called the Server Library) that was provided with the custom tag. You should not change the default value of the Procedure field unless the documentation for the tag indicates otherwise. The Keep Library Loaded option, when enabled, causes the tag to be retained in memory to improve performance of the tag. Of course, with large numbers of custom tags it may not be possible to maintain them all in memory.

After you are finished configuring the tag, click the Add button. The tag will then appear in the list of CFX tags on the main Registered CFX Tags screen, where you can click the name of a tag to alter its configuration or delete it from the list.

Applets

The Registered Applets screen shown in Figure 35.19 is used to register new applets for use with the CFAPPLETS tag. The CFAPPLETS tag allows the easy integration of Java applets into pages generated by ColdFusion.

To add a new applet, provide the name of the applet in the Applet field and click the Register New Applet button. The Register New Applet screen will be displayed, as in Figure 35.20.

FIGURE 35.19
The Registered Applets
screen

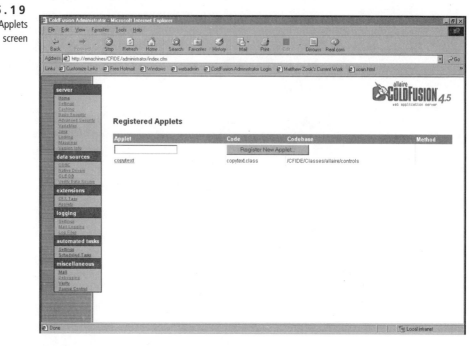

FIGURE 35.20
The Register New Applet
screen

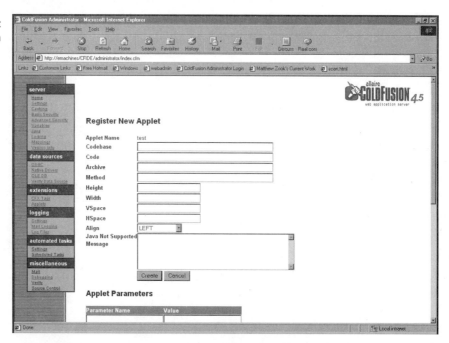

To register an applet, you need to provide all the information that would normally be provided when using the applet with a standard APPLET tag. This includes:

Codebase   The URL of the directory containing the applet.

Code   The filename of the applet. The `*.class` extension is not needed.

Archive   The filename of the ZIP archive of the applet for Microsoft Internet Explorer.

Method   The name of a method in the applet that returns a string value. Can be left blank if there is none. This is used to populate a form variable with the method's value in your templates.

Height   The height in pixels used to display the applet.

Width   The width in pixels used to display the applet.

Vspace   The space above and below the applet in pixels.

Hspace   The space on either side of the applet in pixels.

Align   Alignment of the applet relative to the surrounding HTML text.

Java Not Supported Message   A message to display on browsers that do not support Java.

In addition to these values, you need to specify the parameters required by the applet and a default value for the parameter. This is done in the list of parameter and value fields at the bottom of the screen.

After you provide all the necessary information, hit the Create button to create the entry. It will appear on the list of applets at the bottom of the main Registered Applets screen. Click the name of the applet to edit or delete it from the list.

Logging

The Logging section provides control over the way in which ColdFusion creates logs of its activities for the purposes of tracking activity and debugging problems. Logging is controlled through three screens:

- Settings
- Mail Logging
- Log Files

Settings

The General Error Logging screen, shown in Figure 35.21, allows control over the basic log settings, including:

Administrator E-Mail   The e-mail address that should appear under each error message displayed for users.

Log Directory   The directory where ColdFusion will store its log files.

Log Slow Pages   When enabled, pages that take longer than the specified number of seconds to complete will be logged in the `server.log` log file.

System Logging   When enabled, some ColdFusion log messages will be logged to both the ColdFusion log files and to the system logging facility. On Windows NT, this facility is the Event Log.

FIGURE 35.21
The General Error Logging
screen

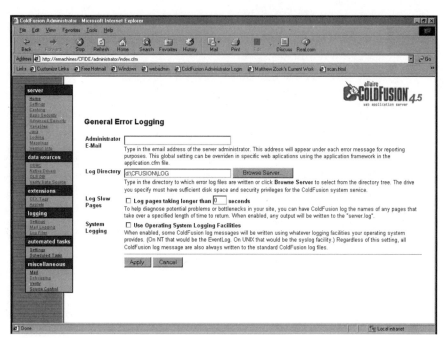

Mail Logging

The Mail Logging screen, shown in Figure 35.22, allows the specification of two simple settings related to the logging of sending of e-mail messages via ColdFusion. The first setting indicates which level of severity should be logged. Severity levels for messages are Information, Warning, and Error. The second setting indicates whether the content of all messages should be saved to the log files.

FIGURE 35.22

The Mail Logging screen

Log Files

The Log Files screen, shown in Figure 35.23, displays the name, size, and last modification date of existing ColdFusion log files. You can click the names of any log files to view them. This leads to a supplementary screen where you can choose to view the file in the Web browser or download it for offline viewing. If you choose to view a log file online, it will look like Figure 35.24.

FIGURE 35.23

The Log Files screen

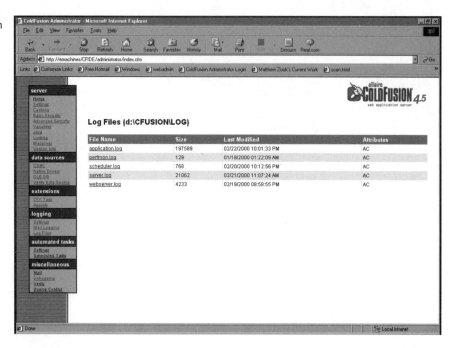

FIGURE 35.24

Viewing a log file

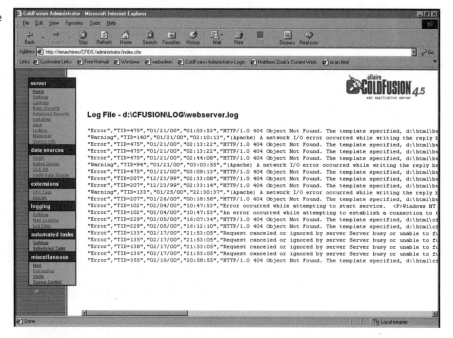

Automated Tasks

The Automated Tasks section enables you to schedule templates to execute automatically and to manage events after they are scheduled. Use of this section of the ColdFusion Administrator is covered in depth in Chapter 28, "Scheduling Events."

Miscellaneous

The final section of the ColdFusion Administrator brings together several screens that don't belong directly in other sections:

- Mail
- Debugging
- Verity
- Source Control

Use of the Mail screen is covered in Chapter 21, "Sending Mail." The Verity screen is covered in Chapter 29, "Implementing a Search Engine."

Debugging

The Debug Settings screen, shown in Figure 35.25, provides settings that can help developers debug their applications and templates.

FIGURE 35.25
The Debug Settings screen

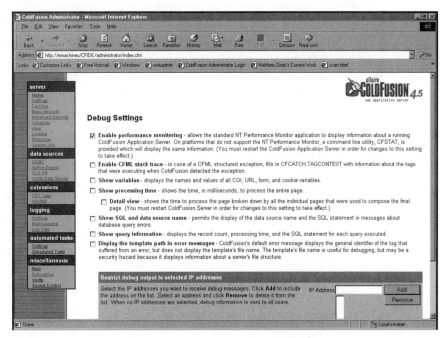

Five main settings are on the page:

Enable Performance Monitoring   Enables ColdFusion performance information to be viewed in the Windows NT Performance Monitor. This is known to create system overhead on the server and can affect the performance of heavily used systems. Therefore, it is wise to use it for testing and statistics purposes but to leave it disabled during normal system use.

Enable CFML stack trace   If enabled, when a CFML structured exception occurs, the CFCATCH.TAGCONTEXT variable will be populated with information about tags executing when the exception occurred.

Show Variables   Causes the name and value of CGI, URL, form, and cookie variables to be displayed at the bottom of every template.

Show Processing Time   Causes the time in milliseconds used to process a page to be displayed at the bottom of every template. If you enable the Detailed view sub-option in ColdFusion 4.5, the time to process a page will be broken down by individual pages used to build the complete page. If you enable this sub-option, you will need to restart the ColdFusion server process to cause it to take effect.

Show SQL and Data Source Name   Causes the data source name and SQL statement to be displayed at the bottom of messages about database query errors.

Show Query Information   Displays the SQL statement, processing time, and record count of every query in a template at the bottom of the template.

Display the template path in error messages   When this setting is enabled in ColdFusion 4.5, error messages will include the path of the template. This is useful for debugging but poses security concerns because it exposes information about the structure of the ColdFusion server to users who view error messages. Care should be taken in using this option.

Figure 35.26 shows a template being displayed with Show Variables, Show Processing Time, and Show Query Information enabled.

Of course, this type of information is useful for Web developers but need not be displayed for every user of your Web site. By default, all users will receive the debugging information at the bottom of pages unless you explicitly restrict this information to a selected group of IP addresses. Then, only users connecting from the specified IP addresses will see the data. To do this, simply add IP addresses to the list in the green box at the bottom of the screen.

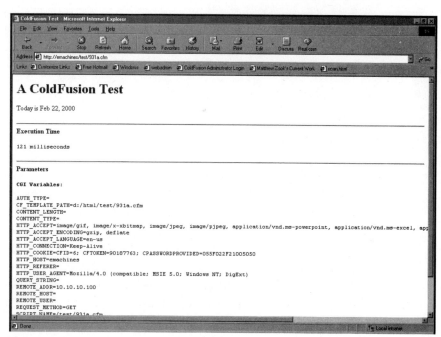

Source Control

If you have a network version of Microsoft SourceSafe installed on the same server as your ColdFusion server, then you can use ColdFusion Studio to access SourceSafe through the ColdFusion server. This is configured through the Source Control screen. Here you need to provide the complete path of the directory containing the Src-Safe.ini file as well as a working directory where files being edited are kept.

Performance Tuning

Web application environments such as ColdFusion, which are used to deploy dynamic pages to the Web, generally demand far more of your hardware than simply serving up static HTML pages and GIF files. Therefore, it is essential to maintain a strong program of performance monitoring and to be aware of options to scale ColdFusion as performance concerns demand.

Performance Monitoring

As the load on your ColdFusion server grows, monitoring its performance is important so that you can pinpoint bottlenecks and other potential sources of slowness before they become critical issues. To understand how resources on your system are being used, you need to do a couple of things:

- Analyze your log files
- Use the Windows NT Performance Monitor

Analyzing Your Log Files

The first step in determining possible sources of performance problems is to track certain types of errors being generated by the ColdFusion server. These errors are written to the `Application.log` file that can be accessed through the Logging section of the ColdFusion Administrator, as discussed earlier in this chapter.

Specifically, Request Timed Out messages may signal different types of performance problems. If the same document (or documents) is consistently generating this error in the log, it is highly suggestive that it may be the culprit in any performance problems on the server. If templates take a long time to execute and still don't finish, then it is likely that some aspect of the code (a query to a problematic database or an endless loop, for example), is causing the template to use excessive system resources.

At the same time, if you see Request Timed Out messages regularly being generated by all the templates on your server, then you may face a different problem, such as:

- A specific bottleneck that affects all your templates. These bottlenecks could include a query to a specific database that is used in all your templates or a physical problem, such as a slow hard disk that needs to be replaced with a faster one.
- You server may simply be reaching its limits. If you can't identify a clear bottleneck affecting your templates, then it may be time to either upgrade your server by adding memory and additional processors or to scale to multiple servers and use load balancing (which is discussed later in this chapter).

Using the Windows NT Performance Monitor

The Windows NT Performance Monitor is a tool for graphically displaying a wide range of information about system resources that determine the overall performance of a Windows NT system. Although we won't provide the details of using the Performance Monitor (refer to your Windows NT documentation for this), we will discuss the ColdFusion-related information that can be tracked with the Performance Monitor.

ColdFusion 4.5 provides a ColdFusion object for use with the Windows NT Performance Monitor. This object provides the following counters, which can be displayed and tracked:

Avg DB Time   The cumulative average of time in milliseconds taken for individual ColdFusion-initiated database operations to finish executing

Avg Queue Time   The cumulative average of the time in milliseconds that requests spend waiting in the queue

Avg Request Time   The cumulative average of the time in milliseconds that it took for requests to finish executing

Bytes In/Sec   The number of bytes received each second by the server

Bytes Out/Sec   The number of bytes pushed out each second by the server

DB Hits/Sec   The number of database operations performed each second by the server

Page Hits/Sec   The number of pages processed each second by the server

Queued Requests   The number of requests queued for processing at any given time

Running Requests   The number of requests being processed by the server at any given time

Timed Out Requests   The number of requests that timed out while being executed by the server

In addition to monitoring the ColdFusion counters, you may want to monitor the % Processor Time counter. Correlation between this counter and some of ColdFusion's counters (such as Running Requests) may help you adjust the server's settings for optimum performance. For instance, setting the number of simultaneous requests that ColdFusion will accept to too high a value can cause performance degradation. This counter can help catch these problems.

Performance Enhancement with the ColdFusion Administrator

As you saw in the "Using the ColdFusion Administrator" section, some Administrator settings can be used to optimize performance for your applications. Specifically, these are:

- Limit Simultaneous Requests to X on the Server Settings screen of the Server section
- Template Cache Size on the Server Settings screen of the Server section

Limiting Simultaneous Request

Web servers and their associated application environments are designed to simultaneously handle multiple requests from browsers. Given this, the initial idea of many new Web administrators is to allow far too many simultaneous connections.

Although at first this seems logical (after all, allowing a large number of simultaneous requests should mean that most incoming requests will be answered and processing will start as soon as they arrive), too many simultaneous requests can overload a system's resources, rendering performance so poor that all the requests being handled take an interminably long time to finish. By limiting the simultaneous requests being handled to a reasonable number, sufficient resources are then available to handle all the requests. Meanwhile, new requests are queued until the current number of requests being processed drops below the limit.

Consider a hypothetical example: You have a server capable of handling five simultaneous requests comfortably and completing them in an average of 10 milliseconds per request. At the same time, if the system is asked to handle 10 simultaneous requests, performance drops dramatically and each requests now takes 100 milliseconds to complete.

If you allow 10 simultaneous requests and 10 do arrive at the same time, then all of them will take 100 milliseconds to complete. The first completes in 100 milliseconds at roughly the same time the tenth is done. However, if you limit the number of simultaneous requests to five, the first five are immediately processed and the remaining five are queued up. Table 35.1 shows roughly when each request is completed relative to the time that all the requests arrive.

TABLE 35.1:   The Effect of Limiting Simultaneous Requests

Request	Completion Time
1	10 milliseconds
2	10 milliseconds
3	10 milliseconds
4	10 milliseconds
5	10 milliseconds
6	20 milliseconds
7	20 milliseconds
8	20 milliseconds
9	20 milliseconds
10	20 milliseconds

Notice that all the requests are completed at least 80 seconds earlier than they were when 10 simultaneous requests were allowed.

This example is an exaggeration of the reality of hardware and software performance on most Web servers, but it clearly illustrates that increasing the number of simultaneous requests allowed on a ColdFusion server does not guarantee better performance but can instead drastically reduce performance.

Unfortunately, simple formula cannot tell you how many simultaneous requests to allow. If performance on your server is suffering and analysis of the `Application.log` file suggests this is related to the numbers of simultaneous requests or the length of time requests take to complete, then you should try adjusting this value to see whether it has any effect. If you see large numbers of simultaneous requests in the log, try reducing the value to see whether pages return any faster. If you have pages that, even when they are the sole request, take a long time to complete, try increasing the value slightly so that other, quicker templates can be processed while the longer ones are running.

Adjusting the Template Cache Size

In terms of performance, dynamic pages require the most resources. Next, static pages served from the system's disk offer notably fewer demands on system resources. Finally, pages served from the system's RAM offer the best performance and least demand on system resources.

This is where the cache size comes into play. The cache size indicates how much RAM to make available to retain copies of the most recently processed templates. As new templates are processed and the cache is full, older templates are removed to make way for the new.

At first, it might seem that this offers a quick and easy solution to performance problems: Set the cache size high enough so that all your templates can fit in the cache. If you have enough system RAM, this will definitely have a marked effect on performance.

However, the formula is not so simple. You need to take the amount of available physical RAM and other software running on your system into consideration. Remember, all running applications and services require RAM. When physical RAM is used up, the system reverts to using virtual memory, treating hard-disk space as additional RAM. This allows for more applications to load than physical memory renders possible but, as more and more virtual memory is used more and more often, the performance of the system can grind to a halt because it is constantly accessing the hard drive for information that should be in physical RAM.

You need to keep this problem with virtual memory in mind when setting your cache size. You may have enough RAM at first glance to create a cache for storing all your templates. But you may not have enough to do this and still allocate enough physical RAM to other processes that require it, and the end result will be drastically decreased performance. On Windows NT systems you can get a sense of your system's current usage of physical and virtual memory from the Task Manager. If your system consistently has large amounts of physical RAM free, then you can probably use a good portion of it for your ColdFusion cache. However, if your system is regularly using large amounts of virtual memory, the best path to improved performance may be to add more physical memory to your server.

Limiting Dynamic Requests with *CFCACHE*

With a Web application environment such as ColdFusion, the dynamic nature of most pages is the source of many performance problems that arise. However, in many cases pages are built out of queries against data sources that do not change frequently.

For instance, consider a site that displays an online catalog based on a products database that is updated weekly. Every time a user views a page in the catalog, a unique query is made of the products database even though the results of the query (and the resulting HTML that is generated by the template) will be identical to the results generated by the request from the preceding user to access the page.

The CFCACHE tag provides a way to cache dynamically generated pages in static files that can be returned to the user instead of the dynamic pages. In our example, this would mean that the first person to access a page being cached would receive the dynamically generated content, but subsequent users would receive the cached static page, greatly reducing demands on the server's resources.

This is all oversimplified, of course. For instance, you need to ensure that the cached document is regenerated at frequent enough intervals to ensure that it reflects the most recent updates to the data sources it accesses. Fortunately, the CFCACHE tag makes this easy to achieve.

CFCACHE maintains a mapping file called `cfcache.map`, which is used to associate requested templates with static cache files. The file is stored in the same directory as the cached files it relates to and contains entries similar to a Windows INI file:

```
[test.cfm]
Mapping=C:\html\CFCBD.tmp
SourceTimeStamp=02/28/1999 03:37:45 PM
```

To use the CFCACHE tag, you simply need to include it in the templates you wish to cache as static pages. The tag takes the following attributes:

ACTION   The CFCACHE tag can perform two possible actions: CACHE, which causes the page to be cached, or FLUSH, which forces a cached page to be refreshed. The default action is CACHE.

PROTOCOL   Either the HTTP or HTTPS protocol can be used to create cached pages. This attribute indicates which protocol to use by taking either HTTP:// or HTTPS:// as its value. The default value for the attribute is HTTP://.

TIMEOUT   This attribute specifies a DateTime object indicating the oldest acceptable cached page for the document being cached. If the cached page being requested is older than the date, then the page is refreshed in the cache. For instance, to indicate that a cached page should be no older that 24 hours, you could use #DateAdd("h","-24",Now())# as the value of the TIMEOUT attribute. By default there is no timeout, which means that you will need to manually refresh pages by using the FLUSH action.

DIRECTORY   This attribute is used with the FLUSH action to indicate the directory where the cfcache.map file to be used in the FLUSH action is stored.

EXPIREURL   This attribute is used with the FLUSH action to indicate filenames in the cfcache.map file that should be refreshed. These filenames can be specified with wildcards so that test.cfm* matches test.cfm as well as test.cfm?attribute=value.

Because all the attributes of the CFCACHE tag are optional and have reasonable default values, to cache pages it is often enough to include a basic CFCACHE tag at the top of all documents to be cached. The only attribute that you may want to set manually is the TIMEOUT attribute—to give it a value that makes sense for the data sources being used by the pages being cached. Alternately, instead of specifying timeouts in all your CFCACHE tags, you can simply build a separate template that flushes the necessary cached files and then schedule that template to run as needed by using the scheduling feature of ColdFusion (see Chapter 28, "Scheduling Events").

Load Balancing Using ClusterCATS

At some point, a popular or heavily used ColdFusion server is going to hit a ceiling where additional hardware becomes necessary to improve performance. When this happens, several factors come into the decision, but ultimately the question at hand will be: Do you increase the power of your existing server or move to multiple servers? The answer is never easy, but the experience of many Web administrators suggests the following:

- When originally purchasing your server, purchase server-class hardware that supports multiple processors (but initially you may want to install only one processor).

- If you need to upgrade, consider adding a second processor to your system if it has only one. This generally provides a cost-effective but significant boost in server CPU performance of roughly 70 percent.
- If your current server already has two processors, consider adding a second two-processor server rather than adding two more processors to your server. Each additional processor in a multi-processor system offers less of a performance gain than the preceding processor. In fact, a four-processor system offers about 2.5 times the CPU performance of a single processor system whereas a two-processor system offers about 1.75 times the performance of the single-processor system. Two two-processor systems will offer about 3.5 times the performance of the single-processor system, a significant improvement over a single four-processor system.

If you have reached the point where you are deciding to implement multiple Cold-Fusion and Web servers, you need to consider several points in your deployment:

- Keeping your systems consistent
- Replicating data between your systems
- Balancing traffic between your systems

Keeping Your Systems Consistent

Generally, if you are installing multiple ColdFusion servers for your applications, you will want to install and run the same set of applications on all your systems. This helps keep your systems consistent and easy to manage. If your systems have widely differing installed applications and configuration settings, managing the systems becomes extremely difficult. Instead, to ease your management task and ensure that the user experience is consistent, try to keep system configurations as close as possible to one another across your multiple Web/ColdFusion servers.

Replicating Data between Your Systems

If you plan to run the same applications on multiple servers, you need a system for keeping the content of your applications synchronized across your servers. There are several approaches to doing this:

- Use a replication application such as Robocopy, which is part of the Windows NT Resource Kit.
- Maintain a separate development copy of your sites and then use an integrated development tool such as ColdFusion Studio or NetObjects Fusion to publish your content to multiple production servers.

- Use the built-in replication service provided by ClusterCATS (assuming that you decide to use this component of ColdFusion server). ClusterCATS is discussed later in this chapter.

Balancing Traffic between Your Systems

When deciding to run multiple Web servers, the general practice is to implement some form of load balancing. Under this scenario, all your Web servers serve identical content, but as far as the Web-browsing public is concerned, your site is accessed through a single host name.

You then implement a system for causing user requests to your site to be distributed across the multiple servers in some fashion, with the goal of evenly spreading load across the servers. From the user's perspective, there is a single server (or address) and they don't need to know that they could be receiving each page during their visit to your site from a different server.

Several techniques can be used for load balancing:

- Round-robin DNS
- Load-balancing software
- Load-balancing hardware

Round-Robin DNS

DNS is the domain name service. This is an Internet-wide distributed database that translates host names such as www.landegg.edu into IP addresses such as 194.148.43.194. This is important because computers on the Internet use IP addresses to direct communication to the correct destination.

Generally, each organization that owns its domain name runs its own name server for the domain to handle translation of host names within their domain. DNS can be extended to implement basic load-balancing. Through special changes to a DNS server, you can make it deliver different IP addresses each time a name is looked up. For instance, if you have two Web servers, then each time a name lookup is received for your Web server host name, alternating IP addresses will be provided during the name lookup.

At first glance this may seem like a simple way to evenly distribute load across multiple servers. However, this technique does not take into account actual load on the servers. It is not unlikely that one server will end up handling a disproportionate number of CPU-intensive requests, resulting in distinctly unbalanced loads across the servers. Also, if a system is down, the DNS server doesn't detect this and at least some of the attempts to connect to your site will be directed to the system that is down, resulting in failed connection attempts.

Load-Balancing Software

Specialized load-balancing software exists that takes things a step beyond the crude functionality of round-robin DNS. ColdFusion Server includes Bright Tiger's Cluster-CATS load-balancing software (the name comes from the concept of a cluster: multiple servers appearing to act as one server). Other products are also available.

Specialized load-balancing software can perform several jobs:

- Replicating content across multiple servers in a cluster
- Handling situations in which a server suffers failure or a state of massive load imbalance occurs
- Monitoring actual load on the various servers to ensure the optimal distribution of incoming requests on the basis of available server resources on different servers

However, load-balancing software has its limits. These include the need for one server in the cluster to play the central role of managing the cluster, which introduces a single point of failure (if the primary server goes down, the cluster ceases to function), and lack of built-in support for security features such as network address translation.

Load-Balancing Hardware

The most complete form of load balancing comes in dedicated hardware systems such as Cisco's Local Director or HydraWeb. These systems completely hide a cluster from the outside world, masking the cluster behind a single IP address. The hardware manages the distribution of requests by negotiating with servers in the cluster to find one that appears to be most ready to handle a new request.

Of all load-balancing approaches, this is the most complex to install and manage but offers the best capabilities for large-scale Web installations. Hardware load balancing offers many advantages, including the best distribution of load across servers, extra security in the form of network address translation, and the best capability to handle system failures. It is also possible to provide redundancy of the cluster management system, which is generally not possible with software-based solutions. On the other hand, hardware systems generally don't handle content replication and tend to be pricey.

An Overview of ClusterCATS

The Enterprise edition of ColdFusion Server 4.5 ships with ClusterCATS from Bright Tiger software. This is a software-based load-balancing solution integrated into the ColdFusion server environment.

ClusterCATS works through URL redirection: Your application server is monitored and requests are redirected to another server in the cluster when load gets too high. This is a fairly basic form of load balancing but it generally works. The version of ClusterCATS bundled in ColdFusion 4.5 is not a full version; it lacks replication capabilities that are available in the full version of ClusterCATS.

A major disadvantage of the URL redirection approach used by ClusterCATS is that your cluster appears to the end user as a large collection of identical Web servers. When they are redirected to another server, users see the change in the URL of the page displayed in their browser. This contrasts with other solutions, which make the cluster appear to be one large server with a single IP address.

ClusterCATS consists of a server component for Windows NT and Solaris. This component controls how a machine plays its role in the cluster and runs on all machines in the cluster.

The ClusterCATS Explorer is a Windows NT–based tool for managing a cluster. This can run on any member of the cluster and is used to create a cluster, add and remove servers from a cluster, define load limitations for clusters, and more.

To learn to use the ClusterCATS software, refer to the documentation that comes with ClusterCATS.

Where Do We Go from Here?

In this chapter, we have covered the details of the ColdFusion Administrator that allows you to manage all aspects of the ColdFusion server's behavior. This information is essential if you manage a ColdFusion server in addition to simply developing applications for it.

In the next chapter, we will cover a topic new to ColdFusion 4.5: the installation and use of ColdFusion for Linux. Until version 4.5, ColdFusion was only available for Windows systems and commercial Unix environments such as Solaris. Allaire has responded to the widespread popularity of Linux as a Web server platform even in larger corporate environments that use other operating systems for the rest of their networks. We will look at the installation and basic management of ColdFusion on Linux systems.

ColdFusion for Linux

- An Overview of ColdFusion for Linux

- Installing ColdFusion for Linux

- Starting and Stopping ColdFusion for Linux

- Databases and ColdFusion for Linux

Starting with ColdFusion 4.5.1, Allaire is porting ColdFusion to the Linux platform. This is a significant move designed to take advantage of the widespread popularity of Linux as a platform for Web servers. Many Linux Web server administrators have, until now, hesitated to adopt ColdFusion because of the need to deploy Windows NT, which is seen as less stable than Linux, or purchase expensive commercial Unix systems such as Solaris.

In this chapter, we will take a brief look at ColdFusion for Linux and look more closely at the two places where it differs most from ColdFusion for Windows NT: installation and database support.

An Overview of ColdFusion for Linux

ColdFusion for Linux is almost identical to ColdFusion for Windows NT, implementing almost all features found in the Windows version. It is available in both the Professional and Enterprise Editions for Linux. The primary differences between the two platforms are:

- A different installation procedure
- Different management procedures
- Support for a different set of database drivers
- No COM support

In addition, ColdFusion 4.5 for Windows is currently available while version 4.5.1 for Linux (and Windows) is currently in beta testing at the time of printing. ColdFusion 4.5 is not available for Linux.

In addition, ColdFusion Studio is a Windows-only product and is not available for any Unix platform on which ColdFusion is available. However, a Windows-based Cold-Fusion Studio installation can connect to a Linux-based ColdFusion Server for remote development purposes.

ColdFusion for Linux is designed to be used with RedHat Linux 6.0 or higher. Nonetheless, an advanced Linux administrator can probably make ColdFusion work on most modern Linux distributions. The minimum requirements for ColdFusion for Linux are:

- 64 MB RAM; 128 MB recommended; 128 MB required for clustering support
- 70 MB disk space; 100MB required for clustering support
- Apache 1.3.6 or higher; Apache 1.3.6 or Apache 1.3.9 recommended

Because the current release of ColdFusion for Linux is a beta version, not all features are currently implemented or supported, although most will be by the time the final release is available for Linux. In particular, the following features are currently not supported:

- The `LSParseDateTime` function only works in the English locale.
- The `CFOBJECT` tag currently only supports Java objects.
- Verity is not supported so the `CFINDEX`, `CFSEARCH`, and `CFCOLLECTION` tags do not work.

Installing ColdFusion for Linux

These installation instructions assume you are familiar with your Linux system and have installed the Apache Web server and it is operational before proceeding. Before installing beta 1 of ColdFusion 4.5.1 for Linux, you need to note the following:

1. You should install RedHat Linux in either Server or Custom modes rather than GNOME or KDE Workstation mode in order to ensure that all packages needed are installed.

2. Make sure that the `ServerName` directive in `/etc/httpd/conf/httpd.conf` file is uncommented and specifies your Web server's host and domain name.

3. The Apache development package must be installed; you can use the command `rpm -qa | grep apache-devel` to check if the package if installed

The current beta of ColdFusion is distributed as a compressed tape archive file named `coldfusion-451b1-linux.tar.gz`. Before installing, extract the file to the `coldfusion-451b1-linux` subdirectory and then change your current directory to that directory with the following commands:

```
# tar xzvf coldfusion-451b1-linux.tar.gz
# cd coldfusion-451b1-linux
```

To install ColdFusion for Linux, use the following steps:

1. Launch the installation script with the command:

   ```
   # ./cfinstall
   ```

   The installation script will prompt you for your registration ID:

   ```
   ********************************************************************
   *   Welcome to the ColdFusion 4.5.1 Installation for Linux
   *
   *                 Thank you for choosing ColdFusion!
   ********************************************************************

   Please enter your ColdFusion registration ID [Evaluation]:
   ```

2. Press the Enter key to accept the evaluation registration ID. The installation script will prompt you for the directory where ColdFusion will be installed:

   ```
   Please enter the absolute path of the directory where you'ld like
   ColdFusion installed. ColdFusion will be installed into a subdirectory,
   named 'coldfusion', of the directory you specify here. You do not need
   to create the 'coldfusion' subdirectory (this install will create it
   for you), but the parent directory you specify here must already exist.

   Enter the installation directory for ColdFusion [/opt]:
   ```

3. ColdFusion will be installed in the `coldfusion` subdirectory under the specified directory. If you enter a directory other than /opt, ColdFusion will be installed where you specify and a link will be created from `/opt/coldfusion` to the final ColdFusion installation directory.

4. Press the Enter key to accept the default installation directory (/opt) or enter the desired directory and then press the Enter key. The installation script will prompt you to specify the type of Web server you are running:

```
In order for ColdFusion to be able to receive requests your web server must be
configured to recognize CFML files.

For Apache, a ColdFusion dynamically loaded module must be configured.
For a Netscape server, the installation can install a NSAPI plugin to do this.
If you are running another web server, you must configure a CGI program.

What type of web server are you running (apache netscape other) [apache]:
```

5. Press the Enter key to install ColdFusion with the Apache Web server. ColdFusion will detect your version of Apache and then will prompt you to indicate if you want to configure Apache automatically:

```
It appears you have Apache 1.3.9 installed.

Automatically configure your Apache server [y]:
```

6. Press the Enter key to allow the installation script to automatically configure Apache for ColdFusion. The installation script will prompt you for your Web server's document root directory:

```
In order to install the ColdFusion Administrator and the ColdFusion
documentation, files must be copied in to the document directory
(usually called the document root) of your web server.

Enter your web server's document root directory [/home/httpd/html]:
```

7. Press the Enter key to accept the default directory (/home/httpd/html) or enter your Apache server's document root directory and press the Enter key. The installation script will prompt you to indicate if you want to install the ColdFusion documentation:

```
Do you want the ColdFusion documentation (HTML files) installed? [y]:
```

8. Press the Enter key to allow the documentation to be installed. The installation script will prompt you to indicate if you want the sample applications to be installed. They should not be installed on a production system:

    ```
    It is not recommended that the ColdFusion example applications be installed
    on a production server due to potential security concerns.

    Do you want the ColdFusion example applications installed? [n]:
    ```

9. Press the Enter key to make sure the sample applications are not installed. The installation script will prompt you to enter the user account under which ColdFusion will run:

    ```
    Please enter the user name of the account under which you would
    like ColdFusion to run. This must be a valid, existing user
    account.  Is is a good idea to create an account specifically
    for ColdFusion.

    It is not recommended the ColdFusion server run as root.

    Enter an existing login name [nobody]:
    ```

    As with the Apache Web server, you should not run ColdFusion as the root user. Instead, you should run it as the nobody user or a user account you specifically create for the purpose of running the ColdFusion server.

10. Enter the user account for running ColdFusion and press the Enter key. The installation script will prompt you to indicate if you want to install ClusterCATS support:

    ```
    ClusterCATS for ColdFusion is software which will allow you to
    configure multiple server machines in to a cluster for load
    balancing and high-availability.

    Do you want to install ClusterCATS for ColdFusion [n]:
    ```

    ClusterCATS provides support for multiple-server clusters for load balancing and redundancy and only needs to be installed if you run that type of high-volume site.

11. Press the Enter key to indicate you do not wish to install ClusterCATS. The installation script will indicate it is ready to install ColdFusion:

    ```
    Ready to begin the installation.  Press ENTER to continue..
    ```

12. Press the Enter key. The installation script will install ColdFusion and start it:

```
Preserving user-modified files from the existing installation...

Copying files.......
Setting up uninstall links...
Initializing ColdFusion Settings...
ColdFusion registry initialized.
Customizing ColdFusion startup scripts...
        Restoring saved start script
        Restoring saved odbc.ini
Configuring the ColdFusion Apache Module
cp /opt/coldfusion/webserver/apache/mod_coldfusion.so /etc/httpd/modules/
mod_col
dfusion.so
chmod 755 /etc/httpd/modules/mod_coldfusion.so
Restarting Apache...
Shutting down http: [  OK  ]
Starting httpd: [  OK  ]
Starting ColdFusion servers...

ColdFusion installation completed successfully.

The ColdFusion Application Server is now running!
```

Starting and Stopping ColdFusion for Linux

ColdFusion for Linux includes a script you can use to start and stop ColdFusion. To start ColdFusion, use the following command:

 # /etc/rc.d/init.d/coldfusion start

Similarly, to stop ColdFusion for Linux, use the following command:

 # /etc/rc.d/init.d/coldfusion stop

When ColdFusion is running, you can access the ColdFusion Administrator from your Web browser using the URL: `http://localhost/cfide/administrator/index.cfm`.

Databases and ColdFusion for Linux

ColdFusion for Linux supports a smaller set of databases than ColdFusion for Windows. At the current time the following database drivers are provided with ColdFusion for Linux:

- PostgreSQL (ODBC)
- Informix 7.x (ODBC)

- Informix 9.x (ODBC)
- Sybase 11 (ODBC)
- Sybase 11 (Native)
- Oracle 8.0 (Native)
- Informix 7.3 (Native)
- DB2 (Native)

Use of these drivers is similar to their counterparts in Windows versions of ColdFusion. The PostgreSQL driver is not available in ColdFusion for Windows. PostgreSQL is a popular, freely available client-server database platform for Unix systems including Linux. Most major Linux distributions, including RedHat Linux, include PostgreSQL, which makes it an attractive choice for a cost-effective client-server database platform.

In addition to these platforms, numerous Linux systems use the freely available MySQL database for their applications. While a MySQL driver does not currently ship with ColdFusion for Linux, ColdFusion for Linux is reported to support the myODBC driver for MySQL available from `http://www.mysql.com/downloadmyodbc.html`.

You should build the myODBC driver following the instructions included with the software and then copy the `libmyodbc.so` library to `/opt/coldfusion/lib/`. After installing the myODBC driver library to the ColdFusion library directory, MySQL should be available from the ODBC driver drop-down list in the ColdFusion Administrator and ColdFusion should work with MySQL.

Where Do We Go from Here?

Congratulations! You've reached the end of your essential training for ColdFusion. This doesn't mean there isn't anything left to learn. To the contrary, you now have the knowledge and skills to tackle most ColdFusion tasks and have positioned yourself so that you can continue learn new, specialized knowledge when it is needed to complete a task.

In your on-going ColdFusion education, you will find several of this book's appendices useful. Our Appendix B, "ColdFusion Tag Reference," and Appendix C, "ColdFusion Function Reference," provide useful references for daily use when you are programming. Appendix E, "SQL Function Reference," will help you when you need to build sophisticated database queries for your ColdFusion applications, and Appendix F, "Additional Resources," will help you find useful information on the Internet when you are researching new problems and strategies for your work.

Installing ColdFusion

Installing ColdFusion on a new system requires the three following steps:

1. Installing an appropriate Web server
2. Installing the ColdFusion Application Server
3. Installing ColdFusion Studio

We will look at these in turn.

Installing a Web Server

The following Web servers work best with ColdFusion on the Windows platform:

- Microsoft Internet Information Server
- Netscape Enterprise Server
- Apache

On a development system, Microsoft's Personal Web Server can also be used. Because Apache is included on the CD-ROM with this book, we will take quick look at Web server installation with Apache.

To launch the Apache installation program from the CD-ROM, insert the disc into your CD-ROM drive. On most systems, this launches the main installation menu of the CD-ROM from which you can choose to install the Apache Web server. Alternately, you can launch the following application from the CD-ROM: `d:\Apache\apache_1_3_11_win32.exe` (this assumes your CD-ROM drive is drive D).

Either method launches the Apache installation program. Installation is fairly straightforward. After accepting the license and reading the welcome screen, the first choice you have to make is where to install the software. By default, the Apache server software is installed at `C:\Program Files\Apache Group\Apache`. You can change this by clicking the Browse button next to the default path.

Next, you choose the type of setup you prefer. Your choices are:

Typical   The most commonly used components are installed.
Compact   The minimum required components are installed.
Custom   You can specify the component to install.

For most users, Typical is the best choice which provides the Web server, documentation and modules needed to run Apache. If you select Custom, then you are presented with the following components to choose from:

Web Server Application Files   Installs the actual Apache software. You need this to use Apache. This is a required option.
Web Server Source Code   Installs the Apache source code. Apache is a freely distributed Web server. The distribution includes the full source code so that if you want to alter the functionality of the server, you can do so by changing the source code and re-compiling the application. For most users, this option is not necessary. In order to take advantage of the source code, you need to have extensive programming experience and access to Windows development tools and compilers.
Web Server Manual   Installs the Apache documentation. If you are short on disk space, you can leave this out because the documentation is available at `http://www.apache.org`. Installing the documentation is recommended if you have sufficient space.
Additional Modules   Installs modules that add functionality to the core program. The Apache distribution comes with a small collection of modules.
Web Server Icons   Installs several useful icons for Apache.

The next choice you have to make is what to name the program group that you will install the Apache icons in. The default is Apache Web Server, but you can change this.

After you choose the program group, the installation program installs the Apache components you selected, creates the program group if it doesn't exist, and creates icons for Apache. Then your installation is complete.

To test your installation, you first need to launch the Apache server. To do this, double-click the Start Apache as a Console App icon in the Apache Web Server program group (or the group that you specified during installation). You can get to this program group from the Programs submenu of the Windows Start menu. You should see a window displayed with the current date and text similar to "Apache/1.3.6 (Win32) running…". If you see this, then the server is installed correctly and works. Every time you start your PC you can double-click the icon to start your Web server.

If, for some reason, the window quickly disappears, refer to the Apache documentation for troubleshooting information. If you installed the documentation, you can open it by double-clicking the Apache Documentation icon in the Apache Web Server program group. The documentation also contains complete instructions about configuring your Apache server.

NOTE   If you are using Apache on Windows NT, you can install Apache as a service so that it starts every time you reboot your system. This prevents you from having to use the Start Apache as a Console App icon to start Apache each time you start your system. To do this, double-click the Install Apache as a Service icon in the Apache Web Server program group. Apache can run as a service only in Windows NT. This will not work in Windows 95 or 98, but you place a shortcut to the Apache Web server in your StartUp group so that Windows will launch the server every time it starts.

Installing the ColdFusion Application Server

The next step, after you have a working Web server, is to install the ColdFusion Application Server.

To launch the ColdFusion Application Server installation program from the CD-ROM, insert the disc into your CD-ROM drive. On most systems, this launches the main installation menu of the CD-ROM from which you can choose to install the ColdFusion Application Server. Alternately, you can launch the following application from the CD-ROM: `d:\ColdFusion45_Eval\cf45enterprise_eval.exe` (this assumes your CD-ROM drive is drive D).

Either method launches the ColdFusion Application Server installation program. After accepting the license and reading the welcome screen, provide your name and company and, if you are installing a full version (an evaluation version comes on the CD-ROM with this book), a serial number.

Then, the first choice you have to make is where to install the software. By default, ColdFusion Application Server is installed at `C:\CFUSION`. You can change this by clicking the Browse button next to the default path.

Next, indicate the type of Web server you are using. ColdFusion attempts to determine the type of Web server you are using and presents a list of servers it finds. If your server appears on the list, select it. Otherwise, choose Other Server. In the case of the Apache Web server, select Other Server.

Then, indicate the location of your Web server's document directory. With some Web servers, this is detected automatically and presented for verification. With others, you need to click the Browse button and select the directory. If you are unsure of the correct directory, refer to your server's documentation. In the case of a default Apache installation, this directory should be `c:\program files\apache group\apache\htdocs`.

After that, select the components to install. You can install the three following components:

ColdFusion program files   These files are necessary for the Application Server to work.

Documentation   These are the complete ColdFusion documentation. It is a good idea to install them.
Examples   A set of example ColdFusion applications and templates. There are security concerns regarding the ColdFusion examples and you should not install the examples on a publicly-accessible Web server.
CFXAPI Tag Development Kit   If you plan to develop ColdFusion custom tags by using Visual C++, you will need this kit. Otherwise, you don't need to install it.
Advanced Security Services   Advanced security services in addition to the basic security features of ColdFusion server.

After you select the components you wish to install, provide a password that will be used to control access to the ColdFusion Administrator. Then provide a password for limiting remote development access to the server through ColdFusion Studio. Because the ColdFusion development and administration environment has limited security, it is advisable to select a difficult password of at least eight characters which combines upper and lower case letters with numbers and punctuation symbols.

The next choice to make is the name of the program group to install the ColdFusion icons in. The default is ColdFusion Server 4.5, but you can change this.

The installation program then installs the components you selected, creates the program group if it doesn't exist, and creates the necessary icons in the program. In addition, the ColdFusion Application Server starts. After this is done, your installation is complete and you are prompted to restart your PC. Restarting ensures that all configuration and installation is complete. If everything went well, the Cold-Fusion server should start automatically when you start Windows. If you are running Windows 95 or 98, an icon for it should appear on the taskbar. If you are using the Apache server, there are two steps left to finish configuring ColdFusion Application Server:

1. Install the ColdFusion Apache module by copying the file `c:\cfusion\bin\ApacheModuleCold-Fusion.dll` to `c:\Program Files\Apache Group\Apache\modules\ApacheModuleColdFu-sion.dll` (these paths assume the default installation locations for both ColdFusion and Apache).

2. Edit the Apache configuration file, `C:\Program Files\Apache Group\Apache\conf\httpd.conf`. Inside the file, add the line `LoadModule coldfusion_module modules/ApacheModule-ColdFusion.dll` to the end of the file.

After you have completed these steps, you can stop your Apache server if it is running and restart it to enable ColdFusion support. Consult the Apache documentation for information on starting and restarting the Apache server.

To test whether ColdFusion is working properly, launch the ColdFusion Administrator from the ColdFusion Server 4.5 program group. If your Web server is running and ColdFusion is installed properly and is also running, then you should see a login form for the ColdFusion administrator in your browser.

Another way to test your installation is by using a special application provided by Allaire for that purpose. You can find it at `http://127.0.0.1/CFDOCS/testinstallation/test.htm`. Follow the directions displayed in the browser for performing the installation verification test. If the preceding URL does not exist, or if you receive an error after performing the test, then the ColdFusion server is not installed or has installation problems. If this is the case, please refer to "Troubleshooting Your Cold-Fusion Installation" later in this appendix.

NOTE   If you have installed ColdFusion on Windows NT, it is advisable to install the latest service pack for Windows NT after installing ColdFusion to avoid exposing your server to known security exploits. Remember to regularly check the Allaire Web site at `http://www.allaire.com` for updates to ColdFusion so that you have the latest bug fixes and security patches on your server.

Installing ColdFusion Studio

The final step in installing a complete ColdFusion environment is to install ColdFusion Studio.

To launch the ColdFusion Studio installation program from the CD-ROM, insert the disc into your CD-ROM drive. On most systems, this launches the main installation menu of the CD-ROM from which you can choose to install ColdFusion Studio. Alternately, you can launch the following application from the CD-ROM: `d:\ColdFusionStudio45_Eval\cfstudio45_eval.exe` (this assumes your CD-ROM drive is drive D).

Either method launches the Studio installation program. After accepting the license and reading the welcome screen, provide your name and company and, if you are installing a full version (an evaluation version comes on the CD-ROM with this book), a serial number.

Then, the first choice you have to make is where to install the software. By default, ColdFusion Studio is installed at `C:\Program Files\Allaire\ColdFusion Studio 4.5`. You can change this by clicking the Browse button next to the default path.

> **NOTE**   If you already have the full version of TopStyle installed on your system and you allow ColdFusion to install TopStyle Lite, then you will need to reinstall the full version again.

Next, select the components to install. You have two components to choose from:

ColdFusion Studio program files   These files are necessary for Studio to work.

Documentation   These files comprise the complete ColdFusion Studio documentation. It is a good idea to install them.

Next, choose the name of the program group to install the Studio icons in. The default is ColdFusion Studio 4.5, but you can change this.

The installation program then installs the components you selected, creates the program group if it doesn't exist, and creates the necessary icons in the program group. After this is done, your installation is complete and you are prompted to restart your PC. Restarting ensures that all configuration and installation is complete.

Troubleshooting Your ColdFusion Installation

If, after installing the ColdFusion Application Server, it doesn't appear to be working, you need to check the following:

1. Is your Web server running? The way to check this depends on your Web server. Check the Web server's documentation, and if the server is not running, start it. You can check if your Web server is running by pointing a browser on the Web server system to `http://127.0.0.1/`.
2. Is the ColdFusion Application Server running? In Windows NT, you can check this in the Services Applet of the Control Panel and restart the service from there if it isn't running. In Windows 95 and 98, look for the ColdFusion icon on the taskbar. If it isn't there, restart the ColdFusion server by choosing the ColdFusion icon in the ColdFusion Server 4.5 program group.
3. Is your network properly configured? Check your Windows documentation for more details.

If, after performing these steps, you still can't get your ColdFusion server running properly, consult the ColdFusion documentation. In addition, you can search the Allaire Knowledge Base for relevant technical articles at `http://www1.allaire.com/Support/KnowledgeBase/SearchForm.cfm`. You can also post a query to the ColdFusion Support that is offered by Allaire at `http://forums.allaire.com/devconf/`. Finally, Allaire offers a general support Web site at `http://www1.allaire.com/support/index.cfm`.

ColdFusion Tag Reference

The following reference is extracted from the ColdFusion Language Reference, which ships with the ColdFusion Server distribution. The complete reference is available in the online documentation on the CD-ROM or in the Cold-Fusion Language Reference manual in the boxed set of ColdFusion Server.

ColdFusion Tags by Function

In the following section, we will be going over ColdFusion tags by their functions.

Database Manipulation Tags

CFINSERT	CFQUERYPARAM
CFPROCPARAM	CFSTOREDPROC
CFPROCRESULT	CFTRANSACTION
CFQUERY	CFUPDATE

Data Output Tags

CFCOL	CFHEADER	CFTABLE
CFCONTENT	CFOUTPUT	

Exception Handling Tags

CFERROR
CFRETHROW
CFTHROW
CFTRY CFCATCH

Variable Manipulation Tags

CFCOOKIE	CFSCHEDULE
CFPARAM	CFSET

Flow-Control Tags

CFABORT	CFLOOP
CFBREAK	CFSWITCH CFCASE
CFEXECUTE	CFDEFAULTCASE
CFIF CFELSEIF CFELSE	CFTHROW
CFLOCATION	CFTRY CFCATCH

Internet Protocol Tags

CFFTP	CFMAIL
CFHTTP	CFMAILPARAM
CFHTTPPARAM	CFPOP
CFLDAP	

Java Servlet and Java Object Tags

CFOBJECT   CFSERVLETPARAM
CFSERVLET

File Management Tags

CFDIRECTORY   CFFILE

Web Application Framework Tags

CFAPPLICATION   CFERROR
CFASSOCIATE   CFLOCK
CFAUTHENTICATE

ColdFusion Forms Tags

CFAPPLET   CFINPUT
CFFORM   CFSELECT
CFGRID   CFSLIDER
CFGRIDCOLUMN   CFTEXTINPUT
CFGRIDROW   CFTREE
CFGRIDUPDATE   CFTREEITEM

Extensibility Tags

CFCOLLECTION   CFSEARCH
CFEXECUTE   CFSERVLET
CFINDEX   CFSERVLETPARAM
CFOBJECT   CFWDDX
CFREPORT

Other Tags

CFASSOCIATE   CFREPORT
CFCACHE   CFSCHEDULE
CFHTMLHEAD   CFSETTING
CFINCLUDE   CFSILENT
CFLOCK   CFWDDX

Alphabetical List of Tags

CFABORT	CFFORM	CFLOOP	CFSELECT
CFAPPLET	CFFTP	CFMAIL	CFSERVLET
CFAPPLICATION	CFGRID	CFMAILPARAM	CFSERVLETPARAM
CFASSOCIATE	CFGRIDCOLUMN	CFMODULE	CFSET
CFAUTHENTICATE	CFGRIDROW	CFOBJECT	CFSETTING
CFBREAK	CFGRIDUPDATE	CFOUTPUT	CFSILENT
CFCACHE	CFHEADER	CFPARAM	CFSLIDER
CFCASE	CFHTMLHEAD	CFPOP	CFSTOREDPROC
CFCATCH	CFHTTP	CFPROCESSINGDIRECTIVE	CFSWITCH
CFCOL	CFHTTPPARAM	CFPROCPARAM	CFTABLE
CFCOLLECTION	CFIF CFELSEIF CFELSE	CFPROCRESULT	CFTEXTINPUT
CFCONTENT	CFIMPERSONATE	CFQUERY	CFTHROW
CFCOOKIE	CFINCLUDE	CFQUERYPARAM	CFTRANSACTION
CFDEFAULTCASE	CFINDEX	CFREGISTRY	CFTREE
CFDIRECTORY	CFINPUT	CFREPORT	CFTREEITEM
CFERROR	CFINSERT	CFRETHROW	CFTRY CFCATCH
CFEXECUTE	CFLDAP	CFSCHEDULE	CFUPDATE
CFEXIT	CFLOCATION	CFSCRIPT	
CFFILE	CFLOCK	CFSEARCH	

CFABORT

The CFABORT tag stops processing of a page at the tag location. ColdFusion simply returns everything that was processed before the CFABORT tag. CFABORT is often used with conditional logic to stop processing a page because of a particular condition.

Syntax

```
<CFABORT SHOWERROR="text">
```

SHOWERROR

Optional. Specify the error you want to display when CFABORT executes. This error message appears in the standard ColdFusion error page.

CFAPPLET

Used in a CFFORM, CFAPPLET allows you to reference custom Java applets that have been previously registered using the ColdFusion Administrator.

To register a Java applet, open the ColdFusion Administrator and click the Applets button.

Syntax

```
<CFAPPLET APPLETSOURCE="applet_name"
    NAME="form_variable_name"
    HEIGHT="pixels"
    WIDTH="pixels"
    VSPACE="pixels"
    HSPACE="pixels"
    ALIGN="alignment"
    NOTSUPPORTED="text"
    param_1="value"
    param_2="value"
    param_n="value">
```

APPLETSOURCE

Required. The name of the registered applet.

NAME

Required. The form variable name for the applet.

HEIGHT

Optional. The height in pixels.

WIDTH

Optional. The width in pixels.

VSPACE

Optional. Space above and below applet in pixels.

HSPACE

Optional. Space on each side of the applet in pixels.

ALIGN

Optional. Alignment. Valid entries are the following:

- Left
- Right
- Bottom
- Top
- TextTop
- Middle
- AbsMiddle
- Baseline
- AbsBottom

NOTSUPPORTED

Optional. The text you want to display if the page containing a Java applet-based CFFORM control is opened by a browser that does not support Java or has Java support disabled. For example:

```
NOTSUPPORTED="<B>Browser must support Java to
view
ColdFusion Java Applets</B>"
```

By default, if no message is specified, the following message appears:

```
<B>Browser must support Java to <BR>
view ColdFusion Java Applets!</B>
```

paramn

Optional. The valid name of a registered parameter for the applet. Specify a parameter only if you want to override parameter values already defined for the applet using the ColdFusion Administrator.

CFAPPLICATION

Defines scoping for a ColdFusion application, enables or disables storing client variables, and specifies a client variable storage mechanism. By default, client variables are disabled. Also, used to enable session variables and to set timeouts for both session and application variables. Session and application variables are stored in memory.

Syntax

```
<CFAPPLICATION NAME="Name"
    CLIENTMANAGEMENT="Yes/No"
    CLIENTSTORAGE="Storage Type"
    SETCLIENTCOOKIES="Yes/No"
    SESSIONMANAGEMENT="Yes/No"
    SESSIONTIMEOUT=#CreateTimeSpan(days,
hours,
      minutes, seconds)#
    APPLICATIONTIMEOUT=#CreateTimeSpan(days,
hours,
      minutes, seconds)#
    SETDOMAINCOOKIES="Yes/No"
>
```

NAME

The name you want to give your application. This name can be up to 64 characters long. Required for application and session variables to work. Optional for client variables.

CLIENTMANAGEMENT

Optional. Yes or No. Enables client variables. Default is No.

CLIENTSTORAGE

Optional. Specifies the mechanism for storing client variables:

Datasourcename   ColdFusion stores client variables in the specified ODBC or native data source. To use this option you must create a client variable storage repository using the Variables page of the Cold-Fusion Administrator.

Registry   ColdFusion stores client variables in the system registry. This is the default.

Cookie   ColdFusion stores client variables on the client machine in a cookie. Storing client data in a cookie is scalable to large numbers of clients, but this storage mechanism has some limitations. Chief among them is that if the client turns off cookies in the browser, client variables won't work.

SETCLIENTCOOKIES

Optional. Yes or No. Yes enables client cookies. Default is Yes.

If you set this attribute to "NO", ColdFusion does not automatically send the CFID and CFTOKEN cookies to the client browser; you must manually code CFID and CFTOKEN on the URL for every page that uses Session or Client variables.

SESSIONMANAGEMENT

Optional. Yes or No. Yes enables session variables. Default is No.

SESSIONTIMEOUT

Optional. Enter the CreateTimeSpan function and the values you want in days, hours, minutes, and seconds, separated by commas to specify the lifespan of any session variables that are set. The default value is specified in the Variables page of the ColdFusion Administrator.

APPLICATIONTIMEOUT

Optional. Enter the CreateTimeSpan function and the values you want in days, hours, minutes, and seconds, separated by commas to specify the lifespan of any application variables that are set. The default value is specified in the Variables page of the ColdFusion Administrator.

SETDOMAINCOOKIES

Optional. Yes or No. Sets the CFID and CFTOKEN cookies for an entire domain not just a single host. Applications that are running on clusters must set this value to Yes. The default is No.

CFASSOCIATE

The CFASSOCIATE tag allows sub-tag data to be saved with the base tag. This applies to custom tags only.

Syntax

```
<CFASSOCIATE BASETAG="tagname"
    DATACOLLECTION="collectionname">
```

BASETAG

Specifies the name of the base tag.

DATACOLLECTION

Optional. Specifies the name of the structure in which the base tag stores sub-tag data. The default is AssocAttribs.

CFAUTHENTICATE

The CFAUTHENTICATE tag authenticates a user, setting a security context for the application. See the descriptions of the functions IsAuthenticated and Authenticated-Context.

Syntax

```
<CFAUTHENTICATE SECURITYCONTEXT="context"
    USERNAME="user ID"
    PASSWORD="password"
    SETCOOKIE="yes/no"
    THROWONFAILURE="yes/no">
```

SECURITYCONTEXT

Required. Security context with which the specified user is authenticated. This context must have been previously defined in the security system.

USERNAME

Required. User to be authenticated.

PASSWORD

Required. Password for the user.

SETCOOKIE

Optional. Default is Yes. Indicates whether ColdFusion sets a cookie to contain authentication information. This cookie is encrypted and its contents include user name, security context, browser remote address, and the HTTP user agent.

THROWONFAILURE

Optional. Default is Yes. Indicates whether ColdFusion throws an exception (of type SECURITY) if authentication fails.

CFBREAK

Used to break out of a CFLOOP. See Breaking out of a loop, later in this chapter, for more information.

Syntax

<CFBREAK>

CFCACHE

CFCACHE allows you to speed up pages considerably in cases where the dynamic content doesn't need to be retrieved each time a user accesses the page. To accomplish this, it creates temporary files that contain the static HTML returned from a particular run of the ColdFusion page.

You can use CFCACHE for simple URLs and URLs that contain URL parameters.

Syntax

```
<CFCACHE
     ACTION="action"
     PROTOCOL="protocol name"
     TIMEOUT="timeout date-time"
     DIRECTORY="directory name for map file"
     CACHEDIRECTORY="directory name for cached
pages"
     EXPIREURL="wildcarded URL reference"
     PORT= "port-number">
```

ACTION

Optional. Specifies one of the following:

> **CACHE**   Specifies server-side caching. The default is CACHE.
>
> **FLUSH**   Refresh the cached page. If you specify FLUSH, you can also specify the DIRECTORY and EXPIREURL attributes.
>
> **CLIENTCACHE**   Specifies browser caching.
>
> **OPTIMAL**   Specifies optimal caching through a combination of server-side and browser caching.

PROTOCOL

Optional. Specifies the protocol used to create pages from cache. Specify either HTTP:// or HTTPS://. The default is HTTP://.

TIMEOUT

Optional. DateTime that specifies the oldest acceptable cached page. If the cached page is older than the specified datetime, ColdFusion refreshes the page. By default, ColdFusion uses all cached pages. For example, if you want a cached file to be no older than 4 hours, code the following:

```
<CFCACHE TIMEOUT="#DateAdd("h", "-4", Now()
)#">
```

DIRECTORY

Optional. Used with ACTION=FLUSH. Specifies the fully qualified path of a directory containing the cfcache.map to be used when ACTION=FLUSH. The default is the directory of the current page.

CACHEDIRECTORY

Optional. Specifies the fully qualified path of the directory where the pages are to be cached. The default is the directory of the current page.

EXPIREURL

Optional. Used with ACTION=FLUSH, EXPIREURL takes a wildcarded URL reference that ColdFusion matches against all mappings in the cfcache.map file. The default is to flush all mappings. For example, "foo.cfm" matches "foo.cfm," "foo.cfm?*" matches "foo.cfm?x=5" and "foo.cfm?x=9."

PORT

Optional. The port number of the web server from which the page is being requested. The port number defaults to 80. The port number is useful because the CFCACHE code calls CFHTTP. If the port number is specified correctly in the internal call to CFHTTP, the URL of each retrieved document is resolved to preserve links.

CFCOL

Defines table column header, width, alignment, and text. Only used inside a CFTABLE.

Syntax

```
<CFCOL HEADER="text"
    WIDTH="number"
    ALIGN="position"
    TEXT="text">
```

HEADER

The text to use for the column's header.

WIDTH

The width of the column in characters (the default is 20). If the length of the data displayed exceeds the width value, the data is truncated to fit.

ALIGN

Column alignment: Left, Right, or Center.

TEXT

Double-quote delimited text that determines what displays in the column. The rules for the text attribute are identical to the rules for CFOUTPUT sections, meaning that it can consist of a combination of literal text, HTML tags, and query record set field references. This means you can embed hyperlinks, image references, and even input controls within table columns.

CFCOLLECTION

The CFCOLLECTION tag allows you to create and administer Verity collections.

Syntax

```
<CFCOLLECTION ACTION="action"
    COLLECTION="collection"
    PATH="implementation directory"
    LANGUAGE="language">
```

ACTION

Required. Specifies the action to perform:

CREATE Creates a new collection using the specified path and optionally specified language.

REPAIR Fixes data corruption in the collection.

DELETE Destroys the collection.

OPTIMIZE Purges and reorganizes data for efficiency.

MAP Assigns an alias to an existing Verity collection.

COLLECTION

Required. Specifies a collection name or an alias if the ACTION is MAP.

PATH

Required for CREATE and MAP. Specifies a path to the Verity collection. The effect of the PATH attribute depends on the ACTION that you specify.

ACTION	What happens?
CREATE	CFCOLLECTION creates a directory for the use of Verity. The directory path is composed of the directory path specified in the "PATH attribute with the name specified in the COLLECTION attribute appended to it. Thus, the full directory path is path_name\collection_name\." For example, if the path name is "C:\Col\," and the collection name is " myCollection," the full directory path is "C:\Col\myCollectin\."
MAP	The MAP action provides a name with which ColdFusion can reference an existing collection. This name is specified with the COLLECTION attribute. It is an alias for the collection, which can be used in CFINDEX, and to re-instate a collection after you have re-installed ColdFusion. The directory path specified with the PATH attribute is the full path name of the Verity directory. Therefore, to reference the directory created in the previous example, specify "C:\Col\myCollection\."

LANGUAGE

Optional for CREATE. To use the LANGUAGE attribute you must have the ColdFusion International Search Pack installed. Valid entries are:

- English (default)
- German
- Finnish
- French
- Danish
- Dutch
- Italian
- Norwegian
- Portuguese
- Spanish
- Swedish

CFCONTENT

Defines the MIME type returned by the current page. Optionally, allows you to specify the name of a file to be returned with the page.

NOTE The ColdFusion Server Basic security settings may prevent **CFCONTENT** from executing. These settings are managed using the ColdFusion Administrator Basic Security page. In order for **CFCONTENT** to execute, it needs to be enabled on the Basic Security page. Please refer to Administering ColdFusion Server for more information about securing ColdFusion tags.

Syntax

```
<CFCONTENT TYPE="file_type"
    DELETEFILE="Yes/No"
    FILE="filename"
    RESET="Yes/No">
```

TYPE
Required. Defines the File/MIME content type returned by the current page.

DELETEFILE
Optional. Yes or No. Yes deletes the file after the download operation. Defaults to No. This attribute only applies if you are specifying a file with the FILE attribute.

FILE
Optional. Denotes the name of the file being retrieved.

RESET
Optional. Yes or No. Yes discards any output that precedes the call to CFCONTENT. No preserves the output that precedes the call. Defaults to Yes. The RESET and FILE attributes are mutually exclusive. If you specify a file, the RESET attribute has no effect. See Note.

NOTE You should consider setting RESET to "No " if you are calling **CFCONTENT** from a custom tag and do not want the tag to have the side effect of discarding the current page whenever it is called from another application or custom tag.

CFCOOKIE

Defines cookie variables, including expiration and security options.

Syntax

```
<CFCOOKIE NAME="cookie_name"
    VALUE="text"
    EXPIRES="period"
    SECURE="Yes/No"
    PATH="urls"
    DOMAIN=".domain">
```

NAME
Required. The name of the cookie variable.

VALUE
Optional. The value assigned to the cookie variable.

EXPIRES
Optional. Schedules the expiration of a cookie variable. Can be specified as a date (as in, 10/09/97), number of days (as in, 10, 100), NOW, or NEVER. Using NOW effectively deletes the cookie from the client's browser.

SECURE
Optional. Indicates the variable has to transmit securely. If the browser does not support Secure Socket Layer (SSL) security, the cookie is not sent.

PATH
Optional. Specifies the subset of URLs within the specified domain to which this cookie applies:

```
PATH="/services/login"
```

Separate multiple entries with a semicolon (;).

DOMAIN
Specifies the domain for which the cookie is valid and to which the cookie content can be sent. An explicitly specified domain must always start with a dot. This can be a subdomain, in which case the valid domains will be any domain names ending in this string.

For domain names ending in country codes (such as .jp, .us), the subdomain specification must contain at least three periods, for example, .mongo.stateu.us. In the case of special top level domains, only two periods are needed, as in .allaire.com.

When specifying a PATH value, you must include a valid DOMAIN.

Separate multiple entries with a semicolon (;).

CFDIRECTORY

Use the CFDIRECTORY tag to handle all interactions with directories.

NOTE The ColdFusion Server Basic security settings may prevent CFDIRECTORY from executing. These settings are managed using the ColdFusion Administrator Basic Security page. In order for CFDIRECTORY to execute, it needs to be enabled on the Basic Security page.

If you write ColdFusion applications designed to run on a server that is used by multiple customers, you need to consider the security of the files and directories that could be uploaded or otherwise manipulated by CFDIRECTORY. Please refer to Administering Cold-Fusion Server for more information about securing ColdFusion tags.

Syntax

```
<CFDIRECTORY ACTION="directory action"
    DIRECTORY="directory name"
    NAME="query name"
    FILTER="list filter"
    MODE="permission"
    SORT="sort specification"
    NEWDIRECTORY="new directory name">
```

ACTION
Optional. Defines the action to be taken with directory(ies) specified in DIRECTORY. Valid entries are:

- List (default)
- Create
- Delete
- Rename.

DIRECTORY
Required for all ACTIONs. The name of the directory you want the action to be performed against.

NAME
Required for ACTION="List". Ignored for all other actions. Name of output query for directory listing.

FILTER
Optional for ACTION="List". Ignored for all other actions. File extension filter to be applied to returned names, for example: *.cfm. Only one mask filter can be applied at a time.

MODE
Optional. Used with ACTION="Create" to define the permissions for a directory on Solaris or HP-UX.

Ignored in Windows. Valid entries correspond to the octal values (not symbolic) of the UNIX chmod command. Permissions are assigned for owner, group, and other, respectively. For example:

MODE=644

Assigns all, owner read/write permission, group and other read/write permissions.

MODE=666

Assigns read/write permissions for owner, group, and other.

MODE=777

Assigns read, write, and execute permissions for all.

SORT
Optional for ACTION="List". Ignored for all other actions. List of query columns to sort directory listing by. Any combination of columns from query output can be specified in comma separated list. ASC or DESC can be specified as qualifiers for column names. ASC is the default. For example:

SORT="dirname ASC, filename2 DESC, size, datelastmodified"

NEWDIRECTORY
Required for ACTION="Rename". Ignored for all other actions. The new name of the directory specified in the DIRECTORY attribute.

ACTION=LIST
When using the ACTION=LIST, CFDIRECTORY returns five result columns you can reference in your CFOUTPUT:

Name   Directory entry name.

Size   Size of directory entry.

Type   File type: File or Dir for File or Directory.

DateLastModified   Date an entry was last modified.

Attributes   File attributes, if applicable.

Mode **(Solaris and HP-UX only)**   The octal value representing the permissions setting for the specified directory. For information about octal values, refer to the UNIX main pages for the chmod shell command.

You can use the following result columns in standard CFML expressions, preceding the result column name with the name of the query:

```
#mydirectory.Name#
#mydirectory.Size#
#mydirectory.Type#
#mydirectory.DateLastModified#
#mydirectory.Attributes#
#mydirectory.Mode#
```

CFERROR

Provides the ability to display customized HTML pages when errors occur. This allows you to maintain a consistent look and feel within your application even when errors occur.

Syntax
```
<CFERROR
    TYPE="Request" or "Validation" or
"Monitor" or "Exception"
    TEMPLATE="template_path"
    MAILTO="email_address"
    EXCEPTION="exception_type">
```

TYPE
Required. The type of error that this custom error page is designed to handle:

- Specify Exception to handle exceptions.
- Specify Validation to handle data input validation errors that occur when submitting a form. A validation error handler is only useful if placed inside the Application.cfm file.
- Specify Monitor to set up an exception monitor.
- Specify Request to handle errors that occur during the processing of a page. Request is the default.

See the table under CFERROR Error Variables for information about the variables and other constructs available from the templates used to handle each type of error.

TEMPLATE
Required. The relative path to the custom error handling page. The following table describes the template to use for each type of error.

Types and Their Corresponding Custom Error Pages

Type	Custom Error Page
Exception	An exception-handling template that is dynamically invoked by the CFML language processor when it detects an unhandled exception condition. Exception-handling templates may be specified as part of an application, via the <CFERROR TYPE= "Exception"> tag, or may be set via the ColdFusion Administrator. An exception-handling template can use the full range of CFML tags, making it significantly more powerful than <CFERROR TYPE="Request">. This template also has access to the error variables in the table under CFERROR Error Variables.
Request	This template can include only the error variables described in the table under CFERROR Error Variables and cannot include CFML tags. It is useful as a backup error handler for sites with high user interface requirements.
Validation	A validation error handler. It handles data input validation errors that occur when submitting a form. It is useful only if placed inside the Application.cfm file.
Monitor	An exception-monitoring template is dynamically invoked by the CFML language processor when it first detects an exception condition, before it searches for <CFTRY>/ <CFCATCH> or <CFERROR> handlers for the exception. Exception-monitoring templates are useful for monitoring and debugging exception handling within complex applications.

MAILTO
Optional. The email address of the administrator who should be notified of the error. This value is available to your custom error page using the MailTo property of the error object, such as #Error.MailTo#.

EXCEPTION
Required if the type is specified as Exception or Monitor. The type of exception.

CFEXECUTE

Enables ColdFusion developers to execute any process on the server machine.

Syntax

```
<CFEXECUTE
    NAME=" ApplicationName "
    ARGUMENTS="CommandLine Arguments"
    OUTPUTFILE="Output file name"
    TIMEOUT="Timeout interval in seconds">
```

NAME

Required. The full path name of the application that is to be executed.

NOTE On Windows systems, you must specify the extension, for example, .exe, as part of the application's name.

ARGUMENTS

Optional. Any command-line arguments that should be passed to the program.

If ARGUMENTS is specified as a string, it is processed as follows:

- On Windows systems, the entire string is passed to the Windows process control subsystem for parsing.
- On UNIX, the string is tokenized into an array of arguments. The default token separator is a space; arguments with embedded spaces may be delimited by double quotes.

If ARGUMENTS is passed as an array, it is processed as follows:

- On Windows systems, the array elements will be concatenated into a string of tokens, separated by spaces. This string is then passed to the Windows process control subsystem as above.
- On UNIX, the elements of the ARGUMENTS array is copied into a corresponding array of exec() arguments.

OUTPUTFILE

Optional. The file where the output of the program is to be directed. If this is not specified, the output appears on the page from which it was called.

TIMEOUT

Optional. Indicates how long in seconds the ColdFusion executing thread will wait for the spawned process. Indicating a timeout of 0 is equivalent to the non-blocking

mode of executing. A very high timeout value is equivalent to a blocking mode of execution. The default is 0; therefore, the ColdFusion thread spawns a process and immediately returns without waiting for the process to terminate.

If no output file is specified, and the timeout value is zero, then the program's output will be directed to the bit bucket.

CFEXIT

CFEXIT can be used to:

- Abort the processing of the currently executing CFML custom tag.
- Exit the template within the currently executing CFML custom tag.
- Re-execute a section of code within the currently executing CFML custom tag.

Syntax

```
<CFEXIT METHOD="method">
```

METHOD

Optional. Specifies one of the following:

ExitTag **(default)** Aborts processing of the currently executing CFML custom tag.

ExitTemplate Exits the template of the currently executing CFML custom tag.

Loop Re-executes the body of the currently executing CFML custom tag.

CFFILE

Use the CFFILE tag to handle all interactions with files. The attributes you use with CFFILE depend on the value of the ACTION attribute. For example, if the ACTION is "Write, " ColdFusion expects the attributes associated with writing a text file. See the individual CFFILE topics below for details about which attributes apply to which ACTIONs.

NOTE The Basic Security settings may prevent CFFILE from executing. These settings are managed using the Basic Security page in the ColdFusion Administrator. In order for CFFILE to execute, it needs to be enabled on the Basic Security page.

If you write ColdFusion applications designed to run on a server that is used by multiple customers, you need to consider the security of the files that could be uploaded or otherwise manipulated by CFFILE. See Administering ColdFusion Server for more information about securing ColdFusion tags.

CFFILE Topics

- CFFILE ACTION="Upload"
- CFFILE ACTION="Move"
- CFFILE ACTION="Rename"
- CFFILE ACTION="Copy"
- CFFILE ACTION="Delete"
- CFFILE ACTION="Read"
- CFFILE ACTION="ReadBinary"
- CFFILE ACTION="Append"

CFFILE ACTION Attributes

Depending on the value you assign to the ACTION attribute of CFFILE, there are several additional attributes you can set. This table shows which attributes you can use with each CFFILE ACTION.

Attributes Used with CFFILE ACTIONs

ACTION	Attributes
Upload	ACCEPT, DESTINATION, FILEFIELD, NAMECONFLICT, MODE, ATTRIBUTES
Move	SOURCE, DESTINATION, ATTRIBUTES
Rename	SOURCE, DESTINATION, ATTRIBUTES
Copy	SOURCE, DESTINATION, ATTRIBUTES
Delete	FILE
Read	FILE, VARIABLE
ReadBinary	FILE, VARIABLE
Write	OUTPUT, FILE, MODE, ADDNEWLINE, ATTRIBUTES
Append	OUTPUT, FILE, MODE, ADDNEWLINE, ATTRIBUTES

Sections that follow describe these values and attributes in greater detail.

CFFILE ACTION="Upload"

Use CFFILE with the Upload action to upload a file specified in a form field to a directory on the Web server.

NOTE   The MODE attribute applies to ColdFusion on Solaris and HP-UX, only.

Syntax

```
<CFFILE ACTION="Upload"
    FILEFIELD="formfield"
    DESTINATION="full_path_name"
    NAMECONFLICT="behavior"
    ACCEPT="mime_type/file_type"
    MODE="permission"
    ATTRIBUTES="file_attributes">
```

FILEFIELD

Required. The name of the form field that was used to select the file.

WARNING   Do not use pound signs (#) to specify the field name.

DESTINATION

Required. The full path name of the destination directory on the Web server where the file should be saved. A trailing slash must be included in the target directory when uploading a file. Use the backward slash (\) on Windows ; use the forward slash (/) on UNIX.

NOTE   The directory does not need to be beneath the root of the Web server document directory.

NAMECONFLICT

Optional. Default is error. Determines how the file should be handled if its name conflicts with the name of a file that already exists in the directory. Valid entries are:

Error   Default. The file will not be saved, and ColdFusion will stop processing the page and return an error.

Skip   Neither saves the file nor throws an error. This setting is intended to allow custom behavior based on inspection of FILE properties.

Overwrite   Replaces an existing file if it shares the same name as the CFFILE destination.

MakeUnique   Automatically generates a unique filename for the upload. This name will be stored in the FILE object variable "ServerFile." You can use this variable to record what name was used when the file was saved.

ACCEPT

Optional. Use to limit what types of files will be accepted. Enter one or more MIME types, each separated by comma, of the file types you want to accept. For example, to allow uploads of GIF and Microsoft Word files, enter:

```
ACCEPT="image/gif, application/msword"
```

Note that the browser uses the file extension to determine file type.

MODE

Optional. Defines permissions for an uploaded file on Solaris or HP-UX. Ignored in Windows. Valid entries correspond to the octal values (not symbolic) of the UNIX chmod command. Permissions are assigned for owner, group, and other, respectively. For example:

```
MODE=644
```

Assigns the owner read/write permissions and group/other read permission.

```
MODE=666
```

Assigns read/write permissions for owner, group, and other.

```
MODE=777
```

Assigns read, write, and execute permissions for all.

ATTRIBUTES

Optional. A comma-delimited list of file attributes to be set on the file being uploaded. The following file attributes are supported:

- ReadOnly
- Temporary
- Archive
- Hidden
- System
- Normal

If ATTRIBUTES is not used, the file's attributes are maintained. If Normal is specified as well as any other attributes, Normal is overridden by whatever other attribute is specified.

Individual attributes must be specified explicitly. For example, if you specify just the ReadOnly attribute, all other existing attributes are overwritten.

CFFILE ACTION="Move"

The CFFILE MOVE action can be used to move a file from one location on the server to another.

Syntax

```
<CFFILE ACTION="Move"
    SOURCE="full_path_name"
    DESTINATION="full_path_name"
    ATTRIBUTES="file_attributes">
```

SOURCE

Required. The full path name of the file to move.

DESTINATION

Required. The full path name of the directory to which the file will be moved. If you do not specify the file name, a trailing slash must be included in the target when moving a file. Use the backward slash (\) on Windows; use the forward slash (/) on UNIX.

ATTRIBUTES

Optional. A comma-delimited list of file attributes to be set on the file being moved. The following file attributes are supported:

- ReadOnly
- Temporary
- Archive
- Hidden
- System
- Normal

If ATTRIBUTES is not used, the file's attributes are maintained. If Normal is specified as well as any other attributes, Normal is overridden by whatever other attribute is specified.

Individual attributes must be specified explicitly. For example, if you specify just the ReadOnly attribute, all other existing attributes are overwritten.

CFFILE ACTION="Rename"

Use CFFILE with the Rename action to rename a file that already exists on the server.

Syntax

```
<CFFILE ACTION="Rename"
    SOURCE="full_path_name"
    DESTINATION="full_path_name"
    ATTRIBUTES="file_attributes">
```

SOURCE

Required. The full path name of the file to rename.

DESTINATION

Required. The full path name, including the new name, of the file.

ATTRIBUTES

Optional. A comma-delimited list of file attributes to be set on the file being renamed. The following file attributes are supported:

- ReadOnly
- Temporary
- Archive
- Hidden
- System
- Normal

If ATTRIBUTES is not used, the file's attributes are maintained. If Normal is specified as well as any other attributes, Normal is overridden by whatever other attribute is specified.

Individual attributes must be specified explicitly. For example, if you specify just the ReadOnly attribute, all other existing attributes are overwritten.

CFFILE ACTION="Copy"

The CFFILE tag can be used to copy a file from one directory to another on the server.

Syntax

```
<CFFILE ACTION="Copy"
    SOURCE="full_path_name"
    DESTINATION="full_path_name"
    ATTRIBUTES="file_attributes">
```

SOURCE

Required. The full path name of the file to copy.

DESTINATION

Required. The full path name of the directory where the copy of the file will be saved. If you do not specify a file name, you must include the trailing slash. On Windows, use the backward slash (\). On UNIX, use the forward slash (/).

ATTRIBUTES

Optional. A comma-delimited list of file attributes to be set on the file being copied. The following file attributes are supported:

- ReadOnly
- Temporary
- Archive
- Hidden

- System
- Normal

If ATTRIBUTES is not used, the file's attributes are maintained. If Normal is specified as well as any other attributes, Normal is overridden by whatever other attribute is specified.

Individual attributes must be specified explicitly. For example, if you specify just the ReadOnly attribute, all other existing attributes are overwritten.

CFFILE ACTION="Delete"

The CFFILE tag can be used to delete a file on the server.

Syntax

```
<CFFILE ACTION="Delete"
    FILE="full_path_name">
```

FILE

Required. The full path name of the file to delete.

CFFILE ACTION="Read"

You can use the CFFILE tag to read an existing text file. The file is read into a dynamic parameter you can use anywhere in the page like any other dynamic parameter. For example, you could read a text file and then insert its contents into a database. Or you could read a text file and then use one of the find and replace functions to modify its contents.

Syntax

```
<CFFILE ACTION="Read"
    FILE="full_path_name"
    VARIABLE="var_name">
```

FILE

Required. The full path name of the text file to be read.

VARIABLE

Required. The name of the variable that will contain the contents of the text file after it has been read.

CFFILE ACTION="ReadBinary"

You can use the CFFILE tag to read an existing binary file, such as an executable or image file. The file is read into a binary object parameter you can use anywhere in the page like any other parameter. If you would like to send it through one of the Web protocols, such as HTTP or SMTP, or store it in a database, you should first convert it to Base 64 (see ToBase64).

Syntax

```
<CFFILE ACTION="ReadBinary"
    FILE="full_path_name"
    VARIABLE="var_name">
```

FILE

Required. The full path name of the file to be read.

VARIABLE

Required. The name of the variable that will contain the contents of the binary file after it has been read.

CFFILE ACTION="Append"

Use CFFILE with the Append action to append additional text to the end of an existing text file, for example, when creating log files.

Syntax

```
<CFFILE ACTION="Append"
    FILE="full_path_name"
    OUTPUT="string"
    ATTRIBUTES="file_attributes">
```

FILE

Required. The full path name of the file to which the content of the OUTPUT attribute is appended.

OUTPUT

Required. The string to be appended to the file designated in the DESTINATION attribute.

ADDNEWLINE

Optional. Yes or No. If this attribute is set to Yes, a new line character is appended to the text that is written to the file. If this attribute is set to No, no new line character is appended to the text. The default value is Yes.

ATTRIBUTES

Optional. A comma-delimited list of file attributes to be set on the file being appended. The following file attributes are supported:

- ReadOnly
- Temporary
- Archive
- Hidden
- System
- Normal

If ATTRIBUTES is not used, the file's attributes are maintained. If Normal is specified as well as any other attributes, Normal is overridden by whatever other attribute is specified.

Individual attributes must be specified explicitly. For example, if you specify just the ReadOnly attribute, all other existing attributes are overwritten.

CFFORM

CFFORM allows you to build a form with CFML custom control tags that provide much greater functionality than standard HTML form input elements.

Syntax

```
<CFFORM NAME="name"
    ACTION="form_action"
    ENABLECAB="Yes/No"
    ONSUBMIT="javascript"
    TARGET="window_name"
    ENCTYPE="type"
    PASSTHROUGH="HTML_attributes">

...
</CFFORM>
```

NAME

Optional. A name for the form you are creating.

ACTION

Required. The name of the ColdFusion page that will be executed when the form is submitted for processing.

ENABLECAB

Optional. Yes or No. Allows users to download the Microsoft cabinet (*.cab) file(s) containing the Java classes used for Java applet-based CFFORM controls. If Yes, on opening the page, users are asked if they want to download the CAB file.

ONSUBMIT

Optional. JavaScript function to execute after other input validation returns. Use this attribute to execute JavaScript for preprocessing data before the form is submitted.

TARGET

Optional. The name of the window or window frame where the form output will be sent.

ENCTYPE

Optional. The MIME type used to encode data sent via the POST method. The default value is application /x-www-form-urlencoded. It is recommended that you accept the default value. This attribute is included for compatibility with the HTML FORM tag.

PASSTHROUGH

Optional. HTML attributes that are not explicitly supported by CFFORM. If you specify an attribute and its value, the attribute and value are passed to the HTML code that is generated for the CFINPUT tag.

CFFTP

CFFTP allows users to implement File Transfer Protocol operations.

NOTE The CFFTP tag is for moving files between a ColdFusion server and an FTP server. CFFTP cannot move files between a ColdFusion server and a browser (client). Use CFFILE ACTION="UPLOAD" to transfer files from the client to a ColdFusion server; use CFCONTENT to transfer files from a ColdFusion server to the browser.

Note also that ColdFusion Server Basic security settings may prevent CFFTP from executing. These settings are managed using the ColdFusion Administrator Basic Security page. If you write ColdFusion applications designed to run on a server that is used by multiple customers, you need to consider the security of the files that the customer can move. Please refer to Administering ColdFusion Server for more information about securing ColdFusion tags.

CFFTP Topics

Here are some of the following FFFTP topics:

- Establishing a Connection with CFFTP
- File and Directory Operations with CFFTP
- Accessing the Columns in a Query Object
- CFFTP.ReturnValue Variable
- Connection Caching

Establishing a Connection with CFFTP

Use the CONNECTION attribute of the CFFTP tag to establish a connection with an FTP server.

If you use connection caching to an already active FTP connection, you don't need to respecify the connection attributes:

- USERNAME
- PASSWORD
- SERVER

NOTE Changes to a cached connection, such as changing RETRYCOUNT or TIMEOUT values, may require reestablishing the connection.

Syntax

```
<CFFTP ACTION="action"
    USERNAME="name"
    PASSWORD="password"
    SERVER="server"
    TIMEOUT="timeout in seconds"
    PORT="port"
    CONNECTION="name"
    PROXYSERVER="proxyserver"
    RETRYCOUNT="number"
    STOPONERROR="Yes/No"
    PASSIVE="Yes/No">
```

ACTION

Required. Determines the FTP operation to perform. To create an FTP connection, use Open. To terminate an FTP connection, use Close. See Connection Caching for more information.

USERNAME

Required for Open. User name to pass in the FTP operation.

PASSWORD

Required for Open. Password to log in the user.

SERVER

Required for Open. The FTP server to connect to, as in ftp.myserver.com

TIMEOUT

Optional. Value in seconds for the timeout of all operations, including individual data request operations. Defaults to 30 seconds.

PORT

Optional. The remote port to connect to. Defaults to 21 for FTP.

CONNECTION

Optional. The name of the FTP connection. Used to cache a new FTP connection or to reuse an existing connection. If the USERNAME, PASSWORD, and SERVER attributes are specified, a new connection is created if no connection exists for the specified user. All calls to CFFTP with the same connection name will reuse the same FTP connection information.

PROXYSERVER

Optional. A string that contains the name of the proxy server (or servers) to use if proxy access was specified.

RETRYCOUNT

Optional. Number of retries until failure is reported. Default is one (1).

STOPONERROR

Optional. Yes or No. When Yes, halts all processing and displays an appropriate error. Default is Yes.

When No, three variables are populated:

CFFTP.Succeeded   Yes or No.

CFFTP.ErrorCode   Error number (See following Note for critical information.)

CFFTP.ErrorText   Message text explaining error type.

NOTE   Use CFFTP.ErrorCode for conditional operations. Do not use CFFTP.ErrorText for this purpose.

PASSIVE

Optional. Yes or No. Defaults to No. Indicates whether to enable passive mode.

File and Directory Operations with *CFFTP*

Use this form of the CFFTP tag to perform file and directory operations with CFFTP.

If you use connection caching to an already active FTP connection, you don't need to respecify the connection attributes:

- USERNAME
- PASSWORD
- SERVER

Syntax
```
<CFFTP
    ACTION="action"
    USERNAME="name"
    PASSWORD="password"
    NAME="query_name"
    SERVER="server"
    ASCIIEXTENSIONLIST="extensions"
    TRANSFERMODE="mode"
    FAILIFEXISTS="Yes/No"
    DIRECTORY="directory name"
    LOCALFILE="filename"
    REMOTEFILE="filename"
    ITEM="directory or file"
    EXISTING="file or directory name"
    NEW="file or directory name"
    PROXYSERVER="proxyserver"
    PASSIVE="Yes/No">
```

ACTION

Required if connection is not already cached. If connection caching is used, the ACTION attribute is not required. Determines the FTP operation to perform. Can be one of the following:

- ChangeDir
- CreateDir
- ListDir
- GetFile
- PutFile
- Rename
- Remove
- GetCurrentDir
- GetCurrentURL
- ExistsDir
- ExistsFile
- Exists

USERNAME

Required if the FTP connection is not already cached. If connection caching is used, the USERNAME attribute is not required. User name to pass in the FTP operation.

PASSWORD

Required if the FTP connection is not already cached. If connection caching is used, the PASSWORD attribute is not required. Password to log the user.

NAME

Required for ACTION="ListDir". Specifies the query name to hold the directory listing.

SERVER

Required if the FTP connection is not already cached. If connection caching is used, the SERVER attribute is not required. The FTP server to connect to.

TIMEOUT

Optional. Value in seconds for the timeout of all operations, including individual data request operations. Defaults to 30 seconds.

PORT

Optional. The remote port to connect to. Defaults to 21 for FTP.

CONNECTION

Optional. The name of the FTP connection. Used to cache a new FTP connection or to reuse an existing connection. If the USERNAME, PASSWORD, and SERVER attributes are specified, a new connection is created if no connection exists for the specified user. All calls to CFFTP with the same connection name will reuse the same FTP connection information.

ASCIIEXTENSIONLIST

Optional. A semicolon delimited list of file extensions that force ASCII transfer mode when TRANSFER-MODE="AutoDetect". Default extension list is:

txt;htm;html;cfm;cfml;shtm;shtml;css;asp;asa

TRANSFERMODE

Optional. The FTP transfer mode you want to use. Valid entries are ASCII, Binary, or AutoDetect. Defaults to AutoDetect.

FAILIFEXISTS

Optional. Yes or No. Defaults to Yes. Specifies whether a GetFile operation will fail if a local file of the same name already exists.

DIRECTORY

Required for ACTION=ChangeDir, CreateDir, ListDir, and ExistsDir. Specifies the directory on which to perform an operation.

LOCALFILE

Required for ACTION=GetFile, and PutFile. Specifies the name of the file on the local file system.

REMOTEFILE

Required for ACTION=GetFile, PutFile, and Exists-File. Specifies the name of the file on the FTP server's file system.

ITEM

Required for ACTION=Exists, and Remove. Specifies the object, file or directory, of these actions.

EXISTING

Required for ACTION=Rename. Specifies the current name of the file or directory on the remote server.

NEW

Required for ACTION=Rename. Specifies the new name of the file or directory on the remote server.

RETRYCOUNT

Optional. Number of retries until failure is reported. Default is one (1).

STOPONERROR

Optional. Yes or No. When Yes, halts all processing and displays an appropriate error. Default is No.

When No, three variables are populated:

CFFTP.Succeeded	Yes or No
CFFTP.ErrorCode	Error number (See STOPONERROR variables, below.)
CFFTP.ErrorText	Message text explaining error condition

PROXYSERVER

Optional. A string that contains the name of the proxy server (or servers) to use if proxy access was specified.

PASSIVE

Optional. Yes or No. Defaults to No. Indicates whether to enable passive mode.

Accessing the Columns in a Query Object

When you use CFFTP with the ListDir action, you must also specify a value for the NAME attribute. The value of the NAME attribute is used to hold the results of the ListDir action in a query object. The query object consists of columns you can reference in the form:

queryname.columnname[row]

Where queryname is the name of the query as specified in the NAME attribute and columnname is one of the columns returned in the query object as shown in the following table. Row is the row number for each file/directory entry returned by the ListDir operation. A separate row is created for each entry.

CFFTP Query Object Columns

Column	Description
Name	Filename of the current element
Path	File path (without drive designation) of the current element
URL	Complete URL for the current element (file or directory)
Length	Number indicating file size of the current element
LastModified	Unformatted date/time value of the current element

CFFTP Query Object Columns *(continued)*

Column	Description
Attributes	String indicating attributes of the current element: Normal or Directory.
IsDirectory	Boolean value indicating whether object is a file or directory
Mode	An octal string representing UNIX permissions, when running on UNIX, for example, "rwxrwxrwx" in a directory listing is represented as "777".

NOTE Previously supported query column values that pertain to system- specific information are no longer supported, for example, "Hidden" and "System."

Connection Caching

Once you've established a connection with CFFTP, you can reuse the connection to perform additional FTP operations. To do this, you use the CONNECTION attribute to define and name an FTP connection object that stores information about the connection. Any additional FTP operations that use the same CONNEC-TION name automatically make use of the information stored in the connection object. This facility helps save connection time and drastically improves file transfer operation performance.

If you need to keep the connection open throughout a session or longer, you can use a session or application variable as the connection name. However, if you do this, you must explicitly specify the full variable name with the Close action when you are finished. Note that keeping a connection open prevents others from using the FTP server; therefore, you should close the connection as soon as possible.

NOTE Changes to a cached connection, such as changing RETRYCOUNT or TIMEOUT values, may require reestablishing the connection.

CFGRID

Used inside CFFORM, CFGRID allows you to place a grid control in a ColdFusion form. A grid control is a table of data divided into rows and columns. CFGRID column data is specified with individual CFGRIDCOLUMN tags.

See also CFGRIDROW and CFGRIDUPDATE tags.

Syntax

```
<CFGRID NAME="name"
    HEIGHT="integer"
    WIDTH="integer"
    VSPACE="integer"
    HSPACE="integer"
    ALIGN="value"
    QUERY="query_name"
    INSERT="Yes/No"
    DELETE="Yes/No"
    SORT="Yes/No"
    FONT="column_font"
    FONTSIZE="size"
    ITALIC="Yes/No"
    BOLD="Yes/No"
    HREF="URL"
    HREFKEY="column_name"
    TARGET="URL_target"
    APPENDKEY="Yes/No"
    HIGHLIGHTHREF="Yes/No"
    ONVALIDATE="javascript_function"
    ONERROR="text"
    GRIDDATAALIGN="position"
    GRIDLINES="Yes/No"
    ROWHEIGHT="pixels"
    ROWHEADERS="Yes/No"
    ROWHEADERALIGN="position"
    ROWHEADERFONT="font_name"
    ROWHEADERFONTSIZE="size"
    ROWHEADERITALIC="Yes/No"
    ROWHEADERBOLD="Yes/No"
    ROWHEADERWIDTH="col_width"
    COLHEADERS="Yes/No"
    COLHEADERALIGN="position"
    COLHEADERFONT="font_name"
    COLHEADERFONTSIZE="size"
    COLHEADERITALIC="Yes/No"
    COLHEADERBOLD="Yes/No"
    BGCOLOR="color"
    SELECTCOLOR="color"
    SELECTMODE="mode"
    MAXROWS="number"
    NOTSUPPORTED="text"
    PICTUREBAR="Yes/No"
    INSERTBUTTON="text"
    DELETEBUTTON="text"
    SORTASCENDINGBUTTON="text"
    SORTDESCENDINGBUTTON="text">

</CFGRID>
```

NAME

Required. A name for the grid element.

HEIGHT

Optional. Height value of the grid control in pixels.

WIDTH

Optional. Width value of the grid control in pixels.

VSPACE

Optional. Vertical margin spacing above and below the grid control in pixels.

HSPACE

Optional. Horizontal margin spacing to the left and right of the grid control in pixels.

ALIGN

Optional. Alignment value. Valid entries are: Top, Left, Bottom, Baseline, Texttop, Absbottom, Middle, Absmiddle, Right.

QUERY

Optional. The name of the query associated with the grid control.

INSERT

Optional. Yes or No. Yes allows end users to insert new row data into the grid. Default is No.

DELETE

Optional. Yes or No. Yes allows end users to delete row data in the grid. Default is No.

SORT

Optional. Yes or No. When Yes sort buttons are added to the grid control. When clicked the sort buttons perform a simple text sort on the selected column. Default is No.

FONT

Optional. Font name to use for all column data in the grid control.

FONTSIZE

Optional. Font size for text in the grid control, measured in points.

ITALIC

Optional. Yes or No. Yes presents all grid control text in italic. Default is No.

BOLD

Optional. Yes or No. Yes presents all grid control text in boldface. Default is No.

HREF

Optional. URL to associate with the grid item or a query column for a grid that is populated from a query. If HREF is a query column, then the HREF value that is displayed is populated by the query. If HREF is not recognized as a query column, it is assumed that the HREF text is an actual HTML HREF.

HREFKEY

Optional. The name of a valid query column when the grid uses a query. The column specified becomes the Key no matter what the select mode is for the grid.

TARGET

Optional. Target attribute for HREF URL.

APPENDKEY

Optional. Yes or No. When used with HREF, Yes passes the CFGRIDKEY variable along with the value of the selected tree item in the URL to the application page specified in the CFFORM ACTION attribute. Default is Yes.

HIGHLIGHTHREF

Optional. Yes highlights links associated with a CFGRID with an HREF attribute value. No disables highlight. Default is Yes.

ONVALIDATE

Optional. The name of a valid JavaScript function used to validate user input. The form object, input object, and input object value are passed to the specified routine, which should return True if validation succeeds and False otherwise.

ONERROR

Optional. The name of a valid JavaScript function you want to execute in the event of a failed validation.

GRIDDATAALIGN

Optional. Enter Left, Right, or Center to position data in the grid within a column. Default is Left.

GRIDLINES

Optional. Yes or No. Yes enables rules (lines) in the grid control, No suppresses row and column rules. Default is Yes.

ROWHEIGHT

Optional. Enter a numeric value for the number of pixels to determine the minimum row height for the grid control. Used with CFGRIDCOLUMN TYPE="Image," you can use ROWHEIGHT to define enough room for graphics you want to display in the row.

ROWHEADER

Optional. Yes or No. Yes displays row labels in the grid control. Defaults to Yes.

ROWHEADERALIGN

Optional. Enter Left, Right, or Center to position data within a row header. Default is Left.

ROWHEADERFONT

Optional. Font to use for the row label.

ROWHEADERFONTSIZE

Optional. Size font for row label text in the grid control, measured in points.

ROWHEADERITALIC

Optional. Yes or No. Yes presents row label text in italic. Default is No.

ROWHEADERBOLD

Optional. Yes or No. Yes presents row label text in boldface. Default is No.

ROWHEADERWIDTH

Optional. The width, in pixels, of the row header column.

COLHEADERS

Optional. Yes or No. Yes displays column headers in the grid control. Defaults to Yes.

COLHEADERALIGN

Optional. Enter Left, Right, or Center to position data within a column header. Default is Left.

COLHEADERFONT

Optional. Font to use for the column header in the grid control.

COLHEADERFONTSIZE

Optional. Size font for column header text in the grid control, measured in points.

COLHEADERITALIC

Optional. Yes or No. Yes presents column header text in italic. Default is No.

COLHEADERBOLD

Optional. Yes or No. Yes presents column header text in boldface. Default is No.

BGCOLOR

Optional. Background color value for the grid control. Valid entries are: `black`, `magenta`, `cyan`, `orange`, `dark gray`, `pink`, `gray`, `white`, `light gray`, `yellow`.

A hex value can be entered in the form:

`BGCOLOR="##xxxxxx"`

where x is 0–9 or A–F. Use either two pound signs or no pound signs.

SELECTCOLOR

Optional. Background color for a selected item. See BGCOLOR for color options.

SELECTMODE

Optional. Selection mode for items in the grid control. Valid entries are:

Edit   Users can edit grid data.

Single   User selections are confined to the selected cell.

Row   User selections automatically extend to the row containing selected cell.

Column   User selections automatically extend to column containing selected cell.

Browse   User can only browse grid data.
Default is Browse.

MAXROWS

Optional. Specifies the maximum number of rows you want to display in the grid.

NOTSUPPORTED

Optional. The text you want to display if the page containing a Java applet-based CFFORM control is opened by a browser that does not support Java or has Java support disabled. For example:

`NOTSUPPORTED="<B> Browser must support Java to view ColdFusion Java Applets</B>"`

By default, if no message is specified, the following message appears:

`<B>Browser must support Java to <BR> view ColdFusion Java Applets!</B>`

PICTUREBAR

Optional. Yes or No. When Yes, image buttons are used for the Insert, Delete, and Sort actions rather than text buttons. Default is No.

INSERTBUTTON

Optional. Text to use for the Insert action button. The default is Insert.

DELETEBUTTON

Optional. Text to use for the Delete action button. The default is Delete.

SORTASCENDINGBUTTON

Optional. The text to use for the Sort button. The default is "A -> Z".

SORTDESCENDINGBUTTON

Optional. The text to use for the Sort button. The default is "Z <- A".

CFGRIDCOLUMN

Used with CFGRID in a CFFORM, you use CFGRIDCOLUMN to specify individual column data in a CFGRID control. Font and alignment attributes used in CFGRIDCOLUMN override any global font or alignment settings defined in CFGRID.

Syntax

```
<CFGRIDCOLUMN NAME="column_name"
    HEADER="header"
    WIDTH="column_width"
    FONT="column_font"
    FONTSIZE="size"
    ITALIC="Yes/No"
    BOLD="Yes/No"
    HREF="URL"
    HREFKEY="column_name"
    TARGET="URL_target"
    SELECT="Yes/No"
    DISPLAY="Yes/No"
    TYPE="type"
    HEADERFONT"font_name"
    HEADERFONTSIZE="size"
    HEADERITALIC="Yes/No"
    HEADERBOLD="Yes/No"
    DATAALIGN="position"
    HEADERALIGN="position"
    NUMBERFORMAT="format">
```

NAME

Required. A name for the grid column element. If the grid uses a query, the column name must specify the name of a query column.

HEADER

Optional. Text for the column header. The value of HEADER is used only when the CFGRID COLHEADERS attribute is Yes (or omitted, since it defaults to Yes).

WIDTH

Optional. The width of the column in pixels. By default the column is sized based on the longest column value.

FONT

Optional. Font name to use for data in the column. Defaults to browser-specified font.

FONTSIZE

Optional. Font size for text in the column. Defaults to browser-specified font size.

ITALIC

Optional. Yes or No. Yes presents text in the column in italic. Default is No.

BOLD

Optional. Yes or No. Yes presents text in the column in boldface. Default is No.

HREF

Optional. URL to associate with the grid item. You can specify a URL that is relative to the current page:

`../mypage.cfm`

Or an absolute URL:

`http://myserver.com/mydir/mypage.cfm.`

HREFKEY

Optional. The name of a valid query column when the grid uses a query. The column specified becomes the Key no matter what the select mode is for the grid.

TARGET

Optional. The name of the frame in which to open the link specified in HREF.

SELECT

Optional. Yes or No. Yes allows end users to select a column in a grid control. When No, the column cannot be edited, even if the CFGRID INSERT or DELETE attributes are enabled. The value of the SELECT attribute is ignored if the CFGRID SELECTMODE attribute is set to Row or Browse.

DISPLAY

Optional. Yes or No. Use to hide columns. Default is Yes to display the column.

TYPE

Optional. Enter Image, Numeric, or String_NoCase. When TYPE="Image", the grid attempts to display an image corresponding to the value in the column, which can be a built in ColdFusion image name, or an image of your choice in the cfide\classes directory or a subdirectory, referenced with a relative URL. Built-in image names are as follows:

- cd
- computer
- document
- element

- folder
- floppy
- fixed
- remote

If an image is larger than the column cell where it is being placed, the images is clipped to fit the cell.

When TYPE="Numeric", data in the grid can be sorted by the end user as numeric data rather than as simple character text.

When TYPE="String_NoCase", data in the grid can be sorted by the end user as case insensitive text data like an Excel spreadsheet rather than as case sensitive character text.

HEADERFONT

Optional. Font to use for the column header. Defaults to browser-specified font.

HEADERFONTSIZE

Optional. Font size to use for the column header in pixels. Defaults to browser-specified font size.

HEADERITALIC

Optional. Yes or No. Yes presents column header text in italic. Default is No.

HEADERBOLD

Optional. Yes or No. Yes presents header text in boldface. Default is No.

DATAALIGN

Optional. Alignment for column data. Valid entries are: Left, Center, or Right. Default is Left.

HEADERALIGN

Optional. Alignment for the column header text. Valid entries are: Left, Center, or Right. Default is Left.

NUMBERFORMAT

Optional. The format for displaying numeric data in the grid.

NUMBERFORMAT Mask Characters

Mask characters you can use in the NUMBERFORMAT attribute correspond with those used in the Number-Format CFML function. For more information about the NumberFormat function, see Chapter 2 of this book.

NumberFormat **Mask Characters**

Character	Meaning
_ (underscore)	Optional digit placeholder.
9	Optional digit placeholder. Same as _, but shows decimal places more clearly.
.	Specifies the location of a mandatory decimal point.
0	Located to the left or right of a mandatory decimal point, to force padding with zeros.
( )	Places parentheses around the mask if the number is less than 0.
+	Places + in front of positive numbers, - (minus sign) in front of negative numbers.
-	Place " " (space) in front of positive, - (minus sign) in front of negative numbers.
,	Separates thousands with commas.
L,C	Specifies left-justify or center-justify a number within the width of the mask column. L or C must appear as the first character of the mask. By default, numbers are right-justified.
$	Places a dollar sign in front of the formatted number. $ must appear as the first character of the mask.
^	Separates left from right formatting.

CFGRIDROW

CFGRIDROW allows you to define a CFGRID that does not use a QUERY as source for row data. If a QUERY attribute is specified in CFGRID, the CFGRIDROW tags are ignored.

Syntax

```
<CFGRIDROW DATA="col1, col2, ...">
```

DATA

Required. A comma-separated list of column values. If a column value contains a comma character, it must be escaped with a second comma character.

CFGRIDUPDATE

Used in a CFGRID, CFGRIDUPDATE allows you to perform updates to data sources directly from edited grid data. CFGRIDUPDATE provides a direct interface with your data source.

CFGRIDUPDATE first applies DELETE row actions followed by INSERT row actions and finally UPDATE row actions. Row processing stops if any errors are encountered.

Syntax

```
<CFGRIDUPDATE GRID="gridname"
    DATASOURCE="data source name"
    DBTYPE="type"
    DBSERVER="dbms"
    DBNAME="database name"
    TABLENAME="table name"
    USERNAME="data source username"
    PASSWORD="data source password"
    TABLEOWNER="table owner"
    TABLEQUALIFIER="qualifier"
    PROVIDER="COMProvider"
    PROVIDERDSN="datasource"
    KEYONLY="Yes/No">
```

GRID

Required. The name of the CFGRID form element that is the source for the update action.

DATASOURCE

Required. The name of the data source for the update action.

DBTYPE

Optional. The database driver type:

ODBC (default)   ODBC driver.

Oracle73   Oracle 7.3 native database driver. Using this option, the ColdFusion Server computer must have Oracle 7.3.4.0.0 (or greater) client software installed.

Oracle80   Oracle 8.0 native database driver. Using this option, the ColdFusion Server computer must have Oracle 8.0 (or greater) client software installed.

Sybase11   Sybase System 11 native database driver. Using this option, the ColdFusion Server computer must have Sybase 11.1.1 (or greater) client software installed. Sybase patch ebf 7729 is recommended.

OLEDB   OLE DB provider. If specified, this database provider overrides the driver type specified in the ColdFusion Administrator.

DB2   DB2 5.2 native database driver.
Informix73~MSInformix73 native database driver.

DBSERVER

Optional. For native database drivers and the SQLOLEDB provider, specifies the name of the database server machine. If specified, DBSERVER overrides the server specified in the data source.

DBNAME

Optional. The database name (Sybase System 11 driver and SQLOLEDB provider only). If specified, DBNAME overrides the default database specified in the data source.

TABLENAME

Required. The name of the table you want to update. Note the following:

- ORACLE drivers—This specification must be in uppercase.
- Sybase driver—This specification is case-sensitive and must be in the same case as that used when the table was created

USERNAME

Optional. If specified, USERNAME overrides the username value specified in the ODBC setup.

PASSWORD

Optional. If specified, PASSWORD overrides the password value specified in the ODBC setup.

TABLEOWNER

Optional. For data sources that support table ownership (such as SQL Server, Oracle, and Sybase SQL Anywhere), use this field to specify the owner of the table.

TABLEQUALIFIER

Optional. For data sources that support table qualifiers, use this field to specify the qualifier for the table. The purpose of table qualifiers varies across drivers. For SQL Server and Oracle, the qualifier refers to the name of the database that contains the table. For the Intersolv dBase driver, the qualifier refers to the directory where the DBF files are located.

PROVIDER

Optional. COM provider (OLE-DB only).

PROVIDERDSN

Optional. Data source name for the COM provider (OLE-DB only).

KEYONLY

Optional. Yes or No. Yes specifies that in the update action, the WHERE criteria is confined to just the key values. No specifies that in addition to the key values, the original values of any changed fields are included in the WHERE criteria. Default is Yes.

CFHEADER

CFHEADER generates custom HTTP response headers to return to the client.

Syntax

```
<CFHEADER
    NAME="header_name"
    VALUE="header_value">
```
or
```
<CFHEADER
    STATUSCODE="status_code"
    STATUSTEXT="status_text">
```

NAME

Required if you do not specify the STATUSCODE attribute. A name for the header.

VALUE

Optional. A value for the HTTP header. This attribute is used in conjunction with the NAME attribute.

STATUSCODE

Required if you do not specify the NAME attribute. A number that sets the HTTP status code.

STATUSTEXT

Optional. Text that explains the status code. This attribute is used in conjunction with the STATUSCODE attribute.

CFHTMLHEAD

CFHTMLHEAD writes the text specified in the TEXT attribute to the <HEAD> section of a generated HTML page. CFHTMLHEAD can be useful for embedding Java-Script code, or placing other HTML tags such as META, LINK, TITLE, or BASE in an HTML page header.

Syntax

```
<CFHTMLHEAD TEXT="text">
```

TEXT

The text you want to add to the <HEAD> area of an HTML page. Everything inside the quotation marks is placed in the <HEAD> section.

CFHTTP

The CFHTTP tag allows you to execute POST and GET operations on files. Using CFHTTP, you can execute standard GET operations as well as create a query object from a text file. POST operations allow you to upload MIME file types to a server, or post cookie, form field, URL, file, or CGI variables directly to a specified server.

Syntax

```
<CFHTTP URL="hostname"
    PORT="port_number"
    METHOD="get_or_post"
    USERNAME="username"
    PASSWORD="password"
    NAME="queryname"
    COLUMNS="query_columns"
    PATH="path"
    FILE="filename"
    DELIMITER="character"
    TEXTQUALIFIER="character"
    RESOLVEURL="Yes/No"
    PROXYSERVER="hostname"
    PROXYPORT="port_number"
    USERAGENT="user_agent"
    THROWONERROR="Yes/No"
    REDIRECT="Yes/No"
    TIMEOUT="timeout_period">
</CFHTTP>
```

> **NOTE** Terminate CFHTTP POST operations with </CFHTTP>. Termination is not required with CFHTTP GET operations.

URL

Required. Full URL of the host name or IP address of the server on which the file resides.

PORT

Optional. The port number on the server from which the object is being requested. Default is 80. When used with RESOLVEURL, the URLs of retrieved documents that specify a port number are automatically resolved to preserve links in the retrieved document.

METHOD

Required. GET or POST. Use GET to download a text or binary file, or to create a query from the contents of a text file. Use POST to send information to a server page or a CGI program for processing. POST requires the use of a CFHTTPPARAM tag.

USERNAME

Optional. When required by a server, a valid username.

PASSWORD

Optional. When required by a server, a valid password.

NAME

Optional. The name to assign to a query when a query is to be constructed from a file.

COLUMNS

Optional. The column names for a query. If no column names are specified, the query returns all rows in the query except for the first row. To get all the rows in a query, you must specify column names.

PATH

Optional. The path to the directory in which a file is to be stored. If a path is not specified in a POST or GET operation, a variable is created (CFHTTP.FileContent) that you can use to present the results of the POST operation in a CFOUTPUT.

FILE

Required in a POST operation if PATH is specified. The filename to be used for the file that is accessed. For GET operations, defaults to the name specified in URL. Enter path information in the PATH attribute.

DELIMITER

Required for creating a query. Valid characters are a tab or comma. Default is a comma (,).

TEXTQUALIFIER

Required for creating a query. Indicates the start and finish of a column. Should be appropriately escaped when embedded in a column. For example, if the qualifier is a quotation mark, it should be escaped as " ". If there is no text qualifier in the file, specify a blank space as " ". Default is the quote mark (").

RESOLVEURL

Optional. Yes or No. Default is No. For GET and POST operations, when Yes, any page reference returned into the FileContent internal variable will have its internal URLs fully resolved, including port number, so that links remain intact. The following HTML tags, which can contain links, will be resolved:

- IMG SRC
- A HREF
- FORM ACTION
- APPLET CODE
- SCRIPT SRC
- EMBED SRC
- EMBED PLUGINSPACE
- BODY BACKGROUND
- FRAME SRC
- BGSOUND SRC
- OBJECT DATA
- OBJECT CLASSID
- OBJECT CODEBASE
- OBJECT USEMAP

PROXYSERVER

Optional. Host name or IP address of a proxy server.

PROXYPORT

Optional. The port number on the proxy server from which the object is being requested. Default is 80. When used with RESOLVEURL, the URLs of retrieved documents that specify a port number are automatically resolved to preserve links in the retrieved document.

USERAGENT

Optional. User agent request header.

THROWONERROR

Optional. Boolean indicating whether to throw an exception that can be caught by using the CFTRY and CFCATCH tags. The error code and its associated message can be viewed in the variable CFHTTP.StatusCode. The default is NO.

REDIRECT

Optional. Boolean indicating whether to redirect execution or stop execution. The default is YES. If set to NO and THROWONERROR is set to YES, execution stops if CFHTTP fails, and the status code and associated error message are returned in the variable CFHTTP.StatusCode. To see where execution would have been redirected, use the variable CFHTTP.ResponseHeader[LOCATION]. The key LOCATION identifies the path of redirection.

TIMEOUT

Optional. Timeout period in seconds. By default, the ColdFusion server processes requests asynchronously; that is, the ColdFusion server uses the timeout set on the URL in the browser, the timeout set in the Cold-Fusion Administrator, and the timeout set in the tag to determine the timeout period for the CFHTTP request.

When a URL timeout is specified in the browser, this timeout setting will take precedence over the ColdFusion Administrator timeout. The ColdFusion server then takes the lesser of the URL timeout and the timeout passed in the TIMEOUT attribute so that the request will always time out before or at the same time as the page times out. Likewise, if there is no URL timeout specified, ColdFusion takes the lesser of the Cold-Fusion Administrator timeout and the timeout passed in the TIMEOUT attribute.

If there is no timeout set on the URL in the browser, no timeout set in the ColdFusion Administrator, and no timeout set with the TIMEOUT attribute, ColdFusion processes requests synchronously; thus, ColdFusion waits indefinitely for the CFHTTP request to process.

Note that you must enable the timeout set in the Cold-Fusion Administrator in order for the ColdFusion Administrator timeout and the URL timeout to take effect. This setting is on the ColdFusion Administrator Server Settings page. Please refer to Administering ColdFusion Server for more information about Cold-Fusion settings.

CFHTTPPARAM

Required for CFHTTP POST operations, CFHTTPPARAM is used to specify the parameters necessary to build a CFHTTP POST.

Syntax

```
<CFHTTPPARAM NAME="name"
    TYPE="type"
    VALUE="transaction type"
    FILE="filename">
```

NAME

Required. A variable name for the data being passed.

TYPE

Required. The transaction type. Valid entries are:

- URL
- FormField
- Cookie
- CGI
- File

VALUE

Optional for TYPE="File." Specifies the value of the URL, FormField, Cookie, File, or CGI variable being passed.

FILE

Required for TYPE="File."

CFIF CFELSEIF CFELSE

Used with CFELSE and CFELSEIF, CFIF lets you create simple and compound conditional statements in CFML. The value in the CFIF tag can be any expression.

Syntax

```
<CFIF expression>
    HTML and CFML tags
<CFELSEIF>
    HTML and CFML tags
<CFELSE expression>
    HTML and CFML tags
</CFIF>
```

CFIMPERSONATE

Allows you to impersonate a user defined in a security context defined in Advanced Security. The ColdFusion Application Server enforces all the privileges and restrictions that have been set up for that user with the Advanced Security rules.

Syntax

```
<CFIMPERSONATE
    SECURITYCONTEXT="SecurityContext"
    USERNAME="Name"
    PASSWORD="Password"
    TYPE= "CF" or "OS">
    ...
    HTML or CFML code to execute
    ...
</CFIMPERSONATE>
```

SECURITYCONTEXT

Required. The security context in which the user should be authenticated. If the impersonation type is "CF ," then you should specify a security context that has already been defined using the ColdFusion Advanced Security Administrator. If the impersonation type is "OS," then you should specify an NT domain as the security context.

USERNAME

Required. The user name of the user you want to impersonate. You can create a rule within ColdFusion Advanced Security to restrict a user from being impersonated within a security context.

PASSWORD

Required. The password of the user that you want to impersonate.

TYPE

Required. The type of impersonation needed. This attribute can have the value—"CF" for impersonation at the application level or "OS" for impersonation at the operating system level. Operating System level impersonation means that the impersonation is of a user known to the operating system. Currently, this type of impersonation is available only for Windows NT and not for UNIX. When this type of impersonation is in effect, the operating system will automatically perform access control for access to any resources managed by the operating system such as files and directories. This is fast, since ColdFusion is not doing any extra checking, the OS is, but the OS is limited since only resources that are protected by the operating systemare protected. For example, the operating system cannot check for resource types such as Application, data sources etc.

CFINCLUDE

CFINCLUDE lets you embed references to ColdFusion pages in your CFML. If necessary, you can embed CFINCLUDE tags recursively.

For an additional method of encapsulating CFML, see the CFMODULE tag, used to create custom tags in CFML.

Syntax
```
<CFINCLUDE TEMPLATE="template_name">
```
TEMPLATE
A logical path to an existing page.

CFINDEX

Use the CFINDEX tag to populate collections with indexed data. CFINDEX and CFSEARCH encapsulate the Verity indexing and searching utilities. Verity collections can be populated from either text files in a directory you specify, or from a query generated by any ColdFusion query. Before you can populate a Verity collection, you need to create the collection using either the CFCOLLECTION tag or the ColdFusion Administrator. Use CFSEARCH to search collections you populate with CFINDEX.

Syntax
```
<CFINDEX COLLECTION="collection_name"
    ACTION="action"
    TYPE="type"
    TITLE="title"
    KEY="ID"
    BODY="body"
    CUSTOM1="custom_value"
    CUSTOM2="custom_value"
    URLPATH="URL"
    EXTENSIONS="file_extensions"
    QUERY="query_name"
    RECURSE="Yes/No"
    EXTERNAL="Yes/No"
    LANGUAGE="language">
```

COLLECTION
Required. Specifies a collection name. If you are indexing an external collection (EXTERNAL is "Yes"), specify the collection name, including fully qualified path:
```
COLLECTION="e:\collections\personnel"
```
You cannot combine internal and external collections in the same indexing operation.

ACTION
Optional. Specifies the index action. Valid entries are:

Update   Uates the index and adds the key specified in KEY to the index if it is not already defined.

Delete   Deletes the key specified in KEY in the specified collection.

Purge   Deletes data in the specified collection leaving the collection intact for repopulation.

Refresh   Clears data in the specified collection prior to re-populating it with new data.

Optimize   Optimizes the specified collection of files. This action is deprecated; use CFCOLLECTION instead.

TYPE
Optional. Specifies the type of entity being indexed. Default is CUSTOM. Valid entries are:

File   Indexes files.

Path   Indexes all files in specified path that pass EXTENSIONS filter.

Custom   Indexes custom entities from a ColdFusion query.

TITLE
Required when TYPE="Custom." Specifies one of the following:

- A title for the collection
- A query column name for any TYPE and a valid query name

The TITLE attribute allows searching collections by title or displaying a separate title from the actual key.

KEY
Optional. A unique identifier reference that specifies one of the following:

- Document filename when TYPE="File"
- Fully qualified path when TYPE="Path"
- A unique identifier when TYPE="Custom," such as the table column holding the primary key
- A query column name for any other TYPE argument

BODY

Optional. ASCII text to index or a query column name. Required if TYPE="Custom". Ignored for TYPE="File" and TYPE="Path." Invalid if TYPE="Delete". Specifies one of the following:

- The ASCII text to be indexed
- A query column name when a valid query name is specified in QUERY

Multiple columns can be specified in a comma-separated list:

BODY="employee_name, dept_name, location"

CUSTOM1

Optional. A custom field you can use to store data during an indexing operation. Specify a query column name for any TYPE and a valid query name.

CUSTOM2

Optional. A second custom field you can use to store data during an indexing operation. Usage is the same as for CUSTOM1.

URLPATH

Optional. Specifies the URL path for files when TYPE="File" and TYPE="Path." When the collection is searched with CFSEARCH, this path name will automatically be prepended to all file names and returned as the URL attribute.

EXTENSIONS

Optional. Specifies the comma-separated list of file extensions that ColdFusion uses to index files when TYPE="Path". Default is HTM, HTML, CFM, CFML, DBM, DBML. An entry of "*." returns files with no extension:

EXTENSIONS=".htm, .html, .cfm, .cfml, *."

Returns files with the specified extensions as well as files with no extension.

QUERY

Optional. Specifies the name of the query against which the collection is being generated.

RECURSE

Optional. Yes or No. Yes specifies that directories below the path specified in KEY when TYPE="Path" will be included in the indexing operation.

EXTERNAL

Optional. Yes or No. Yes indicates that the collection specified in COLLECTION was created outside of Cold-Fusion using native Verity indexing tools.

LANGUAGE

Optional. To use the LANGUAGE attribute you must have the ColdFusion International Search Pack installed. Valid entries are:

- English (default)
- German
- Finnish
- French
- Danish
- Dutch
- Italian
- Norwegian
- Portuguese
- Spanish
- Swedish

CFINPUT

CFINPUT is used inside CFFORM to place radio buttons, checkboxes, or text boxes. Provides input validation for the specified control type.

CFINPUT supports the JavaScript on Click event in the same manner as the HTML INPUT tag:

```
<CFINPUT TYPE="radio"
    NAME="radio1"
    onClick="JavaScript_function">
```

Syntax

```
<CFINPUT TYPE="input_type"
    NAME="name"
    VALUE="initial_value"
    REQUIRED="Yes/No"
    RANGE="min_value, max_value"
    VALIDATE="data_type"
    ONVALIDATE="javascript_function"
    MESSAGE="validation_msg"
    ONERROR="text"
    SIZE="integer"
    MAXLENGTH="integer"
    CHECKED="Yes/No"
    PASSTHROUGH="HTML_attributes"
>
```

TYPE

Optional. Valid entries are:

Text   Creates a text entry box control (default).

Radio   Creates a radio button control.

Checkbox   Creates a checkbox control.

Password   Creates a password entry control.

NAME

Required. A name for the form input element.

VALUE

Optional. An initial value for the form input element.

REQUIRED

Optional. Enter Yes or No. Default is No.

RANGE

Optional. Enter a minimum value, maximum value range separated by a comma. Valid only for numeric data.

VALIDATE

Optional. Valid entries are:

Date   Verifies US date entry in the form mm/dd/yyyy.

Eurodate   Verifies valid European date entry in the form dd/mm/yyyy.

Time   Verifies a time entry in the form hh:mm:ss.

Float   Verifies a floating point entry.

Integer   Verifies an integer entry.

Telephone   Verifies a telephone entry. Telephone data must be entered as ###-###-####. The hyphen separator (-) can be replaced with a blank. The area code and exchange must begin with a digit between 1 and 9.

zipcode **(U.S. formats only)**   Number can be a 5-digit or 9-digit zip in the form #####-####. The hyphen separator (-) can be replaced with a blank.

creditcard   Blanks and dashes are stripped and the number is verified using the mod10 algorithm.

social_security_number   Number must be entered as ###-##-####. The hyphen separator (-) can be replaced with a blank.

ONVALIDATE

Optional. The name of a valid JavaScript function used to validate user input. The form object, input object, and input object value are passed to the specified routine, which should return true if validation succeeds and false otherwise. When used, the VALIDATE attribute is ignored.

MESSAGE

Optional. Message text to appear if validation fails.

ONERROR

Optional. The name of a valid JavaScript function you want to execute in the event of a failed validation.

SIZE

Optional. The size of the input control. Ignored if TYPE is Radio or Checkbox.

MAXLENGTH

Optional. The maximum length of text entered when TYPE is Text.

PASSTHROUGH

Optional. HTML attributes that are not explicitly supported by CFINPUT. If you specify an attribute and its value, the attribute and value are passed to the HTML code that is generated for the CFINPUT tag.

CFINSERT

CFINSERT inserts new records in data sources.

Syntax

```
<CFINSERT DATASOURCE="ds_name"
    DBTYPE="type"
    DBSERVER="dbms"
    DBNAME="database name"
    TABLENAME="tbl_name"
    TABLEOWNER="owner"
    TABLEQUALIFIER="tbl_qualifier"
    USERNAME="username"
    PASSWORD="password"
    PROVIDER="COMProvider"
    PROVIDERDSN="datasource"
    FORMFIELDS="formfield1, formfield2, ...">
```

DATASOURCE

Required. Name of the data source that contains your table.

DBTYPE

Optional. The database driver type:

ODBC (default)   ODBC driver.

Oracle73   Oracle 7.3 native database driver. Using this option, the ColdFusion Server computer must have Oracle 7.3.4.0.0 (or greater) client software installed.

Oracle80   Oracle 8.0 native database driver. Using this option, the ColdFusion Server computer must have Oracle 8.0 (or greater) client software installed.

Sybase11   Sybase System 11 native database driver. Using this option, the ColdFusion Server computer must have Sybase 11.1.1 (or greater) client software installed. Sybase patch ebf 7729 is recommended.

OLEDB   OLE DB provider. If specified, this database provider overrides the driver type specified in the ColdFusion Administrator.

DB2   DB2 5.2 native database driver.

Informix73   Informix73 native database driver.

DBSERVER

Optional. For native database drivers and the SQLOLEDB provider, specifies the name of the database server machine. If specified, DBSERVER overrides the server specified in the data source.

DBNAME

Optional. The database name (Sybase System 11 driver and SQLOLEDB provider only). If specified, DBNAME overrides the default database specified in the data source.

TABLENAME

Required. Name of the table you want the form fields inserted in. Note the following:

ORACLE drivers   This specification must be in uppercase.

Sybase driver   This specification is case-sensitive and must be in the same case as that used when the table was created.

TABLEOWNER

Optional. For data sources that support table ownership (such as SQL Server, Oracle, and Sybase SQL Anywhere), use this field to specify the owner of the table.

TABLEQUALIFIER

Optional. For data sources that support table qualifiers, use this field to specify the qualifier for the table. The purpose of table qualifiers varies across drivers. For SQL Server and Oracle, the qualifier refers to the name of the database that contains the table. For the IntersolvdBase driver, the qualifier refers to the directory where the DBF files are located.

USERNAME

Optional. If specified, USERNAME overrides the username value specified in the ODBC setup.

PASSWORD

Optional. If specified, PASSWORD overrides the password value specified in the ODBC setup.

PROVIDER

Optional. COM provider (OLE-DB only).

PROVIDERDSN

Optional. Data source name for the COM provider (OLE-DB only).

FORMFIELDS

Optional. A comma-separated list of form fields to insert. If this attribute is not specified, all fields in the form are included in the operation.

CFLOCATION

CFLOCATION opens a specified ColdFusion page or HTML file. For example, you might use CFLOCATION to specify a standard message or response that you use in several different ColdFusion applications. Use the ADDTOKEN attribute to verify client requests.

Syntax

```
<CFLOCATION URL="url" ADDTOKEN="Yes/No">
```

URL

The URL of the HTML file or CFML page you want to open.

ADDTOKEN

Optional. Yes or No. CLIENTMANAGEMENT must be enabled (see CFAPPLICATION). A value of Yes appends client variable information to the URL you specify in the URL argument.

CFLOCK

The CFLOCK tag provides two types of locks to ensure the integrity of shared data:

- exclusive lock
- read-only lock

An exclusive lock single-threads access to the CFML constructs in its body. Single-threaded access implies that the body of the tag can be executed by at most one request at a time. A request executing inside a CFLOCK tag has an "exclusive lock" on the tag. No other requests are allowed to start executing inside the tag while a request has an exclusive lock. ColdFusion issues exclusive locks on a first-come, first-served basis.

A read-only lock allows multiple requests to access the CFML constructs inside its body concurrently. Therefore, read-only locks should only be used when the shared data will only be read and not modified. If another request already has an exclusive lock on the shared data, the request will wait for the exclusive lock to be released before it can obtain it.

Syntax

```
<CFLOCK
    TIMEOUT="timeout in seconds "
    SCOPE="Application" or "Server" or
"Session"
    NAME="lockname"
    THROWONTIMEOUT="Yes/No"
    TYPE= "ReadOnly/Exclusive ">
    <!--- CFML to be synchronized --->
</CFLOCK>
```

TIMEOUT

Required. Specifies the maximum amount of time in seconds to wait to obtain an lock. If a lock can be obtained within the specified period, execution will continue inside the body of the tag. Otherwise, the behavior depends on the value of the THROWONTIMEOUT attribute.

SCOPE

Optional. Specifies the scope as one of the following: Application, Server, or Session. This attribute is mutually exclusive with the NAME attribute. See the Scope section for valuable information.

NAME

Optional. Specifies the name of the lock. Only one request will be able to execute inside a CFLOCK tag with a given name. Therefore, providing the NAME attribute allows for synchronizing access to the same resources from different parts of an application. Lock names are global to a ColdFusion server. They are shared between applications and user sessions, but not across clustered servers. This attribute is mutually exclusive with the SCOPE attribute. Therefore, do not specify the SCOPE attribute and the NAME attribute in the same tag. Note that the value of NAME cannot be an empty string.

THROWONTIMEOUT

Optional. Yes or No. Specifies how timeout conditions should be handled. If the value is Yes an exception will be generated to provide notification of the timeout. If the value is No execution continues past the </CFLOCK> tag. Default is Yes.

TYPE

Optional. ReadOnly or Exclusive. Specifies the type of lock: read-only or exclusive. Default is Exclusive. A read-only lock allows more than one request to read shared data. An exclusive lock allows only one request to read or write to shared data. See the following Note.

NOTE　　Limit the scope of code that updates shared data. Exclusive locks are required to ensure the integrity of these updates, but they have a significant impact on performance. Read-only locks are faster. If you have a performance-sensitive application, you should substitute read only locks for exclusive locks wherever it is possible, for example, when reading shared data.

CFLOOP

Looping is a very powerful programming technique that lets you repeat a set of instructions or display output over and over until one or more conditions are met. CFLOOP supports five different types of loops:

- Index Loops
- Conditional Loops
- Looping over a Query
- Looping over a List
- Looping over a COM Collection or Structure

The type of loop is determined by the attributes of the CFLOOP tag.

Index Loops

An index loop repeats for a number of times determined by a range of numeric values. Index loops are commonly known as FOR loops, as in "loop FOR this range of values."

Syntax

```
<CFLOOP INDEX="parameter_name"
    FROM="beginning_value"
    TO="ending_value"
    STEP="increment">
    ...
    HTML or CFML code to execute
    ...
</CFLOOP>
```

INDEX

Required. Defines the parameter that is the index value. The index value will be set to the FROM value and then incremented by 1 (or the STEP value) until it equals the TO value.

FROM

Required. The beginning value of the index.

TO

Required. The ending value of the index.

STEP

Optional. Default is 1. Sets the value by which the loop INDEX value is incremented each time the loop is processed.

Conditional Loops

A conditional loop iterates over a set of instructions while a given condition is TRUE. To use this type of loop correctly, the instructions must change the condition every time the loop iterates until the condition evaluates as FALSE. Conditional loops are commonly known as WHILE loops, as in "loop WHILE this condition is true."

Syntax
```
<CFLOOP CONDITION="expression">
```

CONDITION

Required. Sets the condition that controls the loop. The loop will repeat as long as the condition evaluates as TRUE. When the condition is FALSE, the loop stops.

Looping over a Query

A loop over a query repeats for every record in the query record set. The CFLOOP results are just like a CFOUTPUT. During each iteration of the loop, the columns of the current row will be available for output. CFLOOP allows you to loop over tags that can not be used inside CFOUTPUT.

Syntax
```
<CFLOOP QUERY="query_name"
    STARTROW="row_num"
    ENDROW="row_num">
```

QUERY

Required. Specifies the query that will control the loop.

STARTROW

Optional. Specifies the first row of the query that will be included in the loop.

ENDROW

Optional. Specifies the last row of the query that will be included in the loop.

Looping over a List

Looping over a list offers the option of walking through elements contained within a variable or value returned from an expression. In a list loop, the INDEX attribute specifies the name of a variable to receive the next element of the list, and the LIST attribute holds a list or a variable containing a list.

Syntax
```
<CFLOOP INDEX="index_name"
    LIST="list_items"
    DELIMITERS="item_delimiter">
</CFLOOP>
```

INDEX

Required. In a list loop, the INDEX attribute specifies the name of a variable to receive the next element of the list, and the LIST attribute holds a list or a variable containing a list.

LIST

Required. The list items in the loop, provided directly or with a variable.

DELIMITERS

Optional. Specifies the delimiter characters used to separate items in the LIST.

Looping over a COM Collection or Structure

The CFLOOP COLLECTION attribute allows you to loop over a structure or a COM/DCOM collection object:

- A COM/DCOM collection object is a set of similar items referenced as a group rather than individually. For example, the group of open documents in an application is a type of collection.
- A structure can contain either a related set of items or be used as an associative array. Looping is particularly useful when using a structure as an associative array.

Each collection item is referenced in the CFLOOP by the variable name that you supply in the ITEM attribute. This type of an iteration is generally used to access every object within a COM/DCOM collection or every element in the structure. The loop is executed until all objects have been accessed.

The COLLECTION attribute is used with the ITEM attribute in a CFLOOP. In the example that follows, ITEM is assigned a variable called file2, so that with each cycle in the CFLOOP, each item in the collection is referenced. In the CFOUTPUT section, the name property of the file2 item is referenced for display.

CFMAIL

CFMAIL allows you to send email messages via an SMTP server.

See also CFMAILPARAM.

Syntax

```
<CFMAIL TO="recipient"
    FROM="sender"
    CC="copy_to"
    BCC="blind_copy_to"
    SUBJECT="msg_subject"
    TYPE="msg_type"
    MAXROWS="max_msgs"
    MIMEATTACH="path"
    QUERY="query_name"
    GROUP="query_column"
    GROUPCASESENSITIVE="yes/no"
    STARTROW="query_row"
    SERVER="servername"
    PORT="port_ID"
    MAILERID="headerid"
    TIMEOUT="seconds">
```

TO

Required. The name of the recipient(s) of the email message. This can be either a static address (as in, TO="support@allaire.com"), a variable that contains an address (such as, TO="#Form.Email#"), or the name of a query column that contains address information (such as, TO="#EMail#"). In the latter case, an individual email message is sent for every row returned by the query.

FROM

Required. The sender of the email message. This attribute may be either static (e.g., FROM="support@allaire.com") or dynamic (as in, FROM="#GetUser.EMailAddress#").

CC

Optional. Indicates additional addresses to copy the email message to; "CC" stands for "carbon copy."

BCC

Optional. Indicates additional addresses to copy the email message without listing them in the message header. "BCC" stands for "blind carbon copy."

SUBJECT

Required. The subject of the mail message. This field may be driven dynamically on a message-by-message basis. For example, if you want to do a mailing that updates customers on the status of their orders, you might use a subject attribute like SUBJECT="Status for Order Number #Order_ID#".

TYPE

Optional. Specifies extended type attributes for the message. Currently, the only valid value for this attribute is "HTML". Specifying TYPE="HTML" informs the receiving email client that the message has embedded HTML tags that need to be processed. This is only useful when sending messages to mail clients that understand HTML (such as Netscape 2.0 and above email clients).

MAXROWS

Optional. Specifies the maximum number of email messages you want to send.

MIMEATTACH

Optional. Specifies the path of the file to be attached to the email message. Attached file is MIME-encoded.

QUERY

Optional. The name of the CFQUERY from which you want to draw data for message(s) you want to send. Specify this attribute to send more than one mail message, or to send the results of a query within a single message.

GROUP

Optional. Specifies the query column to use when you group sets of records together to send as a single email message. For example, if you send a set of billing statements out to your customers, you might group on "Customer_ID." The GROUP attribute, which is case sensitive, eliminates adjacent duplicates in the case where the data is sorted by the specified field.

GROUPCASESENSITIVE

Optional. Boolean indicating whether to group with regard to case or not. The default value is YES; case is considered while grouping. If the QUERY attribute specifies a query object that was generated by a case-insensitive SQL query, set the GROUPCASESENSITIVE attribute to NO to keep the recordset intact.

STARTROW

Optional. Specifies the row in the query to start from.

SERVER

Required. The address of the SMTP server to use for sending messages. The server name specified in the ColdFusion Administrator is used if no server is specified.

PORT

The TCP/IP port on which the SMTP server listens for requests. This is almost always 25.

MAILERID

Optional. Specifies a mailer ID to be passed in the X-Mailer SMTP header, which identifies the mailer application. The default is Allaire ColdFusion Application Server.

TIMEOUT

Optional. The number of seconds to wait before timing out the connection to the SMTP server.

CFMAILPARAM

CFMAILPARAM can either attach a file or add a header to a message. If you use CFMAILPARAM, it is nested within a CFMAIL tag. You can use more than one CFMAILPARAM tags within a CFMAIL tag in order to attach one or more files and headers.

See also CFMAIL.

Syntax

```
<CFMAIL
    TO="recipient"
    SUBJECT="msg_subject"
    FROM="sender"
    ...more attibutes...
>
    <CFMAILPARAM
        FILE="file-name"
    >
    or
    <CFMAILPARAM
        NAME="header-name"
        VALUE="header-value"
    >
    ...
</CFMAIL>
```

FILE

Required if you do not specify the NAME attribute. Attaches the specified file to the message. This attribute is mutually exclusive with the NAME attribute.

NAME

Required if you do not specify the FILE attribute. Specifies the name of the header. Header names are case insensitive. This attribute is mutually exclusive with the FILE attribute.

VALUE

Optional. Indicates the value of the header.

CFMODULE

Use CFMODULE to invoke a custom tag for use in your ColdFusion application pages. CFMODULE can help deal with any custom tag name conflicts that might arise.

Use the TEMPLATE attribute to name a ColdFusion page containing the custom tag definition, including its path. Use the NAME attribute to refer to the custom tag using a

dot notation scheme indicating the location of the custom tag in the ColdFusion installation directory.

Syntax

```
<CFMODULE TEMPLATE="template"
    NAME="tag_name"

ATTRIBUTECOLLECTION="collection_structure"
    ATTRIBUTE_NAME1="value"
    ATTRIBUTE_NAME2="value"
    ...>
```

TEMPLATE

Used in place of NAME, defines a path to the application page (.cfm file) implementing the tag. Relative paths are expanded from the current page. Physical paths are not allowed. Absolute paths are expanded using the ColdFusion mappings.

NAME

Used in place of TEMPLATE, defines the name of the custom tag in the form "Name.Name.Name..." that uniquely identifies a subdirectory containing the custom tag page under the root directory for CF custom tags. For example:

```
<CFMODULE
NAME="Allaire.Forums40.GetUserOptions">
```
Identifies the page GetUserOptions.cfm in the directory CustomTags\Allaire\Forums40 under the root directory of the ColdFusion installation.

ATTRIBUTECOLLECTION

Optional. A structure that contains a collection of key-value pairs that represent attribute names and their values. You can specify as many key-value pairs as needed. However, you can specify the ATTRIBUTECOL-LECTION attribute only once.

ATTRIBUTE_NAME

Optional. Attributes you want your custom tag to use. You can use as many attributes as needed to specify the parameters of a custom tag.

CFOBJECT

The CFOBJECT tag allows you to call methods in COM, CORBA, and JAVA objects.

NOTE ColdFusion administrators can disable the CFOBJECT tag in the ColdFusion Administrator Basic Security page.

On UNIX, COM objects are not currently supported by CFOBJECT.

CFOBJECT Topics

- CFOBJECT Type="COM"
- CFOBJECT Type="CORBA"
- CFOBJECT Type="JAVA"

CFOBJECT TYPE Attributes

Depending on the value you assign to the TYPE attribute of CFOBJECT, there are several additional attributes you can set. This table shows which attributes you can use with each CFOBJECT TYPE.

Attributes Used with CFOBJECT TYPEs

TYPE	Attributes
COM	ACTION, CLASS, NAME, CONTEXT, SERVER
CORBA	ACTION, CONTEXT, CLASS, NAME, LOCALE
JAVA	ACTION, TYPE, CLASS, NAME

Sections that follow describe these values and attributes in greater detail.

CFOBJECT Type="COM"

CFOBJECT allows you to create and use COM (Component Object Model) objects. Any automation server object type that is currently registered on a machine can be invoked. You can use a utility like Microsoft's OLEView to browse COM objects. OLEView, as well as information about COM and DCOM, can be found at Microsoft's OLE Development Web site http://www.microsoft.com/oledev/.

To use CFOBJECT, you need to know the program ID or filename of the object, the methods and properties available through the IDispatch interface, and the arguments and return types of the object's methods. The OLEView utility can give you this information for most COM objects.

Syntax

```
<CFOBJECT TYPE="COM"
    ACTION="action"
    CLASS="program_ID"
    NAME="text"
    CONTEXT="context"
    SERVER="server_name">
```

ACTION

Required. One of the following:

Create Use Create to instantiate a COM object (typically a DLL) prior to invoking methods or properties.

Connect Use Connect to connect to a COM object (typically an EXE) that is already running on the server specified in SERVER.

CLASS

Required. Enter the component ProgID for the object you want to invoke.

NAME

Required. Enter a name for the object.

CONTEXT

Optional. InProc, Local, or Remote. Uses Registry setting when not specified.

SERVER

Required when CONTEXT="Remote". Enter a valid server name using UNC (Universal Naming Convention) or DNS (Domain Name Server) conventions, in one of the following forms:

```
SERVER="\\lanserver"
SERVER="lanserver"
SERVER="http://www.servername.com"
SERVER="www.servername.com"
SERVER="127.0.0.1"
```

CFOBJECT Type="CORBA"

CFOBJECT allows you to call methods in CORBA objects. These CORBA objects must already have been defined and registered for use.

Syntax

```
<CFOBJECT TYPE="CORBA"
    CONTEXT="context"
    CLASS="file or naming service"
    NAME="text"
    LOCALE="type-value arguments">
```

CONTEXT

Required. Specifies one of the following:

IOR ColdFusion uses the Interoperable Object Reference (IOR) to access the CORBA server.

NameService ColdFusion uses the naming service to access server. "NameService" is only valid with the Initial Context of a VisiBroker Orb.

CLASS

Required. Specifies different information, depending on the CONTEXT specification:

If CONTEXT is IOR Specifies the name of a file that contains the stringified version of the IOR. Cold-Fusion must be able to read this file at all times; it should be local to ColdFusion server or on the network in an open, accessible location.

If CONTEXT is NameService Specifies a period-delimited naming context for the naming service, such as Allaire.Department.Doc.empobject.

NAME

Required. Enter a name for the object. Your application uses this to reference the CORBA object's methods and attributes.

LOCALE

Optional. Sets arguments for a call to init_orb(..). Use of this attribute is specific to VisiBroker orbs, and is currently available on C++, Version 3.2. The value should be of the form:

```
LOCALE=" -ORBagentAddr 199.99.129.33 -
ORBagentPort 19000."
```

Note that each type-value pair has to start with a leading "-".

CFOBJECT Type="JAVA"

CFOBJECT allows you to create and use JAVA objects, and by extension EJB objects.

This support is currently only for NT, but will be extended to Solaris in the next release.

Syntax

```
<CFOBJECT
    ACTION="Create"
    TYPE="Java"
    CLASS="Java class"
    NAME="object name"
>
```

ACTION

Required. Specifies "Create" in order to create the Java object or the WebLogic Environment.

TYPE

Required. Specifies that the type of object, in this case, this is always "Java."

CLASS

Required. Specifies the Java class.

NAME

Required. The name used within CFML to access the object.

CFOUTPUT

Displays the results of a database query or other operation.

Syntax

```
<CFOUTPUT
    QUERY="query_name"
    GROUP="query_column"
    GROUPCASESENSITIVE="yes/no"
    STARTROW="start_row"
    MAXROWS="max_rows_output">

</CFOUTPUT>
```

QUERY

Optional. The name of the CFQUERY from which you want to draw data for the output section.

GROUP

Optional. Specifies the query column to use when you group sets of records together. Use this attribute if you have retrieved a record set ordered on a certain query column. For example, if you have a record set that is ordered according to "Customer_ID" in the CFQUERY tag, you can group the output on "Customer_ID." The GROUP attribute, which is case sensitive, eliminates adjacent duplicates in the case where the data is sorted by the specified field. See the GROUPCASESENSITIVE attribute for information about specifying a case-insensitive grouping.

GROUPCASESENSITIVE

Optional. Boolean indicating whether to group with regard to case or not. The default value is YES; case is considered while grouping. If the QUERY attribute specifies a query object that was generated by a case-insensitive SQL query, set the GROUPCASESENSITIVE attribute to NO to keep the recordset intact.

STARTROW

Optional. Specifies the row from which to start output.

MAXROWS

Optional. Specifies the maximum number of rows you want displayed in the output section.

CFPARAM

CFPARAM is used to test for a parameter's existence, and optionally test its data type, and provide a default value if one is not assigned.

Syntax

```
<CFPARAM NAME="param_name"
    TYPE="data_type">
    DEFAULT="value">
```

NAME

The name of the parameter you are testing (such as "Client.Email" or "Cookie.BackgroundColor"). If you omit the DEFAULT attribute, an error occurs if the specified parameter does not exist.

TYPE

Optional. The type of parameter that is required. The default value is "any."

Type Values

Type Value	Description
any	Any value.
array	Any array value.
binary	A binary value.
boolean	A Boolean value.
date	A date-time value.
numeric	A numeric value.
query	A query object.
string	A string value or a single character.
struct	A structure.
UUID	A Universally Unique Identifier (UUID) formatted as `XXXXXXXX-XXXX-XXXX-XXXXXXXXXXXXXXXX` where `X` stands for a hexadecimal digit (0–9 or A–F). See CreateUUID.
variable-Name	A valid variable name.

DEFAULT

Optional. Default value to set the parameter to if it does not exist.

CFPOP

CFPOP retrieves and deletes email messages from a POP mail server. See also CFMAIL.

Syntax

```
<CFPOP SERVER="servername"
    PORT="port_number"
    USERNAME="username"
    PASSWORD="password"
    ACTION="action"
    NAME="queryname"
    MESSAGENUMBER="number"
    ATTACHMENTPATH="path"
    TIMEOUT="seconds"
    MAXROWS="number"
    STARTROW="number"
    GENERATEUNIQUEFILENAMES="boolean">
```

SERVER

Required. Host name (biff.upperlip.com) or IP address (192.1.2.225) of the POP server.

PORT

Optional. Defaults to the standard POP port, 110.

USERNAME

Optional. If no user name is specified, the POP connection is anonymous.

PASSWORD

Optional. Password corresponds to user name.

ACTION

Optional. Specifies the mail action. There are three possible values:

GetHeaderOnly **(Default)**   Returns message header information only.

GetAll   Returns message header information, message text, and attachments if ATTACHMENTPATH is specified.

Delete   Deletes messages on the POP server.

NOTE   Two retrieve options are offered to maximize performance. Message header information is typically short and therefore quick to transfer. Message text and attachments can be very long and therefore take longer to process. See the Message Header and Body Columns table, which follows the **CFPOP** attribute descriptions, for information on retrieving header and body information form the query when you specify GetHeaderOnly or GetAll.

NAME

Optional. The name you assign to the index query. Required for ACTION="GetHeaderOnly" and ACTION="GetAll".

MESSAGENUMBER

Optional. Specifies the message number(s) for the given action. MESSAGENUMBER is required for ACTION="Delete". If it is provided for ACTION="GetHeaderOnly" or ACTION="GetAll", only referenced messages will be retrieved. If it is omitted for ACTION="GetHeaderOnly"or ACTION="GetAll", all messages available on the server are returned.

MESSAGENUMBER can contain individual message numbers or a comma-separated list of message numbers. Invalid message numbers will be ignored.

ATTACHMENTPATH

Optional. Allows attachments to be written to the specified directory when ACTION="GetAll". If an invalid ATTACHMENTPATH is specified, no attachment files are written to the server.

TIMEOUT

Optional. Specifies the maximum amount of time in seconds to wait for mail processing. Defaults to 60 seconds.

MAXROWS

Optional. Specifies the maximum number of entries for mail queries. This attribute is ignored if MESSAGE-NUMBER is specified.

STARTROW

Optional. Specifies the first row number to be retrieved. Default is 1. This attribute is ignored if MESSAGENUMBER is specified.

GENERATEUNIQUFILENAMES

Optional. Boolean indicating whether to generate unique file names for the files attached to an email message in order to avoid naming conflicts when the files are saved. The default is NO.

CFPOP Query Variables

The following table describes the query variables that are returned by CFPOP. The example illustrates their use.

CFPOP Query Variables

Variable Names	Description
queryname.RecordCount	The total number of records returned by the query.
queryname.CurrentRow	The current row of the query being processed by CFOUTPUT.
queryname.ColumnList	The list of the column names in the query.

Message Header and Body Columns

The following table lists the message header and body columns that are returned by CFPOP when you specify the ACTION attribute to be either GetHeaderOnly or GetAll. All of the columns are returned if you specify GetAll, but only header information is returned when you specify GetHeaderOnly.

Message Header and Body Columns

Column Name	GetHeader-Only returns	GetAll returns
queryname.date	yes	yes
queryname.from	yes	yes
queryname.messagenumber	yes	yes
queryname.replyto	yes	yes
queryname.subject	yes	yes
queryname.cc	yes	yes
queryname.to	yes	yes
queryname.body	not available	yes
queryname.header	not available	yes
queryname.attachments	not available	yes
queryname.attachmentfiles	not available	yes

CFPROCESSINGDIRECTIVE

Suppresses extraneous white space, and other output, produced by the CFML within the tag's scope.

Syntax

```
<CFPROCESSINGDIRECTIVE
    SUPPRESSWHITESPACE="Yes" or "No">
... any CFML tags here ...
</CFPROCESSINGDIRECTIVE>
```

SUPPRESSWHITESPACE

Required. Boolean indicating whether to suppress the white space and other output generated by the CFML tags within the CFPROCESSINGDIRECTIVE block.

CFPROCPARAM

The CFPROCPARAM tag is nested within a CFSTOREDPROC tag. You use it to specify parameter information, including type, name, value, and length.

Syntax

```
<CFPROCPARAM TYPE="IN/OUT/INOUT"
    VARIABLE="variable name"
    DBVARNAME="DB variable name"
    VALUE="parameter value"
    CFSQLTYPE="parameter datatype"
    MAXLENGTH="length"
    SCALE="decimal places"
    NULL="yes/no">
```

TYPE

Optional. Indicates whether the passed variable is an input, output or input/output variable. Default is IN.

VARIABLE

Required for OUT and INOUT parameters. This is the ColdFusion variable name that you use to reference the value that the output parameter represents after the call is made to the stored procedure.

DBVARNAME

Required if named notation is desired. This is the parameter name. This corresponds to the name of the parameter in the stored procedure.

VALUE

Required for IN and INOUT parameters. This corresponds to the actual value that ColdFusion passes to the stored procedure.

CFSQLTYPE

Required. This is the SQL type that the parameter (any type) will be bound to. The CFSQLTypes are as follows:

CF_SQL_BIGINT	CF_SQL_IDSTAMP	CF_SQL_SMALLINT
CF_SQL_BIT	CF_SQL_INTEGER	CF_SQL_TIME
CF_SQL_CHAR	CF_SQL_LONGVAR-CHAR	CF_SQL_TIMESTAMP
CF_SQL_DATE	CF_SQL_MONEY	CF_SQL_TINYINT
CF_SQL_DECIMAL	CF_SQL_MONEY4	CF_SQL_VARCHAR
CF_SQL_DOUBLE	CF_SQL_NUMERIC	
CF_SQL_FLOAT	CF_SQL_REAL	

MAXLENGTH

Optional. Maximum length of the parameter.

SCALE

Optional. Number of decimal places of the parameter.

NULL

Optional. Specify Yes or No. Indicates whether the parameter is passed as a NULL. If you specify Yes, the tag ignores the VALUE attribute.

CFPROCRESULT

The CFPROCRESULT tag is nested within a CFSTORED-PROC tag. This tag's NAME parameter specifies a result set name that other ColdFusion tags, such as CFOUTPUT and CFTABLE, use to access the result set. It also allows you to optionally identify which of the stored procedure's result sets to return.

Syntax

```
<CFPROCRESULT NAME="query_name"
    RESULTSET="1-n"
    MAXROWS="maxrows">
```

NAME

Required. Name for the query result set.

RESULTSET

Optional. Specify this parameter to identify the desired result set if the stored procedure returns multiple result sets. Default is 1.

MAXROWS

Optional. Specifies the maximum number of rows returned in the result set. The default is to return all rows in the result set.

CFQUERY

CFQUERY passes SQL statements for any purpose to your data source. Not limited to queries.

Syntax

```
<CFQUERY NAME="query_name"
    DATASOURCE="ds_name"
    DBTYPE="type"
    DBSERVER="dbms"
    DBNAME="database name"
    USERNAME="username"
    PASSWORD="password"
    MAXROWS="number"
    BLOCKFACTOR="blocksize"
    TIMEOUT="milliseconds"
    CACHEDAFTER="date"
    CACHEDWITHIN="timespan"
    PROVIDER="COMProvider"
    PROVIDERDSN="datasource"
    DEBUG="Yes/No">

SQL statements

</CFQUERY>
```

NAME

Required. The name you assign to the query. Query names must begin with a letter and may consist of letters, numbers, and the underscore character (spaces are not allowed). The query name is used later in the page to reference the query's record set.

DATASOURCE

Required. The name of the data source from which this query should retrieve data.

DBTYPE

Optional. The database driver type:

ODBC (default) ODBC driver.

Oracle73 Oracle 7.3 native database driver. Using this option, the ColdFusion Server computer must have Oracle 7.3.4.0.0 (or greater) client software installed.

Oracle80 Oracle 8.0 native database driver. Using this option, the ColdFusion Server computer must have Oracle 8.0 (or greater) client software installed.

Sybase11 Sybase System 11 native database driver. Using this option, the ColdFusion Server computer must have Sybase 11.1.1 (or greater) client software installed. Sybase patch ebf 7729 is recommended.

OLEDB OLE DB provider. If specified, this database provider overrides the driver type specified in the ColdFusion Administrator.

DB2 DB2 5.2 native database driver.

Informix73 Informix73 native database driver.

DBSERVER

Optional. For native database drivers and the SQLOLEDB provider, specifies the name of the database server machine. If specified, DBSERVER overrides the server specified in the data source.

DBNAME

Optional. The database name (Sybase System 11 driver and SQLOLEDB provider only). If specified, DBNAME overrides the default database specified in the data source.

USERNAME

Optional. If specified, USERNAME overrides the username value specified in the data source setup.

PASSWORD

Optional. If specified, PASSWORD overrides the password value specified in the data source setup.

MAXROWS

Optional. Specifies the maximum number of rows you want returned in the record set.

BLOCKFACTOR

Optional. Specifies the maximum number of rows to fetch at a time from the server. The range is 1 (default) to 100. This parameter applies to ORACLE native database drivers and to ODBC drivers. Certain ODBC drivers may dynamically reduce the block factor at runtime.

TIMEOUT

Optional. Lets you specify a maximum number of milliseconds for the query to execute before returning an error indicating that the query has timed-out. This attribute is not supported by most ODBC drivers. TIMEOUT is supported by the SQL Server 6.x or above driver. The minimum and maximum allowable values vary, depending on the driver.

CACHEDAFTER

Optional. Specify a date value (for example, 4/16/98, April 16, 1999, 4-16-99). ColdFusion uses cached query data if the date of the original query is after the date specified. Effective only if query caching has been enabled in the ColdFusion Administrator. To use cached data, the current query must use the same SQL statement, data source, query name, user name, password, and DBTYPE. Additionally, for native drivers it must have the same DBSERVER and DBNAME (Sybase only).

Years from 0 to 29 are interpreted as 21st century values. Years 30 to 99 are interpreted as 20th century values.

When specifying a date value as a string, make sure it is enclosed in quotes.

CACHEDWITHIN

Optional. Enter a timespan using the ColdFusion CreateTimeSpan function. Cached query data will be used if the original query date falls within the time span you define. The CreateTimeSpan function is used to define a period of time from the present backwards. Effective only if query caching has been enabled in the ColdFusion Administrator. To use cached data, the current query must use the same SQL statement, data source, query name, user name, password, and DBTYPE. Additionally, for native drivers it must have the same DBSERVER and DBNAME (Sybase only).

PROVIDER

Optional. COM provider (OLE-DB only).

PROVIDERDSN

Optional. Data source name for the COM provider (OLE-DB only).

DEBUG

Optional. Used for debugging queries. Specifying this attribute causes the SQL statement actually submitted to the data source and the number of records returned from the query to be output.

CFQUERYPARAM

CFQUERYPARAM checks the data type of a query parameter. The CFQUERYPARAM tag is nested within a CFQUERY tag. More specifically, it is embedded within the query SQL statement. If you specify its optional parameters, CFQUERYPARAM also performs data validation.

> **NOTE**   For data, you must specify the MAXLENGTH attribute in order to ensure that maximum length validation is enforced.

Syntax

```
<CFQUERY NAME="query_name"
    DATASOURCE="ds_name"
    ...other attributes...
>
    SELECT STATEMENT WHERE column_name=
    <CFQUERYPARAM VALUE="parameter value"
        CFSQLType="parameter type"
        MAXLENGTH="maximum parameter length"
        SCALE="number of decimal places"
        DBNAME="database name"
        NULL="Yes/No"
    >
    AND/OR ...additional criteria of the
WHERE clause...
</CFQUERY>
```

VALUE

Required. Specifies the actual value that ColdFusion passes to the right of the comparison operator in a where clause.

CFSQLTYPE

Optional. This is the SQL type that the parameter (any type) will be bound to. The default value is CF_SQL_CHAR. The CFSQLTypes are as follows:

CF_SQL_BIGINT	CF_SQL_IDSTAMP	CF_SQL_REFCURSOR
CF_SQL_BIT	CF_SQL_INTEGER	CF_SQL_SMALLINT
CF_SQL_CHAR	CF_SQL_LONGVAR- CHAR	CF_SQL_TIME
CF_SQL_DATE	CF_SQL_MONEY	CF_SQL_TIMESTAMP
CF_SQL_DECIMAL	CF_SQL_MONEY4	CF_SQL_TINYINT
CF_SQL_DOUBLE	CF_SQL_NUMERIC	CF_SQL_VARCHAR
CF_SQL_FLOAT	CF_SQL_REAL	

MAXLENGTH

Optional. Maximum length of the parameter. The default value is the length of the string specified in the VALUE attribute.

SCALE

Optional. Number of decimal places of the parameter. The default value is zero. Applicable for CF_SQL_NUMERIC and CF_SQL_DECIMAL.

NULL

Optional. Specify Yes or No. Indicates whether the parameter is passed as a NULL. If you specify Yes, the tag ignores the VALUE attribute. The default value is No.

CFREGISTRY

The CFREGISTRY tag reads, writes, and deletes keys and values in the system registry. CFREGISTRY is supported on all platforms, including Solaris and HP-UX.

> **NOTE**   The ColdFusion Server Basic security settings may prevent CFRegistry from executing. These settings are managed using the ColdFusion Administrator Basic Security page. In order for CFRegistry to execute, it needs to be enabled on the Basic Security page. Please refer to Administering ColdFusion Server for more information about securing ColdFusion tags.

CFREGISTRY Topics

- CFREGISTRY ACTION="GetAll"
- CFREGISTRY ACTION="Get"
- CFREGISTRY ACTION="Set"
- CFREGISTRY ACTION="Delete"

CFREGISTRY ACTION Attributes

Depending on the value you assign to the ACTION attribute of CFREGISTRY, there are several additional attributes you set. This table shows which attributes you can use with each CFREGISTRY ACTION.

Attributes Used with CFREGISTRY ACTIONs

ACTION	Attributes
GetAll	BRANCH, TYPE, NAME, SORT
Get	BRANCH, ENTRY, TYPE, VARIABLE
Set	BRANCH, ENTRY, TYPE, VALUE
Delete	BRANCH, ENTRY

Sections that follow describe these values and attributes in greater detail.

CFREGISTRY ACTION="GetAll"

Use CFREGISTRY with the GetAll action to return all registry keys and values defined in a branch. You can access these values as you would any record set.

Syntax

```
<CFREGISTRY ACTION="GetAll"
    BRANCH="branch"
    TYPE="data type"
    NAME="query name"
    SORT="criteria">
```

BRANCH

Required. The name of the registry branch containing the keys or values you want to access.

TYPE

Optional. The type of data you want to access:

String Return string values (default).

Dword Return DWord values.

Key Return keys.

Any Return keys and values.

NAME

Required. The name of the record set to contain returned keys and values.

SORT

Optional. Sorts query column data (case-insensitive). Sorts on Entry, Type, and Value columns as text. Specify any combination of columns from query output in a comma separated list. ASC (ascending) or DESC (descending) can be specified as qualifiers for column names. ASC is the default. For example:

```
Sort="value DESC, entry ASC"
```

CFREGISTRY ACTION="Get"

Use CFREGISTRY with the Get action to access a registry value and store it in a ColdFusion variable.

Syntax

```
<CFREGISTRY ACTION="Get"
    BRANCH="branch"
    ENTRY="key or value"
    TYPE="data type"
    VARIABLE="variable">
```

BRANCH

Required. The name of the registry branch containing the value you want to access.

ENTRY

Required. The registry value to be accessed.

TYPE

Optional. The type of data you want to access:

String Return a string value (default).

Dword Return a DWord value.

Key Return a key's default value.

VARIABLE

Required. Variable into which CFREGISTRY places the value.

CFREGISTRY ACTION="Set"

Use CFREGISTRY with the Set action to add a registry key, add a new value, or update value data.

Syntax

```
<CFREGISTRY ACTION="Set"
    BRANCH="branch"
    ENTRY="key or value"
    TYPE="value type"
    VALUE="data">
```

BRANCH

Required. The name of the registry branch containing the key or value to be set.

ENTRY

Required. The key or value to be set.

TYPE

Optional. The type of data you want to set:

String Set a string value (default).

Dword Set a DWord value.

Key Create a key.

VALUE

Optional. The value data to be set. If you omit this attribute, CFREGISTRY creates default value data, as follows:

String Default value is an empty string: " "

Dword Default value is 0 (zero).

CFREGISTRY ACTION="Delete"

Use CFREGISTRY with the Delete action to delete a registry key or value.

Syntax

```
<CFREGISTRY ACTION="Delete"
    BRANCH="branch"
    ENTRY="keyorvalue">
```

BRANCH

Required. Specifies one of the following:

For key deletion The name of the registry key to be deleted. To delete a key, do not specify ENTRY.

For value deletion The name of the registry branch containing the value to be deleted. To delete a value, you must specify ENTRY.

ENTRY

Required for value deletion. The value to be deleted.

CFREPORT

CFREPORT runs a predefined Crystal Reports report.

Syntax

```
<CFREPORT REPORT="report_path"
    ORDERBY="result_order"
    USERNAME="username"
    PASSWORD="password"
    FORMULA="formula">

</CFREPORT>
```

REPORT

Required. Specifies the path of the report. Store your Crystal Reports files in the same directories that you store your ColdFusion page files.

ORDERBY

Optional. Orders results according to your specifications.

USERNAME

Optional. The username required for entry into the database from which the report is created. Overrides the default settings for the data source in the ColdFusion Administrator.

PASSWORD

Optional. The password that corresponds to a username required for database access. Overrides the default settings for the data source in the ColdFusion Administrator.

FORMULA

Optional. Specifies one or more named formulas. Terminate each formula specification with a semicolon. Use the following format:

```
FORMULA="formulaname1='formula1';formulaname2
='formula2';"
```

If you need to use a semi-colon as part of a formula, you must escape it by typing the semicolon twice (;;), for example:

```
FORMULA="Name1='Val_1a';;Val_1b';Name2='Val2';"
```

CFRETHROW

Rethrows the currently active exception. <CFRETHROW> preserves the exception's CFCATCH.TYPE and CFCATCH.TAGCONTEXT information.

See also CFTRY CFCATCH.

Syntax

```
<CFRETHROW>
```

CFSCHEDULE

CFSCHEDULE provides a programmatic interface to the ColdFusion scheduling engine. You can run a specified page at scheduled intervals with the option to write out static HTML pages. This allows you to offer users access to pages that publish data, such as reports, without forcing users to wait while a database transaction is performed in order to populate the data on the page.

ColdFusion scheduled events are registered using the ColdFusion Administrator. In addition, execution of CFSCHEDULE can be disabled in the Administrator. Information supplied by the user includes the scheduled ColdFusion page to execute, the time and frequency for executing the page, and if the output from the task should be published. If the output is to be published then a path and file is specified.

The event submission and its success or failure status is written to the \cfusion\log\schedule.log file.

Syntax

```
<CFSCHEDULE ACTION="Update"
    TASK="taskname"
    OPERATION="HTTPRequest"
    FILE="filename"
    PATH="path_to_file"
    STARTDATE="date"
    STARTTIME="time"
    URL="URL"
```

```
      PUBLISH="Yes/No"
      ENDDATE="date"
      ENDTIME="time"
      INTERVAL="seconds"
      REQUESTTIMEOUT="seconds"
      USERNAME="username"
      PASSWORD="password"
      RESOLVEURL="Yes/No"
      PROXYSERVER="hostname"
      PORT="port_number"
      PROXYPORT="port_number"
>
```

```
<CFSCHEDULE ACTION="Delete" TASK="TaskName">
<CFSCHEDULE ACTION="Run" TASK="TaskName">
```

ACTION

Required. Valid entries are:

Delete   Deletes task specified by TASK.

Update   Creates a new task if one does not exist.

Run   Executes task specified by TASK.

TASK

Required. The name of the task to delete, update, or run.

OPERATION

Required when creating tasks with ACTION="Update". Specify the type of operation the scheduler should perform when executing this task. For now only OPERATION="HTTPRequest" is supported for static page generation.

FILE

Required with PUBLISH="Yes." A valid filename for the published file.

PATH

Required with PUBLISH="Yes." The path location for the published file.

STARTDATE

Required when ACTION="Update." The date when scheduling of the task should start.

STARTTIME

Required when creating tasks with ACTION="Update." Enter a value in seconds. The time when scheduling of the task should start.

URL

Required when ACTION="Update." The URL to be executed.

PUBLISH

Optional. Yes or No. Specifies whether the result should be saved to a file.

ENDDATE

Optional. The date when the scheduled task should end.

ENDTIME

Optional. The time when the scheduled task should end. Enter a value in seconds.

INTERVAL

Required when creating tasks with ACTION="Update." Interval at which task should be scheduled. Can be set in seconds or as Once, Daily, Weekly, Monthly, and Execute. The default interval is one hour and the minimum interval is one minute.

REQUESTTIMEOUT

Optional. Customizes the REQUESTTIMEOUT for the task operation. Can be used to extend the default timeout for operations that require more time to execute.

USERNAME

Optional. Username if URL is protected.

PASSWORD

Optional. Password if URL is protected.

PROXYSERVER

Optional. Host name or IP address of a proxy server.

RESOLVEURL

Optional. Yes or No. Specifies whether to resolve links in the result page to absolute references.

PORT

Optional. The port number on the server from which the task is being scheduled. Default is 80. When used with RESOLVEURL, the URLs of retrieved documents that specify a port number are automatically resolved to preserve links in the retrieved document.

PROXYPORT

Optional. The port number on the proxy server from which the task is being requested. Default is 80. When used with RESOLVEURL, the URLs of retrieved documents that specify a port number are automatically resolved to preserve links in the retrieved document.

NOTE   You cannot use CFSCHEDULE and apply the Secure Sockets Layer (SSL) to your application.

CFSCRIPT

The CFSCRIPT tag encloses a code segment containing CFScript.

Syntax

```
<CFSCRIPT>
 CFScript code goes here
</CFSCRIPT>
```

CFSEARCH

Use the CFSEARCH tag to execute searches against data indexed in Verity collections. Collections can be created by calling the CFCOLLECTION tag, by using the ColdFusion Administrator, or through native Verity indexing tools. Collections are populated with data either with the CFINDEX tag, or externally, using native Verity indexing tools. Collections must be created and populated before any searches can be executed.

Syntax

```
<CFSEARCH NAME="search_name"
     COLLECTION="collection_name"
     TYPE="criteria"
     CRITERIA="search_expression"
     MAXROWS="number"
     STARTROW="row_number"
     EXTERNAL="Yes/No"
     LANGUAGE="language">
```

NAME

Required. A name for the search query.

COLLECTION

Required. Specifies the logical collection name that is the target of the search operation or an external collection with fully qualified path. Collection names are defined either through the CFCOLLECTION tag or in the ColdFusion Administrator, Verity page.

Multiple ColdFusion collections can be specified in a comma-separated list:

```
COLLECTION="CFUSER, CFLANG"
```

If you are searching an external collection (EXTERNAL="Yes") specify the collection name, including fully qualified path:

```
COLLECTION="e:\collections\personnel"
```

If multiple collections are specified in COLLECTION and EXTERNAL is Yes, the specified collections must all be externally generated. You cannot combine internal and external collections in the same search operation.

TYPE

Optional. Specifies the criteria type for the search. Valid entries are:

SIMPLE   By default the STEM and MANY operators are used.

EXPLICIT   All operators must be invoked explicitly.

CRITERIA

Optional. Specifies the criteria for the search following the syntactic rules specified by TYPE.

MAXROWS

Optional. Specifies the maximum number of entries for index queries. If omitted, all rows are returned.

STARTROW

Optional. Specifies the first row number to be retrieved. Default is 1.

EXTERNAL

Optional. Yes or No. Yes indicates that the collection you are searching was created outside of ColdFusion using native Verity indexing tools. The default is No.

LANGUAGE

Optional. To use the LANGUAGE attribute you must have the ColdFusion International Search Pack installed. Valid entries are:

- English (default)
- German
- Finnish
- French
- Danish
- Dutch
- Italian
- Norwegian
- Portuguese
- Spanish
- Swedish

CFSELECT

Used inside CFFORM, CFSELECT allows you to construct a drop-down list box form control. You can populate the drop-down list box from a query, or using the OPTION tag. Use OPTION elements to populate lists. Syntax for the OPTION tag is the same as for its HTML counterpart.

Syntax

```
<CFSELECT NAME="name"
     REQUIRED="Yes/No"
     MESSAGE="text"
     ONERROR="text"
```

```
SIZE="integer"
MULTIPLE="Yes/No"
QUERY="queryname"
SELECTED="column_value"
VALUE="text"
DISPLAY="text"
PASSTHROUGH="HTML_attributes">
```

</CFSELECT>

NAME

Required. A name for the form you are creating.

SIZE

Optional. Size of the drop-down list box in number of entries.

REQUIRED

Optional. Yes or No. If Yes, a list element must be selected when the form is submitted. Default is No.

MESSAGE

Optional. Message that appears if REQUIRED="Yes" and no selection is made.

ONERROR

Optional. The name of a valid JavaScript function you want to execute in the event of a failed validation.

MULTIPLE

Optional. Yes or No. Yes permits selection of multiple elements in the drop-down list box. The default is No.

QUERY

Optional. Name of the query to be used to populate the drop-down list box.

SELECTED

Optional. Enter a value matching at least one entry in VALUE to preselect the entry in the drop-down list box.

VALUE

Optional. The query column value for the list element. Used with the QUERY attribute.

DISPLAY

Optional. The query column displayed. Defaults to the value of VALUE. Used with the QUERY attribute.

PASSTHROUGH

Optional. HTML attributes that are not explicitly supported by CFSELECT. If you specify an attribute and its value, the attribute and its value are passed to the HTML code that is generated for the CFSELECT tag.

CFSERVLET

Executes a Java servlet on a JRun engine. This tag is used in conjunction with the CFSERVLETPARAM tag, which passes data to the servlet.

Syntax

```
<CFSERVLET
    CODE="class name of servlet"
    JRUNPROXY="proxy server"
    TIMEOUT="timeout in seconds"
    WRITEOUTPUT="Yes/No"
    DEBUG="Yes/No">
    <CFSERVLETPARAM
    NAME="parameter name"
    VALUE="value"
    >
    ...
</CFSERVLET>
```

CODE

Required. The class name of the Java servlet to execute.

JRUNPROXY

Optional. Specifies a remote machine where the JRun engine is executing. By default, the JRun engine is assumed to be on the host running ColdFusion. To indicate the name of a remote host, specify the IP address of the remote host followed by a colon and the port number at which JRun is listening. By default, JRun listens at port 8081.

TIMEOUT

Optional. Specifies how many seconds JRun should wait for the servlet to complete before timing out.

WRITEOUTPUT

Optional. Boolean specifying if the text output of the tag should appear as inline text on the generated page or if it should be returned inside a ColdFusion variable for further processing. The default value, Yes, means output is returned as text to appear inline on the generated page. Setting it to No means no visible text is returned but, instead, the text is returned as the value of the CFSERVLET.OUTPUT variable.

DEBUG

Optional. Boolean specifying whether additional information about the JRun connection status and activity is to be written to the JRun error log. The error log is in JRunHome/jsm-default/logs/stderr.log. Reading this log is helpful for debugging server-side problems. The default is No.

CFSERVLETPARAM

The CFSERVLETPARAM is a child of CFSERVLET. It is used to pass data to the servlet. Each CFSERVLETPARAM tag within the CFSERVLET block passes a separate piece of data to the servlet.

See also CFSERVLET.

Syntax

```
<CFSERVLET
    ...>
    <CFSERVLETPARAM
    NAME="servlet parameter name"
    VALUE="servlet parameter value"
    >
    ...
    <CFSERVLETPARAM
    NAME="servlet attribute name"
    VARIABLE="ColdFusion variable name"
    TYPE="INT" or "DOUBLE" or "BOOL" or
"DATE" or "STRING"
    >
    ...
</CFSERVLET>
```

NAME

Required. If used with the VALUE attribute, it is the name of the servlet parameter. If used with the VARIABLE attribute, it is the name of the servlet attribute.

VALUE

Optional. The value of a name-value pair to be passed to the servlet as a parameter.

VARIABLE

Optional. The name of a ColdFusion variable. The value of which will appear in the servlet as an attribute. See the TYPE attribute for a way to pass data type information to the Java servlet.

TYPE

Optional. The data type of the ColdFusion variable being passed. By default, ColdFusion usually passes variables as strings; however, to ensure that the data is correctly type on the Java side, you can specify any of the following types: INT, DOUBLE, BOOL, DATE, or STRING.

CFSET

Use the CFSET tag to define a ColdFusion variable. If the variable already exists, CFSET resets it to the specified value.

Syntax

```
<CFSET variable_name=expression>
```

Arrays

The following example assigns a new array to the variable "months."

```
<CFSET months=ArrayNew(1)>
```

This example creates a variable "Array_Length" that resolves to the length of the array "Scores."

```
<CFSET Array_Length=ArrayLen(Scores)>
```

This example assigns to index position two in the array "months" the value "February."

```
<CFSET months[2]="February">
```

Dynamic Variable Names

In this example, the variable name is itself a variable.

```
<CFSET myvariable="current_value">
<CFSET "#myvariable#"=5>
```

COM Objects

In this example, a COM object is created. A CFSET defines a value for each method or property in the COM object interface. The last CFSET creates a variable to store the return value from the COM object's "SendMail" method:

```
<CFOBJECT ACTION="Create"
    NAME="Mailer"
    CLASS="SMTPsvg.Mailer">

<CFSET MAILER.FromName=form.fromname>
<CFSET MAILER.RemoteHost=RemoteHost>
<CFSET MAILER.FromAddress=form.fromemail>
<CFSET MAILER.AddRecipient("form.fromname",
"form.fromemail")>
<CFSET MAILER.Subject="Testing CFOBJECT">
<CFSET MAILER.BodyText="form.msgbody">
<CFSET Mailer.SMTPLog="logfile">

<CFSET success=MAILER.SendMail()>

<CFOUTPUT> #success# </CFOUTPUT>
```

CFSETTING

CFSETTING is used to control various aspects of page processing, such as controlling the output of HTML code in your pages. One benefit of this option is managing whitespace that can occur in output pages that are served by ColdFusion.

Syntax

```
<CFSETTING ENABLECFOUTPUTONLY="Yes/No"
    SHOWDEBUGOUTPUT="Yes/No"
    CATCHEXCEPTIONBYPATTERN="Yes/No">
```

ENABLECFOUTPUTONLY

Required. Yes or No. When set to Yes, CFSETTING blocks output of all HTML that resides outside CFOUT-PUT tags.

SHOWDEBUGOUTPUT

Optional. Yes or No. When set to No, SHOWDEBUGOUT-PUT suppresses debugging information that would otherwise display at the end of the generated page. Default is Yes.

CATCHEXCEPTIONSBYPATTERN

Optional. Yes or No. When set to Yes, it overrides the structured exception handling introduced in 4.5. Default is No.

> **NOTE** Structured exception handling introduces a subtle upwards incompatibility. In 4.0.x, an exception was handled by the first **CFCATCH** block that could handle that type of exception. In 4.5, the structured exception manager searches for the best-fit **CFCATCH** handler.

CFSILENT

CFSILENT suppresses all output that is produced by the CFML within the tag's scope.

See also CFSETTING.

Syntax

```
<CFSILENT>
```

CFSLIDER

Used inside CFFORM, CFSLIDER allows you to place a slider control in a ColdFusion form. A slider control is like a sliding volume control. The slider groove is the area over which the slider moves.

> **NOTE** CFSLIDER incorporates a Java applet, so a browser must be Java-enabled for **CFSLIDER** to work properly.

Syntax

```
<CFSLIDER NAME="name"
    LABEL="text"
    REFRESHLABEL="Yes/No"
    IMG="filename"
    IMGSTYLE="style"
    RANGE="min_value, max_value"
    SCALE="uinteger"
    VALUE="integer"
    ONVALIDATE="script_name"
    MESSAGE="text"
    ONERROR="text"
    HEIGHT="integer"
    WIDTH="integer"
    VSPACE="integer"
    HSPACE="integer"
    ALIGN="alignment"
    GROOVECOLOR="color"
    BGCOLOR="color"
    TEXTCOLOR="color"
    FONT="font_name"
    FONTSIZE="integer"
    ITALIC="Yes/No"
    BOLD="Yes/No"
    NOTSUPPORTED="text">
```

NAME

Required. A name for the CFSLIDER control.

LABEL

Optional. A label that appears with the slider control, for example:

```
LABEL="Volume %value%"
```

You can use %value% to reference the slider value. If % is omitted, the slider value appears immediately following the label.

REFRESHLABEL

Optional. Yes or No. If Yes, the label is not refreshed when the slider is moved. Default is Yes.

IMG

Optional. Filename of the image to be used in the slider groove.

IMGSTYLE

Optional. Style of the image to appear in the slider groove. Valid entries are:

- Centered
- Tiled
- Scaled

Default is Scaled.

RANGE

Optional. Determines the values of the left and right slider range. The slider value appears as the slider is moved.

Separate values by a comma, for example:

RANGE="1,100"

Default is "0,100." Valid only for numeric data.

SCALE

Optional. An unsigned integer. SCALE defines the slider scale within the value of RANGE. For example, if RANGE=0,1000 and SCALE=100, the incremental values for the slider would be 0, 100, 200, 300, and so on.

VALUE

Optional. Determines the default slider setting. Must be within the values specified in RANGE. Defaults to the minimum value specified in RANGE.

ONVALIDATE

Optional. The name of a valid JavaScript function used to validate user input, in this case, a change to the default slider value.

MESSAGE

Optional. Message text to appear if validation fails.

ONERROR

Optional. The name of a valid JavaScript function you want to execute in the event of a failed validation.

HEIGHT

Optional. Height value of the slider control, in pixels.

WIDTH

Optional. Width value of the slider control, in pixels.

VSPACE

Optional. Vertical margin spacing above and below slider control, in pixels.

HSPACE

Optional. Horizontal margin spacing to the left and right of slider control, in pixels.

ALIGN

Optional. Alignment value. Valid entries are:
- Top
- Left
- Bottom
- Baseline
- TextTop
- AbsBottom
- Middle
- AbsMiddle
- Right

GROOVECOLOR

Optional. Color value of the slider groove. The slider groove is the area in which the slider box moves. Valid entries are:
- black
- magenta
- cyan
- orange
- darkgray
- pink
- gray
- white
- lightgray
- yellow

A hex value can be entered in the form:

GROOVECOLOR="##xxxxxx"

Where x is 0–9 or A–F. Use either two pound signs or no pound signs.

BGCOLOR

Optional. Background color of slider label. See GROOVE-COLOR for color options.

TEXTCOLOR

Optional. Slider label text color. See GROOVECOLOR for color options.

FONT

Optional. Font name for label text.

FONTSIZE

Optional. Font size for label text measured in points.

ITALIC

Optional. Enter Yes for italicized label text, No for normal text. Default is No.

BOLD

Optional. Enter Yes for bold label text, No for medium text. Default is No.

NOTSUPPORTED

Optional. The text you want to display if the page containing a Java applet-based CFFORM control is opened by a browser that does not support Java or has Java support disabled. For example:

NOTSUPPORTED="<B> Browser must support Java to
view ColdFusion Java Applets</B>"

By default, if no message is specified, the following message appears:

```
<B>Browser must support Java to <BR>
view ColdFusion Java Applets!</B>
```

CFSTOREDPROC

The CFSTOREDPROC tag is the main tag used for executing stored procedures via an ODBC or native connection to a server database. It specifies database connection information and identifies the stored procedure.

Syntax

```
<CFSTOREDPROC PROCEDURE="procedure name"
     DATASOURCE="ds_name"
     USERNAME="username"
     PASSWORD="password"
     DBSERVER="dbms"
     DBNAME="database name"
     BLOCKFACTOR="blocksize"
     PROVIDER="COMProvider"
     PROVIDERDSN="datasource"
     DEBUG="Yes/No"
     RETURNCODE="Yes/No">
```

PROCEDURE

Required. Specifies the name of the stored procedure on the database server.

DATASOURCE

Required. The name of an ODBC or native data source that points to the database containing the stored procedure.

USERNAME

Optional. If specified, USERNAME overrides the username value specified in the data source setup.

PASSWORD

Optional. If specified, PASSWORD overrides the password value specified in the data source setup.

DBSERVER

Optional. For native database drivers, specifies the name of the database server machine. If specified, DBSERVER overrides the server specified in the data source.

DBNAME

Optional. The database name (Sybase System 11 driver only). If specified, DBNAME overrides the default database specified in the data source.

BLOCKFACTOR

Optional. Specifies the maximum number of rows to fetch at a time from the server. The range is 1 (default) to 100. The ODBC driver may dynamically reduce the block factor at runtime.

PROVIDER

Optional. COM provider (OLE-DB only).

PROVIDERDSN

Optional. Data source name for the COM provider (OLE-DB only).

DEBUG

Optional. Yes or No. Specifies whether debug info will be listed on each statement. Default is No.

RETURNCODE

Optional. Yes or No. Specifies whether the tag populates CFSTOREDPROC.STATUSCODE with the status code returned by the stored procedure. Default is No.

CFSWITCH CFCASE CFDEFAULTCASE

Used with CFCASE and CFDEFAULTCASE, the CFSWITCH tag evaluates a passed expression and passes control to the CFCASE tag that matches the expression result. You can optionally code a CFDEFAULTCASE tag, which receives control if there is no matching CFCASE tag value.

Syntax

```
<CFSWITCH EXPRESSION="expression">
     <CFCASE VALUE="value"
DELIMITERS="delimiters">
        HTML and CFML tags
     </CFCASE>
     additional <CFCASE></CFCASE> tags
     <CFDEFAULTCASE>
        HTML and CFML tags
     </CFDEFAULTCASE>
</CFSWITCH>
```

EXPRESSION

Required. Any ColdFusion expression that yields a scalar value. ColdFusion converts integers, real numbers, Booleans, and dates to numeric values. For example, TRUE, 1, and 1.0 are all equal.

VALUE

Required. One or more constant values that CFSWITCH compares to the specified expression (case-insensitive comparison). If a value matches the expression,

CFSWITCH executes the code between the CFCASE start and end tags.

Separate multiple values with a comma or an alternative delimiter, as specified in the DELIMITERS parameter. Duplicate value attributes are not allowed and will cause a runtime error.

DELIMITERS

Optional. Specifies the character that separates multiple entries in a list of values. The default delimiter is the comma (,).

CFTABLE

Builds a table in your ColdFusion page. Use the CFCOL tag to define column and row characteristics for a table. CFTABLE renders data either as preformatted text, or, with the HTMLTABLE attribute, as an HTML table. Use CFTABLE to create tables if you don't want to write your own HTML TABLE tag code, or if your data can be well presented as preformatted text.

Syntax

```
<CFTABLE QUERY="query_name"
    MAXROWS="maxrows_table"
    COLSPACING="number_of_spaces"
    HEADERLINES="number_of_lines"
    HTMLTABLE
    BORDER
    COLHEADERS
    STARTROW="row_number">

</CFTABLE>
```

QUERY

Required. The name of the CFQUERY from which you want to draw data.

MAXROWS

Optional. Specifies the maximum number of rows you want to display in the table.

COLSPACING

Optional. Indicates the number of spaces to insert between columns (default is 2).

HEADERLINES

Optional. Indicates the number of lines to use for the table header (the default is 2, which leaves one line between the headers and the first row of the table).

HTMLTABLE

Optional. Renders the table as an HTML 3.0 table.

BORDER

Optional. Adds a border to the table. Use only when you specify the HTMLTABLE attribute for the table.

COLHEADERS

Optional. Displays headers for each column, as specified in the CFCOL tag.

STARTROW

Optional. Specifies the query row from which to start processing.

CFTEXTINPUT

The CFTEXTINPUT form custom control allows you to place a single-line text entry box in a CFFORM. In addition to input validation, the tag gives you control over all font characteristics.

> **NOTE** CFTEXTINPUT incorporates a Java applet, so a browser must be Java-enabled for CFTEXTINPUT to work properly.

Syntax

```
<CFTEXTINPUT NAME="name"
    VALUE="text"
    REQUIRED="Yes/No"
    RANGE="min_value, max_value"
    VALIDATE="data_type"
    ONVALIDATE="script_name"
    MESSAGE="text"
    ONERROR="text"
    SIZE="integer"
    FONT="font_name"
    FONTSIZE="integer"
    ITALIC="Yes/No"
    BOLD="Yes/No"
    HEIGHT="integer"
    WIDTH="integer"
    VSPACE="integer"
    HSPACE="integer"
    ALIGN="alignment"
    BGCOLOR="color"
    TEXTCOLOR="color"
    MAXLENGTH="integer"
    NOTSUPPORTED="text">
```

NAME

Required. A name for the CFTEXTINPUT control.

VALUE

Optional. Initial value that appears in the text control.

REQUIRED
Optional. Yes or No. If Yes, the user must enter or change text. Default is No.

RANGE
Optional. Enter a minimum value, maximum value range separated by a comma. Valid only for numeric data.

VALIDATE
Optional. Valid entries are:

Date   Verifies US date entry in the form mm/dd/yy.

Eurodate   Verifies valid European date entry in the form dd/mm/yyyy.

Time   Verifies a time entry in the form hh:mm:ss.

Float   Verifies a floating point entry.

Integer   Verifies an integer entry.

Telephone   Verifies a telephone entry. Telephone data must be entered as ###-###-####. The hyphen separator (-) can be replaced with a blank. The area code and exchange must begin with a digit between 1 and 9.

zipcode **(U.S. formats only)**   Number can be a 5-digit or 9-digit zip in the form #####-####. The hyphen separator (-) can be replaced with a blank.

Creditcard   Blanks and dashes are stripped and the number is verified using the mod10 algorithm.

social_security_number   Number must be entered as ###-##-####. The hyphen separator (-) can be replaced with a blank.

ONVALIDATE
Optional. The name of a valid JavaScript function used to validate user input. The form object, input object, and input object value are passed to the specified routine, which should return TRUE if validation succeeds and FALSE otherwise. When used, the VALIDATE attribute is ignored.

MESSAGE
Optional. Message text to appear if validation fails.

ONERROR
Optional. The name of a valid JavaScript function you want to execute in the event of a failed validation.

SIZE
Optional. Number of characters displayed before horizontal scroll bar appears.

FONT
Optional. Font name for text.

FONTSIZE
Optional. Font size for text.

ITALIC
Optional. Enter Yes for italicized text, No for normal text. Default is No.

BOLD
Optional. Enter Yes for boldface text, No for medium text. Default is No.

HEIGHT
Optional. Height value of the control, in pixels.

WIDTH
Optional. Width value of the control, in pixels.

VSPACE
Optional. Vertical spacing of the control, in pixels.

HSPACE
Optional. Horizontal spacing of the control, in pixels.

ALIGN
Optional. Alignment value. Valid entries are:

- Top
- Left
- Bottom
- Baseline
- TextTop
- AbsBottom
- Middle
- AbsMiddle
- Right

BGCOLOR
Optional. Background color of the control. Valid entries are:

- black
- magenta
- cyan
- orange
- darkgray
- pink
- gray
- white
- lightgray
- yellow

A hex value can also be entered in the form:

BGCOLOR="##xxxxxx"

Where x is 0–9 or A–F. Use either two pound signs or no pound signs.

TEXTCOLOR

Optional. Text color for the control. See BGCOLOR for color options.

MAXLENGTH

Optional. The maximum length of text entered.

NOTSUPPORTED

Optional. The text you want to display if the page containing a Java applet-based CFFORM control is opened by a browser that does not support Java or has Java support disabled. For example:

```
NOTSUPPORTED="<B> Browser must support Java
to
view ColdFusion Java Applets</B>"
```

By default, if no message is specified, the following message appears:

```
<B>Browser must support Java to <BR>
view ColdFusion Java Applets!</B>
```

CFTHROW

The CFTHROW tag raises a developer-specified exception that can be caught with CFCATCH tag having any of the following type specifications:

- CFCATCH TYPE="custom_type"
- CFCATCH TYPE="APPLICATION"
- CFCATCH TYPE="ANY"

Syntax

```
<CFTHROW
    TYPE= "exception_type "
    MESSAGE="message"
    DETAIL= "detail_description "
    ERRORCODE= "error_code "
    EXTENDEDINFO= "additional_information ">
```

TYPE

Optional. A custom type or the predefined type APPLICATION. None of the other predefined types should be specified because these types are not generated by ColdFusion applications. If you specify the exception type APPLICATION, you need not specify a type for CFCATCH, because the APPLICATION type is the default CFCATCH type.

MESSAGE

Optional. A message that describes the exceptional event.

DETAIL

Optional. A detailed description of the event. The ColdFusion server appends the position of the error to this description; the server uses this parameter if an error is not caught by your code.

ERRORCODE

Optional. A custom error code that you supply.

EXTENDEDINFO

Optional. A custom error code that you supply.

CFTRANSACTION

Use CFTRANSACTION to group multiple queries into a single unit. CFTRANSACTION also provides commit and rollback processing.

Syntax

```
<CFTRANSACTION
    ACTION="BEGIN" or "COMMIT" or "ROLLBACK"
    ISOLATION="Read_Uncommitted" or
                "Read_Committed" or
                "Repeatable_Read" >
</CFTRANSACTION>
```

ACTION

Optional. The actions are as follows:

- BEGIN, which indicates the start of the block of code to be executed. It is the default value.
- COMMIT, which commits a pending transaction.
- ROLLBACK, which rolls back a pending transaction.

ISOLATION

Optional. ODBC lock type. Valid entries are:

- Read_Uncommitted
- Read_Committed
- Repeatable_Read
- Serializable

CFTREE

The CFTREE form custom control allows you to place a tree control in a CFFORM. User selections can be validated. Individual tree items are created with CFTREE-ITEM tags inside the CFTREE tag block.

> **NOTE** CFTREE incorporates a Java applet, so a browser must be Java-enabled for CFTREE to work properly.

Syntax
```
<CFTREE NAME="name"
    REQUIRED="Yes/No"
    DELIMITER="delimiter"
    COMPLETEPATH="Yes/No"
    APPENDKEY="Yes/No"
    HIGHLIGHTHREF="Yes/No"
    ONVALIDATE="script_name"
    MESSAGE="text"
    ONERROR="text"
    FONT="font"
    FONTSIZE="size"
    ITALIC="Yes/No"
    BOLD="Yes/No"
    HEIGHT="integer"
    WIDTH="integer"
    VSPACE="integer"
    HSPACE="integer"
    ALIGN="alignment"
    BORDER="Yes/No"
    HSCROLL="Yes/No"
    VSCROLL="Yes/No"
    NOTSUPPORTED="text">
```

`</CFTREE>`

NAME
Required. A name for the CFTREE control.

REQUIRED
Optional. Yes or No. User must select an item in the tree control. Default is No.

DELIMITER
Optional. The character used to separate elements in the form variable PATH. The default is "\".

COMPLETEPATH
Optional. Yes passes the root level of the `treename.path` form variable when the CFTREE is submitted. If omitted or No, the root level of this form variable is not included.

APPENDKEY
Optional. Yes or No. When used with HREF, Yes passes the CFTREEITEMKEY variable along with the value of the selected tree item in the URL to the application page specified in the CFFORM ACTION attribute. The default is Yes.

HIGHLIGHTHREF
Optional. Yes highlights links associated with a CFTREEITEM with a URL attribute value. No disables highlight. Default is Yes.

ONVALIDATE
Optional. The name of a valid JavaScript function used to validate user input. The form object, input object, and input object value are passed to the specified routine, which should return true if validation succeeds and false otherwise.

MESSAGE
Optional. Message text to appear if validation fails.

ONERROR
Optional. The name of a valid JavaScript function you want to execute in the event of a failed validation.

FONT
Optional. Font name to use for all data in the tree control.

FONTSIZE
Optional. Font size for text in the tree control, measured in points.

ITALIC
Optional. Yes or No. Yes presents all tree control text in italic. Default is No.

BOLD
Optional. Yes or No. Yes presents all tree control text in boldface. Default is No.

HEIGHT
Optional. Height value of the tree control, in pixels.

WIDTH
Optional. Width value of the tree control, in pixels.

VSPACE
Optional. Vertical margin spacing above and below the tree control in pixels.

HSPACE
Optional. Horizontal spacing to the left and right of the tree control, in pixels.

ALIGN
Optional. Alignment value. Valid entries are:

- Top
- Left
- Bottom
- Baseline
- TextTop
- AbsBottom
- Middle
- AbsMiddle
- Right

BORDER

Optional. Places a border around the tree. Default is Yes.

HSCROLL

Optional. Permits horizontal scrolling. Default is Yes.

VSCROLL

Optional. Permits vertical scrolling. Default is Yes.

NOTSUPPORTED

Optional. The text you want to display if the page containing a Java applet-based CFFORM control is opened by a browser that does not support Java or has Java support disabled. For example:

```
NOTSUPPORTED="<B> Browser must support Java
to
view ColdFusion Java Applets</B>"
```

By default, if no message is specified, the following message appears:

```
<B>Browser must support Java to <BR>
view ColdFusion Java Applets!</B>
```

CFTRY CFCATCH

Used with one or more CFCATCH tags, the CFTRY tag allows developers to catch and process exceptions in ColdFusion pages. Exceptions include any event that disrupts the normal flow of instructions in a ColdFusion page such as failed database operations, missing include files, and developer-specified events.

Syntax

```
<CFTRY>
... Add code here
<CFCATCH TYPE="exceptiontype">
... Add exception processing code here
</CFCATCH>
... Additional CFCATCH blocks go here
</CFTRY>
```

TYPE

Optional. Specifies the type of exception to be handled by the CFCATCH block:

- APPLICATION (default)
- Database
- Template
- Security
- Object
- MissingInclude
- Expression
- Lock

- Custom_type
- Any (default)

CFUPDATE

The CFUPDATE tag updates existing records in data sources.

Syntax

```
<CFUPDATE DATASOURCE="ds_name"
    DBTYPE="type"
    DBSERVER="dbms"
    DBNAME="database name"
    TABLENAME="table_name"
    TABLEOWNER="name"
    TABLEQUALIFIER="qualifier"
    USERNAME="username"
    PASSWORD="password"
    PROVIDER="COMProvider"
    PROVIDERDSN="datasource"
    FORMFIELDS="field_names">
```

DATASOURCE

Required. Name of the data source that contains your table.

DBTYPE

Optional. The database driver type:

ODBC (default)   ODBC driver.

Oracle73   Oracle 7.3 native database driver. Using this option, the ColdFusion Server computer must have Oracle 7.3.4.0.0 (or greater) client software installed.

Oracle80   Oracle 8.0 native database driver. Using this option, the ColdFusion Server computer must have Oracle 8.0 (or greater) client software installed.

Sybase11   Sybase System 11 native database driver. Using this option, the ColdFusion Server computer must have Sybase 11.1.1 (or greater) client software installed. Sybase patch ebf 7729 is recommended.

OLEDB   OLE DB provider. If specified, this database provider overrides the driver type specified in the ColdFusion Administrator.

DB2   DB2 5.2 native database driver.

Informix73   Informix73 native database driver.

DBSERVER

Optional. For native database drivers and the SQLOLEDB provider, specifies the name of the database server machine. If specified, DBSERVER overrides the server specified in the data source.

DBNAME

Optional. The database name (Sybase System 11 driver and SQLOLEDB provider only). If specified, DBNAME overrides the default database specified in the data source.

TABLENAME

Required. Name of the table you want to update. Note the following:

ORACLE drivers   This specification must be in uppercase.

Sybase driver   This specification is case-sensitive and must be in the same case as that used when the table was created

TABLEOWNER

Optional. For data sources that support table ownership (for example, SQL Server, Oracle, and Sybase SQL Anywhere), use this field to specify the owner of the table.

TABLEQUALIFIER

Optional. For data sources that support table qualifiers, use this field to specify the qualifier for the table. The purpose of table qualifiers varies across drivers. For SQL Server and Oracle, the qualifier refers to the name of the database that contains the table. For the Intersolv dBase driver, the qualifier refers to the directory where the DBF files are located.

USERNAME

Optional. If specified, USERNAME overrides the user-name value specified in the ODBC setup.

PASSWORD

Optional. If specified, PASSWORD overrides the pass-word value specified in the ODBC setup.

PROVIDER

Optional. COM provider (OLE-DB only).

PROVIDERDSN

Optional. Data source name for the COM provider (OLE-DB only).

FORMFIELDS

Optional. A comma-separated list of form fields to update. If this attribute is not specified, all fields in the form are included in the operation.

CFWDDX

The CFWDDX tag serializes and de-serializes CFML data structures to the XML-based WDDX format. You can also use it to generate JavaScript statements instantiating JavaScript objects equivalent to the contents of a WDDX packet or some CFML data structures.

Syntax

```
<CFWDDX ACTION="action"
    INPUT="inputdata"
    OUTPUT="resultvariablename"

TOPLEVELVARIABLE="toplevelvariablenameforjava
script"
    USETIMEZONEINFO="Yes/No">
```

ACTION

Specifies the action taken by the CFWDDX tag. Use one of the following:

CFML2WDDX   Serialize CFML to WDDX format

WDDX2CFML   Deserialize WDDX to CFML

CFML2JS   Serialize CFML to JavaScript format

WDDX2JS   Deserialize WDDX to JavaScript

INPUT

Required. The value to be processed.

OUTPUT

The name of the variable to hold the output of the operation. This attribute is required for ACTION=WDDX2CFML. For all other actions, if this attribute is not provided, the result of the WDDX processing is outputted in the HTML stream.

TOPLEVELVARIABLE

Required when ACTION=WDDX2JS or ACTION=CFML2JS. The name of the top-level JavaScript object created by the deserialization process. The object created by this process is an instance of the WddxRecordset object, explained in WddxRecordset Object .

This attribute applies only when the ACTION is WDDX2JS or CFML2JS.

USETIMEZONEINFO

Optional. Indicates whether to output time-zone information when serializing CFML to WDDX. If time-zone information is taken into account, the hour-minute off-set, as represented in the ISO8601 format, is calculated in the date-time output. If time-zone information is not taken into account, the local time is output. The default is Yes.

ColdFusion Function Reference

The following reference is extracted from the ColdFusion Language Reference, which ships with the ColdFusion Server distribution. The complete reference is available in the online documentation on the CD-ROM or in the Cold-Fusion Language Reference manual in the boxed set of ColdFusion Server.

ColdFusion Functions by Type

Array Functions

ArrayAppend	ArrayMax	ArraySum	ArrayAvg	ArrayMin
ArraySwap	ArrayClear	ArrayNew	ArrayToList	ArrayDeleteAt
ArrayPrepend	IsArray	ArrayInsertAt	ArrayResize	ListToArray
ArrayIsEmpty	ArraySet	ArrayLen	ArraySort	

Authentication Functions

AuthenticatedContext	IsAuthenticated
AuthenticatedUser	IsAuthorized

Date and Time Functions

CreateDate	DatePart	IsLeapYear	CreateDateTime	Day
IsNumericDate	CreateODBCDate	DayOfWeek	Minute	CreateODBCDateTime
DayOfWeekAsString	Month	CreateODBCTime	DayOfYear	MonthAsString
CreateTime	DaysInMonth	Now	CreateTimeSpan	DaysInYear
ParseDateTime	DateCompare	FirstDayOfMonth	Quarter	DateConvert
GetTimeZoneInfo	Second	DateDiff	Hour	Week
DateFormat	IsDate	XMLFormat		

Decisions Functions

IsArray	IsNumericDate	IsAuthenticated	IsProtected	IsAuthorized
IsSimpleValue	IsBinary	IsStruct	IsDate	LSIsCurrency
IsDebugMode	LSIsDate	IsDefined	LSIsNumeric	IsLeapYear
ParameterExists	IsNumeric			

Display and Formatting Functions

DateFormat	LSEuroCurrency-Format	DateFormat	DecimalFormat	LSNumberFormat
DecimalFormat	DollarFormat	LSTimeFormat	DollarFormat	FormatBaseN
NumberFormat	FormatBaseN	HTMLCodeFormat	ParagraphFormat	HTMLCodeFormat

Dynamic Evaluation Functions

DE	IIf
Evaluate	SetVariable

International Functions

DateConvert	LSIsNumeric	GetLocale	LSNumberFormat	GetTimeZoneInfo
LSParseCurrency	LSCurrencyFormat	LSParseDateTime	LSDateFormat	LSParseEuroCurrency
LSEuroCurrencyFormat	LSParseNumber	LSIsCurrency	LSTimeFormat	LSIsDate
SetLocale				

List Functions

ArrayToList	ListLast	ListAppend	ListLen	ListChangeDelims
ListPrepend	ListContains	ListQualify	ListContainsNoCase	ListRest
ListDeleteAt	ListSetAt	ListFind	ListSort	ListFindNoCase
ListToArray	ListFirst	ListValueCount	ListGetAt	ListValueCountNoCase
ListInsertAt				

Mathematical Functions

Abs	ACos	ASin	Atn	BitAnd
BitMaskClear	BitMaskRead	BitMaskSet	BitNot	BitOr
BitSHLN	BitSHRN	BitXor	Ceiling	Cos
DecrementValue	Exp	Fix	IncrementValue	InputBaseN
Int	Log	Log10	Max	Min
Pi	Rand	Randomize	RandRange	Round
Sgn	Sin	Sqr	Tan	

Query Functions

IsQuery	QuerySetCell	QueryAddColumn	QuotedValueList	QueryAddRow
ValueList	QueryNew			

String Functions

Asc	Chr	CJustify	Compare	CompareNoCase
DayOfWeekAsString	FormatBaseN	Find	FindNoCase	FindOneOf
GetToken	Insert	JSStringFormat	Left	Len
LJustify	ListValueCount	ListValueCount-NoCase	LSParseCurrency	LSParseDateTime
LSParseEuroCurrency	LSParseNumber	LTrim	Mid	MonthAsString
ParseDateTime	REFind	REFindNoCase	RemoveChars	Replace
ReplaceList	ReplaceNoCase	REReplace	REReplaceNoCase	Reverse
Right	RJustify	RTrim	SpanExcluding	SpanIncluding
ToBase64	UCase	Val		

Structure Functions

IsStruct	StructClear	StructCopy	StructCount	StructDelete
StructFind	StructIsEmpty	StructKeyArray	StructKeyExists	StructKeyList
StructNew	StructUpdate			

System Functions

DirectoryExists	ExpandPath	FileExists	GetCurrentTemplatePath	GetFileFromPath
GetMetricData	GetTempFile	GetTemplatePath	SetProfileString	

Miscellaneous Functions

CreateObject	CreateUUID	Decrypt	DeleteClient-Variable	Encrypt
GetBaseTagData	GetBaseTagList	GetClientVariables-List	GetTickCount	PreserveSingleQuotes
QuotedValueList	StripCR	URLEncodedFormat	ValueList	WriteOutput

Alphabetical List of Functions

Abs	ACos	ArrayAppend	ArrayAvg	ArrayClear
ArrayDeleteAt	ArrayInsertAt	ArrayIsEmpty	ArrayLen	ArrayMax
ArrayMin	ArrayNew	ArrayPrepend	ArrayResize	ArraySet
ArraySort	ArraySum	ArraySwap	ArrayToList	Asc
ASin	Atn	Authenticated-Context	Authenticated-User	BitAnd
BitMaskClear	BitMaskRead	BitMaskSet	BitNot	BitOr
BitSHLN	BitSHRN	BitXor	Ceiling	Chr
CJustify	Compare	CompareNoCase	Cos	CreateDate
CreateDateTime	CreateObject	CreateODBCDate	CreateODBCDate-Time	CreateODBCTime
CreateTime	CreateTimeSpan	CreateUUID	DateAdd	DateCompare
DateConvert	DateDiff	DateFormat	DatePart	Day
DayOfWeek	DayOfWeekAsString	DayOfYear	DaysInYear	DE
DecimalFormat	DecrementValue	Decrypt	DeleteClient-Variable	DirectoryExists
DollarFormat	Encrypt	Evaluate	Exp	ExpandPath
FileExists	Find	FindNoCase	FindOneOf	FirstDayOfMonth
Fix	FormatBaseN	GetBaseTagData	GetBaseTagList	GetBaseTemplatePath
GetClientVariables-List	GetCurrentTemplate-Path	GetDirectory-FromPath	GetFileFromPath	GetFunctionList
GetLocale	GetMetricData	GetProfileString	GetTempDirectory	GetTempFile
GetTemplatePath	GetTickCount	GetTimeZoneInfo	GetToken	Hour

HTMLCodeFormat	HTMLEditFormat	IIf	IncrementValue	InputBaseN
Insert	Int	IsArray	IsAuthenticated	IsAuthorized
IsBinary	IsBoolean	IsDate	IsDebugMode	IsDefined
IsLeapYear	IsNumeric	IsNumericDate	IsProtected	IsQuery
IsSimpleValue	JSStringFormat	LCase	Left	Len
ListAppend	ListChangeDelims	ListContains	ListContainsNo-Case	ListDeleteAt
ListFind	ListFindNoCase	ListFirst	ListGetAt	ListInsertAt
ListLast	ListLen	ListPrepend	ListQualify	ListRest
ListSetAt	ListSort	ListToArray	ListValueCount	ListValueCountNoCase
LJustify	Log	Log10	LSCurrencyFormat	LSDateFormat
LSEuroCurrency-Format	LSIsCurrency	LSIsDate	LSIsNumeric	LSNumberFormat
LSParseCurrency	LSParseDateTime	LSParseEuro-Currency	LSParseNumber	LSTimeFormat
LTrim	Max	Mid	Min	Minute
Month	MonthAsString	Now	NumberFormat	ParagraphFormat
ParameterExists	ParseDateTime	Pi	PreserveSingle-Quotes	Quarter
QueryAddColumn	QueryAddRow	QueryNew	QuerySetCell	Rand
Randomize	RandRange	REFind	REFindNoCase	RemoveChars
RepeatString	Replace	ReplaceList	ReplaceNoCase	REReplace
REReplaceNoCase	Reverse	Right	RJustify	Round
RTrim	Second	SetLocale	SetProfileString	SetVariable
Sgn	Sin	SpanExcluding	SpanIncluding	Sqr
StripCR	StructClear	StructCopy	StructCount	StructDelete
StructFind	StructInsert	StructIsEmpty	StructKeyArray	StructKeyExists
StructKeyList	StructNew	StructUpdate	Tan	TimeFormat
ToBase64	ToBinary	ToString	Trim	UCase
URLDecode	URLEncodedFormat	Val	ValueList	Week
WriteOutput	XMLFormat	Year	YesNoFormat	

Abs

Returns the absolute value of a number. The absolute value of a number is the number without its sign.

See also Sgn.

Syntax
Abs(*number*)

number
Any number.

ACos

Returns the arccosine of a number in radians. The arccosine is the angle whose cosine is *number*.

See also Cos, Sin, ASin, Tan, and Pi.

Syntax
ACos(*number*)

number
Cosine of the angle that is to be calculated. This value must be between -1 and 1, inclusive.

Usage
The range of the result is 0 to .

To convert degrees to radians, multiply degrees by /180. To convert radians to degrees, multiply radians by 180/.

ArrayAppend

Appends an array index to the end of the specified array. Returns a Boolean TRUE on successful completion.

See also ArrayPrepend.

Syntax
ArrayAppend(*array*, *value*)

array
Name of the array to which you want to append an index.

value
The value you want to place into the specified array in the last index position.

ArrayAvg

Returns the average of the values in the specified array.

Syntax
ArrayAvg(*array*)

array
Name of the array containing values you want to average.

ArrayClear

Deletes all data in the specified array. Returns a Boolean TRUE on successful completion.

See also ArrayDeleteAt.

Syntax
ArrayClear(*array*)

array
Name of the array in which you want to delete data.

ArrayDeleteAt

Deletes data from the specified array at the specified index position. Note that when an array index is deleted, index positions in the array are recalculated. For example, in an array containing the months of the year, deleting index position (5) removes the entry for May. If you then want to delete the entry for November, you delete index position (10), not (11), since the index positions were recalculated after index position (5) was removed.

Returns a Boolean TRUE on successful completion.

See also ArrayInsertAt.

Syntax
ArrayDeleteAt(*array*, *position*)

array
Name of the array in which you want to delete index data specified in position.

position
Array position containing the data you want to delete.

ArrayInsertAt

Inserts data in the specified array at the specified index position. All array elements with indexes greater than the new position are shifted right by one. The length of the array increases by one index.

Returns a Boolean TRUE on successful completion.

See also ArrayDeleteAt.

Syntax
ArrayInsertAt(*array*, *position*, *value*)

array
Name of the array in which you want to insert data.

position
The index position in the specified array where you want to insert the data specified in value.

value

The value of the data you want to insert into the array.

ArrayIsEmpty

Determines whether the specified array is empty of data.

Returns a Boolean TRUE if specified array is empty, FALSE if not empty.

See also `ArrayLen`.

Syntax

`ArrayIsEmpty(array)`

array

Name of the array you want to check for data.

ArrayLen

Returns the length of the specified array.

See also `ArrayIsEmpty`.

Syntax

`ArrayLen(array)`

array

Name of the array whose length you want to return.

ArrayMax

Returns the largest numeric value in the specified array.

Syntax

`ArrayMax(array)`

array

Name of the array from which you want to return the largest numeric value.

ArrayMin

Returns the smallest numeric value in the specified array.

Syntax

`ArrayMin(array)`

array

Name of the array from which you want to return the smallest numeric value.

ArrayNew

Creates an array of between 1 and 3 dimensions. Array elements are indexed with square brackets: [ ].

Note that ColdFusion arrays expand dynamically as data is added.

Syntax

`ArrayNew(dimension)`

dimension

An integer value between 1 and 3.

ArrayPrepend

Adds an array element to the beginning of the specified array. Returns a Boolean TRUE on successful completion.

See also `ArrayAppend`.

Syntax

`ArrayPrepend(array, value)`

array

Name of the array to which you want to prepend data.

value

The value you want to add to the beginning of the specified array.

ArrayResize

Resets an array to a specified minimum number of elements. ArrayResize can provide some performance gains if used to size an array to its expected maximum. Use ArrayResize immediately after creating an array with ArrayNew for arrays greater than 500 elements.

Note that ColdFusion arrays expand dynamically as data is added.

Returns a Boolean TRUE on successful completion.

Syntax

`ArrayResize(array, minimum_size)`

array

Name of the array you want to resize.

minimum_size

Minimum size of the specified array.

ArraySet

In a one-dimensional array, sets the elements in a specified range to the specified value. Useful in initializing an array after a call to ArrayNew. Returns a Boolean TRUE on successful completion.

See also `ArrayNew`.

Syntax

`ArraySet(array, start_pos, end_pos, value)`

array

Name of the array you want to change.

start_pos

Starting position in the specified array.

end_pos

Ending position in the specified array. If this value exceeds the array length, elements are accordingly added to the array.

value

The value you want to add to the range of elements in the specified array.

ArraySort

Returns the specified array with elements numerically or alphanumerically sorted.

Syntax

`ArraySort(array, sort_type [, sort_order ])`

array

Name of the array you want to sort.

sort_type

The type of sort to execute. Sort type can be:

- `numeric`—Sorts numerically
- `text`—Sorts text alphabetically, uppercase before lowercase
- `textnocase`—Sorts text alphabetically; case is ignored

sort_order

The sort order you want to enforce:

- `asc`— (Default) Ascending sort order
- `desc`—Descending sort order

ArraySum

Returns the sum of values in the specified array.

Syntax

`ArraySum(array)`

array

Name of the array containing values you want to add together.

ArraySwap

Swaps array values for the specified array at the specified positions. ArraySwap can be used with greater efficiency than multiple CFSETs.

Returns a Boolean TRUE on successful completion.

Syntax

`ArraySwap(array, position1, position2)`

array

Name of the array whose elements you want to swap.

position1

Position of the first element you want to swap.

position2

Position of the second element you want to swap.

ArrayToList

Converts the specified one dimensional array to a list, delimited with the character you specify.

Syntax

`ArrayToList(array [, delimiter ])`

array

Name of the array containing elements you want to use to build a list.

delimiter

Specify the character(s) you want to use to delimit elements in the list. Default is comma (,).

Asc

Returns the ASCII value (character code) of the first character of a string. Returns 0 if string is empty.

See also `Chr`.

Syntax

`Asc(string)`

string

Any string.

ASin

Returns the arcsine of a number in radians. The arcsine is the angle whose sine is *number*.

See also `Sin`, `Cos`, `Pi`, and `Tan`.

Syntax

`ASin(number)`

number
Sine of the angle that is to be calculated. This value must be between 1 and -1.

Usage
The range of the result is -/2 to /2 radians. To convert degrees to radians, multiply degrees by /180. To convert radians to degrees, multiply radians by 180/.

Atn

Returns the arctangent of a number. The arctangent is the angle whose tangent is *number*.

See also Tan, Sin, Cos, and Pi.

Syntax
`Atn(number)`

number
Tangent of the angle you want.

Usage
The range of the result is -/2 to /2 radians. To convert degrees to radians, multiply degrees by /180. To convert radians to degrees, multiply radians by 180/.

AuthenticatedContext

Returns the name of the security context.

See also IsAuthenticated, AuthenticatedUser, IsAuthorized, and CFAUTHENTICATE.

Syntax
`AuthenticatedContext()`

AuthenticatedUser

Returns the name of the authenticated user.

See also IsAuthenticated, AuthenticatedContext, and CFAUTHENTICATE.

Syntax
`AuthenticatedUser()`

BitAnd

Returns the bitwise AND of two long integers.

See also BitNot, BitOr, and BitXor.

Syntax
`BitAnd(number1, number2)`

number1, number2
Any long integers.

Usage
Bit functions operate on 32-bit integers.

BitMaskClear

Returns *number* bitwise cleared with *length* bits beginning from *start*.

See also BitMaskRead and BitMaskSet.

Syntax
`BitMaskClear(number, start, length)`

number
Long integer to be masked.

start
Integer specifying the starting bit for masking.

length
Integer specifying the length of mask.

Usage
Parameters *start* and *length* must be in the range from 0 to 31.

Bit functions operate on 32-bit integers.

BitMaskRead

Returns the integer created from *length* bits of *number* beginning from *start*.

See also BitMaskClear and BitMaskSet.

Syntax
`BitMaskRead(number, start, length)`

number
Long integer to be masked.

start
Integer specifying the starting bit for reading.

length
Integer specifying the length of mask.

Usage
Parameters *start* and *length* must be in the range from 0 to 31.

Bit functions operate on 32-bit integers.

BitMaskSet

Returns *number* bitwise masked with *length* bits of *mask* beginning from *start*.

See also BitMaskClear and BitMaskRead.

Syntax
`BitMaskSet(`*number*`,` *mask*`,` *start*`,` *length*`)`

number
Long integer to be masked.

mask
Long integer specifying the mask.

start
Integer specifying the starting bit in number for masking.

length
Integer specifying the length of mask.

Usage
Parameters *start* and *length* must be in the range from 0 to 31.

Bit functions operate on 32-bit integers.

BitNot
Returns the bitwise NOT of a long integer.

See also `BitAnd`, `BitOr`, and `BitXor`.

Syntax
`BitNot(`*number*`)`

number
Any long integer.

Usage
Bit functions operate on 32-bit integers.

BitOr
Returns the bitwise OR of two long integers

See also `BitAnd`, `BitNot`, and `BitXor`.

Syntax
`BitOr(`*number1*`,` *number2*`)`

number1, number2
Any long integers.

Usage
Bit functions operate on 32-bit integers.

BitSHLN
Returns *number* bitwise shifted without rotation to the left by *count* bits.

See also `BitSHRN`.

Syntax
`BitSHLN(`*number*`,` *count*`)`

number
Long integer to be shifted to the left.

count
Integer specifying number of bits the number should be shifted.

Usage
Parameter *count* must be in the range from 0 to 31.

Bit functions operate on 32-bit integers.

BitSHRN
Returns *number* bitwise shifted without rotation to the right by *count* bits.

See also `BitSHLN`.

Syntax
`BitSHRN(`*number*`,` *count*`)`

number
Long integer to be shifted to the right.

count
Integer specifying number of bits the number should be shifted.

Usage
Parameter *count* must be in the range from 0 to 31.

Bit functions operate on 32-bit integers.

BitXor
Returns bitwise XOR of two long integers.

See also `BitAnd`, `BitNot`, and `BitOr`.

Syntax
`BitXor(`*number1*`,` *number2*`)`

number1, number2
Any long integers.

Usage
Bit functions operate on 32-bit integers.

Ceiling
Returns the closest integer greater than a given number.

See also `Int`, `Fix`, and `Round`.

Syntax
`Ceiling(`*number*`)`

number
Any real number.

Chr

Returns a character of a given ASCII value (character code).

See also Asc.

Syntax
Chr(*number*)

number
Any ASCII value (a number in the range 0 to 255 inclusive).

Usage
Numbers from 0 to 31 are the standard, nonprintable ASCII codes. For example, Chr(10) returns a linefeed character and Chr(13) returns a carriage return character. Therefore, the two-character string Chr(13) & Chr(10) is the newline string.

CJustify

Centers a string in the specified field length.

See also LJustify and RJustify.

Syntax
CJustify(*string*, *length*)

string
Any string to be centered.

length
Length of field.

Compare

Performs a case-sensitive comparison of two strings. Returns a negative number if *string1* is less than *string2*; 0 if *string1* is equal to *string2*; or a positive number if *string1* is greater than *string2*.

See also CompareNoCase and Find.

Syntax
Compare(*string1*, *string2*)

string1, string2
Strings to be compared.

Usage
The comparison is performed on the ASCII values (character codes) of corresponding characters in *string1* and *string2*.

If many strings are sorted in increasing order based on the Compare function, they appear listed in dictionary order.

CompareNoCase

Performs a case-insensitive comparison of two strings. Returns a negative number if *string1* is less than *string2*; 0 if *string1* is equal to *string2*; or a positive number if *string1* is greater than *string2*.

See also Compare and FindNoCase.

Syntax
CompareNoCase(*string1*, *string2*)

string1, string2
Strings to be compared.

Cos

Returns the cosine of a given angle in radians.

See also Sin, Tan, and Pi.

Syntax
Cos(*number*)

number
Angle in radians for which you want the cosine.

Usage
The range of the result is -1 to 1.

To convert degrees to radians, multiply degrees by /180. To convert radians to degrees, multiply radians by 180/.

CreateDate

Returns a valid date/time object.

See also CreateDateTime and CreateODBCDate.

Syntax
CreateDate(*year*, *month*, *day*)

year
Number representing the year in the range 100-9999. Years from 0 to 29 are interpreted as 21st century values. Years 30 to 99 are interpreted as 20th century values.

month
Number representing the month of the year, ranging from 1 (January) to 12 (December).

day
Number representing the day of the month, ranging from 1 to 31.

Usage

CreateDate is a subset of `CreateDateTime`.

Time in the returned object is set to 00:00:00.

CreateDateTime

Returns a valid date/time object.

See also `CreateDate`, `CreateTime`, `CreateODBCDateTime`, and `Now`.

Syntax

`CreateDateTime(year, month, day, hour, minute, second)`

year
Number representing the year in the range 100-9999.

month
Number representing the month of the year, ranging from 1 (January) to 12 (December).

day
Number representing the day of the month, ranging from 1 to 31.

hour
Number representing the hour, ranging from 0 to 23.

minute
Number representing the minute, ranging from 0 to 59.

second
Number representing the second, ranging from 0 to 59.

Usage

Years from 0 to 29 are interpreted as 21st century values. Years 30 to 99 are interpreted as 20th century values.

CreateObject

Allows you to create COM, CORBA, and JAVA objects.

> **NOTE**   ColdFusion administrators can disable the CFOBJECT tag in the ColdFusion Administrator Basic Security page, which also disables this function. On UNIX, COM objects are not currently supported by CreateObject.

CreateObject topics

- COM
- CORBA
- JAVA

Object Types

Depending on the value of the *type* parameter, there are several additional parameters you can use. This table shows which parameters you can use with each object type.

Parameters Used with Object Types

TYPE	Parameters
COM	TYPE
	CLASS
	CONTEXT
	SERVER
CORBA	TYPE
	CONTEXT
	CLASS
	LOCALE
JAVA	TYPE
	CLASS

Sections that follow describe these values and parameters in greater detail.

COM

CreateObject allows you to create and use COM (Component Object Model) objects. Any automation server object type that is currently registered on a machine can be invoked. You can use a utility like Microsoft's OLEView to browse COM objects. OLEView, as well as information about COM and DCOM, can be found at Microsoft's OLE Development Web site `http://www.microsoft.com/oledev/`.

To create COM objects, you need to know the program ID or filename of the object, the methods and properties available through the IDispatch interface, and the arguments and return types of the object's methods. The OLEView utility can give you this information for most COM objects.

Syntax

`CreateObject("COM", class, context, , serverName)`

class
Required. Enter the component ProgID for the object you want to invoke.

context

Optional. "InProc", "Local", or "Remote". Uses Registry setting when not specified.

serverName

Required when CONTEXT="Remote". Enter a valid server name using UNC (Universal Naming Convention) or DNS (Domain Name Server) conventions, in one of the following forms:

```
SERVER="\\lanserver"
SERVER="lanserver"
SERVER="http://www.servername.com"
SERVER="www.servername.com"
SERVER="127.0.0.1"
```

CORBA

CreateObject allows you to call methods in CORBA objects. These CORBA objects must already have been defined and registered for use.

Syntax

CreateObject("CORBA", *class*, *context*, *locale*, **)**

class

Required. Specifies different information, depending on the CONTEXT specification:

- If CONTEXT is IOR—Specifies the name of a file that contains the string version of the IOR. ColdFusion must be able to read this file at all times; it should be local to ColdFusion server or on the network in an open, accessible location.
- If CONTEXT is NameService—Specifies a period-delimited naming context for the naming service, such as Allaire.Department.Doc.empobject.

context

Required. Specifies one of the following:

- "IOR"—ColdFusion uses the Interoperable Object Reference (IOR) to access the CORBA server.
- "NameService"—ColdFusion uses the naming service to access server. "NameService" is only valid with the InitialContext of a VisiBroker Orb.

locale

Optional. Sets arguments for a call to init_orb(..). Use of this attribute is specific to VisiBroker orbs, and is currently available on C++, Version 3.2. The value should be of the form:

"ORBagentAddr 199.99.129.33—ORBagentPort 19000"

Note that each type-value pair has to start with a leading "–".

Usage

ColdFusion Enterprise version 4.0 and above supports CORBA through the Dynamic Invocation Interface (DII). To use CreateObject with CORBA objects, you need to know either the name of the file containing a string version of the IOR or the object's naming context in the naming service. You also need to know the object's attributes, method names and method signatures.

User-defined types (for example, structures) are not supported.

JAVA

CreateObject allows you to create and use JAVA objects, and by extension EJB objects.

This support is currently only for NT, but will be extended to Solaris in the next release.

Syntax

CreateObject("JAVA", *class***)**

class

Required. Specifies the Java class.

Usage

To be able to call Java CFXs or Java objects, ColdFusion uses a JVM embedded in the process. The loading, location and the settings for the JVM are configurable using the ColdFusion Administrator pages.

Any Java class available in the class path specified in the CF Administrator can be loaded and used from ColdFusion using the CreateObject function.

Use the following steps to access Java methods and fields:

1. Call CreateObject or CFOBJECT to load the class.
2. Use the init method with appropriate arguments to call a constructor explicitly. For example:

```
<CFSET ret = myObj.init(arg1, arg2)>
```

Calling a public method on the object without first calling the "init" method results in an implicit call to the default constructor. Arguments and return values can be any valid Java type (simple, arrays, objects). ColdFusion does the appropriate conversions when strings are passed as arguments, but not when they are received as return values.

Overloaded methods are supported as long as the number of arguments are different. Future enhancements will let you use cast functions that will allow method signatures to be built more accurately.

CreateODBCDate

Returns a date in ODBC date format.

See also `CreateODBCDateTime`.

Syntax
`CreateODBCDate(date)`

date
Date/time object in the period from 100 AD to 9999 AD. Years from 0 to 29 are interpreted as 21st century values. Years 30 to 99 are interpreted as 20th century values.

CreateODBCDateTime

Returns a date/time object in ODBC timestamp format.

See also `CreateDateTime`, `CreateODBCDate`, `CreateODBCTime`, and `Now`.

Syntax
`CreateODBCDateTime(date)`

date
Date/time object in the period from 100 AD to 9999 AD. Years from 0 to 29 are interpreted as 21st century values. Years 30 to 99 are interpreted as 20th century values.

Usage
When passing a date/time value as a string, make sure it is enclosed in quotes. Otherwise, it is interpreted as a number representation of a date/time object, returning undesired results.

CreateODBCTime

Returns a time object in ODBC time format.

See also `CreateODBCDateTime` and `CreateTime`.

Syntax
`CreateODBCTime(date)`

date
Date/time object in the period from 100 AD to 9999 AD.

Usage
When passing a date/time value as a string, make sure it is enclosed in quotes. Otherwise, it is interpreted as a number representation of a date/time object, returning undesired results.

CreateTime

Returns a valid time variable in ColdFusion.

See also `CreateODBCTime` and `CreateDateTime`.

Syntax
`CreateTime(hour, minute, second)`

hour
Number representing the hour, ranging from 0 to 23.

minute
Number representing the minute, ranging from 0 to 59.

second
Number representing the second, ranging from 0 to 59.

Usage
CreateTime is a subset of `CreateDateTime`.

Time variables are special cases of date/time variables. The date portion of a time variable is set to December 30, 1899.

CreateTimeSpan

Creates a date/time object for adding and subtracting other date/time objects.

See also `CreateDateTime`, `DateAdd`, and `DateConvert`.

Syntax
`CreateTimeSpan(days, hours, minutes, seconds)`

days
Number representing the number of days.

hours
Number representing the number of hours.

minutes
Number representing the number of minutes.

seconds
Number representing the number of seconds.

Usage
The CreateTimeSpan function creates a special date/time object that should only be used to add and subtract from other date/time objects or with the CFQUERY CACHEDWITHIN attribute.

CreateUUID

Returns a Universally Unique Identifier (UUID) formatted as 'XXXXXXXX-XXXX-XXXX-XXXXXXXXXXXXXXXX' where 'X' stands for a hexadecimal digit (0-9 or A-F).

Syntax
`CreateUUID()`

Usage
Each UUID returned by the CreateUUID function is a 35-character-string representation of a unique 128-bit integer. Use the CreateUUID function when you need a unique string that you will use as a persistent identifier in a distributed environment. To a very high degree of certainty, this function returns a unique value; no other invocation on the same or any other system should return the same value.

UUIDs are used by distributed computing frameworks, such as DCE/RPC, COM+, and CORBA. With Cold-Fusion, you can use UUIDs as primary table keys for applications where data is stored on a number of shared databases. In such cases, using numeric keys may cause primary key constraint violations during table merges. By using UUIDs, you can eliminate these violations because each UUID is unique.

DateAdd
Returns a date to which a specified time interval has been added.

See also `DateConvert`, `DatePart`, and `CreateTimeSpan`.

Syntax
`DateAdd(datepart, number, date)`

datepart
One of the following strings:

- yyyy—Year
- q—Quarter
- m—Month
- y—Day of year
- d—Day
- w—Weekday
- ww—Week
- h—Hour
- n—Minute
- s—Second

number
Number of units of *datepart* to add to *date* (positive to get dates in the future or negative to get dates in the past).

date
Date/time object in the period from 100 AD to 9999 AD. Years from 0 to 29 are interpreted as 21st century values. Years 30 to 99 are interpreted as 20th century values.

Usage
The *datepart* specifiers "y," "d," and "w" perform the same function—add a certain number of days to a given date.

When passing a date/time value as a string, make sure it is enclosed in quotes. Otherwise, it is interpreted as a number representation of a date/time object, returning undesired results.

DateCompare
Performs a full date/time comparison of two dates. Returns -1 if *date1* is less than *date2*; returns 0 if *date1* is equal to *date2*; returns 1 if *date1* is greater than *date2*. See the description of *datePart* for information on specifying the precision of the comparison.

See also `CreateDateTime` and `DatePart`.

Syntax
`DateCompare(date1, date2 [, datePart])`

date1
Date/time object in the period from 100 AD to 9999 AD.

date2
Date/time object in the period from 100 AD to 9999 AD.

datePart
Optional. The precision of the comparison. This parameter can have any of the following values:

- s—precise to the second
- n—precise to the minute
- h—precise to the hour
- d—precise to the day
- m—precise to the month
- yyyy—precise to the year

By default, precision is to the second.

Usage
When passing a date/time value as a string, make sure it is enclosed in quotes. Otherwise, it is interpreted as a number representation of a date/time object, returning undesired results.

Years from 0 to 29 are interpreted as 21st century values. Years 30 to 99 are interpreted as 20th century values.

DateConvert

Converts local time to Universal Coordinated Time (UTC) or UTC to local time based on the specified parameters. This function uses the daylight savings settings in the executing machine to compute daylight savings time, if required.

See also GetTimeZoneInfo, CreateDateTime, and DatePart.

Syntax

DateConvert(*conversion-type*, *date*)

conversion-type

There are two conversion types: "local2Utc" and "utc2Local." The former converts local time to UTC time. The later converts UTC time to local time.

date

Any ColdFusion date and time string. In order to create a ColdFusion date and time, use CreateDateTime.

Usage

When passing a date/time value as a string, make sure it is enclosed in quotes. Otherwise, it is interpreted as a number representation of a date/time object, returning undesired results.

DateDiff

Returns the number of intervals in whole units of type *Datepart* by which *Date1* is less than *Date2*.

See also DateAdd, DatePart, and CreateTimeSpan.

Syntax

DateDiff(*datepart*, *date1*, *date2*)

datepart

One of the following strings:

- yyyy—Year
- q—Quarter
- m—Month
- y—Day of year
- d—Day
- w—Weekday
- ww—Week
- h—Hour
- n—Minute
- s—Second

date1

Date/time object in the period from 100 AD to 9999 AD.

date2

Date/time object in the period from 100 AD to 9999 AD.

Usage

If you want to know the number of days between *date1* and *date2*, you can use either Day of Year ("y") or Day ("d").

When *datepart* is Weekday ("w"), DateDiff returns the number of weeks between the two dates. If *date1* falls on a Monday, DateDiff counts the number of Mondays until *date2*. It counts *date2* but not *date1*. If interval is Week ("ww"), however, the DateDiff function returns the number of calendar weeks between the two dates. It counts the number of Sundays between *date1* and *date2*. DateDiff counts *date2* if it falls on a Sunday; but it doesn't count *date1*, even if it does fall on a Sunday.

If *Date1* refers to a later point in time than *date2*, the DateDiff function returns a negative number.

When passing date/time value as a string, make sure it is enclosed in quotes. Otherwise, it is interpreted as a number representation of a date/time object returning undesired results.

Years from 0 to 29 are interpreted as 21st century values. Years 30 to 99 are interpreted as 20th century values.

DateFormat

Returns a formatted date/time value. If no mask is specified, DateFormat function returns date value using the *dd-mmm-yy* format.

See also Now, CreateDate, and ParseDateTime.

Syntax

DateFormat(*date* [, *mask*])

date

Date/time object in the period from 1601 AD to 9999 AD.

mask

Set of characters that are used to show how ColdFusion should display the date:

- d—Day of the month as digits with no leading zero for single-digit days.
- dd—Day of the month as digits with a leading zero for single-digit days.
- ddd—Day of the week as a three-letter abbreviation.
- dddd—Day of the week as its full name.
- m—Month as digits with no leading zero for single-digit months.

- mm—Month as digits with a leading zero for single-digit months.
- mmm—Month as a three-letter abbreviation.
- mmmm—Month as its full name.
- y—Year as last two digits with no leading zero for years less than 10.
- yy—Year as last two digits with a leading zero for years less than 10.
- yyyy—Year represented by four digits.
- gg—Period/era string. Currently ignored, but reserved for future use.

Usage

When passing a date/time value as a string, make sure it is enclosed in quotes. Otherwise, it is interpreted as a number representation of a date/time object, returning undesired results. On UNIX, there is a switch that provides fast date-time parsing. If you have enabled this switch, you must refer to dates in expressions in the following order: month, day, and year. For example, consider the following:

```
<CFIF "11/23/1998" GT "11/15/1998">
```

If this switch is set, the default date format returned by the DateFormat() function cannot be parsed in an expression. However, if you specify a mask, indicating the correct order, such as, mm/dd/yyyy, the date returned by this function can be parsed.

The Fast Date/Time Parsing switch is set on the Cold-Fusion Administrator Server Settings page. Please refer to *Administering ColdFusion Server* for more information about ColdFusion settings.

DatePart

Returns the specified part of a date as an integer.

See also DateAdd and DateConvert.

Syntax

DatePart(*datepart*, *date*)

datepart

One of the following strings:

- yyyy—Year
- q—Quarter
- m—Month
- y—Day of year
- d—Day
- w—Weekday
- ww—Week

- h—Hour
- n—Minute
- s—Second

date

Any date.

Usage

Years from 0 to 29 are interpreted as 21st century values. Years 30 to 99 are interpreted as 20th century values.

When passing a date/time value as a string, make sure it is enclosed in quotes. Otherwise, it is interpreted as a number representation of a date/time object, returning undesired results.

Day

Returns the ordinal for the day of the month, ranging from 1 to 31.

See also DayOfWeek, DayOfWeekAsString, DayOfYear, DaysInMonth, DaysInYear, and FirstDayOfMonth.

Syntax

Day(*date*)

date

Any date.

Usage

Years from 0 to 29 are interpreted as 21st century values. Years 30 to 99 are interpreted as 20th century values.

When passing a date/time value as a string, make sure it is enclosed in quotes. Otherwise, it is interpreted as a number representation of a date/time object, returning undesired results.

DayOfWeek

Returns the ordinal for the day of the week. The day is given as an integer ranging from 1 (Sunday) to 7 (Saturday).

See also Day, DayOfWeekAsString, DayOfYear, Days-InMonth, DaysInYear, and FirstDayOfMonth.

Syntax

DayOfWeek(*date*)

date

Any date.

Usage

Years from 0 to 29 are interpreted as 21st century values. Years 30 to 99 are interpreted as 20th century values.

When passing a date/time value as a string, make sure it is enclosed in quotes. Otherwise, it is interpreted as a number representation of a date/time object, returning undesired results.

DayOfWeekAsString

Returns the day of the week corresponding to *day_of_week*, an integer ranging from 1 (Sunday) to 7 (Saturday).

See also Day, DayOfWeek, DayOfYear, DaysInMonth, DaysInYear, and FirstDayOfMonth.

Syntax
DayOfWeekAsString(*day_of_week*)

day_of_week
Integer representing the day of the week, where 1 is Sunday, 2 is Monday, and so on.

Usage
Years from 0 to 29 are interpreted as 21st century values. Years 30 to 99 are interpreted as 20th century values.

DayOfYear

Returns the ordinal for the day of the year.

See also Day, DayOfWeek, DayOfWeekAsString, DaysInMonth, DaysInYear, and FirstDayOfMonth.

Syntax
DayOfYear(*date*)

date
Any date.

Usage
DayofYear is aware of leap years.

Years from 0 to 29 are interpreted as 21st century values. Years 30 to 99 are interpreted as 20th century values.

When passing a date/time value as a string, make sure it is enclosed in quotes. Otherwise, it is interpreted as a number representation of a date/time object, returning undesired results.

DaysInMonth

Returns the number of days in the specified month (*Date*).

See also Day, DayOfWeek, DayOfWeekAsString, DayOfYear, DaysInYear, and FirstDayOfMonth.

Syntax
DaysInMonth(*date*)

date
Any date.

Usage
Years from 0 to 29 are interpreted as 21st century values. Years 30 to 99 are interpreted as 20th century values.

When passing a date/time value as a string, make sure it is enclosed in quotes. Otherwise, it is interpreted as a number representation of a date/time object, returning undesired results.

DaysInYear

Returns the number of days in a year.

See also Day, DayOfWeek, DayOfWeekAsString, DayOfYear, DaysInMonth, DaysInYear, FirstDayOfMonth, and IsLeapYear.

Syntax
DaysInYear(*date*)

date
Any date.

Usage
DaysInYear is aware of leap years.

Years from 0 to 29 are interpreted as 21st century values. Years 30 to 99 are interpreted as 20th century values.

When passing a date/time value as a string, make sure it is enclosed in quotes. Otherwise, it is interpreted as a number representation of a date/time object, returning undesired results.

DE

Returns its argument with double quotes wrapped around it and all double quotes inside it escaped. The DE (Delay Evaluation) function prevents the evaluation of a string as an expression when it is passed as an argument to IIf or Evaluate.

See also Evaluate and IIf.

Syntax
DE(*string*)

string
String to be evaluated with delay.

DecimalFormat

Returns *number* as a string formatted with two decimal places and thousands separator.

See also `DollarFormat` and `NumberFormat`.

Syntax
`DecimalFormat(number)`

number
Number being formatted.

DecrementValue

Returns integer part of *number* decremented by one.

See also `IncrementValue`.

Syntax
`DecrementValue(number)`

number
Number being decremented.

Decrypt

Decrypts an encrypted string.

See also `Encrypt`.

Syntax
`Decrypt(encrypted_string, key)`

encrypted_string
String to be decrypted.

key
String specifying the key used to encrypt *encrypted_string*.

DeleteClientVariable

Deletes the client variable specified by *name*. Returns a Boolean TRUE when variable is successfully deleted, even if variable did not previously exist. To test for the existence of a variable, use IsDefined.

See also `GetClientVariablesList`.

Syntax
`DeleteClientVariable("name")`

name
Name of a client variable to be deleted, surrounded by double quotes.

Usage
If the client variable specified by *name* does not exist, an error is returned.

DirectoryExists

Returns YES if the directory specified in the argument does exist; otherwise, it returns NO.

See also `FileExists`.

Syntax
`DirectoryExists(absolute_path)`

absolute_path
Any absolute path.

DollarFormat

Returns *number* as a string formatted with two decimal places, thousands separator, dollar sign. Parentheses are used if *number* is negative.

See also `DecimalFormat` and `NumberFormat`.

Syntax
`DollarFormat(number)`

number
Number being formatted.

Encrypt

Encrypts a string.

See also `Decrypt`.

Syntax
`Encrypt(string, key)`

string
String to be encrypted.

key
String specifying the key used to encrypt *string*.

Evaluate

The function evaluates all of its arguments, left to right, and returns the result of evaluating the last argument.

See also `DE` and `IIf`.

Syntax
`Evaluate(string_expression1 [, string_expression2 [, ... ] ] )`

string_expression1, string_expression2
Valid expressions to be evaluated.

Usage
String expressions can be arbitrarily complex. Note, however, that they are somewhat more complicated to write because they are inside a string. In particular, if

the string expression is double-quoted, double-quotes inside the expression must be escaped.

Exp

Returns e raised to the power of *number*. The constant e equals 2.71828182845904, the base of the natural logarithm.

See also Log and Log10.

Syntax

Exp(*number*)

number

Exponent applied to the base e.

Usage

To calculate powers of other bases, use ^ (the exponentiation operator). Exp is the inverse of Log, the natural logarithm of *number*.

ExpandPath

Returns a path equivalent to the *relative_path* appended to the base template path. Note the following:

- ExpandPath creates a platform-appropriate path. You can use either a slash (/) or a back slash (\) in the specified relative path.
- The return value contains a trailing slash (or back slash) if the specified relative path contains a trailing slash (or back slash).

See also FileExists, GetCurrentTemplatePath, and GetFileFromPath.

Syntax

ExpandPath(*relative_path*)

relative_path

Any relative path. ExpandPath converts relative directory references (.\ and ..\)to an absolute path. The function throws an error if this argument or the resulting absolute path is invalid.

FileExists

Returns YES if the file specified in the argument does exist; otherwise, it returns NO.

See also DirectoryExists, ExpandPath, and Get-TemplatePath.

Syntax

FileExists(*absolute_path*)

absolute_path

Any absolute path.

Find

Returns the first index of an occurrence of a *substring* in a *string* from a specified starting position. Returns 0 if *substring* is not in *string*. The search is case-sensitive.

See also FindNoCase, Compare, FindOneOf, REFind, and Replace.

Syntax

Find(*substring, string* [, *start*])

substring

String being sought.

string

String being searched.

start

Starting position for the search.

FindNoCase

Returns the first index of an occurrence of a *substring* in a *string* from a specified starting position. Returns 0 if *substring* is not in *string*. The search is case-insensitive.

See also Find, CompareNoCase, FindOneOf, REFind, and Replace functions.

Syntax

FindNoCase(*substring, string* [, *start*])

substring

String being sought.

string

String being searched.

start

Starting position for the search.

FindOneOf

Return the first index of the occurrence of any character from *set* in *string*. Returns 0 if no characters are found. The search is case-sensitive.

See also Find, Compare, and REFind functions.

Syntax

FindOneOf(*set, string* [, *start*])

set

String containing one or more characters being sought.

string
String being searched.

start
Starting position for the search.

FirstDayOfMonth

Returns the ordinal (the day's number in the year) for the first day of the specified month.

See also Day, DayOfWeek, DayOfWeekAsString, DayOfYear, DaysInMonth, and DaysInYear.

Syntax
FirstDayOfMonth(*date*)

date
Any date.

Usage
Years from 0 to 29 are interpreted as 21st century values. Years 30 to 99 are interpreted as 20th century values.

When passing a date/time value as a string, make sure it is enclosed in quotes. Otherwise, it is interpreted as a number representation of a date/time object, returning undesired results.

Fix

Returns the closest integer less than *number* if *number* is greater than or equal to 0. Returns the closest integer greater than *number* if *number* is less than 0.

See also Ceiling, Int, and Round.

Syntax
Fix(*number*)

number
Any number.

FormatBaseN

Converts a *number* to a string in the base specified by *radix*.

See also InputBaseN.

Syntax
FormatBaseN(*number*, *radix*)

number
Number to be converted.

radix
Base of the result.

GetBaseTagData

Returns an object that contains data (variables, scopes, etc.) from a specified ancestor tag. By default the closest ancestor is returned. If there is no ancestor by the specified name, or if the ancestor does not expose any data (for example, CFIF), an exception will be thrown.

See also GetBaseTagList.

Syntax
GetBaseTagData(*tagname* [, *instancenumber*])

tagname
Required. Specifies the ancestor tag name for which the function returns data.

instancenumber
Optional. Specifies the number of ancestor levels to jump before returning data. The default is 1.

GetBaseTagList

Returns a comma-delimited list of uppercase ancestor tag names. The first element of the list is the parent tag. If you call this function for a top-level tag, it returns an empty string.

See also GetBaseTagData.

Syntax
GetBaseTagList()

GetBaseTemplatePath

Returns the fully specified path of the base template.

See also GetCurrentTemplatePath, FileExists and ExpandPath.

Syntax
GetBaseTemplatePath()

GetClientVariablesList

Returns a comma-delimited list of non-readonly client variables available to a template.

See also DeleteClientVariable.

Syntax
GetClientVariablesList()

GetCurrentTemplatePath

Returns the fully specified path of the template containing the call to this function.

See also GetBaseTemplatePath, FileExists and ExpandPath.

Syntax
`GetCurrentTemplatePath()`

Usage
This function differs from GetBaseTemplatePath in that it will return the template path of an included template if the call is made from a template included with a CFINCLUDE tag; whereas GetBaseTemplatePath returns the template path of the top-level template even when the call to GetBaseTemplatePath is actually made from an included template.

GetDirectoryFromPath
Extracts the directory (with a \ (backslash)) from a fully specified path.

See also ExpandPath and GetFileFromPath.

Syntax
`GetDirectoryFromPath(path)`

path
Fully specified path (drive, directory, filename, and extension).

GetFileFromPath
Extracts the filename from a fully specified path.

See also ExpandPath and GetCurrentTemplatePath.

Syntax
`GetFileFromPath(path)`

path
Fully qualified path (drive, directory, filename, and extension).

GetFunctionList
Returns a structure of functions that are available in ColdFusion.

Syntax
`GetFunctionList()`

GetLocale
Returns the locale for the current request. Locales are determined by the native operating system.

A locale is an encapsulation of the set of attributes that govern the display and formatting of international date, time, number, and currency values.

See also SetLocale.

Syntax
`GetLocale()`

Locale Support
ColdFusion can be expected to support the following locales with a default Windows NT installation. The following locales are supported by ColdFusion:

Dutch (Belgian)
Dutch (Standard)
English (Australian)
English (Canadian)
English (New Zealand)
English (UK)
English (US)
French (Canadian)
French (Standard)
French (Swiss)
German (Austrian)
German (Standard)
German (Swiss)
Italian (Standard)
Italian (Swiss)

> **NOTE** The variable Server.ColdFusion.SupportedLocales is initialized at startup with a comma-delimited list of the locales that ColdFusion and the operating system support. GetLocale( ) will return an entry from that list. SetLocale will fail if called with a locale name not on that list.

GetMetricData
On Windows NT, GetMetricData returns all the internal data that is otherwise displayed in the Windows NT PerfMonitor. On UNIX, GetMetricData returns all of the internal data found by using CFStat. For it to work on NT you need to have turned on the PerfMonitor feature from the ColdFusion Administrator. See the Usage section for details of the structure that this function returns.

Syntax
`GetMetricData(monitor_name)`

monitor_name
The name of the performance monitor. On Windows NT, the performance monitor is PerfMonitor. On UNIX, it is CFStat.

Usage
On Windows NT, the function returns a ColdFusion structure with the following data fields:

- InstanceName
- PageHits
- ReqQueued
- DBHits
- ReqRunning
- ReqTimedOut
- BytesIn
- BytesOut
- AvgQueueTime
- AvgReqTime
- AvgDBTime
- CachePops

GetProfileString

Returns the value of an entry in an initialization file or an empty string if the value does not exist. An *initialization file* assigns values to configuration variables, also known as entries, that need to be set when the system boots, the operating system comes up, or an application starts. An initialization file is distinguished from other files by its .ini suffix, for example, boot.ini, Win32.ini, and setup.ini.

See also `SetProfileString`.

Syntax
`GetProfileString(`*iniPath*`, `*section*`, `*entry*`)`

iniPath
Fully qualified path (drive, directory, filename, and extension) of the initialization file, for example, `C:\boot.ini`.

section
The section of the initialization file from which you would like to extract information.

entry
The name of the value that you would like to see.

GetTempDirectory

Returns the full path name of a directory, including the trailing slash. The directory that is returned depends on the account under which ColdFusion is running as well as a variety of other factors. Before using this function in an application, test to see the directory it returns under your account.

See also `GetTempFile`.

Syntax
`GetTempDirectory()`

GetTempFile

Creates and returns the name of a temporary file in a directory whose name starts with (at most) the first three characters of *prefix*.

See also `GetTempDirectory`.

Syntax
`GetTempFile(`*dir*`, `*prefix*`)`

dir
Directory name.

prefix
Prefix of a temporary file to be created in the directory specified by *dir*.

GetTemplatePath

Returns the fully specified path of the base template.

> **NOTE** For backward compatibility, GetTemplatePath is still supported. However, `GetBaseTemplatePath` supersedes this function, and should be used in place of it in all code written after the release of ColdFusion 4.0.

See also `GetBaseTemplatePath`, `FileExists` and `ExpandPath`.

Syntax
`GetTemplatePath()`

GetTickCount

Returns a millisecond clock counter that can be used for timing sections of CFML code or any other aspects of page processing.

Syntax
`GetTickCount()`

Usage
The absolute value of the counter has no meaning. Generate useful timing values by taking differences between the results of GetTickCount() at specified points during page processing.

GetTimeZoneInfo

Returns a structure containing time zone information for the machine on which this function is executed. The structure contains four elements with the following keys.

- utcTotalOffset—total offset of the local time in minutes from UTC (Universal Coordinated Time). A plus sign (+) indicates that a time zone is west of UTC, such as all of the time zones in North and South America. A minus sign (-) indicates that a time zone is east of UTC, such as the time zones in Germany.
- utcHourOffset—offset in hours of local time from UTC.
- utcMinuteOffset—offset in minutes after the hours offset is taken into account. For North America, this will always be zero. However, for some countries that do not land exactly on the hour offset, the number will be between 0 and 60. For example, standard time in Adelaide, Australia has an offset of 9 hours and 30 minutes from UTC.
- isDSTOn—True if Daylight Savings Time (DST) is on in the host machine; False if DST is off.

See also `DateConvert`, `CreateDateTime` and `DatePart`.

Syntax
`GetTimeZoneInfo()`

GetToken

Returns the specified token in a string. Default delimiters are spaces, tabs, and newline characters. If *index* is greater than the number of tokens in *string*, GetToken returns an empty string.

See also `Left`, `Right`, `Mid`, `SpanExcluding`, and `SpanIncluding`.

Syntax
`GetToken(string, index [, delimiters ])`

string
Any string.

index
Any integer > 0 that indicates position of a token.

delimiters
String containing sets of delimiters.

Hour

Returns the ordinal value for the hour, ranging from 0 to 23.

See also `DatePart`, `Minute`, and `Second`.

Syntax
`Hour(date)`

date
Any date.

Usage
Years from 0 to 29 are interpreted as 21st century values. Years 30 to 99 are interpreted as 20th century values.

When passing a date/time value as a string, make sure it is enclosed in quotes. Otherwise, it is interpreted as a number representation of a date/time object, returning undesired results.

HTMLCodeFormat

Returns HTML escaped *string* enclosed in <PRE> and </PRE> tags. All carriage returns are removed from *string*, and all special characters (> < " &) are escaped.

See also `HTMLEditFormat`.

Syntax
`HTMLCodeFormat(string [, version ])`

string
String being HTML escaped and preformatted.

version
The specific HTML version to use in replacing special characters with their entity references. Valid entries are:

- -1—The latest implementation of HTML
- 2.0—For HTML 2.0 (Default)
- 3.2—For HTML 3.2

HTMLEditFormat

Returns HTML escaped *string*. All carriage returns are removed from *string*, and all special characters (> < " &) are escaped.

See also `HTMLCodeFormat`.

Syntax
`HTMLEditFormat(string [, version ])`

string
String being HTML escaped.

version
The specific HTML version to use in replacing special characters with their entity references. Valid entries are:

- –1—The latest implementation of HTML
- 2.0—For HTML 2.0 (Default)
- 3.2—For HTML 3.2

Usage
By escaping all special characters, this function increases the length of the specified string. This can cause unpredictable results when performing certain

string functions (Left, Right, and Mid, for example) against the expanded string.

IIf

The function evaluates its *condition* as a Boolean. If the result is TRUE, it returns the value of Evaluate(*string_expression1*); otherwise, it returns the value of Evaluate(*string_expression2*).

Prior to using IIf, please read the Usage section and Note carefully. The IIf function is primarily intended for the conditional processing of dynamic expressions.

> **NOTE**   For general conditional processing, see CFIF CFELSEIF CFELSE. For error handling, see CFTRY CFCATCH. See also DE and Evaluate.

Syntax
```
IIf(condition, string_expression1,
string_expression2)
```

condition

Any expression that can be evaluated as a Boolean.

string_expression1

Valid string expression to be evaluated and returned if condition is TRUE.

string_expression2

Valid string expression to be evaluated and returned if condition is FALSE.

Usage
The IIf function is a shortcut for the following construct:

```
<CFIF condition>
    <CFSET
result=Evaluate(string_expression1)>
<CFELSE>
    <CFSET
result=Evaluate(string_expression2)>
</CFIF>
```

returning *result*.

The expressions *string_expression1* and *string_expression2* must be string expressions, so that they do

not get evaluated immediately as the arguments of IIf. For example:

```
IIf(y is 0, DE("Error"), x/y)
```

will generate error if y=0 because the third argument is the value of x/0 (not a valid expression).

Remember that ColdFusion evaluates *string_expression1* and *string_expression2*. To return the string itself instead of evaluate the expression, use the DE (delay evaluation) function.

> **NOTE**   If you use pound signs (#) in either *string_expression1* or *string_expression2*, ColdFusion evaluates the part of the expression that is in pound signs first. By misusing pound signs, you can skew the results of the IIf function. In particular, if you use pound signs around the whole expression in *string_expression1*, it can cause the function to fail with the error 'Error Resolving Parameter' if there is an undefined variable in *string_expression1*.

For example, "LocalVar" is undefined, however, the following logic functions as you would expect if you do not use pound signs around "LocalVal:"

```
<CFOUTPUT>
#IIf(IsDefined("LocalVar"), "LocalVar",
DE("The variable is not
defined."))#
</CFOUTPUT>
```

The output is:

```
The variable is not defined.
```

Whereas, the pound signs around "LocalVar" in the following code cause it to fail with the error message 'Error Resolving Parameter', because ColdFusion never has a chance to evaluate the original condition IsDefined("LocalVar").

```
<CFOUTPUT>
#IIf(IsDefined("LocalVar"),
DE("#LocalVar#"), DE("The variable is not
defined."))#
</CFOUTPUT>
```

The error message would be:

```
Error resolving parameter LOCALVAR
```

The DE function has no impact on the evaluation of LocalVal, since the pound signs cause it to be evaluated immediately:

```
<!--- This example shows IIf --->
<HTML>
<HEAD>
<TITLE>
IIf Example
</TITLE>
</HEAD>

<BODY bgcolor=silver>
<H3>IIf Function</H3>

<P>IIf evaluates a condition, then  performs
an Evaluate on
string expression 1 or string expression 2
depending on the
Boolean outcome <I>(TRUE = run expression 1;
FALSE = run
expression 2)</I>.
</P>

<P>The result of the expression
IIf( Hour(Now()) GT 12,
  DE("It is afternoon or evening"),
    DE("It is morning"))
is:<BR>
<CFOUTPUT>
#IIf( Hour(Now()) GT 12,
  DE("It is afternoon or evening"),
    DE("It is morning"))#
</CFOUTPUT>
</P>

</BODY>
</HTML>
```

IncrementValue

Returns integer part of *number* incremented by one.

See also DecrementValue.

Syntax
IncrementValue(*number*)

number
Number being incremented.

InputBaseN

Returns the number obtained by converting *string* using the base specified by *radix*, an integer ranging from 2 to 36.

See also FormatBaseN.

Syntax
InputBaseN(*string*, *radix*)

string
Any string representing number in base specified by radix.

radix
Base of number represented by string ranging from 2 to 36.

Insert

Inserts a *substring* in a *string* after a specified character *position*. Prepends the *substring* if *position* is equal to 0.

See also RemoveChars and Len.

Syntax
Insert(*substring*, *string*, *position*)

substring
String to be inserted.

string
String to be inserted into.

position
Integer that indicates the character position in string where the substring will be inserted.

Int

Returns the closest integer smaller than a number.

See also Ceiling, Fix, and Round.

Syntax
Int(*number*)

number
Real number you want to round down to an integer.

IsArray

Returns TRUE if value is an array.

See also "Array Functions".

Syntax
IsArray(*value* [, *number*])

value

Variable name or array name.

number

Tests if the array has exactly the specified dimension.

IsAuthenticated

Returns TRUE if the user has been authenticated for any ColdFusion security context. If you specify the name of the security context, IsAuthenticated returns TRUE if the user has been authenticated for the specified ColdFusion security context.

See also CFAUTHENTICATE, AuthenticatedContext, AuthenticatedUser, and IsAuthorized.

Syntax

`IsAuthenticated([security-context-name ])`

security-context-name

The security context name.

IsAuthorized

Returns TRUE if the user is authorized to perform the specified action on the specified ColdFusion resource.

See also IsAuthenticated.

Syntax

`IsAuthorized(resourcetype, resourcename [, action ])`

resourcetype

String specifying the type of resource:

- Application
- CFML
- File
- DataSource
- Component
- Collection
- CustomTag
- UserObject

resourcename

String specifying the name of the resource. The value specified varies depending on the resource type:

The following are resourcetype specifications:

- APPLICATION
- CFML
- FILE
- DATASOURCE
- COMPONENT
- COLLECTION
- CUSTOMTAG

The following are resourcename specifications:

- Application name
- CFML tag name
- File name
- Data source name
- Component name
- Verity collection name
- Custom tag name
- Object name

Resourcename is the actual resource that is protected, not to be confused with the rule name, which you specify in the ColdFusion Administrator.

action

String specifying the action for which authorization is requested. Do not specify this parameter for COMPONENT and CUSTOMTAG. For all other resource types, this parameter is required.

resourcetype Specification	Possible ACTIONs
APPLICATION	ALL USECLIENTVARIABLES
CFML	Valid actions for the tag specified by resourcename
FILE	READ
	WRITE
DATASOURCE	ALL
	CONNECT
	SELECT
	INSERT
	UPDATE
	DELETE
	SP (stored procedure)
COMPONENT	No actions for this resource type
COLLECTION	DELETE
	OPTIMIZE
	PURGE
	SEARCH
	UPDATE
CUSTOMTAG	No actions for this resource type
USEROBJECT	Action specified via the ColdFusion Administrator

Usage

If you specify THROWONFAILURE=Yes in the CF-AUTHENTICATE tag, you can enclose IsAuthorized in a CFTRY/CFCATCH block to handle possible exceptions programmatically.

IsBinary

Returns TRUE if *value* is binary; otherwise, the function returns FALSE.

See also ToBinary, ToBase64, IsNumeric and YesNoFormat.

Syntax
IsBinary(*value*)

value
Any value.

IsBoolean

Returns TRUE if *value* can be converted to a Boolean; otherwise, FALSE.

See also IsNumeric and YesNoFormat.

Syntax
IsBoolean(*value*)

value
Any number or string.

IsDate

Returns TRUE if *string* can be converted to a date/time value; otherwise, FALSE. Note that ColdFusion converts the Boolean return value to its string equivalent, "Yes" and "No."

See also ParseDateTime, CreateDateTime, and IsNumericDate.

Syntax
IsDate(*string*)

string
Any string value.

Usage
Years from 0 to 29 are interpreted as 21st century values. Years 30 to 99 are interpreted as 20th century values.

IsDebugMode

Returns TRUE if debugging mode was set via the ColdFusion Administrator and FALSE if debugging mode is disabled.

Syntax
IsDebugMode()

IsDefined

Evaluates a string value to determine if the variable named in the string value exists. IsDefined returns TRUE if the specified variable is found, FALSE if not found.

IsDefined provides an alternative to the Parameter-Exists function, eliminating the need for cumbersome expressions used to test for the existence of a variable:

Evaluate("ParameterExists(#var_name#)")
See also Evaluate.

Syntax
IsDefined("*variable_name*")

variable_name
A string value, the name of the variable you want to test for. This value must always be enclosed in quotation marks.

IsLeapYear

Returns TRUE if the *year* is a leap year; otherwise, FALSE.

See also DaysInYear.

Syntax
IsLeapYear(*year*)

year
Number representing the year.

IsNumeric

Returns TRUE if *string* can be converted to a number; otherwise, FALSE.

See also IsBinary.

Syntax
IsNumeric(*string*)

string
Any string value.

IsNumericDate

Evaluates "real value" of date/time object. Returns TRUE if the number represents "real value" of the date/time object; otherwise, FALSE.

See also IsDate and ParseDateTime.

Syntax
`IsNumericDate(number)`

number

Real number.

IsProtected

Returns TRUE if the resource is protected in the security context of the authenticated user.

See also `IsAuthorized`.

Syntax
`IsProtected(resourcetype, resourcename [, action])`

resourcetype

String specifying the type of resource:

- Application
- CFML
- File
- DataSource
- Component
- CustomTag
- UserObject

resourcename

String specifying the name of the resource. Resourcename is the actual resource that is protected, not to be confused with the rule name, which you specify in the ColdFusion Administrator. The value specified varies depending on the resource type.

The following are `resourcetype` specifications:

- APPLICATION
- CFML
- FILE
- DATASOURCE
- COMPONENT
- COLLECTION
- CUSTOMTAG

The following are `resourcename` specifications:

- Application name
- CFML tag name
- File name
- Data source name
- Component name
- Verity collection name
- Custom tag name
- Object name

action

String specifying the action for which authorization is requested. Do not specify this parameter for

COMPONENT and CUSTOMTAG. For all other resource types, this parameter is required.

resourcetype Specification	Possible ACTIONs
APPLICATION	ALL
	USECLIENTVARIABLES
CFML	Valid actions for the tag specified by resourcename
FILE	READ
	WRITE
DATASOURCE	ALL
	CONNECT
	SELECT
	INSERT
	UPDATE
	DELETE
	SP (stored procedure)
COMPONENT	No actions for this resource type
COLLECTION	DELETE
	OPTIMIZE
	PURGE
	SEARCH
	UPDATE
CUSTOMTAG	No actions for this resource type
USEROBJECT	Action specified via the ColdFusion Administrator

Usage
The `IsProtected` function only returns true if the resource is protected by a rule in the security context or sandbox within which a request is being processed. An application may need to determine if a resource is protected and if the current user is authorized to use the resource. If a resource is not protected, then the `IsAuthorized` function returns true. In order to determine if a resource is explicitly protected with a rule, you must use the `IsProtected` function.

IsQuery

Returns TRUE if *value* is a query.

See also `QueryAddRow`.

Syntax
IsQuery(*value*)

value
Query variable.

IsSimpleValue

Returns TRUE if value is a string, number, Boolean, or date/time value.

Syntax
IsSimpleValue(*value*)

value
Variable or expression.

IsStruct

Returns TRUE if *variable* is a structure.

See also "Structure Functions."

Syntax
IsStruct(*variable*)

variable
Variable name.

JSStringFormat

Returns a string that is safe to use with JavaScript.

Syntax
JSStringFormat(*string*)

string
Any string.

Usage
JSStringFormat escapes special JavaScript characters, such as the single quote ('), double quotes ("), and new-line character so that you can put arbitrary strings safely into JavaScript.

LCase

Returns *string* converted to lowercase.

See also UCase.

Syntax
LCase(*string*)

string
String being converted to lowercase.

Left

Returns the count of characters from the beginning of a string argument.

See also Right, Mid, and Len.

Syntax
Left(*string, count*)

string
String from which the leftmost characters are retrieved.

count
Positive integer indicating how many characters to return.

Len

Returns the length of a string or a binary object.

See also ToBinary, Left, Right, and Mid.

Syntax
Len(*string or binary object*)

string
Any string or binary object.

ListAppend

Returns *list* with *value* appended behind its last element.

See also ListPrepend, ListInsertAt, and ListSetAt.

Syntax
ListAppend(*list, value* [, *delimiters*])

list
Any list.

value
Number or list being appended.

delimiters
Set of delimiters used in list.

Usage
When appending an element into a list, ColdFusion needs to insert a delimiter. If *delimiters* contains more than one delimiter, ColdFusion defaults to the first delimiter in the string, or, (comma) if *delimiters* was omitted.

If you intend to use list functions on strings that are delimited by the conjunction ", " (comma-space), as is common in HTTP header strings such as the COOKIE header, we recommend that you specify *delimiters* to include both comma and space because ColdFusion Server does not skip white space. For example,

```
ListAppend(List, "MyCookie", "," & CHR(32))
```

ListChangeDelims

Returns *list* with all delimiter characters changed to *new_delimiter* string.

See also `ListFirst` and `ListQualify`.

Syntax

`ListChangeDelims(list, new_delimiter [, delimiters ])`

list
List of delimiters being changed.

new_delimiter
String being used as a new delimiter.

delimiters
Set of delimiters used in list.

ListContains

Returns the index of the first item that contains the specified substring. The search is case-sensitive. If the substring is not found in any of the list items, it returns zero (0).

See also `ListContainsNoCase` and `ListFind`.

Syntax

`ListContains(list, substring [, delimiters ])`

list
List being searched.

substring
String being sought in elements of list.

delimiters
Set of delimiters used in list.

ListContainsNoCase

Returns the index of the first element of a list that contains the specified substring within elements. The search is case-insensitive. If no element is found, returns 0.

See also `ListContains` and `ListFindNoCase`.

Syntax

`ListContainsNoCase(list, substring [, delimiters ])`

list
List being searched.

substring
String being sought in elements of list.

delimiters
Set of delimiters used in list.

ListDeleteAt

Returns *list* with element deleted at the specified position.

See also `ListGetAt`, `ListSetAt`, and `ListLen`.

Syntax

`ListDeleteAt(list, position [, delimiters ])`

list
Any list.

position
Positive integer indicating the position of the element being deleted. The starting position in a list is denoted by the number 1, not 0.

delimiters
Set of delimiters used in list.

ListFind

Returns the index of the first occurrence of a value within a list. Returns 0 if no value is found. The search is case-sensitive.

See also `ListContains` and `ListFindNoCase`.

Syntax

`ListFind(list, value [, delimiters ])`

list
List being searched.

value
Number or string that is to be found in the items of the list.

delimiters
Set of delimiters used in the list.

ListFindNoCase

Returns the index of the first occurrence of a value within a list. Returns 0 if no value was found. The search is case-insensitive.

See also `ListContains` and `ListFind`.

Syntax
`ListFindNoCase(list, value [, delimiters ])`

list
List being searched.

value
Number or string being sought among elements of list.

delimiters
Set of delimiters used in list.

ListFirst

Returns the first element of the list.

See also `ListGetAt`, `ListLast`, and `ListQualify`.

Syntax
`ListFirst(list [, delimiters ])`

list
List whose first element is being retrieved.

delimiters
Set of delimiters used in list.

ListGetAt

Returns the element at a given position.

See also `ListFirst`, `ListLast`, `ListQualify`, and `ListSetAt`.

Syntax
`ListGetAt(list, position [, delimiters ])`

list
List whose element is being retrieved.

position
Positive integer indicating the position of the element being retrieved.

delimiters
Set of delimiters used in *list*.

Usage
The first position in a list is denoted by the number 1, not 0.

ListInsertAt

Returns *list* with *value* inserted at the specified position.

See also `ListDeleteAt`, `ListAppend`, `ListPrepend`, and `ListSetAt`.

Syntax
`ListInsertAt(list, position, value [, delimiters ])`

list
Any list.

position
Position where the value is being inserted. The first position in a list is denoted by the number 1, not 0.

value
Number or list being inserted.

delimiters
Set of delimiters used in list.

Usage
When inserting elements into a list, ColdFusion needs to insert a delimiter. If *delimiters* contain more than one delimiter, ColdFusion defaults to the first delimiter in the string, or, (comma) if *delimiters* was omitted.

If you intend to use list functions on strings that are delimited by the conjunction "," (comma-space), as is common in HTTP header strings such as the COOKIE header, we recommend that you specify *delimiters* to include both comma and space because ColdFusion Server does not skip white space.

ListLast

Returns the last element of the list.

See also `ListGetAt` and `ListFirst`.

Syntax
`ListLast(list [, delimiters ])`

list
List whose last element is being retrieved.

delimiters
Set of delimiters used in list.

ListLen

Returns the number of elements in the list.

See also `ListAppend`, `ListDeleteAt`, `ListInsertAt`, and `ListPrepend`.

Syntax
`ListLen(list [, delimiters ])`

list
Any list.

delimiters

Set of delimiters used in list.

ListPrepend

Returns *list* with *value* inserted at the first position, shifting all other elements one to the right.

See also `ListAppend`, `ListInsertAt`, and `ListSetAt`.

Syntax
`ListPrepend(list, value [, delimiters ])`

list

Any list.

value

Number or list being prepended.

delimiters

Set of delimiters used in list.

Usage

When prepending an element to a list, ColdFusion needs to insert a delimiter. If *delimiters* contain more than one delimiter, ColdFusion defaults to the first delimiter in the string, or, (comma) if *delimiters* was omitted.

If you intend to use list functions on strings that are delimited by the conjunction "," (comma-space), as is common in HTTP header strings such as the COOKIE header, we recommend that you specify *delimiters* to include both comma and space because ColdFusion Server does not skip white space.

ListQualify

Returns a list with a qualifying character around each item in the list, such as double or single quotes.

See the `List Functions` table.

Syntax
`ListQualify(list, qualifier [, delimiters ] [, elements ])`

list

Any list of items or a variable that names a list.

qualifier

The character that is to be placed at the beginning and end of each item in the list.

delimiters

Set of delimiters used in *list*.

elements

Either the keyword "ALL" or "CHAR." If you specify "ALL," the function qualifies all items in the list. If you specify "CHAR," the function qualifiers only items comprised of alphabetic characters; it does not qualify numeric items.

Usage

The new list may not preserve all of the delimiters in the previous list.

ListRest

Returns *list* without its first element. Returns an empty list (empty string) if *list* has only one element.

See also `ListFirst`, `ListGetAt`, and `ListLast`.

Syntax
`ListRest(list [, delimiters ])`

list

List whose elements are being retrieved.

delimiters

Set of delimiters used in list.

ListSetAt

Returns *list* with *value* assigned to its element at specified position.

See also `ListDeleteAt`, `ListGetAt`, and `ListInsertAt`.

Syntax
`ListSetAt(list, position, value [, delimiters ])`

list

Any list.

position

Any position. The first position in a list is denoted by the number 1, not 0.

value

Any value.

delimiters

Set of delimiters.

Usage

When assigning an element to a list, ColdFusion needs to insert a delimiter. If *delimiters* contain more than one delimiter, ColdFusion defaults to the first delimiter in the string, or, (comma) if *delimiters* was omitted.

If you intend to use list functions on strings that are delimited by the conjunction ", " (comma-space), as is common in HTTP header strings such as the COOKIE header, we recommend that you specify *delimiters* to include both comma and space because ColdFusion Server does not skip white space.

ListSort

Sorts and delimits the items in a list according to the specified sort type and sort order.

Syntax

`ListSort(list, sort_type [, sort_order]`
`[, delimiter ])`

list

List to be sorted. The items in the list must be separated by commas or otherwise delimited.

sort_type

The type of sort to be executed. You can specify any of the following sort types:

- Numeric—sorts numbers.
- Text—sorts text alphabetically.
- Textnocase—sorts text alphabetically. The case is ignored.

sort_order

The order to be followed. You can specify any of the following:

- Asc—(Default) Ascending sort order.
- Desc—Descending sort order.

delimiter

Specify the character(s) used to delimit elements in the list. Default is comma (,).

ListToArray

Converts the specified list into an array.

See also `ArrayToList`.

Syntax

`ListToArray(list [, delimiter ])`

list

Name of the list variable that contains the elements to be used to build an array. You can define a list variable with a CFSET statement. The items in the list must be separated by commas or otherwise delimited.

delimiter

Specify the character(s) used to delimit elements in the list. Default is comma (,).

ListValueCount

Returns the number of instances of a specified value in a list. The underlying search that finds the instances is case-sensitive.

See also `ListValueCountNoCase`.

Syntax

`ListValueCount(list, value [, delimiters ])`

list

A list or the name of a list that is to be searched.

value

The string or number that the function is to find and count.

delimiter

Optional. Specify the character(s) used to delimit elements in the list. The default is a comma (,).

ListValueCountNoCase

Returns the number of instances of a specified value in a list. The underlying search that finds the instances is not case-sensitive.

See also `ListValueCount`.

Syntax

`ListValueCountNoCase(list, value [,`
`delimiters ])`

list

A list or the name of a list that is to be searched.

value

The string or number that the function is to find and count.

delimiter

Optional. Specify the character(s) used to delimit elements in the list. The default is a comma (,).

LJustify

Returns left-justified *string* of the specified field length.

See also `CJustify` and `RJustify`.

Syntax
LJustify(*string*, *length*)

string
String to be left-justified.

length
Length of field.

Log
Returns the natural logarithm of a number. Natural logarithms are based on the constant e (2.71828182845904).

See also Exp and Log10.

Syntax
Log(*number*)

number
Positive real number for which you want the natural logarithm.

Log10
Returns the logarithm of *number* to base 10.

See also Exp and Log.

Syntax
Log10(*number*)

number
Positive real number for which you want the logarithm.

LSCurrencyFormat
Returns a currency value using the locale convention. Default value is "local."

See, also, LSEuroCurrencyFormat.

Syntax
LSCurrencyFormat(*number* [, *type*])

number
The currency value.

type
Currency type. Valid arguments are:

- none—(For example, 10.00)
- local—(Default. For example, $10.00)
- international—(For example, USD10.00)

Currency Output

The following table shows sample currency output for some of the locales supported by ColdFusion in each of the format types: local, international, and none.

Currency Output by Locale

Locale	Format Type Output
Dutch (Belgian)	Local: 100.000,00 BF
	International: BEF100.000,00
	None: 100.000,00
Dutch (Standard)	Local: fl 100.000,00
	International: NLG100.000,00
	None: 100.000,00
English (Australian)	Local: $100,000.00
	International: AUD100,000.00
	None: 100,000.00
English (Canadian)	Local: $100,000.00
	International: CAD100,000.00
	None: 100,000.00
English (New Zealand)	Local: $100,000.00
	International: NZD100,000.00
	None: 100,000.00
English (UK)	Local: £100,000.00
	International: GBP100,000.00
	None: 100,000.00
English (US)	Local: $100,000.00
	International: USD100,000.00
	None: 100,000.00
French (Belgian)	Local: 100.000,00 FB
	International: BEF100.000,00
	None: 100.000,00
French (Canadian)	Local: 100 000,00 $
	International: CAD100 000,00
	None: 100 000,00
French (Standard)	Local: 100 000,00 F
	International: FRF100 000,00
	None: 100 000,00
French (Swiss)	Local: SFr. 100'000.00

Currency Output by Locale *(continued)*

	International: CHF100'000.00
	None: 100'000.00
German (Austrian)	Local: öS 100.000,00
	International: ATS100.000,00
	None: 100.000,00
German (Standard)	Local: 100.000,00 DM
	International: DEM100.000,00
	None: 100.000,00
German (Swiss)	Local: SFr. 100'000.00
	International: CHF100'000.00
	None: 100'000.00
Italian (Standard)	Local: L. 10.000.000
	International: ITL10.000.000
	None: 10.000.000
Italian (Swiss)	Local: SFr. 100'000.00
	International: CHF100'000.00
	None: 100'000.00
Norwegian (Bokmal)	Local: kr 100 000,00
	International: NOK100 000,00
	None: 100 000,00
Norwegian (Nynorsk)	Local: kr 100 000,00
	International: NOK100 000,00
	None: 100 000,00
Portuguese (Brazilian)	Local: R$100.000,00
	International: BRC100.000,00
	None: 100.000,00
Portuguese (Standard)	Local: R$100.000,00
	International: BRC100.000,00
	None: 100.000,00
Spanish (Mexican)	Local: $100,000.00
	International: MXN100,000.00
	None: 100,000.00

Currency Output by Locale *(continued)*

Spanish (Modern)	Local: 10.000.000 Pts
	International: ESP10.000.000
	None: 10.000.000
Spanish (Standard)	Local: 10.000.000 Pts
	International: ESP10.000.000
	None: 10.000.000
Swedish	Local: 100.000,00 kr
	International: SEK100.000,00
	None: 100.000,00

LSDateFormat

Formats the date portion of a date/time value using the locale convention. Like DateFormat LSDateFormat returns a formatted date/time value. If no mask is specified, LSDateFormat returns a date value using the locale-specific format.

Syntax
`LSDateFormat(date [, mask ])`

date

Date/time object in the period from 100 AD to 9999 AD.

mask

Set of characters that are used to show how ColdFusion should display the date:

- d—Day of the month as digits with no leading zero for single-digit days
- dd—Day of the month as digits with a leading zero for single-digit days
- ddd—Day of the week as a three-letter abbreviation
- dddd—Day of the week as its full name
- m—Month as digits with no leading zero for single-digit months
- mm—Month as digits with a leading zero for single-digit months
- mmm—Month as a three-letter abbreviation
- mmmm—Month as its full name
- y—Year as last two digits with no leading zero for years less than 10
- yy—Year as last two digits with a leading zero for years less than 10
- yyyy—Year represented by four digits

- gg—Period/era string. Currently ignored, but reserved for future use

Usage

When passing date/time value as a string, make sure it is enclosed in quotes. Otherwise, it is interpreted as a number representation of a date/time object returning undesired results.

LSEuroCurrencyFormat

Returns a currency value using the convention of the locale and the Euro as the currency symbol. Default value is "local."

NOTE   The locale is set with the SetLocale function.

See, also, LSParseEuroCurrency, LSCurrencyFormat, and SetLocale.

Syntax

LSEuroCurrencyFormat(*currency-number* [, *type*])

currency-number
The currency value.

type
Currency type. Valid arguments are:

- none—(For example, 10.00)
- local—(Default. For example, 10.00 _)
- international—(For example, EUR10.00)

Usage

The LSEuroCurrencyFormat function can display the Euro symbol (_) only on Euro-enabled computers, such as Windows NT 4.0 SP4, that have Euro-enabled fonts installed.

This function is similar to LSCurrencyFormat except that LSEuroCurrencyFormat displays the Euro currency symbol (_) or the international Euro sign (EUR) if you specify the type as local or international, respectively, and the Euro is the accepted currency of the locale.

Currency Output

The following table shows sample currency output for some of the locales supported by ColdFusion in each of the format types: local, international, and none.

Currency Output by Locale

Locale	Format Type Output
Dutch (Belgian)	Local: 100.000,00 €
	International: EUR100.000,00
	None: 100.000,00
Dutch (Standard)	Local: € 100.000,00
	International: EUR100.000,00
	None: 100.000,00
English (Australian)	Local: €100,000.00
	International: EUR100,000.00
	None: 100,000.00
English (Canadian)	Local: €100,000.00
	International: EUR100,000.00
	None: 100,000.00
English (New Zealand)	Local: €100,000.00
	International: EUR100,000.00
	None: 100,000.00
English (UK)	Local: €100,000.00
	International: EUR100,000.00
	None: 100,000.00
English (US)	Local: €100,000.00
	International: EUR100,000.00
	None: 100,000.00
French (Belgian)	Local: 100.000,00 €
	International: EUR100.000,00
	None: 100.000,00
French (Canadian)	Local: 100 000,00 €
	International: EUR100 000,00
	None: 100 000,00
French (Standard)	Local: 100 000,00 €
	International: EUR100 000,00
	None: 100 000,00

Currency Output by Locale *(continued)*

French (Swiss)	Local: € 100'000.00
	International: EUR100'000.00
	None: 100'000.00
German (Austrian)	Local: € 100.000,00
	International: EUR100.000,00
	None: 100.000,00
German (Standard)	Local: 100.000,00 €
	International: EUR100.000,00
	None: 100.000,00
German (Swiss)	Local: € 100'000.00
	International: EUR100'000.00
	None: 100'000.00
Italian (Standard)	Local: € 10.000.000
	International: EUR10.000.000
	None: 10.000.000
Italian (Swiss)	Local: € 100'000.00
	International: EUR100'000.00
	None: 100'000.00
Norwegian (Bokmal)	Local: € 100 000,00
	International: EUR100 000,00
	None: 100 000,00
Norwegian (Nynorsk)	Local: € 100 000,00
	International: EUR100 000,00
	None: 100 000,00
Portuguese (Brazilian)	Local: €100.000,00
	International: EUR100.000,00
	None: 100.000,00
Portuguese (Standard)	Local: €100.000,00
	International: EUR100.000,00
	None: 100.000,00
Spanish (Mexican)	Local: €100,000.00
	International: EUR100,000.00

Currency Output by Locale *(continued)*

	None: 100,000.00
Spanish (Modern)	Local: 10.000.000 €
	International: EUR10.000.000
	None: 10.000.000
Spanish (Standard)	Local: 10.000.000 €
	International: EUR10.000.000
	None: 10.000.000
Swedish	Local: 100.000,00 €
	International: EUR100.000,00
	None: 100.000,00

LSIsCurrency

Checks whether a string is a locale-specific currency string. Returns TRUE if *string* is a currency string, FALSE otherwise.

Syntax
LSIsCurrency(*string*)

string
The locale-specific currency string.

LSIsDate

Like the IsDate function, LSIsDate returns TRUE if *string* can be converted to a date/time value in the current locale, FALSE otherwise.

Syntax
LSIsDate(*string*)

string
Any string value.

Usage
Years less than 100 are interpreted as 20th century values.

LSIsNumeric

Like the IsNumeric function, LSIsNumeric returns TRUE if *string* can be converted to a number in the current locale; otherwise, FALSE.

Syntax
LSIsNumeric(*string*)

string
Any string value.

LSNumberFormat

Formats a number using the locale convention. If mask is omitted, the number is formatted as an integer.

Syntax
LSNumberFormat(*number* [, *mask*])

number
The number you want to format.

mask
All LSNumberFormat mask characters apply except that ($) dollar, (,) comma, and (.) dot are mapped to their locale-specific counterparts.

LSNumberFormat Mask Characters

Character	Meaning
_ (underscore)	Optional digit placeholder.
9	Optional digit placeholder. Same as _, but shows decimal places more clearly.
.	Specifies the location of a mandatory decimal point.
0	Located to the left or right of a mandatory decimal point, to force padding with zeros.
( )	Places parentheses around the mask if the number is less than 0.
+	Places + in front of positive numbers, - (minus sign) in front of negative numbers.
-	Place " " (space) in front of positive, - (minus sign) in front of negative numbers.
,	Separates thousands with commas.
L,C	Specifies left-justify or center-justify a number within the width of the mask column. L or C must appear as the first character of the mask. By default, numbers are right-justified.
$	Places a dollar sign in front of the formatted number. $ must appear as the first character of the mask.
^	Separates left from right formatting.

NOTE   If you do not specify a sign for the mask, positive and negative numbers will not align in columns. As a result, if you expect to display both positive and negative numbers in your application, use either the space or use a hyphen (–) to force a space in front of positive numbers and a minus sign in front of negative numbers.

Usage

The position of codes in format masks determines where those codes will have effect. For example, if you place a dollar sign character at the far left of a format mask, ColdFusion displays a dollar sign at the very left edge of the formatted number. If you separate the dollar sign on the left edge of the format mask by at least one underscore, ColdFusion displays the dollar sign just to the left of the digits in the formatted number.

In all examples below, the numbers under the masks and the formatted output are used to clearly show the positions of characters.

Number	Mask	Result
4.37	$____.__	"$ 4.37"
4.37	_$____.__	" $4.37"
	12345678	12345678

This positioning idea can also be used to show where to place the - (minus sign) for negative numbers.

Number	Mask	Result
-4.37	-____.__	"- 4.37"
-4.37	_-____.__	" -4.37"
	12345678	12345678

There are four possible positions for any code character: far left, near left, near right, and far right. The left and right positions are determined by the side of the decimal point the code character is shown on. For formats that do not have a fixed number of decimal places, you can use a ^ (caret) to separate the left fields from the right.

Whether the code is placed in the far or near position is determined by the use of _ (underscore). Most code characters will have their effect determined by which of these of fields they are located in. The following example shows how to use the field to determine exactly where to place parentheses to display negative numbers:

Number	Mask	Result
3.21	C(__^__)	"(3.21)"
3.21	C__(^__)	" (3.21)"
3.21	C(__^)__	"(3.21) "
3.21	C__(^)__	" (3.21) "
	12345678	12345678

LSParseCurrency

Converts a locale-specific currency string to a number. Attempts conversion through each of the three default currency formats (none, local, international). Returns the number matching the value of *string*.

See, also, LSCurrencyFormat and LSParseEuroCurrency.

Syntax
LSParseCurrency(*string*)

string
The locale-specific string you want to convert to a number.

Currency Output

The following table shows sample currency output for some of the locales supported by ColdFusion in each of the format types: local, international, and none.

Currency Output by Locale

Locale	Format Type Output
Dutch (Belgian)	Local: 100.000,00 BF
	International: BEF100.000,00
	None: 100.000,00
Dutch (Standard)	Local: fl 100.000,00
	International: NLG100.000,00
	None: 100.000,00
English (Australian)	Local: $100,000.00
	International: AUD100,000.00
	None: 100,000.00
English (Canadian)	Local: $100,000.00
	International: CAD100,000.00
	None: 100,000.00

Currency Output by Locale *(continued)*

English (New Zealand)	Local: $100,000.00
	International: NZD100,000.00
	None: 100,000.00
English (UK)	Local: £100,000.00
	International: GBP100,000.00
	None: 100,000.00
English (US)	Local: $100,000.00
	International: USD100,000.00
	None: 100,000.00
French (Belgian)	Local: 100.000,00 FB
	International: BEF100.000,00
	None: 100.000,00
French (Canadian)	Local: 100 000,00 $
	International: CAD100 000,00
	None: 100 000,00
French (Standard)	Local: 100 000,00 F
	International: FRF100 000,00
	None: 100 000,00
French (Swiss)	Local: SFr. 100'000.00
	International: CHF100'000.00
	None: 100'000.00
German (Austrian)	Local: öS 100.000,00
	International: ATS100.000,00
	None: 100.000,00
German (Standard)	Local: 100.000,00 DM
	International: DEM100.000,00
	None: 100.000,00
German (Swiss)	Local: SFr. 100'000.00
	International: CHF100'000.00
	None: 100'000.00
Italian (Standard)	Local: L. 10.000.000
	International: ITL10.000.000
	None: 10.000.000
Italian (Swiss)	Local: SFr. 100'000.00
	International: CHF100'000.00
	None: 100'000.00

Currency Output by Locale *(continued)*

Norwegian (Bokmal)	Local: kr 100 000,00
	International: NOK100 000,00
	None: 100 000,00
Norwegian (Nynorsk)	Local: kr 100 000,00
	International: NOK100 000,00
	None: 100 000,00
Portuguese (Brazilian)	Local: R$100.000,00
	International: BRC100.000,00
	None: 100.000,00
Portuguese (Standard)	Local: R$100.000,00
	International: BRC100.000,00
	None: 100.000,00
Spanish (Mexican)	Local: $100,000.00
	International: MXN100,000.00
	None: 100,000.00
Spanish (Modern)	Local: 10.000.000 Pts
	International: ESP10.000.000
	None: 10.000.000
Spanish (Standard)	Local: 10.000.000 Pts
	International: ESP10.000.000
	None: 10.000.000
Swedish	Local: 100.000,00 kr
	International: SEK100.000,00
	None: 100.000,00

LSParseDateTime

A locale-specific version of the ParseDateTime function, except that there is no option for POP date/time object parsing. Returns a date/time object.

See also ParseDateTime and SetLocale.

Syntax

LSParseDateTime(*date-time-string*)

date-time-string

String being converted to date/time object. This string must be in a form that is readable in the current locale setting. By default the locale is set to English (US).

Usage

When passing a date/time value for the English (US) locale, the date-time string can be in any of the following forms in this table.

Date-Time Formats for the English (US) Locale

Date-Time Composition	Example
dd mmmm yyyy	"25 January 1999"
hh:mm:ss	"8:30:00"
hh:mm:ss	"20:30:00"
mmmm dd, yyyy hh:mm:ss	"January 25, 1999 8:30:00"
hh:mm:ss mmm. dd, yyyy	"8:30:00 Jan. 25, 1999"
m/dd/yyyy hh:mm:ss	"1/25/1999 8:30:00"

Note that if you specify a year in the date, you should specify the full year.

If the date is formatted for a locale other than the English (US) locale, add or subtract the conversion time, depending on the locale. LSParseDateTime does not accept POP dates, nor does it have the capacity to convert dates to Greenwich Mean Time.

Years from 0 to 29 are interpreted as 21st century values. Years 30 to 99 are interpreted as 20th century values.

LSParseEuroCurrency

Converts a locale-specific currency string that contains the Euro symbol (_) or sign (EUR) to a number. Attempts conversion through each of the three default currency formats (none, local, international). Returns the number matching the value of *string*.

See, also, LSParseCurrency, LSEuroCurrencyFormat and SetLocale.

Syntax

LSParseEuroCurrency(*currency-string*)

currency-string

The locale-specific string you want to convert to a number.

Usage

The LSParseEuroCurrency function can read the Euro symbol (€) only on Euro-enabled computers, such as Windows NT 4.0 SP4, that have Euro-enabled fonts installed.

This function is similar to LSParseCurrency except that LSParseEuroCurrency parses only the Euro currency symbol (€) or the international Euro sign (EUR), not other currency symbols such as the dollar sign ($) or the pound sign (£).

LSParseNumber

Converts a locale-specific string to a number. Returns the number matching the value of *string*.

Syntax
LSParseNumber(*string*)

string
String being converted to a number.

LSTimeFormat

Returns a custom-formatted time value using the locale convention.

See also LSParseDateTime.

Syntax
LSTimeFormat(*time* [, *mask*])

string
Any date/time value or string convertible to a time value.

mask
A set of masking characters determining the format:

- h—Hours with no leading zero for single-digit hours. (Uses a 12-hour clock.)
- hh—Hours with a leading zero for single-digit hours. (Uses a 12-hour clock.)
- H—Hours with no leading zero for single-digit hours. (Uses a 24-hour clock.)
- HH—Hours with a leading zero for single-digit hours. (Uses a 24-hour clock.)
- m—Minutes with no leading zero for single-digit minutes.
- mm—Minutes with a leading zero for single-digit minutes.
- s—Seconds with no leading zero for single-digit seconds.
- ss—Seconds with a leading zero for single-digit seconds.
- t—Single-character time marker string, such as A or P. Ignored by some locales.
- tt—Multiple-character time marker string, such as AM or PM

Usage
When passing date/time value as a string, make sure it is enclosed in quotes. Otherwise, it is interpreted as a number representation of a date/time object returning undesired results.

LTrim

Returns *string* with leading spaces removed.

See also RTrim and ToBase64.

Syntax
LTrim(*string*)

string
String being left-trimmed.

Max

Returns the maximum, or higher, value of two numbers.

See also Min.

Syntax
Max(*number1*, *number2*)

number1, number2
Any numbers.

Mid

Returns *count* characters from *string* beginning at *start* position.

See also Left, Len, and Right.

Syntax
Mid(*string*, *start*, *count*)

string
Any string.

start
Starting position for count.

count
Number of characters being returned.

Min

Returns the minimum, or smaller, value of two numbers.

See also Max.

Syntax
Min(*number1*, *number2*)

number1, number2
Any numbers.

Minute

Returns the ordinal for the minute, ranging from 0 to 59.

See also DatePart, Hour, and Second.

Syntax
Minute(*date*)

date

Any date.

Usage
Years from 0 to 29 are interpreted as 21st century }values. Years 30 to 99 are interpreted as 20th century values.

When passing a date/time value as a string, make sure it is enclosed in quotes. Otherwise, it is interpreted as a number representation of a date/time object, returning undesired results.

Month
Returns the ordinal for the month, ranging from 1 (January) to 12 (December).

See also DatePart, MonthAsString, and Quarter.

Syntax
Month(*Date*)

date

Any date.

Usage
Years from 0 to 29 are interpreted as 21st century values. Years 30 to 99 are interpreted as 20th century values.

When passing a date/time value as a string, make sure it is enclosed in quotes. Otherwise, it is interpreted as a number representation of a date/time object, returning undesired results.

MonthAsString
Returns the name of the month corresponding to *month_number*.

See also DatePart, Month, and Quarter.

Syntax
MonthAsString(*month_number*)

month_number

An integer ranging from 1 to 12.

Now
Returns the current date and time as a valid date time object.

See also CreateDateTime and DatePart.

Syntax
Now()

NumberFormat
Creates a custom-formatted number value. If no mask is specified, returns the value as an integer with a thousands separator.

See also DecimalFormat, DollarFormat, and IsNumeric.

Syntax
NumberFormat(*number* [, *mask*])

number

The number you want to format.

mask

Set of characters that are used to show how ColdFusion should display the number.

Mask Characters

Character	Meaning
_ (underscore)	Optional digit placeholder.
9	Optional digit placeholder. Same as _, but shows decimal places more clearly.
.	Specifies the location of a mandatory decimal point.
0	Located to the left or right of a mandatory decimal point, to force padding with zeros.
( )	Places parentheses around the mask if the number is less than 0.
+	Places + in front of positive numbers, - (minus sign) in front of negative numbers.
-	Place " " (space) in front of positive, - (minus sign) in front of negative numbers.
,	Separates thousands with commas.
L,C	Specifies left-justify or center-justify a number within the width of the mask column. L or C must appear as the first character of the mask. By default, numbers are right-justified.
$	Places a dollar sign in front of the formatted number. $ must appear as the first character of the mask.
^	Separates left from right formatting.

NOTE If you do not specify a sign for the mask, positive and negative numbers will not align in columns. As a result, if you expect to display both positive and negative numbers in your application, use either the space or use a minus sign (–) to force a space in front of positive numbers and a minus sign in front of negative numbers.

Usage

The position of codes in format masks determines where those codes will have effect. For example, if you place a dollar sign character at the far left of a format mask, ColdFusion displays a dollar sign at the very left edge of the formatted number. If you separate the dollar sign on the left edge of the format mask by at least one underscore, ColdFusion displays the dollar sign just to the left of the digits in the formatted number.

In all examples below, the numbers under the masks and the formatted output are used to clearly show the positions of characters.

Number	Mask	Result
4.37	$___.__	"$ 4.37"
4.37	_$___.__	" $4.37"
	12345678	12345678

This positioning idea can also be used to show where to place the - (minus sign) for negative numbers:

Number	Mask	Result
-4.37	-___.__	"- 4.37"
-4.37	_-___.__	" -4.37"
	12345678	12345678

There are four possible positions for any code character: far left, near left, near right, and far right. The left and right positions are determined by the side of the decimal point the code character is shown on. For formats that do not have a fixed number of decimal places, you can use a ^ (caret) to separate the left fields from the right.

Whether the code is placed in the far or near position is determined by the use of _ (underscore). Most code characters will have their effect determined by which of these of fields they are located in. The following

example shows how to use the field to determine exactly where to place parentheses to display negative numbers:

Number	Mask	Result
3.21	C(__^__)	"(3.21)"
3.21	C__(^__)	" (3.21)"
3.21	C(__^)__	"(3.21) "
3.21	C__(^)__	" (3.21) "
	12345678	12345678

ParagraphFormat

Returns *string* with converted single newline characters (CR/LF sequences) into spaces and double newline characters into HTML paragraph markers (<P>).

See also StripCR.

Syntax
ParagraphFormat(*string*)

string
String being converted to the HTML paragraph format.

Usage
ParagraphFormat is useful for displaying data entered into TEXTAREA fields.

ParameterExists

Returns True if the specified parameter has been passed to the current template or has already been created during execution of the current template. Otherwise returns NO.

This function is provided for backward compatibility with previous versions of ColdFusion. You should use the function IsDefined instead.

See also GetClientVariablesList and IsDefined.

Syntax
ParameterExists(*parameter*)

parameter
Any syntactically valid parameter name.

ParseDateTime

Returns a date/time object from a string.

See also LSParseDateTime, IsDate and IsNumeric-Date.

Syntax

`ParseDateTime(date-time-string [, pop-conversion ] )`

date-time-string

String being converted to date/time object.

pop-conversion

POP or STANDARD. If you specify POP, the function takes the date/time string passed from a POP mail server and converts it to GMT (Greenwich Mean Time) for the English (US) locale. If you specify STANDARD or nothing, the function provides no conversion. See the Note for more information about parsing date-time strings that are not from the English (US) locale.

Usage

ParseDateTime is similar to CreateDateTime except that it takes a string instead of specifically enumerated date/time values.

Both ParseDateTime and CreateDateTime are provided primarily to increase the readability of code in compound expressions.

Years from 0 to 29 are interpreted as 21st century values. Years 30 to 99 are interpreted as 20th century values.

When passing a date/time value as a string, make sure it is enclosed in quotes. Otherwise, it is interpreted as a number representation of a date/time object, returning undesired results.

NOTE If the date is formatted for a locale other than the English (US) locale, you need to use the `LSParseDateTime()` function, then add or subtract the conversion time, depending on the locale. `LSParseDateTime` does not accept POP dates, nor does it have the capacity to convert dates to Greenwich Mean Time.

Pi

Returns the number 3.14159265358979, the mathematical constant , accurate to 15 digits.

See also `ASin`, `Cos`, `Sin`, and `Tan`.

Syntax

`Pi()`

PreserveSingleQuotes

Prevents ColdFusion from automatically "escaping" single quotes contained in *variable*.

Syntax

`PreserveSingleQuotes(variable)`

variable

Variable containing the string for which single quotes are preserved.

Usage

PreserveSingleQuotes is useful in SQL statements.

Quarter

Returns the number of the quarter, an integer ranging from 1 to 4.

See also `DatePart` and `Month`.

Syntax

`Quarter(date)`

date

Any date.

Usage

Years from 0 to 29 are interpreted as 21st century values. Years 30 to 99 are interpreted as 20th century values.

When passing a date/time value as a string, make sure it is enclosed in quotes. Otherwise, it is interpreted as a number representation of a date/time object, returning undesired results.

QueryAddColumn

Adds a new column to a specified query and populates the column's rows with the contents of a one-dimensional array. Returns the query object with the additional column. Padding is added, if necessary, on the query columns to ensure that all columns have the same number of rows.

See also `CFQUERY`, `QueryNew`, `QueryAddRow`, and `QuerySetCell`.

Syntax

`QueryAddColumn(query, column-name, array-name)`

query

Name of a query that was created with QueryNew.

column-name

The name of the new column.

array-name

The name of the array whose elements are to populate the new column.

Usage

You can add columns to any type of query object, such as queries retrieved with CFQUERY or queries created with QueryNew. The only type of query that you cannot use QueryAddColumn on is a cached query.

This function is particularly useful if you are an Oracle developer and would like to generate a query object from the arrays of output parameters which Oracle stored procedures can generate. Padding is added, if necessary, on the query columns to ensure that all columns have the same number of rows.

QueryAddRow

Adds a specified number of empty rows to the specified query. Returns the total number of rows in the query that you are adding rows to.

See also `QueryNew`, `QueryAddColumn` and `QuerySetCell`.

Syntax

`QueryAddRow(query [, number ])`

query
Name of the query already executed.

number
Number of rows to add to the query. Default is 1.

QueryNew

Returns an empty query with a set of columns or an empty query with no columns. See Usage for more information.

See also `QueryAddColumn`, `QueryAddRow`, and `QuerySetCell`.

Syntax

`QueryNew(columnlist)`

columnlist
Comma-separated list of columns you want to add to the new query or an empty string.

Usage

If you specify an empty string, you can add a new column to the query and populate its rows with the contents of a one-dimensional array using QueryAddColumn.

QuerySetCell

Sets the cell in a specified column to a specified value. If no row number is specified, the cell on the last row will be set. Returns TRUE.

See also `QueryAddColumn` and `QueryAddRow`.

Syntax

`QuerySetCell(query, column_name, value [, row_number ])`

query
Name of the query already executed.

column_name
Name of the column in the query.

value
Value to set in the specified cell.

row_number
Number of the row. Defaults to last row.

QuotedValueList

Returns a comma-separated list of the values of each record returned from a previously executed query. Each value in the list is enclosed in single quotes.

See also `ValueList`.

Syntax

`QuotedValueList(query.column [, delimiter ])`

query.column
Name of an already executed query and column. Separate query name and column name with a period (.).

delimiter
A string delimiter to separate column data.

Rand

Returns a random decimal number in the range 0 to 1.

See also `Randomize` and `RandRange`.

Syntax

`Rand()`

Usage

To ensure even greater randomness, call `Randomize` before calling Rand.

Randomize

Seeds the random number generator in ColdFusion with the integer part of a *number*. By seeding the random number generator with a variable value, you help to ensure that the Rand function generates highly random numbers.

See also Rand and RandRange.

Syntax

Randomize(*number*)

number

Any number.

Usage

Call this function before calling Rand. Although this function returns a decimal number in the range 0 to 1, it is not a random number and you should not use it.

RandRange

Returns a random integer between two specified numbers. Note that requests for random integers greater than 100,000,000 will result in non-random behavior. This restriction prevents overflow during internal computations.

See also Rand and Randomize.

Syntax

RandRange(*number1*, *number2*)

number1, number2

Integer numbers less than 100,000,000.

REFind

Returns the position of the first occurrence of a regular expression in a string starting from the specified position. Returns 0 if no occurrences are found. This search is case sensitive.

Returns the position and length of the first occurrence of a regular expression in a string if the *returnsubexpressions* parameter is set to True. See the description of the *returnsubexpressions* parameter and the "Usage" section for details.

See also Find, REFindNoCase, and REReplace.

Syntax

REFind(*reg_expression*, *string* [, *start*]
    [, *returnsubexpressions*])

reg_expression

Regular expression used for search. This regular expression can include POSIX-specified character classes (for example, [[:alpha:]], [[:digit:]], [[:upper:]], and [[:lower:]]).

string

String being searched.

start

Optional. Starting position for the search. Default is 1.

returnsubexpressions

Optional. A Boolean value indicating whether a substring is returned. If you set this parameter to TRUE, the function returns a CFML structure composed of two arrays containing the position and length of the first substring that matches the criteria of the search. You can retrieve the position and length of the matching subexpression by using the keys "pos" and "len." If there are no occurrences of the regular expression, the "pos" and the "len" arrays each contain one element that has a value of zero. If you set this parameter to FALSE, a scalar value is returned indicating the position of the first occurrence of a regular expression. The default value of this parameter is FALSE.

Usage

In order to find multiple instances of a substring, you must call REFind more than once, each time with a different starting position. To determine the next starting position for the function, use the *returnsubexpressions* parameter and add the value returned in the position key to the value in the length key.

If you do not use parentheses in the regular expression, the *returnsubexpressions* parameter returns single element arrays that denote the position and length of the first match found in the string.

If you do use parentheses to denote subexpressions within the regular expression, the *returnsubexpressions* parameter returns the position and length of the first match of the regular expression in the first element of the respective arrays; the position and length of the first instance of each subexpression within the regular expression are returned in subsequent elements of the arrays.

REFindNoCase

Returns the position of the first occurrence of a regular expression in a string starting from the specified position if the *returnsubexpressions* parameter is not set to True. Returns 0 if no occurrences are found. The search is case-insensitive.

Returns the position and length of the first occurrence of a regular expression in a string if the *returnsubexpressions* parameter is set to True. See the description of the *returnsubexpressions* parameter and the "Usage" section for details.

See also Find, FindNoCase, REReplace, and REReplaceNoCase.

Syntax

REFindNoCase(*reg_expression, string* [, *start*] [, *returnsubexpressions*] **)**

reg_expression
Regular expression used for search. This regular expression can include POSIX-specified character classes (for example, [[:alpha:]], [[:digit:]], [[:upper:]], and [[:lower:]]).

string
String being searched.

start
Optional. Starting position for the search. Default is 1.

returnsubexpressions
Optional. A Boolean value indicating whether a substring is returned. If you set this parameter to TRUE, the function returns a CFML structure composed of two single-element arrays containing the position and length of the first substring that matches the criteria of the search. You can retrieve the position and length of the matching subexpression by using the keys "pos" and "len." If there are no occurrences of the regular expression, the "pos" and the "len" arrays each contain one element that has a value of zero. If you set this parameter to FALSE, a scalar value is returned indicating the position of the first occurrence of a regular expression. The default value of this parameter is FALSE.

Usage

In order to find multiple instances of a substring, you must call REFind more than once, each time with a different starting position. To determine the next starting position for the function, use the *returnsubexpressions* parameter and add the value returned in the position key to the value in the length key.

If you do not use parentheses in the regular expression, the *returnsubexpressions* parameter returns single element arrays that denote the position and length of the first match found in the string.

If you do use parentheses to denote subexpressions within the regular expression, the *returnsubexpressions* parameter returns the position and length of the first match of the regular expression in the first element of the respective arrays; the position and length of the

first instance of each subexpression within the regular expression are returned in subsequent elements of the arrays.

RemoveChars

Returns *string* with *count* characters removed from the specified starting position. Return 0 if no characters are found.

See also Insert and Len.

Syntax

RemoveChars(*string, start, count* **)**

string
Any string.

start
Starting position for the search.

count
Number of characters being removed.

RepeatString

Returns a string created from *string* being repeated a specified number of times.

See also CJustify, LJustify, and RJustify.

Syntax

RepeatString(*string, count* **)**

string
String being repeated.

count
Number of repeats.

Replace

Returns *string* with occurrences of *substring1* being replaced with *substring2* in the specified scope.

See also Find, ReplaceNoCase, ReplaceList, and REReplace.

Syntax

Replace(*string, substring1, substring2* [, *scope*] **)**

string
Any string.

substring1
String to be replaced.

substring2
String that should replace occurrences of substring1.

scope

Defines how to complete the replace operation:

- ONE—Replace only the first occurrence (default).
- ALL—Replace all occurrences.

ReplaceList

Returns *string* with all occurrences of the elements from the specified comma-delimited list being replaced with their corresponding elements from another comma-delimited list. The search is case-sensitive.

See also Find, Replace, and REReplace.

Syntax

ReplaceList(*string*, *list1*, *list2*)

string

Any string.

list1

Comma-delimited list of substrings to be replaced.

list2

Comma-delimited list of replace substrings.

Usage

Note that the list of substrings to be replaced is processed one after another. In this way you may experience recursive replacement if one of your *list1* elements is contained in *list2* elements. The second example listed below demonstrates such replacement.

ReplaceNoCase

Returns *string* with occurrences of *substring1* being replaced regardless of case matching with *substring2* in the specified scope.

See also Find, Replace, ReplaceList, and REReplace.

Syntax

ReplaceNoCase(*string*, *substring1*, *substring2* [, *scope*])

string

Any string.

substring1

String to be replaced.

substring2

String that should replace occurrences of substring1.

scope

Defines how to complete the replace operation:

- ONE—Replace only the first occurrence (default).

- ALL—Replace all occurrences.

REReplace

Returns *string* with a regular expression being replaced with *substring* in the specified scope. This is a case-sensitive search.

See also REFind, Replace, ReplaceList, and REReplaceNoCase.

Syntax

REReplace(*string*, *reg_expression*, *substring* [, *scope*])

string

Any string.

reg_expression

Regular expression to be replaced. This regular expression can include POSIX-specified character classes (for example, [:alpha:], [:digit:], [:upper:], and [:lower:]).

substring

String replacing reg_expression.

scope

Defines how to complete the replace operation:

- ONE—Replace only the first occurrence (default).
- ALL—Replace all occurrences.

REReplaceNoCase

Returns *string* with a regular expression being replaced with *substring* in the specified scope. The search is case-insensitive.

See also REFind, REFindNoCase, Replace, and ReplaceList.

Syntax

REReplaceNoCase(*string*, *reg_expression*, *substring* [, *scope*])

string

Any string.

reg_expression

Regular expression to be replaced. This regular expression can include POSIX-specified character classes (for example, [:alpha:], [:digit:], [:upper:], and [:lower:]).

substring

String replacing *reg_expression*.

scope

Defines how to complete the replace operation:

- ONE—Replace only the first occurrence (default).
- ALL—Replace all occurrences.

Reverse

Returns *string* with reversed order of characters.

See also Left, Mid, and Right.

Syntax
Reverse(*string*)

string
String being reversed.

Right

Returns the rightmost *count* characters of a string.

See also Left, Len, and Mid.

Syntax
Right(*string*, *count*)

string
String from which the rightmost characters are retrieved.

count
Integer indicating how many characters to return.

RJustify

Returns right-justified *string* in the specified field length.

See also CJustify and LJustify.

Syntax
RJustify(*string*, *length*)

string
String to be right-justified.

length
Length of field.

Round

Rounds a number to the closest integer.

See also Ceiling, Fix, and Int.

Syntax
Round(*number*)

number
Number being rounded.

RTrim

Returns *string* with removed trailing spaces.

See also LTrim and Trim.

Syntax
RTrim(*string*)

string
String being right-trimmed.

Second

For a date/time value, returns the ordinal for the second, an integer from 0 to 59.

See also DatePart, Hour, and Minute.

Syntax
Second(*date*)

date
Any date.

Usage
When passing a date/time value as a string, make sure it is enclosed in quotes. Otherwise, it is interpreted as a number representation of a date/time object, returning undesired results.

SetLocale

Sets the locale to the specified new locale for the current session.

> **NOTE** SetLocale returns the old locale in case it needs to be restored.

See also GetLocale.

Syntax
SetLocale(*new_locale*)

new_locale
The name of the locale you want to set.

Locale Support

ColdFusion can be expected to support the following locales in a default Windows NT installation:

Dutch (Belgian)
Dutch (Standard)
English (Australian)
English (Canadian)
English (New Zealand)
English (UK)
English (US)
French (Canadian)
French (Standard)
French (Swiss)

German (Austrian)
German (Standard)
German (Swiss)
Italian (Standard)
Norwegian (Bokmal)
Norwegian (Nynorsk)
Portuguese (Brazilian)
Portuguese (Standard)
Spanish (Mexican)
Spanish (Modern)
Spanish (Standard)
Swedish

NOTE   The variable Server.ColdFusion.SupportedLocales is initialized at startup with a comma-delimited list of the locales that ColdFusion and the operating system support. `GetLocale` ( ) will return an entry from that list. `SetLocale` will fail if called with a locale name not on that list.

SetProfileString

Sets the value of a profile entry in an initialization file. This function returns an empty string if the operation succeeds or an error message if the operation fails.

See also `GetProfileString`.

Syntax
`SetProfileString(iniPath, section, entry, value)`

iniPath
Fully qualified path (drive, directory, filename, and extension) of the initialization file.

section
The section of the initialization file in which the entry is to be set.

entry
The name of the entry that is to be set.

value
The value to which to set the entry.

SetVariable

The function sets the variable specified by *name* to *value* and returns the new value of the variable.

See also `DeleteClientVariable` and `GetClient-VariablesList`.

Syntax
`SetVariable(name, value)`

name
Valid variable name.

value
String or number assigned to the variable.

Usage
When setting client variables, it is required that the client variable exists prior to the using of this function and the ClientManagement attribute of CFAPPLICATION tag has been set to "Yes" for this template.

Sgn

Determines the sign of a number. Returns 1 if *number* is positive; 0 if *number* is 0; and -1 if *number* is negative.

See also `Abs`.

Syntax
`Sgn(number)`

number
Any number.

Sin

Returns the sine of the given angle.

See also `ASin`, `Atn`, `Cos`, `Pi`, and `Tan`.

Syntax
`Sin(number)`

number
Angle in radians for which you want the sine. If the angle is in degrees, multiply it by PI()/180 to convert it to radians.

SpanExcluding

Returns all characters from *string* from its beginning until it reaches a character from the *set* of characters. The search is case-sensitive.

See also `GetToken` and `SpanIncluding`.

Syntax
`SpanExcluding(string, set)`

string
Any string.

set
String containing one or more characters being sought.

SpanIncluding

Returns all characters from *string* from its beginning until it reaches a character that is not included in the specified *set* of characters. The search is case-sensitive.

See also GetToken and SpanExcluding.

Syntax
SpanIncluding(*string*, *set*)

string
Any string.

set
String containing one or more characters being sought.

Sqr

Returns a positive square root.

See also Abs.

Syntax
Sqr(*number*)

number
Number for which you want the square root.

Usage
Number must be greater than or equal to 0.

StripCR

Returns *string* with all carriage return characters removed.

See also ParagraphFormat.

Syntax
StripCR(*string*)

string
String being formatted.

Usage
Function StripCR is useful for preformatted HTML display of data (PRE) entered into TEXTAREA fields.

StructClear

Removes all data from the specified structure. Always returns Yes.

See also StructDelete, StructFind, StructInsert, StructIsEmpty, StructKeyArray, StructCount, StructKeyArray, and StructUpdate.

Syntax
StructClear(*structure*)

structure
Structure to be cleared.

StructCopy

Returns a new structure with all the keys and values of the specified structure.

See also StructClear, StructDelete, StructFind, StructInsert, StructIsEmpty, StructKeyArray, StructKeyArray, and StructUpdate.

Syntax
StructCopy(*structure*)

structure
Structure to be copied.

Usage
This function throws an exception if *structure* does not exist.

StructCount

Returns the number of keys in the specified structure.

See also StructClear, StructDelete, StructFind, StructInsert, StructIsEmpty, StructKeyArray, StructKeyArray, and StructUpdate.

Syntax
StructCount(*structure*)

structure
Structure to be accessed.

Usage
This function throws an exception if *structure* does not exist.

StructDelete

Removes the specified item from the specified structure.

See also StructClear, StructFind, StructInsert, StructIsEmpty, StructKeyArray, StructCount, StructKeyArray, and StructUpdate.

Syntax
StructDelete(*structure*, *key* [, *indicatenotexisting*])

structure
Structure containing the item to be removed.

key
Item to be removed.

indicatenotexisting

Indicates whether the function returns FALSE if *key* does not exist. The default is FALSE, which means that the function returns Yes regardless of whether *key* exists. If you specify TRUE for this parameter, the function returns Yes if *key* exists and No if it does not.

StructFind

Returns the value associated with the specified key in the specified structure.

See also StructClear, StructDelete, StructInsert, StructIsEmpty, StructKeyArray, StructCount, StructKeyArray, and StructUpdate.

Syntax

StructFind(*structure*, *key***)**

structure

Structure containing the value to be returned.

key

Key whose value is returned.

Usage

This function throws an exception if *structure* does not exist.

StructInsert

Inserts the specified key-value pair into the specified structure. Returns Yes if the insert was successful and No if an error occurs.

See also StructClear, StructDelete, StructFind, StructIsEmpty, StructKeyArray, StructCount, StructKeyArray, and StructUpdate.

Syntax

StructInsert(*structure*, *key*, *value* [, *allowoverwrite*]***)**

structure

Structure to contain the new key-value pair.

key

Key that contains the inserted value.

value

Value to be added.

allowoverwrite

Optionally indicates whether to allow overwriting an existing key. The default is FALSE.

Usage

This function throws an exception if *structure* does not exist or if *key* exists and *allowoverwrite* is set to FALSE.

StructIsEmpty

Indicates whether the specified structure contains data. Returns TRUE if *structure* is empty and FALSE if it contains data.

See also StructClear, StructDelete, StructFind, StructInsert, StructKeyArray, StructCount, StructKeyArray, and StructUpdate.

Syntax

StructIsEmpty(*structure***)**

structure

Structure to be tested.

Usage

This function throws an exception if *structure* does not exist.

StructKeyArray

Returns an array of the keys in the specified Cold-Fusion structure.

See also StructClear, StructDelete, StructFind, StructInsert, StructIsEmpty, StructKeyList, StructKeyExists, StructCount, and StructUpdate.

Syntax

StructKeyArray(*structure***)**

structure

Structure from which the list of keys is to be extracted.

Usage

The array of keys returned by StructKeyArray is not in any particular order. In order to sort keys alphabetically or numerically, use ArraySort.

Note that this function throws an exception if *structure* does not exist.

StructKeyExists

Returns TRUE if the specified key is in the specified structure and FALSE if it is not.

See also StructClear, StructDelete, StructFind, StructInsert, StructIsEmpty, StructCount, StructKeyArray, and StructUpdate.

Syntax

StructKeyExists(*structure*, *key***)**

structure
Structure to be tested.

key
Key to be tested.

Usage

This function throws an exception if *structure* does not exist.

StructKeyList

Returns the list of keys that are in the specified Cold-Fusion structure.

See also `StructKeyArray`, `StructClear`, `Struct-Delete`, `StructFind`, `StructInsert`, `StructIsEmpty`, `StructCount`, and `StructUpdate`.

Syntax

`StructKeyList(structure, [delimiter])`

structure
Structure from which the list of keys are to be extracted.

delimiter
Optional. The value of this parameter indicates the character that will separate the keys in the list. By default, a comma (,) is used.

Usage

The list of keys returned by `StructKeyList` is not in any particular order. In order to sort keys alphabetically or numerically, use `ListSort`.

Note that this function throws an exception if *structure* does not exist.

StructNew

Returns a new structure.

See also `StructClear`, `StructDelete`, `StructFind`, `StructInsert`, `StructIsEmpty`, `StructKeyArray`, `StructCount`, and `StructUpdate`.

Syntax

`StructNew()`

StructUpdate

Updates the specified key with the specified value. Returns Yes if the function is successful and throws an exception if an error occurs.

See also `StructClear`, `StructDelete`, `StructFind`, `StructInsert`, `StructIsEmpty`, `StructKeyArray`, `StructCount`, and `StructKeyArray`.

Syntax

`StructUpdate(structure, key, value)`

structure
Structure to be updated.

key
Key whose value is updated.

value
New value.

Usage

This function throws an exception if *structure* does not exist.

Tan

Returns the tangent of a given angle.

See also `Atn`, `ASin`, `Cos`, `Sin`, and `Pi`.

Syntax

`Tan(number)`

number
Angle in radians for which you want the tangent. If the angle is in degrees, multiply it by PI()/180 to convert it to radians.

TimeFormat

Returns a custom-formatted time value. If no mask is specified, the TimeFormat function returns time value using the *hh:mm tt* format.

See also `CreateTime`, `Now`, and `ParseDateTime`.

Syntax

`TimeFormat(time [, mask ])`

time
Any date/time value or string convertible to a time value.

mask
A set of masking characters determining the format:

- h—Hours with no leading zero for single-digit hours. (Uses a 12-hour clock.)
- hh—Hours with a leading zero for single-digit hours. (Uses a 12-hour clock.)
- H—Hours with no leading zero for single-digit hours. (Uses a 24-hour clock.)
- HH—Hours with a leading zero for single-digit hours. (Uses a 24-hour clock.)
- m—Minutes with no leading zero for single-digit minutes

- mm—Minutes with a leading zero for single-digit minutes
- s—Seconds with no leading zero for single-digit seconds
- ss—Seconds with a leading zero for single-digit seconds
- t—Single-character time marker string, such as A or P
- tt—Multiple-character time marker string, such as AM or PM

Usage

When passing a date/time value as a string, make sure it is enclosed in quotes. Otherwise, it is interpreted as a number representation of a date/time object, returning undesired results.

ToBase64

Returns the Base 64 representation of the *string or binary object. Base64 is a format that uses printable characters, allowing binary data to be sent in forms and Email, and stored in a database or file.*

See also CFFILE for information about loading and reading binary data, CFWDDX for information about serializing and deserializing binary data, and IsBinary and ToBinary for checking for binary data and converting a Base 64 object to binary form.

Syntax

ToBase64(*string or binary_object*)

string or binary_object
String or binary object that is to be converted to Base 64.

Usage

Base 64 provides 6 bit encoding of 8-bit ASCII characters. Because high ASCII values and binary objects are not safe for transport over Internet protocols such as HTTP and SMTP, ColdFusion offers Base 64 as a means to safely send ASCII and binary data over these protocols.

In addition, Base 64 allows you to store binary objects in a database if you convert the data into Base 64 first.

ToBinary

Returns the binary representation of Base64 encoded data.

See CFFILE for information about loading and reading binary data, CFWDDX for information about serializing and deserializing binary data, and IsBinary and ToBase64 for checking for binary data and converting

it into printable form. See also Len for determining the length of a binary object.

Syntax

ToBinary(*string_in_Base64 or binary_value*)

string_in_Base64 or binary_value
String in Base 64 that is to be converted to binary or binary value that is to be tested to ensure that it is an acceptable binary value.

Usage

Base 64 provides 6 bit encoding of 8-bit ASCII characters.If you receive data in Base 64, you can re-create the actual binary object that it represents, such as a .gif, .jpeg, or executable file, by using the ToBinary function.

ToString

Attempts to convert a value of any type, including a binary value, into a string.

Syntax

ToString(*any_value*)

any_value
The value that is to be converted into a string.

Usage

If ToString cannot convert the value into a string, it throws an exception. All simple values can be converted into a string, even binary values that do not contain byte zero can be converted.

Trim

Returns *string* with both leading and trailing spaces removed.

See also LTrim and RTrim.

Syntax

Trim(*string*)

string
String being trimmed.

UCase

Returns *string* converted to uppercase.

See also LCase.

Syntax

UCase(*string*)

string
String being converted to uppercase.

URLDecode

Decodes a URL-encoded string.

See also URLEncodedFormat.

Syntax
URLDecode(urlEncodedString)

urlEncodedString
A string that has been URL-encoded.

Usage

URL encoding refers to a data format where all high ASCII and non-alphanumeric characters are encoded using a percent sign followed by the two character hexadecimal representation of the character code. For example, a character with code 129 will be encoded as %81. In addition, spaces can be encoded using the plus sign (+).

Query strings in HTTP are always URL-encoded.

URL-encoded strings can be created using the URL-EncodedFormat function.

URLEncodedFormat

Returns a URL-encoded *string*. Spaces are replaced with + and all non-alphanumeric characters with equivalent hexadecimal escape sequences. This function enables you to pass arbitrary strings within a URL, because ColdFusion automatically decodes all URL parameters that are passed to the template.

See also URLDecode.

Syntax
URLEncodedFormat(*string*)

string
String being URL encoded.

Usage

URL encoding refers to a data format where all high ASCII and non-alphanumeric characters are encoded using a percent sign followed by the two character hexadecimal representation of the character code. For example, a character with code 129 will be encoded as %81. In addition, spaces can be encoded using the plus sign (+).

Query strings in HTTP are always URL-encoded.

URL-encoded strings can be created using the URL-EncodedFormat function.

Val

Returns a number that the beginning of a string can be converted to. Returns 0 if conversion is not possible.

See also IsNumeric.

Syntax
Val(*string*)

string
Any string.

ValueList

Returns a comma-separated list of the values of each record returned from a previously executed query.

See also QuotedValueList.

Syntax
ValueList(*query.column* [, *delimiter*])

query.column
Name of an already executed query and column. Separate query name and column name with a period (.).

delimiter
A string delimiter to separate column data.

Week

Returns the ordinal for the week number in a year; an integer ranging from 1 to 53.

See also DatePart.

Syntax
Week(*date*)

date
Any date/time value or string convertible to date.

Usage

Years from 0 to 29 are interpreted as 21st century values. Years 30 to 99 are interpreted as 20th century values.

When passing date as a string, make sure it is enclosed in quotes. Otherwise, it is interpreted as a number representation of a date returning undesired results.

WriteOutput

Appends text to the page output stream. Although you can call this function anywhere within a page, it is most useful inside a CFSCRIPT block.

When within the CFQUERY and CFMAIL tags, the WriteOutput function does not output to the current page, but instead writes to the current SQL statement or mail text. Do not use WriteOutput within CFQUERY and CFMAIL.

This function writes to the page output stream regardless of conditions established by the CFSETTING tag.

Syntax
WriteOutput(*string*)

string
Text to be appended to the page output stream.

XMLFormat

Returns a string that is safe to use with XML.

Syntax
XMLFormat(*string*)

string
Any string.

Usage
XMLFormat escapes special XML characters so that you can put arbitrary strings safely into XML. The characters that are escaped by XMLFormat include the following:

- greater than sign (>)
- less than sign (<)
- single quotation mark (')
- double quotation mark (")
- ampersand (&)

Year

Returns the year corresponding to *date*.

See also DatePart and IsLeapYear.

Syntax
Year(*date*)

date
Any date/time value or string convertible to date.

Usage
Years from 0 to 29 are interpreted as 21st century values. Years 30 to 99 are interpreted as 20th century values.

When passing a date as a string, make sure it is enclosed in quotes. Otherwise, it is interpreted as a number representation of a date returning, undesired results.

YesNoFormat

Returns Boolean data as YES or NO.

See also IsBinary and IsNumeric.

Syntax
YesNoFormat(*value*)

value
Any number or Boolean value.

Usage
The YesNoFormat function returns all non-zero values as YES and zero values as NO.

Differences between ColdFusion and Traditional Server-Side Programming

Traditionally, server-side Web applications used to deploy interactive Web sites have been developed using the Common Gateway Interface (commonly known as CGI). Cgi-bin. CGI is a simple mechanism whereby scripts or programs written in most languages can process data received from a Web user (usually though a form) and return data in dynamic Web pages.

Generally, under the CGI model, server-side applications are built out of stand-alone scripts or programs that communicate with the Web server by using a standard method of passing information between them. However, CGI programs and scripts run as independent processes from the Web server. This introduces additional layers of inefficiency into the model, and this inefficiency may become an issue in sites with a large dynamic component and heavy usage or when using interpreted languages for CGI programming.

Web application platforms such as ColdFusion offer a closer integration into Web servers and provide numerous benefits over traditional CGI programming. ColdFusion offers the following benefits over CGI:

- Better performance than interpreted CGI programming
- Tighter integration with HTML, allowing applications to be deployed more easily and more efficiently
- Simplification of the processes for accessing and manipulating outside data sources such as relational databases, e-mail systems, and LDAP directory servers
- Simpler programming language and syntax to enable non-programmers to develop interactive applications

In this appendix, you will look at the mechanics of how CGI and ColdFusion work.

The CGI Model

Essentially, CGI defines a standard method for passing information from the Web server to an external program, which then has a standard method for passing information back to the Web server.

CGI programs can generally be written in any standard programming language available for the platform on which the Web server is running. Common languages for developing Web applications using CGI include:

- Perl
- C
- C++
- Java
- Unix shell scripting languages such as the Bourne Shell

This ability to choose from a wide range of standard programming and scripting languages lends CGI a great deal of flexibility, but it is this flexibility that helps make CGI a difficult environment to work in for the non-programmer. All the languages in the preceding list, and most others used in CGI programming, are general-purpose languages that require a minimum level of programming skill to use efficiently.

In addition, because of the general-purpose nature of the languages, none are optimized for writing applications that perform tasks common in interactive Web applications, such as:

- Inserting and retrieving data from relational databases
- Quickly formatting output based on the results of a query
- Working with outside data sources such as e-mail and LDAP servers
- Integrating easily with standard HTML

At the same time, though, the very fact that these languages are general purpose provides capabilities often lacking in ColdFusion such as:

- Easy integration with other applications and system services
- Powerful constructs for creating custom data types, hash tables, and linked lists
- The capability to create full-blown object-oriented programs with inheritance, classes, and all other features commonly found in object-oriented programming languages
- The capability to access the system at a low level, potentially addressing individual memory locations, stacks, and registers

Of course, for most purposes, these features are not needed in interactive Web applications. Where they are, however, access to these features is available through CGI.

Technically, CGI interacts with the Web server as outlined in Figure D.1

FIGURE D.1
A typical CGI flow of information

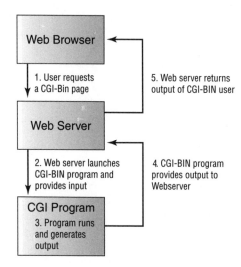

Figure D.2 shows the typical architecture of a Web server using CGI to create interactive applications and dynamic pages.

Step-by-step, the information flow is as follows:

1. A user makes a request for a page that is generated by a CGI script or program.
2. The Web server launches the program and passes input data from the user to the program.
3. The program runs, processes any input data, and generates output data in the form of HTML code.
4. The HTML code is sent by the program to the Web server.
5. The Web server sends the HTML code it receives from the CGI program back to the user.

FIGURE D.2
A CGI architecture

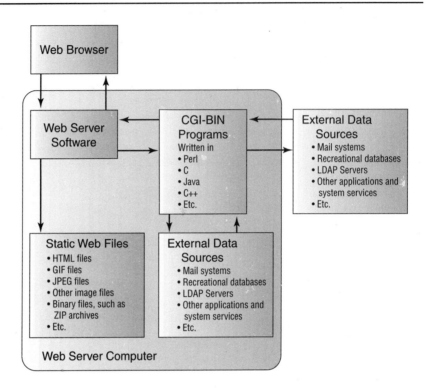

The ColdFusion Model

In contrast, ColdFusion leverages the power of the application programmer's interface to link more closely with the Web server. All major Web servers including Apache, Netscape Enterprise Server, and Microsoft Internet Information Server offer APIs, and ColdFusion is designed to work with all of these. API's are application program interfaces which provide a set of standard mechanisms a programmer can use to access the features of an application, development environment or platform.

By using the API to connect with the Web server, several benefits are automatically achieved:

- The ColdFusion server essentially becomes part of the Web server.
- A separate program is not launched each time a dynamic page is requested; instead, the pages are interpreted by the ColdFusion server and returned to the user.
- ColdFusion can access capabilities of the Web server to directly return data to the user without the extra stage of passing it to the Web server for the Web server to, in turn, resend to the user.
- Tight integration with the security and authentication model used by the Web server.

In terms of language, ColdFusion offers less flexibility than the CGI environment: ColdFusion is an integrated system using mechanisms for communicating with the Web server through the API, a server for parsing the content of ColdFusion templates, and a proprietary, tag-based programming language designed to directly leverage the capabilities of the ColdFusion server.

The ColdFusion environment is also designed to allow tight integration with HTML. A ColdFusion template can include both HTML tags and ColdFusion tags. When a user requests a file, the following process occurs:

1. The Web server retrieves the ColdFusion template from the collection of HTML and ColdFusion files available to the server.
2. The file is identified as a ColdFusion template by its extension.
3. The file is interpreted by the ColdFusion server, the API, and all ColdFusion tags are processed and converted into the resulting HTML code.
4. The result is then passed to the web server.
5. The completed HTML file is passed to the user by the Web server.

Architecturally, this looks like the design in Figure D.3.

FIGURE D.3
The ColdFusion
architecture

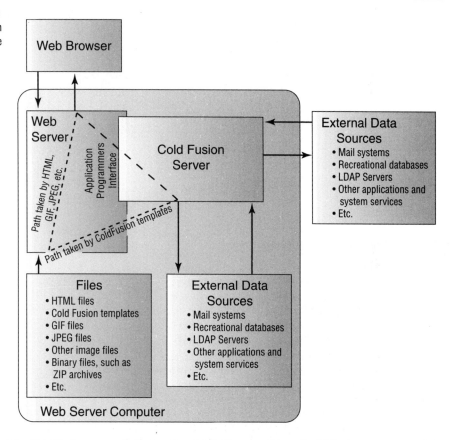

Notice that the ColdFusion server is depicted as tightly integrated into the Web server as opposed to being a collection of individual programs that the Web server launches as independent processes each time they are requested by a user (which is how things work in the CGI model).

A single collection of files, including static HTML and image files, exists as well as ColdFusion templates. The route the file takes (directly through the Web server to the client, or to the client via the API and the ColdFusion server) depends on the type of file requested by the user.

Final Notes

It is important to remember that ColdFusion and CGI are not mutually exclusive technologies. A Web server that has ColdFusion installed can still use CGI programs, and the use of CGI programs does not prevent the use of ColdFusion templates. Some applications can use both technologies where they are best suited to achieve results beyond what could be achieved with either technology on its own.

ColdFusion can be used to:

- Quickly deploy database interfaces
- Generate sophisticated HTML based on dynamic data
- Access external data sources, including mail systems and LDAP servers

At the same time, CGI programs could be accessed where applications need some or all of the following capabilities:

- Sophisticated data processing requiring advanced data types
- Direct access to external applications and system services
- Features of a specific language such as object-oriented capabilities
- Extensive mathematical capabilities and performance

As your interactive applications grow in complexity, study the ways in which ColdFusion can be combined with other server-side technologies including CGI to achieve the best results possible.

SQL Functions and
Data Types

This appendix will provide a brief listing of SQL functions and data types available for use when coding your SQL queries. This listing contains functions and data types that may or may not be supported by your particular database. Where possible, it has been indicated which versions of SQL support each particular function and data type. You should check your database documentation for additionally supported functions and data types. The following codes are used to indicate support for the functions and data types for various products:

- A–Access
- T–Transact SQL (SQL Server)
- P–PL/SQL (Oracle)
- 0–ODBC supported (You may need to use special function parameters when passing ODBC functions)
- S–SQL-92 ANSI Supported

SQL Functions

This section will cover a variety of functions supported by various versions of SQL. The functions are split up into categories. Functions perform an operation on a value and then return a single value result. Mainly, SQL functions are used to format data in a column before it is returned in the query results.

When using functions in your SQL statements, you can use them in both the SELECT and WHERE clauses. Most of the time you can just explicitly insert the function into your SQL statement with no problem. But there are cases where you may need to tell the ODBC driver that you are passing a function statement in order for it to be interpreted correctly. To do this you can add the function call symbols around your function: SELECT {fn curdate()} AS Day. This will indicate to the ODBC driver that the text within the function parameters is a function. Usually you only need to do this with the ODBC supported functions as indicated by the 0 in the support column of each table.

Aggregate Functions

Aggregate functions perform a calculation on a set of rows and return a single result. Null values are ignored, except when using COUNT(), and they are often used with the GROUP BY clause of the SQL statement. For more information on using aggregate function please refer to Chapter 10, "Using CFQUERY and SQL to Interact with the Database." The most commonly used aggregate functions are listed in Table E.1. Your database may support additional aggregate functions not listed here.

TABLE E.1:   SQL Aggregate Functions

Function	Support	Description
AVG(column)	A,T,P,S	Calculates the average value of a group. Null values are ignored.
COUNT(column)	A,T,P,S	Returns the count of rows. Null values are ignored.
COUNT(*)	A,T,P,S	Returns the total number of rows in a table including Nulls.
MAX()	A,T,P,S	Returns the maximum value of a group. Character fields are based on sort sequence. Null values are ignored.
MIN()	A,T,P,S	Returns the minimum value of a group. Character fields are based on sort sequence. Null values are ignored.
SUM()	A,T,P,S	Calculates the sum of the values in a group. Can only be used on numeric fields. Null values are ignored.

Date/Time Functions

Date and Time functions perform an action on a date or time value. If the column you are performing the function on is not a date column, you may receive an error. The most commonly used Date and Time functions are listed in Table E.2. Always enclose Date and Time values in single quotes.

T A B L E E . 2 : SQL Date/Time Functions

Function	Support	Description
Add_Months(date,x)		Adds a number of months (x) to a date (date).
Convert(datatype, value)	A,T,P,O	The function returns the specified **value** converted to the specified **datatype**.
CurDate()	A,T,O	Returns the current date.
CurTime()	A,T,O	Returns the current local time.
Current_Timestamp	T,S	Returns the current date and time.
DateAdd(datepart, number, date)	T	Adds an interval (**number**) to the specified part (**datepart**) of the date value (**date**) and returns a new date and time value. *
DateDiff(datepart, startdate, enddate)	T	Subtracts the specified part (**datepart**) of the first date (**startdate**) from the second date (**enddate**) and returns the result as a new date/time value. *
DateName(datepart, date)	T	Returns the character equivalent of the specified part (**datepart**) of a date value (**date**). *
DatePart(datepart, date)	T	Returns the numerical equivalent of the specified part (**datepart**) of a date value (**date**). *
Day(date)	A,T	Returns the day part of the specified date (**date**) as an integer.
DayName(date)	T,O	Returns the string equivalent of the day part of a date value (**date**).
DayOfMonth(date)	T,O	Returns the numerical equivalent of the day of the month part of a date value (**date**). Possible results are from 1-31.
DayOfWeek(date)	T,O	Returns the numerical equivalent of the day of the week part of a date value (**date**). Possible results are from 1-7, where 1 is Sunday.
DayOfYear(date)	T,O	Returns the numerical equivalent of the day of the year part of a date value (**date**). Possible results are from 1-366.
Format(date)	A	Returns the specified date (**date**) in the format of: yyyy dd mm
GetDate()	T	Returns the current system date and time.
Hour(time)	A,T,O	Returns the hour as an integer value in the range of 0-23.
Last_day(month)	P	Returns the last day of a month (**month**).
Minute(time)	A,T,O	Returns the minute as a value in the range of 0-59.

TABLE E.2: SQL Date/Time Functions *(continued)*

Function	Support	Description
Month(date)	A,T,O	Returns the month part of a date (**date**) as an integer within the range of 1 to 12.
MonthName(date)	A,T,O	Returns the character equivalent of the month specified by the date (**date**).
Months_Between(date1, date2)	P	Returns the number of months between **date1** and **date2**.
New_Time(date, timezone1, timezone2)	P	Returns the date and time in **timezone2** when date and time in **timezone1** are the **date** specified. Check documentation for available time zones.
Next_Day(date, weekday)	P	Returns the name of the **weekday** specified by the **date**.
Now()	A,T,O	Returns the current timestamp.
Quarter(date)	A,T,O	Returns the quarter of the **date** as a value in the range of 1-4.
Round(date)		Returns date rounded to the nearest day.
Second(time)	A,T,O	Returns the seconds of the time value in the range of 1-59.
SysDate		Returns the system date and time.
TimeStampAdd(interval, integer, timestamp)	T,O	Calculates a new timestamp by adding an integer (**integer**) of the interval type (**interval**) to the specified timestamp (**timestamp**). Available intervals can be found in your database documentation.
TimeStampDiff(interval, timestamp1, timestamp2)	T,O	Calculates the difference specified by the interval (**interval**) between two timestamp values (**timestamp1** and **timestamp2**).
Trunc(date)	P	Returns **date** with the time portion of the day truncated to the nearest day.
Week(date)	A,T,O	Returns the week part of the **date** as an integer value in the range of 1-53.
Year(date)	A,T,O	Returns the year part of a specified date.

*Valid options for the datepart are: year, yy, yyyy quarter, qq, q, month, mm, m, dayofyear, dy, y, day, dd, d, week, wk, ww, hour, hh, minute, mi, n, second, ss, s, millisecond, ms.

Number/Mathematical Functions

Mathematical functions perform a calculation using numerical arguments and return a numeric result. The arguments can be supplied as a column, another function, or a specific numeric value. If the column or value you are performing the function on is not a numeric data type, you may receive an error. The most commonly used mathematical functions are listed in Table E.3.

TABLE E.3: SQL Number/Mathematical Functions

Function	Support	Description
Abs(numeric_value)	A,T,P,O	Returns the absolute and positive value of the provided numeric value (numeric_value).
Acos(float_value)	A,T,P,O	Returns the arccosine of the given value (float_value) as an angle, expressed in radians.
Asin(float_value)	A,T,P,O	Returns the arcsine of the given value (float_value) as an angle, expressed in radians.
Atan(float_value)	A,T,P,O	Returns the arctangent of the given value (float_value) as an angle, expressed in radians.
Atan2(float_value1, float_value2)	P,O	Returns the arc tangent of float_value1 and float_value2 as an angle, expressed in radians.
Atn2(float_value1, float_value2)		Returns the arc tangent of float_value1 and float_value2 as an angle, expressed in radians.
Ceil(numeric_value)		Returns the smallest integer greater than or equal to the numeric value (numeric_value).
Ceiling(numeric_value)	A,T,O	Returns the smallest integer greater than or equal to the numeric value (numeric_value).
Convert(datatype, value)	A,T,P,O	The function returns the specified value converted to the specified datatype.
Cos(float_value)	A,T,P,O	Returns the cosine of an angle expressed in radians (float_value).
Cosh(float_value)	P	Returns the hyperbolic cosine of the given value (float_value).
Cot(float_value)	A,T,O	Returns the cotangent of an angle expressed in radians (float_value).
Degrees(numeric_value)	T,O	Calculates an angle in degrees based upon an angle in radians (numeric_value).
Exp(float_value)	A,T,P,O	Returns e (2.71828183) raised to the power of the given value (float_value).
Floor(numeric_value)	A,T,P,O	Returns the largest integer less than or equal to the numeric value (numeric_value).
Ln(positive_value)		Returns the natural logarithm of the positive given value (positive_value).
Log(float_value)	A,T,P	Returns the natural logarithm of the given float expression (float_value).
Log10(float_value)	T,O	Returns the base-10 logarithm of the given float expression (float_value).

T A B L E E.3: SQL Number/Mathematical Functions *(continued)*

Function	Support	Description
Mod(integer1, integer2)	A,T,P,O	Returns the remainder of integer1 divided by integer2. Also known as modulus.
Pi()	T,O	Returns the constant value of Pi.
Power(numeric_value, integer)	A,T,P,O	Returns the calculation of the numeric_value to the power of the integer.
Radians(numeric_value)	T,O	Returns radians calculated from a given numeric expression in degrees.
Rand(integer)	A,T,O	Returns a random float value between 0 and 1.
Round(numeric_value, decimal_places)	A,T,P,O	Returns the calculation of the value (numeric_value) rounded to the number of decimal places (decimal_places). If no value is given for decimal_places then the numeric_value is rounded to the nearest integer.
Sign(numeric_value)	A,T,P,O	Returns the sign of the given value (numeric_value).
Sin(float_value)	A,T,P,O	Returns the sine of an angle expressed in radians (float_value).
Sinh(float_value)		Returns the hyperbolic sine of the given value (float_value).
Square(float_value)		Returns the square of the given value (float_value).
Sqrt(float_value)	A,T,P,O	Returns the square of the positive given value (float_value).
Tan(float_value)	A,T,P,O	Returns the tangent of an angle expressed in radians (float_value).
Tanh()		Returns the hyperbolic tangent of the given value (float_value).

String Functions

String functions perform an action on a character string and return a result. The arguments can be supplied as a column, another function, or a specific string value. If the column or value you are performing the function on is not a character data type, you may receive an error or the value may be automatically converted. When specifying a literal character string as an argument to a function you must enclose the value in single quotes. The most commonly used string functions are listed in Table E.4.

T A B L E E.4: SQL String Functions

Function	Access	Description
ASCII(string)	A,T,P,O	Returns the ASCII code value of the first character of the given string (string).

TABLE E.4: SQL String Functions *(continued)*

Function	Access	Description
Char(code)	A,T,O	Returns the character as specified by the ASCII code value (**code**). The value of **code** should be between 0 and 255.
Chr(n)	A,P	Returns the character as specified by the ASCII code value (**code**). The value of **code** should be between 0 and 255.
Concat(string1, string2)	A,T,P,O	Concatenates two strings (**string1** and **string2**) and returns the result as a character string.
Convert(datatype, value)	A,T,P,O	The function returns the specified **value** converted to the specified **datatype**.
Difference(string1, string2)	T,O	Indicates the difference as an integer value between the Soundex values for **string1** and **string2**.
InitCap(string)		Converts the string to initial caps.
Insert(string1, start, length, string2)	T,O	Returns a character string where length characters have been deleted from string1 beginning at start, and where string2 has been inserted into string1 beginning at start.
Instr(string1,string2)	A,T,P,O	Returns the numerical position in **string1** where **string2** begins.
Lcase(string)	A,T,O	Converts **string** to lowercase characters.
Left(string, Count)	A,T,O	Returns the total characters of the **string** indicated by **count**, starting with the first character and going forward.
Len(string)	A,T	Returns the number of characters in the given **string**.
Length(string)	A,T,P,O	Returns the number of characters in the given **string**.
Locate(string1, string2)	A,T,O	Returns the numerical position of the first occurrence of **string1** within **string2**.
Lower(string)	T,P,S	Converts **string** to lowercase characters.
Lpad(string1, length, string2)		Pads **string1** on the left with the character specified in **string2** to a length specified by **length**.
Ltrim(string)	A,T,P,O	Returns **string** with blank characters on the left side removed.
PatIndex(string1, string2)	T	Returns the numerical position in **string2** where **string1** begins.
Repeat(string, count)	T,O	Returns a string where the given **string** value is repeated **count** times.

TABLE E.4: SQL String Functions *(continued)*

Function	Access	Description
Replace(string1, string2, string3)	P,O	Replaces all occurrences of **string2** in **string1** with **string3**.
Replicate(string, count)	T	Returns a string where the given **string** value is repeated **count** times.
Reverse(string)	T,P	Reverses the order of characters in the given **string**.
Right(string, count)	A,T,O	Returns the total characters of the **string** indicated by **count**, starting with the last character going backward.
Rpad(string, length, string2)	P	Pads **string1** on the left with the character specified in **string2** to a length specified by **length**.
Rtrim(string)	A,T,P,O	Returns **string** with blank characters on the right side removed.
Soundex(string)	T,P,O	Returns a character string representing the sound of the words in the given **string**. Consult your database documentation for a full explanation.
Space(count)	A,T,O	Returns a character string consisting of the number of spaces as specified by **count**.
Substr(string, length, position)	P	Extracts the total characters from the given **string** as indicated by **length** starting at the given **position**.
Substring(string, position, length)	A,T,O	Extracts the total characters from the given **string** as indicated by **length** starting at the given **position**.
Translate(string, list1, list2)	P	Takes all occurrences in the given **string** of characters specified in **list1** and replaces them with the equivalent characters specified in **string2**.
Ucase(string)	A,T,O	Converts **string** to uppercase characters.
Upper(string)	T,P,S	Converts **string** to uppercase characters.

SQL Data Types

Each column (field) in your database has a specific data type assigned to it. This data type is assigned when the column is created. You can assign data types to columns by using the CREATE and ALTER SQL statements. The CREATE and ALTER SQL clauses are discussed in Chapter 11, "Using Advanced Query Techniques."

The data type enforces a fixed set of rules or properties on the data entered into that column. For example, if you try to enter text into a numeric column, you will receive an error. The data types can vary from column to column as well as from database to database. You should consult your database documentation to see a full listing of supported data types. A brief listing has been included here.

Date and Time Data Types

Date and Time columns are used to store valid date and time values. The recognized date and time formats vary with each database. When inserting date and time values you can make sure that they follow your database's recognized formats by using the DateFormat() and CreateODBCDate()

functions provided by ColdFusion. Inserting data into a database is explained in Chapter 10,"Using CFQUERY and SQL to Connect to a Database." The most common Date and Time data types are described in Table E.5.

TABLE E.5: Date Data Types

Data Type	Support	Description
Date	A,P,S	Stores the date value with the year in a four-digit format.
DateTime	A,T,0	Stores date and time values for a specified range as determined by your database.
SmallDateTime	T	Stores date and time values (with less precision than the DateTime data type) from January 1, 1900, through June 6, 2079, accurate to the minute.
Time	A,S	Stores the time value.
TimeStamp	A,T,S	Stores the date and time value. Can be automatically set as a unique incremented value depending upon the database.

Binary Data Types

Binary columns are used to store binary data including Microsoft documents, images, or very large text files. The most common Binary data types are described in Table E.6.

TABLE E.6: Binary Data Types

Data Type	Support	Description
Binary(length)	A,T,0	Stores data in two-byte pairs with a fixed length. Maximum lengths vary depending on database.
Blob	P	A large binary object. Maximum size is four gigabytes.
Image	A,T	Stores image data in two-byte pairs with a variable length. Maximum lengths vary depending on database.
OLEObject	A	Objects created using OLE can be stored as longbinary data with a variable length.
VarBinary (length)	A,T,0	Stores data in two-byte pairs with a variable length. Maximum lengths vary depending on database.

BOOLEAN Data Types

The BOOLEAN data type is used to store ON/OFF, YES/NO, TRUE/FALSE, or 1/0 values. The supported BOOLEAN data types are listed in Table E.7.

TABLE E.7: BOOLEAN Data Types

Data Type	Support	Description
Bit	A,T,S	An integer value of 1, 0, or NULL. Often used as yes/no, true/false, or on/off columns. Bit columns cannot be indexed.
Logical	A	Same as Bit
YesNo	A	Same as Bit

Exact Numeric Data Types

Exact numeric data type columns store values with fixed precision and scale. Calculations performed on these numbers are done in infinite precision. The most common exact numeric data types are listed in Table E.8.

T A B L E   E . 8 :   Exact Numeric Data Types

Data Type	Support	Description
Byte	A	Stores whole number values (no decimal points). Supported range is from 0 to 255.
Dec	T,P,S	Stores exact numeric information with decimal precision. Allowable range varies for each database.
Decimal	T,P,S	Same as **Dec**.
Int	A,T,P,S	Stores whole number values (no decimal points). Storage size is four bytes. Supported range varies according to database.
Integer	A,T,P,S	Stores whole number values (no decimal points). Storage size is four bytes. Supported range varies according to database.
Long	A,P	Stores whole number values (no decimal points). Storage size is four bytes. Supported range varies according to database.
Numeric	A,T,P,S	Same as **Dec**.
Short	A	Stores whole number values (no decimal points). Storage size is two bytes.
SmallInt	A,T,P,S	Stores whole number values (no decimal points). Storage size is two bytes. Supported range varies according to database.
TinyInt	T,0	Stores whole number values (no decimal points) in the range of 0 to 255. Storage size is one byte.

Approximate Numeric Data Types

Approximate numeric data type columns store values with floating point numeric data. Calculations performed on these numbers are done in finite precision and are approximate. The most common approximate numeric data types are listed in Table E.9.

T A B L E   E . 9 :   Approximate Numeric Data Types

Data Type	Support	Description
Float(number)	A,T,P,S	Stores approximate numeric information with decimal point precision as indicated by the given **number**. Allowable range varies for each database.
Real	A,T,P,S	Stores approximate numeric information based on a specific small decimal point value. Allowable range varies for each database.
Single	A	Same as **Real**.
Double	A	Stores approximate numeric information based on a specific large decimal point value. Allowable range varies for each database.
Number	A,P	Same as **Double**.

Character Data Types

Character data type columns store data in text format with either fixed-length or variable-length values. When referring to these data types remember enclose the value single quotes. The most common character data types are listed in Table E.10.

T A B L E E . 1 0 : Character Data Types

Data Type	Support	Description
char(length)	A,T,P,S	Stores character strings with the length specified. Maximum length values vary depending on the database.
Character(length)	T,P,S	Stores character strings with the length specified. Maximum length values vary depending on the database.
Varchar(length)	A,T,P,S	Stores character strings with a variable length not to exceed the maximum specified by length. Maximum length values vary depending on the database.
Varchar2(length)	P	Stores character strings with a variable length not to exceed the maximum specified by length. The maximum length available is 2000 bytes.
String(length)	A	Stores character strings with the length specified. Maximum length is 255 characters.
Text(length)	A,T	Stores large character strings with a variable length not to exceed the maximum specified by length. Maximum length values vary depending on the database.
Memo(length)	A	Stores large character strings with a variable length not to exceed the maximum specified by length. Maximum length is 65,535 characters. This field cannot be indexed.

Money Data Types

Monetary data type columns are used to store various monetary or currency values. Check your database documentation for specifics on the data format. The money data types are listed in Table E.11.

T A B L E E . 1 1 : Money Data Types

Data Type	Support	Description
money	A,T	Represents monetary or currency values. Storage size is eight bytes.
Smallmoney	T	Represents monetary or currency values. Storage size is four bytes.
Currency	A	Represents monetary or currency values and is accurate to 15 digits to the left of the decimal and four digits to the right. Storage size is eight bytes.

Uniquely Identified Data Types

The columns with uniquely identified data types provide a unique value used to distinguish each record in a table and/or database. These columns are often used as the primary keys of a table. In most cases these columns can be set to automatically increment each time a record is added tot he database. These fields cannot be updated. The most common of these data types is listed in Table E.12.

TABLE E.12: Uniquely Identified Data Types

Data Type	Support	Description
Identity	T	Stores a database-wide unique value used to distinguish each record.
GUID	A	Used as a replication ID.
Counter	A	A unique sequential number in the format of a long integer.
AutoIncrement	A	Same as Counter.

Reference Sites

- T-SQL Functions: http://msdn.microsoft.com/library/psdk/sql/fa-fz_15.htm
- T-SQL Datatypes: http://msdn.microsoft.com/library/psdk/sql/da-db_1.htm
- ANSI Standards: http://www.ansi.org/
- Database jump site: http://www.pcslink.com/~ej/dbweb.html
- SQL glossary: http://www-act.ucsd.edu/trn/datawhse/glossary.html
- SQL glossary: http://mysql.com/crash-me-choose.html

Additional Resources

This appendix provides lists of selected ColdFusion-related resources available on the Internet. The number of Web sites dedicated to ColdFusion and related topics is always growing, so these lists are intended to provide a glimpse into the breadth and depth of the information available.

General Resources, Support, and Custom Tags

The following Web sites offer useful, general information related to ColdFusion and ColdFusion development:

`Allaire home page` http://www.allaire.com/
`ColdFusion documentation` http:// www2.allaire.com/handlers/index.cfm?ID=13381
`ColdFusion support` http://www.allaire.com/Support/
`ColdFusion Support Forum` http://forums.allaire.com/devconf/
`ColdFusion Developer Center` http://www.allaire.com/developer/ReferenceDesk/
`ColdFusion Tag Gallery` http://www.allaire.com/developer/taggallery/
`Allaire Alive` http://alive.allaire.com/
`ColdFusion Code Factory` http://www.geocities.com/SiliconValley/Campus/7521/coldfusionhelp.htm
`CodeBits` http://www.codebits.com/
`FuseBox` http://www.fusebox.org/
`House of Fusion` http://www.houseoffusion.com/
`Serendipity` http://members.dca.net/rbilson/cold_fusion.htm
`Miscellaneous custom tags` http://lsanin.ne.mediaone.net/misc.htm
`Introfoundation Software Freeware` http://www.intrafoundation.com/freeware.html
`CF_Code` http://www.cfcode.com/
`ColdFusion Frontier` http://psyberspace.net/coldfusion/
`CFScripts.com` http://www.cfscripts.com/
`CF Tips` http://www.systemanage.com/cff/cftips.cfm
`ColdCuts` http://www.teratech.com/coldcuts/
`CF_Tutorial` http://www.cftutorials.com/

Publications

The following is a list of some of the ColdFusion publications (both print and electronic) that are currently available:

`ColdFusion Developer's Journal` http://www.coldfusionjournal.com/
`Defusion` http://www.defusion.com/
`ColdFusion Advisor` http://www.cfadvisor.com/

Users Groups

The list of ColdFusion users groups worldwide is constantly growing. This list represents known groups with Web sites at the time of publication. For more complete lists of groups, check the *Cold-Fusion Advisor*'s list of users groups at http:// http://post.cfadvisor.com/UserGroups/info_UG.cfm or Allaire's list of users groups at http://www.allaire.com/developer/UG.cfm.

`Albany NY ColdFusion Users Group` http://www.anycfug.org/
`Atlanta ColdFusion Users Group` http:// www.acfug.org/
`Australia ColdFusion Users Group` http://www.cfug.org.au/
`Bay Area ColdFusion Users Group` http://www.bacfug.org/

Belgium ColdFusion Users Group http://www.cfug-be.org/
Birmingham ColdFusion Users Group http://www.birminghamcoldfusion.com/
Boston Area ColdFusion Users Group http:// www.cfugboston.org/
Central Europe ColdFusion Users Group http://cfug.interlake.net/
Dallas-Fort Worth ColdFusion Users Group http:// www.dfwcfug.org/
Kansas City ColdFusion Users Group http://www.beachcreative.com/cfug/index.cfm
Maryland ColdFusion Users Group http://www.cfug-md.org/
New Jersey ColdFusion Users Group http://www.njcfug.org/
Northern Colorado ColdFusion Users Group http://www.nccfug.org/
Ohio Area ColdFusion Users Group http://www.oacfug.org/
Phoenix ColdFusion Users Group http://www.azcfug.org/
Portland Area ColdFusion Users Group http:// www.pdxcfug.org/
San Antonio ColdFusion Users Group http://www.sacfug.org/
Seattle ColdFusion Users Group http://cfseattle.org/
Southern California ColdFusion Users Group http://www.sccfug.org/p/
HomePage.cfm
Taiwan ColdFusion Users Group http://www.coldfusion.leetide.net/
Tampa Bay ColdFusion Users Group http://cfug.etais.com/
Toronto ColdFusion Users Group http://www.cfugtoronto.org/CFUGTorontoCore.cfm
Twin Cities ColdFusion Users Group http://coldfusion.twincities.com/
United Kingdom ColdFusion Users Group http:// www.cfug.co.uk/

INDEX

Note to the Reader: Page numbers in **bold** indicate the principal discussion of a topic or the definition of a term. Page numbers in *italic* indicate illustrations.

F

G

W

What's on the CD?

The companion CD-ROM contains the code for many of the examples in this book. It also contains evaluation software, custom tags, and an electronic version of the book. A breakdown of the contents is as follows:

- Electronic source code matching the code provided in the book.
- Access database used in conjunction with the source code.
- Evaluation version of ColdFusion Application Server 4.5: A fully-functional, time-limited evaluation version of the software used to run the applications developed in this book.
- Evaluation version of ColdFusion Studio 4.5: A fully-functional, time-limited evaluation version of the integrated development environment for creating ColdFusion-based templates.
- ColdFusion Express 4.0: A scaled-down version of ColdFusion Application Server freely distributed.
- Evaluation version of Allaire Jrun 2.3.3: JRun allows you to develop server-side Java-based applications that incorporate Java Servlets and JavaServer Pages.
- Evaluation version of Allaire Jrun 2.3.3 for Unix.
- Custom Tags: A collection of custom tags (from the most recognized ColdFusion names) that you can use to extend the functionality of your ColdFusion templates.
- Apache Server: A freely-available Web server that can be used to support the operation of the ColdFusion Application Server.
- Searchable electronic PDF version of Mastering ColdFusion 4.5.
- IE5 (Internet Explorer 5).